Thermoplastic Elastomers

Edited by N. R. Legge, G. Holden, H. E. Schroeder

Thermoplastic Elastomers

A Comprehensive Review

Edited by
N. R. Legge, G. Holden, H. E. Schroeder

With Contributions from

R. K. Adams, J. K. Bard, A. T. Chen, C. I. Chung,
S. L. Cooper, A. Y. Coran, S. Davison, G. Deleens,
R. Fayt, W. P. Gergen, W. Goyert, T. Hashimoto,
G. K. Hoeschele, G. Holden, R. Jérôme, N. R. Legge,
R. D. Lundberg, R. G. Lutz, W. J. MacKnight,
J. E. McGrath, W. Meckel, D. J. Meier, J. A. Miller,
M. Morton, R. G. Nelb, K. Onder, D. R. Paul,
R. W. Rees, G. Riess, H. E. Schroeder, C.-K. Shih,
A. C. L. Su, Ph. Teyssié, G. Wegner, W. Wieder,
J. R. Wolfe, Jr.

Hanser Publishers, Munich Vienna New York

Distributed in the United States of America by
Macmillan Publishing Company, New York
and in Canada by
Collier Macmillan Canada, Inc., Ontario

Editors:

Dr. N. R. Legge, Consultant, 19 Barkentine Rd., Rancho Palos Verdes, CA 90274

Dr. G. Holden, Shell Development Co., Houston, Texas 77001

Dr. H. E. Schroeder, Consultant, 74 Stonegates, 4031 Kennett Pike, Greenville, Delaware 19807

Distributed in USA by
Scientific and Technical Books
Macmillan Publishing Company
866 Third Avenue, New York, N. Y. 10022

Distributed in Canada by
Collier Macmillan Canada, Inc.
1200 Eglington Ave. E, Suite 200, Don Mills, Ontario M3C 3N1 Canada

Distributed in all other countries by
Carl Hanser Verlag
Kolbergerstr. 22
D-8000 München 80

CIP-Kurztitelaufnahme der Deutschen Bibliothek

Thermoplastic elastomers: a comprehensive
review / ed. by N. R. Legge . . . With
contributions from R. K. Adams . . . – Munich;
Vienna; New York: Hanser; New York:
Macmillan, 1987.
    ISBN 3-446-14827-2 (Hanser)
    ISBN 0-02-949531-8 (Macmillan)

NE: Legge, Norman R. [Hrsg.]; Adams, Rowland K.
[Mitverf.]

ISBN 3-446-14827-2 Carl Hanser Verlag, Munich, Vienna, New York
ISBN 0-02-949531-8 Macmillan Publishing Company, New York
Library of Congress Catalog Card Number 87-060395

PREFACE

The editors planned this volume to cover the entire field of Thermoplastic Elastomers — history, chemistry, polymer structure, morphology, rheology, physical properties, and typical applications — a comprehensive review as of 1987. Among the authors are technical experts of major companies which have developed and now produce the numerous types of Thermoplastic Elastomers. In addition we have included contributions of leading Directors of academic research laboratories throughout the world.

We are very grateful to the authors and their secretarial staffs for their excellent contributions and their courtesy in working with us in meeting deadlines for publication. We also gratefully acknowledge the cooperation of the various companies who provided time and facilities for completion of the chapters requested. These are: Atochem, Bayer A. G., Dow Chemical USA, E. I. du Pont de Nemours and Co., Exxon Chemical Co., Monsanto Polymer Products Co., and Shell Development Co.

The attention of the reader is drawn to our indexing method which is unusual, but will, we believe, make this volume much more useful as a reference. The Table of Contents on page VI lists the Chapter Titles and Authors. The Index, commencing on page 547, is arranged by chapter number. Under each chapter we have listed the sub-sections by title in numerical order as found in each chapter of the.book. Within each sub-section we have listed the keywords alphabetically with a page number for each.

Thus to locate a keyword in the Index, turn to the chapter number covering the Thermoplastic Elastomer, or subject, of interest, run your eye down the sub-section list to find the area of your interest and look for the keyword and page number.

We have arranged the Index this way because, for example, the "hard segments" of a semi-crystalline TPE, say a Polyester Elastomer (Chapter 8) are quite different from the "hard segments" of Polystyrene-Polydiene Block Copolymers (Chapter 3). In the normal index method "hard segment" would easily run to 20 page numbers, which would not facilitate the use of the book as a reference volume.

The editors, particularly NRL, acknowledge with their gratitude, the assistance of Jean Legge in typing, word processing, proof reading, indexing and, most importantly, in literary criticism.

July, 1987

N. R. Legge
G. Holden
H. E. Schroeder

The figures on the cover show schematic representations of Thermoplastic Elastomers.
Front cover: example of (A–B)$_n$ morphology
Back cover: example of S–B–S morphology

CONTENTS

Chapter 1

INTRODUCTION AND PLAN

N. R. Legge, G. Holden, H. E. Schroeder

The editors had a number of reasons for bringing forth this volume on Thermoplastic Elastomers – A Comprehensive Review. The growth of the thermoplastic elastomer industry has now reached a high level of commercial importance, involving many new products and industrial participants, and a large number of strong academic research groups. From the discovery of the elastomeric character of plasticised PVC in 1926 by Waldo Semon, and the first academic work on block copolymers by Bolland and Melville in 1938, through the discovery of the polyurethanes by Otto Bayer, and all the practical industrial thermoplastic polyamides, copolyesters and polyester amides of the 30's and 40's, to the contributions of Flory, Mark, Tobolsky and many others, there has been an interaction of academic and industrial research enlivened by happy serendipitous discoveries which resulted in great advances.

The main objective of the book is to record in one volume the research and development status of the thermoplastic elastomer systems from the beginning up to the most recent academic research. To place these in the proper time frame, the order of the chapters will be chronological insofar as this is possible.

A second objective is to stimulate further research and development interest in these systems, since it is now apparent that there are very many new ways of arriving at thermoplastic elastomers. There is now a second tremendous upsurge of interest, activity, and progress in this area. The consequences of this forward movement will be important technically and economically.

In Chapter 12, Research on Thermoplastic Elastomers, eight academic research directors were invited to describe recent research in their fields of interest. This will be a valuable contribution to research and development personnel.

Finally, two of the editors with many years of experience in directing research on elastomers, having reviewed in detail the contributions to the book, discuss future trends in thermoplastic elastomer research.

A brief survey of the events leading up to the present status of thermoplastic elastomers, as described in the chapters of the book, will aid in orienting the reader.

In early research the term "thermoplastic elastomer" is seldom found. Nevertheless, polymeric products with both thermoplastic and elastomeric properties were discovered and utilized. For example, the plasticization of polyvinylchloride, PVC, by high boiling liquids, to give a flexible material resembling rubber or a leather, was recognized by Waldo Semon[1] of B. F. Goodrich in 1926. Plasticized PVC was later marketed by Goodrich under the tradename Koroseal.

N. R. Legge, Consultant, 19 Barkentine Rd., Rancho Palos Verdes, CA 90274

G. Holden, Shell Development Co., Houston, Texas

H. E. Schroeder, Consultant, 74 Stonegates, 4031 Kennett Pike, Greenville, Delaware 19807

A composition of matter patent covering vulcanized and unvulcanized blends of poly(acrylo-nitrile-co-butadiene) rubber, NBR, and PVC was applied for in 1940 by D. E. Henderson[2] of Goodrich (see Chapter 6). In 1947 Goodrich offered NBR/PVC blends under the tradename Geon Polyblend. A typical blend having a composition 45 % NBR/55 % PVC had a tensile strength of 13 MPa, and elongation at break of 450 %.

The basic diisocyanate polyaddition reaction was discovered by Professor Otto Bayer[3] in the I. G. Farben laboratories in Leverkusen in 1937 and used to make a polyurethane fiber trademarked as Perlon. Then the elastomeric properties of some polyurethanes were recognized independently by chemists at Du Pont[4,5] and ICI[6]. Many of the polymers they obtained were thermoplastic but lacked adequate melt stability to function as practical thermoplastic elastomers. In the early 1950's chemists at Bayer, Du Pont, Goodyear and other companies were making and offering to their customers thermoplastic gum elasto-mers, but these did not have a sufficiently high concentration of hard segments to have good properties unless vulcanized.

In the late 1940's Coleman of ICI was attempting to impart dyeability to polyethylene terephthalate by copolymerizing small amounts of poly(oxyalkylene) glycols. Snyder of Du Pont was using a somewhat similar approach in a program aimed at elastic fibers. In 1952 Snyder received a US Patent[7], applied for in 1950, on elastic linear copolyesters prepared by melt copolymerizing, for example, terephthalic acid, suberic acid and trimethylene glycol; melt copolymerizing separately a copolyester of terephthalic acid and ethylene glycol, and finally performing a carefully controlled melt-ester interchange reaction between the two polymers. The resulting linear copolyester had a higher strength and higher stretch modulus than any natural rubber threads. These copolyester elastic fibers had that essential property of natural rubber threads, lacking in most synthetic materials, a very quick elastic recovery (snap!). The fibers could be extruded from the melt or spun from solvents. The former is a thermoplastic processing step and the latter indicates solubility, i.e., no cross-linking. Thus, these elastic fibers can be classified as thermoplastic elastomers, possibly the first random block copolymers in which the relation between structure and property was clearly deline-ated.

Moncrief[8] notes a 1954 patent by Du Pont[9] which describes a polyurethane spandex fiber based on copolymerizing polyethylene glycol and tolylene-2,4-diisocyanate in the presence of water and a small amount of acid chloride. It had a tensile strength of 13.8 MPa and and elongation at break of 500 %.

In April of 1958 Du Pont[10] introduced to the trade an experimental segmented polyurethane identified as Fiber K. This fiber was commercialized in 1959 under the Lycra trademark and was later revealed to be a segmented polyether urethane from methylene bis (4-phenyl isocyanate).

In 1957 Schollenberger[11] presented a paper on Polyurethan VC, a "virtually crosslinked elastomer". This was a linear polymer prepared from diphenylmethan-p,p'-diisocyanate, adipic acid and butanediol-1,4. The polymer was completely soluble with high elasticity, high extensibility, and excellent resistance to tear and abrasion. There was no explanation of the virtual cross-linking mechanism.

Charch and Shivers[12] in 1959 published a paper on elastomeric condensation block copoly-mers which gave a very useful discussion of the stress-decay and tensile recovery properties of condensation block copolymers that had different amounts of hard-crystalline and soft low-melting copolymer blocks. The authors viewed these as prototypes of a very large family of condensation elastomers which combine stiff and flexible segments in the same polymer chain. More detailed discussions of this paper are presented in Chapters 2 and 8. It is interesting to note that the paper, which came close to describing the essentials of elastomeric, multisegmented thermoplastic elastomers, was oriented to elastic fibers and published in the Textile Research Journal.

However, it was not until 1966 that Cooper and Tobolsky[13] compared the properties of Polyurethan VC with those of an anionically polymerized, triblock poly(styrene-b-butadiene-b-styrene) copolymer (S-B-S). They concluded that the presence of the segregated hard and soft blocks in the polyurethane, rather than the hydrogen bonding, was the source of the thermoplastic elastomer behavior.

In addition to Goodrich at least five other companies have manufactured and sold thermoplastic polyurethane elastomer in the U.S.A. These products have processed well in thermoplastic equipment and have shown very good elastomeric properties. Abrasion and tear resistance have been outstanding and the materials have been very successful commercially.

Professor Otto Bayer and his coworkers at Bayer A. G. in Leverkusen have accomplished major developments in polyurethane elastomers and thermoplastic polyurethane elastomers. The editors were delighted when Dr. W. Meckel, Dr. W. Goyert and Dr. W. Wieder of Bayer A. G. agreed to write Chapter 2 – Thermoplastic Polyurethane Elastomers.

The majority of thermoplastic elastomers are block or graft polymers. During the late 60's and through the 70's there was a very active interest in block polymers as evidenced by the number of comprehensive texts and proceedings of symposia[14-21]. The most commonly applied terminology for block polymers uses A to represent a block of A mer units and similarly, B, C, and etc. Thus A–B represents a diblock polymer, A–B–C a triblock polymer in which all the segments are polymerized from different monomers, and A–B–A represents two terminal A blocks and a B center block.

The following representations are widely used:

$$A\text{--}B \qquad A\text{--}B\text{--}A \qquad\qquad A\text{--}B\text{--}C$$
$$(A\text{--}B)_n \qquad (A\text{--}B)_n x \qquad \text{where } x = \text{coupling agent}$$
$$n = 2,3,4 \ldots$$

$$B \ldots B\text{--}B\text{--}\begin{bmatrix} B \\ | \\ A \end{bmatrix}_n\text{--}B\text{--}B \ldots B$$

where there are n random grafts of
A block on B block

Most authors in discussing block polymers will use the first letter of the monomer unit to describe the block. For example, a three-block copolymer, poly(styrene-b-butadiene-b-styrene) will be represented by S–B–S.

The first academic reference to block polymer formation that we have noted was reported in 1938 by Bolland and Melville[22] who found that a film of polymethylmethacrylate, deposited on the walls of an evacuated tube, could initiate the polymerization of chloroprene. Melville later concluded[23] that trapped free radicals in the film initiated the second polymerization.

Early $(A\text{--}B)_n$ type block copolymers were made by Hanford and Holmes[5] by reaction of diisocyanate with difunctional polymer. Bayer's Vulcolan elastomer of the early 40's was a diisocyanate/alkylene adipate condensation polymer (see Chapter 2).

An $(A\text{--}B)_n$ block polymer was reported in 1946 by Baxendale et al[24], who linked low molecular weight polystyrene and polymethylacrylate with diisocyanate to form a high molecular weight, multiblock polymer.

Non-ionic detergents based on a triblock A–B–A type polymer with polyethylene oxide end blocks and a polypropylene oxide center block were introduced in 1951 by Lundsted[25].

In 1953 H. F. Mark[26] published a paper on multiblock and multigraft polymers in which the blocks were of the order of 50 monomer units in length. Potential applications of these block polymers were considered mainly from the point of view of detergency and of surface treatment of fibers and films. The preparation of the multiblock and multigraft polymers was also discussed.

A comprehensive review of graft and block copolymers and their syntheses was published by E. H. Immergut and H. F. Mark[27] in 1956. The research of Bateman and coworkers[28] at the British Rubber Producers Research Association showed that graft copolymers of methyl-methacrylate (PMMA) on natural rubber (NR) could exist in two physical forms depending on the precipitation method used. If precipitated by a non-solvent for NR, the NR polymer chains were collapsed and the PMMA chains extended, the resulting material was hard, stiff and non-tacky. If precipitated by a non-solvent for PMMA, the NR chains were extended and the PMMA chains collapsed, the material was soft and flabby. Both of these forms were stable under heavy milling. Merrett[29] discussed these observations in terms of the microsep-aration of phases. He pointed out that once this occurred any attempt to approach homogeneity would be improbable. He postulated that either form of the dry polymer would consist of domains of collapsed chains as a discrete phase in a continuous phase of extended chains. Merrett's comments constitute a precursor event to the domain theory of two phase thermoplastic elastomers which was not postulated as such until several years later.

It is interesting to note Ceresa's comment on our state of knowledge of block and graft polymers in 1962[30]. His book covered the syntheses of 1,400 block or graft polymers. He stated that less than 5 % of the block and graft copolymers described had been isolated with any reasonable purity and that fewer than 20 species had been analysed and characterized fully. He attributed this to the contamination of the product block or graft copolymers with homopolymers. In many cases the block or graft copolymers comprised only a small percentage of the final mixture.

Anionic polymerization systems have been widely used in block polymerizations. However, as Halasa[31], has pointed out, Ziegler and his coworkers[32–35] in the late 1920's and early 1930's laid the foundation for living polymerization by their research on alkali metal and organic derivatives (lithium and alkyllithium), with butadiene, isoprene and piperylene in polar media. These were shown to be "nontermination" systems. The polymeric products were low in molecular weight and high in 1,2-addition polybutadiene, or 3,4-addition polyiso-prene. Thus, the polymers had high Tg's and were resinous in nature.

An economic polymerization system which would produce a high cis-1,4-polyisoprene (the structure of natural rubber) had been a long term objective of the U.S. Synthetic Rubber Research Program. In 1955 Firestone Research reported to the Office of Synthetic Rubber, U.S. Federal Facilities Corporation, a lithium metal catalyst polymerization system which produced high cis-1,4-polyisoprene. The following publication[36], as well as the Goodrich announcement[37] of a high cis-1,4-polyisoprene prepared via a Ziegler coordination catalyst system, aroused a great interest in other rubber research groups. Since the Firestone report was distributed to the operators of the U.S. government owned synthetic rubber plants there is little doubt that those with adequate research facilities quickly turned to an examination of lithium metal initiated polymerizations of isoprene during the years 1955–56.

Shell Development commenced research on lithium metal initiators for isoprene polymeri-zation in 1956. It is apparent that they and others did not go back to the early work of Ziegler. However, it was soon discovered that the initiating species was an alkyllithium and that the system, if sufficiently pure, had no termination step. In 1957 Porter[38], working in a research department with both elastomers and plastics responsibility, described a process for the polymerization of styrene-diene block polymers using alkyllithium initiators. At this point the experimental polymers were not recognized as thermoplastic elastomers but the research contributed importantly to in-house background knowledge.

The alkyllithium polymerization of high cis-1,4-polyisoprene was taken through benchscale process development at Shell Development and then directly to plant scale in a modified styrene-butadiene-rubber (SBR) plant. This resulted in the first commercial production of high cis-polyisoprene in 1959[39].

Crouch and Short[40] of Phillips discussed the use of S–B block copolymers, although not identified as such, in 1961. The polymers were produced commercially in 1962 and identified[41] as S–B block polymers in 1964.

Szwarc, Levy and Milkovich[42, 43, 44] rediscovered the anionic living polymer systems in 1956, using sodium naphthalene diinitiators in tetrahydrofuran (THF) to prepare styrene-isoprene block copolymers. By the time the Szwarc papers appeared most of the major research groups working with isoprene polymerizations based on alkyllithium initiators were aware of the living polymer nature of these systems. Sodium naphthalene diinitiators required polar solvents such as THF. This resulted in very high 3,4-addition polyisoprene which was not useful as an elastomer. Thus, the Szwarc results were not directly applicable in the ongoing elastomer research projects.

In 1961 the staff of the Synthetic Rubber Research Laboratory of Shell Chemical were examining solutions to problems of excessive flow and poor green strength of high cis-1,4-polyisoprene, which was in commercial production at that time, and of alkyllithium polybutadiene. As a part of the experimental program low molecular weight polyisoprene and polybutadienes were prepared with very short end blocks of polystyrene, that is poly-styrene-polyisoprene-polystyrene (S–I–S) triblock copolymers, and the corresponding S–B–S. These polymers were pressed into flat sheets for determination of green strength. When tested the sheets were found to have very high tensile strength, high elongations at break, and very rapid elastic returns (snap), without any vulcanization step. The sheets were soluble in toluene, that is no chemical cross-links had been formed.

The Research Laboratory at that time fortunately also housed a polystyrene research group fully equipped with thermoplastic forming processes. The combined research groups were quick to recognize the potential of thermoplastic elastomers and to evolve an explanation – the domain theory. Physical properties and thermoplastic processability of the S–I–S and S–B–S samples were so outstanding that the incentives to carry through the commercialization were clear.

The discovery of the S–I–S and S–B–S triblock thermoplastic elastomers was clearly serendipitous and drew on much research background[39]. Three factors of importance leading up to this discovery can be identified;

1. The in-house development and commercialization of alkyllithium polymerization of high cis-1,4-polyisoprene.
2. Early scouting research, also in-house, on a styrene-diene block polymer process.
3. Existence at the discovery location of an R&D staff with long experience in both elastomers and plastics.

The triblock styrene-diene thermoplastic elastomers were announced in October 1965[45] and the domain theory described in a paper presented in 1967[46].

Chapter 3, Thermoplastic Elastomers Based on Polystyrene-Polydiene Block Copolymers, is written by Geoffrey Holden and N. R. Legge, both members of the research team who discovered these materials in the 60's.

Following the announcement[45] of these styrene-diene thermoplastic elastomers and the publication of papers on the domain theory[47, 48] there was a tremendous surge of interest in thermoplastic elastomers and in the two phase systems[49]. One of the most active of the academic research groups which studied the anionic polymerization systems and polymer properties of the block copolymers was at the University of Akron. The editors invited Professor Maurice Morton, Regents Professor Emeritus of Polymer Science, and Retired Director of the Institute of Polymer Science of the University of Akron, to write Chapter 4, Research on Anionic Three-Block Copolymers. The editors were pleased that he accepted and agreed to fit this project into his busy schedule of retirement. In Chapter 4 Professor Morton has covered most of the research done on this subject at the Institute of Polymer Science.

A. V. Tobolsky in 1958[50] predicted that "new block polymers might be synthesized, one block being composed of linear polyethylene, or isotactic polypropylene and the other block being a random copolymer of ethylene and propylene. Such a polymer would . . . have high melting crystalline regions, and amorphous regions of low Tg. Blends of different varieties of ethylene propylene polymers may also prove interesting." E. G. Kontos of Uniroyal had done some thought provoking research on "living α-olefin polymerizations"[51–54]. These polymers were composed of random amorphous ethylene/propylene blocks and linear homopolymer polyethylene blocks, or isotactic polypropylene blocks. The semi-crystalline stereo-block copolymers were said to have "plastic-rubber properties"[53]. Although these polymer systems were not commercialized the editors believed that it would be useful to have this area reviewed. We were very fortunate in locating Dr. C.-K. Shih and Dr. A. C. L. Su of Du Pont who have done some recent research and offered to review the previous studies as part of Chapter 5, Poly α-Olefin Based Thermoplastic Elastomers.

The next segment of our preliminary agenda was the melt-mixed blends of EPDM and polypropylene. Here the editors were attracted by the excellent series of papers, commencing in 1978 and continuing through 1985[55–64], presented by A. Y. Coran et al, of Monsanto, on EPDM-Polypropylene Thermoplastic Vulcanizates.

However, before proceeding to discuss these melt-mixed blends in which the elastomer was dynamically vulcanized (during the melt-mixing), the editors decided to cover the area of elastomer-thermoplastic blends without dynamic vulcanization. We invited Dr. James R. Wolfe, Jr. of Du Pont to review this subject for us in Chapter 6, Elastomer-Thermoplastic Blends as Thermoplastic Elastomers. Dr. Wolfe has provided us a very careful review of this subject which we believe will surprise our readers by the wealth of information to which we have paid little attention in recent years. In this area there is mention of some very early thermoplastic elastomers.

The editors are grateful to A. Y. Coran for agreeing to write Chapter 7, Thermoplastic Elastomers Based on Elastomer-Thermoplastic Blends Dynamically Vulcanized, and for including also a discussion of the earlier work by others. Coran's research is outstanding in coverage of the polymers examined, the breadth of the physical evaluations, the application of the results to guidelines for these systems and in the commercialization of several very useful new products.

From the time of their early work on segmented liquid and solid elastomeric polyurethane gums (1950–1960), and throughout the studies of the high modulus elastomeric fibers such as Lycra, Du Pont scientists had been seeking a unique species of thermoplastic elastomer to round out their line of specialty elastomeric polymers. When their research showed that the urethanes had relatively poor melt stability because of a tendency to revert to mac-romonomer segments, and that this deficiency could not be corrected through use of economical structural variations, they turned back to the early work on segmented conden-sation polymers. These had produced polyamides and polyesters of great interest as elastic fibers and had given indications that high modulus rubbers could be made from segmented polymers with hard and soft segments.

In 1968 Witsiepe[65] discovered an outstanding new variant of this class in the form of a segmented copolyester based on poly(tetramethylene terephthalate) and poly(oxytetra-methylene)glycol. In Chapter 8, Thermoplastic Polyester Elastomers, Dr. G. K. Hoeschele and Dr. R. K. Adams describe the background for this discovery, and then review the structure, morphology, and the physical and mechanical properties of these materials. The morphology has been of special interest because these polymers appear to have an entirely different structure from the S–B–S triblock copolymers. In the copolyester there seem to be two interpenetrating, more or less co-continuous phases, made up of a network of crystalline polybutylene terephthalate domains in a co-continuous polyether terephthalate matrix. Because of the unusual structure they have extraordinary physical properties. Drs. R. K. Adams and G. K. Hoeschele have had long experience with high performance polyuretha-nes and esters in the Du Pont Products Research Laboratory from which Dr. Adams is now retired.

When the copolyesters revealed the virtues of crystalline hard segments in thermoplastic elastomers others were quick in the search for new polymers which might show special advantages[66,67]. In Chapter 9A Drs. R. G. Nelb II, A. T. Chen and K. Onder of the Research staff of Dow Chemical Company describe the synthesis of a class of copoly-etheramides or copolyesteramides through condensations involving the reaction of an aromatic isocyanate with a carboxylic acid to form an aromatic amide. When applied to suitable macromonomers and carboxylic acids a variety of structures results. Hard segments of high melting point are accessible through proper choice of diisocyanate and carboxylic acid. The resulting polymers have good high temperature mechanical properties.

Then in Chapter 9B Dr. G. Deleens describes the synthesis and properties of a new class of polyetheramides prepared by polycondensation of polyether diols with dicarboxylated polyamides. These products have fine mechanical properties somewhat like the copolyesters and are said to possess good thermal stability. The upper use temperature is determined by the particular polyamide hard segment employed. Dr. Deleens is the discoverer of these products and directs research on them by the staff of ATOCHEM in France.

In a recent review[68] of research and patent activity in thermoplastic elastomers, ionomeric systems were prominent in both areas. The editors decided that this was another case in which some of the early work should be set forth as a preamble. We asked R. W. Rees of Du Pont to describe the early research on these products, including Surlyn. The result is Chapter 10A, Ionomeric Thermoplastic Elastomers: Early Research – Surlyn and Related Products. R. W. Rees is the discoverer of the Surlyn polymers and the first to postulate, in 1964[69], the clustering of the ionic structures in these systems. He and his collaborators noted the differences in cross-links produced by different ion pairs, e.g., the ionomers based on Na, K, NH_4 were thermally reversible; similar materials based on Zn and Mg were very high melting and intractable.

For a review of ionomeric systems overall we invited Professor W. J. MacKnight of the University of Massachusetts and Dr. R. D. Lundberg of Exxon Company to contribute. Their comprehensive discussion is found in Chapter 10B, Research on Ionomeric Systems.

At this point in the book we have included chapters on the research and development of the major types of thermoplastic elastomers. We now turn to an essential element, Chapter 11,

Theoretical Aspects of Block Copolymers, by. Dr. Dale J. Meier, Professor of Polymer Physics, Michigan Molecular Institute. Dr. Meier was very active in formulating and expanding the theoretical basis of the domain theory in the triblock polystyrene-polydiene copolymers in the early 60's, and has continued his interest in the theory of block copolymers over the past twenty years.

The objective of Chapter 12, Research on Thermoplastic Elastomers, was to invite a number of outstanding academic research directors to describe recent research of their laboratories. The editors did not request specific topics but rather suggested that the research leaders might describe a single project, or summarize work done by the laboratory in recent years. The choice was theirs.

It was difficult to decide on the order of the sections. Finally the editors selected an order, secure in the knowledge that most readers would approach Chapter 12 with their own specific interest firmly in mind, and decide their own order of reading by title and author. Following are some comments:

Section 1 – Modeling the Elastic Behavior of Poly(Styrene-b-Butadiene-b-Styrene) Block
          Copolymers
          J. K. Bard and C. I. Chung

Professor C. I. Chung is Director of the Materials Engineering Department of Rensselaer Polytechnic Institute; Dr. J. K. Bard is now at the Research Center of Hercules Inc., in Wilmington, Delaware.

The paper is a study of the mechanical properties of phase separated polymer systems. The material is considered as a filled elastomer. Concepts of the theories of rubberlike elasticity, modified to account for the presence of the phase separated structure, are used to model the mechanical behavior.

Section 2 – Interfacial Activity of Block Copolymers
          G. Riess

Professeur Riess is Director of the Laboratoire de Chimie Macromoleculaire, Ecole Nationale Superieure de Chimie de Mulhouse in France.

In Section 2 Professeur Riess presents a survey of the work done in his laboratory on block copolymers. This has been the principal research area there for some 25 years. Some specific synthesis techniques, to produce polymers with thermoplastic elastomer properties are first described. Professeur Riess then discusses the interfacial activity of block copolymers in the presence of solvents and in polymeric emulsions. Finally, he shows how the interfacial characteristics can be used to understand the behavior of polymer blends and their morphology.

Section 3 – Order-Disorder Transition in Block Copolymers
          T. Hashimoto

Professor Takeji Hashimoto is Director of the Department of Polymer Chemistry of Kyoto University in Kyoto, Japan.

The nature of the order-disorder transition in block copolymers has been explored extensively in recent years. Professor Hashimoto and his coworkers have been active contributors. He has pointed out that this problem bears on such industrial applications of block copolymers as thermoplastic elastomers, pressure sensitive hot-melt adhesives, viscosity stabilizers for oils, etc. For example, if the block copolymers are in the disordered state at processing temperatures their viscosities are low – an advantage in processability. On the other hand, if they are in the ordered state at processing temperatures they exhibit high viscosity and remarkable non-Newtonian behavior.

The order-disorder transition of block copolymers is also of great theoretical importance. It is related to structure and structure evolution (ordering) and dissolution (disordering) in a cooperative system – a fundamental problem in equilibrium and non-equilibrium statistical physics in the condensed state.

Section 4 – Chain Conformation in Block Copolymers by Small Angle Neutron Scattering
             J. A. Miller and S. L. Cooper

Professor Stuart L. Cooper is Chairman of the Department of Chemical Engineering, The University of Wisconsin in Madison, Wisconsin. Dr. J. A. Miller is located at 3M Center in St. Paul, Minnesota.

Miller and Cooper have applied small angle neutron scattering (SANS) to phase separated block copolymer systems. They review the theory of applying SANS to evaluate chain conformation in these systems and describe experimental results on polyether polyurethanes and on polyether-polyesters.

Section 5 – Compatibilization of Polymer Blends by Styrene/Hydrogenated Butadiene
             Block Copolymers
             D. R. Paul

Dr. D. R. Paul is The T. Brockett Hudson Professor and Chairman of the Department of Chemical Engineering at the University of Texas at Austin.

Professor Paul in 1978[70] presented a comprehensive review of the expected action of block copolymer molecules as interfacial agents in immiscible polymer mixtures. In Section 5 he provides a more focused review of results which have been published since then. The discussion here is limited to the use of styrene/hydrogenated butadiene block copolymers (S–EB–S) as the compatibilizing agents. The systems considered are those in which these block copolymers are added to mixtures of polystyrene (PS) with low density polyethylene (LDPE), high density polyethylene (HDPE), and polypropylene (PP). One example is included in which the block copolymer segments are not miscible with either homopolymer – HDPE and poly(ethylene terephthalate) (PET). In addition to results from his own laboratory, Professor Paul has included results from Teyssie and Heikens. Throughout the discussions of these systems Professor Paul attempts to reach conclusions concerning mechanisms and the optimum structure for compatibilizing block copolymers.

Section 6 – Novel Block Copolymers, Thermoplastic Elastomers and Polymer Blends
             R. Jerome, R. Fayt and Ph. Teyssie

This section is a contribution from the Laboratoire de Chemie Macromoleculaire et de Catalyse Organique of the Universite de Liege, under the direction of Professeur Ph. Teyssie.

The review illustrates the broad scope of this field of research through examples developed in this laboratory. It should be noted that Professeur Teyssie's group and the group in Dr. D. R. Paul's laboratory both worked with the polystyrene-polyethylene blends. When we informed these gentlemen of our plans for Chapter 12, they indicated that this might be an overlap between their contributions. After some discussion Professeur Teyssie suggested that Professor Paul include this area in his section and that Professeur Teyssie's group would not dwell on this area except for reference. The editors much appreciate Professeur Teyssie's courtesy.

Professeur Teyssie's review of the research done in his laboratory covers a very broad range of subjects. The synthesis techniques described have extensive application in block polymer research and development and illustrate the potential of macromolecular engineering.

Section 7 – Relation Between Molecular Structure-Morphology-Properties in Segmented
             Thermoplastic Block Copolymers
             G. Wegner

Professor G. Wegner is the Director of the Max-Planck Institut for Polymerforschung in Mainz.

Professor Wegner describes the work of his research group on model compounds (oligomers), phase formation and morphology, mechanical and thermal properties of polyetheresters, polyetheresteramides and, to some extent, polyurethanes.

Section 8 – Thermoplastic Elastomer Studies 1968–1988
             James E. McGrath

Professor James E. McGrath directs a large research group at the Department of Chemistry, and Polymers Materials and Interfaces Laboratory at Virginia Polytechnic Institute and State University in Blacksburg, Virginia.

In his review of research from 1968, extending through 1988, Professor McGrath discusses: diene containing block copolymers, urea and urethane systems, and siloxane containing block copolymers.

Chapter 13, Applications of Thermoplastic Elastomers, by Dr. Geoffrey Holden of Shell Development Company, Houston, Texas covers applications of most of the commercially available thermoplastic elastomers and their physical properties. Dr. Holden has been active in the field of thermoplastic elastomer research since the early 60's, and has written many papers on the rheology, physical properties, compounding and applications of thermoplastic elastomers.

In Chapter 14, S. Davison, W. P. Gergen and R. G. Lutz discuss Hydrogenated Block Copolymers in Thermoplastic Interpenetrating Networks. The authors have been active in Shell Development Company thermoplastic elastomer research for over twenty years, specializing in rheology, morphology and physical properties of the polymers and blends. The authors describe the structure and properties of hydrogenated diene block copolymers, poly(styrene-b-ethylene-co-butylene-b-styrene), S–EB–S, compared to those of poly(styrene-b-butadiene-b-styrene) S–B–S, of comparable block lengths. They then go on to discuss the morphology and properties of interpenetrating network blends of S–EB–S with polypropylene, polybutylene, nylon, polybutylene terephthalate, polycarbonate and other thermoplastics.

Chapter 15, Future Trends, by H. E. Schroeder and N. R. Legge, reviews the potential research advance in thermoplastic elastomers based on the requirements for new product properties on the one hand, and on the opportunities which may be possible in view of the contributions described in the preceding pages. Both of these authors have previously presented views of the futures of thermoplastic elastomers[71,68].

References

1. W. L. Semon, US 1, 929, 453 (Oct. 10, 1933) (to B. F. Goodrich Co.); W. L. Semon, *Ann. Tech. Conf. Soc. Plast. Eng. 30,* 693 (1972)
2. D. E. Henderson, US 2, 330, 353 (Sept. 28, 1943) (to B. F. Goodrich Co.)
3. Otto Bayer, et al., Ger Patent 728, 981 (1937) (to I. G. Farben)
4. A. E. Christ, W. E. Hanford US 2, 333, 639 (1940) (to Du Pont)
5. W. E. Hanford, D. F. Holmes, US 2, 284, 896 (June 2, 1942) (to Du Pont)
6. (to ICI) Brit. Pat. 580, 524 (1941) 574, 134 (1942)
7. M. D. Snyder, US 2, 632, 031 (1952) (to Du Pont)
8. R. W. Moncrief, *Man-Made Fibers,* 6th Edn., 1975, Halsted Press, John Wiley and Sons, New York, p. 489
9. Ibid., p. 489, US 2, 692, 873 (1954) (to Du Pont)
10. B. P. Corbman, *Textiles: Fibers to Fabric,* 4th Edn., McGraw-Hill, New York, 1975, p. 462
11. C. S. Schollenberger, US 2, 871, 218 (1955) (to B. F. Goodrich). C. S. Schollenberger, H. Scott and G. R. Moore, paper presented at the ACS Rubber Div. Mtg., Sept. 13, 1957, *Rubber World, 137* 549 (1958), *Rubber Chem. Tech. 35* 742 (1962)
12. W. H. Charch, J. C. Shivers, *Textile Research Jour. 29,* 536 (1959)
13. S. L. Cooper, A. V. Tobolsky, *Textile Research Jour. 36,* 800 (1966)
14. *Block Polymers;* S. L. Aggarwal, Ed.; Proc. Am. Chem. Soc. Symposium, New York, 1969; Plenum Press, New York, 1970
15. *Colloidal and Morphological Behavior of Block and Graft Copolymers;* G. E. Molau, Ed.; Plenum Press, New York, 1971
16. *Block Polymers;* D. C. Allport, W. H. Janes, Eds.; John Wiley and Sons, New York, 1972
17. *Block and Graft Polymerization;* R. J. Ceresa, Ed.; John Wiley and Sons, New York, 1972
18. *Block and Graft Copolymers;* J. J. Burke, V. Weiss, Eds.; Syracuse Univ. Press, 1973
19. *Block Copolymers;* A. Noshay and J. E. McGrath: Academic Press, New York, 1977
20. *Multiphase Polymers;* S. L. Cooper, G. M. Estes, Eds.; Advances in Chemistry Series No. 176, Am. Chem. Soc., Washington, D. C., 1979
21. *Handbook of Thermoplastic Elastomers;* B. M. Walker, Ed., Van Nostrand Reinhold, New York, 1979
22. J. H. Bolland, H. W. Melville, Proc. *First Rubber Technology Conference,* London; W. Heffer, London, 1938, p. 239
23. H. W. Melville, *J. Chem. Soc.* 414 (1946)
24. J. H. Baxendale, M. G. Evans and G. S. Parks; *Trans. Faraday Soc. 42,* 155 (1946)
25. L. G. Lundsted; *J. Am. Oil Chem. Soc. 28,* 294 (1951)
26. H. F. Mark; *Textile Research Jour. 23,* 294 (1953)
27. E. H. Immergut, H. F. Mark; *Makromolekular Chem. 18/18,* 322 (1956)
28. L. C. Bateman; *Ind. Eng. Chem. 49,* 704 (1957)
29. F. M. Merrett; *J. Polymer Science 24,* 462 (1957)
30. R. J. Ceresa, Ed., *Block and Graft Copolymers,* Butterworths, Washington, D. C., 1962
31. A. F. Halasa, *Rubber Chem. Tech. 54,* 627 (1981)
32. K. Ziegler, K. Bahr, *Chem. Ber. 61,* 253 (1928)
33. K. Ziegler, H. Colonius and O. Schater, *Ann. Chem. 473,* 36 (1929)
34. K. Ziegler, O. Schater, *Ann. Chem. 479,* 150 (1930)
35. K. Ziegler, et al., *Ann. Chem. 511,* 64 (1934)
36. F. E. Stavely, et al., Paper presented to the ACS Rubber Division, Philadelphia, PA, Nov. 1955, *Ind. Eng. Chem. 48,* 778 (1956)
37. S. E. Horne, et al., *Ind. Eng. Chem. 48,* 784 (1956)
38. L. M. Porter, US 3, 149, 182, 1964 (to Shell Oil Co.), filed Oct. 28, 1957
39. N. R. Legge; *Thermoplastic Elastomers Based on Three-Block Copolymers – A Successful Innovation,* presented at a meeting of the ACS Rubber Division, May 4, 1982; *Chemtech 13,* p. 630–639 (1983)
40. W. W. Crouch, J. N. Short, *Rubber and Plastics Age 42,* 276 (1961)
41. H. E. Railsback, C. C. Beard and J. R. Haws, *Rubber Age 94,* 583 (1964)
42. M. Szwarc, M. Levy and R. Milkovich, *Jour. Am. Chem. Soc. 78,* 2656 (1956)
43. M. Szwarc, *Nature 178,* 1168 (1956)

44. M. Szwarc, *Polym. Prepr. 26,* (1) 198 (1985)
45. J. T. Bailey et al., *Thermoplastic Elastomers,* presented at a meeting of the ACS Rubber Disvision, October 22, 1965; *Rubber Age* 1966, Oct. p. 69
46. G. Holden, E. T. Bishop and N. R. Legge, *Proceedings International Rubber Conference,* 1967; Maclaren and Sons, London (1968), p. 287–309; *J. Polym. Sci. Part C 26,* 37 (1969)
47. E. T. Bishop, S. Davison, *J. Polym. Sci. Part C 26,* 54 (1969)
48. D. J. Meier, *J. Polym. Sci. Part C 26,* 81 (1969)
49. N. R. Legge et al., "Block Polymers and Related Materials", in *Applied Polymer Science,* Second Edn., R. W. Tess and G. W. Poehlein, Eds., ACS Symp. Series 285 (1985), p. 186

50. A. V. Tobolsky, *Rubber World 138,* 857 (1959)
51. E. G. Kontos, E. K. Easterbrook and R. D. Gilbert, *J. Polym. Sci. 61,* 69 (1962)
52. E. G. Kontos, US 3, 378, 606 (1968) (to Uniroyal)
53. E. G. Kontos, US 3, 853, 969 (1974) (to Uniroyal)
54. D. Puett, K. J. Smith, A. Ciferri and E. G. Kontos, *J. Chem. Phys. 40,* (1) 253 (1964)
55. A. Y. Coran, R. P. Patel, paper presented at the International Rubber Conference, Kiev, USSR, October 1978
56. A. Y. Coran, R. P. Patel, Rubber-Thermoplastic Compositions, Part I EPDM-Polypropylene Thermoplastic Vulcanizates, *Rubber Chem. Tech. 53,* 141 (1980)
57. A. Y. Coran, R. P. Patel, Rubber-Thermoplastic Compositions, Part II NBR-Nylon Thermoplastic Elastomeric Compositions, *Rubber Chem. Tech. 53,* 781 (1980)
58. A. Y. Coran, R. P. Patel, Rubber-Thermoplastic Compositions, Part III Predicting Elastic Moduli of Melt-Mixed Rubber-Plastic Blends, *Rubber Chem. Tech. 54,* 91 (1981)
59. A. Y. Coran, R. P. Patel, Rubber-Thermoplastic Compositions, Part IV Thermoplastic Vulcanizates from Various Rubber-Plastic Combinations, *Rubber Chem. Tech. 54,* 892 (1981)
60. A. Y. Coran, R. P. Patel and D. Williams, Rubber-Thermoplastic Compositions, Part V Selecting Polymers for Thermoplastic Vulcanizates, *Rubber Chem. Tech. 55,* 116 (1982)
61. A. Y. Coran, R. P. Patel and D. Williams, Rubber-Plastic Compositions, Part VI The Swelling of Vulcanized-Plastic Compositions in Fluids, *Rubber Chem. Tech. 55,* 1063 (1982)
62. A. Y. Coran, R. P. Patel, Rubber-Thermoplastic Compositions, Part VII, Chlorinated Polyethylene Rubber-Nylon Compositions, *Rubber Chem. Tech. 56,* 210 (1983)
63. A. Y. Coran, R. P. Patel, Rubber Thermoplastic Compositions, Part VIII Nitrile Rubber Polyolefin Blends with Technological Compatibilization, *Rubber Chem. Tech. 56,* 1045 (1983)
64. A. Y. Coran, R. P. Patel and D. Williams-Headd, Rubber-Thermoplastic Compositions, Part IX Blends of Dissimilar Rubbers and Plastics with Technological Compatibilization, *Rubber Chem. Tech. 58,* 1014 (1985)
65. W. K. Witsiepe, US 3, 651, 014 (Mar. 21, 1972) (to Du Pont)
66. A. T. Chen et al, US 4, 129, 715 (Dec. 12, 1978) (to Dow Chemical Co.)
67. R. G. Nelb II, et al, *SPE Ann. Tech. Conf. (ANTEC),* Boston (May 4–7, 1981), p. 421
68. N. R. Legge, *Elastomerics 117,* (10) 17 (1985)
69. R. W. Rees, "Chemistry of Surlyn A Ionomers", *Mod. Plastic 42,* 209 (1964)
70. D. R. Paul, Chapter 12 in *Polymer Blends, Vol. 2,* D. R. Paul and S. Newman, Eds., Academic, New York, 1978
71. H. E. Schroeder, *Kautschuk Gummi Kunststoffe 35,* 661 (1982)

Chapter 2

THERMOPLASTIC POLYURETHANE ELASTOMERS

W. Meckel, W. Goyert, W. Wieder

Contents

W. Meckel, W. Goyert, W. Wieder, Bayer AG, KA-Forschung, D-4047 Dormagen, West Germany

1   INTRODUCTION

Polyurethane chemistry opened the way to a new class of high performance materials such as coatings, adhesives, elastomers, fibres and foams. Based on a simple polyaddition reaction, the polyurethanes proved to be very versatile polymers. Materials with tailor-made properties can be produced from the broad variety of the chemicals used. Today, thermoplastic polyurethane elastomers play an important role within the rapidly growing family of thermoplastic elastomers. Since thermoplastic polyurethane elastomers (TPU) were the first, homogeneous, thermoplastically processable elastomers, let us consider the history, which led to the discovery and development of TPU.

Pioneering polyurethane work was done by Otto Bayer and his coworkers of I.G. Farbenindustrie at Leverkusen, Germany (now Bayer AG) in 1937[1]. Their original target was to duplicate or improve the properties of synthetic polyamide fibres. Subsequently, the elastomer properties of polyurethanes were recognized by DuPont[2] and by ICI[3]. By the 1940's polyurethanes were produced on an industrial scale[4]. This first so-called "I-rubber", however, had very poor properties. To overcome the deficiencies which were supposed to stem from a non-regular elastomeric network, a polyurethane elastomer was synthesized which consisted of linear polyesters and 2-nitro-4,4'-diisocyanato-biphenyl[5]. In a second step the nitro groups were to be reduced to form azo linkages. Surprisingly, this later step proved to be unnecessary, because the original polymer, which was chain extended by water, already showed interesting elastomeric behaviour. A similar result was obtained when the nitrodiisocyanate was replaced by naphthalene-1.5-diisocyanate[6]. These unexpected results were explained in terms of the following reaction sequence[7]: First the strictly linear hydroxyl terminated polyester reacts with an excess diisocyanate to form a diisocyanate prepolymer. This prepolymer is subsequently chain extended by water, leading to urea linkages. The urea linkages react with further diisocyanate to build an elastomeric network. Chain extension by short chain diols proved to be the breakthrough to polyurethane elastomers, which were tradenamed by Bayer as Vulkollan®. In the USA, Chemigum SL® was an early Vulkollan-type polyester urethane elastomer which was developed by Seeger et al. of the Goodyear Tire and Rubber Co.[8]. DuPont marketed Adiprene® a polyether urethane.

Early polyurethane elastomers consisted of basically three components:

1. a polyester- or polyether macrodiol,
2. a chain extender such as water, a short-chain diol, or a diamine
3. a bulky diisocyanate, e. g. naphthalene-1.5-diisocyanate (NDI).

However, these polyurethane elastomers were not yet real thermoplastic polyurethane elastomers in the proper sense of the term, since their melting temperature was higher than the decomposition temperature of the urethane linkages.

Great progress was achieved when NDI was replaced by diphenylmethane-4.4'-diisocyanate (MDI) in the above mentioned three component system. Schollenberger of B. F. Goodrich described[10] a TPU in 1958. Somewhat earlier DuPont announced a Spandex fiber called Lycra®, a polyurethane based on MDI. By the early 1960's Goodrich marketed Estane®, Mobay Texin®, Upjohn Pellethane® in the USA. Bayer and Elastogran marketed Desmopan® and Elastollan® respectively in Europe.

In the following years much effort was spent to elucidate the nature of bonding, structure-property-relationship, etc. Today it is well established that TPU owe their unique properties to a domain structure which is achieved by the phase separated systems of these multi-block polymers.

One type of block, the hard segment, is formed by addition of the chain extender, e. g. butanediol, to the diisocyanate, e. g. MDI. The other type is the soft segment and consists of the long flexible polyether or polyester chains which interconnect two hard segments, Figure 1.

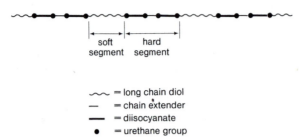

soft   hard
segment   segment

∿ = long chain diol
— = chain extender
▬ = diisocyanate
● = urethane group

Figure 1   Schematic representation of a TPU composed of diisocyanate, long chain diol, and chain extender

At room temperature, the low melting soft segments are incompatible with the polar high melting hard segments, which leads to a microphase separation. A part of the driving force for phase separation is the development of crystallinity of the hard segments. Upon heating above the melting temperature of the hard segments, the polymer forms a homogeneous viscous melt which can be processed by thermoplastic techniques such as injection molding, extrusion, blow molding, etc. Subsequent cooling leads again to segregation of hard and soft segments.

Usually, the soft segments form an elastomer matrix which accounts for the reversibly elastic properties of TPU, with the hard segments acting as multifunctional tie points functioning both as physical crosslinks and reinforcing fillers. However, these crosslinks can be reversibly overcome by heat or by solvation. Then by cooling or on desolvation a TPU network is reformed. Thus, the TPU network was described as "virtually crosslinked"[10]. To obtain thermoplasticity, the sum of functionalities of the raw materials should be close to 2.00. This ensures formation of high molecular weight linear chains with no or only very few branch points[11-13].

2   RAW MATERIALS

Thermoplastic polyurethanes are generally made from long chain polyols with an average molecular weight of 600 to 4000, chain extenders with a molecular weight of 61 to 400 and polyisocyanates.

Among the broad variety of possible starting materials only a limited number of raw materials are of practical interest. However, as a result of the wide range of hard to soft segment variations possible, TPU can be formulated which range from soft flexible, elastomeric materials to more brittle, high modulus plastics.

The most common raw materials and their most typical influence on the properties of TPU are as follows.

2.1 Soft Segments

The long flexible soft segment largely controls the low temperature properties, the solvent resistance and the weather resistant properties of TPU.

There are two types of flexible segments of importance: the hydroxyl terminated polyesters and the hydroxyl terminated polyethers.

2.1.1 Polyesters

The typical hydroxyl terminated polyester is made from adipic acid and an excess of glycol such as ethylene glycol, butanediol-1,4, hexanediol-1,6, neopentyl glycol or mixtures of these diols[14].

The reaction is carried out at temperatures up to 200 °C and the resulting polyester should have an acid number of less than two. As in all polymeric structures, the polyesters are composed of all possible oligomers ranging from the monomeric glycol to high molecular weight species: the distribution follows a Flory-probability[15]. The properties of the elastomer are governed mainly by the overall molecular weight of the polyester and only to a minor degree by the molecular weight distribution[16].

Starting from adipic acid and straight chain diols, the resulting polyesters are crystalline products with melting points up to 50–60 °C. The crystallinity can be easily reduced either by using mixtures of diols, e. g. butanediol-1,4 with ethylene glycol or hexanediol-1,6 and hexanediol-1,6 with neopentyl glycol or by using mixtures of polyesters.

The use of other acids has also been reported, e. g. azelaic acid, ortho- or terephthalic acid either alone or in mixture with adipic acid. Generally, the presence of aromatic or cycloaliphatic rings in the acid or in the diol increases the glass transition temperature of the polyester.

There are two special classes of polyesters of commercial interest, the polycaprolactones and the aliphatic polycarbonates.

The polycaprolactones are made from ε-caprolactone and a bifunctional initiator, e. g. hexanediol-1,6[17]. The properties of these polyesters are very similar to poly(butanediol-1,4 hexanediol-1,6 adipate) glycols.

The polycarbonates offer excellent hydrolytic stability[18]. They are made from diols, e. g. hexanediol-1,6, and phosgene or by transesterification with low molecular weight carbonates like diethyl or diphenyl carbonate.

2.1.2 Polyethers

There are two classes of polyethers of technical importance, the poly(oxypropylene) glycols and the poly(oxytetramethylene) glycols.

The poly(oxypropylene) glycols are made by the base catalyzed addition of propylene oxide and/or ethylene oxide to bifunctional initiators, e. g. propylene glycol or water[19]. By using propylene oxide the resulting polyethers have predominantly secondary hydroxyl groups at the ends. Primary hydroxyl groups are introduced by using higher proportions of ethylene oxide especially at the end ("tipping") of the reaction. Due to side reactions, the functionality of poly(oxypropylene) glycols is always lower than the functionality of the initiator. Increasing amounts of allylic and isopropylidene endgroups are generated with increasing molecular weight of the polyether. For example, a poly(oxypropylene) glycol with a molecular weight of 2000 has a functionality of about 1.96 instead of 2.00.

Poly(oxytetramethylene) glycols are made by cationic polymerisation of tetrahydrofuran[20]. The functionality is about 2.00.

The molecular weight distribution of the polyether oligomers follows the Poisson probability equation yielding a less broad distribution compared to the thermodynamically controlled Flory probability[15] of analogous polyesters.

Special polyethers have been claimed in the patent literature to have advantages, however, they have made no major breakthrough in the market for TPU.

Examples are:

Mixed polyethers of tetrahydrofuran and ethylene or propylene oxide[21].

Poly(oxypropylene) glycols grafted with ethylenically unsaturated monomers, e. g. styrene and acrylonitrile[22, 23], polyethers with high proportion of primary hydroxyl groups made by "tipping" with ethylene oxide[24] and mixtures of such polyethers with poly(oxytetramethylene) glycols[25]. Another type of polyether is obtained by the acid catalyzed condensation of bis (2-hydroxyethyl) sulfide and is characterized by the general formula

$$HO-CH_2-CH_2-S(CH_2-CH_2-O-CH_2-CH_2-S-)_x-CH_2-CH_2-OH$$

However, the resulting elastomers, despite their good properties, were not successful due to the generation of a strong odor on processing[26].

Polyacetals from glycols, e. g. hexanediol-1,6, and formaldehyde were also used but with no major success[27]. Mixtures of polyethers and polyesters are of economic interest and TPU with very useful combinations of properties have been obtained[28, 29].

Diene polymers containing hydroxyl groups have attracted some interest[30], however, the distribution of the functionalities within these polyols is too broad, and the physical properties of derived urethanes are deficient at the present time. To overcome polyol functionality deficiencies (< 2.00) or to achieve slight branching in the final polymer, branched polyesters and trifunctional polyethers can be used. However, the average functionality of the raw materials should be close to 2.00.

As mentioned before, the character of the soft segment mainly governs low-temperature flexibility and the longtime ageing properties of TPU. Table I shows the general trends of the more important soft segments.

Despite the fact that the melting points of the polyols are mostly above room temperature, the soft segment in the TPU is normally in the amorphous state. The soft segments crystallize only at very low levels of hard segments or on prolonged cooling. The crystalliza-

TABLE I   Important Polyols[a] and Corresponding Thermoplastics Polyurethane Elastomers[b]

	Polyols		Elastomers	
Polyol Nomenclature	T_e	T_m	T_e	Hydrolytic Stability
Poly(ethylene adipate) glycol	− 46	52	−25	fair
Poly(butylene-1.4 adipate) glycol	− 71	56	−40	good
Poly(ethylene butylene- -1.4 adipate) glycol	− 60	17	−30	fair/good
Poly(hexamethylene 2.2-di-methylpropylene adipate) glycol	− 57	27	−30	good
Polycaprolactone glycol	− 72	59	−40	good
Poly(diethylene glycol adipate) glycol	− 53	/	−30	poor
Poly(hexanediol-1.6 carbonate) glycol	− 62	49	−30	very good
Poly(oxytetramethylene) glycol	−100	32	−80	very good

[a] molecular weight 2000
[b] ca. 85 Shore hardness
T_e: Lower end of glass transition range T_m: melting point
After ref. 31 with permission

tion is noticable as an increase in hardness. However, the crystallization tendency of the soft segment is very well observed during low and medium elongations of polyurethanes, Figure 2. This induced crystallization leads to a self reinforcing effect which is noticed as a higher modulus, compared to elastomers with noncrystalline soft segments. This effect disappears at temperature above the melting points of the soft segment[32, 33]. On the other hand, the induced crystallization leads to a higher permanent set and compression set.

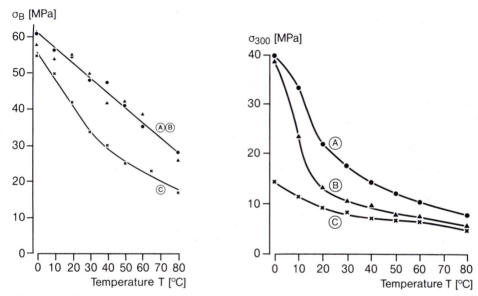

Figure 2   Influence of the soft segment crystallinity on the temperature dependence of the tensile strength at 300 % elongation and the ultimate tensile strength. From ref. 31 with permission; (A) Poly(butylene-1,4 adipate), (B) polycaprolactone, (C) Poly(diethylene glycol adipate)

Thus, the character of the soft segment must be carefully adjusted to match the required property profile of the final application.

The low temperature properties of TPU are governed by the broadness and the location of the glass transition range, defined by starting with the very first melting of the glassy soft segment at T_e and ending at the temperature where the complete soft segment is molten.

The lower end, T_e, of the glass transition temperature range in a low to medium hardness TPU is normally 20–30° above the corresponding temperature of pure soft segment which has a rather narrow glass transition range.

The broadness of the glass transition range depends on the amount of hard segment and the separation of hard and soft segments, increasing with concentration of the hard segments and their resulting intrusions into soft segments. This leads to poorer low temperature properties. Improved low temperature flexibility[34, 35], characterized by a T_e well below room temperature and a narrow glass transition temperature range, is obtained through the use of soft segments which are less compatible with the hard segment as by the use of polyethers. The incompatibility is also increased by increasing the molecular weight of the soft segment[34, 36, 37] or by annealing the elastomer[38].

2.2 Hard Segments

2.2.1 Polyisocyanates

Among the technical polyisocyanates[39] only a very few are suitable for TPU[35].

The most important diisocyanate is 4,4'-diphenylmethane diisocyanate (MDI).

$$OCN-\!\!\left<\!\bigcirc\!\right>\!\!-CH_2-\!\!\left<\!\bigcirc\!\right>\!\!-NCO$$

Other diisocyanates being used or having attracted some interest are the following:

Hexamethylene diisocyanate (HDI).

$$OCN-\!\left(CH_2\right)_{\!6}\!-NCO$$

1-Isocyanato-3-isocyanatomethyl-3,5,5-trimethylcyclohexane (isophorone diisocyanate or IPDI)

$$\begin{array}{c} NCO \\ | \\ H_3C \diagdown \\ H_3C \diagup \end{array}\!\!\!\!\!\!\!\!\begin{array}{c} CH_2-NCO \\ CH_3 \end{array}$$

4,4'-Dicyclohexylmethane diisocyanate (H$_{12}$-MDI),

$$OCN-\!\!\left<\!\bigcirc\!\right>\!\!-CH_2-\!\!\left<\!\bigcirc\!\right>\!\!-NCO$$

3,3'-Dimethyl-4,4'-biphenyl diisocyanate (TODI)[40],

$$OCN-\!\!\left<\!\bigcirc\!\right>\!\!-\!\!\left<\!\bigcirc\!\right>\!\!-NCO$$
$$CH_3 \qquad\qquad CH_3$$

2,4 and 2,6-Toluene diisocyanate (TDI)[41],

$$\begin{array}{cc} CH_3 & CH_3 \\ \bigcirc\!-NCO \ OCN\!\!-\!\!\bigcirc\!-NCO \\ NCO \end{array}$$

1,4-Benzene diisocyanate and trans-Cyclohexane-1,4-diisocyanate[42],

$$\begin{array}{cc} NCO & NCO \\ \bigcirc & \bigcirc \\ NCO & NCO \end{array}$$

1,5-Naphthalene diisocyanate[43]

2.2.2 Chain Extenders

The choice of chain extender and diisocyanate determines the characteristics of the hard segment and to a large extent the physical properties of TPU.

The most important chain extenders for TPU are the linear glycols such as ethylene glycol, 1,4-butanediol, 1,6-hexanediol and hydroquinone bis(2-hydroxyethyl) ether.

With diisocyanates these glycols form urethanes which are mostly well crystallized and melt without decomposition on thermoplastic processing.

The use of ethylene glycol as a chain extender should be avoided for a TPU with a high hard segment content because of thermal instability at higher temperature[44, 45].

Butanediol-1,4 and hydroquinone bis(2-hydroxyethyl) ether are the most suitable diols for TPU. The latter gives better high and low temperature properties and reduced compression set.

Table II gives a survey of the most important hard segments.

Other diols mentioned in the literature for use in TPU are: 1,4-Dimethylol benzene[46, 47].

Diols derived from sugar alcohols by ring closure reaction under dehydrating conditions[48].

Nonlinear diols are normally not suitable for TPU because the urethanes do not form well crystallized hard segments and therefore exhibit poor low and high temperature properties. A chain extender mixture of straight chain diols is sometimes recommended to produce a hard segment of lower order. This is especially valuable in extrusion grade TPU to provide a broader processing range[49].

With increasing hard segment content, the polymers generally show an increase in hardness accompanied with an increase in the glass transition temperature[50]. At levels of 60–70 % by weight of hard segment a phase transition occurs, which leads to a change in the overall behavior from that of an elastomeric polymer to a more brittle, high modulus plastic[51, 52].

Although diamines are excellent chain extenders, they normally cannot be used for TPU, because the urea groups melt well above the processing range of TPU and undergo some decomposition on melting. Sterically hindered diamines, e. g. 1-amino-3-aminomethyl-

TABLE II   Melting Temperatures T_m of Diisocyanates, Chain Extenders and Corresponding Hard Segments Ascertained by DSC Measurements

Diisocyanate		chain extender		X-ray[1]	Hard segments Melting point determined by		
	T_m (°C)		T_m (°C)		DSC measurement Curve profile	T_{max} (°C)	Visual evaluation in the melting tube
Naphthylene-1,5-diiso-cyanate (NDI)	131	butanediol-1,4	19,5	K	thermal effects as from 190 °C, no real melting up to 320 °C	–	sintering as from about 260 °C, no melting up to 320 °C
Diphenylmethane-4,4′-diiso-cyanate (MDI)	42	butanediol-1,4	19,5	K		230	initial softening at about 120 °C, melting at 230 to 237 °C[2]
Hexamethylene-diiso-cyanate (HDI)	11	butanediol-1,4	19,5	K	step at 75 to 100 °C	165	initial softening up to about 100 and 148 °C, melting at 166 °C to 172 °C
2,4-TDI	24	butanediol-1,4	19,5	A	step at 70 to 110 °C	217[2]	initial softening at 78 to 120 °C, melting at 220 °C[2)]
NDI	131	1,4-bis(β-hydroxy-ethoxy)-benzene	104	K	step at 133 and 210 °C	302	brown discoloration as from 288 °C, melting at 298 to 302 °C
MDI	42	1,4-bis(β-hydroxy-ethoxy)-benzene	104	K		252	initial softening at 243 °C, melting at 247 to 260 °C[2]
HDI	11	1,4-bis(β-hydroxy-ethoxy)-benzene	104	K		214	initial softening at 140 to 150 °C, melting at 212 to 226 °C[2]
2,4-TDI	24	1,4-bis(β-hydroxy-ethoxy)-benzene	104	K	step at 140 °C	197	initial softening at 140 °C, melting at 200 to 216 °C, breakdown as from 250 °C)

[1] X-ray wide angle study   K = crystalline   A = amorphous
[2] melts with breakdown
After ref. 31 with permission

3,5,5-trimethylcyclohexane (isophorone diamine), can be used in combination with aromatic and aliphatic diisocyanates[53, 54]. The use of a sterically hindered amine and a glycol as co-chain extender produces a hard segment that is not well crystallized. The polymer exhibits poor elastomeric properties but this makes it especially suitable for energy absorbing applications[54].

Water was the very first chain extender used for making elastomeric polyurethanes. One urea group is formed from two isocyanate groups. This reaction has been studied recently[30, 55], and the resulting polymers may allow melt processing because this reaction leads to hard blocks with a lower accumulation of urea groups as compared to the use of diamines.

2.3   Additives

The following compounds are the most widely used additives for TPU.

Mold release agents are the most commonly employed additives and are necessary for fast and economic cycle times. Chemically they belong to the class of fatty acid derivatives like esters and amides, and silicones or fluoroplastics. The amount of mold release agent is about 0.1 to 2 %-by weight.

Polyester based TPU are stabilized against hydrolytic degradation by adding 1–2 % by weight of sterically hindered aromatic carbodiimides. The carbodiimide group reacts with acid residues, generated by the hydrolysis of ester groups, which otherwise would catalyse further hydrolysis[56, 57].

$$\text{Ar}-\text{N}=\text{C}=\text{N}-\text{Ar} + \text{R}-\text{C} \overset{\text{O}}{\underset{\text{OH}}{\diagdown}} \longrightarrow [\text{Ar}-\text{N}=\overset{\text{H}}{\underset{\overset{\text{O}}{\underset{\overset{\text{C}=\text{O}}{\underset{\text{R}}{|}}}{|}}}{\text{C}}}-\text{N}-\text{Ar}] \longrightarrow \text{Ar}-\overset{\text{H}}{\underset{\overset{\text{C}=\text{O}}{\underset{\text{R}}{|}}}{\text{N}}}-\overset{\text{O}}{\overset{||}{\text{C}}}-\overset{\text{H}}{\text{N}}-\text{Ar}$$

Sterically hindered phenols and certain amines are the preferred stabilizers against degradation by light, oxidation and higher temperatures[45, 58, 59].

Inorganic materials, e. g. calcium carbonate, talc or silicates are added for better release properties in molding operations or in film production. They act either as crystallization promoters or surface rougheners.

Certain minerals, e. g. mica, organic fibers[60] and especially glass fibers[61] are used to reinforce TPU.

The friction coefficient of TPU can be markedly reduced by adding small amounts of graphite, molybdenum sulfide, fluorinated hydrocarbon or silicone oil as well as mixtures thereof[62].

Soft grades of TPU may be obtained by adding small amounts of plasticizers, however, no major success has been achieved yet.

3   SYNTHESIS

In general TPU are made by mixing all of the ingredients together at temperatures above 80 °C. For optimum results, the ratio of isocyanate groups to the sum of isocyanate reactive groups should be close to 1.0.

Polymers with insufficient molecular weight are obtained at ratios below 0.96, whereas thermoplastic processing becomes increasingly difficult at ratios above 1.1 due to crosslinking reactions.

At an average molecular weight M_n of 40,000 sufficient property development has occurred[11]. This M_n is easily obtained at ratios of 0.98 and higher.

The reaction can be carried out in different ways. The so called "one-shot method" involves mixing all the ingredients together. In the "prepolymer method" the polyol is reacted first with the diisocyanate to give an isocyanate containing prepolymer, which is then reacted with the chain extender. The reaction can be done batchwise[63] or continuously in a mixing chamber or reaction extruder[64–66].

For large scale industrial production mainly two methods are used, the belt process and the reaction extruder process. In the belt process all ingredients are mixed together. The liquid mixture is then poured on to a belt where it is allowed to solidify. The slab is granulated. The granulated material can be used as such but it is most often blended and extruded into more uniform pellets.

If a reaction extruder is used, the urethane reaction is almost complete at the end of the extruder and uniform pellets are obtained immediately.

The heat history during production is of extreme importance because the separation of the hard and soft segment, and hence the properties of TPU, is temperature dependant. Thus, starting from the same raw materials, the physical properties of the resulting polymers can be very different.

Various methods of influencing the properties of TPU are given in the literature[67–73].

4   MORPHOLOGY

It is evident that morphology of multiphase systems plays an important role in determining the final properties of a product. By controlled variation of the morphology, desired properties of a material can be obtained. Hence, a profound knowledge of the morphology is essential for understanding structure-property-relationships. However, this has proved to be a formidable challenge, since the morphology of urethane block polymers is complicated by physical phenomena such as crystallization, interphase mixing, hydrogen bonding in both segments, dependence of properties on thermal history, etc.

Theoretically, phase separation occurs due to thermodynamic incompatibility of the phases. A model to predict phase separation phenomena on a thermodynamic approach has been developed by Krause[74, 75]. Phase separation becomes more difficult as the number of blocks increases in a copolymer molecule of given length. On the other hand, an increase in molecular weight at fixed copolymer composition and number of blocks per molecule would favor phase separation. Generally a higher degree of phase separation is predicted for a copolymer system where one component is crystallizable. Both soft and hard domains in polyurethanes can be amorphous or partially crystalline.

4.1   Structure of Hard Segments

Considerable efforts have been made to elucidate the nature of TPU hard-segment domains[76–80]. Hard segments which are formed by linear glycols and MDI should be expected to be crystalline. Under normal conditions, however, crystallinity as evidenced by wide angle X-ray scattering (WAXS) techniques appears to be inhibited[76]. Initial proposals for the structure of hard segments, based on small angle X-ray scattering (SAXS) results, were made by Bonart and co-workers[77–79], and by Wilkes and Yusek[80]. Clough et al.[81, 82] also used SAXS to study domain structures in polyurethane blockpolymers. The ordered state of TPU hard segment domains has been referred to as paracrystalline[77]. Bonart developed two-dimensional and three-dimensional models of MDI/butanediol hard segment crystals[78, 79, 83]. Arrangements were constructed that provide optimum hydrogen bonding. Adequate heat treatment transformed the structure from paracrystalline into crystalline[78]. Relatively high temperature and long annealing times (190 °C, 12 h) are reportedly required to produce significant hard segment crystallinity[84].

Blackwell et al. extensively studied the structure of hard segments in MDI/diol/polytetramethylene adipate polyurethanes by X-ray diffraction. They used butanediol (BDO), propanediol (PDO), and ethylene glycol (EDO) as chain extenders[85, 86]. Poly (MDI/BDO) was found to be the most crystalline hard segment. Based on conformational analysis and model compound considerations, it was concluded that poly (MDI/BDO) existing in its fully extended chain conformation can form a hydrogen bonded network in two dimensions perpendicular to the chain axis. In contrast, poly (MDI/PDO) and poly (MDI/EDO) crystallize in higher energy contracted conformations, which are necessary for a non-staggered packing of the chains. The above findings were confirmed by the recent results of Eisenbach[87] who reported on the synthesis and analysis of a series of soft and hard segments under strictly controlled conditions. Oligomers from MDI and BDO were synthesized and endcapped. By SAXS measurements it was shown that MDI/BDO based oligourethanes crystallize in an extended chain without chain folding. Recently, Blackwell and Lee[88] found hard segment polymorphism in MDI/diol based polyurethane elastomers. In a MDI/polyester urethane, the authors varied the chain length of the extender from EDO to hexanediol (HDO) and observed crystallization phenomena by X-ray analyses. The HDO- and BDO-extended polyurethanes clearly showed polymorphism of the crystalline state. These findings were supported by DSC traces. The appearance of a second crystalline structure is accompanied by another melting point. The HDO-extended TPU is not very crystalline in the melt-pressed film, but develops high crystallinity on stretching and annealing. In contrast, EDO-based polyurethane seems to show no polymorphism at all. An X-ray analysis on single crystals formed by MDI/methanol bisurethanes furnished a model for the arrangement of MDI/BDO polyurethane chains within the hard segment domains[89], Figure 3. This model compound was proved to exist in two crystal modifications[90].

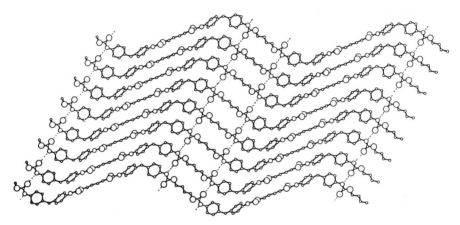

Figure 3   Chain arrangement of MDI/BDO hard-segments derived from X-ray studies of a model compound. Reference 89 with permission

Analogous studies were performed on model compounds which were obtained by reaction of diphenylmethane-4-mono-isocyanate and glycols of the $HO-(CH_2)_n-OH$ structure with n = 2 to 6[91]. X-ray analyses on single crystals of these compounds revealed a more stable arrangement of hydrogen bonds between neighboring molecules in urethanes with "even" chain extenders, while urethanes containing "odd" chain extenders exhibited significant strains which result in reduced stability of the physical crosslinking system. In a more recent paper, Born[92] published additional crystal structure data on some of these model compounds. Similarly, Born and Hespe[93] studied a bis-urea produced by reacting diphenyl-methane-4-isocyanate with 1.4-butane diamine. They found that the hydrogen bonds in this system were bifurcated, which accounts for the greater heat stability of the bis-urea crystals compared with those of the corresponding bis-urethane. Based on single crystal X-ray data, Blackwell et al.[94] derived structural parameters, such as bond lengths, bond angles, and bond torsion angles, for the prediction of polyurethane structures.

4.2 Thermal Transitions

Differential scanning calorimetry (DSC) is a common tool to determine changes in the state of organization of the molecules in a sample, e. g., phase segregation, glass transitions and melting. The practical use of DSC in analyzing thermal response of a TPU with respect to engineering properties has been illustrated by Goyert and Hespe[31]. The effect of hard segment content on thermal response is shown in Figure 4. The specimens of this series were prepared from the same components, but with differing molar ratios of polyesterdiol, BDO, and MDI (see Table III). The glass transition is broadened and shifted toward higher temperatures with increasing hard segment content. The observed glass transition shift may be explained by an increasing amount of hard segments which are "dissolved" in the soft matrix. Consequently, it seems plausible that a concentration gradient of hard segments exists near the phase interface. This assumption agrees with earlier explanations, where the observed phenomena were attributed to irregular structures at the phase interfaces[95].

This structure can be represented schematically by the model shown in Figure 5 (left). As a result of these irregularities, which have also been observed by SAXS[34, 79], parts of the soft segments are heavily restricted in mobility and therefore, only appear as flexible components at elevated temperatures. The increasing content of chain extender results not only in more but also in larger hard segments, see Table III.

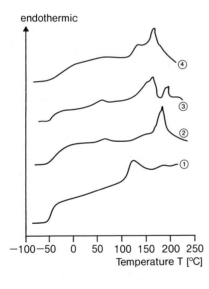

Figure 4   DSC scans of TPU samples with different hard segment content. Ref. 31 with permission. For sample designation see Table III

TABLE III   TPU-Samples with Various Hard Segment Content

Sample N°	Molar Ratio polyester[a]	BDO	MDI	Hard-Segment content (weight %)	Mean Hard Segment Length (calculated) (μm)
1	1	: 1,77	: 2,8	31	5,0
2	1	: 3,55	: 4,6	40	8,6
3	1	: 5,55	: 6,6	52	12,7
4	1	: 10	: 11	65	21,7

[a] Soft segment: poly(ethylene butylene adipate)glycol M_n = 2000.
Reference 31 with permission

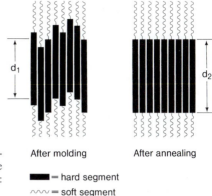

Figure 5   Model illustrating schematically the arrangement of the hard segments; left: after molding/cleavage of interfaces; right: after additional annealing. d_1, d_2: crystal thickness. Ref. 31 with permission

After molding   After annealing

■■■ = hard segment
〰〰 = soft segment

The length of the hard segment blocks forms the upper limit to the size of the hard segment crystals in the chain direction, which, in turn, determines the melting point and, thus, the thermal stability. In Figure 4 the temperature range in which most hard segment crystals melt (maximum of the DSC curve) is seen to shift towards higher temperature as the content of hard segment increases. The maximum is achieved at ca. 190 °C (specimen No. 2 was prepared under different conditions). Moreover, the graphs show transitions over a broad temperature range, which suggests a wide distribution of the hard segment crystal thickness[96].

The crystallite size distribution, which results when a TPU is cooled from the melt, is governed not only by the length distribution of the hard segment but also by the crystallization kinetics. Figure 6 (curve 1) shows the DSC trace of a TPU based on MDI, BDO and ethanediol-butanediol-polyadipate, prepared at the initial molar ratio of about 6:5:1. The material was molded into a panel. Several melting maxima are recognized, of which the most pronounced occurs at 205 °C. By thermal treatment at 118, 135, 180 and 205 °C for 5 min. each (curves 2 to 5), the primary melting region can be shifted to a limit of ca. 230 °C. The

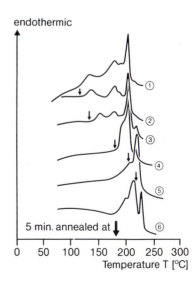

Figure 6   Effect of annealing on DSC transitions. Curves 2 to 5 illustrate the effect of thermal treatment at 118, 135, 180 and 205 °C for 5 minutes each. Ref. 31 with permission

melting range narrows at the same time. This effect is attributable to a partial melting of the hard segment crystals as well as to re-crystallization towards larger crystals of a better order. This process can be imagined as follows: On rapid cooling, the hard segment blocks corresponding to their arrangement in the melt, form crystals, which are statistically displaced with respect to one another. The thermodynamically effective crystal thickness d_1, is small while the phase interface is large (Figure 5, left). Upon annealing, the structure rearranges, resulting in a thermodynamically more favorable arrangement (Figure 5, right). The melting point subsequently rises because of the increased crystal thickness d_2. Naturally, additional improvements of the crystalline order in the lateral direction cannot be excluded. The uniform block length shown in Figure 5 is also a simplification. When the annealing temperatures exceed a limit of ca. 210 °C, the melting temperatures decrease again (curve 6 in Figure 6). In this case the existing crystals are largely molten and the hard segments cannot form new crystals within the storage period. Crystallization will only occur on subsequent cooling to form lower-melting aggregates of relatively poor order.

The kinetics of phase separation have been investigated by Wilkes et al.[97, 98]. Polyester TPU were quickly heated, then rapidly quenched to room temperature. Changes in phase separation were monitored by SAXS and DSC measurements as a function of time. It was shown that, as a result of kinetic and viscous effects, as much as several days were required to regain equilibrium.

Interphase mixing phenomena, as studied by thermal analysis and SAXS measurements, have been explained in terms of soft-segment hydrogen bonding ability[81, 82, 99]. For the same molecular weight polyol (M_n = 1000) a $1:2:1$ polyester : MDI : BDO system was single phased (compatible) whereas a $1:2:1$ polyether : MDI : BDO system was phase separated[14]. The former material was much more transparent, in agreement with smaller crystallites or a much lower degree of crystallinity. A DSC transition at 60–80 °C was ascribed to urethane polyester or urethane polyether hydrogen bond disruption. More recent studies have shown, however, that the intermediate DSC transitions are not attributable to hydrogen bond-dissociation[100]. The observed transition could alternatively be described as the glass transition of the hard phase for the particular block length employed, combined with a plasticizer effect of the soft segments. IR studies indicate that it is the chain mobility, or T_g of the hard blocks, that controls hydrogen bond dissociation[96, 101–103]. Thus, hydrogen bonds serve to increase the cohesion of the hard domains. Within the hard domains, hydrogen bonds appear to determine the arrangement of urethane groups[77–79]. However, the importance of hydrogen bonds in TPU should not be overemphasized. This is demonstrated in the example of polyetherester elastomers, where no hydrogen bonding exists. Witsiepe[160] prepared them by condensation of chloroformates of short chain glycols and of polytetramethylene or other long chain ether diols with piperazine. The resulting "secondary" urethane elastomers have no urethane hydrogen for bonding yet have physical properties fully comparable with the isocyanate derived materials. In addition, since the reversion reaction to isocyanate and alcohol is not possible, they are much more stable thermally and have a wider processing "window". Others attribute an important influence to π-electron interactions between parallel oriented rings.

Schneider and co-workers have extensively studied TDI-based polyurethanes[102–105]. Block polyurethanes were prepared from 2,4- and 2,6-TDI isomers. Thermomechanical studies, DSC, X-ray scattering, and IR analysis were applied to elucidate the structural organization and thermal transitions in these products. It was found that the degree of phase segregation strongly depended on the TDI-symmetry and the soft segment molecular weight. The T_g of 2,4-TDI polyurethanes with polyether soft segment of M_n ca. 1000 showed a strong dependence on composition, indicating extensive phase mixing occurred. In contrast, comparable 2,6-TDI-based polyurethanes displayed a highly ordered structure as revealed by a concentration independent T_g and a high temperature transition attributed to melting of the crystallizable hard segment.

Changing the soft-segment molecular weight from 1000 to 2000 led to phase segregation in the 2.4-TDI series and further improved phase segregation in the 2.6-TDI series. The results are in agreement with similar results obtained with a polycaprolactone diol-based TPU[35, 50].

It can be concluded, that the soft segment T_g is a sensitive measure of the degree of phase separation. Recently, the above described findings of Schneider et al. were confirmed by a paper of Senich and MacKnight[106]. From a technical standpoint, as hardness is increased by increasing the hard block content the extent of phase mixing also increases. This shows up as a decrease of low temperature flexibility. This drawback can be reduced by incorporation of soft segments with higher molecular weight or the use of pre-extended polyols.

4.3   Dynamic Mechnical Property Measurements

The dynamic mechanical behavior of segmented polyurethanes has been studied by many research groups[35, 50, 95, 99, 107, 108]. An example is illustrated in Figure 7, which represents the effect of a differing content of hard segments on the dynamic mechanical behavior. The curves for the samples designated in Table III clearly show the glass transitions of the soft segments, which starts at ca. -40 °C and accounts for the pronounced decrease of the shear modulus. A severe drop of the modulus occurs for specimen No. 1. With increasing hard segment content, this drop becomes less pronounced, demonstrating the function of hard segment domains as reinforcing filler. Sample 1 maintains a rubbery plateau over a reasonable temperature range. A second drop in modulus occurs when the temperature is increased to the hard-segment transition point. The two transitions depend strongly upon block length, composition, phase mixing and thermal history.

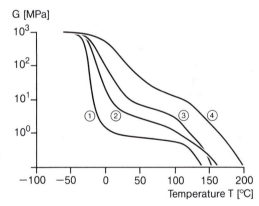

Figure 7   Shear modulus curves of TPU with various hard segment contents. Reference 31 with permission. For sample designation see Table III

Cooper[84, 109] and Wilkes[107] reported on extensive studies of dynamic mechanical properties on hydrogen-bonded and nonhydrogen-bonded TPU. In addition to the hard segment transition and the soft segment T_g, several relaxations were found, which could be assigned to low temperature transitions of the soft segment. The comparison between hydrogen-bonded and nonhydrogen-bonded[110] polyurethanes revealed a pronounced influence of hydrogen bonds on soft segment mobility. Low temperature dynamic mechanical properties of MDI/BDO/polyether based polyurethanes with various soft segments were studied by Schneider and co-workers[99]. They found that with increasing urethane concentration the soft segment glass transition remained almost constant, but the crystallization of the soft segment was inhibited above a certain urethane content. Koleske et al.[35, 50] studied the dynamic mechanical properties of a polycaprolactonediol (PCP) /MDI/BDO polyurethane system. The hard segment concentration was varied as well as the PCP molecular weight. With a PCP M_n lower than 3000 a compatible noncrystalline system was observed. A two phase morphology with soft segment crystallization was found for higher M_n PCP. The low molecular weight PCP system was very sensitive to hard segment content whereas the T_g of the higher M_n PCP system was much less affected over the same range of hard segment concentration, i.e. about 40 to 60 % hard segment content.

4.4 Sample History

As mentioned repeatedly, sample history is always an important factor in determining TPU properties. Chang and Thomas[111] compared the "as-reacted" to the DMF solution cast properties of a PCP/MDI/BDO system. DSC scans revealed two broad endothermic transition regions – a very broad and weak transition near 77 °C and a narrower, stronger transition below 227 °C . The high-temperature peak occurs at a significantly higher temperature for the "as-reacted" than for the solvent-cast sample (217 °C vs. 182 °C). Both peaks shift to higher temperatures with increasing hard-segment content. Recently, Cooper et al.[112] reported on the microstructure of "as-polymerized" TPU. These "as-reacted" products were obtained by reaction of the previously homogenized components in the mold. This procedure corresponds to a reaction injection molding (RIM) process, in contrast to techniques where the already formed polymer is shaped after polymerization, e. g. by extrusion. A different morphology for these various techniques might be expected. Thus, a series of polyether TPU were prepared, varying the polyether segment, with respect to molecular weight, and molecular weight distribution, and the molar ratios of MDI/chain extender/polyether glycol. The products were analyzed by DSC, dynamic mechanical measurements, X-ray diffraction, and polarized light microscopy. It was found that the degree of ordering of the polyether sequences increases dramatically with the average degree of polymerization of the sequences. The breadth of the distribution of polyether

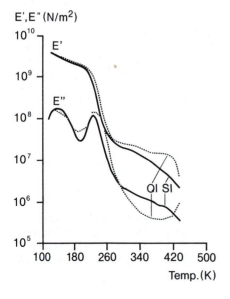

Figure 8   Dynamic tensile storage and loss moduli data for an as-reacted (Q 1) and solvent-cast (S 1) sample at 110 Hz and 2K min[-1]. Reprinted with permission from ref. 112

sequences was not strongly correlated with the measured properties. The comparison of "as-reacted" TPU with similar solvent-cast samples showed better dynamic mechanical properties of the former as a result of a higher level of organization. Figure 8 shows dynamic mechanical data of an "as-reacted" (Q 1) and solvent-cast (S 1) TPU of nearly equal chemical composition, i. e. MDI/BDO/Poly (tetramethyleneether) glycol = 2/1/1. The most striking difference is the slower decrease of the storage modulus of Q 1 and a different curve shape of loss modulus. As this example demonstrates, correlating molecular data with engineering properties is somewhat difficult, due to the complex nature and the multitude of reaction parameters, common in usual bulk polyurethane reactions.

4.5   Stress-strain and Ultimate Properties

The thermomechanical behavior of linear block copolyurethanes is basically different from the behavior of chemically crosslinked products. Applied mechanical stress causes orientation phenomena, which in turn lead to disruption and recombination of hydrogen bonds in an energetically more favorable position. These phenomena may explain typical features of TPU such as high tensile strength, tear strength, and elongation, and also high permanent set. Studies of orientation using infrared dichroism[113, 114] showed that the soft segments may be readily oriented by an applied stress but return to the unoriented state when the stress is removed. The hard blocks, however, show a more complex behavior of orientation and relaxation. This behavior is dependent on the magnitude of the applied stress, the molecular weight of the soft blocks and the crystallinity of the hard blocks. Harrell[110] systematically studied the effect of segment size distribution on mechanical properties in a non-hydrogen-bonded piperazine-based TPU. Hard and soft segment molecular weight distribution were varied and their combined effects on stress-strain and permanent set were described. It was observed that the ultimate stress-strain properties were significantly better in the case of a narrow size distribution, in particular for the hard segment. In contrast, permanent set is better when the size distribution is broad. Apparently, a more regular physical network and a higher degree of hard segment domain perfection[109], accompanied by strain-induced crystallization, is responsible for the better ultimate properties. Strain-induced crystallization, however, accounts for an increase in permanent set[115], if the sample temperature is below the melting point of the soft segment. Cooper and co-workers, in a recent paper[116] examined the influence of hard segment lengths and hard segment distribution on orientation phenomena using infrared dichroism experiments. In contrast to soft segment distribution, hard segment size distribution was found to exert a pronounced influence on the orientation tendency. In comparison to the orientation behavior of non-hydrogen bonded TPU containing monodisperse hard segment lengths[117], the MDI based hard segments oriented to a much lower degree than piperazine- based hard segments at high strains.

5   PROPERTIES

TPU were the first polymeric materials to combine both rubber elasticity and thermoplastic characteristics. The comparison of the Young's moduli of TPU to those of other materials is shown in Figure 9[118]. The Young's moduli of TPU range from 8 MPa up to about 2000 MPa depending on hard segment concentration[119, 120]. The stiffness of TPU can also be increased by inorganic and organic fillers, especially by glass fibers[61].

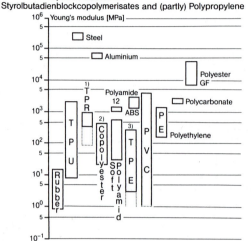

Young's modulus of various materials

1) TPR = Thermoplastic Rubber (EPDM + Polypropylene)
2) Copolyester = Polybutylene terephtalate polytetraoximethylene
3) TPE = Thermoplastic elastomers
   Styrolbutadienblockcopolymerisates and (partly) Polypropylene

Figure 9   Comparison of the Young's moduli of TPU with other similar plastic materials. Ref. 118 with permission

5.1 Mechanical Properties

TPU offer excellent physical properties, e. g., high tensile strength and elongation, see Figure 10. Depending on their chemical structures and Shore hardness, the tensile strengths of TPU vary from 25 to 70 MPa. Softer grades (70–85 Shore A) show lower tensile strength, while harder grades (50–83 Shore D) exhibit higher values, Figure 10. One of the main advantages of TPU is its high abrasion resistance. Therefore, polyurethanes, especially

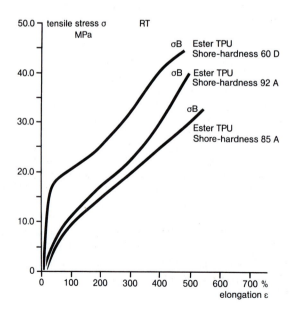

Figure 10   Stress diagram of three TPU with different Young's moduli (Shore D-hardness), ref. 118 with permission

ester- or ether-ester-polyurethanes are the materials of choice for shoe soles, screen section and cable jacketing. The tear propagation resistance is so high, that even skiboot-buckles don't tear. TPU exhibit flexibility over a wide temperature range and good resistance to many oils and greases. TPU do not contain any plasticizers and are thus preferred for sandwich constructions with other materials, such as polycarbonate and ABS.

The soft segment (polyol) determines the behavior at low temperatures and is responsible for many other properties as shown in Table IV. The major quantity of TPU is ester based. Ester-TPU show better abrasion and cut resistance, tensile and tear strength than ether-TPU. Ester-TPU also swell less in oil, grease and water than ether-TPU, Table IV. Ether-TPU are recommended if special properties such as resistance to hydrolysis and microbiological degradation or good low temperature flexibility are required. Further advantages can be often expected when using ether-ester-TPU produced by a special synthesis procedure[29]. Ether-ester-TPU are often a good compromise with respect to many properties. Therefore they have been used in applications such as fire hoses, cable jacketing and films.

TABLE IV   Comparison of Properties of TPU Prepared from Different Polyols

	Ester (Adipate or Caprolactone)	Ester with Carbodiimide	Ether	Ether-Special Ester
Tensile strength	+ +	+ +	0	+
Abrasion resistance	+ +	+ +	0	+
Low swelling in oil, grease, water	+	+	0	+
Wheathering	+	+	0	+
Stability to energic radiation	+	+	0	+
Tear strength, Graves	+ +	+ +	0	+
Rebound resilience	+ + → +	+ + → +	+ + → +	+
Microbe and fungus resistance	+ → −	0 → −	+ +	+ +
Low temperature impact resistance	+ → 0	+ → 0	+ + → +	+
Hydrolysis resistance	0	+ / 0	+	+

++ excellent,   favorable
+ good,
0 indifferent,   ↓
− poor,   unfavorable

5.2 Thermal Properties

TPU can be used within a wide range of temperatures[121]. The majority of articles made of TPU can be used from −40 °C up to 80 °C for both long and short-term applications. TPU have a short-term resistance to temperatures up to 120 °C, though in some cases even higher temperatures can be tolerated as by the use of secondary urethanes based on piperazine. The hard segment is the main contributor to high service temperature performance[122]; the harder the product (more isocyanate and chain extender) the higher the service temperature, Figure 7. Besides being a function of the amount of chain extender, TPU high temperature performance is also influenced by the type of chain extender, Figure 7. Hydroquinone bis (2-hydroxyethyl) ether yields TPU with higher service temperature than butanediol-1,4 or hexanediol-1,6.

The diisocyanate type also effects the high temperature performance[122]. As is seen in Table II the hard segments produced from different diisocyanates and chain extenders show different melting points. The melting points of urethanes derived from TDI are so low, that polyurethanes based on TDI are not used for TPU.

All mechanical properties, e. g. stiffness, and elasticity, are dependent on temperature. This is demonstrated by plotting the shear moduli of four different TPU at a wide range of temperatures, Figure 7.

The Shore hardness of two different TPU show a similar dependance on temperature, Figure 11.

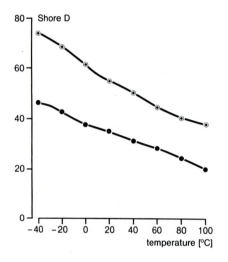

Figure 11   Dependance of the Shore hardness on temperature in case of two different TPU, ref. 118 with permission

5.3 Hydrolytic Stability

TPU can be used in pure water over a period of several years at room temperature without any significant changes of the properties. At 80 °C, however, the mechanical properties are affected after exposure for some weeks or months, see Figure 12. The hydrolytic stability is dependant on the structure of the polyol. Ester-TPU are less resistant than ester-TPU

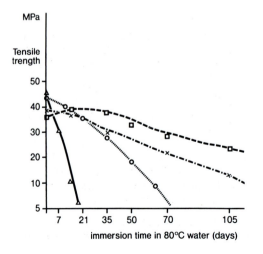

Figure 12   Effect of immersion in water at 80 °C on the tensile strength of different TPU of about 87 Shore A hardness: △ : Ester-TPU without carbodiimide, ○: Ester-TPU with carbodiimide, × : Ether-TPU (Tetramethyleneoxide), □ : Propylenglycol ether-carbonate-TPU

protected by carbodiimide[123, 124]. The highest resistance to water at elevated temperatures is shown by ether-ester-TPU or pure ether-TPU, Figure 12.

With increasing hardness, TPU becomes more hydrolytically stable due to the hydrophobic character of the hard segment.

Polyurethanes are sensitive to acids and bases. They are attacked slowly by diluted acids and bases at room temperature. They cannot withstand concentrated acids and alkalies at higher temperatures. Every acid behaves differently in contact with various urethanes. Immersion tests under simulated conditions are therefore recommended, to approve a TPU for a special application.

5.4 Oil, Grease and Solvent Resistance

Non-polar solvents such as hexane, heptane and paraffin oil have almost no effect on the polar polyurethanes. Even at high temperatures only a slight swelling may be observed.

TPU exhibit excellent resistance to pure mineral oils (Diesel oils) and greases. Some technical oils and greases can attack TPU at elevated temperatures due to the additives they may contain. Therefore it is advisable to test the influence of the oil to the TPU under service conditions.

Chlorinated hydrocarbons or aromatic components like toluene cause a very severe swelling of TPU[125]. The degree of swelling is dependant on the structure of the polyurethane. Ester-types swell less than ether-types and hard polyurethanes swell less than soft ones.

Some polar solvents, e. g. tetrahydrofuran, methylethylketone or dimethylformamide are capable of partially or completely dissolving TPU. For example soft linear polyurethanes can be dissolved in methylethylketone acetone mixtures and applied as adhesives, while harder linear polyurethanes are dissolved and applied as textile and leather coatings. These topics are not covered in this book but further information is available in a recent publication by Oertel[126].

Polyurethanes are generally stable in contact with petroleum hydrocarbons if they do not contain alcohol. Fuels that contain aromatics or alcohols cause a reversible swelling of the polymer; the extent of the swelling depends on the amount of such ingredients.

5.5 Micro-organism Resistance

Soft ester-TPU can be attacked by micro-organisms after long contact with moist earth. Soft and hard ether-, ether-ester-TPU or hard TPU are normally resistant to such attack. A slight discoloration at the surface of the articles can be caused by fungus, but it does not indicate a mechanical damage of the material.

6   PROCESSING

Thermoplastic Urethanes are normally supplied as granules in moisture proof containers. They can be processed by the usual methods for thermoplastic materials such as injection molding, extrusion, blow molding and calendering without any pretreatment.

The TPU as well any additives, when stored incorrectly may become moist, and must be dried prior to the processing. Moist granules should be dried at 100–110 °C in a circulating air oven or in a flash drier for 12 hours. The moisture content of the granules should be below 0.1%.

After processing the articles achieve nearly their final properties by storage at room temperature for 4–6 weeks. If some special properties (e. g. low compression set at elevated temperatures) are desired, annealing at 100–130 °C for 12 hours is recommended.

6.1 Injection Molding

Thermoplastic polyurethanes can be injection molded similarly to other thermoplastic materials.

Three zone screws with non return valves have proved to be the most suitable. The compression ratio should be about 1:2, with screw length:diameter ratio of ca. 17:1, see Figure 13. The barrel temperatures of the injection molding machine for a TPU of a medium Shore hardness should increase from the feed zone to the metering zone and then decrease by 5–10 °C from the metering zone to the nozzle to avoid running out the melt, see Figure 14; the temperatures for softer TPU types should be 10 °C lower, for harder types they are up to 30 °C higher. The size and type of the machine will also influence the processing result.

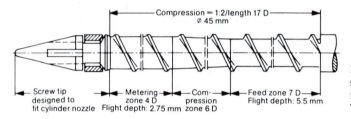

Figure 13   A profile of a screw design recommended for injection molding of TPU

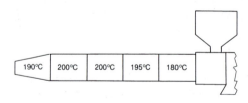

Figure 14   Temperature profile recommended for injection molding of TPU

The shrinkage of the molded articles is dependant on the TPU grade, wall thickness and processing conditions. More information is given in the literature[127].

6.2 Extrusion

Thermoplastic urethanes up to a Shore hardness of about 95 A can be extruded.

Figure 15 shows a temperature profile for an extruder with a screw up to 90 mm diameter. The temperature range for processing TPU is between 170 °C and 230 °C depending on the hardness and viscosity of the TPU. The screw speed for injection molding and extrusion should not be too high, otherwise material degradation will occur.

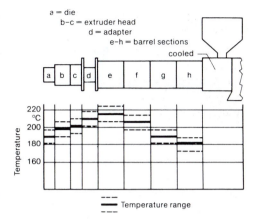

Figure 15 Temperature profile recommended for extrusion of TPU

Good results are obtained with screws having a length : diameter ratio of 18–25. The compression ratio should be from 1:2.5 to 1:3.5, Figure 16. Short compression screws are not suitable.

The melt pressure during processing depends on the width of the die or the cross section and the melt temperature. If a flat film or a tubular film is extruded, the melt pressure is between 100 and 500 bar; in the case of profiles, hoses and sheetings, values up to 250 bar are measured. Shear pins on the screw are not suitable for extrusion of thermoplastic polyurethanes, because they can degrade the material. The homogeneity of colored material can be improved by mixing pins.

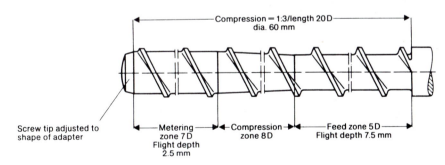

Figure 16 Screw recommended for extrusion of TPU

One can extrude TPU films with a thickness of 0,03 to 3 mm. The films with 0,03 to 0,3 mm thicknesses should be fabricated by a blown film extruder. Higher wall thicknesses should be extruded as flat films.

Many TPU articles are formed by the blow molding process. The Figure 17 shows the typical production process of bellows by blow molding. A special range of viscosities of TPU are required for this technique. It is also necessary to adapt trimming and demolding techniques due to the flexibility and high tear (cut) strength of TPU[127].

The melt calender process can be used to coat various substrates with special types of TPU.

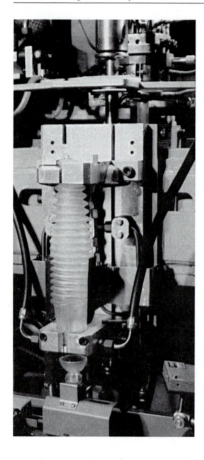

Figure 17   The production of TPU bellows by extrusion blow moulding

6.3 Welding – Bonding

The following techniques[127] are used to weld TPU with TPU:

– Heated mirror welding
– Hot air or nitrogen welding
– Heating tool and thermal impulse welding
– High frequency welding
– Friction welding

TPU can be bonded with itself using solvents such as N-methyl-pyrrolidone or dimethyl-formamide as long as the surface is small. Two component polyurethane adhesives are suitable for bonding TPU with itself and other polar plastic materials, metals, wood, leather etc.[126]. Other adhesives that may be applied are epoxy resins.

7   BLENDS

The literature dealing with blends of TPU with other polymers is quite large[128–130].

Except for very unpolar resins, like polyethylene or polypropylene, TPU can be blended with many other resins in wide ratios, as long as the processing temperatures are below ca.

280 °C. Depending on the portion of TPU, the blends can be formally divided into three areas:

7.1 TPU as the Minor Component

In this case TPU is acting as a modifier. Especially softer grades of TPU are used to modify higher modulus plastics, e. g. unsaturated polyester resins, epoxy resins, poly(oxymethylene)[131] or poly(butylene terephthalate)[132]. The main improvement gained by adding small amounts of TPU is an increase in impact strength and low temperature flexibility without impairing the other properties.

TPU is also used as a nonmigrating, nonvolatile plasticizer for PVC and can be blended in any ratio with PVC[133].

7.2 TPU as an Equal Component with Other Resins

Blending equal amounts of TPU with other thermoplastics usually results in additive mechanical properties. Examples for such blends are: TPU/Polycarbonate[134]: The addition of polycarbonate results in a higher modulus and the blends exhibit excellent processing properties making them useful for automotive applications.

TPU/ABS: These two resins can be blended in any ratio. Increasing the ABS-proportion results in a higher modulus and lower abrasion resistance and tear strength. The blends may offer cost advantages because of the lower ABS-costs[135]. Blends of copolymers such as styrene and maleic anhydride[136] or styrene and maleimides[137] with TPU exhibit improved impact strength at still high Vicat-temperatures.

The blends of TPU with the following compounds are basically comparable to TPU/ABS blends:
copolymers of styrene, methacrylic acid and alkadienes[138] and e. g. styrene and acrylonitrile or methacrylic acid ester[139] or rubbery copolymers of styrene, butadiene and acrylonitrile or methylmethacrylate[140].

Examples for ternary blends are:
TPU/polycarbonate/ABS: These blends are claimed to have better processing properties[141] and better fuel resistance[142].
TPU/polycarbonate/polybutyleneterephthalate: These blends show less stress cracking with solvents[143].

7.3 TPU as the Major Component

The use of ABS as an impact modifier for higher modulus TPU or a phase compatibilizer for polyether based TPU has been described in the patent literature and proved to be successful in the market[119, 144, 145].

Certain acrylic polymers can serve as processing aids for TPU[146].

Neutralized salts of ethylene acrylic acid copolymer have been described to improve the processing of TPU in blow molding operations[147]. Generally, ionic groups in nonpolar resins are acting as compatibilizers[148].

Besides blending TPU with other polymers, the mixing with a different TPU is often practiced, e. g.:
Blends of hard and soft grades have been used to obtain TPU with medium hardness or to achieve TPU of better processing properties. These blends are especially useful for filled TPU. Polyester and polyether grades have been blended to obtain special properties[149].

Blending of TPU with different intrinsic melt indexes and hardnesses, is claimed to produce better demolding properties and less blocking in blow molding operations[150].

8   APPLICATIONS

8.1 Film and Sheet

Films and sheet of thermoplastic polyurethanes can be extruded in thicknesses ranging from few µm to several mm. Films of TPU have outstanding properties regarding abrasion, puncture and tear propagation resistance in combination with high elasticity, bondability and weldability. Therefore, films of TPU are being used for conveyor belts and exhibit excellent abrasion resistance. They may also be pigmented in any color. Depending on the grade of TPU used, these conveyor belts may be used for contact with dry, aqueous and fatty foods. Special TPU types meet the requirements for food contact of the Federal German Health office (BGA)[151]. Some special grades of TPU meet the corresponding regulations of the United States (FDA)[152].

TPU has low air permeability and may be used for many other applications where these properties are required. Other applications for TPU films include:

– Welded hollow bodies
– Textile lamination
– Protective coverings
– Sealing of foams
– Abrasion resistant coatings.

8.2 Hose

Many different types of hoses are made from thermoplastic polyurethanes. The high elongation, good hydrolysis and microbe resistance and the high mechanical properties (e. g. tensile strength and resistance to tear propagation) of ether-ester or ether polyurethanes are an ideal combination for the inner liner of fire hoses. The high tensile strength of TPU allows a thinner wall thickness to be used in comparison to conventional hoses[153]. Fire hoses made with an inner lining of TPU are lighter than conventional hoses and thus allow a fireman to operate more effectively.

Tubes with an inner layer of TPU are very helpful in the transport of sand and stone slurries. The excellent abrasion and cut resistance of polyurethanes guarantees a relatively long service life of such tubes.

8.3 Shoes

Today the outer materials of ski boot are made primarily from thermoplastic polyurethanes. The polyurethane properties of good abrasion and cut resistance, permanent buckling strength and the high impact strength at low temperatures are particularly useful for ski boots. No other plastic material has this high resistance to tear and tear propagation, so the buckles cannot tear out. Thermoplastic polyurethanes of varying stiffnesses are used for skiboots, with E-(Young's)-moduli ranging from 100–600 MPa (50–66 Shore D). Various TPU must be used to meet the property requirements of the different shoe parts.

Ice hockey boots, which are similar to ski boots, are often also made from thermoplastic polyurethanes. They must show a very high impact strength at low temperatures.

Many sport shoe soles are manufactured from TPU. The largest application is soccer shoes. They are made mostly from ester polyurethanes of a Shore hardness of 85–90 Shore A. The excellent abrasion and cut resistance of ester polyurethanes is the main reason to use this material.

8.4 Automotive

Exterior automotive body parts can be injection-molded of pure TPU, TPU-PC blends and, recently, glass reinforced TPU. Parts with Young's (E-) modulus up to 2,000 MPa can be produced. The good recovery of TPU after deformation, the cut resistance, the good weathering properties and the resistance to oils and fuels are decisive factors contributing to the use of TPU for this application. Other automotive applications include bearing bushings and gaskets for wheel components, tie rods and suspension link pivots, membranes for hydropneumatic suspension systems, bellows for steering assemblies and shock absorbers, tank bleeding tubes and catches and seals for door locks[153].

8.5 Mechanical Goods and Other Applications

The high E-Modulus in comparison to rubber and the high dynamic load-bearing capacity of TPU are some useful properties for toothed belts. These can be produced from ester-TPU of a Shore hardness from 85–93 Shore A by extrusion techniques[153].

TPU is used for couplings. Depending upon the application and the size of the part, ester-TPU in a Shore hardness range of 85 Shore A up to 60 Shore D are used. The high E-modulus of the polyurethane elastomer enables the transmission of high energies.

Precision cogged wheels are molded from ester-TPU. The vibration damping of poly-urethane elastomers can be used in modern business machines.

Screens made of polyurethanes can classify dry and wet materials, e. g. gravel, coal and coke, or can be applied for sorting, washing and separating. Screens of TPU, with its high abrasion resistance, exhibit a longer lifetime in comparison to rubber and steel elements.

TPU sheathing for geophysical measuring cables shows high abrasion, cut and tear resistance. Other sheathing applications are connecting leads for electrical tools (in industry and in the home) and spiral leads.

Ear tags of TPU ensure a reliable identification of different animals. These ear tags must have a high tensile strength and tear propagation resistance as well as good weathering properties. TPU based on aromatic isocyanates exhibit yellowing, although that only minimally influences the properties of the polymer. Special UV-absorbers can be used to minimize the yellowing.

8.6 Medical

Polyurethane elastomers show a good compatibility to human skin. The good compatibility of ether-polyurethane elastomers with human blood and tissues[154] allows catheters and tubes for blood to be made from TPU[155]. Even a microporous, biodegradable, compliant and blood compatible vascular prothesis was developed[156]. More information about this topic is given in the literature[157–159].

9   FUTURE TRENDS

In addition to the continuing need to improve quality, it will be necessary to broaden the range of applications for TPU beyond the current limits. This means producing TPU with lower hardness and greater long term temperature resistance as well as TPU with higher hardness which still retain good low temperature properties.

To achieve these goals it will be necessary to have a deeper understanding of the morphology of TPU and its influence on properties. The development of new and better building blocks, will allow the production of polymers with tailor-made properties using polyurethane chemistry.

The major object of research will be the development of more sophisticated blends with other resins to gain the best combination of properties needed.

10 ACKNOWLEDGEMENTS

The authors thank J. F. Dormish, H. Hespe, H. G. Hoppe, B. Krüger, B. Quiring, N. Schön, H. Wagner, Bayer AG and E. C. Ma, Mobay Chemical Corp. for helpful discussions.

References

1. O. Bayer, H. Rinke, W. Siefken, L. Ortner, H. Schild, (to I.G. Farben), Ger. Pat. 728 981 (1937)
2. A. E. Christ, W. E. Hanford (to DuPont), US Pat. 2333 639 (1940)
3. Brit. Pat. 580 524 (1941). (to ICI). Brit. Pat. 574 134 (1942)
4. P. Pinten (to Dynamit AG), Ger. Pat. 932 633 (1943)
5. E. Müller, S. Petersen, O. Bayer, (to Bayer), Ger. Pat. 896 413 (1944)
6. S. Petersen, E. Müller, O. Bayer, (to Bayer), Ger. Pat. 883 347 (1944)
7. O. Bayer, E. Müller, S. Petersen, H. F. Piepenbrink, E. Windemuth, *Angew. Chem. 62*, 57 (1950)
8. T. G. Mastin, N. V. Seeger, (to Goodyear), US Pat. 2625535 (1953)
9. F. B. Hill, C. A. Young, J. A. Nelson, R. G. Arnold, *Ind. Eng. Chem. 48,* 927 (1956)
10. C. S. Schollenberger, H. Scott, G. R. Moore, *Rubber World 137,* 549 (1958)
    C. S. Schollenberger, (to B. F. Goodrich), US Pat. 2871218 (1955)
11. C. S. Schollenberger and K. Dinbergs, *J. Elastoplastics 5*, 222 (1973); 7, 65 (1975)
12. C. S. Schollenberger and K. Dinbergs, *ACS Polymer Preprints 20* (1), 532 (1979)
13. R. Becker and H. U. Schimpfle, *Plaste und Kautschuk 22*, 15 (1975); J. H. Saunders and K. C. Frisch, High Polymers XVI:*"Polyurethanes, part I, Chemistry"*, Intersci. Publ., New York, 1962
14. J. Rohr, K. Koenig, H. Koepnick and K.-H. Seemann, *"Polyester"*, Ullmanns Encyklopaedie der technischen Chemie, 4. Auflage, Verlag Chemie, Weinheim, 1980

15. P. J. Flory, *"Principles of Polymer Chemistry"*, Cornell University Press, Ithaca, N. Y., 1953
16. G. L. Lunardon, Y. Sumida, and O. Vogl, *Ang. Makrom. Chem. 87,* 1 (1980)
17. F. Hostettler (to Union Carbide), US Pat. 2933477 (1956)
18. E. Mueller, *Ang. Makrom. Chem. 14,* 75 (1970)
19. E. Windemuth, H. Schnell and O. Bayer (to Bayer), Ger. Pat. 974371 (1951)
20. F. B. Hill (to DuPont), US Pat. 2929800 (1953)
21. E. Pechold (to DuPont), US Pat. 4120850 (1977)
22. C. G. Seefried, jun., R. D. Whitman and R. van Cleve (to Union Carbide), Ger. Pat. Appl. 2550830 (1975)
23. F. X. O'Shea and C. L. Mao (to Uniroyal), US Pat. 4041105 (1976)
24. H. W. Bonk and T. M. Shah (to Upjohn), Ger. Pat. Appl. 2537775 (1975)
25. D. D. Russel and G. Shkapenko (to Samuel Moore), US Pat. 4010146
26. H. Holtschmidt (to Bayer), Ger. Pat. 1039232 (1956)
    H. Schwarz, W. Kallert, C. Muehlhausen and H. Holtschmidt (to Bayer), US Pat. 2844566 (1958)
27. E. Mueller and G. Braun (to Bayer), Ger. Pat. 1039744 (1955)
    W. Thoma, H. Rinke, H. Oertel and E. Mueller (to Bayer), Ger. Pat. 1149520 (1961)
28. E. G. Kolycheck (to B. F. Goodrich), Ger. Pat. 1720843 (1967)
29. E. Meisert, A. Awater, C. Muehlhausen and U. J. Doebereiner (to Bayer), Ger. Pat. 1940181 (1969)
30. G. L. Statton (to Atlantic Richfield), US Pat. 3987012 (1975)
31. W. Goyert and H. Hespe, *Kunststoffe 68,* 819 (1978)
32. L. Morbitzer and R. Bonart, *Kolloid Z. und Z. Polymere 232,* 764 (1969)
33. L. Morbitzer and H. Hespe, *J. Appl. Polym. Sci. 27,* 2891 (1982)
34. R. Bonart and E. H. Mueller, *J. Macromol. Sci. 10,* 177 and 345 (1974)
35. C. G. Seefried, jr., J. V. Koleske and F. E. Critchfield, *J. Appl. Polym. Sci. 19,* 2493 and 3185 (1975)
36. R. J. Zdrahala, S. L. Hager, R. M. Gerkin and F. E. Critchfield, *J. Elast. and Plast. 12,* 225 (1980)
37. N. E. Rustad and R. G. Krawiec, *J. Appl. Polym. Sci. 18,* 4101 (1974)
38. T. K. Kwei, *J. Appl. Polym. Sci. 27,* 2891 (1982)
39. Becker/Braun, *"Kunststoffhandbuch"*, 2. Auflage, VII; 63, Carl Hanser Verlag, (1983)
40. H. W. Bonk and T. M. Shah (to Upjohn), US Pat. 3899467 (1974)
41. R. Roberts (to Union Carbide), US Pat. 4055549 (1976)
42. H. Schulze, H. Zengel, W. Brodowski, F. Huntjems, J. Schutijer and P. Hentschel (to AKZO), Ger. Pat. Appl. 2829199 (1978)
43. W. Goyert (to Bayer), Ger. Pat. Appl. 3329775 (1983)
44. K. J. Vorhees and R. P. Lattimer,
    J. Polym. Sci., Polym. Chem. Ed. 20, 1457 (1982)
45. H. J. Fabris, Adv. in *Ureth. Chem. and Techn. 6,* 173 (1978)
46. T. M. Shah (to Upjohn), US Pat. 3901852 (1974)
47. Y. Camberlin, J. P. Pascault, J. M. Letoffe and P. Claude, *J. Polym. Sci., Polym. Chem. Ed. 20,* 1445 (1982)
48. H. Salzburg, H. Meyborg, W. Goyert and J. M. Barnes (to Bayer), Ger. Pat. Appl. 3111093 (1981), 3302603 (1983)
49. B. Quiring, H. G. Niederdellmann, W. Goyert and H. Wagner (to Bayer), Europ. Pat. Appl. 4393 (1978)
50. C. G. Seefried, jr., J. V. Koleske and F. E. Critchfield, *J. Appl. Polym. Sci. 19,* 2503 (1975)
51. R. J. Zdrahala, R. M. Gerkin, S. L. Hager and F. E. Critchfield, *J. Appl. Polym. Sci. 24,* 2041 (1979)
52. S. Abouzahr, L. C. Wilkes and Z. Ophir, *Polymer 23,* 1077 (1982)
53. B. Quiring, J. Wulff and A. Eitel (to Bayer), Ger. Pat. Appl. 2423764 (1974)
54. H. P. Mueller, W. Oberkirch, K. Wagner and B. Quiring (to Bayer), Ger. Pat. Appl. 2644434 (1976)
55. B. Quiring, W. Wenzel, H. G. Niederdellmann, H. Wagner and W. Goyert (to Bayer), Ger. Pat. Appl. 2925944 (1979)
56. W. Neumann and P. Fischer, *Ang. Chem. 74,* 806 (1962)
57. W. Neumann et al. (to Bayer), Belg. Pat. 610969 and 612040 (1961)
58. C. S. Schollenberger and F. D. Stewart, *J. Elastoplastics 4,* 294 (1972)

59. J. E. Kresta, *Polymer Additives,* Plenum Press, New York and London, 1984, p. 49 and 135
60. S. Inoue, S. Shibata, Y. Kaneko, T. Nishi and T. Matsunaga (to Bridgestone Tire), Ger. Pat. Appl. 2220306 (1972)
61. W. Goyert, W. Grimm, A. Awater, H. Wagner and B. Krüger (to Bayer), Ger. Pat. Appl. 2854406 (1978)
62. J. W. Britain and G. J. Schexnayder (to Mobay), Ger. Pat. Appl. 2740711 (1976)
63. J. H. Saunders and K. A. Piggot (to Mobay), US Pat. 3214411 (1965)
64. B. F. Frye, K. A. Piggot and J. H. Saunders (to Mobay), US Pat. 3233025 (1966)
    K. W. Rausch, jr. and T. R. McClellan (to Upjohn), US Pat. 3642964 (1969)
65. E. Meisert, U. Knipp, B. Stelte, M. Hederich, A. Awater and R. Erdmenger (to Bayer), Ger. Pat. 1964834 (1969)
66. R. M. Erdmenger, M. Ulrich, M. Hederich, E. Meisert, B. Stelte, A. Eitel and R. Jacob (to Bayer), Ger. Pat. Appl. 2302564 (1973)
67. J. A. Obal and I. S. Megna (to American Cyanamid), Ger. Pat. Appl. 2648246 (1976)
68. K. H. Illers and H. Stutz (to BASF), Ger. Pat. Appl. 2547864 (1975)
69. K. H. Illers and H. Stutz (to BASF), Ger. Pat. Appl. 2547866 (1975)
70. S. Abouzahr and G. L. Wilkes, *J. Appl. Polym. Sci. 29,* 2695 (1984)
71. G. Heinz, H.-J. Maas, P. Herrmann and H.-D. Schumann (to VEB Chemieanlagen), Ger. Pat. Appl. 2523987 (1975)
72. J. W. Britain and W. Meckel (to Mobay), Ger. Pat. appl. 2323393 (1973)
73. H. Meisert, W. Goyert, A. Eitel and W. Krohn (to Bayer), Ger. Pat. Appl. 2418075 (1974)
74. S. Krause, *Block and Graft Copolymers,* J. J. Burke, V. Weiss, Eds., Syracuse University, Syracuse, 1973
75. S. Krause, P. A. Reismiller, *J. Polym. Sci. A-2,* 13, 1975 (1975)
76. S. L. Cooper, A. V. Tobolsky, *J. Appl. Polym. Sci.,* 10, 1837 (1966)
77. R. Bonart, *J. Macromol. Sci. B 2,* 115 (1968)
78. R. Bonart, L. Morbitzer, G. Hentze, *J. Macromol. Sci., B 3,* 337 (1969)
79. R. Bonart, L. Morbitzer, E. H. Müller, *J. Macromol. Sci., B 9,* 447 (1974)
80. C. W. Wilkes, C. Yusek, *J. Macromol. Sci. B 7,* 157 (1973)
81. S. B. Clough, N. S. Schneider, *J. Macromol. Sci. B 2,* 553 (1968)
82. S. B. Clough, N. S. Schneider, A. O. King, *J. Macromol. Sci. B 2,* 641 (1968)
83. R. Bonart, *Angew. Makromol. Chemie, 58/59,* 259 (1977)
84. D. S. Huh, S. L. Cooper, *Polym. Eng. Sci., 11,* 369 (1971)
85. J. Blackwell, M. R. Nagarajan, *Polymer, 22,* 202 (1981)
86. J. Blackwell, M. R. Nagarajan, T. B. Hoitink, *ACS Symp. Ser., 172,* 179 (1981)
87. C. D. Eisenbach, C. Guenther, *Am. Chem. Soc., Org., Coat. Appl. Sci. Proc. 49,* 239 (1983)
88. J. Blackwell, C. D. Lee, *J. Polym. Sci. Phys., 22,* 759 (1984)
89. J. Blackwell, K. H. Gardner, *Polymer 20,* 13 (1979)
90. J. Hocker, L. Born, *J. Polym. Sci., Polym. Lett. Ed., 17,* 723 (1979)
91. L. Born, H. Hespe, J. Crone, K. H. Wolf, *Colloid Polym. Sci., 260,* 819 (1982)
92. L. Born, *Z. Kristallographie, 167,* 145 (1984)
93. L. Born, H. Hespe, *Colloid Polym. Sci., 263,* 335 (1985)
94. J. Blackwell, J. R. Quay, M. R. Nagarajan, L. Born, H. Hespe, *J. Polym. Sci., Phys. Ed., 22,* 1247 (1984)
95. H. Hespe, E. Meisert, U. Eisele, L. Morbitzer, W. Goyert, *Kolloid-Z. 250,* 797 (1972)
96. R. W. Seymour, S. L. Cooper, *Macromolecules, 6,* 48 (1973)
97. G. L. Wilkes, S. Bagrodia, W. Humphries, R. Wildnauer, *Polymer Letters Ed., 13,* 321 (1975)
98. G. L. Wilkes, J. A. Emerson, *J. Appl. Phys., 47,* 4261 (1976)
99. J. L. Illinger, N. S. Schneider, F. E. Karasz, *Polym. Eng. Sci., 12,* 25 (1972)
100. C. S. Schollenberger, L. E. Hewitt, *Polym. Prepr., Am. Chem. Soc, Div. Polym. Chem., 19,* 17 (1978)
101. R. W. Seymour, G. M. Estes, S. L. Cooper, *Macromolecules, 3,* 579 (1970)
102. C. S. Paik Sung, N. S. Schneider, *Macromolecules, 8,* 68 (1975)
103. C. S. Paik Sung, N. S. Schneider, *Macromolecules, 10,* 452 (1977)
104. N. S. Schneider, C. S. Paik Sung, *Polym. Eng. Sci., 17,* 73 (1977)
105. N. S. Schneider, C. S. Paik Sung, R. W. Matton, J. L. Illinger, *Macromolecules, 8,* 62 (1975)
106. G. A. Senich, W. J. MacKnight, *Advan. Chem. Ser., 176,* 97 (1979)

107. S. L. Samuels, G. L. Wilkes, *J. Polym. Sci., C 43*, 149 (1973)
108. R. W. Seymour, S. L. Cooper, *Rubber Chem. Technol., 47*, 19 (1974)
109. H. N. Ng., A. E. Allegrezza, R. W. Seymour, S. L. Cooper, *Polymer, 14*, 255 (1973)
110. L. L. Harrell, *Macromolecules, 2*, 607 (1969)
111. A. L. Chang, E. L. Thomas, *Advan. Chem. Ser., 176*, 31 (1979)
112. M. A. Vallance, J. L. Castles, S. L. Cooper, *Polymer 25*, 1734 (1984)
113. R. W. Seymour, A. E. Allegrezza, S. L. Cooper, *Macromolecules, 6*, 896 (1973)
114. S. L. Cooper, G. M. Estes, R. W. Seymour, *Macromolecules, 4*, 452 (1971)
115. L. Morbitzer, H. Hespe, *J. Appl. Polym. Sci., 16*, 2697 (1972)
116. S. B. Lin, K. S. Hwang, S. Y. Tsay, S. L. Cooper, *Colloid Polymer Sci., 263*, 128 (1985)
117. A. E. Allegrezza, R. W. Seymour, H. N. Ng, S. L. Cooper, *Polymer, 15*, 433 (1974)
118. W. Goyert, *Swiss Plastics 4*, 7 (1982)
119. W. Goyert, J. Winkler, H. Wagner and H. G. Hoppe (to Bayer), Eur. Pat. Appl. 15049 (1984)
120. D. J. Goldwasser, K. Onder (to Upjohn), US 4376 834 (1981)
121. Desmopan, Thermoplastic polyurethane elastomer, Order No. Pu 52016 a/e, Edition 10/84, Bayer AG, 5090 Leverkusen, W.-Germany
122. G. Oertel, *Polyurethane Handbook*, Carl Hanser Verlag, Munich 1985, page 412 and following; W. Goyert, Thermoplastic PU-Elastomers, Properties
123. W. Neumann, H. Holtschmidt, J. Peter and P. Fischer (to Bayer), US 3193522, (1965)
124. C. S. Schollenberger and F. D. Stewart, Angew. *Makromol. Chemie 29/30*, 413 (1973)
125. Technische Information; "Beständigkeit von Elastollan-Typen (= TPU) gegenüber Chemikalien", Elastogran-Chemie, Lemförde, W.-Germany
126. G. Oertel, *Polyurethane Handbook*, Carl Hanser Verlag, Munich 1985, page 548 and following; 510 and following
127. G. Oertel, *Polyurethane Handbook*, Carl Hanser Verlag Munich 1985, page 408 and following pages by B. Krüger
128. C. G. Seefried, jr., J. V. Koleske and F. E. Critchfield, *Polym. Eng. and Sci. 16*, 771 (1976)
129. R. D. Deanin, S. B. Driscoll and J. T. Krowchun, jr., *Org. Coat. Plast. Chem. Preprints 40*, 664 (1979)
130. J. M. Buist, *"Developments in Polyurethanes-1"*, 54, Applied Science Publ. Ltd., London, 1978
131. T. J. Dolce, F. Berardinelli and D. E. Hudgin (to Celanese), US Pat. 3144431 (1959)
     G. W. Miller (to Mobay), Can. Pat. 842325 (1969)
     P. N. Richardson (to DuPont), Eur. Pat. Appl. 117748 (1984)
     E. A. Flexman (to DuPont), Eur. Pat Appl. 116456, 117667, 120711 and 121407 (1984)
     E. Reske and E. Wolters (to Hoechst), Ger. Pat. Appl. *330376* (1983)
132. M. Cramer and A. D. Wambach (to General Electric), US Pat. 4279801 (1975)
133. C. B. Wang and S. L. Cooper, *J. Appl. Polym. Sci. 26*, 2989 (1981)
134. K. B. Goldblum (to General Electric), US Pat. 3431224 (1962)
135. C. N. Georgacopoulos and A. A. Sardanopoli, *Mod. Plastic Intern.* May, 96 (1982)
     G. Demma, E. Martuscelli, A. Zanetti and M. Zarzetto, *J. Materials Sci. 18*, 89 (1983)
136. M. Freifeld, G. S. Mills and R. J. Nelson (to GAF) Ger. Pat. Appl. 1694315 (1967)
137. R. A. Fava (to ARCO Polymers), US Pat. 4287314 (1980)
138. C. E. Chaney (to ARCO Polymers), US Pat. 4284734 (1980)
139. H. Sakano, F. Nakai and Y. Tomari (to Sumitomo Naugatuck), US Pat. 4373063 (1981)
140. K. H. Tan and J. L. de Greef (to Borg Warner), US Pat. 4251642 (1979)
141. W. J. O'Connell (to General Electric), US Pat. 3813358 (1972)
142. E. J. Frencken, N. G. M. Hoen and T. B. R. Drummen (to Stamicarbon), Eur. Pat. Appl. 104695 (1983)
143. A. L. Baron and J. V. Bailey (to Mobay), US Pat. 4034016 (1976)
144. T. S. Grabowski (to Borg Warner), US Pat. 3049505 (1962)
145. R. Roxburgh and D. M. Aitken (to ICI), GB Pat. 2021600 (1978)
146. R. P. Carter (to Mobay), US Pat. 4179479 (1978)
147. I. S. Megna (to American Cyanamid), US Pat. 4238574 (1979)
148. M. Rutkowska and A. Eisenberg, *J. Appl. Polym. Sci. 29*, 755 (1984)
149. R. Roxburgh, J. P. Aitken and D. M. Brown (to ICI), GB Pat. Appl. 2021603 (1978)
150. G. Zeitler, F. Werner, G. Bittner and H. M. Rombrecht (to BASF), Eur. Pat. Appl. 111682 (1983)

151. "Empfehlung XXXIX der Kunststoffkommission" of the Federal German Health Office (BGA)
152. Title 21, § 177.2600 of the FDA, USA: "Rubber articles for repeated use"
153. G. Oertel, *Polyurethane Handbook,* Carl Hanser Verlag, Munich 1985, page 424 and following pages:
     H.-G. Hoppe – Application for Polyurethane Elastomers
154. K. C. Frisch, D. Klempner, *Advances in Urethane Science and Technology,* Volume 9 (1984), page 130, *"Biomedical uses of Polyurethane"* by A. J. Coury, K. E. Cobian, P. T. Cahalan and A. J. Jevne
155. H. Ulrich and H. W. Bonk, *"Emerging Biomedical Applications of Polyurethane Elastomers",* presented at Proceedings of the SPI 27th Annual Technical/Marketing Conference
156. Gogolewski, S., abstract and lecture presented at *"Internationales Kolloquium: Polyurethane in der Medizin-Technik",* Stuttgart, Germany, January 27–29, 1983, Nr. 29
157. H. M. Leeper and R. W. Wright, *Rubber Chem. Technol., 56,* 523 (1983)
158. G. S. Pande, *Elastomerics, 116,* Nr. 7, 17 (1984)
159. M. Szycher, *Elastomerics, 116,* Nr. 7, 20 (1984)
160. W. K. Witsiepe (to DuPont) US Pat. 3,377,322 Apr. 9 (1968)

Chapter 3

THERMOPLASTIC ELASTOMERS BASED ON POLYSTYRENE-POLYDIENE BLOCK COPOLYMERS

G. Holden, N. R. Legge

Contents

G. Holden, Shell Development Co., Houston, Texas
N. R. Legge, Consultant, 19 Barkentine Rd., Rancho Palos Verdes, California

1   INTRODUCTION

Of the various types of thermoplastic elastomers described in this book, those based on tri-block copolymers of polystyrene and polydienes are the largest (in terms of commercial production[1]) and one of the earliest to be investigated. Because of their relatively simple molecular structure and the fact that this structure is uniform, unequivocal and reproducible, they have served as model polymers from which the properties of other block copolymers could be deduced by analogy. In one of the earliest papers dealing with their properties[2], the explanation of these properties, the domain theory (see later), was generalized to include "any block copolymer having or containing the structure A–B–A, where A represents a block which is glassy or crystalline at service temperatures but fluid at higher temperatures, and B represents a block which is elastomeric at service temperatures". In serving as model polymers for the whole spectrum of polymers covered by this definition, the polystyrene/polydiene block copolymers have acted as a paradigm[3], that is, their obvious technical and commercial importance combined with a reasonable and simple explanation of their properties has spurred the development of a new field of polymer science. Thus we note that since 1967, the date of the first symposium[4] on block copolymers – a symposium largely devoted to the polystyrene/polydiene type – numerous texts[5–20], symposia[4, 21–26] and review articles[27–30] have been devoted either to block copolymers or to the related subject of thermoplastic elastomers.

2   HISTORICAL REVIEW

The roots from which the tri-block polystyrene-polydiene thermoplastic elastomers grew are described in Chapter 1. Details of this innovation have been given in an recent article[31] and the various steps which led to it are as follows.

First, it is necessary to consider the state of research in the synthetic rubber industry about 1960. For many years the prime objective of this research was the economic polymerization of polyisoprene with a high cis-1,4 structure – that is, the production of a synthetic version of natural rubber. In the mid-1950's this work was stimulated by papers describing synthesis on a semi-commercial scale using both Ziegler type catalysts[32] and lithium metal catalysts[33]. About this time, workers at the Shell Development Company investigated lithium metal initiators for isoprene polymerization and found that alkyllithiums were better initiators than the metal itself, a conclusion duplicated at other industrial research laboratories[34]. With these lithium based catalysts and with properly purified monomer, there were no chain termination or chain transfer steps. Thus when all the original monomer was consumed the polymer chain still remained active – that is, it could initiate further polymerization if more monomer (either of the same or of a *different* species) was added. In 1957[35], a process was described for the manufacture of polystyrene-polydiene block copolymers using alkyllithium initiators. Although at the time these polymers were not recognized as thermoplastic elastomers, this research contributed to our background knowledge. About this time tri-block copolymers were also reported in which the polymerization initiator was difunctional[36, 37]. These were produced under condition which gave polydiene segments with relatively low 1,4 content and so the products had very poor elastomeric properties. Somewhat later a new SBR type rubber was described for use in blends with conventional vulcanized rubbers[38]. This polymer was later revealed to be an polystyrene-polybutadiene diblock polymer[39] in which one block tapered into the other.

In parallel with these developments, the melt rheology of polybutadiene[40] and polyisoprene[41] was being investigated. Both (especially polybutadiene) show Newtonian behavior, that is, the viscosities of the pure polymers approach constant values as the shear rate approaches zero. Thus even at room temperature, bales of these elastomers, although they appear to be solids, are in fact very viscous liquids. This gives serious problems in their commercial manufacture and subsequent storage. In the course of Shell Chemical research directed at this problem, these polydiene elastomers were polymerized at lower molecular weights and with short blocks of polystyrene, first at only one end and later at each end. In contrast to the diene homopolymers, these block copolymers showed non-Newtonian behavior, in that their viscosities tended towards infinity as the shear rate approached zero. In addition, their viscosities were anomalously high at other shear rates[2]. An even more striking anomaly was given by the physical properties of the triblock copolymers. When pressed into tensile sheets they showed properties in the *unvulcanized* state which were very similar to those of conventional elastomeric vulcanizates – that is, they had high tensile strength, high elongations and rapid and almost complete recovery after elongation. These examples of anomalous behavior led to the development of the domain theory. This is the theory that in the bulk state, the polystyrene short end segments of these block copolymers agglomerate. At temperatures significantly below the glass transition temperature of polystyrene, these agglomerations (the "domains") act as strong, multifunctional junction points and so the triblock copolymers behave as though they are joined in a cross-linked network[42].

When this discovery was made, the laboratory also housed a polystyrene research group who were able to contribute much expertise on the processing of thermoplastics. The combined research groups were thus able to quickly recognize that the combination of properties – thermoplasticity and elasticity – possessed by these block polymers was so outstanding that the incentives to carry the work through to commercialization were very clear. Within days of the original discovery, potential applications in injection molded footwear, solution based adhesives and injection molded mechanical goods were foreseen.

It is important to note that the discovery of these thermoplastic elastomers was serendipitous and drew on much research background. In retrospect we may identify four essential elements as contributing to this innovation. They are:

1. The in-house development and commercialization of alkyllithium polymerization systems for the manufacture of polyisoprene.
2. Early scouting research on a polystyrene-polydiene block copolymer process.
3. The existence at the discovery location of an R&D staff with much experience in both elastomers and plastics and with thermoplastics processing equipment.
4. The domain theory was very rapidly defined by this joint R&D group.

3   STRUCTURE

Most of the polystyrene/polydiene block copolymers that are thermoplastic elastomers have the basic structure poly(styrene-b-butadiene-b-styrene) or poly(styrene-b-isoprene-b-styrene), using the nomenclature of Ceresa[43]. For convenience, they will be referred to here as S–B–S and S–I–S respectively. The most important result of this structure is that they are phase separated systems, quite unlike the corresponding random copolymers. The two phases, polystyrene and polydiene, retain many of the properties of the respective homopolymers. For example, such block copolymer have two glass transition temperatures, (T_g) characteristic of the respective homopolymers whereas the equivalent random copolymers have a single intermediate T_g[2, 44–48] as shown in Figure 1. This means that in S–B–S and S–I–S block copolymers, at room temperature the polystyrene phase is strong and rigid while the polydiene phase is soft and elastomeric. If the polystyrene phase is only a minor part of the total volume, it is reasonable to postulate a phase structure shown (in idealized

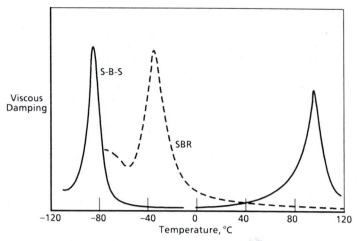

Figure 1   Viscous damping of S–B–S and SBR copolymers

form) in Figure 2. In this structure, the polystyrene phase consists of separate spherical regions (domains). Since both ends of each polydiene chain are terminated by polystyrene segments, these rigid polystyrene domains act as multifunctional junction points to give a crosslinked elastomer network similar to that of a conventional vulcanized rubber. However, in this case the cross links are formed by a physical rather than a chemical process and so are labile. At room temperature, a block copolymer of this type has many of the properties of a vulcanized rubber. However, when it is heated, the domains soften, the network loses its strength and eventually the block copolymer can flow. When the heated block copolymer is cooled down, the domains become hard again and original properties are regained. Similarly, such a block copolymer will be soluble in many solvents (generally, those which are solvents for both of the respective homopolymers) but it will regain its original properties when the solvent is evaporated.

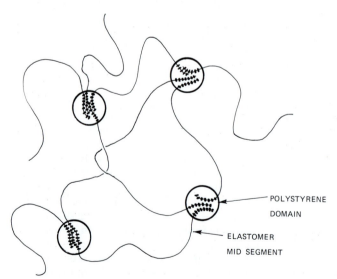

POLYSTYRENE DOMAIN

ELASTOMER MID SEGMENT

Figure 2   Phase structure of S–B–S and S–I–S block copolymers

This explanation has been given in terms of S–I–S and S–B–S block copolymers but it should apply (with similar restrictions on relative phase volumes) to other block copolymers such as S–I–S–I–S–I ... and (S–B)$_n$x (where x represents a multifunctional junction point), since these should be able to form continuous network structures similar to that shown in Figure 2. On the other hand, block copolymers such as S–I and B–S–B cannot form these structures, since only one end of each polydiene chain is terminated by a polystyrene segment. Because of this, these block copolymers are weak materials with no resemblance to conventional vulcanized rubbers.

When this explanation was first postulated, it was generalized to include all block copolymers with alternating hard and soft segments and specifically it was applied to polycarbonate/polyether and poly(dimethyl siloxane)/poly(silphenylene siloxane) block copolymers[2]. A similar explanation was applied by analogy to segmented polyurethanes[49, 50] and it is now accepted as the underlying mechanism which gives most thermoplastic elastomers their valuable properties.

4   SYNTHESIS

S–B–S, S–I–S and similar block copolymers are made by anionic polymerization[51,52]. This reaction is limited to only three common monomers – styrene (including substituted styrenes), butadiene and isoprene. It is usually carried out in an inert hydrocarbon solvent such as cyclohexane or toluene and it is necessary to rigorously exclude oxygen, water or any impurity that can react with the highly reactive propagating species. Under these conditions the polymeric molecular weights can be precisely controlled. This is in contrast to other block and graft copolymers which generally contain a broad distribution both of the segment molecular weights and also of their arrangements in the polymer molecule. The preferred initiators are organolithiums, although others can be used[51]. There are three basic methods:

1. Sequential. i.e., start polymerization at one end of the molecule and continue to the other.
2. Coupling. i.e., start polymerization at each end of the molecule and then join the reactive chains together by a coupling or linking agent.
3. Multi-functional Initiation. i.e., start polymerization at the center of the molecule and continue to the ends, using initiators which have more than one active group.

In the first two polymerization methods, sec-butyl lithium is the preferred initiator because it initiates the polymerization very readily[34]. That is to say, the rate of the initiation reaction is high compared to that of the subsequent polymerization. This initiator first reacts with one molecule of styrene monomer. This is known as the initiation reaction.

$$R^-Li^+ + CH_2{=}CH \longrightarrow RCH_2CH^-Li^+ \tag{1}$$

The product can then continue polymerization of the styrene and this is known as the propagation reaction.

$$RCH_2CH^-Li^+ + nCH_2{=}CH \longrightarrow R(CH_2CH)_nCH_2CH^-Li^+ \tag{2}$$

The new end product is termed polystyrol lithium (the effects of the terminal sec-butyl radical are ignored) and we will denote it as S^-Li^+. If a diene (in this case butadiene) is added, the S^-Li^+ can initiate further polymerization:

$$S^-Li^+ + nCH_2=CHCH=CH_2 \longrightarrow S(CH_2CH=CHCH_2)_{n-1}CH_2CH=CHCH_2{}^-Li^+ \qquad (3)$$

In the above example, the polymerization is shown to take place exclusively through the end or 1,4 carbon atoms. Polymerization in hydrocarbon solvents which are inert and non-polar gives at least 90% of the polymer in this arrangement. The remaining material is polymerized through either the 1,2 carbon atoms (in the case of butadiene) or through the 3,4 carbon atoms (in the case of isoprene). For the above reaction, we will denote the product $S-B^-Li^+$. It also is an initiator, so that if more styrene monomer is now added, it will polymerize onto the "living" end of the polymer chain:

$$S-B^-Li^+ + nCH_2=CH \longrightarrow S-B(CH_2CH)_{n-1}CH_2CH^-Li^+ \qquad (4)$$

This can give some difficulty because the rate of initiation of styrene polymerization by the $S-B^-Li^+$ is slow compared to the rate of the subsequent propagation reaction. This effect broadens the molecular weight distribution of the second polystyrene segment. In extreme cases there may even be some $S-B^-Li^+$ molecules still unreacted when all the added styrene monomer is consumed. The problem can be avoided by adding solvating agents, such as ethers, just before the styrene is added. This increases the initiation rate and gives a much narrower molecular weight distribution to second polystyrene segment. It is important not to add solvating agents before this step because they also alter the microstructure of the polydiene, reducing the amount of 1,4 enchainment.

When this last reaction is complete, the product ($S-B-S^-Li^+$) can be inactivated by the addition of a protonating species such as an alcohol. This terminates the reaction:

$$S-B-S^-Li^+ + ROH \longrightarrow S-B-SH + ROLi \qquad (5)$$

If the polymer is to be made by coupling, the first three reactions shown above are unchanged, but instead of the $S-B^-Li^+$ initiating further polymerization of styrene, in this case it is reacted with a coupling agent:

$$2S-B^-Li^+ + X-R-X \longrightarrow S-B-R-B-S + 2LiX \qquad (6)$$

Many coupling agents have been described, including esters, organohalogens and silicon halides[27-29]. The example above shows the reaction of a difunctional coupling agents but those of higher functionality (for example $SiCl_4$) can also be used and give branched or star-shaped molecules $(S-B)_nX$. If divinyl benzene is added at the end of the reaction the products are highly branched, i.e., the value of n is very large[28, 29].

The third method of producing these block copolymers uses multifunctional initiation. In this method a multifunctional initiator ($Li^+{}^-R^-Li^+$) is first reacted with the diene (in this case butadiene).

$$nCH_2=CHCH=CH_2 + Li^+{}^-R^-Li^+ \longrightarrow Li^+{}^-B-R-B^-Li^+ \qquad (7)$$

The final two steps are similar to the corresponding steps in the sequential polymerization described above. When the reaction to produce the $Li^{+-}B–R–B^-Li^+$ is completed, styrene monomer is added and the $Li^{+-}B–R–B^-Li^+$ in turn initiates its polymerization onto the "living" chain ends to give $Li^{+-}S–B–R–B–S^-Li^+$. A protonating species is then added to terminate the reaction and give the S–B–R–B–S polymer. This example shows the use of a difunctional initiator. There is no reason in principle why initiators of higher functionality could not be used but none appears to have been reported in the literature.

Multifunctional initiation has received less attention than the preceding two methods, although early workers used a sodium napthalene diinitiator[36, 37]. In addition, multifunctional initiation has the serious deficiency that "living" chain ends associate when the polymerization is carried out in hydrocarbon solvent. This causes such multifunctionally initiated polymers to gel as soon as the reaction starts, which gives significant problems with heat removal etc. Although this association can be prevented by the use solvating agents such as ethers, as noted above, these in turn alter the microstructure of the polydiene. For these reasons elastomer research groups have done little work with sodium napthalene diinitiators.

S–I–S and S–B–S block copolymers are the precursors of styrenic block copolymers with saturated elastomer center segments (see Chapter 14). If S–B–S polymers are used, they are polymerized in the presence of a structure modifier to give elastomer segments which are a mixture of 1,4 and 1,2 isomers and these are subsequently hydrogenated to give ethylene-butylene copolymers, (EB):

$$-CH_2-CH=CH-CH_2\!\!+\!\!CH-CH_2- \xrightarrow{H_2} -CH_2-CH_2-CH_2-CH_2\!\!+\!\!CH-CH_2- \qquad (8)$$

		CH			CH₂
		‖			
		CH₂			CH₃
1,4		1,2	E		B

Similarly polyisoprene elastomer segments can be hydrogenated to give ethylene-propylene copolymers, (EP). The resultant S–EB–S and S–EP–S block copolymers have improved resistance to degradation.

All the above block copolymers have polystyrene end segments. This has been the preferred material for this type of block copolymer but substituted polystyrenes can be used also. Among those used are poly(alpha-methyl-styrene)[53], copolymers of alpha-methylstyrene and styrene[54,55] and poly(para tert. butylstyrene)[56]. The attractive feature of all three is their relatively high T_g. However, alpha-methylstyrene is difficult to polymerize[57] because it has a slow reaction rate and a low ceiling temperature. (This is the temperature at which the rate of the depolymerization reaction is the same as the rate of the polymerization reaction). Poly(para tert. butylstyrene) is apparently rather compatible with the polydienes and so only forms a phase separated system at relatively high molecular weights[56].

5   PROPERTIES

5.1   Tensile Properties

From a commercial point of view, the most interesting property of these polymers is their resemblance, at least at room temperatures, to vulcanized rubbers. This was shown in very early work[58], where the stress-strain behavior of an S–B–S was compared to that of vulcanized natural rubber and vulcanized SBR, see Figure 3. This and similar block copolymers typically have tensile strengths of about 30 MPa (about 4000 psi) and elongations of up to 800%. These values (particularly tensile strength) are much higher than those obtained from unreinforced vulcanizates of SBR or polybutadiene. This apparent anomaly has been explained by two possible mechanisms[2]. The first postulates that the domains act as reinforcing filler and the second takes account of the increased tensile strength resulting from the slippage of entangled chains. It is quite possible that both apply. What is clear is that for materials of constant polystyrene content, the tensile moduli and tensile strengths of both S–B–S[2] and S–I–S[30] polymers are not molecular weight dependent, so long as the polystyrene molecular weight is high enough to cause the formation of strong, well separated domains under the conditions of the test.

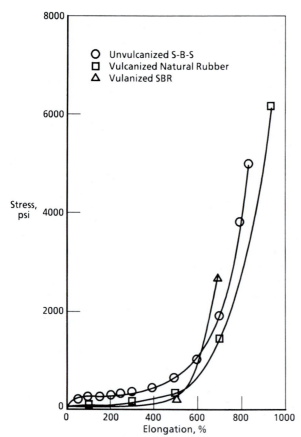

Figure 3   Stress-strain properties of elastomers

These observations lead to the interesting and still unresolved question of the mechanism of tensile failure in styrenic block copolymers. There appears to be three possible mechanisms:

1. Ductile failure in the styrenic domains.
2. Brittle fracture in the styrenic domains.
3. Elastic failure in the polydiene center segments.

The case for the first mechanism has been put very strongly[30]. It is supported by the fact that in otherwise similar polymers, when the end segments were changed from polystyrene to poly(alpha methylstyrene), both the tensile strength and the tensile modulus were almost doubled[59]. This suggests that the glass transition temperature of the styrenic phase, which for poly(alpha methylstyrene) is about 70 °C higher than for polystyrene[55], is the controlling parameter. This of course is exactly what would be expected if ductile flow of the domains is the mechanism leading to failure. Against this may be argued the fact that the tensile properties are not affected by molecular weight (see above), a factor which must strongly influence such ductile flow. Both ductile flow and rupture of the domains have been observed in electron micrographs. The failure envelope (the locus of the point defining the tensile strength and elongation at break under various test conditions) has been measured for an S–B–S polymer, Figure 4, and appeared to go through some kind of transition at about 40 °C[59]. It was suggested that failure took place in the domains and at about this temperature the mode changed from brittle to ductile. The case for failure taking place in the elastomer phase rests with the fact that as S–B–S or S–I–S triblock polymers are diluted by S–B or S–I diblocks, tensile strength and tensile modulus both decrease.

It is possible that which of the mechanisms will apply in a particular case depends on the conditions. At high temperatures, as the domains soften, they will be the "weak link in the chain" and ductile failure will predominate. The same effect will apply when the time scale of the test is long. At lower temperatures or shorter times one of the other two mechanisms will take over. For relatively pure S–I–S or S–B–S polymers, it is hard to say which of these

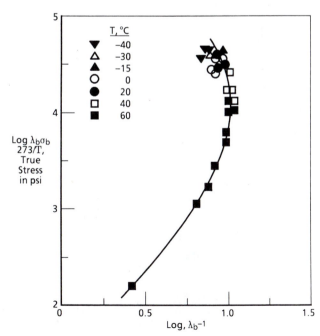

Figure 4   Failure envelope of an S–B–S block copolymer

two mechanisms will predominate but as more diblock is added, this will weaken the elastomer phase to the point where it will clearly be the site of failure.

The analogy between the domains in these block copolymers and the reinforcing fillers such as carbon black in conventional vulcanizates also extends to the stress-softening or Mullins effect (see later). Thus most block copolymers show a loss in modulus between the first and subsequent extensions[60, 61].

Another interesting point is the elastic modulus of these materials. It is anomalously high and does not vary with molecular weight. In a simple approach, this is attributed to trapped entanglements in the elastomer center segments acting as cross links. If this is the case, the molecular weight between entanglements is the critical parameter. This value (rather than the segmental molecular weight) can used to calculate both the elastic modulus[2] and the degree of swelling in solvents which are incompatible with the polystyrene phase but compatible with the elastomer phase[62]. This gives much better agreement and also predicts that at constant styrene content, the elastic modulus of otherwise similar block copolymers should increase in the order S–I–S, S–B–S, S–EB–S[63]. The subject is reviewed in much more detail in an article by Bard and Chung (see Chapter 12) but the basic conclusion – that by far the largest contribution to the modulus derives from trapped entanglements – remains the same.

5.2   Viscous and Viscoelastic Properties

A very striking feature of S–B–S and S–I–S block copolymers is their melt viscosities[2, 64]. Under low shear conditions, these are much higher than those of either polybutadiene[40],

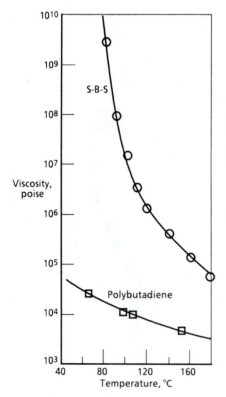

Figure 5   Viscosities of polymers at constant shear stress

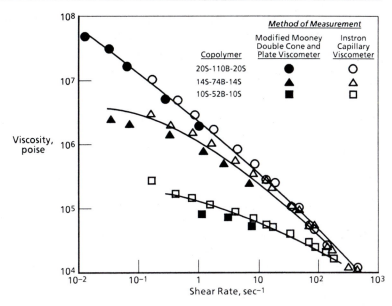

Figure 6   Viscosities of S–B–S block copolymers at 175 °C. From reference 2 with permission

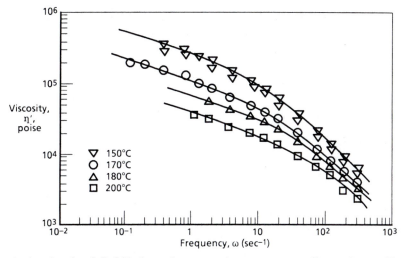

Figure 7   Dynamic viscosity of an S–B–S block copolymer at various temperatures. From reference 67 with permission

polyisoprene[41] or random copolymers of styrene and butadiene[65] of equivalent molecular weights. Figure 5, for example, shows a comparison of the viscosities of an S–B–S and a polybutadiene each of about 75,000 molecular weight. Moreover, these block copolymers show non-Newtonian behavior, that is their viscosities increase as the shear is decreased and apparently approach infinite values at zero shear. This behavior is shown both under steady state[2, 64] and dynamic conditions[66, 67], see Figures 6 and 7. It is attributed[2, 66] to the persistence of a two phase structure in the melt similar to that shown in Figure 1. In such a structure, flow can only take place by the polystyrene segments at the ends of the elastomer chains being pulled out of the domains. Above a critical molecular weight (see later), the polystyrene segments are phase separated at all temperatures of practical importance and so even though the polystyrene is above its T_g (and therefore fluid), it requires an extra amount of energy to bring it into the elastomer phase. This energy is manifested as an increased viscosity. It should increase with the degree of incompatibility between the end and center segments and therefore the viscosity should also increase with the segmental incompatibility. This is seen to a very striking degree in similar S–EB–S block copolymers, which have very high (and very non-Newtonian) viscosities because of their extreme segmental incompatibility (see Chapter 14). Conversely, in similar polymers with polyethylene end segments (i.e., E–EB–E) the end and center segments are sufficiently compatible so that there is apparently no phase separation in the melt. For this reason E–EB–E block copolymers have very low melt viscosities[68].

The dynamic mechanical behavior of these block copolymers is also unusual. For most polymers the results can be expressed by using the WLF[69] approach. In this method the dynamic mechanical properties are measured at various fixed temperatures and over a range of frequencies. The data are plotted on a master curve by applying appropriate shift factors, which depend on the difference between the temperature of measurement and a reference temperature. This reference temperature is related to the T_g of the polymer. As noted previously, these block copolymers have two T_gs[2, 44–48] and so this technique cannot be directly applied. Several modifications have been used. In one the shift factors for these block copolymers at low temperatures were calculated using a reference temperature appropriate for polybutadiene and at high temperatures using one appropriate for polystyrene. At other temperatures they can be calculated using a "sliding" T_g intermediate between the two[70]. In another approach, an extra factor at higher temperatures was added to reflect the viscoelastic response of the polystyrene domains[71] and in later work it was concluded that shift factors dependent both on temperature and on frequency were necessary to describe the behavior of S–B–S block copolymers with both high and low 1,2 content in the polybutadiene segments[72].

From a practical point of view, one of the most interesting aspects of the viscoelastic behavior of block copolymers is in their application as pressure sensitive adhesives (see Chapter 13). Here, the concept of using resins to both soften the polymer by diluting the elastomer phase and also to modify its viscoelastic response has resulted in a most fruitful and elegant explanation of the adhesive behavior.

5.3   Solution Properties

The properties of dilute solutions of these polymers in relatively good solvents are quite normal. Of course, there are some difficulties applying theories of molecular behavior that apply to theta solvents, since no solvent can simultaneously provide theta conditions for both the elastomer and the polystyrene segments. Nevertheless, good approximations can be made to such dilute solution properties as intrinsic viscosity, which has been measured in a range of solvents, see Figure 8[73]. It was maximized when then solubility parameter of the solvent was about 8.6 $(cal/cc)^{1/2}$. In contrast, the viscosities of concentrated (24.8% w/v) solutions were minimized in the same region, Figure 9. Allowances must be made for the fact that there is some interference between the coils of the two segmental types and also that the environment surrounding each segmental chain is not just that of the solvent alone but also that of the other segments in the same molecule.

As the solutions become more concentrated phase separation begins and evidence of ordered structures is observed. The first indications were given by the iridescence of these solutions[74], and in later work small angle X-ray scattering was used to establish domain sizes, interdomain distances and morphologies[75–79]. The domain sizes depend on the polystyrene molecular weights and on the thermal histories of the solutions[80].

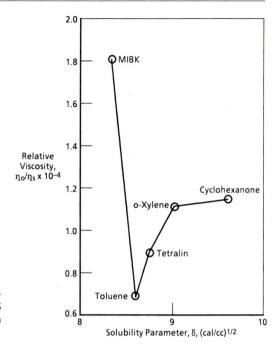

Figure 8   Effect of solvent solubility parameter on the solution viscosity of an S–B–S block copolymer. From reference 73 with permission

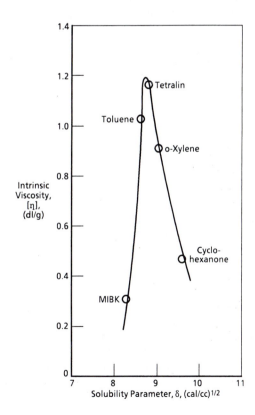

Figure 9   Effect of solvent solubility parameter on the intrinsic viscosity of an S–B–S block copolymer. From reference 73 with permission

5.4 Morphology

The morphology of the systems is one of their most interesting features. The idealized structure shown in Figure 1 was postulated from the mechanical and rheological behavior of S—I–S and S–B–S block copolymers – there were no direct observations to support it. At the same time changes in phase arrangement with the relative proportions of the two segmental types were also postulated – again without any direct observations[2]. One problem was that the domains are too small to be observed by visible light, which is why these block copolymers are transparent. However, the development of a staining technique using osmium tetroxide[81] allowed the morphologies to be established by electron microscopy[46] and this work confirmed that the postulated structures were at least conceptually correct. Later, a more detailed picture of the morphological changes with block copolymer composition was proposed[82], see Figure 10 in which, as the styrene content is increased, the morphology of the polystyrene phase changes from spheres to cylinders, both dispersed in a continuous elastomer phase. When the volume fractions of the elastomer and polystyrene phase are about equal, the two form alternating lamellae. With further increase in the styrene content a continuous polystyrene phase forms in which either cylinders of spheres of the elastomer are dispersed. This picture was supported by electron micrographs showing regularly spaced lamellae in block copolymers of intermediate (i.e. about 50 %) styrene content[83]. Later work showed that at lower (about 30 %) styrene content, a remarkably regular hexagonal array of polystyrene domains dispersed in the elastomer matrix could be obtained, especially if the sample was slowly cast from the solvent[84, 85], see Figure 11. Rods containing hexagonally packed cylindrical polystyrene domains were produced by extrusion under carefully controlled conditions and shown by small angle X-ray scattering to have almost "single crystal" perfection. Electron microscopy of ultra thin sections of these rods showed the dramatic regularity and effectively infinite length of these cylindrical polystyrene domains[86]. Application of an oscillating shear field was found to be even more effective in ordering block copolymer domains into either hexagonally packed cylindrical arrays or alternating lamellae[87, 88]. Which was formed in a particular case depended on the polystyrene content of the polymer, with the formation of lamellae being favored when the volume fractions of the polystyrene and the elastomer were about equal.

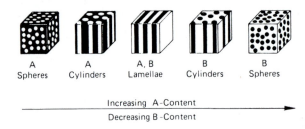

A   A   A, B   B   B
Spheres   Cylinders   Lamellae   Cylinders   Spheres

Increasing A-Content
Decreasing B -Content

Figure 10   Changes in the morphology of an A–B–A block copolymer as a function of composition. From reference 82 with permission

When samples are cast from solution, the morphologies of the resultant films depend on the nature of the solvent. Good solvents for the polystyrene segments favor the formation of a continuous polystyrene phase. This gives products which are relatively stiff and inelastic. Conversely, good solvents for the elastomer segments favor the formation of a dispersed polystyrene phase and this gives softer, more elastic products[89, 90]. When these block copolymers (particularly those with a continuous polystyrene phase) are extended, there is an obvious stress-softening, similar to the Mullins effect in conventional reinforced vulcanizates[90, 91]. Thus when the polymer is stretched to an elongation below its ultimate elongation, allowed to retract and then restretched, it shows much higher modulus during the first extension than during the second and subsequent ones. This behavior appears to be caused by rupture of the continuous polystyrene phase during elongation to give discrete domains[92] and has been investigated by both electron microscopy and small angle X-ray scattering.

Figure 11   Electron micrograph of an (S–I)$_4$x block copolymer. The polyisoprene phase is stained black. From reference 85, Macromolecules, © 1975, Am. Chem. Soc.

5.5   Stress-Optical Properties

Birefringence measurements during elongation of S–B–S block copolymers at several temperatures supported the view that below temperatures of about 70 °C, the decrease in strength and modulus were not caused by flow of the polystyrene segments but rather by increased mobility of the polybutadiene chains[91]. In an unstrained S–B–S sample, the difference between calculated and observed birefringence was attributed to residual stresses in the domains[93]. However, when the samples were stretched, clamped and annealed below the polystyrene T$_g$, molecular orientation caused a very large increase in the birefringence[94]. Increasing the annealing temperature removed this effect.

5.6   Critical Molecular Weights for Domain Formation

In block copolymers complete miscibility of the segments will take place if the free energy of mixing (ΔG_m) is favorable, i.e. negative. This free energy can be expressed as:

$$\Delta G_m = \Delta H_m - T\Delta S_m \tag{9}$$

where ΔH_m and ΔS_m are the enthalpy and entropy of mixing and T is the absolute temperature. Thus the condition for domain formation is that:

$$\Delta H_m > T \, \Delta S_m \tag{10}$$

For hydrocarbon polymers, ΔH_m is positive, since there are no strongly interacting groups, and will increase as the structures of the two polymers forming the segments become less alike. ΔS_m will always be positive but will approach zero as the molecular weights of the segments become large. Thus we can expect domain formation to be favored by several factors:

1. A high degree of structural difference between the segments
2. High segmental molecular weight
3. Low temperatures.

Using this approach, the theory of domain formation has been extensively developed and quantified (see Chapter 11). In experimental work, the effects of structural differences are shown by the fact that E–EB–E block copolymers are apparently not phase separated in the melt[69] whereas a strong separation exists for corresponding S–EB–S copolymers (see Chapter 14). The effects of molecular weight and temperature have been demonstrated by work on an experimental S–B–S with end segments molecular weights of 7,000. Measurements of both the steady state[95] and dynamic viscosities[96] showed that for this polymer the critical temperature for domain formation was about 150 °C. Another S–B–S block copolymer with end segments molecular weights of 8,000 was reported to show Newtonian behavior at 160 °C[96] and so is apparently not phase separated at this temperature. On the other hand, similar block copolymers with end segment molecular weights of 10,000 and greater appeared to be phase separated at temperatures up to 200 °C[2, 66]. These values of the critical molecular weights and temperatures for domain formation agree quite well with the predictions of the theory. In an extension of the original theory, the effects of adding homopolymers to block copolymers were also accounted for[97]. It was shown that even if the homopolymer is structurally identical to one segment of the block copolymer, significant amounts will not be miscible unless the homopolymer molecular weight is much less than that of the corresponding segment in the block copolymer. This has also been at least qualitatively confirmed[98]. In n-tetradecane, a good solvent for polybutadiene but a poor one for polystyrene, an S–B–S copolymer with higher segmental molecular weights gave a phase separated gel at lower temperatures but an apparently homogeneous solution at higher temperatures. The temperature at which the solution became homogeneous depended strongly on concentration[99].

5.7 Structural Variations

Almost all of the work described above has dealt with triblock copolymers having terminal polystyrene segments and center elastomer segments. Commercially these are the most important, but other types have been prepared.

In early work linear multiblock copolymers with the general structure $(S–I)_n$ and having a total of up to nine segments were reported[100]. Later the rheological properties of a series of linear and branched polymers having 30% polystyrene content and with the structures S–B–S, $(S–B)_3x$, $(S–B)_4x$, B–S–B and $(B–S)_3x$ were compared[101]. At the same total molecular weight, polymers of the first three types (i.e. those with terminal polystyrene segments) showed much higher viscosities than those of the last two types (those with terminal polybutadiene segments). At equal *total* molecular weights, the linear polymers (S–B–S and B–S–B) were much more viscous than the branched equivalents. However, if the linear polymers were considered as di-branched materials (i.e. $(S–B)_2x$ and $(B–S)_2x$ respectively), then at equal arm length there was little difference between the viscous or visco-elastic responses of equivalent linare and branched polymers. Solution viscosities and Melt Flows[102] of a series of S–B–S, $(S–B)_3x$ and $(S–B)_4x$ polymers with 25% styrene content also showed the same tendency[103], i.e., the polymers behaved very similarly if they were compared at equal arm length. The behavior in the melt state supports the view that in this state these polymers are phase separated[2, 66]. In the case of an S–B–S or (S–B)$_n$x polymer, flow will take place by disruption of the disperse polystyrene phase and extra energy will be required for this. This extra energy will depend on the molecular weight of the polystyrene segments and branching in the polybutadiene phase will not have much effect on it. Conversely, for B–S–B and (B–S)$_n$x polymers, flow can take place in the continuous polybutadiene phase without disruption of the polystyrene domains. The energy required for this will be much less and so the viscosity will be lower.

References

1. R. School, *Rubber Plast. News 49,* (May 7, 1984)
2. G. Holden, E. T. Bishop, and N. R. Legge, *"Thermoplastic Elastomers"*, Proc. International Rubber Conference, 1967, MacLaren and Sons, London, p. 287 (1968), *J. Polym. Sci., Pt. C 26,* 37 (1969)
3. T. S. Kuhn, *"The Structure of Scientific Revolutions"*, University of Chicago Press, Chicago (1970)
4. J. Moacanin, G. Holden, and N. W. Tschoegl, Eds., Symposium sponsored by the California Institute Technology and the American Chemical Society, Pasadena, CA, 1967; *J. Polym. Sci., Pt. C 26* (1969)
5. *"Block Copolymers"*, D. C. Allport and W. H. Janes, Eds., John Wiley & Sons, New York (1972)
6. R. J. Ceresa, Ed., *"Block and Graft Polymerization"*, John Wiley & Sons, New York (1972)
7. *"Block and Graft Copolymers"*, J. J. Burke and V. Weiss, Eds., Syracuse, New York (1973)
8. G. E. Molau, Ed., *"Colloidal and Morphological Behavior of Block and Graft Copolymers"*, Plenum Press, New York (1970)
9. S. L. Cooper and G. M. Estes, Eds., *"Multiphase Polymers"*, Advances in Chemistry Series, No. 176, American Chemical Society, Washington, D. C., 1979
10. A. Eisenberg and M. King, *"Ion Containing Polymers"*, Academic, New York (1977)
11. A. Noshay and J. E. McGrath, *"Block Copolymers-Overview and Critical Survey"*, Academic, New York (1977)
12. D. Klempner and K. C. Frisch, Eds., *"Polymer Alloys-Blends, Blocks, Grafts and Interpenetrating Networks"*, Plenum, New York (1977)
13. D. Klempner and K. C. Frisch, Eds., *"Polymer Alloys II"*, Plenum, New York (1980)
14. O. Olabisi, L. M. Robeson, and M. T. Shaw, *"Polymer-Polymer Miscibility"*, Academic, New York (1979)
15. D. R. Paul and S. Newman, Eds., *"Polymer Blends"*, Academic, New York Vol. 1 and 2 (1978)
16. N. A. J. Platzer, *"Copolymer, Polyblends, and Composites"*, Advances in Chemistry Series, No. 142, American Chemical Society, Washington, D. C. (1975)
17. L. H. Sperling, *"Interpenetrating Polymer Networks and Related Materials"*, Plenum, New York (1981)
18. Yu. S. Lipatou and L. M. Sergeena, *"Interpenetrating Polymeric Networks"*, Naukova Dumka, Kiev (1979)
19. B. M. Walker, Ed., *Handbook of Thermoplastic Elastomers,* Van Nostrand, New York (1979)
20. A. D. Thorn, *Thermoplastic Elastomers – A Review of Current Information,* Rubber and Plastics Research Association of Great Britain, Shawbury, Shrewsbury, Shropshire SY4 4NR, Great Britain (1980)
21. S. L. Aggarwal, Ed., *"Block Polymers"*, Proc. Am. Chem. Soc. Symposium, New York (1969); Plenum Press, New York (1970)
22. L. H. Sperling, Ed., *"Recent Advances in Polymer Blends, Grafts, and Blocks"*, Proc. Am. Chem. Soc. Symposium, Chicago (1973); Plenum Press, New York (1974)
23. C. E. Rogers and A. Skoulios, Eds., *Poly. Eng. Sci. 17* (8), (1977)
24. R. J. Ambrose and S. L. Aggarwal, Eds., *J. Polym. Sci., Poly. Symp. 60,* (1977)
25. ACS Rubber Div. Symposium on *"Thermoplastic Elastomers"*, Los Angeles, CA. April 25, 1985
26. ACS Symposium on *"Advances in Elastomers and Rubber Elasticity"*, Chicago, IL. Sept. 10, 1985

27. N. R. Legge, G. Holden, S. Davison and H. E. DeLaMare in *"Applied Polymer Science"*, J. K. Craver and R. W. Tess, Eds. Organic Coatings and Plastics Chemistry Division, American Chemical Society, Washington, D.C., 1975, ch. 29

28. N. R. Legge, S. Davison, H. E. DeLaMare, G. Holden and M. K. Martin in *"Applied Polymer Science, 2nd Ed."* R. W. Tess and G. W. Poehlein, Eds. ACS Symposium Series No. 285, American Chemical Society, Washington, D.C., 1985, ch. 9

29. P. Dreyfuss, L. J. Fetters and D. R. Hansen. *Rubber Chem. Technol. 53,* 728 (1980)

30. M. Morton, *Rubber Chem. Technol. 56,* 1069 (1983)

31. N. R. Legge, *"Thermoplastic Elastomers Based on Three-Block Polymers – A Successful Innovation"*, presented at a Symposium on Innovation and Creativity in the Rubber Industry, ACS Rubber Div. Meeting, Philadelphia, PA. May 4, 1982; *Chemtech 13,* 630 (1983)

32. S. E. Horne Jr., et al, *Ind. Eng. Chem. 48,* 784 (1956)

33. F. W. Stavely, et al, *Ind. Eng. Chem. 48,* 778 (1956)

34. L. E. Foreman, *"Polymer Chemistry of Synthetic Elastomers"*, Part II, Kennedy & Tornquist, Eds., John Wiley & Sons, New York, p. 497 (1969)

35. L. M. Porter (to Shell Oil Co.), U.S. Patent 3, 149, 182 (1964), filed 1957

36. M. Szwarc, M. Levy, R. Milkovich, *J. Am. Chem. Soc. 78,* 2656 (1956)

37. M. Szwarc, *Nature 178,* 1168 (1956). See also A. F. Halasa, *Rubber Chem. Technol. 54,* 627 (1981) and M. Szwarc, *Polym. Prep. 26* (1), 198 (1985)

38. W. W. Crouch and J. N. Short, *Rubber Plastics Age 42,* 276 (1961)

39. H. E. Railsback, C. C. Beard, J. R. Haws, *Rubber Age 94,* 583 (1964)

40. J. T. Gruver and G. Kraus, *J. Polym. Sci. Pt. A, 2,* 797 (1964)

41. G. Holden, *J. Appl. Polym. Sci., 9,* 2911 (1965)

42. G. Holden and R. Milkovich, (to Shell Oil Co.), U.S. Patent 3, 265, 765 (1964) filed Jan. 1962

43. R. J. Ceresa, *"Block and Graft Copolymers"*, Butterworth, Washington, D.C. (1962)

44. G. Kraus, C. W. Childers, and J. T. Gruver, *J. Appl. Polym. Sci., 11,* 1581 (1967)

45. R. J. Angelo, R. M. Ikeda, and M. L. Wallach, *Polymer 6,* 141 (1965)

46. H. Hendus, K. H. Illers, and E. Ropte, *Kolloid Z. Z. Polymere 216–217,* 110 (1967)

47. J. F. Beecher, L. Marker, R. D. Bradford, and S. L. Aggarwal, *J. Polym. Sci. Pt. C 26,* 117 (1969)

48. D. G. Fesko and N. W. Tschoegl, *Intern. J. Polym. Mater. 3,* 51 (1974)

49. S. L. Cooper and A. V. Tobolsky, *J. Appl. Polym. Sci. 10,* 1837 (1966)

50. S. L. Cooper and A. V. Tobolsky, *Textile Res. J. 36,* 800 (1966)

51. M. Morton, *"Anionic Polymerization: Principles and Practice"* Academic Press, New York, NY (1983)

52. J. E. McGrath, Ed., *"Anionic Polymerization. Kinetics Mechanics and Synthesis"*, ACS Symposium Series No. 166, American Chemical Society, Washington, D.C. (1981)

53. L. J. Fetters and M. Morton, *Macromolecules 2,* 190 (1969)

54. F. E. Neumann (to Shell Oil Co), *Brit. Patent 1,* 264, 741

55. G. Y. Lo and L. H. Tung, Paper presented at ACS Symposium on "Advances in Elastomers and Rubber Elasticity", Chicago, IL. Sept. 10, 1985. To be published in proceedings of the conference.

56. R. E. Cunningham, *J. Appl. Polym. Sci. 22,* 2907 (1978)

57. p. 256 of Ref. 29

58. J. T. Bailey, E. T. Bishop, W. R. Hendricks, G. Holden and N. R. Legge *Rubber Age, 98* (10), 69 (1966)

59. T. L. Smith and R. A. Dickie, *J. Polym. Sci. Pt. C 26,* 163 (1969)

60. D. Puett, K. J. Smith, and A. Ciferri, *J. Phys. Chem., 69,* 141 (1965)

61. E. Fisher and J. F. Henderson, *Rubber Chem. Technol. 40,* 1313 (1967)

62. E. T. Bishop and S. Davison, *J. Polym. Sci. Pt. C 26,* 59 (1969)

63. G. Holden, Article "Elastomers, Thermoplastic" in *Encyclopedia of Polymer Science and Engineering*, 2nd ed, J. I. Kroschwitz, Ed. John Wiley & Sons, Inc., New York, NY, Vol 15, p 416

64. C. W. Childers and G. Kraus, *Rubber Chem. Technol. 40,* 1183 (1967)

65. G. Kraus and G. T. Gruver, *Trans. Soc. Rheol. 13,* 15 (1969)

66. G. Kraus and G. T. Gruver, *J. Appl. Polym. Sci. 11,* 2121 (1967)

67. K. R. Arnold and D. J. Meier, *J. Appl. Polym. Sci. 14,* 427 (1970)

68. M. Morton, N.-C. Lee and E. R. Terrill, *Polym. Prep. (2),* 136 (1981); ACS Symposium Series No. 193 American Chemical Society, Washington, D.C. 1982, p. 101

69. J. D. Ferry, *Viscoelastic Properties of Polymers,* 2nd. ed. John Wiley & Sons Inc., New York, NY, 1971, p. 344

70. M. Shen and D. H. Kaelble, *Polymer Letters 8,* 149 (1970)

71. C. K. Lim, R. E. Cohen and N. W. Tschoegl, *Advances in Chemistry Series,* No. 99, American Chemical Society, Washington, D.C. (1971)

72. R. E. Cohen and N. W. Tschoegl, *Trans. Soc. Rheol. 20,* 153 (1976)

73. D. R. Paul, J. E. St. Lawrence and J. H. Troell, *Polym. Engr. Sci. 10,* 70 (1970)

74. E. Vanzo, *J. Polym. Sci. Al 4,* 1727 (1966)

75. M. Shibayama, T. Hashimoto and H. Kawai, *Macromolecules 16,* 16 (1983)

76. T. Hashimoto, M. Shibayama, H. Kawai, H. Wanatabe and T. Kotaka, *Macromolecules 16,* 361 (1983)

77. M. Shibayama, T. Hashimoto, H. Hasegawa and H. Kawai, *Macromolecules 16,* 1427 (1983)

78. T. Hashimoto, M. Shibayama and H. Kawai, *Macromolecules 16,* 1093 (1983)

79. M. Shibayama, T. Hashimoto and H. Kawai, *Macromolecules 16,* 1434 (1983)

80. C. J. Stacy and G. Kraus, *Polym. Engr. Sci. 17,* 627 (1977)

81. K. Kato, *Polym. Engr. Sci. 7,* 38 (1967)

82. G. E. Molau, *"Block Polymers",* S. L. Aggarwal, Ed., Plenum Press, New York , NY, p. 79 (1970)

83. E. B. Bradford and E. Vanzo, *J. Polym. Sci. Pt. A-1 6,* 1661 (1968)

84. P. R. Lewis and C. Price, *Polymer 13,* 20 (1972)

85. L. K. Bi and L. J. Fetters, *Macromolecules 8,* 98 (1975)

86. J. A. Odell, J. Dlugosz and A. Keller, *J. Polym. Sci., Polym. Phys. Ed., 14,* 861 (1976)

87. G. Hadziioannou, A. Mathis and A. Skoulios, *Colloid Polym. Sci., 257,* 136 (1979)

88. G. Hadziioannou and A. Skoulios, *Macromolecules 15,* 258 (1982), *15,* 263 (1982), *15,* 267 (1982)

89. J. F. Beecher, L. Marker, R. D. Bradford and S. L. Aggarwal, *J. Polym. Sci., Pt. C 26,* 117 (1969)

90. D. M. Brunwin, E. Fischer and J. F. Henderson, *J. Polym. Sci., Pt. C 26,* 117 (1969)

91. E. Fischer and J. F. Henderson, *J. Polym. Sci., Pt. C 26,* 149 (1969)

92. M. Fujimura, T. Hashimoto and H. Kawai, *Rubber Chem. Technol. 51,* 215 (1978)

93. T. Pakula, K. Saijo, H. Kawai and T. Hashimoto, *Macromolecules 18,* 1294 (1985)

94. T. Pakula, K. Saijo and T. Hashimoto, *Macromolecules 18,* 2037 (1985)

95. C. I. Chung and J. C. Gale, *J. Polym. Sci., Polym. Phys. Ed., 14,* 1149 (1976)

96. E. V. Gouinlock and R. S. Porter, *Polym. Eng. Sci. 17,* 535 (1977)

97. D. J. Meier, *Polym. Prep. 18,* 340 (1977)

98. R.-J. Roe and W.-C. Zin, *Macromolecules 17,* 189 (1984)

99. H. Wanatabe, S. Kuwahara and T. Kotaka, *Trans. Soc. Rheol. 28,* 393 (1974)

100. S. Ye. Bresler, L. M. Pyrkov, S. Ya. Frenkel, L. A. Laius and S. I. Klenin, *Vysokmolekul Soedin., 4,* 250 (1962); *Polym. Sci. (USSR) 4,* 89 (1963)

101. G. Kraus, F. E. Naylor and K. W. Rollman, *J. Polym. Sci. Pt. A-2, 9,* 1839 (1971)

102. ASTM Specification D 1238-57T. American Society for Testing Materials, Philadelphia, PA

103. O. L. Marrs, R. P. Zelinski and R. C. Doss, paper presented at ACS Rubber Div. Meeting, Denver, CO. Oct. 1973

Chapter 4

RESEARCH ON ANIONIC
TRIBLOCK COPOLYMERS

M. Morton

Contents

Maurice Morton, Institute of Polymer Science, The University of Akron, Akron, Ohio
44325

1   INTRODUCTION

This chapter is essentially a review of the research carried out on these types of block copolymers over the past twenty years at our laboratories, much of it in collaboration with Professor L. J. Fetters and his group of investigators. Appropriate reference is, of course, made to work by other investigators which has some bearing on our results and conclusions. The original research project was centered on the styrene-diene-styrene type of triblock copolymers, which first demonstrated the properties of "thermoplastic elastomers", as pointed out in the basic patent (and associated publications)[1] on this composition of matter, and many of the results presented here relate to these materials. However, as will be seen, other variations of triblock (and polyblock) copolymers were also studied by us, and are included herein.

Since the application of these block polymers as thermoplastic elastomers represented a breakthrough in rubber technology, it might be appropriate to define more precisely the meaning of this term. It should first be recognized that, by definition, the term "elastomer" refers to a network of flexible polymer chains. This is because such chains do not exhibit the properties of an elastomer (high degree of retraction after deformation) unless they are crosslinked ("vulcanized") into a network. The latter, then, generally loses the ability to flow. However, the term "thermoplastic elastomer", which may at first seem to be a contradiction in terms, simply refers to a material which, at normal atmospheric conditions, behaves like a crosslinked network, but at elevated temperatures has the ability to flow (hence "thermoplastic").

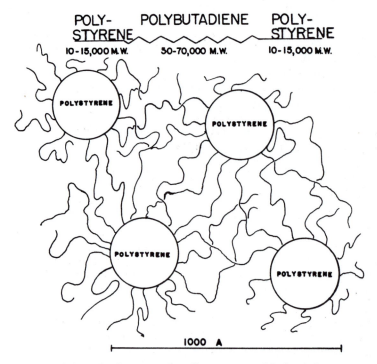

Figure 1   Schematic of a styrene–butadiene–styrene triblock copolymer

The reason why the triblock copolymers, such as the polystyrene–polybutadiene–polystyrene type, exhibit the properties of thermoplastic elastomers can be easily seen by examining the morphology of the resultant material. Because of the basic incompatibility of the polymer blocks, a two–phase morphology is obtained, containing a fine dispersion of polystyrene thermoplastic, chemically bonded to the surrounding elastic polybutadiene chains (which are, of course, not chemically bonded to each other). Thus it can be concluded that, in this type of network, the elastic chains are held together only by the thermoplastic domains.

The morphology described above is illustrated graphically in Figure 1, which shows a schematic for a typical triblock copolymer of the polystyrene–polybutadiene–polystyrene type (S–B–S). Two things should be noted about this representation: 1. the polystyrene is shown as the dispersed phase, since it is the minor constituent, and 2. the polystyrene domains are, presumably, spherical in shape. It turns out that both of these aspects are dependent on the relative proportions of the two constituents, as well as on the method of preparation of the specimens, and this is discussed in a later section.

Because these types of triblock copolymers exhibit the remarkable property of thermoplastic elastomers, the research at our laboratories had, as its prime objective, the elucidation of the structure–property relations of these unusual "networks". The main questions requiring answers could be listed as follows:

1. What is the role of the polystyrene domains (other than as thermoplastic "crosslinks"), and do they also act as reinforcing "fillers"?
2. Does the molecular weight of the polydiene blocks represent the "molecular weight between crosslinks (M_C)" in these networks?
3. In this connection, to what extent do these networks behave like conventional cross-linked (and filled) elastomers, with regard to such parameters as modulus and tensile strength?

Finding the answers to such questions required the preparation of a series of styrene–diene–styrene triblock copolymers. Furthermore, since the structure (and morphology) of these networks is governed by the structure of the triblock copolymers from which they originate, it is obvious that any property measurements can only be as good as the method of synthesis is successful. The synthesis of block copolymers by anionic polymerization involves sophisticated techniques, because of the "living" character of the growing chains, so that a review of methods and problems of synthesis is most appropriate.

2   METHODS AND PROBLEMS IN THE LABORATORY SYNTHESIS OF TRIBLOCK COPOLYMERS

The high vacuum techniques used to carry out carbanionic polymerization in our laboratories have been described in the literature[2, 3]. The application of these techniques to the synthesis of triblock copolymers has also been discussed[4]. The requirements for the synthesis of triblock copolymers of the styrene–diene–styrene (S–D–S) types having predictable molecular weights and a narrow molecular weight distribution (MWD) can be listed as follows:

a) Any possible chain termination reactions must be reduced to a negligible level.
b) The polymerization system must be capable of producing a polydiene block of high 1,4 chain structure, i.e., a soft elastomer.
c) The initiation rate for each block must be much faster than the propagation rate.

Organolithium initiators can fulfill all of these requirements, by suitable choice of solvents, e.g., non-polar solvents to assure high 1,4 content.

In the special case of block copolymer it is necessary not only to assure the absence of impurities in the polymerization "reactor", but to take special pains in purifying the monomers, which are, of course, added sequentially, since each monomer addition may also offer an opportunity for the introduction of impurities which may terminate some of the "living" chains. Bearing this in mind, it is possible to list 3 basic methods for the organolithium polymerization of SDS triblock copolymers:

2.1 Three-Stage Process with Monofunctional Initiator

This is the standard method, used in our laboratories. It requires a rapid initiation of the polystyrene chain in a nonpolar solvent (e.g., with sec–butyl lithium). The "crossover" reaction with the diene is known[5] to be very rapid, assuring a fast initiation of the center polydiene block. Finally, to overcome the well-known slow crossover reaction[5] with the final styrene charge in non-polar media, it is necessary to add a small amount of a polar solvent, e.g., tetrahydrofuran (THF). The excellent results which can be obtained by this method, with rigorous exclusion of impurities, is demonstrated by the Gel Permeation Chromatograms[2] shown in Figure 2 for both S–I–S and S–B–S block copolymers.

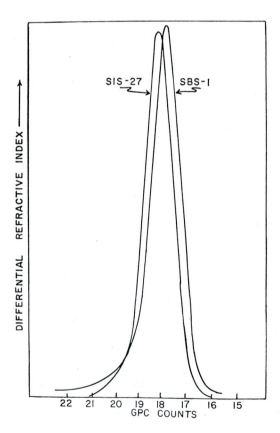

Figure 2   Gel permeation chromatograms of styrene–isoprene–styrene and styrene–butadiene–styrene triblock copolymers[6] (Courtesy of John Wiley & Sons)

2.2   Two-Stage Process with Monofunctional Initiators

This process also uses a monofunctional organolithium initiator, as in the above case, but the polymerization is carried only to the diblock (S–D) stage. The triblock copolymers are then formed by using a linking agent, e.g., a dihalide, to join the lithium chain ends of the diblock. This has the advantage of requiring only two monomer additions, thus avoiding potential introduction of impurities. However, it has the serious disadvantage of requiring very careful adjustment of the ratio of linking agent to chain-end concentration, any deviation from exact stoichiometry leading to formation of free diblocks. The latter have been found[4, 6] to have a dramatic effect on the strength of the material (free chain ends in the network). It is interesting to note, in this connection, that a certain amount of free polystyrene (terminated monoblock) can be easily tolerated[4, 6] since it is apparently incorporated into the polystyrene domains.

2.3   Two-Stage Process with Difunctional Initiators

This process requires a dilithium initiator, so that the center block (D) is formed first, by a dianionic polymerization, followed by addition of the styrene to form the two end blocks. It, too, has the advantage of requiring only two monomer additions. However, it has several serious disadvantages. In the first place, it is difficult to obtain a good dilithium initiator which is soluble in hydrocarbon media, as required for polymerization of dienes, although some success has been reported[7]. Furthermore, any loss of difunctionality, either in the initiator or after the addition of the diene, leads to formation of undesirable diblocks. However, this method can be especially useful in the case of "unidirectional" block copolymerization, i.e., where monomer A can initiate monomer B but not vice versa. One such case has already been demonstrated[7], in the synthesis of an α–methylstyrene–isoprene–α–methylstyrene triblock copolymer.

2.4   "Star" Block Copolymers

No discussion of the synthesis of triblock copolymers would be complete without mention of the "star" (or "radial") type of block copolymers. This can be considered a variant of Method 2 described above, except that the original S–D diblocks are linked by means of a polyfunctional, instead of a difunctional, linking agent. This can be expressed by means of the following chemical equations for the case of a styrene (S)–isoprene(I) star block copolymer:

$$RLi + xS \longrightarrow RS_xLi$$

$$RS_xLi + yI \longrightarrow RS_xI_yLi$$

$$zRS_xI_yLi + R'X_z \longrightarrow (RS_xI_y)_zR' + zLiX$$

where $R'X_z$ is a z–functional linking agent. This, of course, leads to a star-branched structure but the block sequence in all branches is still (S–D–S). The synthesis, morphology, and properties of these systems have been studied extensively by L. J. Fetters and associates in recent years, using first divinyl benzene[8], and later polychlorosilanes[9, 10] as polyfunctional linking systems.

In conclusion, it should be emphasized that, as will be seen later, the experimental precision exercised during the synthesis (and sample preparation) of these polymers has a strong bearing on the morphology and properties of these materials.

3   STRUCTURE–PROPERTY RELATIONS OF TRIBLOCK COPOLYMERS

3.1   Effect of Sample Preparation Methods

The thermoplastic elastomeric behavior of the triblock copolymers depends on phase separation on cooling from the processing and forming temperatures. Therefore, it might be expected that their morphology and resulting mechanical behavior would be influenced by their processing history.

In our earlier work, these polymers were processed like conventional elastomers, i.e., by compression molding. However, it soon became apparent that these composite materials were far from their equilibrium phase separation under these conditions, and that film-casting from solvents allowed a closer approach to the equilibrium state. This is demonstrated in Table I, which compares the tensile strength of molded and cast films of a typical SIS triblock copolymer. It is obvious from these results that films cast from solvent showed superior properties, presumably as a result of better phase separation resulting from this technique, i.e., higher purity of the polystyrene domains, which hold the network together. This effect was corroborated by the experiment in Table I where cast films were remolded, and thereby experienced an actual decrease in strength. It should be noted that proper care had to be taken in the use of film casting to select the best solvent system[6] and to remove the last traces of solvent.

TABLE I   Tensile Properties of Molded and Cast Films of $(S-I-S)$[6]

$(S-I-S)$ Block Mol. Wts. $(\times 10^{-3})$	S %	Tensile Strength, MPa		
		Molded Sample[a]		Cast Film[b]
		0.13 cm	0.03 cm[c]	0.03 cm
13.7−63.4−13.7	30	29.0	25.0	32.0
21.1−63.4−21.1	40	29.0	27.0	34.0

[a] Compression molded 10 min. 140°C
[b] From soln. of 90 % tetrahydrofuran 10 % methylethyl ketone (MEK)
[c] Molded from 0.03 cm cast film

The effect of solvent type and of traces of residual solvent is convincingly shown in Table II. As can be seen, three different solvent systems were used[6]: 90 % tetrahydrofuran/10 % methyl ethyl ketone, 90 % benzene/10 % n–heptane, and carbon tetrachloride. These were chosen because electron microscopy studies[11] had shown that the best phase separation was obtained with the first and second of the above solvents, which represented specific solvents for the polystyrene and polydiene, respectively, whereas the CCl_4 was a mutual solvent. The data in Table II corroborate this effect of the two specific solvents, i.e., higher tensile strengths compared to the CCl_4–cast films. What is even more dramatic, however, is the effect of traces of residual solvent, and the time necessary to vacuum–dry the films. It should, therefore, be noted that all tensile data reported from our laboratories on solvent––cast films of triblock copolymers are based on samples rigorously vacuum–dried for several days. It is of interest also to note the stringent drying and annealing techniques used on solvent–cast films, as described in a recent paper[10] on the equilibrium morphology of "star" block copolymers.

TABLE II   Solution Casting of S−I−S Polymer Films[6] (S−I−S) (13.7−41.1−13.7) × 10³ MW

| Film Treatment | 90/10 THF/MEK | | 90/10 C₆H₆/C₇H₁₆ | | CCl₄ | |
	Wt. % Loss	Tensile Strength (MPa)	Wt. % Loss	Tensile Strength (MPa)	Wt. % Loss	Tensile Strength (MPa)
Air dried	—	25.0	—	27.5	—	26.0
Vacuum dried[a]						
1 day	3.1	29.0	2.5	34.0	7.7	28.0
2 days	0.3	31.0	0.13	33.0	0.42	30.0
3 days	0.09	36.0	∼ 0	35.0	∼ 0	33.0
4 days	∼ 0	36.0	∼ 0	36.0	∼ 0	33.5

Wt.% loss based on polystyrene content
[a] At 1 mm Hg, 25° C

3.2 Morphology

The effect of various factors on the morphology of these two–phase systems has been studied extensively, both theoretically and experimentally[12, 13, 14], and a general picture has emerged. Thus, it is now accepted that, under equilibrium conditions, e.g., in films cast from suitable solvents and well–annealed, the polystyrene domains will assume highly ordered but different morphologies as the polystyrene content is increased, starting from spheres, at less than 20 % polystyrene, and changing to cylinders and then lamellae as the content rises to 50 %. Beyond that, there is apparently a phase inversion, with the polystyrene forming a continuous phase and the polybutadiene dispersion assuming the different shapes described above.

The remarkable order found in the morphology of these polymers is illustrated in the transmission electron microphotographs of ultra–thin (∼ 50 nm) films of a S–I–S triblock copolymer, shown in Figure 3, and of a (S–I)$_X$ "star" block copolymer, shown in Figure 4.

Figure 3   Transmission electron microphotograph of an S–I–S triblock copolymer

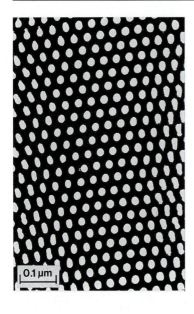

Figure 4   Transmission electron microphotograph of an $(S–I)_x$ "radial" block copolymer. Ultrathin ($\sim$50 nm) section of cast film, stained with OsO_4 (Reprinted with permission from ref. 8, Copyright 1975, American Chemical Society)

The osmium tetroxide "staining" renders the polydiene matrix more opaque to the electron beam, and hence dark, while the polystyrene domains appear lighter. The circular shape of the latter does not necessarily reflect a spherical shape, since it could represent a cylindrical cross section as well.

The remarkable regularity shown in these figures is, of course, a natural outcome of the near monodisperse MWD of the polymer blocks. Since this heterophase morphology results from the incompatibility of the two types of polymer blocks present, it might be instructive to consider the constraints and limitations on block molecular weight imposed by the material considerations, as follows:

a) The styrene–diene ratio controls the modulus of the thermoplastic elastomer (polystyrene domains acting as a "filler").
b) The lower limit of polystyrene block size is set by incompatibility requirements.
c) The upper limit of molecular weights is set by viscosity considerations, which affect both processibility and efficiency of phase separation in the melt.

Because of these considerations, the molecular weights of the polystyrene blocks are generally in the range of 10,000 to 15,000 while the polydiene molecular weights vary from 50,000 to 70,000, as indicated in Figure 1.

In this connection, it might be of interest to consider the difference between phase separation of two amorphous phases, as a result of incompatibility, with the case where one of the components separates by crystallization. In the first instance, i.e., separation of two amorphous phases, it is obvious that this will be enhanced with increasing incompatibility, thus leading to less "phase mixing", and better mechanical properties. However, a greater incompatibility of the two phases would also lead to poorer processibility, i.e., higher melt viscosity, since flow of such a two–phase system involves their free energy of mixing. In contrast, where phase "separation" occurs by crystallization of one of the components, no incompatibility is involved in the melt and the flow properties are those of a homogeneous material, i.e., low melt viscosity.

3.3   Mechanical Properties – Uniaxial Stress–Strain Behavior

3.3.1   S–I–S Triblock Copolymers

To answer the questions raised in the introductory section about the elastic behavior of these polymers, a series of (S–I–S) triblock copolymers was prepared with varying polystyrene content and molecular weight of the polyisoprene center block. The stress–strain properties, up to break, are shown in Figure 5, from which the following conclusions may be drawn:

1. The tensile modulus appears to be mainly dependent on the polystyrene content ("filler" effect) and independent of the molecular weight of the center elastomeric block. Hence the latter cannot be considered as representing the "molecular weight between cross-links" (M_C) of the network. This is really not surprising, since the polyisoprene center block has a molecular weight of at least 40,000, and generally higher, while the "molecular weight between entanglements" $(M_e)^{15}$ is about 7000. Hence there are obviously a number of such chain entanglements between the polystyrene "crosslinks", and the "networks chain" can really be considered as equivalent to the M_e value.
2. The tensile strength (end of each curve) of this series of S–I–S polymers appears to be largely independent of either polystyrene content or molecular weight, with the exception of the polymer having the lowest polystyrene molecular weight, where the strength is cut by almost one–half. The most obvious conclusion is that, in the latter case, the polystyrene MW is too low for good phase separation, so that there is substantial plasticization of the polystyrene domains by the polyisoprene, decreasing their ability to withstand the stress. This is further illustrated in Table III, where the molecular weight of the polystyrene and blocks has been further reduced (below 8400), showing the dramatic effect this has on the tensile strength. It is obvious that, at a molecular weight of 5000–6000, the polystyrene is compatible with the polyisoprene, and no domains can be present.

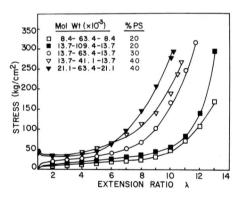

Figure 5   Effect of composition and block size on tensile properties of styrene–isoprene–styrene triblock copolymers[6] (1 kg.cm^{-2} = 0.1 MPa) (Courtesy of John Wiley & Sons)

TABLE III   Effect of Polystyrene Molecular Weight on the Tensile Strength of S−I−S

Wt. % Styrene	Polymer Mol. Wt. S−I−S ($\times 10^{-3}$)	Tensile Stress (MPa) 300 % Elong.	At break
20	13.7−100.4−13.7	1.8	27.0
20	8.4− 63.4− 8.4	1.1	16.0
19	7.0− 60.0− 7.0	1.3	2.2
11	5.0− 80.0− 5.0	∼ 0	∼ 0

One further note should be made about Figure 5. These tensile curves represent the first stretch. The retraction curves exhibit a large hysteresis loop and considerable unrecovered deformation (set), which increases with degree of strain and of polystyrene content. This phenomenon is apparently largely due to a distortion of the polystyrene domains, which has actually been observed by electron microscopy[11] of stretched specimens. The distorted domains can be restored to their original condition either by heating the sample at or above the T_g of the polystyrene, or by swelling in a specific solvent for the polystyrene, namely tetrahydrofurfuryl alcohol (THFA). This type of treatment, of course, also restores the tensile behavior of the prestretched sample, as convincingly demonstrated in Figure 6[6, 16]. Apparently it is the polystyrene phase which is wholly responsible for any unrecovered deformation, swelling by a selective solvent for the polyisoprene (n–decane) not having any effect.

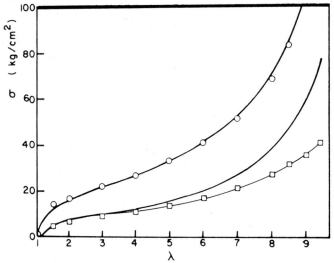

Figure 6   Effect of swelling on stress–softened S–I–S triblock copolymer[16] ($M_w \times 10^{-3}$ = 13.7−63.4−13.7). □ n–decane; ○ tetrahydrofurfuryl alcohol; —— 1st and 2nd cycle unswollen (1 kg.cm^{-2} = 0.1 MPa)

These experiments on the behavior of these polymers under uniaxial stress seem to corroborate the fact that it is the polystyrene domains which are responsible for the integrity and strength of the network, and that the mechanism of tensile failure involves rupture of these domains. As a matter of fact, the exceptionally high strength shown by these polymers is undoubtedly a result of both the regularity of the network, which helps to distribute the stresses more evenly, and to the fact that the polystyrene domains can act as an "energy sink" to absorb the elastic energy and thus delay failure.

This proposed strength mechanism is further supported by experiments involving the introduction of crosslinks[6] in the polyisoprene matrix, using dicumyl peroxide as crosslinking agent. This agent is known[17] to crosslink polyisoprene stoichiometrically without any observed chain scission. The results are shown in Table IV. The swelling data show that crosslinks were indeed introduced, yielding a tighter network. However, this had little effect on the modulus and a very noticeable deleterious effect on the tensile strength. Hence these experiments add further evidence pointing to the polystyrene domains as the key factor in the strength of these materials. The decrease in tensile strength is undoubtedly due to the

TABLE IV   Crosslinking of S–I–S by Dicumyl Peroxide

	Swelling Vol. Ratio[a]	Stress at 300 % Elong. (MPa)	Tensile Stregth (MPa)
Original sample	9.8	5.0	22.5
After crosslinking	5.4	5.3	16.0

[a] In n-decane, 48 hr

action of the fixed crosslinks in preventing stress distribution in the entangled chain network.

One additional feature of the tensile curves in Figure 5 deserves mention. It can be seen that the curves representing the polymers containing 40 % styrene show an initial yield point. It should be noted that this occurs only on the first stretch and not on any subsequent stretch, unless the sample is reheated, or allowed to rest (for several months at room temperature). This is believed to be due to the high concentration of polystyrene domains, which, at 40 % content, are approaching the critical fraction for volume packing. Hence it can be expected that there would be some "connections" between the domains, which would, of course, be broken on the first stretch. In a sense, at this stage, the morphology would be that of two interpenetrating continuous phases. Needless to say, such yield points are also found at higher proportions of styrene.

3.3.2 S–B–S Triblock Copolymers

A similar series of S–B–S triblock copolymers was used to obtain the tensile curves shown in Figure 7. It should be noted that these polymers were of an earlier vintage, from a time when compression molding was used in their preparation, rather than solution casting, and this may account for the somewhat lower tensile strength obtained. However, they also show some similarity in behavior to the S–I–S polymer, at least on two counts, i.e., the styrene content does control the modulus, and the latter is independent of the molecular weights. However, the real difference from the S–I–S polymers lies in the fact that the tensile strength seems to depend greatly on the styrene content. (The difficulties of using compression molding for sample preparation are illustrated in the case of the 40 % styrene–containing

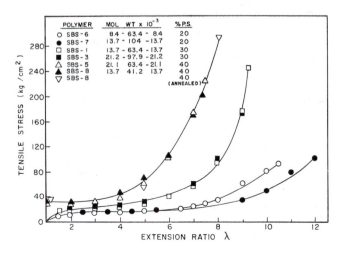

Figure 7   Effect of composition and block size on tensile properties of styrene–butadiene–styrene triblock copolymers[6] (1 kg.cm^{-2} = 0.1 MPa) (Courtesy of John Wiley & Sons)

polymers, where "annealing", i.e., allowing to cool very slowly, at 1 °C per minute, from the molding temperature of 140 °C, increased the tensile strength substantially).

This unexpected effect of styrene content on the tensile strength of S–B–S is in all likelihood related to the question of incompatibility. This becomes apparent from an examination of the solubility parameters (δ) of polystyrene, polyisoprene and polybutadiene, which are, respectively, 9.2, 8.1 and 8.4, as given in the literature[18]. Hence it appears that poly-butadiene is more compatible than polyisoprene with polystyrene (closer values of δ). Furthermore, the incompatibility of two polymers is dependent not only on their basic chemical structure but also on their molecular weights and volume fractions in the mixture, as given by the relations:

$$X_{12} = M_1 (\delta_1 - \delta_2)^2/\varrho_1 RT \tag{1a}[19]$$

and

$$\Delta E_m = V\Phi_1\Phi_2 (\delta_1 - \delta_2)^2 \tag{1b}[20]$$

where X_{12} = interaction parameter of components 1 and 2.

M_1 = molecular weight of component 1.

δ_1 and δ_2 = solubility parameters of components 1 and 2.

ΔE_m = heat of mixing.

Φ_1 and Φ_2 = volume fractions of components 1 and 2.

V   = total volume of mixture

Hence the increase in tensile strength of S–B–S with increasing styrene content shown in Figure 7 is most likely related to a better phase separation of the polystyrene domains at higher volume fractions of this component, i.e., less phase mixing and plasticization by the polybutadiene. In the case of the S–I–S polymers, it appears that the incompatibility of the two phases is already high enough not to be affected very much, at those levels, by the styrene content.

In this connection, it is interesting to note the experimental results we obtained[6] by solution blending polystyrene with S–I–S and S–B–S. For this purpose, a polystyrene was prepared by organolithium polymerization, having approximately the same molecular weight as the polystyrene end blocks in the S–I–S or S–B–S. When this polystyrene was blended into an S–B–S polymer, it was found[6] that the blend had the same tensile properties as an S–B–S with a similar styrene block content, i.e., higher modulus and higher tensile strength than the original S–B–S used in the blend. However, when a similar blend was made of S–I–S and PS, only the modulus was raised, the tensile strength remaining unchanged, just like the results shown in Figure 5. These experiments offered a gratifying confirmation of the results shown in Figures 5 and 7, and of the proposed strength mechanism.

3.3.3 Substituting α–Methylstyrene for Styrene in S–I–S

In view of the temperature limitations imposed by the glass transition temperature of the polystyrene in the triblocks (these materials show a serious loss of strength even at 60 °C), it was of interest to substitute α–methylstyrene for styrene, since poly–α–methylstyrene has a T_g of about 165 °C instead of the 105 °C for polystyrene. Also, the α–methylstyrene is known to be polymerizable by organolithium. Because of its low "ceiling" temperature the polymerization of the α–methylstyrene[7] had to be carried out at reduced temperature, using polar solvents to accelerate the rate. This also then required the use of a dilithium initiator[7] (Method 3 described above), which yielded excellent results and a mS–I–mS triblock of narrow MWD and high purity.

The stress–strain properties of this polymer are shown in Figure 8, compared with those of S–I–S triblock of very similar composition and architecture. It is most interesting to note the substantially higher modulus of the mS–I–mS triblock, providing a strong confirmation of the idea that the plastic domains are the principal stress bearers, since poly–α–methylstyrene has the higher tensile modulus. Furthermore, Figure 9 shows the marked superiority of the mS–I–mS polymer at elevated temperatures, its tensile strength still being substantial (7 MPa) even at 100 °C! The dependence of tensile strength on the temperature also points to the plastic domains as the key factor in the strength of the network.

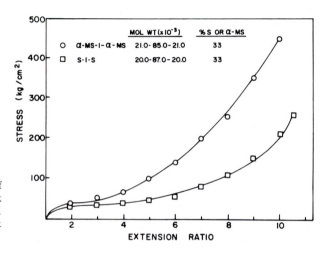

Figure 8 Tensile properties of mS–I—mS and S–I–S triblock copolymers[6] (1 kg.cm^{-2} = 0.1 MPa) (Courtesy of John Wiley & Sons)

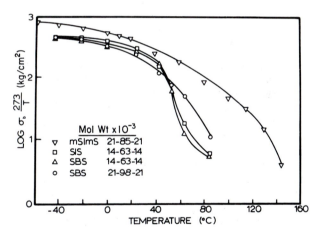

Figure 9 Effect of temperature on tensile strength of triblock polymers[6] (1 kg.cm^{-2} = 0.1 MPa) (Courtesy of John Wiley & Sons)

It is interesting, in this connection, to compare the temperature–dependence of tensile strength of conventional rubber networks with that of these triblock copolymers. Thus, according to the viscoelastic theory of tensile strength of elastomers[21], the latter is inversely dependent on the difference between the test temperature and the glass transition temperature (T_g) of the elastomer, i.e., the S–I–S based on a T_g of about −65 °C for the polyisoprene, should be considerably stronger than the SBS, based on a T_g of −95 °C for the polybutadiene. Yet, as Figure 9 shows, the S–B–S and S–I–S curves lie very close together. In contrast, the tensile strength vs. temperature curves for conventional, sulfur–vulcanized

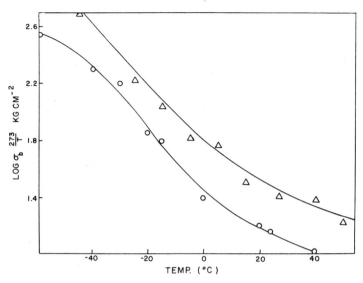

Figure 10   Effect of temperature on tensile strength of gum vulcanizates of SBR ($\triangle$) and polybutadiene ($\bigcirc$)[28] (1 kg.cm^{-2} = 0.1 MPa)

polybutadiene and SBR ($T_g \sim -50$ °C) as shown[22] in Figure 10, show the expected difference. All of these differences in tensile behavior illustrate quite unequivocally the strong dependence of these thermoplastic elastomers on the nature of the plastic domains which hold the network together.

4   RESEARCH ON OTHER ANIONIC TRIBLOCK COPOLYMERS

Since the advent of the S–D–S triblock copolymers as novel thermoplastic elastomers, it was realized that other heterophase polymers containing "hard" thermoplastic domains dispersed in, and chemically bonded to, an elastomer matrix should also behave similarly. In fact, it was soon recognized that some of the polyurethane elastomers, which were developed much earlier, represented similar heterophase systems, with the polyester, or polyether, chains being the soft elastic phase, and the associated urethane aggregates forming the hard, dispersed phase. Since then, of course, there has been a rapid development of several analogous thermoplastic elastomers, based on block or graft polymers such as polyesters, polyamides and polyolefins, amongst others.

We were similarly interested, in our laboratories, in exploring other triblock copolymers which could be prepared by anionic polymerization under rigorous conditions and thus offer new systems for study of their structure–property relations.

4.1   Triblock Copolymers of α–Methylstyrene and Propylene Sulfide

A successful synthesis[23] of a triblock copolymer having poly–α–methylstyrene end blocks and a poly(propylene sulfide) center block (mS–PS–mS) was accomplished. The method involved initiation by ethyl lithium, and sequential addition of α–methylstyrene and propy-

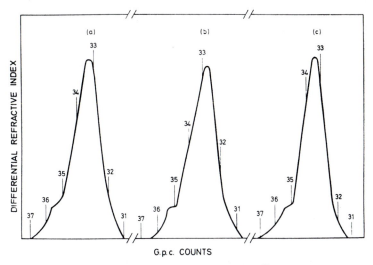

Figure 11   Gel permeation chromatograms of mS–PS–mS triblock copolymers[23], Wt % α–methylstyrene: (a) 20, (b) 30, (c) 40 (Reprinted by permission from ref. 23. Copyright 1971 American Chemical Society)

lene sulfide, followed by coupling of the chain ends by phosgene. This use of Method 2, as described above, was necessary since the lithium thiolate chain ends cannot initiate the polymerization of α–methylstyrene as end block. The success of this method is demonstrated by the gel permeation chromatograms in Figure 11, all of which show a satisfactory narrow MWD but include a very small shoulder corresponding to unlinked diblock.

The uniaxial tensile properties of these triblock copolymers, containing 20, 30 and 40 % end block, are shown in Figure 12, and indicate typical behavior similar to that of the S–I–S triblocks. However, their tensile strength is substantially lower, especially considering that the end blocks consist of poly–α–methylstyrene (see Figure 8). Possibly this is partly due to

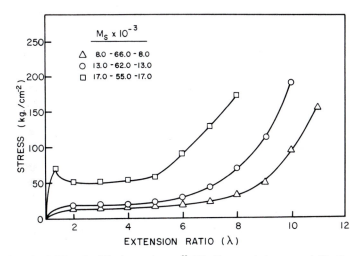

Figure 12   Tensile properties of mS–PS–mS triblock copolymers[23]. Wt % α–methylstyrene: △ 20, ○ 30, □ 40 (kg.cm^{-2} = 0.1 MPa) (Reprinted by permission from ref. 23, Copyright 1971 American Chemical Society)

the small fraction of diblock, visible in Figure 11. However, in the absence of any knowledge about the morphology of these polymers (these saturated polymers were not amenable to osmium tetroxide staining for electron microscopy), it is difficult to draw any definitive conclusions about these differences in tensile strength. Furthermore, other factors, such as interphase adhesion, which is discussed in a later section, may also play a role.

It should be noted here that the test samples used for the data in Figure 12 were, as usual, cut from solution-cast films. However, it was also observed that these polymers could not be compression molded, in view of the high temperature required for flow of the mS−PS−mS triblock copolymer ($\cong 200\,^\circ$C) which led to decomposition. Presumably, the thermally weak link was the central dithiocarbonyl group ($-\text{S}-\overset{\text{O}}{\underset{\|}{\text{C}}}-\text{S}-$) resulting from the coupling reac-

tion. In this respect, these polymers behaved in analogous fashion to the mS−I−mS triblocks, which could also not be compression molded, due to decomposition of the polyisoprene center block.

4.2 Triblock Copolymers Based on Polysiloxanes

Even though it was found that poly–α–methylstyrene end blocks made it possible for triblock copolymers to show good strength at elevated temperatures, this could not be put to practical use because the center blocks (e.g., polydienes) were not able to withstand the higher molding temperatures required. In this connection, a new candidate for the rubbery center block was considered, i.e., a polysiloxane. The anionic polymerization of cyclic siloxanes has been known for some time, but this required the use of strong bases, e.g., KOH, and was notorious for its bond interchange tendencies. However, the more recent discovery[24] that the use of the less well–known cyclic trimer, hexamethylcyclotrisiloxane, instead of the usual tetramer, made it possible to use organolithium initiators and thus to obtain a "living" polymer with no noticeable bond interchange. In view of the known high temperature properties of polysiloxanes, this method was considered as feasible for the synthesis of triblock copolymers based on polysiloxanes[25].

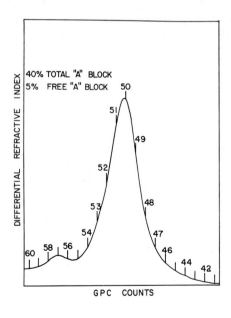

Figure 13 Gel permeation chromatogram of mS–D$_X$–mS–6 triblock copolymer[25] (40 % α–methylstyrene) (Courtesy of John Wiley & Sons)

Because the block copolymerization of vinyl monomers and cyclic siloxanes can only be "unidirectional", Method 2, using sec–butyl lithium as initiator, was used. Either styrene or α–methylstyrene was first added, followed by the cyclic trimer, hexamethylcyclotrisiloxane, to form the diblocks. The latter were then coupled by reacting with dimethyldichlorosilane, so that no heterogeneous chemical groups were introduced in the chain. Experimental details are described elsewhere[25]. A gel permeation chromatogram of a typical copolymer, containing 40 % α–methylstyrene, is shown in Figure 13. The MWD is not quite as narrow as that of the S–D–S triblocks, but still quite satisfactory. It is interesting to note the absence of any unlinked diblocks, which might ordinarily be expected (see Figure 11), and instead to find the presence of a small amount of free poly–α–methylstyrene (at count 57), obviously due to some fortuitous termination occurring during addition of the cyclic trisiloxane.

In this case, it was possible to obtain transmission electron microphotographs of thin films, since the silicon atoms are much denser than carbon atoms. A typical example is shown in Figure 14 for a triblock containing 40 % poly–α–methylstyrene end blocks. Here the white domains represent the poly–α–methylstyrene. These triblocks were given the nomenclature mS–D_X–mS. The same type of orderly phase separation can be noted, but the contrast in the photo is not as good as in the case of the S–D–S polymers. This either represents a less efficient phase separation, or is an artifact of the electron microscopy.

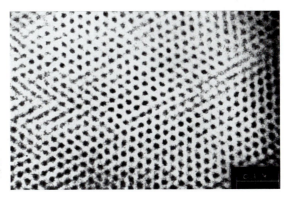

Figure 14   Transmission electron microphotograph of ultrathin (~50 nm) section of cast film of mS–D_X–mS–6 (cut parallel to film surface)[25] (Courtesy of John Wiley & Sons)

The tensile properties of solution–cast films of a series of these triblocks are shown in Figure 15. The increase in modulus and tensile strength with increase in "hard block" content is again observed, but the tensile strength values are disappointingly low, compared to the values obtained for the mS–I–mS triblock (see Figure 8). It is difficult to offer any definitive explanation for the low tensile strengths, since several possibilities may apply. One concerns the efficiency of phase separation, already mentioned above, although the disparity in solubility parameters of poly–α–methylstyrene (8.8)[26, 27] and the polysiloxane (7.5)[18] is even greater than in the case of mS–I–mS triblocks. Another possibility may be based on the much lower viscoelasticity of polysiloxanes, which may make it impossible for the elastic chains to transfer the stress to the "hard domains", thus changing the mechanism of fracture. An alternative explanation may invoke the interphase adhesion between the domains and the matrix, as discussed in a later section. In this connection, it should be noted that the tensile strength of these triblocks, containing 30–40 % end blocks, compares very favorably with that of conventional silicone rubber vulcanizates, reinforced by fine silica fillers.

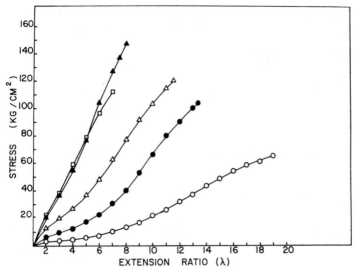

Figure 15   Tensile properties of mS−D$_x$−mS triblock copolymers[25] (Courtesy of John Wiley & Sons)

Mol. Wt. (×10⁻³)	% End Block
○ 12.5−141.3−12.5	15
● 11.9− 80.4−11.9	22
△ 12.9− 60.8−12.9	31
□ 12.5− 38.4−12.5	40
▲	36[a]

Mol. Wt. (×10⁻³) is written as $\times 10^{-3}$

[a] Fractionated sample of 40 end-block polymer, with no free poly-α-MS

5   INCOMPATIBILITY AND PROCESSIBILITY IN TRIBLOCK COPOLYMERS[28]

The various well–characterized A–B–A triblock copolymers described above, all prepared by anionic polymerization under rigorous experimental conditions, offer an opportunity to draw some conclusions about the relation between heterophase incompatibility and processibility of these materials. Thus far, only uniaxial tensile data have been discussed. However, it has also been postulated, in a previous section, that the degree of incompatibility between the two phases affects the flow properties, since this involves the heat of mixing of the two phases. In other words, although incompatibility between the blocks is desirable for phase separation, too high an incompatibility can introduce flow problems.

Because of the greater difference in solubility parameters between polysiloxanes and hydrocarbon polymers, triblock copolymers containing polysiloxane center blocks could conveniently be compared with triblocks containing, say, polyisoprene center blocks. For this purpose, the flow properties were determined by measuring the compliance rate of the polymers from the deformation of a sample compressed between parallel plates. The experimental details are described elsewhere[29]. The results are shown in Table V. In addition to the data shown in this table, it should be noted that the values of M$_e$ (molecular weight between entanglements), which govern the melt viscosity of the elastic center blocks, are 7000 and 12,000, respectively, for polyisoprene[15] and polydimethylsiloxane[30].

TABLE V   Flow Properties of Triblock Copolymers[28]

Polymer[a]	M_n $(\times 10^{-3})$	$\Delta\delta$[b] cal.$^{1/2}$ cm$^{-3/2}$	Temp. °C	Compliance Rate MPa^{-1} s^{-1}
S–I–S	102	1.1	130	0.25
S–D$_x$–S	53	1.7	130	0.04
mS–I–mS	132	0.7	200	0.50
mS–D$_x$–mS	87	1.3	200	0.06

[a] All polymers at 30 wt. % end block
[b] Difference between solubility parameters of blocks

The much poorer flow properties (lower compliance values) of the polysiloxane–containing triblocks are immediately apparent. This despite the much higher M_e values and lower overall molecular weights (M_n) of the polysiloxane center blocks. In other words, because of its higher M_e and lower M_n, a polydimethylsiloxane of the same molecular weight as the center block in the above polymers would have a much lower viscosity than a polyisoprene having the same molecular weight as the center block in the corresponding triblock copolymers.

These data illustrate dramatically how the incompatibility dominates the flow properties of triblock copolymers.

6   INTERPHASE ADHESION AND TENSILE STRENGTH[28]

It has already been pointed out in this discussion that the "hard phase" which separates from the soft, rubbery matrix forms domains which have the dimensions of reinforcing fillers in rubber ($\sim$ 30 nm.). Recent studies in our laboratories[31] have been concerned with the use of model polymeric fillers, e.g., polystyrene, in rubber vulcanizates, and the effect of uniaxial strain on the extent of dewetting of such fillers, using sensitive density measurements to determine the volume dilation. Such measurements have shown that there is an inverse relation between such volume dilation and tensile strength of the composite, indicating a strong influence of the filler–elastomer adhesion.

The poor tensile strength of the polysiloxane–based triblock copolymers described above raises questions about the possible influence of the well–known low surface free energy of polysiloxane on the inter–phase adhesion. To determine whether this inter–phase adhesion does indeed play a role in the tensile strength, volume dilation measurements were carried out, as a function of strain, on a series of triblock copolymers[28]. Experimental details can be found elsewhere[29]. As before[31] the volume dilation ($\Delta V/V$) was found to increase linearly as a function of extension ratio (λ), so that the slopes of the $\Delta V/V$ vs. λ plot, i.e., $\Delta V/V\lambda$, could be defined as the "specific dilation" parameter for any given samples. These can then be considered as an inverse measure of the adhesion between the two phases.

What is even more interesting is to relate the tensile strength, the strain dilation and the calculated work of adhesion between the two phases. The latter, W_a, as defined by Zisman et al[32] is expressed as

$$W_a = (2 + b_d\gamma_d)\gamma_m - b_d\gamma_m^2 \qquad (2)$$

where γ_d and γ_m are the critical surface free energies of the dispersed phase and the matrix, respectively

b_d is defined by the equation $\cos\theta = \text{constant} - b_d\gamma_d$

and θ = contact angle between phases

The required values of W_a for the various block copolymers were calculated from the published values of critical surface free energy (γ) for the polymer blocks, as shown in Table VI.

TABLE VI   Critical Surface Free Energies of Polymers

Polymer	γ mN/m
Polydimethylsiloxane[32]	24
Polybutadiene[32]	31
Polyisoprene[33]	31
Polystyrene[34, 35]	33
Poly-α-methylstyrene[35, 36]	36

The correlation between tensile strength, calculated interphase adhesion (W_a) values, and measured volume dilation ($dV/V\lambda$) values, is shown in Table VII for a series of triblock copolymers. All of the polymers, with the exception of the Kraton 1102, were prepared in our laboratories, and were chosen because they all had a roughly equivalent "end–block" content (hard phase) of about 30 %.

It can be seen from Table VII that, at least qualitatively, there is an excellent correlation between inter–phase adhesion, strain dilation and tensile strength, i.e., better adhesion leads to lower dilation and higher tensile strength. The much lower tensile strength of the S–D$_X$–S–1 sample as compared to the S–D$_X$–S–2 despite the same W_a values, can be easily explained by the much lower molecular weight of the end blocks of the S–D$_X$–S–1 which would lead to more phase mixing, as discussed previously (see Table III). The same type of correlation between low strain dilation and high tensile strength was found in the studies of model fillers in rubber vulcanizates[31].

TABLE VII   Effect of Interphase Adhesion on Tensile Strength of Triblock Copolymers

Polymer	Mol. Wt. ($\times 10^{-3}$)	W_a mJ/m^2	Specific Dilation ($\Delta V/V\lambda \times 10^3$)	Tensile Strength MPa
S–D$_x$–S –1	8–37– 8	54	6.90	0.6
S–D$_x$–S –2	16–76–16	54	—	1.8
mS–D$_x$–mS	13–61–13	57	4.79	7.4
Kraton 1102[a]	10–55–10	64	3.57	26
mS–I–mS	21–85–21	67	2.86	45

[a] S–B–S

7   TRIBLOCK COPOLYMERS WITH CRYSTALLIZABLE END BLOCKS

It has already been pointed out in a previous part of this chapter that triblock thermoplastic elastomers based on an amorphous two–phase system embody an inherent structural balance, because phase separation is caused by incompatibility, and an increase in the latter, while favoring good phase separation, decreases processibility, i.e. melt flow. Some of our most recent work, therefore, concerned the study of structure–property relations of anionic triblock copolymers, where the two types of blocks might be compatible in the melt, but the two end blocks would be capable of crystallizing to form crystalline domains on cooling. Some of this work has been reported recently[28, 37] and one of the systems studied will be discussed here, as illustrative of this type of approach.

This particular triblock involved the organolithium polymerization of a single monomer, butadiene, in such a way that the two end blocks were high in 1,4–structure (>90 %), while the center block had about 45 % of 1,2 chain units. Subsequent hydrogenation of the polymer solution converted the end blocks into "lightly branched" polyethylene, while the center block became a random copolymer of ethylene and butene–1. Hence the end blocks were crystallizable while the center block was an elastomer. The experimental details of synthesis and characterization are described elsewhere[37, 38] but suffice it to say that the original polybutadiene triblock had the desired narrow MWD, that hydrogenation was very close to 100 %, and that no significant chain scission occurred with the special hydrogenation method used. Furthermore, the end blocks were found to crystallize to form spherulites, similar to those of conventional, high pressure polyethylene, and showed a melting point of 107 °C, again very similar to that of commercial polyethylene.

A series of 4 such triblock copolymers was prepared, and their architecture is described in Table VIII. It can be seen that the 4 polymers contained two levels of end–block content ("hard phase") and two levels of molecular weight. The latter variation was thought to be especially important, in view of the known effect of molecular weight on crystallization; and optical microscopy indeed showed[37, 38] that the higher molecular weight end–blocks formed better spherulites.

TABLE VIII   Molecular Structure of Hydrogenated Polybutadiene Triblocks

Polymer	Wt. % End Blocks	Mol. Wt. ($\times 10^{-3}$)
B60−19	60	19− 25−19
B30−18	30	18− 58−18
B60−54	60	54− 72−54
B30−55	30	55−257−55

The uniaxial tensile behavior of these 4 polymers is shown in Figure 16. As expected, the 2 polymers containing 60 % "hard block" showed a higher modulus than the 30 % end–block polymers, regardless of molecular weight, and they also showed more of a yield point at initial stretch. In contrast, however, the 2 polymers with the shorter end blocks B–60–19 and B–30–18 both showed similar (and lower) tensile strengths (end of curves). Since the 2 polymers containing 60 % end blocks (B–60–19 and B–60–54) both exhibited more plastic than elastic behavior, i.e., high unrecovered deformation on stretching, the only real thermoplastic elastomers were those triblocks containing 30 wt. % end blocks; and of these, the B–30–55 (high M. W.) had excellent tensile strength, thus demonstrating the critical

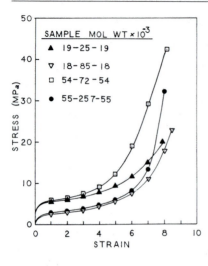

Figure 16   Tensile properties of hydrogenated polybutadiene triblock copolymers[28, 37] (Reprinted with
permission from ref. 37, Copyright 1982 American
Chemical Society)

importance of molecular weight on formation of the crystalline domains. It should be noted
that this effect was not so critical in the amorphous, styrene–based triblocks, except at the
low molecular weights, where phase separation was actually affected.

Two other aspects about the behavior of these crystallizable triblocks are worthy of note.
They seemed to show a somewhat higher degree of tensile "set" (unrecovered deformation
on stretching) than their styrene–based counterparts. Although no direct morphological
data were obtained, it appears that the crystalline domains presumably suffer a greater
distortion than the amorphous, glassy polystyrene domains. This is perhaps not surprising,
considering the tendency of fibers to "cold draw".

The second aspect concerns the tensile strength of these crystalline triblocks at elevated
temperature, where they seem to be somewhat better than the S–I–S or S–B–S triblocks (but
not the mS–I–mS type). Thus, at 60 °C, the tensile strength of the B–30–55 triblock is still at

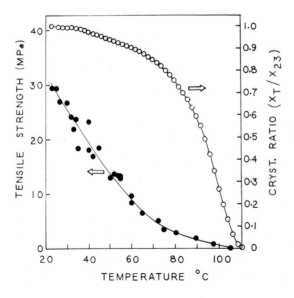

Figure 17   Comparative effect of
temperature on tensile strength and
crystallinity of B30–55 triblock
copolymers[28, 37] (Reprinted with permission from ref. 37, Copyright 1982
American Chemical Society)

the respectable level of 10 MPa, compared to only 2 MPa for a similar S–I–S triblock (see Figure 9). An interesting aspect of the effect of temperature on these crystalline triblocks is shown in Figure 17, where both the tensile strength and the degree of crystallinity (as measured by DTA) of the B–30–55 polymer are plotted against temperature. Thus it can be seen that, at 60 °C, where the sample has lost ⅔ of its strength, it has only lost 10 % of its crystallinity, while at 80 °C, where its strength is only 10 % of the original, it still retains almost 80 % of its original crystalline content. It would be interesting to compare the behavior of highly crystalline materials, e.g., fibers in this regard.

References

1. G. Holden and R. Milkovich, Belgian Patent 627, 652 (July 29, 1963); US 3, 265, 765 (August 9, 1965, Filed Jan. 29, 1962); G. Holden, E. T. Bishop and N. R. Legge, *Proc. Int. Rubber Conf. 1967,* Maclaren and Sons, London, 1968, p. 287–309, *J. Polymer Sci. C 26* 37 (1969); N. R. Legge, *Chemtech 13,* 630 (1983)
2. M. Morton, J. E. McGrath and P. C. Juliano, *J. Polym Sci. C 26* 99 (1969)
3. M. Morton and L. J. Fetters, *Rubber Chem. Technol. 48* 3 (1975)
4. M. Morton, *Block Polymers,* S. L. Aggarwal, Ed., Plenum Press, 1970, p. 1
5. M. Morton and F. R. Ells, *J. Polym. Sci. 61* 25 (1962)
6. M. Morton, *Encyclopedia of Polymer Science and Technology,* John Wiley and Sons, New York, 1971, Vol 15, p. 508
7. L. J. Fetter and M. Morton, *Macromolecules 2* 453 (1969)
8. L.-K. Bi and L. J. Fetters, *Macromolecules 8* 90 (1975); *9* 732 (1976)
9. N. Hadjichristidis and L. J. Fetters, *Macromolecules 13* 191 (1980)
10. L. J. Fetters et al, *Macromolecules 19* 215 (1986)
11. J. F. Beecher et al, *J. Polym Sci. C 26* 117 (1969)
12. G. E. Molau, Ed. *Colloidal and Morphological Behavior of Block and Graft Copolymers,* Plenum Press, New York, 1971
13. B. R. M. Gallot, *Adv. Polym. Sci. 29* 85 (1978)
14. L. Goodman, Ed. *Developments in Block Copolymers* Applied Science, New York, 1982, Vol I
15. L. J. Fetters, *J. Res. Nat. Bur Stand. 69 A* 33 (1965)
16. S. H. Goh, Ph. D. Thesis, Univ. Akron, 1971
17. K. W. Scott, *J. Polym. Sci. 58* 517 (1962)
18. *Polymer Handbook, 2nd Ed.,* J. Brandup and E. H. Immergut, Eds., John Wiley and Sons, New York, 1975, Ch. IV, p. 354
19. R. F. Fedors, *J. Polym. Sci. C 26* 189 (1969)
20. H. Morawetz, *Macromolecules in Solution,* Interscience, New York (1966), p. 41
21. J. C. Halpin, *Rubber Chem Technol. 38* 1007 (1965)
22. M. Morton in *Multicomponent Polymer Systems,* N. A. J. Platzer, Ed., Advances in Chemistry Series No. 99, American Chemical Society, Washington, 1970, p. 490
23. M. Morton, R. F. Kammereck and L. J. Fetters, *Br. Polym. J. 3* 120 (1971); *Macromolecules 4* 11 (1971)
24. J. G. Saam, D. J. Gordon and S. Lindsey, *Macromolecules 3* 1 (1970)
25. M. Morton, Y. Kesten and L. J. Fetters, *Appl. Polym. Symp. No 26,* 113 (1975)
26. P. A. Small, *J. Appl. Chem. 3* 71 (1953)
27. R. F. Fedors, *Polym. Eng. Sci. 14* (2) 147 (1974)
28. M. Morton, *Rubber Chem. Technol. 56* 1096 (1983)
29. M. T. Tse, Ph. D. Dissertation, University of Akron, 1979
30. J. D. Ferry, *Viscoelastic Properties of Polymers,* 2nd Ed., John Wiley and Sons, New York, 1975, p. 406
31. M. Morton, N. K. Agarwal and M. Cizmecioglu, in *Polymer Alloys III,* D. Klempner and K. C. Frisch, Eds., Plenum Press, New York, 1983; M. Morton, R. J. Murphy and T. C. Cheng, in

Copolymers, Polyblends and Composites, Advances in Chemistry Series, No. 142, N. A. J. Platzer,
- Ed., American Chemical Society, Washington, 1975, p. 409
32. E. G. Shafrin and W. A. Zisman, in *Contact Angle, Wettability and Adhesion,* R. F. Gould, Ed.,
    Advances in Chemistry Series No. 43, American Chemical Society, Washington 1964, p. 145
33. L. H. Lee, *J. Polym. Sci. Pt. A2 5* 1103 (1967)
34. W. A. Zisman, Ref. 32, p. 4
35. L. H. Lee, *J. Appl. Polym. Sci. 12* 719 (1968)
36. A. H. Ellison and W. A. Zisman, *J. Phys. Chem. 58* 503 (1954)
37. M. Morton, N–C. Lee and E. R. Terill, in *Elastomers and Rubber Elasticity,* J. E. Mark and J. Lal,
    Eds., ACS Symposium Series No. 193, American Chemical Society, Washington, 1982, p. 101
38. N–C. Lee, Ph. D. Dissertation, University of Akron, 1982

Chapter 5

POLY-α-OLEFIN BASED THERMOPLASTIC ELASTOMERS

C.-K. Shih, A. C. L. Su

Contents

C.-K. Shih, A. C. L. Su, E. I. Du Pont de Nemours & Co., Inc., Polymer Products Department, Du Pont Experimental Station, Wilmington, DE 19898

1 INTRODUCTION

Since the discovery of the segmented thermoplastic polyurethanes and the poly(strene-b-butadiene-styrene) copolymers (S–B–S) it became apparent that one can produce elastomers of high tensile strength through "physical crosslinking" without the use of chemical vulcanizations.

These thermoplastic elastomer molecules need both elastomeric soft segments and thermoplastic hard segments. Proper combinations of the soft and hard segments are required to introduce suitable molecular tie points or the physical crosslinks to produce a network structure similar to those established by the chemical crosslinks. A wide variety of intra- and inter-molecular combinations can be used. The advantage of this class of elastomers is the thermoplastic processability.

The physical crosslink by means of crystallizable hard segments is of particular interest because products of low melt viscosity can be produced readily for easy processing once the melting temperature of the crystallizable segments is exceeded. A great deal of effort has been concentrated in this area. Examples include:

1. Random and block copolymers of α-olefin – e.g. propylene/hexene-1 copolymer, (ethylene)/(ethylene-propylene) block copolymer.
2. Melt blend of thermoplastic elastomer and thermoplastics – e.g., propylene/hexene-1 copolymer and isotactic polypropylene (iPP) blend.
3. Stereoblock homopolymer – e.g. stereoblock polypropylene.
4. Graft copolymerization of crystallizable monomer segments onto elastomer molecules – e.g., pivalolactone-grafted EPDM.
5. Elastomer-thermoplastic blends – e.g., blends of EPDM and iPP.
6. Elastomer-thermoplastic blends, dynamically vulcanized – e.g., EPDM/iPP blends in the presence of EPDM curatives.
7. Segmented copolymers – e.g., copolyetheresters and the thermoplastic polyurethanes.

These efforts have resulted in interesting thermoplastic elastomers of quite different structures and properties. In contrast to the S–B–S block copolymer system, the physical properties of these systems can be maintained at elevated temperatures by the choice of crystallizable segments having a higher melting temperature. For example, the use of polypropylene segments can easily extend the useful temperature range of a thermoplastic elastomer system to beyond 100 °C.

This chapter will deal with thermoplastic elastomers made by a homopolymer and copolymers of poly α-olefins, with α-olefins including ethylene. While other hydrocarbon based thermoplastic elastomers such as the EPDM/iPP blends given in Examples 5 & 6 above are well known, those made by direct polymerization of α-olefins are not. At present there is no commercial product based on this type of polymers. The primary reason for the lack of such product is the difficulty of making block copolymers or stereoblock polymers from these monomers by coordination or Ziegler-Natta catalysts. These types of catalysts unlike anionic polymerization systems have high decay rates[1,2] as well as high propagation rates[3,4]. As a result, methods such as sequential or block copolymerization or even graft copolymerization becomes very difficult to implement. However, there are impressive efforts aiming to produce α-olefin based block copolymers. These are done either through development of very stable coordination catalyst systems or by other direct or indirect[5] technique to create the right distribution of elastomer and rigid segments in a polymer composition. Some of these efforts could lead to commercial products.

Elastomers described in Examples 5, 6 and 7 are covered in detail in other chapters of this book. The random and block copolymers of polyolefins, the stereoblock polypropylene, some of which exhibit an interesting co-crystallization behavior, and a graft copolymer of EPDM will be discussed in the following sections.

2   BLOCK AND RANDOM COPOLYMERS

A number of investigations have tried to synthesize polyolefin block copolymer with molecular structure similar to the S–B–S tri-block copolymer with the S and B blocks replaced with crystallizable, and elastomeric, polyolefin segments, respectively[5-11]. Kontos[6, 9, 10] reported that "living α-olefin polymers" could be produced using certain modified Ziegler-Natta catalyst systems e.g. $TiCl_4/LiAlR_4$ or $VOCl_3/R_2AlCl$. The "living" nature of the polymer allowed him to make a variety of sequentially prepared copolymers from different α-olefins including ethylene. He described three types of such sequentially prepared copolymers which exhibited thermoplastic elastomer behavior. They are

$$(H–C)_n$$
$$(C_1–C_2)_n$$
$$(H_1–H_2)_n$$

where H and C are α-olefin homopolymer and copolymer sequences respectively. 1 and 2 denote sequences of a different homo or co-polyolefins. A number of examples are given, among them:

$$[(E)–(E/P)]_3–(E)$$

$$[(E/P)_1 – (E/P)_2]_3–(E/P)_1$$

$$[(E) – (P)]_3 – (E)$$

where the polyolefin blocks are ethylene (E), propylene (P) and ethylene/propylene (E/P) sequences.

High tensile strength of 8−27 MPa (or 1000−3900 psi) with over 500 % ultimate elongation were reported for these copolymers[9]. These results suggest that crystalline polyolefin phases can indeed provide physical crosslinks during tensile deformation just like the glassy domains in the S–B–S tri-block copolymers. Unfortunately the limited characterizations carried out by the author were not sufficient to establish that the products prepared were single stereoblock compositions as depicted by the multiple block structures shown above.

The true "living" nature of the polymer ends is also subject to question. In a living polymerization the polymer produced should have a molecular weight distribution (MWD) approaching 1 and the molecular weight should be close to the weight of polymer produced per mole of catalyst. In the absence of MWD data and the knowledge of the concentration of the active catalyst species existing during polymerization, it is very difficult to assess the true living nature of the polymerization reaction. Also, without detailed catalyst structural analysis there is no assurance that multiple active catalyst sites do not exist during polymer synthesis. It is entirely possible that the polymers produced are not homogeneous and only a fraction of the polymer consists of the block sequences as depicted by Kontos.

It is of interest to compare the tensile properties of the sequentially prepared copolymers with an unvulcanized, semi-crystalline random copolymer of α-olefin. This is shown in

Figure 1. The random copolymer is an EPDM with a high ethylene content (Nordel® 1560 by E. I. du Pont de Nemours and Co.), hence, the polyethylene crystallinity provided the physical crosslinks to yield a tensile strength of 19.3 MPa (2800 psi). The compression set of the unvulcanized EPDM is very high however. Unfortunately, Kontos did not report any compression or tension set properties with his block copolymers.

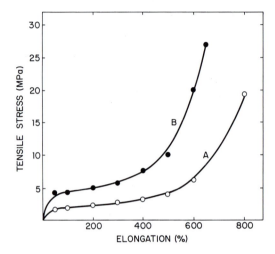

Figure 1   A Comparison of the Tensile Properties of Semicrystalline EPDM (Nordel® 1560), A, with Sequential Polymerized (E) (E/P) Copolymer, B

For systems such as the unvulcanized EPDM with high ethylene content, the phase separation between the crystalline and amorphous segments is rather poor. One invariably observes yielding of the crystalline phase during stretching as evidence by a high initial tensile modulus followed by a sharp reduction of slope in the stress-strain curve. Note, this yielding behavior is also quite evident in the samples reported by Kontos. However, tensile and recoverable properties resembling those of vulcanized rubber can be produced rather easily after yielding has taken place, that is, in the stress hardening zone where the continuous crystalline phase is broken up into small dispersed domains.

It is believed that an α-olefin based block copolymer with a molecular structure as well as phase separations truly resembling those of the S–B–S tri-block copolymer would be an excellent thermoplastic elastomer with mechanical properties, including the compression set resistance, similar to the chemically vulcanized elastomer. The mechanical strength of some of the semicrystalline α-olefin copolymers can be significantly augmented by blending with a homopolyolefin through an unusual phenomenon where the amorphous phases are compatible and merge into one single phase whereas the crystalline phases of the components become co-crystallized[17, 12]. A detailed description of this phenomenon is given in the next section where such a two component blend involving propylene/hexene-1 copolymer and the isotactic polypropylene is discussed. Starkweather reported[12] a blend of EPDM and low density polyethylene exhibits behavior similar to above except that two independent co-crystallized phases were observed.

3   PROPYLENE/α-OLEFIN COPOLYMERS

As discussed in the previous section, copolymers with certain thermoplastic elastomer characteristics can be produced by a sequential polymerization technique. But the process is rather complex and impractical with a relatively low polymerization rate[6,9,10]. Direct polymerization of α-olefins using Ziegler-Natta catalysis to produce homopolymers or copolymers is, however, quite practical with much greater polymerization rate[13–17]. Homopolyolefins are either semicrystalline plastics, e.g. polypropylene or polybutene, etc. or non-crystalline elastomers. The glass transition temperature, Tg of a series of homopoly α-olefins with increasing number of carbon atoms in the monomer is shown in Figure 2. Copolymerization of the α-olefins can produce, in many cases, a semicrystalline polymer with low glass transition temperature which fulfills a prime requirement for thermoplastic elastomers. For example, the propylene/α-olefin copolymer of about 50 weight % propylene are semicrystalline with glass transition temperature ranging from −45 °C to −20 °C depending upon the comonomer used, see Figure 2.

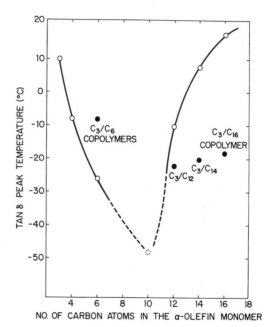

Figure 2   Glass Transition Temperature* of α–Olefins Homopolymers –◯– and, Copolymers –●–

* Tan δ Peak Determined with Dynamic Mechanical Measurements

3.1   Synthesis

In general, direct copolymerization of α-olefins A & B produces a copolymer with a structure of $(A_xB_y)_n$, x and y denote the monomer sequence length in a particular segment n of a chain molecule. By proper choices of monomers A, B and the catalysts, one could produce sufficiently long sequences of A, crystallizable after melt processing, to serve as intermolecular tie points for the non-crystalline sequences which contribute to the elastomeric amorphous phase. Copolymerization of propylene with C_6 to C_{10} α-olefin yields such a semicrystalline copolymer over a broad composition range. Two catalyst systems were reported to produce such polymers. One consists of γ-TiCl₃ with diethylaluminum chloride co-catalyst[18]. The other is a supported system[16, 19] consisting of TiCl₄ absorbed on MgCl₂ with trialkyl aluminum co-catalyst. These system are capable of producing propylene sequences of high isotacticity.

The copolymers can be produced over a wide range of conditions either by a batch or a continuous process. The catalyst efficiency and polymerization rate is quite high especially when the MgCl₂/TiCl₄ supported catalyst is used. The productivity can be in excess of 3×10^5 g of polymer per mole of Ti per hour at 25 °C and one atmosphere[16]. This value can be greatly increased under higher temperature and pressure.

The P/α-olefin copolymers that exhibit thermoplastic elastomer properties contain about 25–60 % by wt of the α-olefin. These copolymers also have different levels of crystallinity with a crystallinity index, defined by the ratio of infrared absorbtivity at 993 cm^{-1} to that at 975 cm^{-1}, ranging from 20−60. Standard iPP has an index of over 80. The DSC thermogram of a typical thermoplastic composition having an index of 25−35 is shown in Figure 3. It has a wide melting range of about 130−150 °C and a crystallization peak temperature of about 80 °C. A glass transition temperature of between −25 to −30 °C is also observed. The polymer properties are influenced by both the crystallinity and the α-olefin content. Increase in α-olefin content always reduces crystallinity, Figure 4.

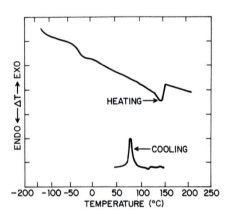

Figure 3   Typical DSC Thermogram of the Propylene/Hexene (PH) Copolymer

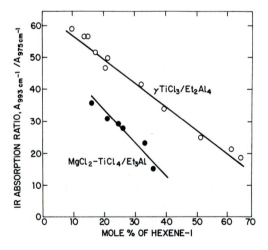

Figure 4   Isotacticity of Propylene/Hexene Copolymers

3.2   Properties

The elastomeric characteristics of a propylene/hexene-1 copolymer (PH) and a propylene/decene-1 copolymer are shown in Table I. They exhibit high tensile strength of 18.3 and 6.6 MPa (2650 and 960 psi) and high ultimate elongation. The tensile stress–strain relationship for the PH copolymer shown in Figure 5 resembles quite closely a chemically vulcanized elastomer. Although there appears to be a slight plastic yielding at about 35 % elongation, the tensile stress at higher deformation continues to increase as the elongation is increased. The strain hardening behavior is probably resulted from the orientation of the crystalline component of the copolymer. The somewhat high compression set and permanent set shown in Table I is probably caused by the yielding of the crystalline component.

TABLE I   Elastomeric Properties of Propylene/α-Olefin Copolymer 25 °C

	P/HEXENE-1	P/DECENE-1
% α-Olefin (mole)	26	22
Crystallinity Index[1]	28	37
Stress (MPa)		
at 100 % Elongation	2.76	1.52
at 300 % Elongation	8.28	3.31
Tensile Strength (MPa)	18.27	6.62
Ultimate Elongation (%)	495	480
Permanent Set (%)	80	32
Compression Set[2] (%)	66	–
Hardness, Shore A	71	49

[1] Defined by the ratio of infrared absorbtivity at 993 cm^{-1} to that at 975 cm^{-1}
[2] Measured after 22 hours at 70 °C

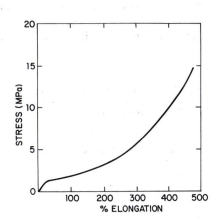

Figure 5   Stress/Strain Curves of a PH Copolymer (50 % H)

The thermoplasticity of these copolymers is demonstrated by their ability to be shaped repeatedly by compression molding at temperature above the crystalline melting point. As discussed previously these copolymers have a rather broad melting temperature. As a result, the high temperature strength e.g., at 70–100 °C decreases in spite of its higher melting peak temperature shown in Figure 3. Another undesirable property noted is the lack of dimensional stability of the injection molded articles. The product tends to warp after molding

TABLE II   Property Comparison of Propylene/Hexene-1 Copolymer and the iPP Blend
(Compression Molded Samples)

	PH Copolymer (41 Wt % H)		80/20 Blend (PH/iPP)	
	25 °C	70 °C	25 °C	70 °C
Stress at 100 % Elongation (MPa)	2.76	0.62	4.48	1.59
Stress at 300 % Elongation (MPa)	8.28	1.03	9.14	2.69
Tensile Strength (MPa)	18.27	1.79	17.59	4.28
Elongation at Break, %	495	470	500	455
Permanent Set at Break %	80	44	90	58
Compression Set % 22 hr/70 °C		66		54

even for materials with low melt viscosity, e.g. Melt Index of 2 to 6. These property deficiencies are significantly improved or eliminated by the addition of isotactic polypropylene through melt blending, Table II.

3.3   Blends of Propylene/Hexene-1 Copolymer and Isotactic Polypropylene

An unusual compatibility was observed with the polymer blend. As shown in Table III a single glass transition temperature as well as a single melting temperature were observed for binary blends of 20 % (wt) iPP with a variety of P/α-olefin copolymers. The compatibility of the blends appears to extend to all proportions. Single glass transition temperatures were observed over the entire composition range for PH Copolymer/iPP blends as shown in Figure 6. A single melting endotherm with considerable narrowing of the melting ranges is also observed as shown in Table IV. All these indicate that the crystalline segments are probably co-crystallized as will be discussed later in this section.

The mechanical properties of the copolymers, especially those at elevated temperatures are significantly improved. This is illustrated in Table II and Figure 7. The storage modulus determined by dynamic mechanical analysis, Figure 8, increases steadily at temperatures

TABLE III   Transition Temperatures of P/α-Olefin Copolymer and Blends with iPP

P/α-Olefin Copolymer				80/20 Blend (Copolymer/iPP)	
α-Olefin Comonomer	α-Olefin Content (mole %)	T_g (°C) Tan δ Peak	T_m (°C)	T_g (°C) Tan δ Peak	T_m (°C)
C_6H_{12}	34	− 8	148	− 6	158
C_8H_{16}	17	−12	140	− 6	155
	20	−12	138	−12	152
$C_{10}H_{20}$	17	−18	143	−10	153
				−18	157
$C_{12}H_{24}$	11	−22	145	−22	158
	15	−26	136	−22	158
$C_{14}H_{28}$	11	−20		−16	157
	15	−22	138	−22	158
$C_{16}H_{32}$	10	−12	145	−14	155

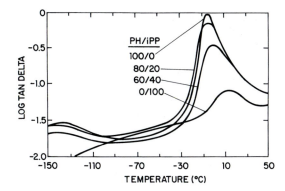

Figure 6   Dynamic Mechanical Properties of PH/iPP Blends

TABLE IV   Characteristics of PH/iPP[1] Blends

% iPP	Melting Endtotherm Range	(°C) Peak	Crystallizing Temp. (°C) Onset	Peak	ΔH$_f$ (cal/G) Obs	Calc	Extractable[2] (Wt %) Obs	Calc
0	40–169	148	86	80	6.1		55	
10	100–165	153	90	85			46	50
23	120–165	158	102	94	15.9	10.4		
50	120–170	164	112	105	18.7	15.3	13	28
100	130–175	166	122	112	24.5		0	

[1] Based on a PH sample with 34 % H, prepared by TiCl$_4$Et$_3$Al catalyst; iPP is a commercial product Amoco 4018
[2] 1 g polymer extracted by 200 g boiling hexane for 1 hour

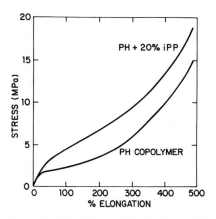

Figure 7   Stress/Strain Relationships of PH and PH/iPP Blend

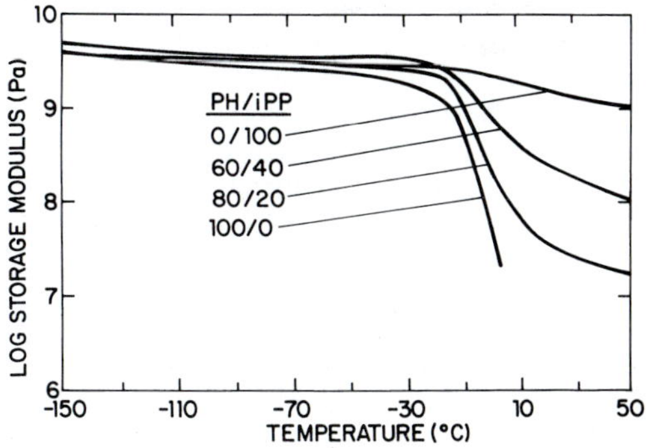

Figure 8   Dynamic Mechanical Properties of PH/iPP Blends

above the glass transition region. And the temperature ranges corresponding to the rubbery plateau are broadened considerably.

The processing problem related to injection molding of the propylene/hexene copolymer was not observed with the binary blends containing as little as 20 wt % of iPP.

TABLE V   Property Comparison of Oriented PH/iPP Blends

Sample	A	B	C (Copolyetherester)
Composition, %			
Copolymer	80	60	–
Isotactic Polypropylene	20	40	–
Draw Ratio	2.9x	3.9x	4.0x
Modulus, M_{200}			
MPa	18	35	30
Tensile Strength at Break, MPa	50	35	150
Elongation at Break, %	130	80	100

These positive changes in properties are attributed to a postulated co-crystallization of the homopolypropylene with the shorter propylene segments in the copolymer, besides the fact that iPP can also serve as a natural reinforcing filler for the copolymer. The increased heat of fusion of the blend, see Table IV, suggests that some non-crystallized propylene segments of the copolymer are incorporated into the crystalline lattice.

The stress/strain behavior of PH copolymer and PH/iPP blend indicates the presence of stretch induced orientation of the polymers. This suggests that the polymers are orientable to improve tensile properties as shown in Table V. Dramatic improvement in modulus and tensile strength as well as tension set was observed. In fact the moduli are comparable to that of a commercial high strength copolyether ester thermoplastic elastomer. Such high strength is unusual for a hydrocarbon based thermoplastic elastomer.

The co-crystallization phenomenon is very unusual and interesting. The remainder of this section will be devoted to discussions of this characteristics.

3.3.1 Melting and Crystallization Behavior

Standard DSC thermograms were obtained with the blends and the components of the PH copolymer and iPP. Closer examination showed that the thermogram of the blend cannot be represented by the weighted average of the components as is shown schematically in Figure 9. The peaks of the individual components cannot be identified, and one sees instead a new peak situated between those of the components for both the heating and cooling thermograms. This behavior occurs over the entire composition range of PH copolymers studied. As shown in Figure 10, the peak melting temperature, T_m, and crystallization

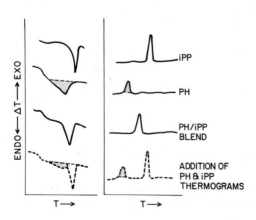

Figure 9   DSC Thermograms of PH, iPP and PH/iPP Blend (Schematic)

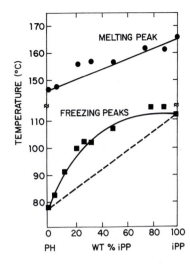

Figure 10   Melting and Crystallization Temperature of PH/ iPP Blends

temperature, T_f (peak of exotherm upon cooling), increases as the iPP content in the blend is increased. As shown in Table IV other characteristics including heat of fusion and solubility of the blend are again different form the expected. The characteristics of the blend can be summarized below.

(1) Single T_m between those of the components.
(2) Single T_f between those of the components.
(3) Heat of fusion greater than that of either of the components and equal to or greater than the weighted average.
(4) Lower hexane extractables than the weighted average.
(5) Slab appearance not opaque but semi-transparent between that of the transparent PH and milky PP.
(6) Reduced tendency to stress whitening observed with homopolypropylene.

The observed thermal characteristics cannot be explained based on a simple nucleation or plasticization phenomenon. The hypothesis is that the isotactic propylene segments from the two component polymers become co-crystallized when the compatible blend is cooled from the molten state. A further demonstration of the affinity of the two systems is shown by monitoring the thermal characteristics of a freeze milled (at liquid nitrogen temperature) powder mixture of PH copolymer and homopolypropylene by subjecting the sample to repeated cycles of heating and cooling between 0° and 200 °C in a differential scanning calorimetric cell. In the first cycle, the melting point, T_m, and freezing point, T_f (peak temperature of the exotherm on cooling), of the individual components are observed as shown in Table VI; but as heating and cooling progresses, the individual values are moving toward each other. Finally, on the 7th cycle, a single valued T_m and a single valued T_f are observed. The values are in close agreement with those observed with the melt blended sample.

These results suggest that crystalline segments of the two polymers are co-crystallized. The X-ray diffraction patterns of the two components are all iPP in origin, but the double peak in 16–17° 2Θ range observed in iPP component turned into a singlet as in PH copolymers whereas the double peak in 23–25° 2Θ range remained in the blend as shown in Figure 11. The results of the repeatedly heated powder blend of PH and PP reinforce the thinking that the two polymer systems can be dispersed and dissolved in each other very readily. Some of

TABLE VI   Thermal Analysis of Freeze Milled PH/iPP Blends

Cycle No.[2]	T_m	(°C)	T_f	(°C)
1	148[1]	163	115	85
2	148[1]	161	115	87
3	148[1]	160	114	88
4		160	114	89
5		160	114	93[1]
6		160	113	94[1]
7		159	107	no shoulder
Melt Blended Sample		157	102	no shoulder
Pure iPP		166	112	
Pure PH	148			84

[1] Shoulder
[2] Sample: ¼ blend ratio of iPP and PH 44% H, Consecutive DSC runs at 10 °C/minute heating and cooling cycles between 0° and 200 °C

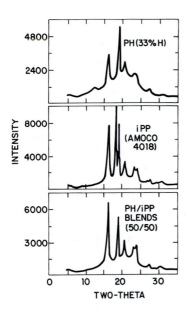

Figure 11   X-Ray Diffraction Pattern of PH Copolymer and iPP Blends

the short amorphous isotactic propylene sequences in the PH copolymer may have been incorporated into the co-crystallized lattice as evidenced by the observed higher heat of fusion and lower extractables as compared to the values of weighted average.

3.3.2 Dynamic Mechanical Behavior

The DSC thermograms do not show very clearly the influence of the added iPP in the glass transition region as the signals are rather weak in these samples. However this influence is revealed more clearly by studying the dynamic mechanical properties. The results are rather striking. As shown in Figure 6 and 8, the tan δ loss peak of the PH copolymer decreases in size and the peak temperature moves higher as the iPP content in the blend is increased; the storage modulus at temperature above the glass transition region also increases and the rubbery plateau zone broadens steadily with the increased iPP content. These data suggest a compatible amorphous phase resulted from blending the components.

3.3.3 Annealing Behavior

Another way to examine the extent of interaction between the crystalline segments of the component polymers is through the thermal characteristics of the annealed samples. The results are shown in Figure 12. The T_m-$T_{annealing}$ relationship suggests strongly the blend is not acting like two separate crystalline phases and in fact no trace of melting for the blend is observed in the temperature range 135–150 °C and 170–173 °C where significant melting was observed for annealed PH copolymer and iPP respectively. This result again demonstrates the possibility of co-crystallization in this system.

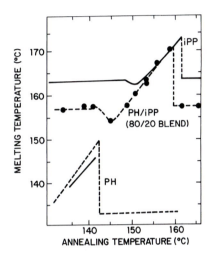

Figure 12   Effect of Annealing on the Melting Temperature of iPP ——, PH (34 % H) Copolymer – – – – and PH/iPP Blends – –●– –

4   HIGH MOLECULAR WEIGHT STEREOBLOCK POLYPROPYLENE

The most recent and interesting development of α-olefin TPE is a composition derived from a homopolymer of polypropylene. Polypropylene so far can only be made by Ziegler Natta type coordination catalyst. Most efforts have been concentrated in developing highly stereoselective catalyst to manufacture isotactic, highly crystalline polypropylene. Thus polypropylene is generelly associated with plastic materials. Although atactic noncrystalline polypropylene is produced as a by-product during the production of crystalline polypropylene, it can be isolated only as low molecular weight gummy material. Natta discovered through his fractionation work of polypropylene (20–22) that low crystalline stereo block polypropylene which existed as a fraction of regular polypropylene can have attractive elastomeric properties. However, he was not able to produce such polymer exclusively. Sutter[5] et al, were able to produce stereo block material by epimerization of isotactic polypropylene using a palladium catalyst. Unfortunately, such process is not very practical. The most recent and possibly the most practical approach is a catalytic polymerization process which produce directly elastomeric stereoblock polymer. This is a unique process and it will be the subject of this section.

4.1 The Catalyst

The key factor which enables the production of an elastic propylene homopolymer or elastomeric polypropylene, abbreviate ELPP, is the discovery of a class of stable catalyst based on absorption of transition metal organometallic compound on Al_2O_3. The transition metal compounds are derived from metal alkyls R_4M (where M is Ti, Zr or Hf and R is an alkyl with no β-hydrogens). These transition metal alkyls alone were relatively inactive for olefin polymerization; and produce only small amounts of predominantly isotactic poly-propylene[23–25]. The lifetime and catalyst efficiencies are dramatically increased when the transition metal alkyl is supported on the surface of a metal oxide such as Al_2O_3[26–30].

A group in Du Pont led by J. W. Collette[13–14] using an improved version of the above type of catalyst developed by Setterquist et al[31–39], also of Du Pont, was able to produce high molecular weight stereoblock elastomeric polypropylene (ELPP) with high catalyst efficiency and rate. This improved type of catalysts consists of group IVB metal alkyls shown in Figure 13, their hydride and chloride derivatives, supported on a non-porous alumina with a fundamental particle size of $10-20$ nm and a surface area of over 100 m^2/g.

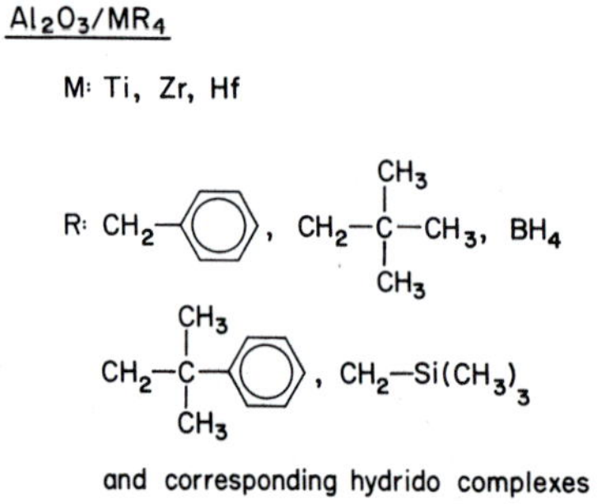

Al_2O_3/MR_4

M: Ti, Zr, Hf

R: $CH_2-C_6H_5$, $CH_2-C(CH_3)_2-CH_3$, BH_4

$CH_2-C(CH_3)_2-C_6H_5$, $CH_2-Si(CH_3)_3$

and corresponding hydrido complexes

Figure 13   Catalyst Systems for Stereoblock Polypropy-lenes

One of the most effective catalysts is tetraneophyll zirconium, TNZ, supported on Al_2O_3. A typical or standard supported catalyst[31–17] is prepared by reacting the organo transition metal complex, e.g. TNZ, with an alumina which contains about $0.4-0.8$ m mole of hydroxide (OH) per g. The concentration of the transition metal on A_2O_3 is usually less than half of the OH content. This supported catalyst is then introduced into the reactor to initiate the polymerization. The catalyst can also be generated in-situ by introducing the Al_2O_3 and the transition metal complex separately into the reactor.

4.2 Polymerization

The polymerization can be carried out, in either batch or continuous, processes, in hydrocarbon medium or in liquid propylene, under a wide range of pressure and temperature (ambient to 150 °C). The catalyst efficiencies are relatively high, ranging up to 6×10^5 g of polymer per mole of the transition metal.

In a typical solution polymerization reaction, 450 ml of cyclohexane is injected into a one liter autoclave followed by 126 g of propylene. Hydrogen can also be added at this stage if desired to regulate the molecular weight. Polymerization is initiated by pressure injection of the catalyst which is suspended as a slurry in 75 ml of cyclohexane and composed of 0.2 mg of TNZ supported on 2 g of Al_2O_3. The reactor temperature was maintained at a desired level somewhere between 25 °C and 70 °C for up to one hour. At the end of the polymerization a viscous solution was obtained from which the polymer was isolated.

When liquid propylene is used as the reaction medium the polymer is not soluble and appeared as a suspension in the medium which can be isolated more readily than in the solvent process.

4.3 The Polymer

The polymer produced under the above condition is reported to be a high molecular weight stereoblock elastomeric material with low isotactic content ($< 20\,\%$ by NMR and IR) and low crystallinity (< 10 J/g by DSC). However, depending on the catalyst make up, the isotactic content can vary from $20-70\,\%$ and the crystallinity from $10-70$ J/g. Only the lower isotacticity and crystallinity polymers exhibit elastomeric properties, Figure 14. Standard isotactic polypropylene has an isotactic content of over 90 % and crystallinity in excess of 100 J/g.

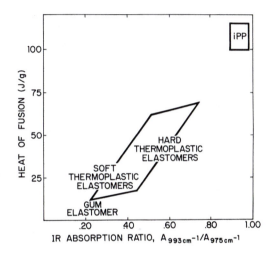

Figure 14 Stereoblock Polypropylenes from R_4M/Al_2O_3. Heat of Fusion vs. IR – Isotacticity

4.4 Catalyst Composition and Polymer Structure

The degree of stereoregularity depends on the types of organotransition metal and the ratio of the transition metal to the Al_2O_3 support. The stereoregularity was determined both by means of the Crystallinity Index (see Footnote, Table I) which measures the isotactic helix[40] and from the 13 C NMR which measures isotactic pentads[41].

For example, in the TNZ/Al_2O_3 system the stereoregulation was strongly dependent on the concentration of the metal on the support surface. As shown in Figure 15, the isotactic content as measured by IR, increases as the Zr/Al_3O_2 ratio increases; catalyst efficiency decreases at the same time. For more detail analysis of reactions between the organometallic compounds and the Al_2O_3 surfaces see the work of Firment[34].

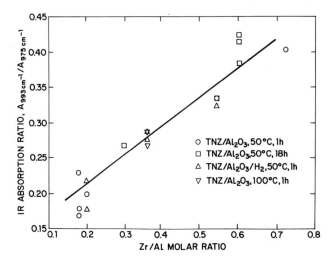

Figure 15   Stereoregularity as a Function of Zr/Al

4.5 Polymer Properties

The most unique feature of these new polypropylenes is their elastomeric behavior. The polymers showed typical properties of an α-olefin thermoplastic elastomer as seen in the preceding sections. This behavior is very interesting since propylene homopolymer is generally associated only with plastic material.

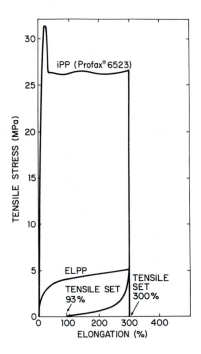

Figure 16   Stress-Strain Properties of Elastomeric Poly-propylene (ELPP) and iPP

A typical stress-strain curve of ELPP as compared to isotactic polypropylene is shown in Figure 16. The isotactic polymer shows a sharp yield at 20 % elongation and essentially no recovery. ELPP has no yield and has significant elastic recovery.

The elastomeric property of the polymer is demonstrated more dramatically in the hysteresis curve, Figure 17, in which the sample is elongated 300 %, and allowed to recover repeatedly until failure.

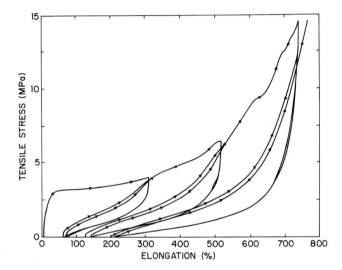

Figure 17   Hysteresis of ELPP

Figure 18 compares the stress strain curve for two samples of ELPP of different crystallinities. The curves suggest that the tensile properties both of a thermoplastic elastomer and a flexibilized plastic can be obtained by varying the isotacticity and molecular weight. The commercial thermoplastic elastomers shown in the same figure are for property comparison only. No structural property comparison is implied.

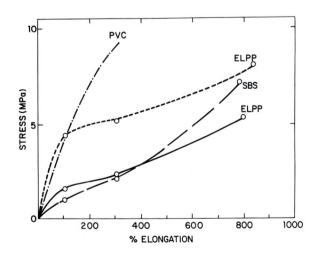

Figure 18   Stress/Strain Properties of ELPP, Plasticized PVC and a Compounded S–B–S (Kraton 2705) Block Copolymer

TABLE VII   Comparison of Polypropylene from Different Catalysts

CATALYST	HYDROGEN PRESSURE (MPa)	YIELD (g)	mmol × M	FRACTION	FRACTION (%)	INHERENT VISCOSITY	T_g (°C)	T_m (°C)	$-\Delta H_f$ (J/g)	M_n	M_w	M_w/M_n
New Catalyst[1]	–	15.0	48.8	Total	100.0	10.2	– 10.1	147.1	13.1	75,500	600,000	8.0
				Ether Sol.	28.2	3.8	– 8.0	52.0	1.6	80,800	604,000	7.5
				Heptane Sol.	17.9	4.8	– 7.8	130.2	27.7	39,300	934,000	23.9
				Heptane Insol.	50.0	15.3	– 7.4	147.7	49.0	455,000	2626,000	5.8
New Catalyst[2]	.034	30.9	92.7	Total	100.0	4.0	– 11.5	151.8	5.0	34,000	370,000	10.9
				Ether Sol.	49.0	2.5	– 8.8	53.0	1.8	22,300	261,000	11.7
				Heptane Sol.	33.0	3.3	– 10.1	137.0	29.2	22,000	478,000	21.6
				Heptane Insol.	24.0	8.0	– 7.5	149.9	68.7	108,000	3460,000	3.2
Standard Catalyst[3]	–	65.5	2680	Total	100.0	2.11	– 3.4	159.6	12.5	22,400	128,000	5.6
				Ether Sol.	21.0	0.82	– 3.6	–	–	19,100	66,800	3.5
				Heptane Sol.	19.3	0.78	– 1.6	140.1	63.0	28,000	110,000	3.7
				Heptane Insol.	53.0	3.45	n.d.	166.3	102.0	531,000	160,000	3.0
Standard Catalyst[4]	.034	64.9	2140	Total	100.0	0.86	– 9.8	159.0	78.1	12,100	42,300	3.5
				Ether Sol.	26.6	0.25	– 10.4	–	–	6,670	16,500	2.5
				Heptane Sol.	24.5	.093	– 1.8	16.4	65.3	10,000	26,700	2.7
				Heptane Insol.	46.7	2.23	n.d.	161.3	105.0	26,800	110,000	4.1

Propylene was polymerized at 60–65 °C for 1 hr. in 100 ml n-heptane. 45 mg MgCl$_2$/Cl$_4$ (2.61 % Ti) activated with 2 ml AlEt$_3$, 200 mg tetraneophyl zirconium was supported on 1 g dry Degussa Alumina C.

[1] TNZ/Al$_2$0$_3$ Catalyst
[2] TNZ/Al$_2$0$_3$ Catalyst and H$_2$
[3] MgCl$_2$/TiCl$_4$/AlET$_3$ Catalyst used in Commercial iPP Manufacturing
[4] MgCl$_2$/TiCl$_4$/AlEt$_3$ Catalyst and H$_2$

4.6 Composition Comparison of ELPP and Isotactic Polypropylene

As mentioned above, the ability to obtain an elastomeric material from homopolymer of propylene is a very important and interesting achievement which can be attributed to the unique property of the new TNZ/Al_2O_3 type catalyst system. Some idea about the factors that contribute to this elasticity is gained from fractionation studies of the polymer. This is done by separating the "as made" polymer into three major fractions by successive extraction with boiling ether, hexane or heptane. Each fraction is then studied separately. In Table VII, the results of these studies are shown together with data obtained from fractionation of normal isotactic polypropylene made by standard catalysts. From the table, one notices immediately that all fractions from ELPP contain polypropylene crystallinity, i.e. they are all stereoblock polymers, with the ether soluble fraction the least crystalline and the heptane insoluble fraction the most crystalline as indicated by the ΔH_f data. Also notable is the very high molecular weight and broad molecular weight distribution (MWD), of both the ether and the heptane soluble fractions, see also Figure 19. On the other hand, the fractions from normal isotactic polypropylene are quite different. The ether soluble fractions are noncrystalline and low molecular weight while the heptane soluble fractions are also of low molecular weight but much higher in crystallinity. The heptane insoluble fractions have much higher crystallinity than the corresponding fractions of ELPP. Thus the main differences between normal isotactic polypropylene and ELPP are that the former lacks high molecular weight stereo block ether and heptane soluble fractions and also has significantly higher crystallinity in both the heptane soluble and heptane insoluble fractions. The results also show that ELPP is actually a mixture of stereo block polypropylene of different crystallinity or block size.

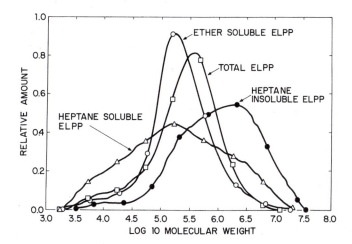

Figure 19 ELPP Molecular Weight Distribution

The stress-strain properties of the various fractions of ELPP have been measured, Figure 20. The ether soluble fraction appeared to be a weak gum elastomer while the heptane insoluble fraction behaves like a semicrystalline plastic which show a plastic yield point. The heptane soluble fraction is elastomeric and comparable to the elastomeric fraction reported by Natta (20−22). Interestingly the elastomeric property of the polymer can almost be duplicated by combining the two extreme fractions (see dotted line in Figure 20) and omitting the middle fraction.

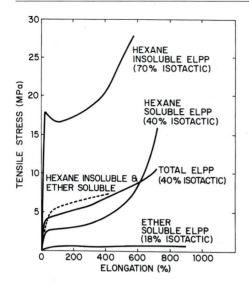

Figure 20   Stress/Strain Relationships of ELPP and ELPP Fractions

4.7 Co-crystallization

The above described properties of various ELPP fractions as well as the DSC data, Figure 21, of the individual fractions and that of the original polymer, strongly suggest the existence of co-crystallization phenomena among the fractions. This co-crystallization can be compared to that observed for blends of propylene-hexene copolymer and isotactic polypropylene as described previously. In this case the ether soluble and the hexane (or heptane) soluble fractions can be compared to the propylene-hexene copolymer and the insoluble fraction can be compared to that of isotactic polypropylene.

Support for the possibility of co-crystallization was obtained by extraction studies shown in Table VIII. The ether soluble fraction can be melt blended with more crystalline fractions or even with isotactic polypropylene so as to obtain a homogeneous mixture. Extraction of these blends repeatedly with ether yields only the low molecular weight portion of the

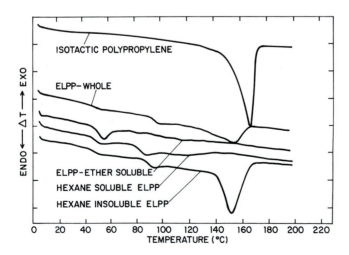

Figure 21   DSC Thermograms of ELPP Fractions

TABLE VIII   Effect of Cocrystallization

Blend	Original Ether Soluble		Blend or Milled Ether Soluble		% of Ether Soluble Fraction Insolubilized in Blend or Milling
	(%)	η_{inh}	(%)	η_{inh}	
Profax® 6523/Afax[1] (1:1)	50	0.21	48	0.17	4
Profax® 6523/ELPP–E (1:1)[2]	50	4.40	23	1.40	55
Profax® 6523/ELPP–E (3:1)	25	4.40	6.7	0.84	73
ELPP	57	6.40	22	1.50	60

[1] Atactic ether soluble fraction of Profax® 6523 isotactic polypropylene
[2] ELPP–E: ether soluble ELPP fraction

original ether soluble fraction; the high molecular weight portion has been insolubilized by co-crystallization. A similar effect is found with the crude polymer. Extraction of the virgin polymer with ether yields a significantly larger fraction than is obtained if the polymer is first melt processed. The melt processing allows a better mixing of the various fractions which in turn enhances the co-crystallization of the individual components. A comparative experiment, in which low molecular weight atactic polypropylene is melt blended with isotactic polypropylene, shows that virtually all the atactic material can be subsequently extracted.

Figure 22 shows the DSC curve for a low molecular weight ELPP (η = 2.2), isotactic polypropylene (Profax 6723), and a 60/40 blend. The observed braodening of the melting range and a lower melting point is consistent with the formation of a homogeneous blend. The result is quite comparable to those obtained for blends of the propylene-hexene copolymer with isotactic polypropylene, Figure 9.

In Figure 23 the dynamic mechanical spectra of ELPP and atactic polypropylene are compared. A definite rubbery plateau extending into the 100 °C region is observed only in the case of ELPP. This is also consistent with the presence of strong crosslinks formed by co-crystallization.

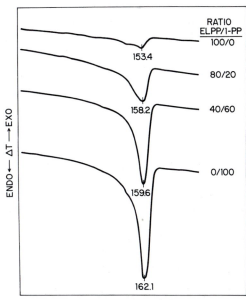

Figure 22   DSC Thermograms of Blends of ELPP and iPP

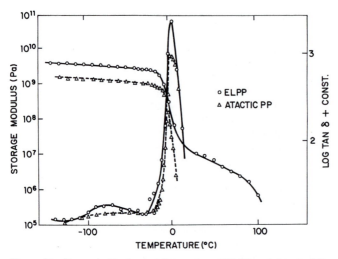

Figure 23   Dynamic Mechanical Properties of ELPP and Atactic PP

In summary one can safely say that the elastomeric nature of ELPP is due to the presence of high molecular weight, low crystalline, rubbery polypropylene fractions which can form co-crystallizable homogeneous blends with higher crystalline, more plastic-like polypropylene fractions produced in the same reaction. In a conventional polypropylene, produced by standard Ziegler-Natta catalyst, the amorphous fraction is a low molecular weight attactic polypropylene, incapable of co-crystallizing with the crystalline fractions and thus cannot contribute to the elastomeric properties of the overall composition.

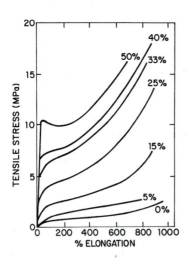

Figure 24   Stress-Strain Properties of Ether Soluble ELPP Fraction/Profax® 6523 Blends. Percentage numbers indicate amount of iPP blended with ether soluble ELPP.

The fact that a low crystalline, high molecular weight propylene homopolymer can induce the formation of rubbery composition by blending with high crystalline polypropylene is best demonstrated in Figure 24. Here, the stress-strain curves of blends of a commercial isotactic polypropylene with only the ether soluble fraction of ELPP are shown. Compositions of varying degree of elasticity can be formed by changing the ratio of the two components.

5   GRAFT COPOLYMER OF EPDM

All the thermoplastic elastomers described including the blends with iPP exhibit distinct yielding during stretching. Although their stress-strain relationships resemble quite closely those of the chemically vulcanized elastomers, the recovery properties and the compression set properties are quite poor. This is most likely due to the existence of a continuous crystalline phase which yields upon deformation. An EPDM backbone grafted with a chemically dissimilar crystalline polypivalolactone is the only known exception where the crystalline phase is distinctly separated from the amorphous phase and the polypivalolactone crystals are dispersed into small discrete domains over a wide composition range. This class of material was first reported in 1976[40–42] where its properties including stress-strain relationships and the compression set resistance resemble closely those of the chemically vulcanized elastomers.

The comb-graft copolymers prepared by ring-opening graft polymerization of pivalolactone, are initiated by carboxylate anions which are randomly located on the backbone of EPDM polymers. Rigorous extraction results suggest 90−98 % of the polypivalolactone (PPVL) formed are grafted onto the EPDM molecules. Grafted polymer with varying PPVL graft length (M_n of 350 to 2870), and concentration (7 to 42 % by weight) were reported. Analysis on these polymers suggest discrete PPVL crystalline domains existing in a continous amorphous EPDM matrix. The domain size, ranging from 10 to about 100 nm, is dependent upon both the MW of the PPVL grafts as well as the molecular weight of the EPDM segments between adjacent graft sites. The melting point of the thermoplastic material ranging from 120 °C to 200 °C is strongly dependent upon the molecular weight of the PPVL grafts and to a lesser degree upon the carboxylate graft site structure.

The mechanical properties of the graft copolymer exhibit many features closely resembling a chemically vulcanized elastomer. This can be attributed to its unique morphological structure, viz. the dispersed crystalline domains as well as the strong phase separation between the hard and soft molecular species. An incipient network with substantial strength occurs at

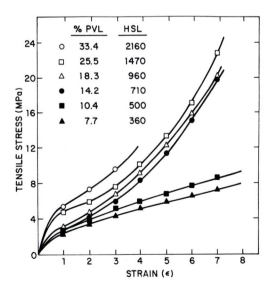

Figure 25   Effect of Hard Segment Length (HSL, Molecular Weight Unit) on Tensile Properties of PPVL-Grafted EPDM (Soft Segment Length is Kept Constant in this Series)

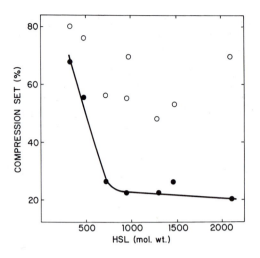

Figure 26 Effect of Hard Segment Length (HSL, Molecular Weight Units) on Compression Set Resistance of PPVL-Grafted EPDM; Soft Segment Length = 3600 Molecular Weight Units. Test Conditions: 70 h at 100 °C under 25 % Compression. ○ As Molded, ● After Annealing 16 h at 115 °C

an average graft molecular weight corresponding to an average degree of polymerization of 3 to 4. When the later is increased beyond 7, the compositions are very strong and resistant to compression set, even at temperatures in excess of 100 °C. The dependence of the stress-strain relationship and the compression set resistance on the PPVL-graft molecular weight and/or PPVL content is shown in Figures 25 and 26.

Annealing at 115−120 °C further improves the tensile strength as well as the compression set resistance. As shown in Figure 26 a constant compression set value of 10−11 % at 70 °C and 20−22 % at 100 °C is observed for copolymers with PPVL graft length of over 10 repeat units (MW over 1000). These values are quite impressive and are equivalent to those exhibited by EPDM vulcanizates, specially compounded and cured by conventional recipe for compression set resistance. The response of the PPVL-grafted EPDM to tensile strain is compared with a sulfur-cured EPDM in Figure 27. The grafted copolymer exhibited higher tensile strength and much greater ultimate elongation than the sulfur-cured and carbon black

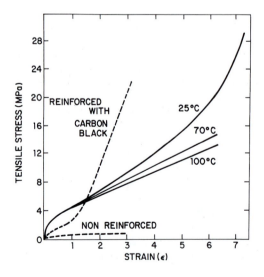

Figure 27 Tensile Properties of PPVL-Grafted EPDM Compared to Conventionally Cured EPDM: (———) PPVL–Grafted EPDM; (−−−−) Sulfur-Cured EPDM

reinforced EPDM. Since sulfur-cured but unreinforced EPDM has a very low strength, the submicron PPVL domains clearly serve as reinforcing particles, as well as interchain tiepoints, a generally recognized property of multiphase thermoplastic elastomers.

The melt viscosity of these graft copolymers is significantly greater than that of the ungrafted backbone EPDM. This is attributed to the existence of a phase-separated structure in the melt where additional energy would be required to remove graft chains from their preferred domains and transport them through the EPDM matrix. Similar behavior, of about the same order of magnitude, has been observed in S–B–S block copolymers[43]. A rather unusual observation with this graft copolymer is its significantly higher viscous activation energy of 112 and 167 KJ/mole in comparison with the 25 KJ/mole for the ungrafted EPDM. This is not observed for S–B–S polymer. Further investigation is required for a full understanding of the flow behavior.

6   SUMMARY

Many attempts were made to synthesize polyolefin-based block copolymers with structure and properties similar to the SBS tri-block copolymer. Some success was reported based on coordination polymerizations using sequential monomer feeds. But additional work is required to establish the structure of the product. The process is very complex and impracitcal.

A wide range of semicrystalline propylene/α-olefin copolymers, and a stereoblock homopolypropylene exhibiting thermoplastic elastomer characteristics can be produced by direct polymerizations via more practical processes. The elastomeric properties, especially the high temperature tensile strength and compression set resistance of these polymers can be improved by melt blending with isotactic polypropylene where the unique blends are compatible and capable of co-crystallization. This class of thermoplastic elastomers, including the blends with isotactic polypropylene also exhibits the stress hardening behavior during stretching. Hence, its tensile strength can be further improved by orientation. Such a behavior is lacking in the simple melt blend of EPDM and iPP including those prepared via dynamic vulcanizations.

The all polyolefin based thermoplastic elastomers reported in this chapter (including the EPDM/iPP blends) rely on the crystalline components to serve as intermolecular tiepoints, or the physical crosslinks. The rather apparent yielding behavior observed during stretching suggests the existence of continuous crystalline phase resulting from poor phase separation. A comb-graft copolymer with EPDM backbone and pendant crystalline polypivalolactone is the only known exception where the crystalline domains are distinctly dispersed in the undeformed state over a wide composition range. Their reported stress-strain relationship and the compression set properties resemble closely those of the chemically vulcanized elastomers.

7   ACKNOWLEDGEMENT

The authors are indebted to Drs. R. C. Thamm and J. W. Collette of E. I. du Pont de Nemours and Company, Inc. for many helpful discussions and cooperation.

References

1. U. Giannini, *Makromol. Chem., Suppl.,* 5, 216 (1981)
2. P. Galli, L. Luciani, and G. Cecchin, *Angew. Makromol. Chem.,* 94, 63 (1981)
3. T. Keii, *Kinetics of Ziegler-Natta Polymerization,* Kodanska, Tokyo, 1972
4. J. Boor Jr., *Ziegler-Natta Catalysts and Polymerizations,* Academic, New York, 1979
5. U. W. Suter, P. Neuenschwander, *Macromolecules 14,* 523 (1981)
6. E. G. Kontos, E. K. Easterbrook, R. D. Gilbert, *J. Polym. Sci., 61,* 69 (1962)
7. G. Natta, *J. Polym. Sci., 34,* 531 (1959)
8. G. Natta, C. Crespi, U. S. Patent 3, 175, 999 (1965)
9. E. G. Kontos, U. S. Patent 3, 378, 606 (1968). Assigned to Uniroyal, Inc.
10. E. G. Kontos, U. S. Patent 3, 853, 969 (1974). Assigned to Uniroyal, Inc.
11. R. Gobran, L. V. Kremer, D. O. Ethier, U. S. Patent 3, 784, 582 (1974)
12 a. R. L. Morgan, Du Pont Nordel® 1560 Hydrocarbon Rubber Bulletin No. 8 (1968)
12. H. W. Starkweather, *J. Appl. Polymer Sci., 25,* 139 (1980)
13. J. W. Collette, C. W. Tullock, U. S. 4, 298, 722
14. J. W. Collette, C. W. Tullock, R. N. MacDonald, A. C. L. Su, J. R. Harrell, R. Mulhaupt, ACS Reprint, *Polymeric Material Sci. and Eng. 53,* 488 (1985)
15. C.-K. Shih, U. S. Patent 3, 888, 949, June 1975. Assigned to E. I. du Pont de Nemours and Company, Inc.
16. A. C. L. Su, U. S. Patent 4, 461, 872, July 1984. Assigned to E. I. du Pont de Nemours and Company, Inc.
17. A. C. L. Su and C.-K. Shih, *ACS Polymer Preprint, 26,* 21, 22 (1985)
18. T. R. Manley, British Patent 957, 777, Example 8, May 1964
19. O. Hidekuni et al, Patent 2, 757, 863, June 1978, Fed. Rep. Germany, Example 1, assigned to Mitsui Petrochemical Co., Japan
20. G. Natta et al, U. S. 3, 175, 999 (1965). Assigned to Monticatini Co., Italy
21. G. Natta, *J. Polym. Sci., 34,* 531 (1959)
22. G. Natta, G. Mazzanti, G. Crespi, G. Moraglio, *Chim. Ind., Milano, 39,* 275 (1957)
23. D. G. H. Ballard, P. W. Van Lienden, *Makromol. Chem., 154,* 177 (1972)
24. P. Pino, G. Consiglio, H. J. Ringger, *Justus Liebigs Ann. Chem.,* 509 (1975)
25. K. Soga, K. Izumi, S. Ikeda, T. Keii, *Makromol. Chem.,* 178, 337 (1977)
26. D. G. H. Ballard, *Adv. Catal., 23,* 299 (1973)
27. D. G. H. Ballard, *Catalysis Proc. Int. Symp.,* 521, Elsevier, Amsterdam (1975)
28. D. G. H. Ballard, *J. Polym. Sci. Polym. Chem. Ed., 132,* 191 (1975)
29. D. G. H. Ballard, *J. Catal., 44,* 116–125 (1976)
30. D. G. H. Ballard et al, U. S. 3, 969, 386, ICI (1976)
31. R. A. Setterquist, U. S. 3, 950, 269 (1976). Assigned to E. I. du Pont de Nemours and Company, Inc.
32. R. A. Setterquist, F. N. Tebbe, W. G. Peet, *Polym. Sci. Techn., 19,* 167, Plenum Press, New York (1983)
33. W. G. Peet, F. N. Tebbe, R. A. Setterquist, G. W. Parshall, in *"Coordination Polymerization",* Edited by C. C. Price and E. J. Vanderberg, Plenum Press, 1983
34. L. E. Firment, *J. Catal., 77,* 491 (1982); *82,* 196 (1983)
35. R. A. Setterquist, U. S. 3, 392, 307 (1976), Assigned to E. I. du Pont de Nemours and Co., Inc.
36. R. A. Setterquist, U. S. 4, 017, 525 (1977). Assigned to E. I. du Pont de Nemours and Co., Inc.
37. R. A. Setterquist, U. S. 3, 971, 767 (1976). Assigned to E. I. du Pont de Nemours and Company, Inc.
38. J. P. Luongo, *J. Appl. Polym. Sci., 3,* 302 (1960)
39. J. W. Collette, D. W. Ovenall, W. H. Buck, et al, in press
40. S. A. Sundet, R. C. Thamm, J. M. Meyer, W. H. Buck, S. W. Caywood, P. M. Subramanian, B. C. Anderson, *Macromolecules, 9,* 371 (1976)
41. R. C. Thamm, W. H. Buck, *J. Polym. Sci.* (Polymer Chem. Ed), *16,* 539 (1978)
42. R. C. Thamm, W. H. Buck, S. W. Caywood, J. M. Meyer, B. C. Anderson, *Die Angew. Makromol. Chemie, 58/58,* 345 (1977)
43. G. Holden, E. T. Bishop, N. R. Legge in "Block Copolymers", *J. Polymer Sci. C 26,* J. Moacain, G. Holden and N. W. Tschoegl, Eds., Wiley, New York 1969, p. 37

Chapter 6

ELASTOMER-THERMOPLASTIC BLENDS AS THERMOPLASTIC ELASTOMERS

James R. Wolfe, Jr.

Contents

James R. Wolfe, Jr., Polymer Products Department, Experimental Station, E. I. Du Pont de Nemours and Company, Wilmington, Delaware 19898

1   INTRODUCTION

This chapter is concerned with thermoplastic elastomer compositions prepared by mixing elastomers with thermoplastics. Compositions in which the elastomeric component is itself a thermoplastic elastomer are not included. Thermoplastic elastomers prepared by the dynamic vulcanization technique in which the elastomeric component is tightly crosslinked while subjecting the elastomer-thermoplastic mixture to high shear mixing are the subject of a subsequent chapter.

The thermoplastic elastomers covered in this review can be divided into two categories: those in which the thermoplastic used contains a low level of crystallinity and derives its rigidity as a plastic from its high glass transition temperature as typified by poly(vinyl chloride) (PVC); and those in which the thermoplastic is a highly crystalline polymer such as polyethylene or isotactic polypropylene. The crystalline thermoplastics are typically mixed with elastomers with which they are not molecularly compatible to form thermoplastic elastomers which are multiphased. PVC and its copolymers are most often converted to thermoplastic elastomers by admixture with plasticizers which are more or less molecularly compatible with the PVC, resulting in a blend having a glass transition temperature intermediate between that of the components. Both polymeric and low molecular weight plasticizers are used with PVC to form elastomeric compositions. Only the polymeric plasticizers are covered in this review.

2   PVC BLENDS

2.1 Nitrile Elastomers with PVC

2.1.1 Research and Development

Elastomeric copolymers of acrylonitrile and 1,3-butadiene (nitrile elastomers or NBR) have been blended with PVC to achieve a number of purposes. Small amounts of nitrile elastomer in PVC can be used to improve the impact strength of rigid PVC compositions. Small amounts of PVC can be added to nitrile elastomers before vulcanization to improve the ozone resistance of the vulcanizates. Blends of comparable amounts of nitrile elastomer and PVC can be used as thermoplastic elastomers or can be vulcanized to form thermoset elastomers. This discussion is limited to those compositions which act as thermoplastic elastomers.

The first use of plasticizers in PVC is attributed to Fritz Klatte[1, 2] for the formation of semirigid sheets. The discovery that PVC could be converted to an elastomer by the addition of plasticizer was made more than ten years later in 1926 by Waldo Semon[1, 3, 4] while trying to dissolve the polymer. This discovery lead to the marketing of rubbery plasticized PVC under the name Koroseal[5]. The plasticizers used were low molecular weight materials.

The first mention of the use of a polymeric plasticizer in PVC in the form of nitrile elastomer is reported to have occurred in 1938 in trade literature from the Advance Solvents and Chemical Corp.[6], a distributor in the U.S. for nitrile elastomers manufactured in Germany by I.G. Farbenindustrie[7]. Badum[8] filed a patent application in Germany in 1937 and in the U.S. in 1938 on ozone resistant blends of PVC and nitrile rubber containing 10–50% PVC. A composition of matter patent covering both vulcanized and unvulcanized blends of 1,3-butadiene/acrylonitrile copolymers with PVC was applied for in 1940 by D.E. Henderson[9] of Goodrich.

The shortage of natural rubber which occurred during World War II stimulated research in the U.S. on the compounding and modification of plastics to form rubber-like materials[10]. This work was pursued after the war ended and resulted in the commercial marketing of NBR/PVC blends by Goodrich in 1947 under the name Geon Polyblend[11, 12]. These materials were prepared by blending NBR and PVC in the colloidal state as opposed to previous blends which had been prepared by mill mixing. The Polyblend products were furnished as light-yellow sheets which were soft, somewhat tacky, and relatively weak. Prior to their end use, they had to be heat treated at some point in the processing operation in order to develop their properties. At temperatures above about 150 °C the colloidal blends become homogeneous thermoplastic materials with good physical properties. An unvulcanized Polyblend having the composition 45 % NBR/55 % PVC has a tensile strength of 13 MPa, an elongation at break of 430 %, and a Shore A hardness equal to 93. Softer products were prepared by adding low molecular weight plasticizers. A latex version of Geon Polyblend also became available[13].

Also in 1947 Young and coworkers[14] at Standard Oil Development Co. reported on thermoplastic blends of nitrile elastomers, produced by Enjay, with 95 % vinyl chloride/5 % vinyl acetate copolymers, manufactured by the Bakelite Corp. Further studies on blends of vinyl chloride/vinyl acetate copolymers with nitrile elastomers were published by Reed and Harding[15]. They evaluated 64 plasticizers, including two nitrile elastomers, in the vinyl chloride copolymers. The use of nitrile elastomers as plasticizers resulted in blends with excellent resistance to swelling and to loss of plasticizer due to extraction or volatility. In a subsequent publication Reed[16] stated that nitrile elastomers plasticize vinyl chloride polymers by a solvation mechanism in the same manner as monomeric ester plasticizers. He pointed out that when powdered vinyl chloride polymer is added to nitrile elastomer and the batch is hot milled, the blend becomes clear and behaves as a normal plasticized compound.

Factors affecting the processability and properties of NBR/PVC blends were addressed by Bolam[17]. For a nitrile elastomer to be an efficient PVC plasticizer, he felt it should posses a minimum of nerve. This calls for nitrile elastomer having a low gel content and a low Mooney viscosity as discussed in a patent by Wheelock[18]. Others advocated an alternative approach claiming that nitrile elastomers having 50–75 % contents of tight gel produce NBR/PVC blends with improved processing properties[19]. Smith[20] reported on the processing and properties of NBR/PVC blends covering both their advantages and shortcomings. In a talk on thermoplastic NBR/PVC compounds Beekley[21] pointed out that difficulties in processing can arise from the long breakdown periods required for the nitrile elastomer, causing excessive frictional heat build-up, leading to degraded PVC and excessively crosslinked nitrile elastomer. To reduce these processing problems Goodyear introduced a low molecular weight PVC and an easy processing nitrile elastomer for the preparation of blends. The mechanical properties of mill–mixed blends of PVC with various amounts of nitrile elastomer containing 40 % acrylonitrile were reported by Byl'ev and Voskresenski[22]. Pedley[23] pointed out the advantages and availability of preblended, prefluxed, easy processing NBR/PVC blends and described the compounding, processing and applications of these materials.

When powdered nitrile elastomers became available, they were combined with powdered PVC compounds to make possible the processing of NBR/PVC blends in powder form. The advantages of powder processing are discussed in several publications which show typical compound formulations useful in thermoplastic applications[24–28]. The use of precrosslinked and powdered nitrile elastomer is reported to be effective in reducing the elastic memory (nerve) of NBR/PVC blends[24, 25, 28].

The properties of PVC plasticized with various polymeric plasticizers including nitrile elastomers, chlorinated polyethylene, an ethylene copolymer and a polyurethane were compared[29]. The effects of various plasticizers including nitrile elastomers on the friction characteristics and abrasion resistance of plasticized PVC have been examined[30]. Jordan and coworkers[31, 32] evaluated the mechanical and viscoelastic properties of blends of several nitrile elastomers with PVC and vinyl chloride/vinyl stearate copolymers.

The status of PVC thermoplastic elastomers in Japan has been reviewed by Kawashima[33]. PVC thermoplastic elastomers are a major force in the Japanese market particularly in automotive applications. New types are being introduced with substantially improved properties. Gel-containing PVC, prepared by polymerizing vinyl chloride in the presence of a polyfunctional monomer, has been mixed with partially crosslinked nitrile elastomer to form NBR/PVC compositions with substantially improved compression set, permanent set, resiliency and high temperature shape retention. The examples shown contain large amounts of low molecular weight plasticizer as well as partially crosslinked nitrile elastomer. Thermoplastic elastomers based on gel-containing PVC are being marketed by Sumitomo Bakelite K. K.

A paper entitled "Design of Alloys of PVC with NBR Copolymers to Produce Thermoplastic Elastomers" was presented at an ACS Rubber Division meeting at the time this review was written[34].

2.1.2 Structure-Property Relationships

Numerous studies have been carried out on thermoplastic NBR/PVC blends[35–57] for the purpose of answering two questions: (1) are the blends one phase or are they multiphase; (2) how are the properties of the blends affected by changing the acrylonitrile content of the nitrile elastomer component. The answer to the first question appears to be that some blends contain only one phase while others are multiphased. The one phase blends have been found to contain regions of microheterogeneity in some instances. An important factor controlling the number of phases present is the acrylonitrile content of the nitrile elastomer in the blend.

Reznikova and coworkers[35–36] studied the effects on the properties of thermoplastic NBR/PVC blends of varying the acrylonitrile content of the nitrile elastomer and the amount of nitrile elastomer in the blends. Nitrile elastomers containing 12–50% of acrylonitrile were mill mixed with PVC over a range of 0–100% PVC. Nitrile elastomers containing 28% or less acrylonitrile had poor compatibility with PVC giving blends which were cloudy, weak, and of poor elasticity. Lel'chuk and Sedlis[37] studied NBR/PVC blends prepared by latex blending followed by coagulation and then milling at 130–140 °C. Nitrile elastomers containing 19–40% acrylonitrile were employed. The effects of varying the molecular weight from 40,000 to 390,000 of a 35% acrylonitrile elastomer were investigated. Nitrile elastomer containing 35–40% acrylonitrile with a low molecular weight gave the best processability and properties. The compatibility of the NBR/PVC mixtures was studied by several methods[37, 38].

Dynamic mechanical test measurements have been a popular method of investigating the compatibility of NBR/PVC blends. In the NBR/PVC blends Nielsen[39, 40] and Breuers and coworkers[41] found that a single maximum in damping occurs at a temperature between the corresponding temperatures of the pure components. They reasoned that the polymers were soluble in each other. Nielsen[42] concluded that the broad damping peak found for an NBR/PVC blend indicated that the two polymers are soluble in each other, but the intermolecular attraction is so weak that considerable association of like segments is taking place in the soluble mixture. Nielsen also pointed out that in plasticized PVC crystallites act as crosslinks preventing the rubbery material from flowing under load even though it is not crosslinked by a chemical reaction as is vulcanized rubber. The presence of a three-dimensional network structure in plasticized PVC in which the tie points are PVC crystallites was elucidated by Alfrey et al[58].

Takayanagi et al[43–45, 47] measured the dynamic viscoelastic behavior of NBR/PVC blends prepared in solution and recovered by evaporation of the solvent. They concluded that even though the two polymers mix molecularly, there is some evidence of microheterogeneity due to the different segmental environments. Matsuo and coworkers[46, 48] examined mill-mixed blends of PVC with nitrile elastomers containing 8–40% acrylonitrile. The results of dynamic viscosity measurements were interpreted to indicate that 20% acrylonitrile elastomer gave two-phase blends with PVC whereas 40% acrylonitrile elastomer gave almost homogenous blends. Electron microscope pictures were interpreted to indicate that microheterogeneity existed even in the blends with the 40% acrylonitrile elastomer. Using differential thermal analysis, Oganesov and coworkers[49] investigated the homogeneity of mill-mixed blends of PVC with nitrile elastomer containing 40% acrylonitrile. They concluded that the blends can be single or two phase depending upon the polymer ratio. Feldman and Rusu[50, 51] examined the compatibility of PVC with nitrile elastomer containing 40% acrylonitrile by viscometric measurements of solutions in cyclohexane. They concluded the polymers were compatible. Krause[59] in her review of polymer compatibility lists the combination of PVC and butadiene-acrylonitrile copolymer as compatible.

Using differential thermal analysis and dynamic mechanical measurements, Jorgensen and coworkers[52] demonstrated the presence of two glass transition temperatures in commercial non-crosslinked nitrile elastomers of less than 35% acrylonitrile content. The two glass transition temperatures were attributed to the presence of two separate phases of different acrylonitrile content. They concluded that for NBR/PVC blends containing 70% NBR the PVC acts as a selective solvent for only that portion of the NBR which is highest in acrylonitrile content. Zakrzewski[53] used phase contrast microscopy, differential scanning calorimetry and torsion pendulum analysis to examine the compatibility of mill-mixed NBR/PVC blends. He concluded that nitrile elastomers containing 23–45% acrylonitrile are compatible with PVC at all PVC levels.

Landi[54] reviewed previous studies on the compatibility of NBR/PVC blends and employed differential scanning calorimetry to measure the glass transition of the blends. When a 29% acrylonitrile elastomer with two glass transitions was mixed with PVC, only the higher glass transition was affected. A single glass transition nitrile elastomer containing 34% acrylonitrile had a single glass transition in its PVC blends. Ranby and his students[55, 56] examined the properties of mill-mixed blends of PVC with nitrile elastomers containing 22–24% acrylonitrile using light scattering, gas permeability, density and dynamic mechanical measurements. Increased amounts of acrylonitrile in the elastomers resulted in increased compatibility with the PVC.

Wang and Cooper[57] investigated the morphology and properties of NBR/PVC blends spin-cast from tetrahydrofuran. Their studies were carried out at various temperatures using differential scanning calorimetry, dynamic mechanical testing, stress-strain, transmission electron microscopy, and infrared dichroism techniques. Nitrile elastomer containing 44% acrylonitrile was found to be incompatible with the PVC employed under the conditions of their blend preparation. Nitrile elastomer containing 31% acrylonitrile was found to be compatible with the PVC with some indication of heterogeneity in the form of microdomains which are rich in either PVC or nitrile elastomer.

The morphological behavior of NBR/PVC blends is complex. There appears to be a window of compatibility whose boundaries are related to the acrylonitrile content of the nitrile elastomer. The locations of the boundaries of this window are not clearly defined. The center of the window appears to lie in the region 30–40% acrylonitrile content in the nitrile elastomer. Jorgensen[52] has shown that all commercial, non-crosslinked butadiene-acrylonitrile elastomers with less than 35% acrylonitrile have two glass transition temperatures. These correlate with fractions of different acrylonitrile content. In blends with these copolymers, PVC tends to solubilize the higher acrylonitrile content fractions.

Even in the region near the center of the window microheterogeneity has been reported in NBR/PVC blends[46, 48, 57]. The occurrence of microheterogeneity in this region may be due to the multiphase nature of the NBR, and to the crystallites and residual "primary particles" of PVC discussed by Terselius and Ranby[60].

A number of reviews have been published covering thermoplastic NBR/PVC blends. Chevassus[61] reviewed work done on vulcanized and nonvulcanized NBR/PVC blends covering both publications and patents up to about 1957. Pedley[23] published a description of the history, preparation and properties of NBR/PVC blends. Bohn[62] summarized the work done on the compatibility of NBR/PVC blends up to about 1963. Published work on both vulcanized and nonvulcanized NBR/PVC blends was reviewed by several authors[60, 63, 64]. Titow[65] included a general overview of NBR/PVC blends in his book. Descriptive listings of commercially available NBR/PVC blends can be found under a variety of trademarks in the Nitrile Elastomers section of "The Blue Book: materials, compounding ingredients, and machinery for rubber", published annually by Bill Communications, Inc., of New York.

2.2 Polyesters with PVC

A variety of polyesters are used in PVC, some as plasticizers for the preparation of elastomeric compositions, others as impact modifiers. Polyesters most commonly employed are oligomeric polyesters of dicarboxylic acids as plasticizers and high molecular weight copolymers of ethylene and ester monomers, such as vinyl acetate, as impact modifiers and as plasticizers. For the remainder of this discussion on polyesters in PVC, the term polyester will refer to the polymeric esters of dicarboxylic acids and diols. The term ethylene copolymer will refer to the high molecular weight copolymers of ethylene with vinyl acetate and other polar monomers.

In 1945 Fligor and Sumner[66] stated that of the polyester plasticizers prepared to date, those derived from sebacic acid have shown the most promise. They reported that Paraplex G-25, a sebacic acid polyester, exhibited good compatibility with PVC and PVC copolymers containing 5–10% vinyl acetate as indicated both by the lack of surface exudation and by the properties of the compositions. Several years later, in 1949, Reed and Harding[15] evaluated 64 plasticizers including 3 polyester plasticizers in a PVC copolymer containing 5% vinyl acetate. PVC copolymer compositions containing 30–45% polyester plasticizer had tensile strengths of 13–24 MPa and elongations at break of 110–330%. They stated that polyester plasticizers and nitrile elastomers were the only high molecular weight materials which had achieved any commercial importance as plasticizers for PVC resins. A number of publications have appeared over the years reporting on the properties of various polyesters as plasticizers for PVC[1, 29, 67].

Not all polyesters are compatible with PVC. Barlow, Paul and coworkers[68, 69] found that PVC formed compatible blends with several different aliphatic polyesters such as poly(butylene adipate) and immiscible mixtures with other aliphatic and aromatic polyesters such as poly(ethylene adipate) and poly(ethylene ortho-phthalate). They concluded that there was an optimum density of ester groups in the polymer chain for achieving maximum interaction with PVC. Too few or too many ester groups results in immiscibility with PVC. A series of aliphatic polyesters having methylene to carboxyl ratios ranging from 2 to 14 in their repeat units were examined for miscibility with PVC[69]. They reported that there is a window of structures in the middle of this range where miscibility is observed. At the high end of the range, phase separation caused by a lower critical solution temperature occurs at progressively lower temperatures as the methylene to carboxyl ratio increases beyond 10.

Prud'homme[70] listed various polyesters which are miscible with PVC and other chlorinated polymers and suggested that the specific interaction between the polyesters and the chlorinated polymers is a dipole-dipole interaction between the carbonyl and the C-Cl groups. Others[71-76] conclude that there is a specific interaction between the α-hydrogens of PVC and the carbonyl groups of polyesters which are compatible with PVC.

2.3   Ethylene Copolymers with PVC

In 1958 Salyer of Monsanto applied for a patent on blends of PVC with ethylene/vinyl acetate (EVA) copolymers including blends in which a portion of the PVC was grafted to the EVA polymer[77]. The compatibility of the EVA with PVC was stated to increase with increasing vinyl acetate content with the higher vinyl acetate content copolymers forming blends with PVC that are clear and transparent. Hardt[78] and Gobel[79] reported on blends of PVC with EVA copolymers containing 18–65 % vinyl acetate. While the EVA copolymers were effective as impact modifiers, particularly copolymers containing about 45 % vinyl acetate at which concentration the copolymers show a minimum glass transition temperature, they stated that in blends with PVC the EVA copolymers have no plasticizing effect. EVA copolymers with high vinyl acetate content, about 60 %, gave blends with improved compatibility, but even these were not considered to be plasticized PVC. There has been a considerable amount of work carried out directed toward determining the compatibility of EVA with PVC[50, 51, 55, 80-92]. There appears to be general agreement that EVA copolymers containing less than 45 % vinyl acetate are not miscible with PVC. EVA copolymers containing 45 % vinyl acetate copolymer have been reported to be incompatible[55, 81-84], semicompatible[87-92], and compatible with PVC[50, 51, 85]. EVA copolymers containing about 65 % vinyl acetate have been reported to be compatible[81] and semicompatible with PVC[86]. A blend of PVC with EVA containing 63 % vinyl acetate was reported to show a lower critical solution temperature[92].

The compatibility of EVA copolymers with PVC increases with increasing vinyl acetate content, however, above 45 % vinyl acetate the glass transition temperature of the copolymers also increases with vinyl acetate content thus limiting the utility of the higher vinyl acetate copolymers as plasticizers for PVC. This sparked research on ethylene copolymers containing more polar monomers which would serve to increase compatibility with PVC at lower levels of polar monomer than required with vinyl acetate. Hammer has been particularly active in this area with a number of patents involving the copolymerization of ethylene with sulfur dioxide and carbon monoxide and various third monomers[93-95]. He has published several papers comparing an ethylene copolymer plasticizer, Elvaloy 742 (Du Pont), to other polymeric plasticizers for PVC[96, 97]. Resin modifiers Elvaloy 741 and 742 are described as ethylene interpolymers having molecular weights of 250,000 useful as permanent plasticizers for PVC[98]. The properties of blends of these materials with PVC have been reported by Tordella[99, 100] and by Bair and coworkers[101-103]. They are reported to be miscible with PVC[92, 99-103]. Resin modifiers PB 3041 and PB 3042, the original designations for Elvaloy 741 and 742, when present in PVC compositions at 80 and 70 parts respectively per 100 parts PVC yield compositions having tensile strengths above 15 MPa and elongations at break above 300 %[99-101]. Hickman and Ikeda[104] have reported on the compatibility of mixtures of PVC with ethylene/vinyl acetate/sulfur dioxide terpolymers.

Robeson and McGrath[105] stated that an ethylene/ethyl acrylate copolymer was not miscible with PVC whereas various terpolymers of ethylene with carbon monoxide and either alkyl acrylate or vinyl acetate monomers were. The increased miscibility of the terpolymers was attributed to interaction of the carbonyl of the terpolymers with the α-hydrogen of the PVC. McGrath and Matzner[106] have claimed compatible blends of PVC with various ethylene copolymers with monomers containing nitrogen. Based on torsional pendulum results, ethylene/N,N-dimethylacrylamide copolymer blends with PVC were found to be incompatible at N,N-dimethylacrylamide contents in the copolymer of 17.7 and 23.4% but were compatible at 26.9 and 28.6%. However, the single glass transition of the compatible blends was sufficiently broad so as to imply a certain level of microheterogeneity persists[107].

2.4 Other Polymeric Plasticizers with PVC

Lutz[108] described elastomers which were PVC compositions containing an acrylic modifier, Acryloid KM-323B (Rohm and Haas), and an experimental plasticizer. Walsh and McKeown[109] reported that n-propyl and n-butyl polyacrylates were compatible with PVC and that the resulting blends exhibited lower critical solution temperatures. Higher chain alkyl polyacrylates were incompatible with PVC.

Chlorosulfonated polyethylene with 43% chlorine and 1% sulfur as sulfonyl chloride gave single phase mixtures with PVC when cast from tetrahydrofuran and 2-butanone and two-phase mixtures from dichloromethane[110]. The single-phase blends exhibit a lower critical solution temperature. Terselius and Ranby[60] reviewed the literature on blends of chlorinated polyethylene with PVC and pointed out that one of the disadvantages of these blends is that they are opaque. Chlorinated polyethylenes with 42% or less chlorine give incompatible blends with PVC and those with 48% chlorine result in semicompatible blends. Titow[65] states that chlorinated polyethylenes at higher chlorine contents (above 40%) are fully compatible with PVC. A number of reviews have included discussions of various polymeric plasticizers for PVC[64, 65, 111, 112, 113].

3   POLYOLEFIN BLENDS

3.1 Butyl Rubber with Polyethylene and Polypropylene

Thermoplastic elastomers based on mixtures of polyolefin elastomers with polyolefin thermoplastics came into commercial prominence long after those based on blends of PVC with nitrile elastomers and other plasticizers. A patent concerned with grafts of synthetic rubbers onto polyolefins by means of reaction with polyfunctional phenolic materials was issued to P. Hartman as a continuation in part of a 1967 filing[114]. In 1970 Hartman and coworkers[115] reported on a series of elastomeric thermoplastics called ET polymers which were prepared by grafting butyl rubber onto polyethylene. Four compositions were available from Allied Chemical Corp. on a developmental basis. They were grafts of butyl rubber onto high and low density polyethylene at two ratios, $\frac{3}{1}$ and $\frac{1}{1}$ butyl rubber/polyethylene. The physical properties of the compositions reflect the type of polyethylene and the proportion of butyl rubber used. Compositions with 25% butyl rubber resemble the polyethylene from which they are prepared but are softer and less stiff. Compositions made from low density polyethylene are more elastomeric, as indicated by lower tensile set, than those made from high density polyethylene. The compositions range in tensile strength from 11 to 23 MPa, in elongation from 375 to 450%, and in compression set, after 22 hrs at 70°C by method B, from 33 to 62%[116]. Dynamic modulus-temperature data were said to be characteristic of polymer mixtures containing mutually immiscible components[115]. Limitations reported for the compositions were the amber color and the lack of "snapback" characteristic of true elastomers. Comments on the properties and uses of these materials have appeared in a number of publications[117–124].

Deanin and coworkers[125] have reported on the properties of blends of butyl rubber with high and low density polyethylene and with polypropylene. The blends were neither vulcanized nor grafted.

Gessler and Haslett[126] of Esso Research and Engineering Co. filed a patent application in 1958 concerning dynamically cured mixtures of polypropylene and chlorinated butyl rubber. Dynamic curing was described as a new process for obtaining a dispersion of elastomeric micro gel in a thermoplastic material to form a thermoplastic elastomer product. Thermoplastic elastomers prepared by dynamic curing are the subject of the next chapter in this book.

3.2 Ethylene/Propylene Copolymers and Terpolymers with Polyethylene and Polypropylene

In 1961 Holzer (Hercules Inc.)[146] filed a patent application concerning blends of crystalline polypropylene and ethylene/propylene copolymers (EPM) in which the EPM contained more than 50% propylene. Mahlman[147], also of Hercules, filed a patent in 1970 covering a process for preparing a blend of natural or synthetic rubber and polypropylene in which polypropylene was the continuous phase.

In 1971 W. K. Fischer of Uniroyal filed patent applications on thermoplastics blends of monoolefin copolymer elastomer such as ethylene/propylene copolymer (EPM) or ethylene/propylene/diene terpolymer (EPDM) elastomer with a polyolefin resin such as polypropylene. The first patent application was concerned with blends prepared by partially curing the elastomer and then blending it with the resin[127]. The second application was concerned with blends which were dynamically partially cured by heating the blend with a curative such as peroxide while shearing the blend[128]. A third patent application filed in 1972 involved blends of high viscosity elastomer with resin[129]. Later in 1972 Uniroyal announced the availability of a new olefinic material called TPR thermoplastic rubber[130] which was said to have been discovered by W. K. Fischer[131]. These thermoplastic rubbers were reportedly prepared by means of a controlled crosslinking process[132–134] using a dynamic curing technique[134]. Various grades of these materials were initially available which ranged in Shore A hardness from 65 to 92, in tensile strength from 5 to 14 MPa, in elongation from 150 to 300%, and in compression set, by ASTM D–395B after 22 hours at room temperature, from 25 to 40%[135, 136]. Additional grades of these materials were added as time passed[123, 137–141]. Not all of the added grades were partially crosslinked blends of EPM or EPDM polymers with polypropylene. For example, TPR 3700 was reportedly based on PVC and nitrile elastomer[121]. A number of papers were published on the properties and applications of these materials[142–144]. Summaries listing the types, properties, and applications of the TPR polymers have been published by Morris[116] and by Thorn[145].

Soon thereafter a host of competitive products appeared, most of which are blends of EPM or EPDM elastomers with polypropylene and/or polyethylene although other polymers and materials may be included in the mixtures. In 1974 Hercules introduced Pro-fax SB-814[120], a high hardness thermoplastic elastomer[116].

Numerous patents have issued covering various mixtures of polyolefin rubber with polyolefin thermoplastic. A patent issued to Von Bodungen and Meredith[148] is concerned with thermoplastic elastomers prepared by subjecting a mixture of EPDM, polyethylene, and a polyolefin homopolymer such as polypropylene to a free radical reaction during hot working. Straub[149] filed a patent application in 1974 on injection moldable, electrostatically paintable polyolefin compositions comprised of blends of ethylene/higher α-olefin copolymer elastomer, crystalline polypropylene, and selected carbon black. In December of 1974 it was reported that DuPont's TPN, a black EPDM based material, was being used in the exterior parts of cars[120]. One of the advantages of TPN was that it could be painted electrostatically. Ford Motor Co. evaluated the properties of four painted thermoplastic elastomers one of which was electrostatically painted TPN while the other three were spray painted polyurethanes. In 1975 DuPont announced the commercial availability of Somel thermoplastic elastomers, polyolefinic materials based on ethylene-propylene chemistry[151–154]. Over the period 1974 to 1976 four patents by Goodrich were concerned with blends of high ethylene content EPM and EPDM polymers with polyethylene and polypropylene[155–158]. Late in 1974 Telcar thermoplastic elastomers were introduced into the market by Goodrich[120, 159]. They are thought to be mechanical blends of EPDM elastomer and polypropylene or polyethylene[116]. Lindsay and coworkers[160] at Goodrich published a paper on blends of partially crystalline EPDM polymers with low density polyethylene. The tensile strengths of the blends can be greater than that of either component. The authors concluded that there was partial miscibility between melts of low density polyethylene and high-ethylene EPDM rubber. Upon cooling from the melt, the low density polyethylene crystallites appear to nucleate crystallization of high-ethylene EPDM segments.

Other polyolefin thermoplastic elastomers have been introduced by a number of companies including: Vistaflex by Exxon Chemical Co.[121], Dutral by Montedison[161], Uneprene by International Synthetic Rubber Co.[162], Keltan TP by DSM[163], and Ren-Flex by Ren Plastics[164]. A number of compounders have introduced versions of the polyolefin thermoplastic elastomers[165]. An article by Garsham[123] lists many of the polyolefin thermoplastic elastomers. Some of the original compositions are now being made by companies other than the original manufacturer. Uniroyal sold its TPR business to Reichold Chemicals, Inc. which in turn has reached an agreement to sell it to a subsidiary of BP Chemicals, Inc.[167]. Goodrich's Telcar products are now being made by Teknor Apex Co. and Ren Plastic's Ren-Flex by Research Polymers[165].

Many articles have been published on the properties and applications of the various commercially available polyolefin thermoplastic elastomers[163, 168–174].

Papers have appeared on the morphology and other properties of elastomeric blends of EPM and EPDM elastomers with polypropylene. Using neutron scattering techniques, Lohse[175] showed that blends of crystalline polypropylene and ethylene/propylene copolymers are immiscible in 50/50 mixtures. Onogi and coworkers[176, 177] carried out rheo-optical studies on blends of ethylene/propylene elastomer with polypropylene. They concluded that in the blends they studied, phase inversion occurs at polypropylene contents of 50–60% based on their analysis of modulus data and infrared dichroism studies. Kresge[124] reported on the results of electron micrograph studies of EPM/polypropylene blends which were found to be cocontinuous in the range 70–85% EPM. Kresge lists a number of patents concerned with thermoplastic elastomers prepared by polymer blending. Danesi and Porter[178] studied blends of ethylene/propylene elastomers with polypropylene to establish relationships between morphology and physical properties and to examine the principles which govern morphological development. An explanation of the microstructure in the blends was developed in terms of the composition ratio and melt properties of the components. The properties of ethylene/propylene elastomer blends with polypropylene have been reviewed by Ranalli[179].

3.3   Natural Rubber with Polypropylene and Polyethylene

Thermoplastic elastomers have been prepared by members of the Malaysian Rubber Producers' Research Association by blending natural rubber with crystalline polyolefins such as polyethylene and polypropylene[180–187]. They have been given the name Thermoplastic Natural Rubber (TPNR). The addition during blending of small amounts of peroxide crosslinking agents has been found to be effective in improving molding behavior[181, 182] and resistance to compression set[185] but is not recommended for blends containing less than 70% rubber due to possible adverse effects on ageing resistance[185]. Properties have been reported for blends based on crystalline polypropylene and/or high density polyethylene[182, 184-187]. Fillers and oil can be included in the compositions. The properties of typical compositions containing 15 to 70 parts of natural rubber per 100 parts total polymer are shown with tensile strengths ranging from 8 to 18 MPa, elongations from 300 to 400%, and Shore D hardnesses from 34 to 68[185].

Thermoplastic elastomers have also been prepared by blending Guayule rubber with polyethylene or polypropylene[188, 189]. Blends with high density polyethylene or with polypropylene have been studied over the range 10 to 90% rubber. Phase inversion occurs at about 60% rubber. The effects of crosslinking during mixing and the addition of carbon black to the rubber component have been investigated.

4   OTHER BLENDS

4.1   Ethylene-Acrylate Copolymers with Polyethylene

Krevsky and coworkers[190] in 1963 reported on blends of high and low density polyethylene with low modulus ethylene-acrylate copolymers which are commercially available. Properties are shown for the entire composition range of 0–100% copolymer. For 50/50 compositions Shore D hardness ranged from about 38 to 53, tensile strength from about 10 to 16 MPa, and elongation from about 160 to 360%, with the high density polyethylene compositions giving the higher hardness and tensile strength and the lower elongation.

4.2   Poly(Dimethylsiloxane) with Polyethylene

Falender and coworkers[191] mixed poly(dimethylsiloxane) copolymers with polyethylene and with a polyethylene resin containing vinyl acetate comonomer under conditions of shear and high temperature to form mixtures consisting of microgelled and grafted particles of silicone polymer dispersed in polyethylene. The polydimethylsiloxane copolymers contained 2.5 to 4 mole percent methylvinylsiloxane units which acted as sites for grafting to polyethylene and for crosslinking of the silicone elastomer. No catalysts were needed to initiate the reaction. To obtain sufficient grafting when the polyethylene copolymer was employed, a temperature of 180 °C or above and simultaneous mixing were required. High-density polyethylene required longer mixing times and a temperature of 220 °C. A 50/50 blend of polyethylene/vinyl acetate resin and poly(dimethylsiloxane) copolymer containing 4% methylvinylsiloxane units had a tensile strength of 9 MPa and an elongation of 550%.

References

1. J. K. Sears and J. R. Darby, *"The Technology of Plasticizers"*, John Wiley and Sons, New York (1982)
2. Ger. Pat. 281, 877 (to Chemische Fabrik Griesheim–Elektron), (Feb. 4, 1915)
3. W. L. Semon, *Annu. Tech. Conf. Soc. Plast. Eng. 30*, 693 (1972)
4. W. L. Semon (to The B. F. Goodrich Co.), U. S. Pat. 1, 929, 453 (Oct. 10, 1953)
5. S. L. Brous and W. L. Semon, *Ind. Eng. Chem. 27*, 667 (1935)
6. D. W. Young, D. J. Buckley, R. G. Newberg, and L. B. Turner, *Ind. Eng. Chem. 41*, 401 (1949); *Rubber Chem. Technol. 22*, 735 (1949)
7. W. L. Semon in *"Synthetic Rubber"*, G. S. Whitby, C. C. Davis, and R. F. Dunbrook, eds., John Wiley & Sons, Inc., New York (1954), pp. 794

8. E. Badum (vested in the Alien Property Custodian), U. S. Pat. 2, 297, 194 (Sep. 29, 1942)
9. D. E. Henderson (to The B. F. Goodrich Co.), U. S. Pat. 2, 330, 353 (Sept. 28, 1943)
10. H. A. Winkelmann, *India Rubber World 113,* 799 (1946)
11. E. Pittenger and G. F. Cohan, *Rubber Age* (N. Y.) *61,* 563 (1947); *Mod. Plast. 25* (1), 81 (1947)
12. M. S. Moulton, *India Rubber World 116,* 371 (1947)
13. G. E. Field, *Mod. Packag. 22,* 149 (Dec. 1948)
14. D. W. Young, R. G. Newberg, and R. M. Howlett, *Ind. Eng. Chem. 39,* 1446 (1947)
15. M. C. Reed and J. Harding, *Ind. Eng. Chem. 41,* 675 (1949)
16. M. C. Reed, *Mod. Plast. 27* (4), 117 (1949)
17. S. E. Bolam, *Rubber Age Synth. 34,* 392 and 436 (1953)
18. G. L. Wheelock (to The B. F. Goodrich Co.), U. S. Pat. 2, 614, 094 (Oct. 14, 1952)
19. H. Romeyn, Jr., and J. F. Petras (to U. S. Rubber Co.), U. S. Pat. 2, 600, 024 (June 10, 1952)
20. W. J. Smith, *India Rubber World 129,* 785 (1954)
21. *Rubber World 139,* 559 (1959)
22. V. A. Byl'ev and V. A. Voskresenskii, *Rubber Chem. Technol. 37,* 770 (1964); *Izr. Vysshikh. Uchebn. Zovedenii i Khim. Tekhnol. 5,* No. 3474–6 (1962); RAPRA translation 1011
23. *K. A. Pedley, Polym. Age 1 (3),* 97 (1970)
24. R. D. DeMarco, M. E. Woods, and L. F. Arnold, *Rubber Chem. Technol. 45,* 1111 (1972)
25. M. E. Woods, R. J. Morsek, and W. H. Whittington, *Rubber World 167* (6), 42 (1973)
26. P. S. Byrne and H. F. Schwarz, *Rubber Age* (N. Y.) *105 (7),* 43 (1973)
27. M. E. Woods and D. G. Frazer, *Annu. Tech. Conf. Soc. Plast. Eng. 32,* 426 (1974)
28. P. Guidici and P. W. Milner, *PRI Conf. Paper Brussels, Cl* (Sept. 1976)
29. F. Roesler and J. McBroom, *Proc. 24th Int. Wire Cable Symp.,* 335 (1975)
30. R. D. Deanin, R. O. Normandin, and I. T. Patel, Am. *Chem. Soc. Div. Org. Coat.·Plast. Prepr. 36* (1), 302 (1976)
31. E. F. Jordan, Jr., B. Artymyshyn, G. R. Riser, and A. N. Wrigley, *J. Appl. Polym. Sci. 20,* 2715 and 2737 (1976)
32. E. F. Jordan, Jr., B. Artymyshyn, and G. R. Riser, *J. Appl. Polym. Sci. 20,* 2757 (1976)
33. G. Kawashima, *J. Soc. Rubber Ind. Jpn. 57,* 736 (1984)
34. H. F. Schwarz and J. W. F. Bley, to be presented at a meeting of the Rubber Div., Am. Chem. Soc., Cleveland, Ohio, Oct. 1–4 (1985)
35. R. A. Reznikova, A. D. Zaionchkovsky, and S. S. Voyutsky, *Colloid J. USSR (Eng. Trans.) 15,* 111 (1953)
36. R. A. Reznikova, S. S. Voyutsky, and A. D. Zaionchovsky, *Colloid J. USSR (Eng. Trans.) 16,* 207 (1954)
37. Sh. L. Lel'chuk and V. I. Sedlis, *J. Appl. Chem. USSR (Eng. Trans.) 31,* 778 (1958)
38. V. I. Alekseyenko, *Polym. Sci. USSR (Eng. Trans.) 3,* 367 (1962)
39. L. E. Nielsen, *J. Am. Chem. Soc. 75,* 1435 (1953)
40. R. Buchdahl and L. E. Nielsen, *J. Polym. Sci. 15,* 1 (1955)
41. W. Breuers, W. Hild, H. Wolff, W. Burmeister, and H. Hoyer, *Plaste Kautsch. 1* (8), 170 (1954)
42. L. E. Nielsen, *"Mechanical Properties of Polymers",* Reinhold Publishing Corp., New York (1962)
43. M. Takayanagi, H. Harima, and Y. Iwata, *Mem. Fac. Eng. Kyushu Univ. 23,* 1 (1963)
44. M. Takayanagi, H. Harima, and Y. Iwata, *J. Jpn. Soc. Test. Mater. 12,* 389 (1963)
45. M. Takayanagi and S. Manabe, *Rep. Prog. Polym. Phys. Jpn. 8,* 285 (1965)
46. M. Matsuo, *Jpn. Plastics 2,* 6 (July 1968)
47. S. Manabe, R. Murakami, and M. Takayanagi, *Mem. Fac. Eng. Kyushu Univ. 28,* 295 (1969)
48. M. Matsuo, C. Nozaki, and Y. Jyo, *Polym. Eng. Sci. 9,* 197 (1969)
49. Yu. G. Oganesov, V. S. Osipchik, Kh. G. Mindiyarov, V. G. Rayevskii, and S. S. Voyutskii, *Polym. Sci. USSR (Eng. Trans.) 11,* 1012 (1969)
50. D. Feldman and M. Rusu, *Eur. Polym. J. 6,* 627 (1970)
51. D. Feldman and M. Rusu, *Rev. Gen. Caoutch. Plast. 48,* 687 (1971)
52. A. H. Jorgensen, L. A. Chandler, and E. A. Collins, *Rubber Chem. Technol. 46,* 1087 (1973)
53. G. A. Zakrzewski, *Polymer 14,* 347 (1973)
54. V. R. Landi, *Appl. Polym. Symp. 25,* 223 (1974)
55. B. G. Ranby, *J. Polym. Sci. Symp. 51,* 89 (1975)
56. Y. J. Shur and B. Ranby, *J. Appl. Polym. Sci. 19,* 2143 (1975)
57. C. B. Wang and S. L. Cooper, *J. Polym. Sci. Polym. Phys. Ed. 21,* 11 (1983)

58. T. Alfrey, Jr., N. Wiederhorn, R. Stein and A. Tobolsky, *J. Colloid Sci. 4,* 211 (1949)
59. S. Krause, *J. Macromol. Sci., Rev. Macromol. Chem. C7(2),* 251 (1972)
60. B. Terselius and B. Ranby, *Pure Appl. Chem. 53,* 421 (1981)
61. F. Chevassus, *Chimie Ind. (Paris) 82,* 690 (1959)
62. L. Bohn, *Rubber Chem. Technol. 41,* 495 (1968); *Koll.–Z. Z. Polym. 213,* 55 (1966)
63. J. R. Dunn, D. C. Coulthard, and H. A. Pfisterer, *Rubber Chem. Technol. 51,* 389 (1978)
64. O. Olabisi, L. M. Robeson, and M. T. Shaw, *"Polymer–Polymer Miscibility",* Academic Press, New York (1979)
65. W. V. Titow, *"PVC Technology",* Fourth Edition, Elsevier Applied Science Publishers, New York (1984)
66. K. K. Fligor and J. K. Sumner, *Ind. Eng. Chem. 37,* 504 (1945)
67. S. H. Goh, D. R. Paul, and J. W. Barlow, *J. Appl. Polym. Sci. 27,* 1091 (1982)
68. J. J. Ziska, J. W. Barlow, and D. R. Paul, *Polymer 22,* 918 (1981)
69. E. M. Woo, J. W. Barlow, and D. R. Paul, *Polymer 26,* 763 (1985)
70. R. E. Prud'homme, *Polym. Eng. Sci. 22,* 90 (1982)
71. O. Olabisi, *Macromolecules 8,* 316 (1975)
72. M. M. Coleman and J. Zarian, *J. Polym. Sci. Phys. Ed. 17,* 837 (1979)
73. M. M. Coleman and D. F. Varnell, *J. Polym. Sci. Phys. Ed. 18,* 1403 (1980)
74. D. F. Varnell and M. M. Coleman, *Polymer 22,* 1324 (1981)
75. M. M. Coleman, E. J. Moskala, P. C. Painter, D. J. Walsh, and S. Rostami, *Polymer 24,* 1410 (1983)
76. D. F. Varnell, E. J. Moskala, P. C. Painter, and M. M. Coleman, *Polym. Eng. Sci. 23,* 658 (1983)
77. I. O. Salyer (to Monsanto Co.), U. S. Pat. 3, 517, 083 (June 23, 1970)
78. D. Hardt, *Br. Polym. J. 1* (5), 225 (1969)
79. W. Gobel, *Kaut. Gummi Kunstst. 22 (3),* 116 (1969)
80. B. Terselius and B. Ranby, *IUPAC Int. Symp. Macromol. Prepr.,* 559 (1970)
81. C. F. Hammer, *Macromolecules 4,* 69 (1971)
82. Y. Jyo, C. Nozaki, and M. Matsuo, *Macromolecules 4,* 517 (1971)
83. H. Storstrom and B. Ranby, *Adv. Chem. Ser. 99,* 107 (1971)
84. K. Marcincin, A. Romanov, and V. Pollak, *J. Appl. Polym. Sci. 16,* 2239 (1972)
85. D. Feldman and M. Rusu, *Eur. Polym. J. 10,* 41 (1974)
86. Y. J. Shur and B. Ranby, *J. Appl. Polym. Sci. 19,* 1337 (1975)
87. C. Elmqvist and S. E. Svanson, *Colloid Polym. Sci. 253,* 327 (1975)
88. C. Elmqvist and S. E. Svanson, *Eur. Polym. J. 11,* 789 (1975)
89. C. Elmqvist and S. E. Svanson, *Eur. Polym. J. 12,* 559 (1976)
90. C. Elmqvist, *Eur. Polym. J. 13,* 95 (1977)
91. S. E. Svanson, C. Elmqvist, Y. J. Shur, and B. Ranby, *J. Appl. Polym. Sci. 21,* 943 (1977)
92. E. Nolley, D. R. Paul, and J. W. Barlow, *J. Appl. Polym. Sci. 23,* 623 (1979)
93. C. F. Hammer and T. F. Sashihara (to E. I. du Pont de Nemours and Co.), U. S. Pat. 3, 657, 202 (Apr. 18, 1972)
94. C. F. Hammer (to E. I. du Pont de Nemours and Co.), U. S. Pat. 3, 684, 778 (Aug. 15, 1972)
95. C. F. Hammer (to E. I. du Pont de Nemours and Co.), U. S. Pat. 3, 780, 140 (Dec. 18, 1973)
96. C. F. Hammer, *Am. Chem. Soc. Div. Org. Coat. Plast. Chem. Prepr. 37* (1), 234 (1977)
97. C. F. Hammer in *"Polymer Blends",* D. R. Paul and S. Newman, eds., Academic Press, New York (1978), pp. 219
98. *"Du Pont Products Book".* J. W. Farr, Jr., ed., E. I. du Pont de Nemours and Co., Wilmington, De. (1981), pp. 101
99. J. P. Tordella, *Annu. Techn. Conf. Soc. Plast. Eng. 33,* 135 (1975)
100. J. P. Tordella, *Mod. Plast. 53* (1), 64 (1976)
101. H. E. Bair, D. Williams, T. K. Kwei, and F. J. Padden, *J. Am. Chem. Soc. Div. Org. Coat. Plast. Chem. Prepr. 37* (1), 240 (1977)
102. H. E. Bair, E. W. Anderson, G. E. Johnson, and T. K. Kwei, *Polym. Prepr. (Am. Chem. Soc., Div. Polym. Chem.) 19* (1), 143 (1978)
103. E. W. Anderson, H. E. Bair, G. E. Johnson, T. K. Kwei, F. J. Padden, Jr., and D. Williams, *Adv. Chem. Ser. 176,* 413 (1979)
104. J. J. Hickman and R. M. Ikeda, *J. Polym. Sci., Polym. Phys. Ed. 11,* 1713 (1973)
105. L. M. Robeson and J. E. McGrath, *Polym. Eng. Sci. 17,* 300 (1977)

106. J. E. McGrath and M. Matzner (to Union Carbide Corp.), U. S. Pat. 3, 798, 289 (Mar. 19, 1974)
107. M. Matzner, L. M. Robeson, E. W. Wise, and J. E. McGrath, *Makromol. Chem. 183,* 2871 (1982)
108. J. T. Lutz, Jr., *Plast. Eng. 9,* 40 (Sept. 1974)
109. D. J. Walsh and J. G. McKeown, *Polymer 21,* 1330 (1980)
110. C. P. Doubé and D. J. Walsh, *Polymer 20,* 1115 (1979)
111. D. R. Paul and J. W. Barlow, *J. Macromol. Sci., Rev. Macromol. Chem. C18* (1), 109 (1980)
112. J. A. Manson, *Pure Appl. Chem. 53,* 471 (1981)
113. G. H. Hofmann in *"Polymer Blends and Mixtures"*, D. J. Walsh, J. S. Higgins and A. Maconnachie, eds., Martinus Nijhoff Publishers, Dordrecht, The Netherlands (1985), pp. 117
114. P. F. Hartman (to Allied Chemical Corp.), U. S. Pat. 3, 909, 463 (Sep. 30, 1975)
115. P. F. Hartman, C. L. Eddy, and G. P. Koo, *SPE J. 26* (5), 62 (1970); *Rubber World 163* (1), 59 (1970)
116. H. L. Morris in *"Handbook of Thermoplastic Elastomers"*, B. M. Walker ed., Van Nostrand Reinhold Co., New York (1979), pp. 5
117. L. L. Scheiner, *Plast. Technol. 19* (5), 36 (1973)
118. S. C. Wells, *J. Elastoplast. 5,* 102 (Apr. 1973); reprinted from *Mach. Des.* (Dec. 28, 1972)
119. H. L. Stephens, *Progr. Rubber Technol. 37,* 65 (1973/4)
120. R. Martino, *Mod. Plast. 51* (12), 50 (1974)
121. A. M. Houston, *Mater. Eng.* (Cleveland) *82* (7), 47 (Dec. 1975)
122. J. E. Theberge and B. Arkles, *Mach. Des. 48* (3), 113 (1976)
123. A. Garshman, *Plast. Technol. 24* (6), 59 (1978)
124. E. N. Kresge in *"Polymer Blends"*, D. R. Paul and S. Newman, eds., Academic Press, New York (1978), pp. 293
125. R. D. Deanin, R. O. Normandin, and C. P. Kannankeril, *Am. Chem. Soc. Div. Org. Coat. Plast. Chem. Prepr. 35* (1), 259 (1975)
126. A. M. Gessler and W. H. Haslett (to Esso Research and Engineering Co.), U. S. Pat. 3, 037, 954 (June 5, 1962)
127. W. K. Fischer (to Uniroyal, Inc.), U. S. Pat. 3, 758, 643 (Sep. 11, 1973)
128. W. K. Fischer (to Uniroyal, Inc.), U. S. Pat. 3, 806, 558 (Apr. 23, 1974)
129. W. K. Fischer (to Uniroyal, Inc.), U. S. Pat. 3, 835, 201 (Sep. 10, 1974)
130. *Chem. Eng. News 50* (42), 7 (Oct. 16, 1972)
131. *Rubber World 167* (5), 49 (1973)
132. E. P. Weaver, *Elastomerics 110* (5), 21 (1978)
133. C. C. Ho and J. R. Johnson, *Elastomerics 111* (6), 19 (1979)
134. L. E. Fithian, *J. Elastomers. Plast. 14,* 222 (Oct. 1982); *Elastomerics 115* (6), 21 (1983)
135. J. R. Johnson and H. L. Morris, *Automot. Eng. 81* (5), 54 (1973); SAE paper 730600 (1973)
136. H. L. Morris, *J. Elast. Plast. 6,* 121 (July, 1974); *Annu. Tech. Conf. Soc. Plast. Eng. 31,* 88 (1973)
137. *Plast. Technol. 22,* 65 (Aug. 1976)
138. *Mod. Plast. 53* (10), 22 (1976)
139. *Rubber Plast. News V (23),* 8 (1976)
140. *Mater. Eng.* (Cleveland) *87 (6),* 11 (1978)
141. *Mod. Plast. 55* (10), 44 (1978)
142. P. Morin and J. R. Johnson, *Plast. Technol. 21* (9), 49 (1975)
143. J. R. Johnson, *Aust. Plast. Rubber 27* (11), 13 (1976)
144. P. R. Morin, *Rubber World 179* (5), 35 (1979)
145. A. D. Thorn, *"Thermoplastic Elastomers – A Review of Current Information"*, Rubber and Plastics Research Institute of Great Britain, Shawbury, Shrewsbury, Shropshire, England (1980)
146. R. Holzer, O. Taunus, and K. Mehnert (to Hercules, Inc.), U. S. Pat. 3, 262, 992 (July 26, 1966)
147. B. H. Mahlman (to Hercules, Inc.), U. S. Pat. 3, 665, 059 (May 23, 1972)
148. G. A. Von Bodungen and C. L. Meredith (to Copolymer Rubber & Chemical Corp.), U. S. Pat. 3, 957, 919 (May 18, 1976)
149. R. M. Straub (to E. I. du Pont de Nemours and Co.), U. S. Pat. 3, 963, 647 (June 15, 1976)
150. L. K. Djiauw and D. G. Fesko, *Rubber Chem. Technol. 49,* 1111 (1976)
151. *Rubber Plast. News IV* (2), 21 (1975)
152. *Mod. Plast. 52* (6), 20 (1975)
153. *Plast. Technol. 21* (7), 25 (1975)

154. *Prod. Eng. 46* (10), 29 (1975)
155. M. Batiuk, R. M. Herman, and J. C. Healy (to The B. F. Goodrich Co.), U. S. Pat. 3, 919, 358 (Nov. 11, 1975)
156. M. Batiuk, R. M. Herman, and J. C. Healy (to The B. F. Goodrich Co.), U. S. Pat. 3, 941, 859 (Mar. 2, 1976)
157. P. T. Stricharczuk (to The B. F. Goodrich Co.), U. S. Pat. 4, 036, 912 (July 19, 1977)
158. C. J. Carman, M. Batiuk, and R. M. Herman (to The B. F. Goodrich Co.), U. S. Pat. 4, 046, 840 (Sep. 6, 1977)
159. *Rubber Plast. News IV* (10), 12 (1974)
160. G. A. Lindsay, C. J. Singleton, C. J. Carman, and R. W. Smith, *Adv. Chem. Ser. 176,* 367 (1979)
161. *Br. Plast. Rubber, 26* (Oct. 1976)
162. *Rubber Age* (N. Y.) *108* (3), 75 (1976)
163. H. Daalmans, *Int. Rubber Conf. Venice,* 281 (Oct. 1979)
164. *Plast. Technol. 22* (12), 127 (1976)
165. S. E. Avery, *Mod. Plast. 62* (4), 75 (1985)
166. *Mod. Plast. 60* (12), 42 (1983)
167. *Plast. Tech. 31* (8), 143 (1985)
168. R. D. Lundberg in *"Handbook of Thermoplastic Elastomers",* B. M. Walker, ed., Van Nostrand Reinhold Co., New York (1979), pp. 247
169. D. A. Booth, *Plastiques Mod. Elastomers 30* (2), 59 (1978)
170. S. A. Banks, J. H. Brillinger, C. A. Coffey, R. C. Puydak, and G. N. Schmit, *Rubber Chem. Technol. 49,* 1355 (1976)
171. G. Bertelli, R. Locatelli, and P. Roma, *Int. Rubber Conf. Venice 924* (Oct. 1979)
172. B. Bozzi, *Int. Rubber Conf. Venice,* 373 (Oct. 1979)
173. S. Danesi and L. Balzani, *Int. Rubber Conf. Venice,* 272 (1979)
174. S. R. Harrison and G. A. Pope, *Ind. Chem. Bull. 1* (5), 156 (1982)
175. D. H. Lohse, *Annu. Tech. Conf. Soc. Plast. Eng. 43,* 301 (1985)
176. S. Onogi, T. Asada, and A. Tanaka, *J. Pol. Sci.,* Part *A–2* 7, 171 (1969)
177. S. Onogi and T. Asada, *Prog. Polym. Sci. Jpn. 2,* 261 (1971)
178. S. Danesi and R. S. Porter, *Polymer 19,* 448 (1978)
179. R. Ranalli, *Dev. Rubber Technol. 3,* 21 (1982)
180. *Rubber Dev. 31* (3), 54 (1978)
181. L. Mullins, *Rubber Dev. 31* (4), 92 (1978)
182. D. S. Campbell, D. J. Elliot, and M. A. Wheelands, *NR Technol. 9* (2), 21 (1978)
183. *Br. Plast. Rubber,* 32 (Sep. 1978)
184. D. J. Elliot, *Dev. Rubber Technol. 1,* 1 (1979)
185. D. J. Elliot, *NR Technol. 12* (3), 59 (1981)
186. D. J. Elliot, Malaysian Rubber Prod. Research Assoc. Publ. 961
187. D. J. Elliot, *Dev. Rubber Technol. 3,* 203 (1982)
188. L. F. Ramos–DeValle and R. R. Ramirez, *Rubber Chem. Technol. 55,* 1328 (1982)
189. L. F. Ramos–DeValle, *Rubber Chem. Technol. 55,* 1341 (1982)
190. B. H. Krevsky, S. Bonotto, and P. R. Junghans, *Plast. Technol. 9,* 34 (1963)
191. J. R. Falender, S. E. Lindsey, and J. C. Saam, *Polym. Eng. Sci. 16* (1), 54 (1976)

Chapter 7

THERMOPLASTIC ELASTOMERS BASED ON
ELASTOMER-THERMOPLASTIC BLENDS
DYNAMICALLY VULCANIZED

A. Y. Coran

Contents

A. Y. Coran, Rubber Chemicals Research Laboratory, Monsanto Polymer Products Company, 260 Springside Drive, Akron, Ohio 44313

1   INTRODUCTION

Elastomer-thermoplastic blends have become technologically useful as thermoplastic elastomers in recent years[1-3]. They have many of the properties of elastomers, but they are processable as thermoplastics[4]. They do not need to be vulcanized during fabrication into end-use parts. Thus, they offer a substantial economic advantage in respect to the fabrication of finished parts.

For many end uses, the ideal elastomer-plastic blend comprises finely divided elastomer particles dispersed in a relatively small amount of plastic. The elastomer particles should be crosslinked to promote elasticity (the ability of the blend composition to retract forcibly from a large deformation). The favorable morphology should remain during the fabrication of the material into parts, and in use. Because of these requirements for the ideal case, the usual methods for preparing elastomer-plastic blends by melt mixing, solution blending or latex mixing[5] are not sufficient.

The best way to produce thermoplastic elastomeric compositions comprising vulcanized elastomer particles in melt-processable plastic matrices is by the method called dynamic vulcanization. It is the process of vulcanizing the elastomer during its melt-mixing with molten plastic[6-9]. This chapter describes the dynamic vulcanization process and the products which can be produced thereby. The scope of applicability of dynamic vulcanization is discussed. End-use applications of some of the products which can be prepared by dynamic vulcanization are also discussed.

Dynamic vulcanization is a route to new thermoplastic elastomers which have properties as good or even, in some cases, better than those of block copolymers. Yet, the new materials are prepared from blends of *existing* polymers. Thus, new, improved thermoplastic elastomers can be prepared from "old" polymers. Entirely new processes and materials can be avoided; moreover, high new-product "entrance fees" (caused by such barriers as environmental concerns, capital costs and the necessity for high-volume polymerization units and competitive divisors) can also be avoided.

There is much commercial interest in dynamic vulcanization since the introduction of proprietary products (e. g., SANTOPRENE® thermoplastic elastomer) prepared by the dynamic vulcanization of blends of olefin rubber with polyolefin resin. If the elastomer particles of such a blend are small enough and if they are fully vulcanized, then the properties of the blend are greatly improved. Examples of the improvements are as follows:

reduced permanent set,
improved ultimate mechanical properties,
improved fatigue resistance,
greater resistance to attack by fluids, e. g., hot oils,
improved high-temperature utility,
greater stability of phase morphology in the melt,
greater melt strength, and
more reliable thermoplastic fabricability.

In short, dynamic vulcanization can provide compositions which are very elastomeric in their performance characteristics. However, these same thermoplastic vulcanizate compositions can be rapidly fabricated into finished parts in thermoplastic processing equipment.

Because of the surprisingly beneficial effects of *complete* dynamic vulcanization (in contrast to prior and *partial* dynamic vulcanization[7]), the work described in this chapter opens a broad new field of thermoplastic-elastomer research.

As stated above, in some respects, the new materials can out-perform block copolymer-type thermoplastic elastomers. This is because the particulate elastomeric domains are comprised of fully vulcanized elastomer. As a result of this, the thermoplastic vulcanizates can perform well in respect to hot-oil resistance, compression set (at elevated temperatures), and high-temperature utility. A factor contributing to the greater high temperature utility is that, during fabrication of a finished part, many of the vulcanized rubber particles physically interact with one another to form a "network" of vulcanized elastomer. Of course, with regrinding and reworking in the melt, the "network" of touching, loosely-bound-together particles disintegrates and melt-processability is restored.

Thermoplastic vulcanizate compositions have been prepared from a great number of plastics and elastomers; however, only a limited number of elastomer-plastic combinations give technologically useful blends, even after dynamic vulcanization. The results of a study of 99 elastomer-plastic combinations (based on 11 kinds of elastomer and 9 kinds of plastic) are reviewed in this chapter. The goal of the work was to define this practical scope of compositions which can be prepared by dynamic vulcanization. This was accomplished by an analysis which related mechanical properties of the dynamically vulcanized blends to characteristics of their elastomeric and plastic components. The conclusion of that work was that the best elastomer-plastic thermoplastic vulcanizates are those in which the surface energies of the plastic and elastomer are matched, when the entanglement molecular length of the elastomer is low, and when the plastic is 15–30 % crystalline.

Were it not for the large difference between the surface energy of acrylonitrile-butadiene copolymer (NBR) and that of polypropylene, a blend of dynamically vulcanized NBR with isotactic polypropylene might be a good choice for an oil-resistant thermoplastic elastomer. In early work with these materials only marginally good compositions were obtained. Now, it has been found that NBR-polypropylene based thermoplastic elastomers, which are resistant to hot oil and have excellent strength-related properties, can be prepared. This can be accomplished by the dynamic vulcanization of technologically compatibilized NBR-polypropylene blends. Technological compatibilization of the blend, before dynamic vulcanization is the result of the presence of a small amount (about 1 %) of compatibilizing agent in the blend. The compatibilizing agent is a block copolymer containing segments similar to each of the polymers which are to be compatibilized. It acts as a macromolecular surfactant and its presence, during mixing, permits the formation of very small droplets of the elastomer which later, during dynamic vulcanization, become very small particles of vulcanized NBR. Research results related to the dynamic vulcanization of technologically compatibilized elastomer-plastic blends, which can lead to a wide variety of new product development opportunities, are considered in this chapter.

2   THE PREPARATION OF ELASTOMER-PLASTIC BLENDS BY DYNAMIC VULCANIZATION

Polymer blends, in general, have been prepared commercially by melt mixing, solution blending, or latex mixing[5]. Elastomer-plastic blends of the type discussed here, containing rather large amounts of elastomer, have generally been prepared by melt-mixing techniques. Melt-mixing avoids problems of contamination, solvent or water removal, etc. In general, Banbury mixers, mixing extruders and the newer twin-screw mixers are suitable for melt-mixing elastomer with plastics. However, for the purposes of this discussion, emphasis will be on laboratory melt-mixing techniques which simulate what can be done in a factory.

The procedures given below are based on the use of either a small Brabender mixer or a Haake Rheomix. In each case the mixer was fitted with cam-type rotors and optimum batch sizes were between 55 and 75 g.

The dynamic vulcanization process was used by Gessler[6] in the preparation of "semi-rigid" elastomer-plastic compositions containing minor proportions of vulcanized elastomer. Fischer[7] used the process to prepare compositions containing varying amounts of partially vulcanized elastomer. Large proportions of elastomer were generally used and soft compositions could be obtained. However, an organic peroxide was used to crosslink the elastomer in the presence of the thermoplastic polypropylene, which was greatly damaged by the action of the peroxide.

More recently, it has been found that very strong, elastomeric compositions of EPDM and polypropylene could be prepared by dynamic vulcanization, provided that peroxide curatives were avoided[8, 9]. If enough plastic phase is present in the molten state, then the compositions are processable as thermoplastics. Plasticizers or extender oils can be used to expand the volume of the elastomer phase. In the molten state, a suitable plasticizer can expand the volume of the plastic or "hard" phase. If the hard phase material is a crystalline material such as polypropylene, then, upon cooling, the crystallization of the hard phase material can force the plasticizer out of the hard phase into the elastomer phase. Thus the plasticizer may be a processing aid at melt temperatures but a softener at the lower temperatures of use.

The dynamic vulcanization process has been applied to many elastomer-plastic combinations. It can be described as follows: Elastomer and plastic are first melt-mixed. After sufficient melt-mixing in the internal mixer to form a well mixed blend, vulcanizing agents (curatives, crosslinkers) are added. Vulcanization then occurs while mixing continues. The more rapid the rate of vulcanization, the more rapid the mixing must be to insure good fabricability of the blend composition. It is convenient to follow the progress of vulcanization by monitoring mixing torque or mixing energy requirement during mixing. After the mixing torque or energy curve goes through a maximum, mixing can be continued somewhat longer to improve the fabricability of the blend. After discharge from the mixer, the blend can be chopped, extruded, pelletized, injection molded, etc.

3   PROPERTIES OF BLENDS PREPARED BY DYNAMIC VULCANIZATION

Dynamic vulcanization is the process of vulcanizing elastomer during its intimate melt-mixing with a non-vulcanizing thermoplastic polymer. Small elastomer droplets are vulcanized to give a particulate vulcanized elastomer phase of stable domain morphology during melt processing and subsequently.

As stated earlier, the effect of the dynamic vulcanization of elastomer-plastic blends is to produce compositions which have the improvements in permanent set, ultimate mechanical properties, fatigue resistance, hot oil resistance, high-temperature utility, melt strength, and thermoplastic fabricability.

Compositions of greatly improved permanent set can be produced by only slight or partial vulcanization of the elastomer. Such compositions can be produced either by the partial vulcanization of the elastomer before its mixture with plastic or by dynamic vulcanization[7] (during mixing with plastic). However, the other improvements can only be obtained (at least in the case of ethylene propylene diene terpolymer (EPDM)-polyolefin compositions) by dynamic vulcanization in which the elastomer is technologically fully vulcanized. The term "fully vulcanized" refers to a state of cure such that the crosslink density is at least 7×10^{-5} moles per ml of elastomer (determined by swelling) or that the elastomer is less than about three percent extractable by cyclohexane at 23 °C[8].

3.1 EPDM-Polyolefin Thermoplastic Vulcanizates

The dynamic vulcanization of blends of EPDM elastomer with polypropylene and with polyethylene have been described[9]. Mechanical properties, hardness, tension set values, and other parameters associated with unfilled compositions are given in Table I. The general recipe of the compositions was as follows:

EPDM (Epsyn® 70A)	100
Polyolefin resin	X
Zinc oxide	5
Stearic acid	1
Sulfur	Y
TMTD (tetramethylthiuram disulfide)	Y/2
MBTS (2-benzothiazolyl disulfide)	Y/4

where X, the number of parts by weight of polyolefin resin, and Y, the amount of sulfur, were varied.

Not all of the compositions of Table I were prepared by dynamic vulcanization, however. In the first four compositions, for comparision purposes, the elastomer was first press cured and then ground, by tight roll-milling, to various particle sizes. The ground elastomer particles were then mixed with molten polypropylene. Composition 5, of Table I, and all of the rest of the compositions were obtained by dynamic vulcanization.

Particle sizes were determined by optical microscopy. However, the particles of the dynamic vulcanizates were so small that their diameters could only be determined to be in the one to two micrometer range. (More recently, electron microscopy has revealed that the commercial grades of EPDM-polypropylene derived thermoplastic elastomer contain elastomer particles in the one to two micrometer range. An example of this is given by Figure 1). For the measurement of the crosslink density of the elastomer, samples of the elastomer alone

Figure 1   Transmission electron microphotograph of Os O_4 stained sample of a 73 Shore A hardness commercial grade of completely vulcanized EPDM-polypropylene derived thermoplastic vulcanizate

TABLE I Properties of Unfilled Thermoplastic Compositions

Composition number	Resin Type/parts per 100 parts of rubber (phr)[a]	Sulfur phr Y	Method of Prep.[c]	Crosslink density, v/2 "moles" × 10^5 per ml of elastomer	Elastomer particle size, μm d_n	d_w	Shore D hardness	Young's modulus MPa	Stress at 100% strain, MPa	Tens. str., MPa	Ult. elong., %	Tens. set, %
1	Polypropylene/66.7	2.0	S	16.4	72	750	43	97	8.2	8.6	165	—
2	Polypropylene/66.7	2.0	S	16.4	39	290	41	102	8.4	9.8	215	22
3	Polypropylene/66.7	2.0	S	16.4	17	96	41	105	8.4	13.9	380	22
4	Polypropylene/66.7	2.0	S	16.4	5.4	30	42	103	8.4	19.1	480	20
5	Polypropylene/66.7	2.0	D	16.4	about 1 to 2		42	58	8.0	24.3	530	16
6	Polypropylene/66.7	1.0	D	12.3	—		40	60	7.2	18.2	490	17
7	Polypropylene/66.7	0.5	D	7.8	—		39	61	6.3	15.0	500	19
8	Polypropylene/66.7	0.25	D	5.4	—		40	56	6.7	15.8	510	19
9	Polypropylene/66.7	0.125	D	1.0	—		35	57	6.0	9.1	407	27
10	Polypropylene/66.7	0.00	—	0.0	—		22	72	4.8	4.9	190	66
11	Polypropylene/33.3	1.00	D	12.3	—		29	13	3.9	12.8	490	7
12	Polypropylene/42.9	2.00	D	16.4	—		34	22	5.6	17.9	470	9
13	Polypropylene/53.8	2.00	D	16.4	—		36	32	7.6	25.1	460	12
14	Polypropylene/81.8	2.00	D	16.4	—		43	82	8.5	24.6	550	19
15	Polypropylene/122	2.00	D	16.4	—		48	162	11.3	27.5	560	31
16	Polypropylene/233	5.00	D	14.5	—		59	435	13.6	28.8	580	46
17	None[b]/0.00	2.00	S	16.4	—		11	2.3	1.5	2.0	150	1
18	Polypropylene[b]/∞	0	—	—	—		71	854	19.2	28.5	530	—
19	Polyethylene/66.7	2.00	D	12.3	—		35	51	7.2	14.8	440	18
20	Polyethylene/66.7	0.0	—	0.0	—		21	46	4.1	3.5	240	24

[a] Polypropylene is Profax® 6723 and polyethylene is Marlex® EHM 6006

[b] Compositions 17 and 18 control compositions purely of cured elastomer or propylene

[c] S = static; D = dynamic

were press cured under conditions selected to simulate the conditions of dynamic vulcaniza-tion. Crosslink densities of the press-cured samples were then determined on the basis of solvent-swelling measurements by using the Flory Rehner equation[10]. It may be argued that the presence of polyolefin might change the crosslink density, especially in the case of the dynamically cured compositions. However, we have determined that the polyolefin is essentially completely extractable from the cured elastomer by boiling decalin or xylene. This would indicate there is little or no resin interaction with the curing system. Mechanical properties and hardness measurements were by usual means.

The effect of the elastomer particle size is given by Figure 2. This is a composite stress-strain curve constructed from the data associated with compositions 1–5 of Table I. Each "X" denotes a stress and strain at rupture or failure. From Figure 1, then, ultimate strength, ultimate elongation and energy to break (area under curve from origin to an appropriate "X") are apparent. The average elastomer particle size associated with each "X" is noted. The ultimate properties are an inverse function of elastomer particle diameter. The best compositions, of course, were prepared by dynamic vulcanization. There appears to be no other means of producing rubber particles of such small size.

Major effects of changes in crosslink density are given by Figure 3. Only a small amount of crosslink formation is required for a large improvement in tension set. Tensile strength

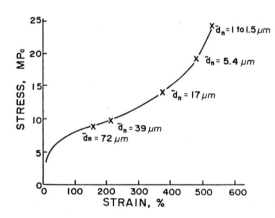

Figure 2   The effect of vulcanized elasto-mer particle size on mechanical properties (X denotes failure). Reproduced with per-mission[9]

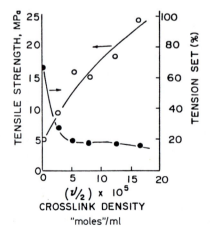

Figure 3   The effect of crosslink density on tensile strength and tension set. Reproduced with permission[9]

improves rather continuously as the crosslink density of the elastomer phase increases, but the compositions remain fabricable as thermoplastics even at high elastomer crosslink densities. However, only small changes in the stiffness of the compositions occur with great changes in the extent of cure.

As the amount of polypropylene resin per amount of elastomer increases, the compositions become less elastomeric and more like the plastic (Figure 4). Modulus, hardness, tension set and strength increase. The shape of the plot of strength against the proportion of polypropylene is interesting. Strengths are low until at least 30 parts of polyolefin resin per 100 parts of elastomer are used. Then as the proportion of resin is further increased, strength rapidly increases until about 50 phr of the polyolefin is used. Further increases in the amount of resin increase the strength only slightly.

Dynamic modulus, as a function of temperature is given by Figure 5. The composition is the same as No. 5 of Table I. The dynamic shear moduli were determined by means of a torsion pendulum[11]. An effect of dynamic vulcanization is to prevent a complete loss of elasticity and strength at the melting point of the resin, polypropylene. The vulcanized composition continues to exhibit sufficient strength for the torsion pendulum modulus measurements even after the plastic phase melting point has been surpassed.

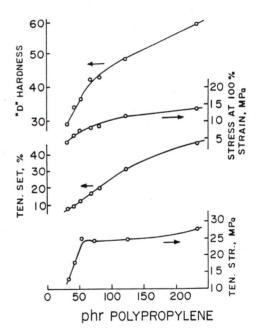

Figure 4   The effect of polypropylene content on EPDM-polypropylene thermoplastic vulcanizate properties. Reproduced with permission[9]

Another effect of dynamic vulcanization, indicated by the results of Figure 5, is a smaller decrease in modulus as the temperature is increased. The unique performance of the thermoplastic vulcanizates even above the plastic melting points suggests a variety of high temperature applications.

The data given for compositions 19 and 20 of Table I indicate that EPDM-polyethylene blends are also greatly improved by dynamic vulcanization. However, on the basis of comparisons between compositions of polyethylene with those of polypropylene, one concludes that the best compositions are prepared from polypropylene.

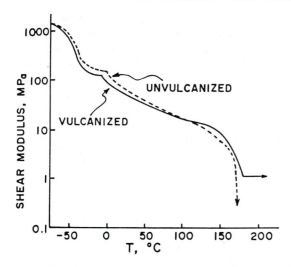

Figure 5   The effect of temperature on the stiffness of EPDM-polypropylene blend compositions. Reproduced with permission[9]

The data of Table II demonstrate the effects of black loading and oil extension. The compositions are variations of No. 15 of Table I. The effect of the filler is to strengthen the composition somewhat and to give some stiffening (in respect to hardness and stress at 100 % strain, but not in respect to the "zero strain". Young's modulus). Both oil extension and carbon black loading can give compositions of lower cost but excellent quality.

From data such as those in Table II, and from measurements of hot oil resistance, fatigue life, etc., it has been concluded that these oil extended, filled compositions will perform similarly to conventional elastomer vulcanizates.

TABLE II   Effect of Carbon Black and Extender Oil[a]

Carbon black, phr	Extender oil, phr	Tensile str., MPa	Stress at 100% strain, MPa	Young's modulus, MPa	Ult. elong., %	Shore hardness	Tension set, %
0.0	0.0	27.5	11.3	162	560	48D	31
80.0	0.0	31.0	14.3	120	410	51D	30
0.0	80.0	15.2	6.4	47	550	29D	19
80.0	80.0	23.0	7.2	23	530	33D	16
80.0	160.0	15.2	4.8	11.5	490	74A	13

[a] Carbon black is N 327, and oil is Sunpar® 2280

3.2 NBR-Nylon Thermoplastic Elastomer Compositions

As in the case of the EPDM-polypropylene compositions, NBR-Nylon compositions were prepared by melt-mixing the polymers and other components in a (Brabender) laboratory size mixer[12]. The temperatures for mixing and molding varied with the melting point of the nylon used in each composition.

Nitrile elastomers can be grouped into two categories: those which are self-curing at elevated mixing temperatures in the absence of curative, and those which are resistant to self curing. (Self-curing at high temperatures is a result of thermal-oxidative instability.) To determine whether or not and elastomer is self-curing, a sample can be mixed at 225 °C (oil-bath temperature). Self-curing elastomers generally gel and crumble (scorch) within 2–8 minutes, whereas nonself-curing samples generally can be mixed for 20 minutes without crumbling.

3.2.1 The Effect of Curatives

The effect of curatives such as m-phenylenebismaleimide is complicated by the fact that some nitrile elastomers tend to self cure at the temperature of mixing. This is particularly true when high-melting nylons are used. In such cases, the effect of adding curative is minimized, since the properties of the composition are improved by the crosslinking of the elastomer which occurs just from mixing. A much greater curative effect is observed with the nonself-curing elastomer, but the best properties are obtained with the self-curing type of NBR.

It was found that the addition of a dimethylol phenolic compound* also substantially improves the properties of NBR-nylon blends. The curative m-phenylenebismaleimide induces considerable gel formation in the elastomer phase and the improved product properties have been associated with gelation of the elastomer phase.

Surprisingly, in the case of dimethylol phenolic curative treatment, high strength blends are obtained even when the gel content of the NBR is as low as 50 %. A portion of the dimethylol phenolic compound is believed to react with the nylon to give chain extension or a small amount of crosslinking. This could increase the viscosity of the molten nylon to where it is more like that of the elastomer and thus, mixing, homogenization and elastomer particle size reduction are greatly improved. In addition, some of the crosslinking can be between molecules of the nylon and those of the elastomer to form nylon-NBR graft molecules. This can also induce better homogenization and interfacial adhesion.

The effect of the curatives on tension set is widely variable. This is suggested by the data of Table III where the various curatives give a wide range of set values. *This is in contrast to what was observed with EPDM-polypropylene compositions.* In that case, curatives invari-

TABLE III   Cured Blends[a] with Different Types of Curatives

Curative type	Tensile Strength, MPa	Stress at 100% strain, MPa	Elon-gation, %	Tension set, %	Shore hardness, D	True stress at break, MPa
None (control)	3.1	2.5	290	72	17	12.3
Accelerated sulfur[b]	8.3	7.4	160	15	35	21.7
Activated bismaleimide[c]	8.5	3.7	310	51	28	34.9
Peroxide[d]	7.9	6.1	220	31	32	25.3

[a] Blends comprise 40 parts of nylon 6–6,6–6 , 10 copolymer (mp = 160 °C) and 60 parts Chemigum® N 365 nonself-curing NBR (39% AN)
[b] Accelerated sulfur system contains 5 parts ZnO, 0.5 parts stearic acid, 2 parts tetramethylthiuramidisulfide, 1 part morpholinothiobenzothiazole, and 0.2 parts of sulfur per 100 parts of elastomer
[c] Activated bismaleamide is 3 parts of *m*-phenylenebismalemide and 0.75 parts of 2,2-bisbenzothiazolyldisulfide per 100 parts of elastomer
[d] Peroxide is 0.5 parts of 2,5-dimethyl-2,5-bis(*t*-butylperoxy)hexane (90% active), L-101

---

* Phenolic resin curative SP-1045 (Schenectady Chemicals, Inc.).

ably reduce set values. The reason for this variation of the effect of curative on tension set is not understood, but it could relate to the extent to which the curatives promote molecular linkages between the nylon and elastomer, rather than cure the elastomer.

3.2.2 The Effect of Elastomer Characteristics

Elastomers of differing viscosities, differing nitrile contents and differing tendencies towards self-curing were studied. There appears to be no simple relationship between the strength of a composition and the characteristics of its elastomer phase. However, as mentioned above, self-curing elastomers tend to give the best strengths, and the effect of curative addition is greatest for the nonself-curing elastomers.

The effect of acrylonitrile content on hot oil resistance is similar to what is observed in the usual NBR vulcanizates (high acrylonitrile content gives low oil swelling). This is true for both the self-curing and nonself-curing types of NBR. Oil swell data for all of the compositions are plotted in Figure 6.

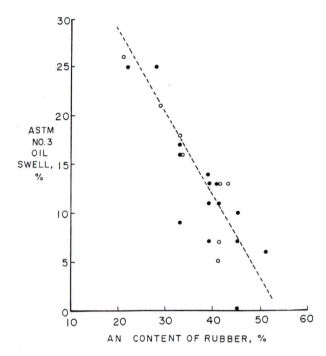

Figure 6 The effect of acrylonitrile (AN) content on hot (150 °C) oil swelling. Self-curing elastomer, O; nonself-curing elastomer. Reproduced with permission[12]

3.2.3 The Effects of NBR-Nylon Proportions

These are similar to those obtained for the EPDM-polyolefin compositions. Increases in the amount of elastomer in the compositions reduce stiffness and strength, but increase resistance to permanent set. Also, extensibility can be increased somewhat. If more than 50 % of the composition is elastomer, compositions having tension set values less than 50 % are obtained. However, excessive amounts of elastomer can result in poor fabricability.

3.2.4 The Effect of Plasticizers

Plasticizers can be added to compositions of NBR and nylon. The effect is to soften the compositions and improve fabricability. Surprisingly, the melting point of the nylon phase

TABLE IV   The Effect of Plasticizers on the Properties of Nylon-NBR Compositions[a]

Plasticizers (compatible phase[b])	Change in Tensile Strength, %	Change in Elongation, %	Change in hardness, "D" units	Change in melting point[c], °C		Change in crystallinity, %
				Peak	Final	
Methyl phthalyl ethylglycolate (R)	−25	+15	− 7	+7	+ 1	−18
Butyl phthalyl butylglycolate (R)	−27	−31	−10	−3	− 7	− 4
C$_7$-C$_9$ trialkyl trimeliate (R)	−28	−35	− 9	−2	− 6	0
Dioctyl phthalate (R)	−26	−38	− 5	+1	− 4	0
Dibutyl sebacate (R)	−34	−23	−10	+1	− 6	−11
N-ethyl-o- and p-toluenesulfonamide (N)	+ 6	+12	− 7	−7	−12	−12
2-propylidene-4,4'-bis-phenol (N)	0	+27	− 7	−8	−12	−22
Nonylphenol (N)	0	+31	− 7	−3	− 6	− 5

[a] Recipe: 50 parts nylon 6-6, 6-6, 10 copolymer (Zyvlel® 63), 50 parts NBR (Hycar® 1092-80), 10 parts plasticizer. 2.5 parts ZnO, and 0.5 parts TMTD. Properties without plasticizer: UTS = 11.6 MPa, UE = 260%, Shore "D" hardness = 45, melting point = 152 °C (peak) or 168 °C (final), heat of fusion (proportional to crystallinity) = 11.6 J/g nylon
[b] The symbols (N or R) indicate primary compatibility with nylon or elastomer, respectively
[c] Melting points and relative crystallinity were determined by differential calorimetry (Perkin Elmer Differential Scanning Calorimeter DSC-IB, 10 °C/min., 20 mg sealed sample)

can increase or decrease, as can the crystallinity. The expected effect is to lower the melting point[13, 14]. However, another expected effect is to decrease the viscosity of the nylon phase. The decrease in viscosity can promote crystallization from the melt and enable formation of more perfect crystals. In some cases these two effects tend to cancel. Plasticizer can either increase or decrease ultimate elongation. Tensile strength generally decreases with the incorporation of plasticizer. Effects of plasticization are indicated by the date in Table IV. Note that plasticizers which are more compatible with the nylon phase tend to give compositions of better mechanical integrity.

3.2.5 The Effect of Filler

Small amounts of clay have little effect on hardness, stiffness or strength, though extensibility is reduced. Young's modulus actually decreases. This is similar to that reported for black filled compositions containing EPDM and polypropylene. Again, it is thought that the filler is in the elastomer phase and it has the effect of both stiffening the elastomer and increasing the volume of its phase. These effects are opposites and largely cancel.

Another effect of filler is to severely reduce the thermoplasticity and therefore to reduce the expected fabricability. To obtain the full benefit of filler, plasticizers can be used to regain both thermoplasticity and extensibility.

3.2.6 Overall Assessment of NBR-Nylon Thermoplastic Elastomeric Compositions

The assessment is complicated by the large number of variations which are possible. There are a number of types of nylon (polyamide) resins of a wide range of melting points, polarities, etc. Also, the variations in the types of NBR are great (nitrile content, viscosity, susceptibility to self-curing, etc.). In addition, the effects of the different curing systems are widely varying. Nevertheless, conclusions can be drawn.

A variety of nylons of differing melting points and NBRs of differing acrylonitrile contents can be used in broad ranges of proportions. The compositions can be further altered by the incorporation of fillers and plasticizers. Thus, a number of types of NBR-nylon based elastomeric materials, fabricable as thermoplastics and exhibiting fairly good strength and excellent hot oil resistance, can be produced in a range of hardnesses.

3.3   Other Thermoplastic Vulcanizates

A large number of elastomer-plastic combinations have been used in the preparation of thermoplastic vulcanizates by dynamic vulcanization. In one study, such compositions were compared in a systematic way[15]. Compositions were prepared as before, by vulcanization of blends during melt-mixing. A variety of curative systems were used, being selected, in the case of each composition, on the basis of at least some optimizational experimentation. Types of curative systems which were used are as follows:

> dimethylolphenolic (P),
> bismaleimide (M),
> bismaleimide-MBTS (M-M),
> bismaleimide-peroxide (M-O),
> organic peroxide (O),
> organic peroxide-coagent (O-C),
> accelerated sulfur (S), and
> soap-sulfur or -sulfur donor (SO-S).

TABLE V   Curatives in Elastomer-Plastic Blends[a]

Elastomers						Plastics			
	PP	PE	PS	ABS	SAN	PMMA	PTMT	PA	PC
IIR	P	P	P	S	S	P	P	P	P
EPDM	S	S	M–O	S	M–O	P	M–O	M–O	M–O
PTPR	P	S	P	P	P	S	M	M	P
NR	P	M–M	M–M	M–M	M–M	M–M	M–M	M–M	M–M
BR	M	M	M	M	M	M	M	M	M
SBR	P	M–M	M	M–M	M–M	M	M	M	M
EVA	O	M–O	M–O	M–O	M–O	M–O	O	O	O
ACM	SO–S	SO–S	SO–S	SO–S	SO–S	SO–S	SO–S	SO–S	SO–S
CPE	M–O	O	O	O	O	O	O	O	O
CR	S	S	M–M	M–M	M–M	S	M	M–M	–
NBR	M–O	M–M	O	O	O	M	–	M	M–M

[a] Each composition is identified corresponding to a elastomer-plastic (row-column) combination. There are 11 elastomers (rows) and 9 plastics (columns) which give 9 × 11 = 99 combinations. Abbreviations for elastomers are standard ASTM D 1418; in addition PTPR is poly-transpentenamer (Bayer), EVA is ethylene-vinyl acetate copolymer elastomer, and CPE is chlorinated polyethylene elastomer. Curative symbols are identified in the text. (IIR = butyl elastomer; EPDM = ethylene-propylene-diene monomer elastomer; NR = natural rubber; BR = butadiene elastomer; SBR = styrene-butadiene elastomer; ACM = acrylate elastomer; CPE = chlorinated polyethylene elastomer; CR = chloroprene elastomer; NBR = nitrile elastomer; PP = polypropylene; PE = polyethylene; PS = polystyrene; ABS = acrylonitrile-butadiene-styrene resin; SAN = styrene-acrylonitrile resin; PMMA = polymethylmethacrylate; PTMT = polytetramethylene terephthalate; PA = polyamide (nylon); and PC = polycarbonate.)

In addition, thermal-oxidative stabilizers were used when appropriate. All of the compositions contained elastomer and plastic in a weight ratio of 60/40. This ratio was chosen for screening of elastomer-plastic pairs because, when good compositions were obtained at the 60/40 elastomer/plastic concentration ratio, they were soft enough and elastic enough (tension set less than 50 %), to be considered elastomeric. The compositions studied are indicated by Table V, in which the types of curing systems are identified by the parenthetic symbols given in the above list of curing systems.

Ultimate tensile strength, ultimate elongation and tension set values which were obtained for the compositions are given in Tables VI, VII and VIII. The values of tensile strength σ_B which are in parentheses for CPE-PTMT, CR-PTMT and CR-PA are in doubt since the elastomers (CPE and CR) are insufficiently stable to withstand processing at the high melt temperatures for PTMT (polyester) and PA (high-melting nylon). The value for EVA-PTMT is in doubt because of the instability of the peroxide curative which was, no doubt, spent before its complete mixture with the molten blend. For similar reasons, other tensile strength values may be low; however, for the purposes of this work only the parenthetic values were removed from consideration in attempts to correlate the measured properties of the elastomer-plastic compositions with characteristics of the elastomer and plastic compo-

TABLE VI   Tensile Strength σ_B of 60–40 Elastomer-Plastic Thermoplastic Vulcanizates[a]

| Elastomers | Plastics | | | | | | | | |
	PP	PE	PS	ABS	SAN	PMMA	PTMT	PA	PC
IIR	21.6	14.9	0.9	1.7	4.3	5.4	1.4	4.0	1.3
EPDM	24.3	16.4	7.9	3.2	5.6	6.0	12.2	7.7	15.7
PTPR	22.7	12.1	6.9	11.0	13.4	4.7	12.1	10.8	2.5
NR	26.4	18.2	6.2	5.8	8.4	1.8	10.9	5.7	6.7
BR	20.8	19.3	11.6	9.9	8.3	3.5	12.8	16.3	2.1
SBR	21.7	17.1	15.8	10.8	8.1	5.7	21.7	14.6	7.3
EVA	17.8	18.9	12.7	9.6	12.9	9.3	(3.4)	10.9	9.6
ACM	4.04	4.21	11.4	9.4	7.7	6.21	14.6	16.1	5.2
CPE	12.3	10.5	14.0	13.7	17.9	17.0	(13.0)	17.3	20.8
CR	13.0	13.8	15.5	12.8	12.5	8.9	(13.5)	(3.2)	14.7
NBR	17.0	17.6	7.7	13.6	25.8	10.8	19.3	21.5	18.2

[a] Values are in MPa; see footnote to Table V

TABLE VII   Ultimate Elongation ε_B of 60–40 Elastomer-Plastic Thermoplastic Vulcanizates[a]

| Elastomers | Plastics | | | | | | | | |
	PP	PE	PS	ABS	SAN	PMMA	PTMT	PA	PC
IIR	380	312	3	18	7	6	156	34	161
EPDM	530	612	69	18	5	6	102	30	66
PTPR	210	280	35	15	10	10	47	60	5
NR	390	360	85	56	14	58	62	42	21
BR	258	229	73	64	12	5	52	121	5
SBR	128	240	89	70	12	15	102	201	19
EVA	319	349	166	102	109	59	(126)	160	81
ACM	18	20	20	144	18	21	135	163	140
CPE	314	221	140	197	151	146	(159)	160	135
CR	141	390	67	96	7	5	(65)	(6)	91
NBR	201	190	20	164	196	56	350	320	130

[a] Values are in %; see footnote to Table V

TABLE VIII   Tension set of 60–40 Elastomer-Plastic Thermoplastic Vulcanizates[a]

Rubbers					Plastics				
---	PP	PE	PS	ABS	SAN	PMMA	PTMT	PA	PC
IIR	23	28	–	–	–	–	–	–	26
EPDM	16	–	–	–	–	–	–	–	–
PTPR	20	27	–	–	–	–	–	–	–
NR	21	–	–	–	–	–	–	–	–
BR	27	–	–	–	–	–	–	–	–
SBR	30	–	–	–	–	–	–	–	–
EVA	36	36	70	–	–	–	(–)	25	–
ACM	–	–	–	–	–	–	41	56	17
CPE	55	58	–	65	91	82	(40)	59	85
CR	33	37	–	–	–	–	(—)	(–)	–
NBR	31	–	–	–	55	–	25	44	–

[a] Values are in %, see footnote to Table 5

nents. Of course, the stability of a component in the presence of the others, in a system of conditions depending thereon, is in itself a characteristic expected to correlate with blend properties. In fact, one might say that an elastomer is technologically incompatible with a plastic if the plastic must be processed at temperatures higher than the temperature range in which the elastomer is stable.

In the case of the ultimate elongation values σ_B given in Table VIII, the parenthetic values are in doubt for the reasons stated above, and again such values were not used in correlations between blend properties and characteristics of the components. Many of the tension set values ε_S are missing from Table VIII because the measurement is impossible with poor compositions which cannot be stretched to an elongation of at least 100 %. Other values are missing because the work was done early in the program, before tension set was routinely measured. The tension set value of 17 % obtained for ACM-PC (acrylate elastomer-polycarbonate resin) appears excessively low (high elastic recovery). Young's modulus for this composition is also very low (1.9 MPa). It would appear that elastomer is the only continuous phase, yet the composition is moldable as a thermoplastic. This could be explained if either the elastomer did not cure in the presence of molten polycarbonate resin, or if the molten polycarbonate decomposed in the presence of the acrylate polymer, possibly by trans-esterification. This would be another type of technological incompatibility.

3.4   Characteristics of Elastomers and Plastics for Correlations with Blend Properties

Properties of elastomer-plastic blends have been correlated with the properties and charac-teristics listed below. Values are given in Table IX.

3.4.1 Dynamic Shear Modulus

This property G' was taken as a measure of stiffness. It was measured by means of a torsion pendulum with specimens whose dimensions were selected to give test frequencies between 0.5 and 2 Hz. This property was selected rather than Young's modulus because of convenience. When considering such widely varying materials as elastomers and hard plastics, it is difficult to find a convenient test condition (rate of loading) appropriate for both elastomers and plastics. The shear moduli of the hard and soft phases (along with elastomer-plastic proportions) were correlated with shear moduli of blends.

TABLE IX   Approximate Polymer Characteristics

	σ_H MPa	G' MPa[a]	γ_c^b	N_c^c	W_c^d
Polypropylene (PP)	30.0	520	28	–	0.63
Polyethylene (PE)	31.7	760	29	–	0.70
Polystyrene (PS)	42	1170	33	–	0.00
ABS	58[e]	926	38	–	0.00
SAN	58	1330	38	–	0.00
Polymethylmethacrylate (PMMA)	61.8	–	39	–	0.00
Polytetramethylene terephthalate (PTMT)	53.3	909	39	–	0.31
Nylon 6, 9 (PA)	46	510	39	–	0.25
Polycarbonate (PC)	66.5	860	42	–	0.00
IIR	–	0.46	27	570	0.00
EPDM	–	0.97	28	460	0.00
Poly-trans-pentenamer Elastomer (PTPR)	–	–	31	417	0.00
IR (NR)	–	0.32	31	454	0.00
BR	–	0.17	32	416	0.00
SBR	–	0.52	33	460	0.00
Ethylene-vinylacetate Elastomer (EVA)	–	0.93	34	342	0.00
ACM	–	–	37	778	0.00
Chlorinated polyethylene (CPE)	–	–	37	356	0.00
CR	–	–	38	350	0.00
NBR	–	0.99	39	290	0.00

[a] Determined by torsion pendulum at about 1 Hz. Rubbers were not vulcanized
[b] γ_c is critical surface tension for wetting, mN/m
[c] N_c is critical molecular length for enlanglement of elastomer molecules, number of chain atoms
[d] W_c is wt. fraction of crystallinity
[e] ABS was considered as SAN containing BR particles: thus ε_H for ABS was considered to be the same as for SAN. The somewhat increased elastomer concentration (over 60 wt. %) should have only a small effect on ultimate properties

3.4.2 Tensile Strength of the Hard-phase Material

This property σ_H was considered because it represents a limit for the strength of the elastomer-plastic blend. Yield stress was used as tensile strength for crystalline materials rather than the stress at break, which occurs only after necking and drawing. (Generally, the elastomeric blends do not exhibit drawing-necking behavior). The values in Table IX were determined in the same way as for the elastomer-plastic blends, by using molded samples which had been equilibrated against laboratory air. For Nylon many of the literature values relate to dried samples and are therefore somewhat higher than the values shown here.

3.4.3 Crystallinity

The weight fractions of crystallinity W_C of many of the plastics are also given in Table IX. The values in the tables are approximations based on the densities of the materials. The reasons for considering crystallinity were empirical; however, interesting correlations between hard-phase crystallinity and certain blend properties have been obtained.

3.4.4 Critical Surface Tension for Wetting

This parameter γ_C has been used as an estimate of polymer surface energy. This was introduced by Zisman[16]. It was estimated by determining contact angles of various liquids against given polymer surface. The contact angles were plotted as functions of the surface tension of test liquids. The surface tension of liquid corresponding to an extrapolated contact angle of zero was taken as the critical surface tension for wetting (or spreading). At one time, it was believed that γ_C was approximately the surface tension γ_S of solid polymer.

At any rate, we thought that the difference between the critical surface tension for wetting (for the elastomer and the plastic) might be a rough estimate of the interfacial tension between the elastomer and plastic during melt mixing. Interfacial tension is a factor which determines, at least in part, the droplet size of one liquid dispersed in another[17]. Lower surface tensions give smaller droplets (which might result in smaller particles of one polymer dispersed in the other after mixing and cooling).

The interfacial tension between two immiscible monomeric liquids is approximated by the difference between the two surface tensions. Unfortunately this is not the case for polymers. However, there is a hypothetical surface tension γ_X which is characteristic of each polymer listed in Wu's review of interfacial tension between molten polymers[18]. If the value of γ_X for one polymer is subtracted from that of the other, the interfacial tension is estimated fairly reliably. The hypothetical values γ_X correlate well weith γ_C. It is also interesting that the critical surface tension for wetting correlates with solubility parameter and that differences between solubility parameters $(\delta_1 - \delta_2)$ of the polymers of a two-phase system correlate with interfacial tension. Indeed, Helfand and Sapse[19] have given a theoretical basis for this.

From all of this we conclude that Δ_C, the difference between critical surface tensions for wetting of each of two polymers may be at least a qualitative estimate of the interfacial tension γ_{12}. The lower the difference Δ_C (which we sometimes call the surface energy mismatch), then, the smaller would be the particles of one molten polymer dispersed in the other. Also a low surface energy mismatch would suggest the possibility of better wetting and interfacial adhesion.

Some of the values of γ_C listed in Table IX were taken from the literature[20]. Those values not available were estimated on the basis of the correlation between solubility parameter δ and γ_C.

3.4.5 Critical Entanglement Spacing

The critical entanglement spacing N_c is measured as the number of polymer chain atoms which corresponds to the molecular weight sufficiently large for entanglements to occur between molecules of undiluted polymer. It has been measured as the molecular weight where the slope of a plot of log viscosity vs. log molecular weight changes from 1.0 to 3.4, the change being associated with intermolecular entanglements. A polymer having a low value of N_C would have a high entanglement density but a low value for the molecular weight between entanglements.

The reason for considering entanglement spacing as a parameter to correlate with blend properties was empirical. It was found that dynamically vulcanized elastomers of high entanglement density (lower values of N_C) gave the higher quality blends with plastics[15]. Although this was an empirical observation, one might speculate why such elastomers give the best blends (in respect to ultimate properties).

It has been observed that, when polymers are blended, one with another, fibrous structures appear which then break up into polymer droplets[21, 22]. We believe it likely that polymer molecules which tend to mutually entangle might be drawn into finer "fibers", during the early phase of mixing, to give emulsions of polymer droplets of smaller size. Of course, after dynamic vulcanization, these droplets would become very small vulcanized rubber particles.

Values of N_C for all of the elastomers, obtained under the same conditions, are not available in the literature. However, it is possible to calculate values of N_C from the chemical structure of the elastomer molecules by using a modified method of Aharoni[23]. The calculated values appear in Table IX.

3.5   The Correlation Between Blend Properties and the Characteristics of the Blend Components

The stress at break was correlated with the component characteristics as a relative ultimate tensile strength σ_B/σ_H, where σ_H is the strength of the hard phase (plastic) material, believed to be a limiting factor.

The effects on relative tensile strength σ_B/σ_H, ultimate elongation ε_B and tension set ε_S are plotted according to regression equations in Figure 7. In each case a property is plotted as a function of one of the three characterizing parameters ($\Delta\gamma_{SH}$, N_C, or W_C) with the other two variables held constant, each at a desirable level.

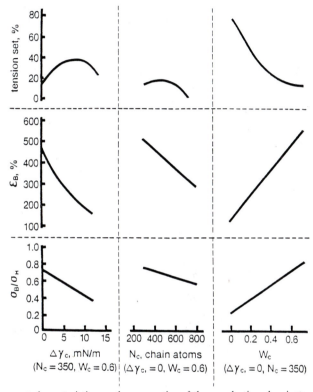

Figure 7   The effect of pure component characteristics on the properties of thermoplastic vulcanizate compositions. σ_B/σ_H is the relative tensile strength. ε_B is the ultimate elongation (%) and ε_S is the tension set (%). $\Delta\gamma_{SH}$ is the difference between the critical surface tension for wetting γ_C (mN/m) of the elastomer and that of the plastic; N_C is the critical molecular length (chain atoms of elastomer molecules) for entanglement; W_c is the weight fraction of crystallinity of the hard phase material. Reproduced with permission[15]

If we accept Figure 7 as an overall view of the effects, certain conclusions can be drawn: (a) An increase in the crystallinity of the plastic material component improves both mechanical integrity and elastic recovery. (b) Elastomers of higher entanglement densities (lower N_C) give compositions of greater mechanical integrity. (c) Compositions, in which the surface energies of the elastomer and plastic phases are closely matched, are strong and extensible. As stated previously, we feel that the matching of surface energies gives lower interfacial tensions, which results in smaller elastomer particles which act as smaller stress concentrator-flaws, thus the high strength and extensibility associated with lower values of $\Delta\gamma_{SH}$.

Thus, based on a few characteristics of the pure elastomers and plastics, elastomer-plastic combinations can be selected, with a good probalitiy of success, to give thermoplastic vulcanizates (by dynamic vulcanization) of good mechanical integrity and elastic recovery. The best compositions are prepared when the surface energies of the elastomer and plastic material are matched, when the entanglement molecular length of the elastomer is low and when the plastic material is crystalline. It is required that neither the plastic, nor the elastomer decomposes in the presence of the other at temperatures required for melt-mixing. Also, a curing system is required, appropriate for the elastomer under the conditions of melt-mixing.

3.6   Technological Compatibilization of NBR-Polyolefin Blends by Elastomer-Plastic Graft Formation

Were it not for their gross mutual incompatibility (in the thermodynamic sense), a combination of a polyolefin resin with NBR might be a good choice of materials from which to prepare oil resistant thermoplastic elastomer compositions by dynamic vulcanization. Early work with these materials demonstrated only marginal success in obtaining good mechanical properties for such compositions[24]. This was likely due to the large surface energy difference between the two types of polymers. Mutual wetting between the polymers appeared incomplete; relatively large particles of cured elastomer dispersed in polyolefin resin formed during mixing and dynamic vulcanization. An approach to technological compatibilization, in addition to dynamic vulcanization, was thus sought[25, 26].

It is now generally accepted that a block copolymer can compatibilize mixtures of the "parent" homopolymers. The block copolymers act as macromolecular surfactants to promote and stabilize the emulsion of the molten homopolymers[27–29]. Figure 8 is an idealized visualization of this.

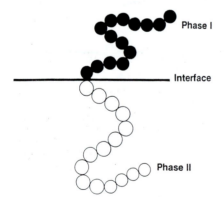

Figure 8   Idealized compatibilizing block copolymers. Reproduced with permission[26]

It has been found that a dimethylol phenolic compound (such as "phenolic resin" curative SP-1045) can be used to technologically compatibilize a mixture of polyolefin and NBR. This compatibilization could be the result of the formation of a block copolymer of the type visualized in Figure 8. Such a compatibilizing block copolymer could be formed by the following reaction scheme:

dimethylol–phenolic compound   quinone methide

phenolic–modified polypropylene

compatibilizing block copolymer

or PP –CH₂... ...CH₂– NBR

The scheme requires the presence of olefinic unsaturation in the polypropylene molecules. Indeed, to satisfy demands of strict polymerization stoichiometry, there is, on the average, one double bond per polyolefin molecule. The scheme is similar to that proposed long ago for the phenolic-resincuring of diene elastomers[30–32].

In practice, the polyolefin resin is treated with about 1–4 parts of a phenolic curative (e. g., SP1045) per 100 parts of polyolefin resin (e. g., polypropylene) in the presence of 0.1–0.5 parts of a Lewis acid (e. g., $SnCl_2$) at a temperature of about 180–190 °C. The phenolic-modified polyolefin is then melt-mixed with NBR for a sufficient time for compatibilization to occur, with the formation of a blend of improved homogenization. Then with continuing mixing, curative for the elastomer is added. (This can be additional dimethylol phenolic resin curative.) If the NBR contains a small amount (ca. 5 %) of an amine terminated liquid NBR (e. g., ATBN 1300X16 – BFGoodrich Co.), then the properties of the compatibilized blend are even more improved.

The formation of polymer-polymer grafts can be accomplished by a number of other chemical means, in addition to the above use of dimethylol phenolic derivatives. In some cases the results are even better. Such a case is the use of maleic-modified polypropylene to form the block-polymeric compatibilizing agent by reaction with the amine terminated liquid NBR. In this case, polypropylene is modified by the action of either maleic acid or maleic anhydride in the presence of decomposing organic peroxide[33, 34]. During the process, the molecular weight of the polypropylene becomes greatly reduced as the molecules thereof acquire pendant succinic anhydride groups:

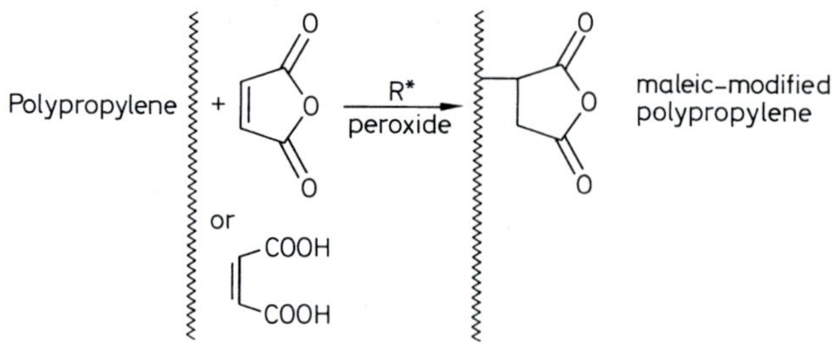

If part of the polypropylene in a NBR-polypropylene composition is maleic-modified, and if part of the NBR is amine terminated, then compatibilizing amounts of NBR-polypropylene block copolymers from *in situ* during melt-mixing:

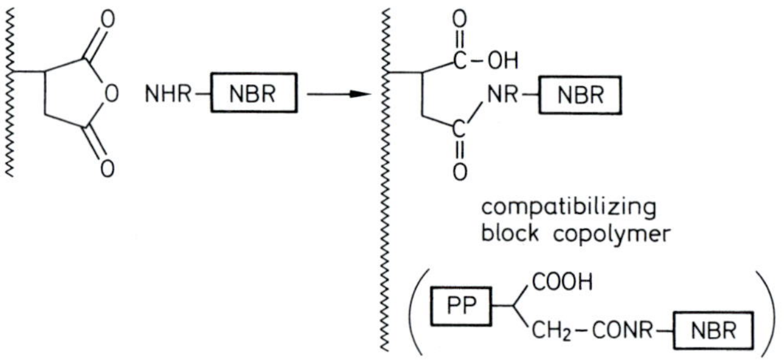

Only a small amount of compatibilizing block copolymer is needed to obtain a substantial improvement in the properties of a blend. The data of Table X relate to compositions in which 10 % of the polypropylene is maleic-modified (by the action of 5 parts of maleic anhydride in the presence of 0.87 parts of L-101 peroxide per 100 parts of polypropylene at 180–190 °C). Varying amounts of the NBR are replaced by amine-terminated liquid NBR. Since the maleic-modified polypropylene is generally in stoichiometric excess, it can be assumed that essentially all of the amine-terminated elastomer is grafted to some of the polypropylene. After each compatibilized blend was prepared, it was dynamically vulcanized and subjected to the usual treatment for molding and testing.

The data of Table X indicate that improved blend properties are obtained when as little as 0.16 % of the elastomer is grafted to polypropylene. Also, after as much as about 2–3 % of the elastomer is grafted to the polyolefin, additional graft formation gives no further improvement. It should be noted that the mechanical properties of the compatibilized dynamically vulcanized blends of NBR and polypropylene can be about as good as those of dynamically vulcanized EPDM and polypropylene.

3.6.1 Resistance to Hot Oil and Brittle Point

The resistance to hot oil and the brittle point of a compatibilized NBR-polypropylene thermoplastic vulcanizate prepared by dynamic vulcanization are given in Table XI. (Stock 1). Though the resistance to hot oil is excellent, low temperature performance is somewhat lacking.

We have found that the low temperature brittle point can be reduced with a minimum sacrifice of hot oil resistance by blending the compatibilized NBR-polypropylene composition with a commercially available thermoplastic elastomer based on polypropylene and

TABLE X   Properties of Compatibilized-Blend Dynamic Vulcanizates as a Function of the Amount of Elastomer Grafted to Plastic

	1	2	3	4	5	6	7	8
Recipe[a]:								
Polypropylene[b]	50	45	45	45	45	45	45	45
Maleic-modified polypropylene[c]	–	5	5	5	5	5	5	5
NBR[b]	50	50	49.22	46.88	43.75	37.5	25	–
NBR master batch[d]	–	–	0.78	3.12	6.25	12.5	25	50
SP-1045[d]	3.75	3.75	3.75	3.75	3.75	3.75	3.75	3.75
$SnCl_2 \cdot 2H_2O$	0.5	0.5	0.5	0.5	0.5	0.5	0.5	0.5
ATBN[b] as % of NBR (% rubber grafted to polypropylene[e])	0	0	0.16	0.62	1.25	2.5	5.0	10.0
Properties:								
Tensile strength, σ_B MPa	8.8	12.0	12.1	15.2	22.0	25.5	25.7	26.7
Stress at 100% strain, σ_{100} MPa	–	12.0	12.1	12.0	12.3	12.3	12.5	12.9
Young's modulus, E, MPa	209	200	212	223	185	188	181	237
Ultimate elongation, ε_B, %	19	110	170	290	400	440	430	540
Tension set, ε_S, %	–	–	45	40	40	40	42	45
True stress at break, σ_B MPa	10	25	33	59	110	138	136	171
Breaking energy[f], J cm^2	1.2	11.0	18.4	34.6	54.9	64.1	61.7	86.5
Improvement in breaking energy due to compatibilization, %	–	–	67	215	399	483	461	686

[a] Parts by weight
[b] Profax® 6723
[c] See text
[d] 90 Wt. percent Hycar® 1092-80, 10 wt. percent Hycar® ATBN 1300 X16
[e] Assuming quantitative reaction between ATBN and maleic-modified polypropylene which is assumed to be present in excess
[f] Determined from stress-strain curves

TABLE XI   Compatibilized NBR-Polypropylene Composition Blended with EPDM-Polypropylene Composition

	1	2	3
Wt. percent NBR-polypropylene composition[a]	100	50	0
Wt. percent EPDM-polypropylene composition[b]	0	50	100
Properties:			
Tensile strength, σ_B, MPa	22.6	15.9	8.6
Stress at 100% strain, σ_{100}, MPa	11.2	7.9	4.4
Ultimate elongation, ε_B, %	585	510	415
Shore A Hardness	93	87	68
Tension set, ε_S, %	48	23	10
True stress at break, σ_B, MPa	155	97	44.3
ASTM #3 oil vol. swell, %[c]	22	32.5	62.5
Brittle point, °C	−24	−47	<−60

[a] Recipe for the NBR-polypropylene compositions is: Profax® 6723 polypropylene, 45 (parts by weight); maleic-modified polypropylene, 5; Hycar® 1092-80 NBR: Hycar® ATBN 1300 X16 liquid NBR (90:10), 50; SP-1045 phenolic curative, 3.75; $SnCl_2 \cdot 2H_2O$, 0.5; Naugard® 495 stabilizer (added after vulcanization), 1.0
[b] Commercially available Santoprene® 201-73 (Monsanto Co.)
[c] Hot oil swelling 70 h at 100 °C

vulcanized EPDM. The two thermoplastic elastomer compositions are mutually compatible, since they are both based on a continuous phase of polypropylene. The results given in Table XI indicate that the blend exhibits average mechanical properties but surprisingly better than the average hot oil resistance.

3.6.2 Overall Assessment of Compatibilized NBR-Polypropylene Thermoplastic Vulcanizates

The mechanical properties of these compatibilized blends can approach those of dynamically vulcanized EPDM-polypropylene blends and, in addition, excellent hot oil resistance can be achieved. The NBR-based compositions may not have good enough resistance to low-temperature embrittlement for some applications, but compositions based on EPDM and polypropylene can be blended with the NBR-polypropylene composition to improve the brittle point without causing severe losses of other attributes.

4   TECHNOLOGICAL APPLICATIONS

The elastomer-plastic blends discussed here are intended for use as thermoplastic elastomers. These are materials which have many of the properties of conventional vulcanized (thermoset) elastomers, but are processable and can be fabricated into parts by the rapid techniques used for thermoplastic materials.

Thermoplastic processing is far more economically attractive than traditional multi-step elastomer processing. In the case of conventional thermoset elastomer processing, the producer of elastomeric articles purchases elastomer, fillers, extender oils or plasticizers, curatives, antidegradants, etc.; these ingredients must then be mixed and uniformly dispersed; after a stock is mixed, it is then shaped by extrusion, calendering, etc.; the crudely shaped preform is then vulcanized in its final shape in a mold contained by a press and

TABLE XII   Properties of Various Types of Elastomer Compositions

	Partially Vulcanized EPDM/Poly-propylene Blend[a]	Completely Vulcanized EPDM/Poly-propylene Blend[b]	Neoprene Vulcani-zate	Polyether-ester Copolymer Thermoplastic Elastomer[c]
Shore A Hardness	77	80	80	92
Tensile Strength, MPa	6.6	9.7	9.7	25.5
Ultimate Elongation, %	200	400	400	450
Volume Swell in ASTM #3 Oil (74 h at 100 °C), %	Disinte-grated	50	35	30
Compression Set (Method B – 22 h at 100 °C), %	70	39	35	33
Use Temperature, °C	100	125	110	125
Type of Processing[d]	TP	TP	CV	TP

[a] TPR-1700 (Uniroyal)
[b] SANTOPRENE® (Monsanto)
[c] HYTREL® (Du Pont)
[d] TP = thermoplastic; CV = conventional thermoset vulcanizate

heated for vulcanization which can take a long period of time. Mold flash or overflow, as well as rejected parts, are not economically reprocessable.

On the other hand, a part produced from a thermoplastic elastomer is shaped or molded into its final shape in a single step. Also mold flash and rejected parts can be simply ground and reused. Detailed comparisons have shown time and again that thermoplastic processing is more economical than thermoset elastomer processing[4].

The lower cost of thermoplastic processing provides the economic incentive for the development of thermoplastic elastomers.

The recently commercialized compositions based on melt-mixed blends of completely dynamically vulcanized EPDM and polypropylene, as described herein, have many of the excellent properties of polyurethane and polyether-ester copolymer thermoplastic elastomers. In addition, the properties of these commerical grades of completely vulcanized EPDM-polypropylene thermoplastic vulcanizate materials compare favorably with those of conventional vulcanized specialty rubbers (CR, EPDM, and CSM). In respect to fatigue life, the commerical EPDM-polypropylene thermoplastic vulcanizates out-perform the conventional specialty elastomers. Comparisons between selected properties of three thermoplastic elastomers and those of a conventional elastomer are given in Table XII.

4.1 Processing-Fabrication Technology

The processing of a rubber-plastic blend composition into a finished part is a function of the melt rheology of the composition, the temperature and shear rate. Processing is also a function of the strength of the molten material under the strain due to its processing, i. e., a function of its resistance to melt fracture. Melt fracture, under the conditions of extrusion, can give rise to very poor surface textures or even functionally useless parts.

The melt rheology of an elastomer-plastic blend composition is related to that of the plastic material. This is illustrated by the idealization given by Figure 9. At high shear rates the viscosity-shear rate profiles are similar for the blend and the plastic material, *per se*. However, at very low shear rates, the viscosity of the blend can be very high. In the case of dynamically vulcanized elastomer-plastic melt-mixed blends containing high levels of elastomer, the viscosity can approach infinity where the shear rate is zero. Under the conditions of melt extrusion, the molten material undergoes rapid flow in the die. Then, as the material

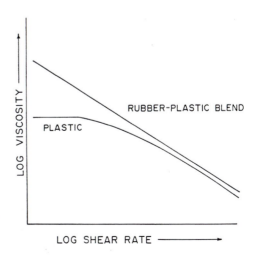

Figure 9   The relationship between viscosity and shear rate for a plastic and for its blend with elastomer

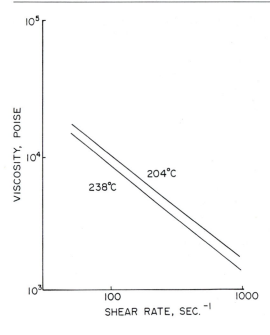

Figure 10   The effect of temperature on the EPDM-polypropylene viscosity-shear rate relationship for a typical thermoplastic vulcanizate

passes out of the die, the rate of deformation drops to zero and, since the viscosity approaches infinity (presumably due to cured elastomer particle-particle interference), little or no die swell is observed. The dimensions of extrusion profiles of such materials are, thus easily controlled.

From Figure 9, it appears that elastomer-plastic blends are highly shear-rate sensitive in respect to melt viscosity. The temperature sensitivity of the viscosity of an EPDM-polypropylene thermoplastic elastomer at high levels of elastomer is illustrated by Figure 10. The viscosity of this type of blend is relatively temperature-*insensitive*. (In compositions based on other types of thermoplastic, the viscosity may indeed be more temperature-sensitive.) Figures 9 and 10 indicate that, in processing certain elastomer-plastic blends by flow techniques, such as extrusion and injection molding, shear rates should be kept high enough to facilitate adequate flow.

TABLE XIII   Injection-Molding Conditions for EPDM-Polypropylene Thermoplastic Elastomers

Barrel temperatures, °C		
Rear zone	180	– 220
Center zone	205	– 220
Nozzle	205	– 220
Mold temperature, °C	20	– 65
Injection Pressure, MPa	35	– 140
Hold Pressure, MPa	30	– 110
Back Pressure, MPa	0.7 –	3.5
Screw Speed, rpm	25	– 75
Injection Speed	Moderate – Fast	
Cycle Times, sec.		
Injection	5	– 25
Hold	15	– 75
Total	20	– 100

TABLE XIV   Extrusion Conditions for EPDM-Polypropylene Thermoplastic Elastomers

Barrel temperatures, °C	
Rear zone	160 – 180
Center zone	175 – 210
Nozzle	190 – 220
Adapter temperature, °C	200 – 225
Die temperature, °C	205 – 225
Melt temperature	205 – 235
Screw Speed, rpm	10 – 150

As O'Connor and Fath[4] have pointed out, the high melt viscosity of these products can be advantageous in processing. The high viscosity can provide high melt integrity or "green strength" and permit the retention of shapes of parts produced by extrusion or blow molding. The high melt viscosity and low die swell are also helpful in calendering sheet and film products. For injection-molded parts, fast injection rates (under high pressure) give lower viscosities due to the high shear rate. This facilitates rapid and complete mold filling. Then, after the mold is filled, the viscosity increases greatly due to shear rate reduction (to zero). This increased viscosity, which can approach infinity, enables more rapid extraction of the part from the mold. The overall effect is a faster injection molding cycle. In addition, the moderate temperature sensitivity of the viscosity of such a composition gives a "broad temperature window" for processing. Typical injection molding and extrusion conditions for an EPDM-polypropylene blend are given by Tables XIII and XIV.

In addition to the above (injection molding, calendering, extrusion, and blow molding), foaming, thermoforming, and compression molding of olefinic elastomer-plastic blends have been reviewed[1]. However, it should be noted that processing conditions vary widely with equipment mold designs, specific blend compositions, etc. The best conditions for the production of a given part must be confirmed by prototype runs in factory equipment.

4.2   End-Use Applications

New techniques of melt-mixing blends of elastomers and plastics, dynamically vulcanized, and employing compatibilizing agents have greatly expanded the number of useful thermoplastic elastomers. It is probable that this expansion will continue and accelerate.

Potential and proven applications of these more recently developed thermoplastic elastomers are:

For mechanical rubber goods applications: caster wheels, convoluted bellows, flexible diaphragms, gaskets, seals, extruded profiles, tubing, mounts, bumpers, housings, glazing seals, valves, shields, suction cups, torque couplings, vibration isolators, plugs, connectors, caps, rollers, oil-well injection lines, handles, and grips.

For under-the-hood automotive applications: air conditioning hose cover, fuel-line hose cover, vacuum tubing, vacuum connectors, body plugs, seals, bushings, grommets, electrical components, convoluted bellows, steering gear boots, emission tubing, protective sleeves, shock isolators, and air ducts.

For industrial hose applications: hydraulic (wire braid), agricultural spray, paint spray, plant air-water, industrial tubing, and mine hose.

For electrical applications: plugs, strain relief, wire and cable insulation and jacketing, bushings, enclosures, connectors and terminal ends.

4.2.1 Emerging Applications

Because of the high level of product-development activity sustained by the industry, a number of new thermoplastic elastomeric compositions are emerging. Efforts are directed towards the development of thermoplastic elastomeric blend compositions which are more resistant to hot oil, compositions which are more resistant to higher temperatures, and, eventually, compositions which are more resistant to both hot oil and higher temperatures. The combination of the two techniques discussed in this chapter have opened the door to many new-product opportunities.

As stated throughout this chapter, dynamic vulcanization greatly improves the properties of elastomer-plastic blends. However, in addition to dynamic vulcanization, technological compatibilization by the incorporation of block-copolymer compatibilizers has greatly increased the number of elastomer-plastic combinations which can give reliably good mechanical properties. It is now not necessary that the elastomer and thermoplastic be of similar surface-energy. Thus, combinations can be selected on the basis of the properties of the *individual* elastomer and thermoplastic components. For example, a high-melting crystalline plastic can, at least in principle, be combined with an elastomer which has a very low brittleness temperature to produce a thermoplastic elastomeric material with a very wide range of end-use temperatures. Alternately, the high-melting crystalline plastic can be combined with an oil resistant elastomer of good thermal-oxidative stability to give a thermoplastic elastomeric material suited for applications in highly aggressive environments.

References

1. H. L. Morris, *Handbook of Thermoplastic Elastomers* (B. M. Walker, ed.), van Nostrand Reinhold, New York, pp. 5–71, (1979)
2. E. N. Kresge, *Polymer Blends,* Vol. 2 (D. R. Paul and S. Newman, ed.), Academic, New York, p. 293 (1978)
3. E. N. Kresge, *J. Appl. Polym. Sci.: Applied Polymer Symposium, 39,* 37 (1984)
4. G. E. O'Connor and M. A. Fath. *Rubber World,* December (1981), January (1982)
5. B. D. Gesner, *Encyclopedia of Polym. Sci. and Technol., Vol. 10,* H. F. Mark and N. G. Gaylord, ed., Interscience, New York, p. 694 (1969)
6. A. M. Gessler, U. S. Patent 3,037,954 (June 5, 1962)
7. W. K. Fischer, U. S. Patent 3,758,643 (Sept. 11, 1973)
8. A. Y. Coran, B. Das, and R. P. Patel, U. S. Patent 4,130,535 (Dec. 19, 1978)
9. A. Y. Coran and R. Patel, *Rubber Chem. Technol., 53,* 141 (1980)
10. P. J. Flory, *Principles of Polymer Chemistry,* Cornell, Ithaca, NY, p. 576 (1953)
11. L. E. Nielson, *Rev. Sci. Instr., 22,* 690 (1951)
12. A. Y. Coran and R. Patel, *Rubber Chem. Technol., 53,* 781 (1980)
13. H. L. Wagner and P. J. Flory, *J. Am. Chem. Soc., 74,* 195 (1952)
14. P. J. Flory, *Principles of Polymer Chemistry,* Cornell, Ithaca, NY, p. 568 (1953)
15. A. Y. Coran, R. Patel and D. Williams, *Rubber Chem. Technol., 55,* 116 (1982)
16. W. A. Zisman, *Advances in Chemistry Ser. 43,* 1 (1964)
17. T. Mikami, R. G. Cox, and S. G. Mason, *Int. J. Multiphase Flow, 2,* 112 (1975)
18. S. Wu, *Polymer Blends Vol. 1,* D. R. Paul and S. Newman, ed., Academic, New York, p. 244 (1978)
19. E. Helfand and A. M. Sapse, *J. Chem. Phys., 62,* 1327 (1975)
20. G. I. Crocker, *Rubber Chem. Technol., 42,* 30 (1969)
21. G. N. Avgeropoulos, F. C. Weissert, P. H. Biddison, and G. G. A. Boehm, *Rubber Chem. Technol., 49,* 93 (1976)
22. G. R. Hamed, *Rubber Chem. Technol., 55,* 151 (1982)
23. S. M. Aharoni, *J. Appl. Polym. Sci., 21,* 1323 (1977)
24. A. Y. Coran and R. Patel, U. S. Patent 4,104,210, (Aug. 1, 1978)
25. A. Y. Coran and R. Patel, U. S. Patent 4,355,139, (Oct. 19, 1982)

26. A. Y. Coran and R. Patel, *Rubber Chem. Technol.*, *56*, 1045 (1983)
27. D. R. Paul, *Polymer Blends, Vol 2*, D. R. Paul and S. Newman ed., Academic, New York, p. 35 (1978)
28. O. Olabisi, L. M. Robeson and M. T. Shaw, *Polymer-Polymer Miscibility*, Academic, New York, p. 321 (1979)
29. N. G. Gaylord, *Adv. Chem. Ser.*, *142*, 76 (1975)
30. S. Vander Meer, *Rev. Gen. Caoutch. Plast.*, *20*, 230 (1943)
31. C. Thelamon, *Rubber Chem. Technol.*, *36*, 268 (1963)
32. A. Giller, *Kant. Gummi. Kunstst.*, *19*, 188 (1966)
33. M. Veda Minoura, S. Mizunuma and M. Oba, *J. Appl. Polym. Sci.*, *13*, 1625 (1969)
34. F. Ide and A. Hasegawa, *J. Appl. Polym. Sci.*, *18*, 963 (1974)

Chapter **8**

THERMOPLASTIC POLYESTER ELASTOMERS

R. K. Adams, G. K. Hoeschele

Contents

Rowland K. Adams, 2142 Haven Road, Wilmington, DE 19809
Guenther K. Hoeschele, E. I. du Pont de Nemours & Co., Polymer Products Department,
Experimental Station, Wilmington, DE 19898

1   INTRODUCTION

The Polyester elastomers are multi-block copolymers which can be represented by generalized formula $(-A-B-)_n$. They are related structurally to the polyurethanes (Chapter 2) and the polyamide elastomers (Chapter 9). Polyester elastomers contain repeating high melting blocks which are capable of crystallization (hard segments) and amorphous blocks having a relatively low glass transition temperature (soft segments). Typically the hard segments are composed of multiple short chain ester units such as tetramethylene terephthalate units and the soft segments are derived from aliphatic polyether or polyester glycols. At useful service temperatures, the polyester elastomers resist deformation because of the presence of a network of microcrystallites formed by partial crystallization of hard segments. The microcrystallites function as physical crosslinks. At processing temperatures, the crystallites melt to yield a polymer melt which after shaping by molding, for example, retains its form upon cooling due to re-crystallization of the hard segments. As in the case of the polyurethanes, a variety of starting materials can be used for the preparation of polyester elastomers. By varying the ratio of hard to soft segments polyesters ranging from soft elastomers to relatively hard elastoplastics can be obtained. Polymers covering the complete hardness spectrum are considered in this chapter even though the hardest polyesters are more plastic than elastomeric in behavior.

Research on block copolyester elastomers started around 1950 with principal effort being directed toward modifying or developing new synthetic fibers based on ethylene glycol or cyclohexanedimethanol and terephthalic acid. While this early work did not lead to any significant commerical applications, it did provide the initial knowledge on the synthesis and nature of this class of polymers. Shortly before 1970, interest in copolyester elastomers intensified with the recognition that the family of polymers prepared from terephthalic acid, tetramethylene glycol and poly(tetramethylene oxide) glycol had outstanding physical properties and processing characteristics, shifting the emphasis of research toward polyester elastomers as polymers for molding and extrusion applications.

In this chapter, the early fiber-related research is reviewed first. This is followed by a more comprehensive discussion of the development and the properties of the commercially successful polymers derived from terephthalic acid, tetramethylene glycol and poly(tetramethylene oxide) glycol. Finally, the effect of structural variations on polymer properties is reviewed.

2   FIBER RESEARCH

In 1949, Coleman[1] undertook a study of block copolymers prepared by copolymerization of ethylene glycol, dimethyl terephthalate and poly(ethylene oxide) glycols having molecular weights ranging from 600–2800. This work was directed toward improving the dye receptivity of poly(ethylene terephthalate) fibers. Previous work by Hill and Edgar[2] with adipic or sebacic acid as a third component had demonstrated that the melting point of poly(ethylene terephthalate) copolymers was a function of the mole fraction of ethylene terephthalate units, in agreement with Flory's predictions[3] relating melting point depression in copolymers to the mole fraction of the principal monomer in a copolymer. The introduction of a third component having a relatively high molecular weight offered the promise of greatly increasing the amorphous regions in the polymer without significantly lowering the melting point of the homopolymer. Coleman found that block copolymers containing up to 30 % by weight by poly(ethylene oxide) units did show only a limited depression in melting point as predicted by Flory's work. The resulting polymers can be considered as random copolyesters of ethylene glycol, poly(ethylene oxide) glycol and terephthalic acid in which blockiness results from the low mole fraction of high molecular weight polyether blocks with the attendant formation of blocks of repeating ethylene terephthalate units. Second order transition points (T_g) were depressed significantly in the block copolymers as shown in Figure 1. Based on this observation and x-ray diffraction diagrams which were substantially identical for oriented samples of both homopolymer and block copolymer, Coleman concluded that the poly(ethylene oxide) blocks were located in the amorphous regions of the polymers and not cocrystallized in the crystalline regions of the polymers.

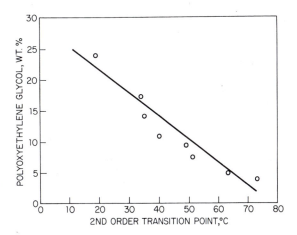

Figure 1   Second order transition points of poly(ethylene terephthalate) copolymers as a function of wt percent poly(ethylene oxide) glycol. Reprinted with permission from J. Polym. Sci., D. Coleman[1], Copyright© 1954 John Wiley & Sons, Inc.

Coleman investigated the mechanical properties of the copolymers only as drawn fibers. The tenacity and elongation of a copolymer containing 7 % by weight poly(ethylene oxide) units did not differ significantly from values for the homopolymer. Based on the decrease in Tg, Coleman recognized that the copolymers were more flexible than the homopolymer but he did not suggest that the more flexible copolymers might be useful as elastomers for fibers or molding resins. The copolymer fibers showed increased dye receptivity, but were found to degrade rapidly when exposed to ultraviolet light.

With thermoplastic copolyester elastomers as our subject, perhaps the most important observation made by Coleman was the large drop in T_g when poly(ethylene oxide) segments were incorporated into poly(ethylene terephthalate). Since polyester homopolymers having sufficiently high melting points to provide a useful range of service temperatures generally have T_g values well above room temperature, the lowering of the T_g by copolymerizing soft segment blocks is necessary to obtain rubbery properties at room temperature and below. The picture suggested by Coleman's work of soft segments being intermingled in the amorphous regions of the crystallizible polyester is still largely accepted at present albeit with some reservations in view of more recent studies of the morphology and properties of commercial copolyester elastomers. At about the same time, Snyder[4] independently prepared similar copolyesters which had improved dyeability.

Following the work by Coleman and Snyder, several investigators set out to develop truly rubbery block copolyesters which when spun into fibers could replace cut rubber thread. This work involved polymers with a much higher percentage of soft segments derived from poly(alkylene oxide) glycols. Since ironing of clothing was still considered important in the fifties, the desired copolyester needed a high stick temperature as well as high elastic recovery and low stress relaxation.

Charch and Shivers[5] described in some detail one approach for selecting the optimum rubbery fiber which could be derived from ethylene glycol, terephthalic acid and poly(ethylene oxide) glycol. It should be noted that Reference 5 is not limited to the aforementioned polymer system but relates to rubbery condensation block copolymers in general regardless of the chemical nature of the soft segments and the hard segments, the latter providing physical tie points by crystallization and/or hydrogen bonding.

Charch and Shivers published a graph of melting points for a series of copolymers containing increasing amounts of soft segments derived from poly(ethylene oxide) glycol, MW 4000, Figure 2. Of significance was the observation that polymer melt temperature (equivalent to polymer stick temperature) fell off only moderately in the elastomer region. The positions of the vertical broken lines which divide the graph into the hard crystalline, elastomer and soft plastic zones apply only to the specific polymer system under study and to the researchers' definition of the term "elastomer". Some degree of elastomeric or rubbery character can be expected as long as sufficient soft segment is present to lower the T_g to about room temperature and there still remain sufficient crystalline tie points to prevent excessive chain slippage.

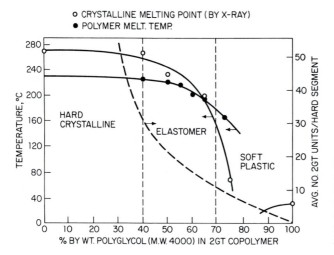

Figure 2   Melting point and average hard segment block length as a function of poly-(ethylene oxide) glycol concentration. Reprinted with permission from Textile Research Journal[5]

Figure 2 has been modified by the addition of the broken curve which represents calculated values of the average number of ethylene terephthalate units (2GT) in the hard segment blocks relative to the weight percent of polyglycol. For the limits of the region designated "elastomer", the average block length is about 31 2GT units at 40 % polyglycol to about 9 2GT units at 70 % polyglycol. Assuming a number average molecular weight of 25,000 for the block copolyester which is typical for present day commercial products, the average polymer molecule containing 40 % polyglycol would contain 2.5 each of hard blocks and soft blocks. At 70 % polyglycol the average polymer molecule would contain 4.4 of each type block. It is clear that harder polymers will at some point no longer have multi-block structure on the average. Even harder compositions will be blends of 2GT homopolymer and copolymers containing an average of one soft segment. At the other extreme, the average hard segment block length is approaching zero and a point is reached where the concentration of hard segment blocks having sufficient length to crystallize is too low to provide the tie points necessary for rubbery character.

Charch and Shivers also studied the tensile recovery and stress decay of fibers prepared from copolyesters containing equal amounts of poly(ethylene oxide) glycol having different molecular weights, Figure 3. The abbreviated description of the copolyester in the caption for Figure 3 represents the most common way to describe the composition of polyester block copolymers. 2GT represents a short chain ester unit derived from ethylene glycol, 2G, and terephthalic acid, T. Tetramethylene glycol would be indicated as 4G with 4GT being a tetramethylene terephthalate unit. PEOT represents a long chain ester unit derived from poly(ethylene oxide) glycol, PEO glycol, and terephthalic acid, T. The numbers in parenthesis indicate the weight percent of short chain and long chain ester units. A copolyester derived from tetramethylene glycol, terephthalic acid and poly(ethylene oxide) glycol having a molecular weight of 1000 would be represented as 4 GT/PEO-1000T (x/100-X) where x is the weight percent of 4GT units.

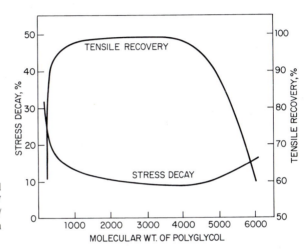

Figure 3 Tensile recovery and stress decay as a function of the MW of PEO glycol in 2GT/PEOT (50/50). Reprinted with permission from Textile Research Journal[5]

Based on Figure 3, Charch and Shivers concluded that PEO-4000 yielded polymers having optimum tensile recovery and stress decay. It should be recognized that the fibers tested probably were oriented by drawing; however, there is no mention of drawing in the reference. At polyglycol molecular weights below 1000 both tensile recovery and stress decay deteriorate probably because of diminished blockiness. An explanation for the decline in tensile recovery and increase in stress decay for polyglycols having a molecular weight in excess of 4000 is not as obvious. The reference indicates that soft segments which are too long may tend to crystallize so as to adversely affect tensile recovery. Another factor which might possibly diminish physical properties is the immiscibility of soft segments with amorphous portions of the hard segments when the molecular weight of the soft segments is relatively high.

Having concluded that PEO having an average molecular weight of 4000 was preferred, Charch and Shivers determined tensile recovery and stress decay for copolymers containing increasing amounts of PEO-4000, Figure 4. Charch and Shivers stress that the system studied in detail is only a prototype. Clearly, other short chain ester units and long chain ester units might be copolymerized to form different systems, each of which would require a separate study if one sought to optimize its properties.

Shivers[6] described the detailed preparation of several copolyester elastomers based on 2GT units and PEOT units as well as copolyesters from 2GT units and poly(tetramethylene oxide) terephthalate [PTMOT] units. With PTMO glycol having molecular weights of

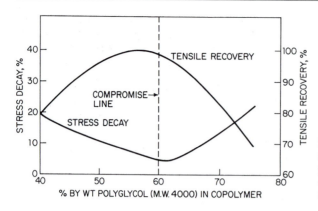

Figure 4 Tensile recovery and stress decay as a function of wt. percent PEO glycol in 2GT/PEO-4000T. Reprinted with permission from Textile Research Journal[5]

800–1800, 40–70 weight percent of PTMOT units gave preferred polymers for elastic fibers. Shivers further noted the high permeability to water vapor of polymers based on PEO glycol. The use of stabilizers to prevent degradation by heat and ultraviolet light was also described.

Bell, Kibler and Smith[7] described the preparation and fiber properties of copolyesters derived from 1,4-cyclohexanedimethanol (CHDM), terephthalic acid and PTMO glycol. Preferred copolyester elastomer fibers contained 7–23 % by weight of short chain ester units, CHDMT, and 77–93 % by weight of long chain ester units, PTMOT, where the PTMO glycol had a molecular weight of 1900–5100. As already observed by Charch and Shivers, with higher melting hard segments such as CHDMT, optimum elastomer fiber properties were obtained at lower concentrations of short chain ester units than were needed with 2GT units.

In preparing their copolyesters by melt condensation of dimethyl terephthalate, CHDM and PTMO glycol, Bell et al. occasionally encountered a condition which they called biphasing – also referred to as melt phasing. When phasing occurs, the polycondensation melt is cloudy or opaque due to the presence of two phases, one rich in PTMOT segments; the other, in CHDMT segments. The presence of two phases in the polymer melt made spinning of fibers very difficult. To eliminate phasing, replacement of up to 20 mole percent of the terephthalic acid with an aliphatic dicarboxylic acid was suggested to increase the solubility of the two phases. Of course, this remedy substantially lowers the melting point of the resulting polyester.

Bell et al. also found that the molecular weight distribution of the PTMO glycol used influenced fiber properties, PTMO glycol of narrow molecular weight distribution yielding fibers with lower permanent set. No explanation was suggested for this improvement. It may be that the presence of very high molecular weight species in PTMO glycol with a broad molecular weight distribution resulted in irreversible crystallization of some of the polyether segments upon extension or possibly, phasing may have been encountered. Recent work[8] has shown that phasing during polyester elastomer preparation can be diminished by using PTMO glycol having a narrow molecular weight distribution. Apparently, the presence of even a small concentration of very high molecular weight PTMO species markedly reduces the miscibility of the long chain segments in the polycondensation melt.

In a continuation of their work, Bell, Kibler and Smith[9] described the use of copolymers of tetrahydrofuran with 8-oxabicyclo(4:3:0) nonane or 3-methyl-8-oxabicyclo (4:3:0) nonane in place of PTMO glycol homopolymer. Elastomers prepared from the copolyether glycols exhibited increased resistance to permanent set, particularly at low temperatures. As noted above, there is a tendency for higher molecular weight PTMO segments to crystallize when extended. The presence of comonomer units in the PTMO chain interferes with this crystallization.

In 1967, Nishimura and Komagata[10] published a study of polyester elastomer fibers based on 4GT units and PTMOT units. The use of 4GT units in the hard segments of these fibers represented a departure from earlier work where hard segments having very high melting points were preferred. Copolyesters containing 9 to 25 percent by weight of 4GT units and soft segments from PTMO glycol having molecular weights from 1940 to 3337 were prepared. At room temperature, fibers made from the copolyesters exhibited elastic recovery of about 99 % after being stretched 200 %. At 100 °C, elastic recovery was poorer, but this property was improved by the use of small amounts of trifunctional monomers.

Looking back from today's viewpoint, one is impressed by how much fundamental knowledge of segmented polyester elastomers was developed during the work directed to fibers. However, because their interests were limited to fibers, the early investigators apparently did not appreciate that thermoplastic polyester elastomers particularly suited for molding and extrusion could be prepared.

3   RESEARCH AND DEVELOPMENT RELATED TO COMMERCIAL POLYESTER ELASTOMERS

Prior to mid-1969, Witsiepe[11, 12, 13] began an investigation of copolyesters derived from terephthalic acid, tetramethylene glycol and PTMO glycol. Compositions containing from about 30 % to 95 % by weight of 4GT units were studied. Additionally, polymers in which a portion of the 4GT units were replaced by tetramethylene isophthalate (4GI) or tetramethylene phthalate (4GP) units were prepared.

This family of polyester elastomers exhibited outstanding elasticity, tear strength, solvent resistance, low temperature flexibility and strength at elevated temperatures. Equally important, they crystallized so rapidly from a melt that they could be processed by typical methods for forming plastics. In 1972, they were commercialized under the trademark HYTREL® polyester elastomer by DuPont[14]. Similar polymers were introduced at about the same time under the trademark PELPRENE by Toyobo[15]. Commercialization of these polymers prompted considerable research directed toward understanding their structure, morphology and chemistry. Many structural variations have been studied and numerous blends with other polymers have been reported.

3.1   Structure and Nature of the Polymers

The copolyesters are readily prepared by melt polymerization. An agitated mixture of dimethyl terephthalate, PTMO glycol and excess tetramethylene glycol is heated in the presence of a titanate catalyst. Methanol resulting from ester exchange is removed by fractional distillation after which the temperature is raised to about 250 °C while the pressure is reduced to less than 133 Pa. Measurement of the viscosity of the reaction mass permits the course of the polymerization to be followed. Temperatures above 260 °C lead to excessive rates of degradation. Hoeschele[16] has discussed in detail the synthesis of these polymers by both melt and solid phase polycondensation.

The resulting linear polymers[17] are random segmented copolymers containing PTMOT units as soft segments and multiple 4GT units as hard segments. The polymers exhibit the

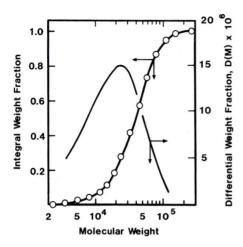

Figure 5   Molecular-weight distribution of polymer containing 58 wt percent tetramethylene
terephthalate (inherent viscosity = 0.15 l/g). Reprinted with permission from ACS Advances in
Chemistry Series 129, 39 (1973), Copyright (1973)
American Chemical Society

expected geometric molecular weight distribution, Figure 5. The copolymers are completely soluble in m-cresol which is a useful solvent for dilute solution polymer characterization.

A more detailed picture of these polymers is provided by Figures 6 and 7. The curves in Figure 6 are calculated, with the average number of segments representing either the hard segments or the soft segments in a polymer having a number average molecular weight of 25,000. The number average molecular weight of the PTMO glycol is 1000 for the polymers described. From Figure 6 it is clear the above 90 wt % 4GT units, the average block length is increasing rapidly and the number of segments per polymer molecular is approaching a region where the polymer is no longer a multi-block copolymer. At some point above 90 %, the product will be a blend of 4GT homopolymer and PTMO-modified 4GT polymer.

Figure 7 presents the calculated block length distribution for a given polymer assuming that equilibrium conditions exist during synthesis and that the resulting polymer is truly random[17]. The distribution was calculated by the method of Frensdorff[18]. At 58 wt % 4GT, the

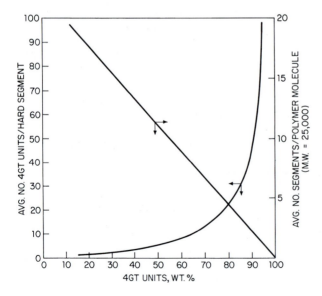

Figure 6   Calculated average hard segment block length and average number of segments/polymer molecule as a function of wt. percent 4GT units in 4GT/PTMO-1000T

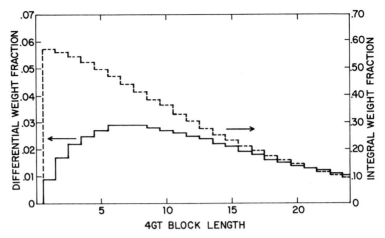

Figure 7   Calculated tetramethylene terephthalate block-length distribution of polymer containing 58 wt percent tetramethylene terephthalate. Reprinted with permission from J. Pol. Sci., Polymer Symposia No. 42, Int. Symp. of Macromol., Helsinki, 1972, No. 2, R. J. Cella, Copyright[©] 1973, John Wiley & Sons, Inc.

polymer on which Figure 7 is based, the average block length is about 7 4GT units and the typical polymer molecule ($\overline{M}_n$=25,000) contains an average of about 9 segments of each type. Figure 7 shows that nearly 45 wt % of the polymer consists of segments having 7 or more 4GT units. This corresponds to about 75 % based only on the weight of 4GT units in the polymer. It follows conversely, that a significant proportion of the hard segments must contain less than the average of seven 4GT units, with some hard segments being so short as to exclude their participation in crystallization. In this connection, Perego, Cesari and Vitali[19] have observed that crystallization is absent in this polymer system when blocks with a length of three or more units of 4GT reach an insignificant level. A consequence of the presence of hard segments having very low block lengths is the joining of two soft segments without the possibility of a tie point existing between them. Thus the block length of the effective hard segments is greater than the calculated average length and the effective length of the soft segments is greater than would be estimated from the molecular weight of the PTMO glycol. These effects help to explain the presence of crystallinity in polymers containing as little as 10 wt % 4GT, where the average block length is less than one 4GT unit[19]. The substitution of PTMO glycol having a higher molecular weight obviously increases both average and actual block lengths of the hard segments and can improve certain properties in polymers with low concentrations of 4GT units. Replacing a portion of the terephthalic acid with a second acid such as isophthalic acid or a portion of the tetramethylene glycol with a second low molecular weight diol, decreases the 4GT hard segment block length. This permits lowering the melting point and reducing the hardness of a polymer while the weight fraction of PTMO glycol is kept constant. The melting points of such mixed polymers are consistent with Flory's predictions.

Evidence of the two-phase structure of this series of polymers has been obtained by differential scanning calorimetry [DSC]. Measurements for polymers varying widely in 4GT content have been made by Cella[20]. Two scans which are typical for this family of polymers are presented in Figure 8. The T_g is characteristic of the amorphous phase which consists of soft segments and amorphous 4GT segments or amorphous portions thereof. The T_m represents melting of the crystalline phase. Both T_g and T_m increase with increasing 4GT content in the polymers due to greater concentrations of amorphous 4GT in the amorphous

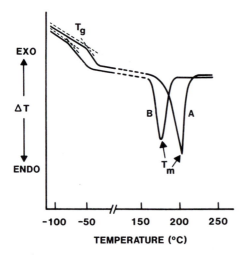

Figure 8   Differential scanning calorimetry curves for A, 4GT/PTMO-1000T (58/42) and B, 4GT/PTMO-1000T (33/67). Reprinted with permission from Reference 46

phase and increased 4GT block length in the crystalline phase. Figure 9 shows the relationship of T_g and T_m to polymer composition[20].

Measurements by dynamic mechanical analysis of the copolyesters based on PTMO-1000 glycol by Lilaonitkul, West and Cooper[21] reveal only a single, relaxation peak in the tan δ curve. The relaxation peak represents the T_g of the amorphous phase. As the concentration of 4GT units increases, the relaxation peak shifts to higher temperatures and broadens significantly. Broadening of the relaxation peak possibly suggests incipient heterogeneity in the amorphous phase of polymers containing more than 80 % 4GT.

The wide angle x-ray diffraction patterns of oriented samples of the block copolyester are identical to the pattern of 4GT homopolymer except for a halo which results from the amorphous phase of the copolymer[20]. These observations are consistent with crystallites being formed exclusively by the 4GT units in the hard segments. Even with the inclusion of a minor amount of a second dicarboxylic acid, such as isophthalic acid, only the 4GT units crystallize[22]. In copolymers where isophthalic acid predominates, the crystalline material is 4GI.

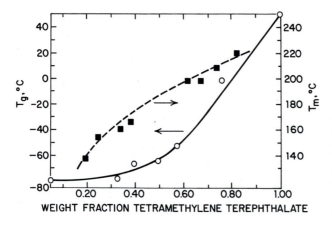

Figure 9   Glass-transition temperature and melting point as a function of 4GT content in 4GT/PTMO-1000T. Reprinted with permission from J. Pol. Sci., Polymer Symposia No. 42, Int. Symp. of Macromol., Helsinki, 1972, No. 2, R. J. Cella, Copyright© 1973, John Wiley & Sons, Inc.

3.2   Crystallinity and Morphology

Cella[20]; Lilaonitikul, West and Cooper[21]; Seymour, Overton and Corley[23]; Wegner, Fugii, Meyer and Lieser[24]; Perego, Cesari and Vitali[19]; and Tanaka, Hiratsuka, Kobayshi and Kitanaka[25] have carried out studies directed to an understanding of the morphology of copolymers having 4GT and PTMOT segments. From a review of this work it is clear, as might be expected, that the supermolecular structure of these polymers depends on many factors including chemical composition, the concentration of nucleating sites and the thermo-mechanical history of the sample. While there are differing view points concerning certain details, it is generally agreed that a lamellar-type morphology in which crystalline lamellae form a more or less continous network extending throughout a continous amorphous phase exists for these polymers. Organization of these lamellae into spherulites under certain conditions has also been observed by most investigators. The formation of spherulites appears to be related to the method of sample preparation, with thermal history being particularly important.

Direct evidence of the lamellar structure is provided by transmission electron micrographs[19, 20]. Figure 10 is a micrograph of a thin cast film stained with phosphotungstic acid[20]. Separate tests show that the stain is preferentially absorbed by the elastomeric phase so that the crystalline material appears as light fibrillar regions in the micrograph. The crystalline lamellae are approximately 100 A in thickness and may be up to several thousand angstroms in length. Micrographs of thin sections of a compression molded sample of copolyester are similar in appearance; however, the crystallites have widths of only 25-30 A and correspondingly shorter lengths. Dimensions of the lamellae in thickness and width appear to be about equal based on many transmission electron micrographs of samples prepared by various procedures and sectioned in several planes[22]. Procedures which provide for slow crystallization such as compression molding, melt casting and solution casting yield larger lamellae, while quenched samples have the smallest lamellae. Organization of lamellae into spherulites having diameters of about 10 µm has been found in melt-cast samples which have

Figure 10 Transmission electron micrograph of solvent-cast polyester elastomer film. Reprinted with permission from J. Pol. Sci., Polymer Symposia No. 42, Int. Symp. of Macromol., Helsinki, 1972, No. 2, R. J. Cella, Copyright© 1973, John Wiley & Sons, Inc.

a thermal history of very slow cooling. Injection-molded samples also exhibit lamellae which are about 60 Å in cross-section and 1000 Å long. The lamellae on the surface of injection-molded samples are arranged substantially parallel to one another, while the lamellae in the interior are smaller and more random in their arrangement.

Examination of oriented and annealed polymer samples by wide-angle X-ray diffraction showed that the repeating 4GT units were aligned parallel to the draw direction. Transmission electron micrographs showed the long axes of the lamellae to be perpendicular to draw direction. Based on these observations, it was concluded that the polymer backbone of 4GT units lies across the crystalline lamellae in a direction perpendicular to the long axes of the lamellae[20]. Figure 11 is a schematic picture which shows the features of the proposed morphology consisting of substantially continous and interpenetrating crystalline and amorphous domains. As drawn, the entire path represents a single polymer molecule. The inclusion of 4GT blocks into more than can crystalline lamella effectively crosslinks the amorphous segments. The diagram indicates that chain folding of longer 4GT segments is possible as is commonly encountered in crystalline homopolymers.

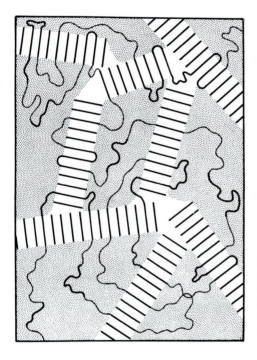

Figure 11   Schematic diagram of the morphology of a copolyester elastomer: (━) 4GT segments; (—) PTMOT segments. Reprinted with permission from J. Pol. Sci., Polymer Symposia No. 42, Int. Symp. of Macromol., Helsinki, 1972, No. 2, R. J. Cella, Copyright© 1973, John Wiley & Sons, Inc.

Cella[20] mentioned the formation of sperulites only for samples prepared by melt casting. Lilaonitkul, West and Cooper[21] observed spherulite formation in compression molded samples and spin-cast films. Seymour, Overton and Corley[23] observed spherulite formation in melt-pressed and solution cast films and in sections of injection-molded bars. Depending on polymer composition and the method of sample preparation, spherulites having diameters of about 2 to 10 μm were observed. The picture suggested in Figure 11 appears to be useful in considering the structure of the copolyester even when spherulites form. Obviously, the lamellar crystallites would be arranged with reference to the radii of the spherulite. However, the possibility of a single polymer molecule meandering from one to another crystallite still exists and the voids between crystallites must be filled with an amorphous mixture of soft segments and uncrystallized 4GT units. Hence, the lamellae would still be effectively linked to one another to provide a network structure.

Long period spacing was determined by small-angle X-ray scattering (SAXS) by several investigators[19, 22, 24]. The long period spacing is assumed to be the distance between crystalline lamellae; i. e., the sum of the thickness of a lamella and the thickness of the amorphous region between lamellae. In rapidly cooled samples the long period spacing is substantially constant at about 130 Å for hard copolyesters containing more than 50 wt % 4GT units. Long term spacing increases for softer polymers up to about 200 Å for polymers in which the concentration of 4GT units is decreasing toward 10 wt %. Annealing causes substantial increases in long term spacing regardless of polymer composition, possibly due to thickening of the lamellae[22]. A sample containing about 50 wt %4GT units had a long term spacing of 274 Å after annealing at a temperature 2 °C below its melting point[24]. Allowing for the thickness of the crystalline lamellae, this distance is so large that several sequences of hard and soft blocks are required to cross the amorphous region between crystalline lamallae.

Surprisingly, a composition containing only 5 wt % 4GT units yielded a SAXS peak even though there was no indication of crystallinity in the sample based on wide-angle X-ray scattering (WAXS) or density measurements. Some ordering in the amorphous phase of hard segments too short to crystallize may explain this observation[19].

It is also interesting to note that an annealed sample having a long-term spacing of 180 Å, when drawn to 5 times its initial length at 25 °C, failed to give a defined SAXS pattern. However, if the stretched sample was annealed at the same temperature used for the undrawn sample, the original long term spacing was observed and the SAXS pattern indicated substantially complete orientation of the crystallites. It appears that cold drawing essentially destroys the original crystalline structure of the polymer[24]. This does not necessarily mean that no crystalline structure exists in cold drawn polymer because cold flow would occur in the absence of some restraining force.

Several investigators have measured the degree of crystallinity in series of copolyesters varying in composition[19, 21, 24, 25]. Measurements employing differential scanning calorimetry[21,24], WAXS[19] and density[19,24] methods have been employed. The results of several of these studies have been compiled by Perego et al.[19] and are presented graphically in Figure 12. An explanation of the units used in Reference 19 is required. This paper describes the composition of copolyesters in terms of W_S, the weight fraction of soft segments, and W_H, the weight fraction of hard segments. These terms differ from conventional descriptions of long chain and short chain ester units in that they recognize that a long

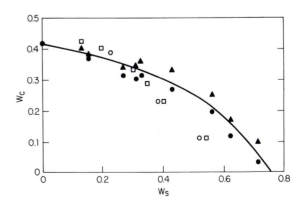

Figure 12   Weight fraction of crystalline 4GT, W_C, as a function of the weight fraction of soft segments, W_S; from density (▲); from WAXS (●); from DSC, References 21 (□) and 24 (○). Reprinted with permission from J. Appl. Polym. Sci., G. Perego, M. Cesari and R. Vitali[19], Copyright© 1984, John Wiley & Sons, Inc.

chain ester unit as conventionally written, PTMOT, contains a 4GT unit consisting of the terminal terphthaloyl radical and the adjacent tetramethylene oxide unit in the PTMO chain. Thus W_S represents the weight fraction of PTMO units reduced by one tetramethylene oxide unit per PTMO unit. W_H represents the fraction of 4GT units conventionally recognized increased by one 4GT unit per PTMO unit. In dealing with theoretical considerations, the description of composition used by Reference 19 probably is preferred because the conventional long chain ester unit includes a crystallizable 4GT unit. A similar situation exists for polymers based on ethylene glycol in combination with poly(ethylene oxide) glycol.

Figure 13 relates the crystallinity of 4GT units to the fraction of soft segments (Curve B). Curve A is a plot of the ratio of the weight of crystalline 4GT units, W_C, to the weight of hard segments having more than 3 4GT units, $W_H(>3)$; versus the weight fraction of soft segments, W_S. The weight fraction of hard segments containing more than three 4GT units, $W_H(>3)$, was calculated according to Sorta and Melis[26] assuming infinite chain length. Relative to 4GT homopolymer, the fraction of crystalline 4GT is greater for the copolyesters up to about 0.65 W_S. Beyond that point, the degree of crystallinity falls rapidly toward zero for a polymer containing 0.76 W_S. The disappearance of crystallinity corresponds to a polymer in which $W_H(>3)$ is approaching zero.

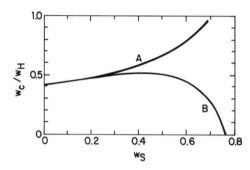

Figure 13   Fraction of 4GT units which are crystalline as a function of the weight fraction of soft segments; curve A, W_C/W_H and curve B, $W_C/W_H(>3)$. Reprinted with permission from J. Appl. Polym. Sci., G. Perego, M. Cesari and R. Vitali[19], Copyright© 1984, John Wiley & Sons, Inc.

From Curve A it is obvious that as the concentration of hard segments having greater than three 4GT units decreases, the crystallinity of such segments increases and approaches unity. As possible explanations for the high crystallinity of 4GT units in copolyesters, increased mobility of hard segments in the presence of soft segments and a driving force due to incompatibility of the segments have been proposed[21].

3.3   Orientation and Stress-Strain Behavior

The commercially important copolyesters based on PTMO glycol and containing about 30-90 wt % 4GT units exhibit largely reversible deformation at very low strain levels below 10 %. With increasing levels of strain up to about 300 %, significant orientation occurs and is accompanied by an irreversible disruption of the crystalline matrix. Samples strained to these intermediate levels exhibit considerable permanent set. At strains beyond about 300 % only very limited increases in orientation occur and the stress in transmitted primarily by the rubbery amorphous phase until the sample breaks.

Figure 14 is a stress-strain curve for a medium hardness copolyester at low strain rate[20]. The high initital modulus in region I results from largely reversible deformation of the interpenetrating crystalline matrix. In region II, the crystalline matrix is disrupted and orientation

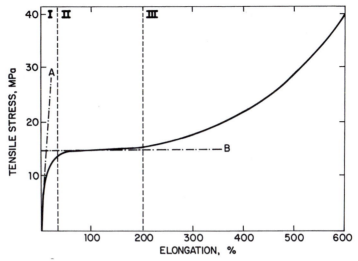

Figure 14   Stress-strain curve for polyester elastomer 4GT/PTMO-1000T (58/42); A, slope = Young's modulus; B, yield stress. Reprinted with permission from J. Pol. Sci., Polymer Symposia No. 42, Int. Symp. of Macromol., Helsinki, 1972, No. 2, R. J. Cella, Copyright© 1973, John Wiley & Sons, Inc.

occurs. In region III, the sample behaves much like a cured elastomer. Figure 15 presents stress-strain curves for a series of copolyesters containing increasing amounts of 4GT units[20]. Both the initial modulus and the yield stress increase with increasing concentrations of crystallizable 4GT units, lending support to the proposal that the initial modulus and the

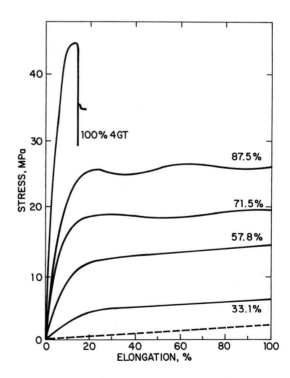

Figure 15   Stress-strain curves of polyester elastomers containing increasing concentrations of 4GT units; strain rate, 0.5 %/min.; (--), typical neoprene vulcanizate. Reprinted with permission from J. Pol. Sci., Polymer Symposia No. 42, Int. Symp. of Macromol., Helsinki, 1972, No. 2, R. J. Cella, Copyright© 1973, John Wiley & Sons, Inc.

yield stress are related to the crystalline matrix. The harder polymers display erratic draw behavior reminiscent of crystalline homopolymers. Necking of the polymers may occur during drawing depending on strain rate and temperature.

Cella studied the degree of orientation in copolyester fibers as a function of elongation by means of wide-angle X-ray diffraction[20]. The results are shown in Figure 16, where orientation angle is defined as the angular half width of the wide-angle X-ray pattern. An isotropic sample yielding circular diffraction rings would correspond to an orientation angle of 180 °. The circular arcs diminish in angular width as orientation increases, so that a perfectly oriented smaple would have an orientation angle approaching zero. Up to about 300 % elongation, substantial increases in orientation take place, but beyond that the increase in orientation is limited.

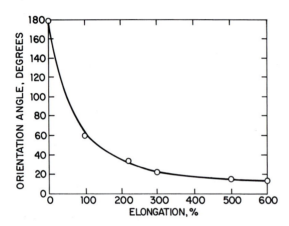

Figure 16   Orientation angle as a function of sample elongation for 4GT/PTMO-1000T (58/42). Reprinted with permission from J. Pol. Sci., Polymer Symposia No. 42, Int. Symp. of Macromol., Helsinki, 1972, No. 2, R. J. Cella, Copyright© 1973, John Wiley & Sons, Inc.

Orientation of several copolyesters differing in 4GT content has been studied by means of infrared dichroism[21]. With this technique it is possible to calculate separate orientation functions, f, for the $C=O$ groups and the C-H groups in the copolyester[27]. These functions have a value of 1.0 for perfect orientation in the stretch direction and -0.5 for perfect transverse orientation. For random orientation the function has a value of zero. The $C=O$ group orientation function appears to be primarily representative of the crystalline 4GT units, but it must be remembered that uncrystallized 4GT units are present in the amorphous phase as well. Likewise, the C-H orientation function is not restricted to the soft segments in the amorphous phase because of the tetramethylene radicals in the 4GT units.

Figure 17 shows the relationship of orientation functions to elongation for copolyesters containing 33,50 and 63 wt % 4GT units. The measurements were made on films which were spin cast from 1,1,2-trichloroethane and possessed a spherulitic morphology. At low extension all of the samples show negative $C=O$ orientation, presumably related to crystalline hard segments. The $C=O$ orientation function is positive at high elongations. The C-H orientation function is always positive. When these measurements were repeated on nonspherulitic samples prepared by casting from chloroform, both $f_{C=O}$ and f_{C-H} were always positive. It has been postulated that the initial negative orientation observed in copolyesters having a spherulitic morphology results from deformation of spherulites which causes the crystalline lamellae to orient as a unit in the stretch direction. Orientation of the crystalline lamellae parallel to the stretch direction would orient the 4GT backbone perpendicular to the stretch direction. With increased elongation, disruption of lamellae apparently becomes the predominate mode of orientation and the orientation function is positive. In samples

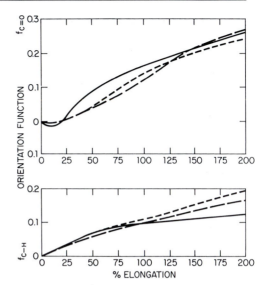

Figure 17   Hard and soft segment orientation functions as a function of elongation for 4GT/PTMO-1000T (x/100-x) for (---) x = 33, (--) x = 50, and (—) x = 63. Reprinted from Reference 21, p. 589 by courtesy of Marcel Dekker, Inc.

having a nonspherulitic morphology, orientation of lamellae as such apparently is not significant compared to disruption of the lamellae even at low extensions.

As previously mentioned, copolyester samples strained to intermediate levels exhibit considerable permanent set when relaxed. Figure 18 presents stress-strain curves for increasing cyclic deformations of a spin-cast sample containing 50 wt % 4GT units[21]. Clearly permanent set increases with increasing strain. It is further noted that subsequent straining results in lower stress at elongations below those previously applied and that at strain levels beyond those previously applied stress levels are essentially independent of the prestraining. Irreversible disruption of the crystalline matrix appears to account for the stress softening observed for these polymers.

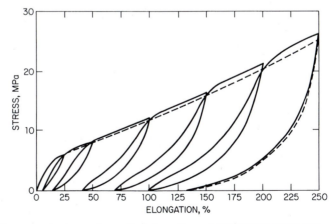

Figure 18   Stress-strain curves for successive increasing cyclic deformations of 4GT/PTMO-1000T (50/50); (--) control single strain cycle. Reprinted from Reference 21, p. 591 by courtesy of Marcel Dekker, Inc.

4   PROPERTIES OF COMMERCIAL THERMO-PLASTIC POLYESTER ELASTOMERS

4.1   Mechanical Properties

A rather complete complitation of mechanical properties, chemical properties and processing information for commercial polyester elastomers can be found in Chapter 4 of the "Handbook of Thermoplastic Elastomers", Benjamin M. Walker, Van Nostrad Reinhold Company (1979). For the purposes of the present chapter, specific details will be omitted and properties will be discussed in general terms only.

Commercial thermoplastic polyester elastomers are available in Shore D hardnesses ranging from 35 to above 75. In terms of hardness, stiffness and resilience, these elastomers bridge the gap between cured elastomers and rigid plastics. Their stress-strain properties in tension have already been discussed and their behavior toward compression and shear is similiar in that distortion from low strains is largely reversible, while higher strains result in permanent distortion. All hardness grades have solenoid brittle temperatures below -70 °C. Surprisingly, a polymer containing 95 % 4GT units exhibits a brittle temperature below -40 °C while 4GT homopolymer has a brittle temperature of 0 °C[13]. All grades exhibit good resistance to impact in the notched Izod test, with the softer grades not breaking even at -40 °C. The softer grades have outstanding resistance to flex cut growth.

4.2   Melt Rheology

The apparent melt viscosity of polyester elastomers decreases only to a limited extent with increasing shear rate. This is particularly true at low shear rates. Figure 19 compares the melt viscosities of 55D polyester (58 wt % 4GT) and a thermoplastic polyurethane of equal hardness[28]. The two curves presented for the polyester at different temperatures give an indication of the temperature dependence of the melt viscosity of the polyester. The polyurethane melt viscosity is obviously more shear sensitive. Because of their low melt viscosity at low shear, the polyester elastomers are readily used in low shear procedures such as calendering, impregnation of porous substrates, melt casting and rotational molding.

Blow molding of standard grades of polyester elastomers suitable for extrusion or injection molding is difficult to carry out because of their low melt viscosity, low melt tension and low die swell. Methods suggested to improve these properties to levels sufficient to facilitate

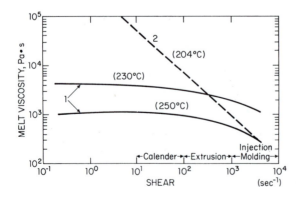

Figure 19   Melt viscosity as a function of shear rate; **1**, copolyester elastomer, 58 % 4GT, 55 Shore D hardness, and **2**, thermoplastic polyesterurethane, 55 Shore D hardness. Reprinted with permission from Reference 46

blow molding have included increasing the molecular weight to high levels by solid phase polycondensation[29], branching during polymer preparation with polyfunctional ester-forming monomers[30], branching of finished polymer by adding controlled amounts of polycarbodiimides[31], polyisocyanates[32] or polyepoxides[33] for end-group reactions and adding sodium salts of aliphatic polycarboxylic acids which form ionic crosslinks with carboxyl end-groups in the polymer[34, 35]. A variety of compositions suitable for blow molding are commercially available.

4.3 Degradation and Stabilization of Polyester Elastomers

In the absence of antioxidants copolyester elastomers are rapidly degraded in air at elevated temperatures[36]. Typically, the drop in inherent viscosity is accompanied by a dramatic increase in the acidity of the polymer, Figure 20. Upon exposing an unstabilized copolyester containing about 58 % 4GT units and PTMO-1000T soft segments to an air stream at 150 °C, Hoeschele found that formic acid was formed as a secondary oxidation product. By incorporation of selected substituted phenolic or secondary aromatic amine antioxidants significant improvement in heat aging is obtained. The addition of a costabilizer containing –NH–(C=X)– linkages (X = O, S, NH) which are capable of reacting with formaldehyde, the precursor of formic acid, greatly prolongs the useful life of polymers stabilized with either amine or phenolic antioxidants. Suitable costabilizers are polyamides[37], polyurethanes[38] and polyureas[39]. Low melting co- and terpolyamides are preferred since they can be readily admixed with the molten polyester. Maximum protection is provided by a secondary aromatic amine antioxidant and a terpolyamide. Following the same reasoning, it has been found that phenolic antioxidants with amide linkages provide superior protection with reference to other phenolic antioxidants[40].

The polyester elastomers are also subject to oxidative degradation when exposed to ultra violet light. In applications where a black stock is acceptable, the addition of carbon black at

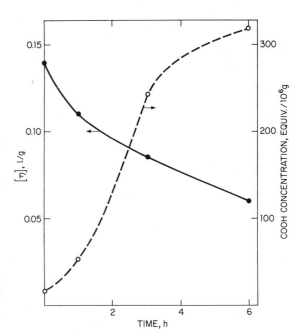

Figure 20   Inherent viscosity and carboxyl content of an unstabilized copolyester elastomer as a function of aging time at 150 °C. Reprinted with permission from Reference 36

0.5 to 3.0 % is very effective as a uv screen. For white or light colored stocks typical uv-absorbers such as substituted benzotriazoles, either alone or in combination with phosphite esters, are useful[41]. Derivatives of 2,2,6,6-tetramethyl-4-piperidinyl alcohol or the corresponding N-methyl derivatives have been shown to provide excellent protection against degradation by light in white or light-colored polyester elastomers; however, the presence of most of these derivatives is highly detrimental to heat aging even in the presence of increased amounts of antioxidants. Pentamethyl-4-piperidinyl esters of malonic acid with one or two 3,5-di-tert-butyl-4-hydroxybenzyl substituents do not reduce thermal stability significantly[42].

Because of their polar nature, polyester elastomers are permeable to water and are subject to degradation by hydrolysis at elevated temperatures even though the rate is much less than that for a polymer containing aliphatic acid ester groups such as a polyesterurethane. The addition of 1 or 2 % of a hindered aromatic polycarbodiimide increases the useful service life of polyester elastomers several fold in the presence of hot water or steam[31].

The melt stability of the polyester elastomers is quite adequate for normal processing. However, in situations where higher than normal processing temperatures and times may be needed; e. g., filling a large mold by melt casting, the melt stability can be improved by incorporating a minor amount of a polyepoxide[33]. The polyepoxide reacts at least partially with carboxyl end-groups already present in the polyester as well as additional carboxyl groups formed by degradation of the melt.

5   STRUCTURAL VARIATIONS

5.1 Hard Segment Modifications

The discussion of commercial thermoplastic polyester elastomers has focused largely on the system of polymers containing 4GT units and PTMO-1000T units in varying amounts. The effects of replacing butanediol with other low molecular weight diols, terephthalic acid partially or completely with other diacids and PTMO-1000 with other soft segments are considered in this section.

As a preliminary to this discussion it is worth noting that the lamellar-network type morphology which was found for the commercial polyesters[20] has been observed for polymers in which (a) tetramethylene glycol was replaced by ethylene glycol, (b) terephthalic acid was replaced by 2,6-naphthalene dicarboxylic acid or (c) PTMO glycol was replaced by poly(1,2-propylene oxide) glycol (PPO)[22]. The same type morphology also has been observed in polymers in which 50 % of the terephthalic acid was replaced by isophthalic acid, with only the 4GT crystallizing on the basis of wide-angle X-ray diffraction studies.

In the course of developing relatively soft polyester elastomers which have outstanding tear strength at high tearing rates, Witsiepe[11, 17] prepared a series of polymers based on mixtures of diacids in which terephthalic acid predominated. The compositions and properties of these polymers are presented in Table I along with two control polymers containing only 4GT units[17]. The tables has been modified by including the calculated average 4GT block length assuming that the polymers are random.

Based on the average hard segment length, it is reasonable to assume that the weight fraction of crystalline 4GT in the samples containing mixed acids is lower than the weight

TABLE I   Physical Properties of 4TG/PTMO−1000T Polymers Containing a Second Short Chain Ester Group[a]

4GT Weight Fraction	0.40	0.40	0.40	0.40	0.50	0.40
Second short chain ester, weight fraction	0.10	0.10	0.10	0.10	—	—
Second short chain ester, structure	4G10	4GP	4GI	4GTP	—	—
Average 4GT block length	2.18	2.03	2.03	2.56	5.14	3.42
η_{inh}, l/g	0.16	0.17	0.18	0.19	0.16	0.16
Stress at 100%, MPa	7.2	7.2	7.6	8.3	12.4	8.3
Stress at 300%, MPa	8.6	9.1	9.8	11.9	15.2	11.0
Tensile strength, MPa	30.9	46.0	51.3	50.7	51.0	17.2
Elongation at break, %	860	760	780	520	780	730
Split tear strength, kN/m	26.3	33.3	38.5	114	50.8	26.3
Clash-Berg $T_{10,000}$, °C	−53	−46	−44	−10	−26	−52
Shore D hardness	41	43	40	49	49	44
Compression set B, (22 h/70°C), %	54	45	70	80	54	53

4G10 = tetramethylene sebacate
4GP = tetramethylene phthalate
4GI = tetramethylene isophthalate
4GTP = tetramethylene m-terphenyl-4,4″-dicarboxylate

[a] Reprinted with permission from ACS Advances in Chemical Series 129, 39 (1973); Copyright 1973 American Chemical Society

fraction of crystalline 4GT in the control containing 40 % 4GT units. Conversely, the proportion of amorphous short chain ester units must be higher in the mixed acid polymers, especially when expressed relative to total amorphous material. From Reference 19 it is possible to estimate the crystalline weight fraction in the two control polymers only 4GT hard segments which is 0.26 for the 40 % 4GT polymer and 0.31 for the 50 % 4GT polymer. From these values it follows that there is about a 20 % increase in the amount of crystalline 4GT in the 50 % polymer relative to the 40 % polymer. At the same time, there is a 45 % increase in the amount of amorphous 4GT based solely on total amorphous material for the 50 % polymer relative to the 40 % polymer.

Returning to Table I, it appears that modulus at 100 % is largely a function of 4GT content (or more correctly a function of the degree of crystallinity). The same is approximately true for the 300 % modulus. The behavior of the polymers with regard to properties involving rupture follows a different pattern which appears to depend on the composition of the amorphous material in the polymers. For those polymers in which there are a relatively high proportion of amorphous short chain ester units, tensile and tear strengths are quite high. These observations are consistent with the poor rupture properties observed for polymers containing only 4GT short chain ester units at concentrations less than about 40 wt %. The properties of these soft polymers containing only 4GT units is highly dependent on their molecular weight and most of their poor properties can be remedied by going to high molecular weights ($\eta_{inh} > 1.9$). However, their tear strength at high tear rates remains poor. Moreover, it is not commercially practical to prepare polymers of such high molecular weight.

The use of mixed acids in preparing the softer polyesters has numerous advantages. All of the properties involving rupture are improved. At a constant 4GT content, the hardness and low temperature stiffness are not significantly changed with the addition of a second acid unless it forms ester units having a high T_g. Resistance to solvents is improved. The properties of polymers based on mixed acids are not highly dependent on molecular weight so that valuable polymers can be prepared readily on a commercial scale. The only significant disadvantages associated with polymers based on mixed acids are their lower melting points and slower rates of crystallization which can make processing more difficult. It should be noted that the effects of using mixed acids are also observed when mixtures of low molecular weight diols; e. g., tetramethylene and trimethylene glycols, are used. However, it is more difficult to control the amount of a second diol which actually enters the polymer because of differing reactivities and volatilities for these monomers.

With the exception of solvent resistance, the use of a second acid or diol provides only limited improvements in properties for polymers containing 50 % or more 4GT units. This is not surprising in view of the above observations, because increased concentrations of 4GT units lead to rapidly increasing concentrations of both crystalline and amorphous 4GT units.

Wolfe[43] has prepared a series of polyester elastomers based on terephthalic acid and PTMO-1000 glycol in which the low molecular weight diol was varied. The properties of these polymers listed in Table II show that both the 2G-based and 4G-based polymers are substantially equivalent in the physical properties listed. This conclusion is supported by another comparative study of slightly harder polymers[44]. The results for the 3G-based polymer are the most surprising. The 3G polymer is very similar to the 2G and 4G polymers except for properties involving rupture of the polymer. The marked deficiency of the tensile and tear strengths of the 3G-based polymer has not been explained. Wolfe has suggested that these results may be related to the findings of other investigators who studied oriented fibers of 2GT, 3GT and 4GT homopolymers in which 3GT crystalline regions were found to respond differently to strain-induced deformation than did 2GT or 4GT crystalline regions[45]. The physical properties of the polymers based on 5G, 6G and 10G are generally inferior to those observed for the polymers based on the lower glycols.

TABLE II   50% Alkylene Terephthalate/PTMO−1000 Terephthalate Copolymers − Properties as a Function of Diol Structure[a]

Diol	2G	3G	4G	5G	6G	10G
Copolymer properties						
Inherent viscosity, l/g	0.13	0.17	0.18	0.16	0.15	0.13
Yield strength, MPa	—	—	—	4.8	—	—
Stress at 100%, MPa	11.4	11.7	11.7	4.5	5.2	6.1
Tensile strength, MPa	45.5	22.8	48.4	15.4	13.5	15.5
Elongation at break, %	675	660	755	880	750	640
Permanent set, %	275	195	370	210	370	370
Split tear strength, kN/m	42	15	48	25	18	7.8
Shore D hardness	46	48	48	32	33	35
Compression set B, %	52	48	52	90	86	81
Class-Berg $T_{10,000}$, °C	−38	−36	−33	−50	−53	−51
Melting point, °C	224	198	189	106	122	106

[a] Reprinted with permission from ACS Advances in Chemical Series 176, 129 (1979); Copyright 1979 American Chemical Society

Based solely on the data in Table II, it would be difficult to choose between 2GT and 4GT based polyester elastomers. The selection of 4GT based polyester elastomers for commercialization involved consideration of other factors; namely, rate of crystallization and to a lesser extent, ease of synthesis of high molecular weight polymers. The 2GT based polymers also have lower moduli at strain levels below 100 %[44]. This is considered to result from a lower degree of crystallinity. Figure 21 compares the hardening rate for 2GT and 4GT based elastomers of about the same hardness[46]. The 4GT based polymer reaches its final hardness almost immediately, while the 2GT based polymer is still increasing in hardness a day and a

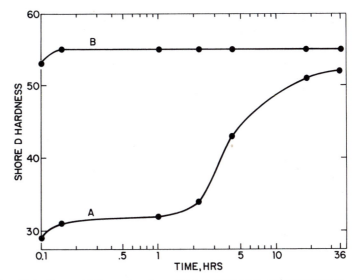

Figure 21   Hardening rate of injection-molded samples of copolyester elastomers; melt temperature, 240 °C; mold temperature, 30 °C; (A), 2GT/PTMO-1000T (56/44); (B), 4GT/PTMO-1000T (58/42). Reprinted with permission from Reference 46

half later. The very rapid hardening rate of 4GT based polyester elastomers facilitates operations such as short cycle injection molding in unheated molds. While the molding of the 2GT based elastomer can be improved with nucleating agents and heated molds, it still does not begin to approach the ease of processing which exists for 4GT based elastomers.

Wolfe[43] also prepared a number of polyester elastomers from tetramethylene glycol and PTMO-1000 in which terephthalic acid was replaced by other dicarboxylic acids. The properties of some of these polymers are presented in Table III. Where rupture is involved

TABLE III   Physical Properties of 50% 4G Dicarboxylate/50% PTMO-1000 Dicarboxylate Copolyesters[a]

	4GT	4GI	4G2,6-N	4GTP
η_{inh}, l/g	0.18	0.16	0.15	0.17
Stress at 100%, MPa	11.7	7.2	10.0	2.8
Tensile strength, MPa	48.4	58.6	51.0	60.3
Elongation at break, %	755	720	660	390
Permanent set, %	370	126	280	3
Split tear strength, kN/m	48	54	117	47
Shore D hardness	48	39	49	31
Compression Set B, (22 hr/70°C), %	52	91	49	100+
Clash-Berg $T_{10,000}$, °C	−33	−31	−14	2
Melting point, °C	189	85/112	202	—

T   = terephthalate
I   = isophthalate
2,6-N = 2,6-naphthalene dicarboxylate
TP   = m-terphenyl-4,4-dicarboxylate

[a] Reprinted with permission after ACS Advances Chemical Series 176, 129 (1979); Copyright 1979 American Chemical Society

the polymer based on isophthalic acid has better physical properties than the terephthalate based control. However, the isophthalate-based elastomer requires several hours to crystallize and in view of its modulus at 100 % strain contains less crystalline material than does the terephthalate control. The percent crystallinity after annealing has been reported as 13 % for 4GI homopolymer versus 39 % for 4GT homopolymer[47]. The presence of a high concentration of amorphous 4GI units may be related to the good rupture properties of the isophthalate polymer. This would be consistent with Witsiepe's observations for polymers derived from mixed diacids.

The elastomer based on 2,6-naphtalene dicarboxylic acid also has excellent properties in general but poorer low temperature stiffening characteristics. The tear strength of the material is more than double that of the terephthalate polymer. Wolfe has prepared the full series of elastomers using 2G through 10G diols in combination with 2,6-naphthalene dicarboxylic acid and PTMO-1000 glycol and all of these polymers exhibit surprisingly good properties[43]. One is reminded of the exceptional properties of polyurethanes based on symmetrical napthalene diisocyanates.

The elastomer prepared from m-terphenyl dicarboxylic acid is slow crystallizing and the values in Table III represent its properties shortly after molding. The polymer is transparent and does not exhibit a melting point. After the polymer is aged for 28 days it is opaque and shows two DSC endotherms at 63° and 158 °C. The 100 % modulus and hardness of the polymer increase upon crystallization, but tensile strength, elongation at break and permanent set remain substantially unchanged. The very low permanent set of 3 % for both samples is most surprising. Wolfe suggested the existence of a glassy hard segment phase to explain the good properties of the uncrystallized polymer. Since permanent set is not increased after crystallization, it must be concluded that the crystallites in this polymer are not disrupted at high elongations.

5.2 Polyether Soft Segment Modification

In a separate study, Wolfe[48] investigated the effects of changing the molecular weight and structure of the ether segment in polyester elastomers. Table IV lists the properties of 4GT-based elastomers containing PTMO-1000, poly(1,2-propylene oxide)-1000 (PPO-1000), poly(ethylene oxide)-1000 (PEO-1000) and ethylene oxide-capped poly(propylene oxide) (EOPPO-1000) soft segments. It should be noted that the data do not take into consideration the fact that each of the soft segments in the PTMO glycol-based elastomer contains a crystallizable 4GT unit[19]. For this reason the 4GT content is actually higher than 57 % for the PTMO glycol-based elastomer. The table has been modified by including the properties of a PPO-1000 glycol-based elastomer prepared by solid phase polymerization by Hoeschele[29]. The secondary hydroxyl groups in PPO glycol are only slowly esterified and the resulting ester groups are thermally labile. As a result, high molecular weight elastomers base on PPO glycol cannot be made by melt condensation. The same problems exist to a lesser extent for EOPPO glycol, because ethylene oxide capping does not convert all of the secondary hydroxyls end groups of the PPO glycol to primary hydroxyl groups unless the amount of ethylene oxide used is excessive. Table IV shows that elastomers based on PTMO-1000, PEO-1000 and PPO-1000 are similar in properties when compared at similar inherent viscosities. However, the PTMO-based polymer has the highest tensile and tear strengths. The EOPPO-1000 polymer appears to be equivalent to the PPO-1000 polymer having about the same inherent viscosity. Undoubtedly the properties of the EOPPO polymer would be improved by increasing its molecular weight. Wolfe investigated the hydrolytic stability of these polymers and found the PTMO and PPO elastomers to be about equivalent and much more resistant to hydrolysis than the PEO-based polymer. The PEO

TABLE IV   57% 4GT/Polyether-T Copolymers: Properties as a Function of Polyether Structure[a]

			Polyether Glycol		
	PTMO	PEO	PPO	PPO	EOPPO[b]
Polyether glycol, MW	975	985	1005	1000	1150
Copolymer properties					
η_{inh}, l/g	0.17	0.17	0.09	0.17	0.11
Stress at 100%, MPa	13.4	13.2	11.7	14.5	11.7
Tensile strength, MPa	47.2	42.6	27.2	42.1	32.4
Elongation, %	660	705	640	600	675
Permanent set, %	365	190	355	—	350
Tear strength, kN/m	62	31	18	56	23

[a] Reprinted with permission after Rubber Chem. and Techn.[48]
[b] 15 wt. % of ethylene oxide units

polymer has a water swell about 10 times that of the PTMO polymer. With regard to oil swell, the PEO polymer is better because it is more polar[49].

In harder polymers containing 76 wt % 4GT, the PTMO-1000 based elastomer is similar to elastomers based on PEO-1000, PPO-1000 and EOPPO-1000 except for a much higher tear strength. When the four glycols are compared in a soft elastomer based on a mixture of terephthalic and isophthalic acid (40 % 4GT/10 % 4GI/50 % poly(alkylene oxide)-1000T/I), the PTMO-1000-based polymer has much better tensile and tear strengths while the stress at 100 % elongation is substantially the same for all polymers.

The properties of polyester elastomers are also influenced by the molecular weight and molecular weight distribution of the polyether soft segments and by the relative proportions of hard and soft segments. Increasing either the molecular weight of the soft segment or the concentration of short chain ester units increases the hard segment chain length. With increasing segment lengths for any given set of reactants, a region is approached where the hard and soft segments are no longer compatible with one another under the conditions of melt condensation. As previously mentioned, this leads to a condition known as melt phasing. Phasing can be very marginal in its effects at the borderline of incompatibility, but it can have profound effects when the segments become highly incompatible. With severe phasing, two liquid phases exist, each of which has a significant volume fraction. One phase is rich in soft segments; the other, ester hard segments. Not surprisingly, when these polymer blends are isolated, they exhibit two glass transition temperatures and two melting points[50]. With marginal phasing, physical and mechanical properties of the resulting polyester do not deviate significantly from the properties anticipated by extrapolation from the properties of polymers just outside the borderline for phasing. With severe phasing, the resulting products have low tensile and tear strengths and are short breaking. For a given hard segment concentration, the tendency for phasing to occur is greatest for PPO glycol, least for PEO glycol with PTMO glycol being intermediate. This is the order which would be predicted from the calculated solubility parameters of the three polymeric glycols versus that of 4GT[51]. Solubility parameters also suggest that phasing would be more likely to occur with 2GT hard segments than with 4GT hard segments and this has been confirmed experimentally[51].

For the commercially important polymers based on 4GT and PTMO the relationship of polymer composition and PTMO molecular weight to phasing is shown in Figure 22[52]. While no phasing occurs with PTMO-1000, it can been seen that phasing does occur in polymers containing less than about 65 % soft segments when PTMO-2000 having a broad molecular weight distribution, representative of the typical commercial product, is used. No phasing is observed in these polymers when specially prepared PTMO-2000 glycol having a relatively

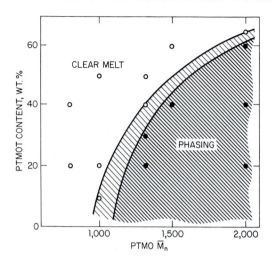

Figure 22   Melt phasing in polycondensations as a function of PTMOT content and PTMO glycol $\overline{M}_n$; (O), clear melt or incipient phasing; (●) melt phasing. Reprinted with permission from Reference 52

narrow molecular weight distribution is used[8]. Since both PEO and PPO glycols have very narrow molecular weight distributions as normally manufactured, control of molecular weight distribution is of no value in avoiding phasing with these glycols. This very narrow distribution may partially explain the absence of phasing with PEO of a molecular weight as high as 4000.

The phasing phenomena which have just been discussed involve the immiscibility of two liquid phases. It seems likely that another type of phasing is possible when the melting point of the homopolymer corresponding to the hard segments is well above the temperature of the melt condensation. Clearly crystallization of such hard segments during the polycondensation is possible once the segment length is great enough. In this situation the chances of phasing would be increased by higher hard segment concentrations and higher polyether glycol molecular weight. Phasing of this type appears to have been encountered by Wolfe[43] in the preparation of elastomers based on 1,4-cyclohexanedimethylene terephthalate [CHDMT] or tetramethylene 4,4'-biphenyldicarboxylate hard segments. The resulting products were short breaking or brittle and not fully soluble in m-cresol, the usual solvent for inherent viscosity determinations. This type of phasing may have been encountered by Bell, Kibler and Smith[7] who also worked with polymers based on CHDMT short chain ester units. Phasing caused by crystallization of hard segments can be alleviated by adding a second diacid or diol to lower the melting point of the hard segments. This procedure would be expected to be of little value in avoiding liquid-liquid phasing unless the second monomer significantly reduced the solubility parameter of the hard segments.

Returning to the effect of polyether glycol molecular weight on polyester elastomers it is found that the relationship is much simpler for elastomers based on polyether glycols having relatively low molecular weights from about 400 to 700. Compared to polymers made from polyethers having molecular weights around 1000, these elastomers show much higher tear strengths, but poor resistance to stiffening at low temperatures while other properties are similar[48]. The T_g of these materials is also higher which is not surprising in view of the observed stiffening behavior[50]. Polymers based on PTMO glycol have better properties than those based on PEO or PPO glycols. The cause of stiffening and improved tear strength probably can be ascribed to a higher concentration of amorphous 4GT in the amorphous phase of these polymers. The shorter path lengths between hard segments may reduce the mobility of hard segments so that they are less likely to enter into crystallites. Phasing has not been observed for any of the polymers based on low molecular weight polyethers. These polymers all exhibit a single T_g and T_m and except for polymers containing very high concentrations of 4GT (about 80 %), the transitions in the DMA scans are sharp, indicating a high compatibility of hard and soft segments within the amorphous phase[50].

In the mid-range of polyether molecular weights, including polymers based on glycols having molecular weights of about 1000, elastomers are obtained which have a good balance of properties. Polymers based on PTMO glycol again excel in properties compared with other polyether glycols. In this intermediate region, elastomers generally have one melting point and one transition which covers a moderately broad temperature range, indicative of some incompatibility. Polymers approaching the borderline where phasing occurs have been observed to have two melting points and show extreme broadening of the β-transition even though they give clear melts. Shih and McKenna[50] have suggested that phasing may occur in these transparent melts with the two separated phases being too finely divided to scatter light or alternatively, separation of phases may occur when the polymer is cooled for isolation.

5.3 Hydrocarbon Soft Segments

Soft segments with a hydrocarbon backbone, terminated with either carboxyl or hydroxyl groups can be used to prepare polyester elastomers. Hoeschele investigated 4GT-based polyester elastomers in which PTMO glycol was replaced with dimer acid[36, 53]. As part of this work, polymers of equal hardness based on PTMO-glycol and dimer acid were compared. For the dimer acid polymer, an ester unit derived from 1 mole of butanediol and 1 mole of dimer acid is considered to be the soft segment. Dimer acid is a mixture of C_{36} alkyl substituted cyclohexenedicarboxylic acids formed by dimerization of C_{18} unsaturated monocarboxylic acids. The dimer acid used in this work was a highly refined commercial product which had been hydrogenated and was substantially free of monomer and trimer fractions. Based on its acid equivalent, a molecular weight of 565 was used for the dimer acid. Table V presents the properties for the two polymers.

TABLE V   Effect of Soft Segment on Physical Properties of Polyester Elastomers[a]

	64 % 4GT/4GD	58 % 4GT/PTMO−1000T
Melting point, °C	195	202
Glass transition temperature, °C	−34	−53
η_{inh}, l/g	0.094	0.152
Melt index, 220°C, g/10 min	5.4	5.8
Shore D hardness	56	55
Tensile strength, MPa	41.4	44.1
Elongation at break, %	620	650
Stress at 5%, MPa	6.48	6.45
Stress at 100%, MPa	14.7	15.1
Stress at 300%, MPa	16.9	16.6
Split tear, kN/m	70.1	70.6
Compression set B, (22 h/70°C), %	46	40
Bashore resilience, %	38	60
Brittle point, °C	<−70	<−70
Notched Izod impact strength, (−40°C), J/m	21	1270
Clash-Berg $T_{10,000}$, °C	−18	−40

4GD = tetramethylene dimerate

[a] Reprinted with permission after Angew. Makromol. Chemie[36]

In spite of the different nature of the soft segments, the two polymers are strikingly similar in physical properties at room temperature with the exception of resilience. The matching values for tensile and tear strengths give reason to consider how stress at high elongations is transmitted by the amorphous phase in polyester elastomers. The poorer low temperature properties of the dimer acid-based polymer follow from its higher T_g. The polymer based on dimer acid has much greater resistance to uv light and thermal degradation in air and to hydrolysis by hot water.

For the purpose of this chapter, the question can be raised as to how long the segments need to be for a material to be classed as a thermoplastic polyester elastomer? With reference to the hard segment length required in a thermoplastic elastomer, the ability of the segments to crystallize might be a useful criterion. For 4GT-based elastomers, the limiting segment length appears to be four 4GT units, recognizing that the calculated average chain length can be much lower[19]. It is more difficult to provide a definitive answer regarding soft segment length. Form a practical standpoint, soft segment length is largely determined by acceptable limits for T_g and T_m.

With reference to soft segment length, an interesting class of random copolyesters has been prepared in which the "soft segment" is provided by long chain alkyl or alkylene substituents on low molecular weight diacids or diols[54]. α-Substituted succinic anhydrides are suitable monomers which are commercially available. The properties of one of these polymers derived from α-docosenylsuccinic anhydride is compared with a polymer based on PEO-400 in Table VI. The two polymers contain the same concentration of 4GT units. The molecular weights of the soft segments in the polymers are similar.

TABLE VI   Comparison of Random Copolyester (57% 4GT/43% 4G α-Docosenylsuccinate) and Block Copolyester (57% 4GT/43% PEO-400T)[a]

	Random	Block[a]
η_{inh}, l/g	0.10	0.13
Melting point, °C	171	181
Stress at 100%, MPa	9.0	14.6
Tensile strength, MPa	38.6	39.3
Elongation at break, %	620	655
Split tear strength, kN/m	124	45
Clash-Berg $T_{10,000}$, °C	12	22

[a] Reprinted with permission from Rubber Chem. and Tech.[48]

The two polymers are surprisingly alike in certain properties even though there are no long flexible chains incorporated into the backbone of the random copolyester. The lack of flexibility between crystallizable hard segments is reflected in the lower degree of crystallinity as evidenced by the lower modulus at 100% elongation. The tear strength of the random copolymer is higher than is generally observed for polyester elastomers based on polyether segments. There may be two factors that account for the high tear strength; namely, the random copolyester backbone free of other segments and the high concentration of amorphous ester moieties in the amorphous phase. The toughening effect of esters is well-known for polyurethanes based on ester soft segments relative to their ether-based counterparts and may be related to the inherently higher T_g of ester soft segments. When these random copolyesters are prepared from succinic acid derivatives having saturated side chains they exhibit outstanding resistance to thermal degradation in air. The low temperature properties of these materials are inferior to those of commerical polyester elastomers.

In contrast to the polymers just discussed in which a large portion of the amorphous phase is provided by hydrocarbon side chains, polymers having an elastomeric hydrocarbon backbone and crystallizable ester side chains (or grafts) have also been described[55]. Poly-(pivalolactone) grafts can be formed in situ on carboxylated ethylene/propylene/hexadiene terpolymer. The resulting graft polymers melt at 120–225 °C depending on the molecular weight of the graft segments. These thermoplastics have physical properties similar to those of cured and reinforced samples of the base polymer but have a much higher initial modulus which increases with the concentration of grafted pivalolactone (see Chapter 5).

Block copolyesters based on hydrocarbon diols and diacids such as hydrogenated derivatives of polybutadiene and polyisoprene have been reported. Little information on the properties of these materials has been published. Polymers based on 2GT which contain up to 15 % weight of hydrogenated polybutadiene glycols are stated to have much better impact strength than 2GT homopolymer[56]. Polymers based on 4GT which contain up to 60 % hydrogenated polydiene glycol or diacid exhibit a higher degree of crystallinity than would be expected from the crystallinity of the homopolymer[57]. This effect has already been mentioned for polyether-based copolyesters. In view of the nonpolar nature of the polyene glycols, phasing during preparation would be anticipated with higher molecular weight glycols and higher hard segment concentrations.

5.4 Polyester Soft Segments

Investigation of low melting polyester glycols as soft segments in polyester elastomers for fibers coincided with early work on polyether glycol-based elastomers. Snyder[58] melt blended poly(ethylene terephthalate) and a rubbery copolyester of ethylene terephthalate and ethylene sebacate and allowed ester interchange to proceed. At intermediate stages, after the melt had become homogeneous but well before complete randomization, block copolymers exhibiting relatively high melting points and elastomeric properties were obtained. Because of the difficulty of controlling the extent of ester interchange, development of commercial products based on polyester glycols lagged behind that of polyether-based products. Perhaps the most significant advance with the ester interchange route has involved the use of titanate ester catalysts for the interchange of high molecular weight hard and soft ester homopolymers followed by deactivation of the catalyst with phosphorus compounds such as phosphonates once the desired amount of randomization has occurred[59]. The formation of a clear homogeneous reaction mass during the interchange is considered the optimum point for stopping the interchange. After deactivation of the catalyst, ester interchange takes place so slowly that it does not represent a problem during processing of the polymer in the melt.

Generally better results have been obtained by coupling preformed hard and soft ester segments with agents such as diacyl-bis-N-lactams or diisocyanates. Coupling of hydroxyl-terminated blocks of poly(tetramethylene terephthalate) with a variety of hydroxyl-terminated rubbery ester blocks by means of terephthaloyl-bis-N-ε-caprolactam has been reported to yield polyester elastomers with melting points in excess of 200 °C[60]. These high melting points suggest that randomization was not a serious problem with this procedure. Reference[60] does not mention randomization and no special steps appear to have been taken to avoid it. Randomization can be substantially avoided with diisocyanate coupling if any catalysts in the preformed ester blocks are deactivated prior to the coupling reaction[61].

Another approach which appears to avoid extensive randomization involves sequential esterification. A high melting polyester of intermediate molecular weight (preferably above 8000) is first formed and in turn reacted in the melt with a lactone, preferably ε-caprolactone. After removal of unreacted lactone, the resulting ester-ester polymer is stated to exhibit useful mechanical properties[62]. To obtain higher molecular weight polymers, coupling of the initial polyesterester molecules can be accomplished with acylating agents such as terephthaloyl-bis-N-ε-caprolactam[63]. Presumably isocyanate coupling could also be employed for this purpose.

Based on these developments, two types of polyesterester elastomers became available commercially in the early eighties. Toyobo introduced a product line which is based on polyesteresters derived from poly(tetramethylene terephthalate) by capping with ε-caprolactone. The stability of the initial polyesterester is improved by post-addition of small amounts of mixtures of mono- and di-epoxides in the presence of a catalyst. At the same time, the melt viscosity of the polymer is increased by chain extension[64].

Akzo introduced polyesterester grades prepared by coupling hydroxyl-terminated tetramethylene teraphthalate oligomers with isocyanate-terminated prepolymers of "soft" polyester glycols such as poly(butylene adipate) glycol[61, 65]. Alternately, a diisocyanate can be added to a mixture of the preformed hard and soft segment glycols[66]. The catalyst used to prepare the 4GT oligomer is deactivated prior to the coupling reaction which is conducted at 240 °C. The properties of these elastomers differ from those based on polyether soft segments in a number of respects. The greater polarity of the ester soft segment increases the compatibility of the hard and soft segments or conversely, decreases the extent of phase separation. This results in a lower degree of crystallinity than is observed for polyether-based elastomers. Crystallinity is even further reduced by partial randomization and from interference of urethane and allophanate groups adjacent to hard segments. The modulus at low strains of ester-based elastomers is generally somewhat lower than for ether-based elastomers. At higher elongations, the draw plateau seen for harder ether-based elastomers in less evident or absent. The stress-strain curves for these diisocyanate-coupled ester-ester elastomers actually bear more similarity to polyesterurethanes than to ether-based polyester elastomers. Some of the ester-based products have lower tensile sets than their ether counterparts.

The poorer low temperature properties observed for polyesterester elastomers are related at least in part to less complete phase separation which in turn raises the glass transition temperature. The ester-based products stiffen more and have poorer impact strength and flex life at low temperatures as well as higher brittle temperatures. The tear strength (ASTM-D624, Die C) of polyesterester elastomers is comparable to that of polyetherester elastomers at equivalent hard segment concentrations. With regard to high temperature properties such as heat sag resistance and Vicat softening temperature, polyesterester elastomers are inferior to comparable polyetherester elastomers, but are superior to polyesterurethanes. The polyesteresters have a broader melting range and a lower rate of crystallization than polyetherester counterparts. The polyesteresters also have higher melt viscosities at low shear rates. A comprehensive discussion of the properties of diisocyanate-coupled polyesterester elastomers is provided in Reference 65.

It is generally known that replacing ether soft segments with ester soft segments substantially improves resistance to oxidative degradation induced by heat or light. The presence of aliphatic ester linkages in the ester soft segments significantly lowers the hydrolytic and chemical stability of polyesterester elastomers relative to ether-based elastomers.

6   POLYMER BLENDS CONTAINING POLYESTER ELASTOMERS

The good melt stability and low melt viscosity of polyester elastomers facilitates their use in polymer blends whenever there is a need to improve resistance to impact, particularly at low temperature, or to provide elastomeric character. Lower melting polyester elastomers with mixed short chain ester units can be blended with temperature sensitive polymers such as poly(vinyl chloride)[67]. A comprehensive review of blends is beyond the scope of this chapter as a large amount of work covering blends with polymers ranging from rigid plastics to conventional elastomers has been reported by both academic and industrial researchers. Only a few oft the more significant developments in the field of blends will be discussed.

Blends of 4GT/PTMOT polyester elastomers with homopolymers corresponding to or closely approaching the structure of the hard or soft segments in the elastomer are of interest from a scientific view point. Blends of 4GT homopolymer containing up to 20 % of relatively soft copolyesters (approx. 40D Shore hardness) show improved impact strength[68]. Blends with other rigid thermoplastics which are mechanically compatible, but not miscible with polyester elastomers, exhibit similar improvements in impact strength[69, 70]. Blends of 4GT with substantial amounts of soft or medium hardness polyester elastomers (4GT/PTMO-1000T) are stiffer and have a higher yield strength at room temperature but have greater flexibility and better impact resistance at low temperatures than do 4GT/PTMO-1000T elastomers having the same total 4GT content as the blend[68, 71, 72]. Such blends have been suggested for use in truck air brake tubing where high burst strength is needed in warm weather and flexibility and resistance to impact are required in cold weather. Good mixing such as provided by a twin-screw extruder is required to achieve optimum properties with these blends. Prolonged mixing should be avoided because ester interchange between 4GT and the elastomer can take place. These blends exhibit two glass-transition temperatures and two melting points as would be anticipated for systems having two phases in the melt[73].

Schroeder and Wolfe[74] described blends of 4GT/PTMOT elastomers with amorphous or low temperature-crystallizing polyesters based on PTMO glycol and a diacid or on PTMO glycol, a diacid and a minor amount of tetramethylene glycol. Blends of crystalline elastomers with these soft amorphous polyesters had melting points nearly as high as the unblended crystalline elastomer. The blends were softer, had reduced stress-strain properties and less tendency to stiffen at low temperature than the starting crystalline elastomers. This approach provides a route to soft compositions which have substantially higher melting points than would be exhibited by unblended copolyester elastomers of equal hardness. Softening of polyester elastomers with conventional low molecular weight plasticizers reduces melting point sharply and results in a greater loss of properties in general. While no conclusive evidence is available, it seems reasonable to assume that the polymers in these blends are not miscible because of the very minimal drop in melting point observed for the crystalline polyester.

Addition of soft polyester elastomers 4GT/PTMO-1000T (33/67) to a flexible poly(vinyl chloride) composition containing conventional low molecular weight plasticizers has been found to improve tensile and tear strength, low temperature flexibility and impact strength, and heat distortion at 121 °C[67, 72]. It is not clear if the polyester elastomer is miscible with the plasticized poly(vinyl chloride) or exists as a separate phase in these blends. Dynamic mechanical properties of blends of soft polyester elastomers with rigid poly(vinyl chloride) in the absence of conventional plasticizers suggest a high degree of miscibility in samples studied directly after mill mixing at 150 °C. Following annealing at 130 °C, the same blends show evidence of phase separation accompanied by a surprising improvement in impact strength[75].

Blends of polyester elastomers with conventional elastomers have also been reported. Shih[76] described blends with ethylene-propylene-diene copolymers which were softer than the starting polyester elastomer but largely retained the melting point and toughness of the polyester. Blends with nitrile rubber provide softer compositions which can be blow molded[77].

It is evident that the commercialization of polyester elastomers in 1972 has led to extensive research in this area by both academic and industrial polymer scientists. Because these polymers offer an unique combination of physical properties and processing characteristics they have gained worldwide acceptance. At present, elastomers based on polyether glycols are manufactured by DuPont in the U.S. and Luxembourg and DuPont-Toray in Japan under the trademark HYTREL®; by GAF in the U.S. under the trademark GAFLEX®; and by General Electric in the U.S. under the trademark LOMOD®. Both polyether-based and polyester-based elastomers are manufactured by Toyobo in Japan under the trademark PELPRENE and by Akzo in the Netherlands under the trademark ARNITEL®. The availability of a wide variety of polymers ranging from relatively soft elastomers to hard elastoplastics with viscosities designed for either low or high shear thermoplastic processing techniques will continue to expand the applications for polyester elastomers.

References

1. D. Coleman, *J. Polym. Sci. 14*, 15 (1954). D. Coleman (to ICI), Brit. 682,866 (November 19, 1952)
2. O. B. Edgar and R. Hill, *J. Polym. Sci. 8*, 1 (1952)
3. P. T. Flory, *J. Chem. Phys. 17*, 233 (1949)
4. M. D. Snyder (to DuPont), US 2,744,087 (May 1, 1956)
5. W. H. Charch and J. C. Shivers, *Text Res. J. 29*, 536 (1959)
6. J. C. Shivers (to DuPont), US 3,023,192 (February 27, 1962)
7. A. Bell, C. J. Kibler and J. G. Smith (to Eastman Kodak), US 3,261,812 (July 19, 1966)
8. C. Tanaka, Y. Futura and N. Naito (to Toray Industries), US 4,251,652 (February 17, 1981)
9. A. Bell, C. J. Kibler and J. G. Smith (to Eastman Kodak), US 3,243,413 (March 29, 1966)
10. A. A. Nishimura and H. Komogata, *J. Macromol. Sci.-Chem. A-1*, 617 (1967)
11. W. K. Witsiepe (to DuPont), US 3,651,014 (March 21, 1972)
12. W. K. Witsiepe (to DuPont), US 3,763,109 (October 2, 1973)
13. W. K. Witsiepe (to DuPont), US 3,755,146 (October 16, 1973)
14. Rubber World, May 1972
15. M. Sumoto, H. Furusawa and T. Takeuchi (to Toyobo), Jap. Patent 1,005,108 (June 30, 1980)
16. G. K. Hoeschele, *Chimia 28*, 544 (1974)
17. W. K. Witsiepe, *ACS Advances in Chemistry Series 129*, 39 (1973)
18. K. H. Frensdorff, *Macromolecules 4*, 369 (1971)
19. G. Perego, M. Cesari and R. Vitali, *J. Appl. Polym. Sci. 29*, 1157 (1984)
20. R. J. Cella, *J. Polym. Sci. Symp. 42* (2), 727 (1973)
21. A. Lilaonitkul, J. West and S. L. Cooper, *J. Macromol Sci.-Phys. B12* (4), 563, Marcel Dekker, Inc., N. Y. (1976)
22. W. H. Buck, R. J. Cella, E. K. Gladding and J. R. Wolfe, Jr., *J. Polym. Sci. Symp. No. 48*, 47 (1974)
23. R. W. Seymour, J. R. Overton and L. S. Corley, *Macromoleculus 8*, 331 (1975)
24. G. Wegner, T. Fujii, W. Meyer and G. Lieser, *Angew. Makromol. Chem. 74*, 295 (1978)
25. C. Tanaka, M. Hiratsuka, H. Kobayshi and M. Kitanaka, *Preprint (G3K04) of Polym. Symp., Soc. Polym. Sci. Japan,* October 1, 1982
26. E. Sorta and A. Melis, *Polymer 19*, 1153 (1978)
27. A. E. Allegrezza, R. W. Seymour, H. N. Ng and S. L. Cooper, *Polymer 15*, 433 (1974)

28. M. Brown and W. K. Witsiepe, *Rubber Age 104/3,* 35 (1972)
29. G. K. Hoeschele (to DuPont), US 3,801,547 (April 2, 1974)
30. G. K. Hoeschele (to DuPont), US 4,013,624 (March 22, 1977); B. Davis, T. F. Gray and H. R. Musser (to Eastman Kodak), US 4,349,469 (September 14, 1982)
31. M. Brown, G. K. Hoeschele and W. K. Witsiepe (to DuPont), US 3,835,098 (September 10, 1974)
32. W. K. Witsiepe (to DuPont), Def. Publ. T 908,011 (March 27, 1973)
33. G. K. Hoeschele (to DuPont), US 3,723,568 (March 27, 1973)
34. C. Shih (to DuPont), US 4,010,222 (March 1, 1977)
35. G. K. Hoeschele (to DuPont), US 4,362,836 (December 7, 1982)
36. G. K. Hoeschele, *Angew. Makromol. Chemie 58/59,* 299 (1977)
37. G. K. Hoeschele (to DuPont), US 3,896,078 (July 22, 1975)
38. G. K. Hoeschele (to DuPont), US 3,904,706 (September 9, 1975)
39. G. K. Hoeschele (to DuPont), US, 3,856,749 (December 24, 1974)
40. G. K. Hoeschele (to DuPont), US 4,221,703 (September 9, 1980)
41. Research Disclosure ?21533, p. 78, March 1982
    G. K. Hoeschele (to DuPont), US 4,185,003 (January 22, 1980)
43. J. R. Wolfe, Jr., *ACS Adv. Chem. Ser. 176,* 129 (1979)
44. A. B. Ijzermans, F. J. Pluijm, F. J. Huntjens and J. F. Repin, *Br. Polym. J. 7,* 211 (1975)
45. R. Jakeways, I. M. ard, M. A. Wilding, I. H. Hall and M. G. Pass, *J. Polym. Sci., Polym. Phys. Ed. 13,* 799 (1975)
46. G. K. Hoeschele and W. K. Witsiepe, *Angew. Makromol. Chemie 29/30,* 267 (1973)
47. M. Gilbert and F. J. Hybart, *Polymer 13,* 327 (1972)
48. J. R. Wolfe, Jr., *Rubber Chem. & Techn. 50,* 688 (1977)
49. G. K. Hoeschele (to DuPont), US 3,784,540 (January 8, 1974)
50. C. Shih and J. M. McKenna, IUPAC Meeting Amherst, Mass. 1982, to be published in *Rubber Chem. and Techn.*
51. W. Meiyan, Z. Dong, C. Chuanfu and Q. Chunqin, *Proc. of China – U.S. Bilateral Symp. on Polym. Chem. and Phys.,* October 5–10, 1979, Beijing Science Press, China 1981, distr. by Van Nostrand Reinhold Co.
52. C. Tanaka and M. Hiratsuka, *Preprint (G3K05) of Polym. Symp., Soc. Polym. Sci. Japan,* October 1, 1982
53. G. K. Hoeschele (to DuPont), US 3,954,689 (May 4, 1976)
54. J. R. Wolfe, Jr. (to DuPont), US 3,890,279 (June 17, 1975)
55. R. C. Thamm, W. H. Buck, S. W. Caywood, J. M. Meyer and B. C. Anderson, *Angew. Makromol. Chemie 58/59,* 345 (1977)
56. L. Brinkmann and H. Froehlich (to Farbwerk Hoechst), US 3,598,882 (August 10, 1971)
57. R. Binsack, K. H. Koehler, L. Morbitzer, L. Bottenbruch and W. Heitz (to Bayer), US 4,382,131 (May 3, 1983)
58. M. D. Snyder (to DuPont), US 2,623,031 (December 23, 1952)
59. N. Saiki, Y. Takeuchi and H. Saiki (to Teijin), US 4,031,165 (June 21, 1977)
60. R. Ca. Waller and M. H. Keck (to Goodyear), US 3,446,778 (May 27, 1969)
61. F. Huntjens (to Akzo), Europ. Pat. 13461 (April 6, 1983)
62. M. Sumoto, S. Minowa and H. Imanaka (to Toyobo), Jap. Pat. Appl. Publ. No. 48–4116 (February 5, 1973)
63. M. Sumoto, S. Minowa and H. Imanaka (to Toyobo), Jap. Pat. Appl. Publ. No. 48–4115 (February 5, 1973)
64. T. Kobayashi, H. Kitagawa and S. Kobayashi (to Toyobo), US 4,500,686 (February 19, 1985)
65. R. W. M. van Berkel, S. A. G. De Graaf, F. J. Huntjens and C. M. F. Vrouenrates, in *"Developments in Block Copolymers-1,* I. Goodman, Ed., Applied Science Publ., London and New York, Ch. 7, p. 261
66. F. J. Huntjens and A. H. J. Brouwer (to Akzo), US 4,483,970 (November 20, 1984)
67. R. W. Crawford and W. K. Witsiepe (to DuPont), U.S. 3,718,715 (February 27, 1973)
68. K. P. Perry, B. Davis and C. J. Kibler, (to Eastman Kodak), German OS 2,338,615 (February 21, 1974)
69. D. L. Dufour and J. S. Holtrop (to Monsanto), U.S. 4,460,741 (July 17, 1984)
70. British 1,509,959 (to Hoechst) published May 10, 1978
71. M. Brown and R. M. Prosser (to DuPont), U.S. 3,907,962 (September 23, 1975)

72. M. Brown, Rubber Industry 9, 102 (1975)
73. C. K. Shih, presented at a meeting of the North American Thermal Analysis Society, Boston, Massachusetts, (1981); to be published in *Rubber Chem. and Techn.*
74. H. E. Schroeder and J. R. Wolfe, Jr. (to DuPont), U.S. 3,917,743 (November 4, 1975)
75. T. Nishi and T. K. Kwei, *J. Applied Polym. Sci., 20,* 1331 (1976)
76. C. K. Shih (to DuPont), U.S. 3,963,802 (June 15, 1976)
77. K. H. Whitlock (to DuPont), U.S. 4,124,653 (November 7, 1978)

Chapter 9A

POLYESTERAMIDES AND POLYETHERESTERAMIDES: THERMOPLASTIC POLYAMIDE ELASTOMERS

R. G. Nelb, A. T. Chen, K. Onder

Contents

Robert G. Nelb II, Augustin T. Chen, and Kemal Onder, Dow Chemical USA, North Haven Laboratories, North Haven, Connecticut 06473

1   INTRODUCTION

The first commercial thermoplastic elastomers (TPE) introduced over four decades ago were the polyvinylchloride blends and plastisols and were designed to replace vulcanized rubber with a suitable material for ease of processing. In the intervening years TPE's have undergone several stages of evolution as the increasing demands of modern technology have required higher performance levels, particularly in the areas of higher use temperatures, better chemical restistance, improved weatherability, and lower compression.

One of the newest additions is a group of thermoplastic polyamide elastomers that have been developed at the North Haven Laboratories of The Dow Chemical Company. These elastomers, polyesteramide and polyetheresteramide, have use temperatures up to 175 °C, have excellent resistance to thermal aging, and have good chemical resistance properties. In this chapter, the ideas leading to the design and development of these polymers will be discussed. How the formulation and morphology allow these properties to be achieved will also be explored. Many of the thermal and mechanical properties will be outlined, and finally, potential application areas for these materials will be identified.

2   SEGMENTED BLOCK COPOLYMERS

2.1 Structure

Polyesteramides (PEA) and polyetheresteramides (PEEA) belong to the class of polymers termed segmented block copolymers whose characteristics are described in Chapters 2 and 8. Other polyetheresteramides, described in Chapter 9B, have polyether based soft segments and hard segments derived from aliphatic polyamides. In contrast, the hard segments of the PEA and PEEA elastomers described in this chapter are based on partially aromatic amides which have higher values for their Tg's and Tm's. In PEA, the soft segments are derived from aliphatic polyesters, while PEEA has aliphatic polyethers linked to the hard segment by an ester group.

2.2 Morphology

In addition to the restraints upon the thermal properties of the two types of segments, the hard and soft segments must be chosen such that the free energy of mixing is positive[1]. Thus, the mutual incompatibility of the segments induces microphase separation in the solid state. The hard segments aggregate to form glassy or semicrystalline hard domains interspersed in the continous soft segment matrix. The boundaries between the two phases are not well defined because there exists some degree of forced compatibility due to the rather short average chain lengths and the molecular weight distributions of the segments.

The soft segments (normally above their Tg) contribute to the flexibility and extensibility of the elastomer. The glassy or semi-crystalline hard segment domains serve as virtual crosslinks, impeding chain slippage and the viscous flow of the polymer. These crosslinks are physical rather than chemical in nature, as in vulcanized rubber, and are therefore thermally reversible. Heating above the softening or melting point of the hard domains causes the hard domains to dissociate. Beginning with the dissolution of the shorter hard segments, phase mixing of the hard segments and soft segments occurs[2]. Without the hard domain tie points, the polymer is able to flow as a thermoplastic material and it can be melt processed. Upon cooling, the hard and soft segments become incompatible again and phase separation into microdomains occurs which leads to the reformation of the physical crosslinks. The rate of the reorganization in the hard segments depends upon the annealing temperature to which the polymer is subjected after solidification.

The mechanical properties of segmented elastomers are dependent upon several factors as described in Chapters 2 and 8. The proportion of the hard segments in the copolymer, their chemical composition, their molecular weight distribution, the method of preparation, and the thermal history of the sample affect the degree of phase separation and domain formation. Increasing the proportion of the hard segment incrases the hardness and the initial modulus while decreasing the ultimate elongation. Increasing the phase separation at equivalent soft/hard segment rations often decreases the hardness and modulus by allowing more freedom of chain motion in the elastomeric domain (lowers the Tg).

The upper use temperature of segmented block elastomers is depentend upon the softening or melting point of the physical crosslinks. For long term aging, the thermal oxidative stability of the soft segment itself is also important. The compatibility of the hard and soft phase at elevated temperatures, the Tg of the hard segments, the concentration of hard segment, and its crystallinity and its associated Tm are important parameters affecting the upper use temperature. These factors influence the amount of phase mixing and the degree of freedom of chain movement in the hard domains, especially for the amorphous portion. At elevated temperatures and with a lower percentage of hard segments acting as physical crosslinks, the modulus and the tensile strength are reduced.

To extend the upper temperature range of a segmented elastomer, it is necessary to introduce physical crosslinks which soften or melt at higher tempreatures. Increasing the amount of hard segment can often accomplish this but it also leads to higher hardnesses and reduces the elastic properties. This, however, can also be accomplished by using a more crystalline hard segment with a higher melting point and one that is less soluble in the soft segment matrix to help maintain the integrity of the hard domains at high temperatures. For crystalline hard segments, the effectiveness of the physical crosslinks is more dependent upon the Tm than the Tg of the hard domains because the crystallinity suppresses the effect of the Tg. Consequently, the use of a high melting, crystalline hard segment was the approach taken in the design and development of the polyesteramide and polyetheresteramide thermoplastic polyamide elastomers.

3   POLYESTERAMIDE AND POLYETHER-ESTERAMIDE THERMOPLASTIC ELASTOMERS

3.1   Synthesis

Polyamides are typically synthesized by the condensation reactions of either diamines with dicarboxylic acids (through the amine salts) or diamines with diacid chlorides (or occasionally esters). These methods either use expensive monomers (acid chlorides), generate corrosive gasses (hydrogen chloride), or generally are limited to aliphatic amines as monomers (aromatic amines have low reactivity in the amine salt or ester processes).

Amides can also be synthesized from isocyanates and carboxylic acids eq 1. The use of an aromatic isocyanate in this reaction affords an amide identical to one which would result

$$R-NCO + R'-COOH \longrightarrow R-NH-CO-R' + CO_2 \tag{1}$$

from an aromatic diamine. The mechanism of this reaction is quite complex and has been reported in the literature[3-10].

Only recently, however, has this reaction been developed into an alternate method for the synthesis of semi-aromatic polyamides[10-15]. With the appropriate reaction conditions[10], this reaction can provide polyamides with no undesirable by-products. The formation of high molecular weight polyamides by this method is evidence of the efficiency of the reaction sequence since greater than 99 % conversion is required in condensation polymerizations to achieve high polymer[16]. The versatility of this reaction has allowed the synthesis of a wide range of polymers ranging from engineering thermoplastics[12, 13] to thermoplastic elastomers[14, 15].

PEA and PEEA are synthesized by the condensation of the aromatic diisocyanate, 4,4'-methylenebis(phenylisocyanate) (MDI), with dicarboxylic acids and a carboxylic acid terminated polyester or polyether prepolymer with a Mn of 500 to 5000 Daltons[14, 15]. Two moles of carbon dioxide are lost for every mole of the diisocyanate consumed in the reaction. The homogeneous polymerization is usually carried out at elevated temperatures in a polar solvent which is nonreactive with isocyanates. The dicarboxylic acid serves as the hard segment chain extender and forms the amide hard segment with the MDI. The carboxylic acid terminated prepolymer, which can be either ester or ether based, forms the soft segment matrix for PEA or PEEA, respectively. The amide content of the elastomer and the

Polymer Reaction Scheme

$$\text{HOOC}\sim\sim\text{COOH} + \text{OCN}\langle\bigcirc\rangle\text{CH}_2\langle\bigcirc\rangle\text{NCO} + n \text{ HOOC}-\text{R}-\text{COOH}$$

polyester

polyether

$$-\text{CO}_2$$

$$\sim\sim\sim\text{CO}\left[\text{NH}\langle\bigcirc\rangle\text{CH}_2\langle\bigcirc\rangle\text{NHCO}-\text{R}-\text{CO}\right]_n\text{NH}\langle\bigcirc\rangle\text{CH}_2\langle\bigcirc\rangle\text{NHCO}\sim\sim\sim$$

soft

hard

crystallinity of the hard domains can be changed by varying the amounts and types of dicarboxylic acid chain extenders in the formulation and/or by changing the molecular weight of the polyester or polyether soft segments. The value of the Tm generally reflects the crystallinity present in the hard domains.

Table I lists several different PEA and PEEA formulations which have been synthesized and characterized. The Shore hardness values, the weight percent amide content, the soft segment Tg, and the amide hard segment Tm are tabulated for later reference.

The PEA and PEEA elastomers produced by this method are transparent and have a yellow-brown color in the finished state. The elastomers are soluble in polar amide solvents such as dimethylformamide (DMF), dimethylacetamide (DMAC), and N-methylpyrollidinone (NMP). The inherent viscosities of these elastomers typically range between 0.8 dl/g and 0.9 dl/g, measured as a 0.5 weight percent solution in N-methylpyrollidinone (NMP).

TABLE I   Glass Transition Temperatures and Melting Points of PEA and PEEA

	Hardness (Shore A)	Hard Segment Extender	Amide (%)	Tg(soft) °C	Tm(hard) °C
PEA−1	88A	Adipic	25	−40	270
PEA−2	94A	Azelaic	35	−28	230
PEA−3	94A	Adipic	33	−34	275
PEA−4	55D	Azelaic/Adipic	37	−33	236
PEA−5	60D	Azelaic/Adipic	39	−33	238
PEA−6	70D	Azelaic/Adipic	42	−34	240
PEEA−1	92A	Azelaic/Adipic	31	−50	251
PEEA−2	92A	Azelaic	31	−40	264

3.2   Morphology

The existence of the domain morphology of PEA and PEEA can be established by differential scanning calorimetry (DSC). Figure 1 shows DSC thermograms for a typical PEA and PEEA. The multiple endotherms for the Tm are commonly observed for semi-crystalline polymers due to the different degrees of crystalline order.

Table I shows the Tg and Tm data for a number of elastomer formulations. If the elastomers were totally phase separated into hard and soft domains, there would be a Tm at 50–100 °C due to the soft segment. Also, the observed soft segment Tg and the hard segment Tm would approach values for the isolated segments. However, the PEA-2 soft segment Tg is 28 °C above that of the pure soft segment and the hard segment Tm is 55 °C lower than the analogous polyamide. These shifts in the Tg and Tm are characteristic of a segmented elastomer which is partially phase separated[17]. The data in Table I also illustrates the effect

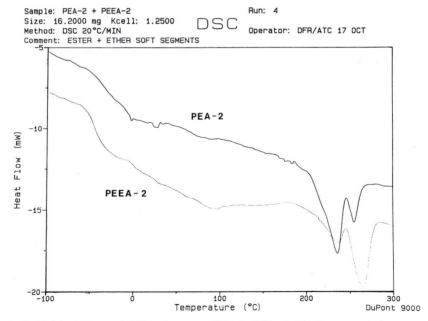

Figure 1   Typical DSC of PEA and PEEA elastomers: PEA-2, PEEA-2. Heating rate: 20 °C

the chemical composition can have upon the phase separation. The polyether based PEEA-2, with an amide content similar to PEA-2, is more phase separated as indicated by the Tg and Tm shifts. The chemical composition of the hard segment, which affects the amount of crystallinity, also effects the phase separation of an elastomer. PEA-3 has a more crystalline amide as the hard segment and the resulting increase in phase separation is indicated by the lowering of the soft segment Tg relative to PEA-2. The average molecular weight of the segments also effects the observed values of the Tg and Tm.

The effect of phase separation upon the polymer hardness is also exemplified in Table I. PEEA-2, which has the same hard segment content and hard segment length as PEA-2, is several Shore hardness points softer because of its greater phase separation.

Infrared dichroism is a technique which can indicate the orientation of the polymer segments when under stress by measuring the infrared absorption of functional groups characteristic of the hard or soft segments[18]. When analyzed by this technique, PEA-2 shows behavior typical of a segmented elastomer which has crystalline hard segments[19]. The soft segments, monitored using the C-H stretch of the methylene group at 2930 and 2860 cm[-1], align parallel to the applied stress resulting in a positive orientation function at all strain levels, Figure 2.

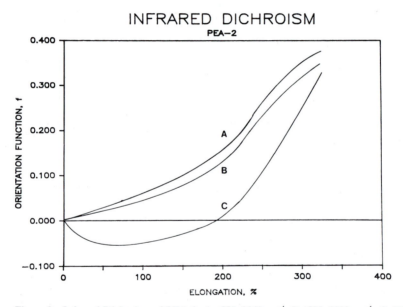

Figure 2   Infrared Dichroism of PEA-2. A, CH_2 2860 cm[-1]; B, CH_2 2930 cm[-1]; C, NH 3310 cm[-1]

Because the hard segments are crystalline, the orientation function observed is quite different. At low strain levels, the crystallites align perpendicularly to the applied stress due to the parallel alignment of the lamellae. This gives rise to a negative orientation function, monitored using the N-H stretch at 3360 cm[-1]. As the stress levels increase, the crystallites are disrupted and the hard segments are able to align parallel to the stress and the orientation function becomes positive. This is in contrast to the less crystalline polyurethanes which show positive orientation functions at all strain levels[19].

The stress induced crystallization of the soft segment can be observed visually by a whitening of the sample when strained above 300 %. A DSC thermogram of a sample, PEA-2, frozen

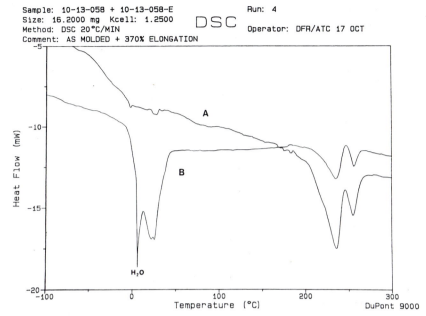

Figure 3   DSC of PEA-2. Heating rate: 20 °C. A, PEA-2 control; PEA-2 elongated to 370 % at 50 cm/min, then frozen at −78 °C before scanning. The H_2O peak is an artifact from the freezing process

while strained, indicates a Tm for the soft segment at 40 °C, Figure 3. Upon heating the frozen sample or relaxing the stress at room temperature, the soft segment readily reverts back to the amorphous state.

Limited experiments with pulsed proton nuclear magnetic resonance (NMR) relaxation experiments, as well as data from small angle light scattering experiments, also result in data supportive of a segmented type of polymer.

4   PHYSICAL PROPERTIES OF PEA AND PEEA

The physical properties exhibited by thermoplastic, segmented block copolymers similar to the PEA's and PEEA's are dependent upon such parameters as the chemical composition of the hard and soft segments and their respective lengths. The following summarizes the major influences exerted by these parameters:

Hard segment chemical composition –
a) polymer melting point
b) degree of phase separation
c) mechanical strength

Soft segment chemical composition –
a) hydrolytic stability
b) chemical and solvent resistance
c) thermal oxidative stability
d) low temperature flexibility

Hard segment molecular weight –
a) polymer melting point
b) polymer hardness
c) thermal stability

Soft segment molecular weight –
a) polymer hardness
b) low temperature flexibility

It is apparent from this summary that the physical properties observed in an elastomer are the result of the complex interaction of many factors. In this section, many of the physical properties of the PEA and PEEA thermoplastic elastomers will be presented. The similarities and differences between the amide elastomers themselves and even other TPE's can often be explained by one or more of these parameters. Since the PEA and PEEA elastomers are relatively new, the data in all categories may not be complete at this writing.

4.1 Tensile Properties

The tensile properties of several formulations of PEA and PEEA are tabulated in Table II and a typical stress-strain curve is shown in Figure 4. The initial moduli of the PEA and PEEA elastomers, which parallel the amide content, are much higher than for many other TPE's in the same hardness range. This is a result of the higher load bearing ability of the crystalline portion of the amide hard segment domains. The deformation of the hard segment in this low strain region is mostly reversible. At higher strain levels, however, disruption and reorganization of the crystalline lamellae occurs and the stress-strain curve levels out as chain slippage relieves some of the stress[20]. This change is irreversible and results in the observed tensile set.

TABLE II   Tensile Properties of PEA and PEEA (ASTM D−412)

Sample	Modulus (MPa)			Tensile Strength (MPa)	Elongation (%)	Tensile Set (%)
	50%	100%	300%			
PEA−1	8.5	10.8	18.2	28.1	470	
PEA−1A[a]	8.7	12.0	21.0	31	495	
PEA−2	11.3	13.2	19.2	26.2	470	50
PEA−2A[b]	12.6	16.4	28.8	31.0	370	40
PEA−4	14.7	18.9	—	36.0	295	34
PEA−5	19.0	22.7	33.1	33.1	300	100
PEA−6	27.0	30.1	—	42.2	265	92
PEEA−2	9.2	11.5	18.4	18.6	300	16
PEEA−2[b]	9.6	12.6	16.7	18.8	410	50

[a] Sample annealed at 175°C for 4 hours
[b] Sample annealed at 200°C for 3 hours

Finally, the load is borne by the soft segment chains which become oriented and crystallize as shown by the DSC studies. This reinforces the elastomer and causes an increase in the stress until catastrophic failure occurs at break. As an indication of the integrity of the crystalline amide hard segment domains on a microscopic scale, PEA does not show a tensile yield even at a hardness of Shore 70D, and therefore it has lower permanent set than some of the other crystalline, thermoplastic elastomers. The tensile set values after a 100 % strain for PEA-2 are 11 % after one minute of relaxation and only 7 % after a ten minute

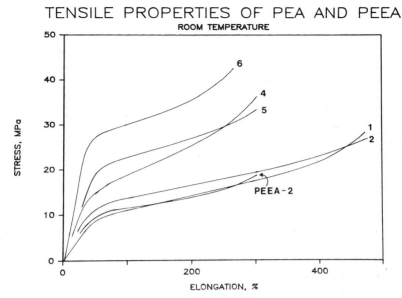

Figure 4   Typical room temperature stress-strain curve for PEA- (1–6) and PEEA-2 elastomers, as indicated. Composition as shown in Table I

relaxation period. A harder material, PEA-4, exhibits only slightly higher set values of 14 % and 12 % for the same conditions.

The tensile properties of PEA and PEEA show an improvement after being annealed above the Tg of the amide hard segment. In addition to the relief of molded-in stresses, annealing also promotes the reorganization of the short range ordered amide segments in the hard segment domains into larger and more perfect crystallites. As a result of this change, the area of the higher melting endotherm in Figure 1 increases at the expense of the lower melting endotherm in the DSC. The net result is often higher modulus values, higher tensile strengths, and better elongations, Table II.

4.2   High Temperature Tensile Properties

The purpose behind the synthesis of polyesteramide and polyetheresteramide was to develop a thermoplastic elastomer suitable for use at elevated temperatures. The success of this endeavor can be determined by performing ring tensile tests in an environmental chamber (ASTM D-412, D-3196) at several test temperatures. Table III lists the tensile properties measured for several PEA formulations and Figure 5 depicts typical stress-strain curves at 150 °C. These data also indicate that the high temperature performance of a segmented elastomer is closely dependent upon the hard segment crystallinity and its melting point. It is also noteworthy that these materials retain useful tensile properties under conditions where most other TPE's could not even be tested. Particularly significant are the properties retained by the lower hardness formulations where high temperature perform-ance is most difficult to achieve in a TPE.

Since many application areas for TPE's do not require high elongations, the initial moduli are often the primary design consideration. The retention of the modulus at several test temperatures is illustrated for PEA-2 in Figure 6 for 10 and 20 percent strain.

TABLE III   Tensile Properties of PEA at Elevated Temperatures (ASTM D−412, D−3196)

Sample	Test Temp.°C	Modulus (MPa) 50%	100%	300%	Tensile Strength (MPa)	Elongation (%)
PEA−1	RT	8.7	12.0	21.0	31.0	495
	150	6.5	8.9	13.3	14.8	340
PEA−2	RT	11.3	13.2	19.2	26.2	470
	100	7.4	8.3	9.7	14.6	480
	150	5.5	5.9	6.3	7.7	320
PEA−4	RT	14.7	18.9	—	36.0	295
	100	5.8	8.1	15.8	20.6	390
	150	3.7	5.1	9.1	9.6	310
PEA−5	RT	22.2	22.7	33.1	33.1	300
	100	7.7	8.4	12.4	20.0	500
	150	3.0	3.2	3.7	5.0	480
PEA−6	RT	27.0	30.1	—	42.2	265
	100	8.1	9.0	14.3	26.9	490
	150	5.7	6.1	9.4	16.2	540

Note: All samples have been annealed for 3 hours at 200°C except PEA−1 which was annealed for 4 hours at 175°C

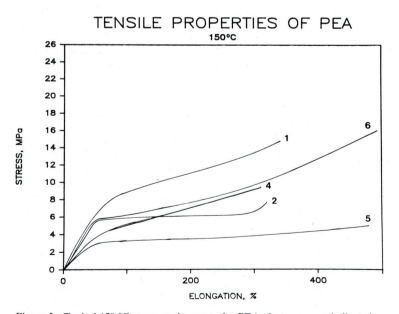

Figure 5   Typical 150 °C stress-strain curves for PEA elastomers, as indicated

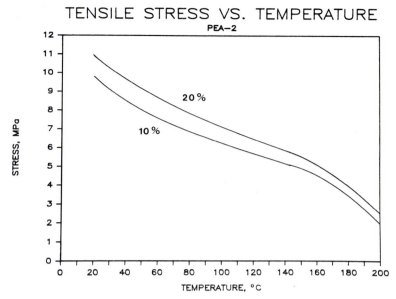

Figure 6   Tensile stress of PEA-2 as a function of temperature at 10 % and 20 % strain levels, as indicated

4.3 Dry Heat Aging

The PEA and PEEA elastomers are also very resistant to long term dry heat aging, even at 150 °C in the absence of any added heat stabilizers. When compared to unaged control samples, some of the room temperature tensile properties actually improved after aging for five days at 150 °C, Table IV. This is due to an annealing effect rather than to any oxidative crosslinking since the samples are still soluble. Similar studies have been carried out for the ester based PEA elastomers at 175 °C with only small losses in properties. Like any other ether based elastomer, the PEEA elastomers do not fare as well at this temperature because of the inherent oxidative instability of the ether linkage. With the addition of stabilizers[21],

TABLE IV   Dry Heat Aging of PEA and PEEA

| Tensile Properties after 120 Hours at 150°C | | | | | |
| Sample | Modulus (MPa) | | | Tensile | Elongation |
	50 %	100 %	300 %	Strength (MPa)	(%)
PEA−1	5.8	8.9	18.0	26.3	430
PEA−2	12.9	16.0	26.2	29.7	390
PEEA−2	10.8	14.6	—	18.0	260

| Tensile properties after 120 hours at 175 °C | | | | | |
| | Modulus (MPa) | | | Tensile | Elongation |
Sample	50 %	100 %	300 %	Strength (MPa)	(%)
PEA−1	3.6	5.8	16.7	19.1	320
PEA−2	12.0	15.9	—	26.9	300

Note: Samples were annealed at 200°C for 3 hours. No added heat stabilizers

TABLE V   Dry Heat Aging of Stabilized PEA−2; Tensile Properties after 120 Hours at 150°C

Sample	Test Temp.°C	Modulus (MPa)			Tensile Strength (MPa)	Elongation (%)
		50%	100%	300%		
Neat	RT	13.7	16.6	—	23.6	275
	100	9.0	11.1	—	13.5	210
	150	7.9	—	—	8.8	80
Stabilized	RT	13.4	16.1	27.4	32.0	350
	100	10.0	12.0	15.7	15.8	315
	150	8.7	10.2	—	10.8	120

Note: Samples were aged, then tested at the indicated temperatures

PEA-2 exhibits improved heat resistance, which becomes clearly evident when the samples are tested at elevated temperatures after the dry heat aging as demonstrated in Table V.

4.4 Humid Aging

The chemical composition of the soft segment is important in determining the resistance of an elastomer to humid aging. Most ester-based TPE's are susceptible to hydrolysis which reduces the properties by lowering the polymer molecular weight and PEA is no exception. However, the presence of a sacrificial stabilizer such as a polymeric carbodiimide based additive does improve the humid aging characteristics of these polymers. The PEA formula-

TABLE VI   Humid Aging of PEA and PEEA; Tensile Properties after Exposure to 100% Relative Humidity at 85°C

Sample	Time Days	Modulus (MPa)			Tensile Strength (MPa)	Elongation (%)	Change	
		50%	100%	300%			% Vol.	% Wt.
PEA−1	Ctrl	8.5	11.1	18.3	28.2	495		
	3	8.1	10.3	15.0	19.0	500		
	7	7.2	9.0	11.2	10.8	280		
PEA−2	Ctrl	13.1	16.1	25.0	27.2	345		
	3	10.4	13.5	17.8	20.0	425	0.32	0.21
	7	—	—	—	8.7	50	0.31	0.23
PEA−2[a]	Ctrl	14.1	20.4	30.0	30.8	305		
	3	11.1	15.6	24.9	27.6	380	0.98	0.26
	7	12.1	13.9	—	14.8	190	0.21	0.08
	10	12.0	15.3	—	18.0	245	0.39	0.28
PEA−4	Ctrl	18.6	22.2	—	30.0	219		
	3	16.7	20.6	—	24.3	210		
PEA−5	Ctrl	28.1	29.1	—	31.4	110		
	3	27.5	27.6	—	27.6	100		
PEEA−1	Ctrl	7.9	11.4	14.9	15.4	310		
	3	8.3	11.0	—	14.5	240	−0.41	−0.45
	7	7.9	11.1	—	13.2	190	−0.72	−0.71
PEEA−2	Ctrl	8.7	12.8	—	17.3	277		
	3	8.8	12.1	—	15.2	220	−0.24	−0.06
	7	9.0	12.2	—	15.7	270	−0.17	−0.22

[a] PEA−2 stabilized with 0.75 Wt % Staboxol P

tions become less susceptible as the hardness increases since the amount of ester present is reduced.

Elastomers which are ether based, such as PEEA, are much less senstitive to the presence of water since the ether linkage does not hydrolyze. The PEEA polymers show excellent retention of their original tensile properties in humid aging tests. Table VI lists the retention of properties for PEA and PEEA after several days at 100 % relative humidity at 85 °C.

4.5   Chemical and Solvent Resistance

The nature of the hard segment has a large effect upon the chemical and solvent resistance of a segmented block elastomer. Since the soft segments commonly used are actually soluble in common organic solvents, it is the hard segment domains which must maintain the integrity of the polymer. The semi-crystalline amide hard segments in PEA have low solubility in many solvents. Thus, PEA-2 has excellent resistance in oil, fuels, and grease. PEA-2 also fares well in phosphate based hydraulic fluids, but chlorinated solvents have a much greater adverse effect. As the proportion of hard segment increases in the harder formulations, the chemical resistance also improves. This effect can be seen in the results of seven day immersion tests in Table VII.

4.6   Tear Strength

PEA-2 has exceptionally good tear strength (ASTM D-624, Die C) with values of 151 and 51 kN/m at room temperature and 150 °C, respectively. Since tear strength generally increases with tensile strength, the harder grades such as PEA-4 have slightly higher values of 169 and 58 kN/m at corresponding test temperatures. PEA also has a value of 31.5 kN/m for split tear strength (ASTM D-470).

TABLE VII   Chemical Resistance of PEA; Seven Day Immersion, Room Temperature (ASTM D−543)

		ASTM #3 Oil	Brake Fluid	Skydrol 500	Toluene	Lithium Grease
PEA−2	% Vol	+1.5	+29	+31	+41	+0.5
	% Wt	+1.3	+27	+29	+31	+0.8
	Hardness	+2	+ 6	− 9	− 5	+3
PEA−4	% Vol	+0.7	+16	+21	+35	+0.3
	% Wt	+0.6	+14	+20	+27	+0.3
	Hardness	+6	− 8	−15	−13	−3
PEA−5	% Vol		+17	+12		
	% Wt		+15	+11		
	Hardness		−20	− 8		

Note: Samples were annealed at 200°C for three hours

4.7   Abrasion Resistance

PEA-2 has good abrasion resistance which is comparable to that of the thermoplastic polyurethanes and the copolyetheresters of similar hardness measured under the same conditions. Table VIII lists the values obtained using several different abrasive wheels in the Taber abrasion test (ASTM D-1044).

TABLE VIII   Abrasion Resistance of PEA−2, Taber Abrasion (ASTM D−1044)

Abrasive Wheel	mg Loss/1000 revs.
CS−17	4
H−18	89
H−22	60

4.8 Compression Set

The PEA elastomers have very good compression set when measured under constant load conditions (ASTM D-395, Method A). This is due to the high modulus and load bearing abilities of these elastomers.

Under test conditions with constant compression (ASTM D-395, Method B), the high modulus is somewhat detrimental because of the very high stress levels generated. Over the course of the test, reorganization in the hard segment domains occurs leading to compression set values somewhat higher than found with a crosslinked rubber material. Factors which favor well organized crystal structures in the hard domains generally help to reduce the compression set. Results are summarized in Table IX.

TABLE IX   Compression Set (ASTM D−395 A, B)

		Set (%)	Temp (°C)
PEA−1	Method A	—	
	Method B	36	RT
		79	100
PEA−2	Method A	2	RT
	Method B	40	RT

4.9 Flex Properties

The Tg of the soft segments relative to the test temperature is an important parameter in the flex fatigue of a TPE since the polymer becomes "leathery" as the Tg is approached. Formulations with greater phase separation usually have lower Tg's and often have improved performance in flex fatigue experiments. This effect is illustrated in Table X where the results of the low temperature Ross flex cut growth test (ASTM D-1052) are compared for PEA-1 (Tg −40°C) and PEA-2 (Tg −28°C).

TABLE X   Ross Flex for PEA (ASTM D−1052)

Sample		Test Temperature	
		−20°C	−35°C
PEA−1	Cycles[a]	1,050,000	1,011,000
	% Cut Growth	0	0
PEA−2	Cycles	26,000	12,300
	% Cut Growth	800	1,000[b]

[a] Test stopped at one million cycles
[b] Sample failed

4.10 Adhesion

The adhesive characteristics of PEA-4 have been measured in a lap shear test using wire brushed, *unprimed* aluminum sheets. The test pieces were prepared by compression molding a 0.18 mm film of the PEA between the aluminum sheets. Lap shear strengths ranging from 7.62 to 9.24 MPa were obtained at room temperature.

4.11 Weatherability

In addition to outdoor exposure to ultraviolet radiation (UV), elastomers used today in indoor applications are also exposed to significant levels of ultraviolet radiation through the increased use of fluorescent lighting. PEA-2, with no additional stabilization, has excellent resistance to UV radiation under moisture condensing conditions (ASTM G-53), Table XI. Since the finished color of PEA is yellow-brown, there was no discernible discoloration after 2500 hours of exposure.

TABLE XI   Weatherability; QUV Exposure of PEA−2 (ASTM G−53)

Time (hr)	Modulus (MPa) 50%	100%	300%	Tensile Strength (MPa)	Elong (%)	Set (%)	Shore Hardness
0	14.3	16.1	25.6	30.5	340	40	93
40	14.3	16.6	—	23.7	280	30	94
100	14.3	16.3	23.6	25.0	300	40	94
300	14.8	16.8	24.1	24.5	300	40	95
500	14.2	16.5	24.2	25.0	320	40	93
1000	15.0	16.5	23.7	25.0	350	50	93
2500	14.8	16.4	22.7	24.1	350	50	93

Note: QUV conditions: repeated 8 hr UV exposure followed by 4 hr condensation at 40 °C

4.12 Electrical Properties

The electrical properties of PEA-2 are summarized in Table XII. These values generally qualify these elastomers for low voltage applications as an insulating material.

TABLE XII   Electrical Properties at 22°C and 50 % Relative Humidity

Dielectric Constant (ASTM D−150)	at 60 Hz	10.26
	10^3 Hz	9.30
	10^6 Hz	5.67
Dissipation Factor (ASTM D−150)	at 60 Hz	0.092
	10^3Hz	0.066
	10^6 Hz	0.100
Surface Resistivity (ASTM D−257)		3.09×10^{12} ohms
Volume Resistivity (ASTM D−257)		8.13×10^{10} ohm-cm

4.13 Processing Characteristics

The PEA and PEEA elastomers have been melt processed on injection molding, blow molding and extrusion equipment, which includes profile, wire coating, and film extrusions. Attributes which facilitate melt processing include a processing window larger than that of thermoplastic polyurethane, and good melt strength. Unlike polyurethanes, however, no

TABLE XIII   Processing Conditions for PEA−2

Injection Molding		Extrusion	
Temperature		*Temperature*	
Zone	°C	Zone	°C
Rear	230−240	Feed	230−240
Middle	240−250	Transition	240−250
Front	240−250	Metering	245−255
Nozzle	250−260	Die	245−255
Mold	75− 85		
Melt	245−255	Melt	250−255
Screw Speed	RPM		RPM
	80−100		50
Pressure	MPa		
Injection	8.3		
Hold	3.4		
Back	0.7		
Cycle Time	Sec		
Injection	2		
Hold	5−8		
Cooling	25		

bond dissociation and recombination occurs during melt processing. Recommended starting conditions for the extrusion and injection molding of PEA-2 are listed in Table XIII. Since the process temperature is related to the polymer Tm (Table I), the zone temperatures must be adjusted accordingly for the other formulations. The apparent melt viscosity as a function of shear rate at several temperatures is shown in Figure 7 for PEA-2.

Mold shrinkage has been measured for PEA-2 using a 125 mm by 125 mm by 1.6 mm plaque. Shrinkage parallel to the flow direction is 0.015 mm/mm and perpendicular shrinkage is 0.010 mm/mm. If the mold surface is kept scrupulously clean, there is no sticking and no need for a mold release.

To obtain the optimum properties, the PEA and PEEA elastomers must be dry prior to processing. As in any amide or ester based polymer, absorbed moisture can lead to hydrolytic chain scission and subsequent loss of molecular weight at the elevated processing temperatures. Thus, it is essential that the resin have a moisture content of less than 0.02 percent before processing. This level can be attained by drying for 4–6 hours at 100–110 °C in a dehumidifying hopper dryer (dew point −30 °C to −40 °C). It is also recommended that the feed hopper be purged with dry nitrogen to maintain the low moisture level.

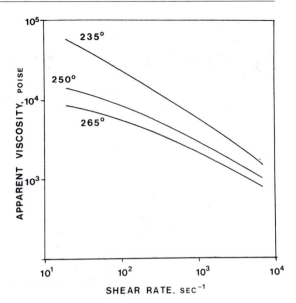

Figure 7   Apparent melt viscosity of PEA-2 as a function of shear rate at indicated temperatures

4.14 Potential Applications

The polyesteramides and polyetheresteramides are members of a new class of thermoplastic polyamide elastomer and, as of this writing, their end use and application areas are just beginning to emerge. Because of the higher service temperatures and the good thermal aging and solvent resistance characteristics, the PEA, and to some extent the PEEA, thermoplastic elastomers are expected to be in the range between the thermoplastic polyurethanes and the silicone polymers. Since the dominant properties of these materials are the heat, oil, and fuel resistance, automotive under-the-hood applications are being explored.

Evaluations are also underway in various industrial applications for use where heat and chemical resistance are required. Extruded films and sheets are also being considered for various applications.

In electrical areas, wire and cable jacketing for high temperature applications are being established. These are primarily for low voltage wiring in confined areas where temperatures are above ambient such as in under-the-hood locations and in the vicinity of various engines and motors.

5   SUMMARY

The effectiveness of the physical crosslinks formed by the hard segment domains in segmented copolymers is illustrated by the upper limit for the use temperature. The goal of increasing the temperature limit of thermoplastic elastomers has been met by the incorporation of high melting, semicrystalline polyamides as the hard segments. This has been accomplished by the reaction of aromatic diisocyanates with dicarboxylic acids and derivatives to provide semiaromatic polyamides. The result is a series of polyesteramide and polyetheresteramide thermoplastic elastomers which have excellent tensile properties at 150 °C continous service temperature, and which can withstand even higher temperature excursions. In addition, these polymers also have good thermal aging and fuel, oil, and grease resistance. Heating above the melting point of the amide hard segments melts the physical crosslinks, allowing the hard segments to flow. Thus, PEA and PEEA can be melt processed readily by conventional means such as extrusion, blow molding, and injection molding into a wide variety of useful end products.

References

1. G. M. Estes, S. L. Cooper, and A. V. Tobolsky, *J. Macromol. Sci., Rev. Macromol. Chem., C4 (2)*, 313 (1970)
2. T. K. Kwei, *J. Applied Polym. Sci., 27*, 2891 (1982) and references cited within
3. W. Dieckmann and F. Breest, *Ber., 39*, 3052 (1906)
4. H. Staudinger, *Helv. Chem. Acta, 5*, 87 (1922)
5. W. D'Olieslager and I. DeAquirre, *Bull. Soc. Chim. Fr., 1*, 179 (1967)
6. P. Babusiaux, R. Longeray, and J. Dreux, *Julius Liebigs Ann. Chem. 3*, 487 (1976)
7. M. F. Sorokin, S. M. Marukhina, and V. N. Stokozenko, *Tr. Mosk. Khim. – Tekhnol. Inst., 86*, 25 (1975)
8. M. F. Sorokin, S. M. Marukhina, and V. N. Stokozenko, *Deposited Doc. 1975, VINITI 1908-75*, p. 33
9. M. F. Sorokin, S. M. Marukhina, J. V. Galkina, and V. N. Stokozenko, *Tr. Mosk. Khim. – Tekhnol. Inst., 86*, 27 (1975)
10. J. T. Chapin, B. K. Onder, and W. J. Farrissey, Jr., *Polymer Preprints, 21 (2)*, 130 (1980)
11. K. B. Onder and C. P. Smith, U. S. Patent 4,156,065 (The Dow Chemical Co.), May 22, 1979
12. K. B. Onder, P. S. Andrews, W. J. Farrissey, Jr., and J. N. Tilley, *Polymer Preprints, 21 (2)*, 132 (1980)
13. K. B. Onder, W. J. Farrissey, Jr., J. T. Chapin, and P. S. Andrews, SPE 39th Annual Technical Conference (ANTEC), Boston, May 4-7, 1981, p. 883.
14. A. T. Chen, W. J. Farrissey, Jr., and R. G. Nelb, II, U.S. Patent 4,129,715 (The Dow Chemical Co.), December 12, 1978
15. R. G. Nelb, II, A. T. Chen, W. J. Farrissey, Jr., and K. B. Onder, SPE 39th Annual Technical Conference (ANTEC), Boston, May 4–7, 1981, p. 421.
16. P. J. Flory, *Principles of Polymer Chemistry*, Cornell University Press, 1953, p. 93.
17. R. Bonart, *Polymer, 20*, 1389 (1979)
18. R. W. Seymour and S. L. Cooper, *Rubber Chem. Technol., 47*, 19 (1977)
19. J. C. West and S. L. Cooper, *J. Polymer Sci., Polym. Symp., 60*, 127 (1977)
20. R. J. Cella, *J. Polymer Sci., Polym. Symp., 42*, 727 (1973)
21. A. T. Chen, R. G. Nelb, II, and K. Onder, U. S. Patent 4,415,693 (The Dow Chemical Co.), November 15, 1983.

Chapter 9B

POLYETHER BLOCK AMIDE THERMOPLASTIC ELASTOMERS

G. Deleens

Contents

G. Deleens, ATOCHEM CERDATO, 27470 Serquigny, France

1   INTRODUCTION

ATOCHEM began research on block copolymers based on polyamide precursors in the early 1970's as an extension of ATOCHEM's position in polyamides 11 and 12.

Before 1970 many laboratories had worked on block copolymers employing several chemical routes. Du Pont in 1954 obtained a patent[1] on a polyurethane spandex fiber which was a thermoplastic elastomer. In 1957 Schollenberger[2] reported on a "virtually cross-linked" elastomer based on polyurethane.

The three-block poly(styrene-b-butadiene-b-styrene) copolymer thermoplastic elastomers were introduced in 1965[3]. In the late 1960's Du Pont commenced research on copolyester thermoplastic elastomers via melt polycondensation. This work resulted in the copolyester TPE's[4]. Toyobo (Japan) introduced similar polymers about the same time.

Polyamide-polyester block copolymers were studied, but preparation of random block copolymers by reaction between ester and amide groups during polymerization resulted in materials with poor consistency and low melting points. Polymers made with polyamide-polyether blocks could not reach a molecular weight high enough to be used as engineering plastics.

Many methods for synthesizing polyamide polyether block copolymers using different linkages between the polyether and polyamide blocks have been studied. Among them are the following:

1.1   Amide Linkage

Several research groups[5,6,7] studied the reaction of dicarboxylic polyamide blocks with diamine polyether blocks or diamine polyamide blocks with dicarboxylic polyether blocks in the molten state.

$$HOOC - PA - COOH + H_2N - PE - NH_2 \longrightarrow HO \left[\underset{O}{\underset{\|}{C}} - PA - \underset{O}{\underset{\|}{C}} - \underset{H}{\underset{|}{N}} - PE - \underset{N}{\underset{|}{N}} \right]_n H$$

$$H_2N - PA - NH_2 + HOOC - PE - COOH \longrightarrow H \left[\underset{H}{\underset{|}{N}} - PA - \underset{H}{\underset{|}{N}} - \underset{O}{\underset{\|}{C}} - PE - \underset{O}{\underset{\|}{C}} \right]_n OH$$

This required modification of polyether diols by cyanoethylation and reduction or hydrolysis, requiring expensive raw material.

1.2   Urethane or Urea Linkage

The reaction of poly (oxyethylene) αω-bischloroformiate with adipyl chloride and piperazine in solution to give a polyamide polyether with urethane linkages between the blocks was reported[8]. Others[9] worked on the reaction, also in solution, of poly (oxyethylene) diisocyanate with a diamine aromatic polyamide to reach polyamide polyether block copolymers with urea linkages.

1.3 Ester Linkage

Just two references were found on the reaction, in the melt, of a dicarboxylic polyamide and a polyether diol. The first[10] covered the reaction of a dicarboxylic acid polyamide based on caprolactam and poly(oxyethylene) dihydroxy at 250 °C with paratoluene sulfonic acid as a catalyst. The second[11] described the reaction of a C-36 fatty acid dimer and a diamine with a polyoxyethylene dihydroxy without catalyst at 250 °C. These two products were low in molecular weight and were used as waxy additives in textile fiber formulations to provide antistatic properties.

ATOCHEM discovered that the use of a particular catalyst family, $Ti(OR)_4$, was the appropriate way to reach a high molecular weight polyamide polyether block copolymer with ester linkages. This catalyst appears to modify the compatibility between the diacid polyamide and dihydroxy polyether segments and allows the possibility of achieving the polymerization in a homogeneous phase which was not possible with any other catalysts. A study of the kinetics of polyesterification was done by Deleens[12] and the first patent was applied for in 1974[13].

A wide study of the combinations between different polyamide blocks and polyether blocks was then made. In addition, research on catalysts, polymerization processes, formulations and applications[14–18] was also undertaken.

In 1981 ATOCHEM launched thermoplastic elastomer products called Polyether Block Amides (PEBA) under the tradename PEBAX[19].

2   CHEMISTRY AND STRUCTURE

2.1 Chemistry

The Polyether Block Amide is obtained by the molten state polycondensation reaction of polyether diol blocks and dicarboxylic polyamide blocks; the general formula of these copolymers is

$$HO - \left[\underset{O}{\overset{\parallel}{C}} - PA - \underset{O}{\overset{\parallel}{C}} - O - PE - O \right]_n H$$

where PA is the polyamide block and PE is the polyether block.

2.1.1 Polyamide Blocks

Dicarboxylic Polyamide blocks are produced by the reaction of polyamide precursors with a dicarboxylic acid chain limitor. The reaction is achieved at high temperature (higher than 230 °C) and generally under pressure (up to 25 bars). The molecular weight of the polyamide block is controlled by the amount of chain limitor. The polyamide precursors can be selected from the following:

– amino acids (aminoundecanoic acid, aminododecanoic acid)
– Lactams (caprolactam, Lauryllactam, ..)
– dicarboxylic acids (adipic acid, azelaic acid, dodecanedioic acid, ..)
– diamines (hexamethylene diamine, dodecamethylene diamine, ..).

2.1.2 Polyether Blocks

Dihydroxy polyether blocks are produced by two different reactions:

– anionic polymerization of ethylene oxide and propylene oxide for polyoxyethylene dihydroxy and polyoxypropylene dihydroxy
– cationic polymerization of tetrahydrofuran for polyoxytetramethylene dihydroxy.

2.1.3 Polyether Block Amides

The block copolymerization is a polyesterfication achieved at high temperature (230–280 °C) under vacuum (0.1 to 10 Torrs) and requires the use of an appropriate catalyst.

Generally, it is necessary to introduce additives, such as an antioxidant or optical brightener during polymerization.

2.2   Structure

The structure of Polyether block amides comprises linear and regular chains of rigid polyamide segments and flexible polyether segments. Since polyamide and polyether segments are not miscible, PEBA present a biphasic structure where each segment offers its own properties to the polymer. Owing to this structure, it is possible to work with four basic chemical criteria:

– the nature of the Polyamide blocks
– the nature of the Polyether blocks
– the length of the Polyamide blocks
– the mass relationship between the Polyamide and Polyether blocks.

These four independent criteria control the properties of the Polyether block amide:

– the nature of the polyamide block influences
  · the melting point of the polymer
  · the specific gravity
  · the chemical resistance
– the nature of the polyether block influences
  · the glass transition temperature
  · the hydrophilic properties
  · the antistatic performance
– the length of the polyamide block influences the melting point of the polymer
– the mass relationship between the polyamide and polyether blocks controls the hardness properties.

2.3   PEBA Range

Because of the wide variety of polyamides and polyethers available it is possible to create a very high number of grades of PEBAX. However, a specific range has been selected to meet defined market needs. With nine basic block copolymers, the range can be expanded through appropriate formulations or by the incorporation of fillers or pigments. Because the chemistry is so versatile, the product range is broad. See Table I.

TABLE I   Product Range of Polyether Block Amides

	Formulation	Designation	Hardness	
			Shore D	Shore A
Extrusion and Molding Grades	Without additives	6333 SA 00	63	—
		5533 SA 00	55	—
		4033 SA 00	40	90
		3533 SA 00	35	83
		2533 SA 00	25	75
	U.V. stabilized	6333 SN 00	63	—
		5533 SN 00	55	—
		4033 SN 00	40	90
		3533 SN 00	35	83
		2533 SN 00	25	75
	U.V. stabilized + mold release agent	5533 SD 00	55	—
		4033 SD 00	40	90
		3533 SD 00	35	83
		2533 SD 00	25	75
	Heat stabilized	6333 ST 01 B[a]	63	—
		5533 ST 01 B[a]	55	—
		4033 ST 01 B[a]	40	90
		3533 ST 01 B[a]	35	83
		2533 ST 01 B[a]	25	75
Molding Grades	U.V. stabilized	6312 MN 00	63	—
		5512 MN 00	55	—
		5512 MN 01 B[a]	55	—
Low Melting Point Molding Grade	Without additives	5562 MA 00	55	—
Antistatic and Hydrophilic Grade	Without additives	4011 MA 00	40	—
Antistatic Extrusion and Molding Grades	Heat stabilized + antistatic fillers	5533 SN 70 B[a]	60	—
		4033 SN 70 B[a]	50	—

[a] Black

3   PROPERTIES

Several major properties characterize this entire family of polymers:

- high mechanical properties
- good performance at low temperatures
- good dynamic properties
- ability to be compounded
- ease of processing

3.1 Physical Properties

The specific gravity of PEBA extends to the lowest values of the high performance thermoplastic elastomers, Table II.

TABLE II   Specific Gravity Comparison

Polymer Grade	Specific Gravity
33 Series	1.01
12 Series	1.10
62 Series	1.06
11 Series	1.10
Thermoplastic Polyurethane	1.16/1.25
Polyether Esters	1.17/1.25
Rubber	>1.20

Moisture absorption is dependent on the nature of the polyamide and also of the polyether blocks. The 33 series grades show very low moisture absorption, which results in dimensional stability and low variation in mechanical and electrical properties. The 4011 grade is a very hydrophilic grade; it absorbs up to 120 % of moisture, Table III.

TABLE III   Moisture Absorption Characteristics of Polyether Block Amide

Condition	Moisture Absorption[a] %			
	33 Series	12 Series	62 Series	11 Series
20 °C – 65 % R. H.	0.5	2.5	1.3	4.5
24 hours in water	1.2	6.5	3.5	120

[a] Test method – ASTM D570

Because of their biphasic structure, PEBA present

– a sharp melting point originating from the polyamide blocks

– a glass transition temperature orginating from the polyether blocks.

Depending on the grade, the melting points can vary from 120 °C to 210 °C, Table IV, however, the glass transition temperature is always close to −60 °C.

TABLE IV   Melting Point of Grades Polyether Block Amide

Grade	Melting Point[a] °C
6333	173
5533	168
4033	168
3533	152
2533	148
6312	205
5512	195
5562	120
4011	195

[a] Test Method – ASTM D2117

3.2 Mechanical Properties

3.2.1 Hardness and Flexibility

PEBA cover a wide range of hardness without the addition of plasticizer. It is possible to synthesize grades with a Shore Hardness between 75 D and 60 A. This range can be compared with other thermoplastics or rubbers, Figure 1.

PEBA shows little variation in flexibility when tested at different temperatures. This is due primarily to the low transition temperature of the polyether blocks, Figure 2, and to same extent to the sharp melting point of the polyamide blocks.

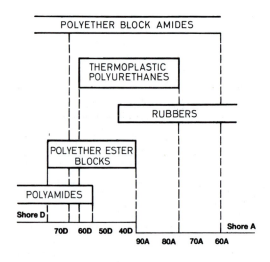

Figure 1   Comparison of the Shore Hardness range of the PEBA polymers with the ranges of other thermoplastics and rubber

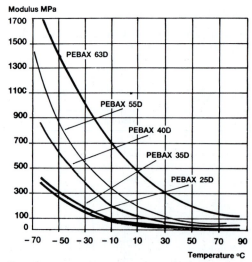

Test pieces injection moulded and conditioned
14 days at 23 ° C and 50 % H.R.

Figure 2   Modulus of elasticity in flexure versus temperature for PEBA of varying Shore D Hardness, ASTM D790

3.2.2 Tensile Strength

The polyether content influences the tensile strength and elastic nature of the block copolymer, Figure 3.

Stress under low deformation, whatever the grade, is higher for PEBA than most thermoplastic materials of the same hardness and higher than elastomers. This is very important for design because one can significantly reduce the thickness of a component in many applications; weight saving, as well as better cost, can result, Figure 4.

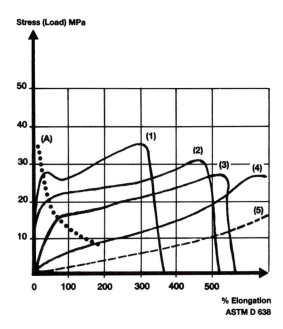

Figure 3   Elastomeric   Character   of PEBA as a function of the polyether content as compared with a Polyamide and an Elastomer, (1) Polyamide, (2) 30 % polyether, (3) 50 % polyether, (4) 80 % polyether, (5) Elastomer. Curve A represents elastic limit

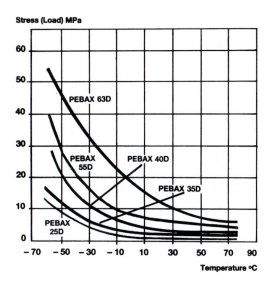

Figure 4   Stress at 5 % Elongation versus temperature for PEBA injection molded samples conditioned 14 days at 23 °C and 50 % relative humidity, ASTM D638

3.2.3 Impact Resistance

These block copolymers have high impact resistance, especially at low temperature (-40 °C). This property is also dependent on the polyether content and the nature of polyamide block, Table V.

TABLE V   Low Temperature Impact Properties of Polyether Block Amide

				Grade			
Test[a]	6333	5533	4033	3533	2533	6312	5512
Izod Impact, Notched (-40 °C)							
J/m of notch	100	NB[b]	NB	NB	NB	35	90

[a] Test Samples of 3.2 mm Thickness, With Notch
[b] NB – No Break

3.3 Dynamic Properties

PEBA present very interesting dynamic properties, which allow them to be used in those applications where the material is subjected to repeated and more or less rapid stresses of limited deformation, see Table VI.

TABLE VI   Dynamic Properties of Polyether Block Amide

Grade	Hysteresis under 10% Extension[a] %	Resilience[b] %	DeMattia Flex Test[c] (Notch Length in mm)	
			20 °C 100,000 Flexes	-20 °C 50,000 Flexes
6333	25.2	56	5	14
5533	22.2	58.8	3	9
4033	17.6	62.5	2	4.5
3533	12.1	70	2	2.5
2533	12.3	75	2	2.5
6312	32.9	49	15,000 Flexes[d]	7,000 Flexes[d]
5512	25.9	54	80,000 Flexes[d]	11

[a] Special ATOCHEM Test – Test Performed at 20 °C
[b] Test Method – BS 903 Part 08, Method A
[c] Test Method – ASTM D813
[d] Length of Crack Reaches 16 mm before, 100,000 Flexes (or 50,000 Flexes at -20 °C)

3.3.1 Hysteresis

The effect of hysteresis may be quantified as a loss of energy during a deformation cycle; the energy which is lost in the form of mechanical energy is coverted into heat. The hysteresis values for PEBA are lower than those for thermoplastic or vulcanized materials of equivalent hardness. This results in a lower temperature rise during dynamic use and hence, a long working life for the parts.

3.3.2 Resilience

The elastic memory of PEBA may be quantified in dynamic terms by the value of the resilience on bouncing. PEBA have high resilience values and show a quick recovery after deformation.

3.3.3 Resistance to Alternating Flexure

The propagation of a notch during alternating flexure shows the ability of a material to withstand repeated deformation under severe conditions. The high resistance of PEBA to alternating flexure, even at low temperature, is one for the reason fo selecting them for use in Nordic ski shoe soles, Table VI.

3.4   Physical Properties of the PEBA Grades

In Table VII are shown the physical properties of five of the 33 series PEBA polymers of decreasing Shore hardness values from 63D to 25D. As might be expected, the melt index increases over the series from 3 to 9–10. The tensile strength decreases from 51 Mpa to 29 MPa, while the elongation at break increases from 380 % to 715 % over the same range of hardness values. These values illustrate high quality physical properties characteristic of the polymers. Heat distortion temperature decreases from 90 °C for the highest hardness sample to 42 °C for the lowest hardness material.

Mechanical properties of the same series of PEBA thermoplastic elastomers are shown in Table VIII. Again we see the expected trends in stress at 25 % extension, tear strength, abrasion resistance and compression set through the series from high to low Shore D Hardness.

TABLE VII   Physical Properties of Polyether Block Amide TPE

Pebax No.	6333	5333	4033	3533	2533
Shore Hardness, D	63	55	40	35	25
Melt Index, ASTM D1238[a]	3	5	5	10	9
Tensile strength, MPa	51	44	36	34	29
Elongation at break, %	380	455	485	710	715
Clash-Berg at −40 °C, MPa[b]	290	155	95	51	46
Heat distortion temp., °C[c]	90	66	52	46	42

[a] 235 °C/1 kg die 2 mm
[b] ASTM D1043, modulus of rigidity in torsion
[c] ASTM D648, under load of 0.46 MPa

TABLE VIII   Physical Properties of Polyether Block Amide TPE

Pebax No.	6333	5333	4033	3533	2533
Stress to 25 % extension, MPa[a]	17.6	11.9	6.5	2.35	1.85
Young's Modulus, PMa[b]	260	145	50	14.6	10.4
Tension Set @ 20 % extension, %[c]	4.9	3.5	2.1	1.9	1.6
Tear, ASTM D624 (C), KN/m[d]	150	115	70	45	38
Abrasion, Taber, ASTM D1242[e]	46	65	70	81	94
Compression Set, %, ASTM D395[f]	5	10	21	54	62

[a] ASTM D638-type IV, Injection molded test pieces
[b] ASTM D638 Epr. type IV, Injection molded test pieces
[c] ASTM D412
[d] notched
[e] mg./1000 cycles
[f] Load = 9.3 MPa, 22 hrs. at 70 °C

3.5 Aging and Chemical Resistance

As with a majority of thermoplastic materials, these block copolymers require specific additives to achieve good resistance to ultraviolet light (U. V.) and high temperature. The photodegradation mechanism is more complex than simple addition of the mechanism of polyamide and polyether degradation, as shown by Gauvin[20]. Thermal degradation is mainly due to the polyether blocks. When block copolymers are well stabilized they show a U. V. resistance without discoloration, higher than other thermoplastics. Thermal resistance can also be improved; because of their melting point, however, PEBA cannot be used at very high temperatures.

The chemical resistance of PEBA is dependent on the grade and on the solvent. Rigid grades that have a low content of polyether have good resistance to a majority of chemical agents. Soft grades can swell in solvent; this is particularly true in chlorinated solvents, alcohol and oils. However, in each case there is no chemical degradation.

3.6 Aptitude for Compounding

Because of their compatibility with pigments, mineral fillers and other polymers, PEBA can be blended or compounded with other materials with good results. Using this attribute it has been possible to develop special grades filled with 30 % $CaCO_3$, 15–20 % carbon black or 30 % glass fibers with good mechanical properties. It is also very easy to color with many types of pigments or dyes. Regarding compounding, the most important fact is that PEBA are compatible with polyamides, PVC, S-B-S and other polymers, such as polyolefins, in various proportions. It is, therefore, possible to create a wide range of new materials.

4   PROCESSING

4.1 Drying

All grades of PEBA must be adequately dried before use, to 0.06 to 0.10 % moisture content. PEBA is shipped in moisture barrier bags with a moisture content below 0.08 %. If the contents should be exposed to moisture before use, it is suggested that the material be dried in a dehumidifying-type dryer. The recommended drying conditions:

For Shore D 40:4 hours at 80 °C
For Shore D 40:6 hours at 70 °C.

4.2 Regrind

In most cases it is possible to recycle PEBA rejects after grinding and drying by incorporating up to 20 % of the reground material into virgin granules of the same grade.

4.3 Conversion Techniques

PEBA are easy to process using conventional thermoplastic converting technology. All grades except for some specialty molding grades, can be processed by normal thermoplastic forming methods – extrusion, molding, rotational molding, thermoforming, etc. The same equipment used for molding and extrusion of polyamides, polyurethanes or PVC can be used. Nevertheless, it is necessary to modify the design of runners and gates for molds, and sizing equipment for tubing extrusion, for the softest grades. These grades have a tendency to stick to metal during processing.

4.4   Extrusion Parameters

The presence of the amorphous elastomer segments in PEBA results in certain rheological differences between PEBA and nylons. For example, there is no need for a high compression ratio screw to obtain a homogeneous melt as is common with most nylons. A compression ratio between 2:1 and 3:1 is suggested. Fine screen packs used in most nylon extrusions to increase melt homogenization are not needed in PEBA extrusion; a screen pack of 40–60–40 mesh should be adequate.

The rheological properties of PEBA and nylon are similar enough to use the nylon-type pin and die which has a longer pin (150 mm) than the one used for PVC. A PIN/DIE ratio to tube dimensions (ID, OD) should be approximately 2 to 1. The softer grades of PEBA may require a ratio of 1.2:1 to 1.5:1.

With the softer grades of PEBA, which have a tendency to stick to metal, it is quite difficult to use differential pressure sizing techniques. It is recommended, for these grades, to proceed with extrusion directly into the cooling tank and then control diameter by:

a) maintaining constant air pressure inside the tube, or
b) maintaining a slight vacuum inside the tube using a differential pressure sizing tank but adjusting the vacuum such that the tube does not contact the entrance to the tank.

Table IX shows recommended temperatures for plasticization of the "33" series of PEBA in extrusion.

TABLE IX   Extrusion

PEBA Grades	Recommended Temperature Range for Plasticization, °C
6333	210 – 230
5533	210 – 230
4033	210 – 230
3533	190 – 220
2533	170 – 210

4.5   Injection Molding

Normal equipment, as used for injection molding of polyamides (screw type press), is suitable. For the more flexible PEBA types it may be advisable to apply the techniques used for polyurethanes as regards to mold design, runner systems. Some examples of molding conditions are shown in Table X. The average shrinkages under optimal molding conditions are of the order of 0.5 to 1 %.

TABLE X   Typical Injection Molding[a] Conditions

PEBA Grade	Cylinder Temp. °C	Injection Pressure, b	Injection Time, s	Cooling Time, s	Injection rate	Mold Temp. °C
5533	220–230–230–225	400	8	20	Average	30
4033	220–260–260–255	430	9	30	Average	30
2533	185–195–200–190	800	10	20	Medium	25

[a] Ankerwerk press, force 65 ton, Moldings: 100×100×1 mm sheets, 12 g

4.6 Assembling

PEBA may be assembled with other materials (rubber, plastics, metal, leather, etc.) by using a variety of techniques:

– insert molding
– bonding
– welding

This good property has been used widely for the design of new items employing PEBA as a unique material.

5   APPLICATIONS

The areas for application of these materials are very wide and can be related to the major properties of the material.

5.1 General Mechanical Goods

PEBA can be used to replace rubber in many applications with a reduction of thickness, weight saving and enhanced mechanical properties (bellows for cars, tubes . . .).

5.2 Dynamic Applications

Conveyor and drive belts, Nordic ski and soccer shoe soles, as well as key pads, have been developed with great success.

5.3 Precision and Noise Reduction Applications

PEBA have been selected for silent gears used in audio and video recorders, cameras, etc., as a result of the ease of molding and enduse properties.

5.4 Transparency

PEBA are used in thin films for packaging or medical applications.

5.5 Antistatic Grades

Specially compounded grades with surface resistivities of 10^3–10^4 ohm-cm are used for car aerials, antistatic paint spray hoses and hair brushes.

Many other applications in the sporting goods, electrical, medical, automotive, agriculture and mechanical handling industries have been developed. The use of PEBA as hot melt adhesives, fine powders for coatings and components for compounds is currently expanding the areas for development of Polyether Block Amides.

6 CONCLUSIONS

The Polyether Block Amide (PEBA) Thermoplastic Elastomers have excellent mechanical, physical and chemical properties over a wide range of flexibility.

Their main characteristics are:

- Flexibility and impact resistance at low temperatures
- Dynamic properties, resilience, hysteresis and alternating flexural properties
- Easy processing
- Compatibility with fillers of various origins (dyes, carbon blacks, heavy fillers, glass fibers).

These properties enable the use of the PEBA TPE's in many fields of applications and in the upper ranges of quality of thermoplastic elastomers.

References

1. Du Pont, US 2,692,873 (1954)
2. C. S. Schollenberger, (to B. F. Goodrich), US 2,871,218 (1955); C. S. Schollenberger, H. Scott and G. R. Moore, presented at ACS Rubber Div. Meeting, Sept. 13, 1957, *Rubber Chem and Tech. 35* 742 (1962)
3. J. T. Bailey, et al., presented at ACS Rubber Division Meeting, Oct. 20, 1965, *Rubber Age 98* 69 (1966);
   G. Holden, E. T. Bishop and N. R. Legge, *J. Poly. Sci., C26* 37 (1969)
4. W. K. Witsiepe (to Du Pont), US 3,651,014 (Mar. 21, 1972);
   W. K. Witsiepe (to Du Pont), US 3,763,109 (Oct. 2, 1973);
   W. K. Witsiepe (to Du Pont), US 3,755,146 (Oct. 16, 1973);
   Du Pont, *Rubber Age,* May 1972
5. Toray, French Patent 1,603,901 (1971);
   Toray, Japan Patent 19,846R (1965)
6. Monsanto, US Patent 3,454,534 (1969).
7. ICI, UK Patent 1,108,812 (1965)
8. Du Pont de Nemours, UK Patent 1,098,475 (1968)
9. Matsushita Electric Works, Japan Patent 24,285 Q (1969)
10. BASF, UK Patent 1,110,394 (1968)
11. Unilever Emery, French Patent 2,178,205 (1973)
12. G. Deleens, Ph. D. Thesis, Rouen (1975).
    G. Deleens, P. Foy, E. Marechal, *Eur. Pol. Journal 13,* pp 337–342, 343–351, 351–360 (1977)
13. G. Deleens, P. Foy, C. Jungblut, French Patent 2,273,021 (1974); US Patent 4,230,838 (1980); US Patent 4,331,786 (1982); US Patent 4,332,920 (1982)
14. G. Deleens, P. Foy, French Patent 2,382,060 (1975)

15. G. Deleens, B. Guerin, C. Poulain, French Patent 2,359,879 (1976)
16. G. Deleens, B. Guerin, C. Poulain, French Patent 2,378,058 (1977)
17. G. Deleens, J. Ferlampin, M. Gonnet, French Patent 2,401,947 (1977)
18. G. Deleens, J. Ferlampin, C. Poulain, French Patent 2,413,417 (1977)
19. G. Deleens, ANTEC-81, p. 419-420 (1981)
20. P. Gauvin, J. L. Philppart, J. Lemaire, *Makromol. Chem. 186* 1167–1180 (1985)

Chapter 10A

IONOMERIC THERMOPLASTIC ELASTOMERS EARLY RESEARCH – SURLYN AND RELATED POLYMERS

R. W. Rees

Contents

R. W. Rees, Polymer Products Dept. Experimental Station, E. I. Du Pont de Nemours & Co., Wilmington, DE 19898

1   INTRODUCTION

The discovery of Surlyn® ionomer resins in 1961 is one of the continuing series of technical advances that has characterized Du Pont's involvement with ethylene polymers for well over forty years. Following the discovery of free-radical polyethylene by I. C. I. in England during the 1930's, both Du Pont and Union Carbide were licensed to produce this polymer during World War II. Small scale equipment for high-pressure experimentation became available and a widely ranging exploratory program on copolymerization of ethylene with other monomers was carried out by members of Du Pont's Central Research Department. It was established that potentially valuable copolymers could be obtained with vinyl acetate[1], vinyl chloride[2], vinylidene chloride[3], vinylidene fluoride[4], carbon monoxide[5], sulfur dioxide[6] and many others[7]. It was recognized that most of these comonomers had the effect of increasing the elastomeric nature of the ethylene polymers.

In the early 1960's, research on specialized polymers, based mainly on ethylene was commenced. Ethylene/vinyl acetate polymers were found to have excellent potential as wax modifiers and ingredients in hot-melt adhesives[10]. J. B. Armitage found that high-quality copolymers of ethylene with methacrylic acid could be obtained by careful control of polymerization conditions[11]. These polymers exhibited excellent adhesion to aluminium foil. Copolymerization work was also in progress with carbon monoxide, sulfur dioxide, acrylamide and acrylic esters. Emphasis was placed on the use of comonomers to enhance adhesion, compatibility with other polymers, and controlled crosslinking.

2   IONOMER DISCOVERY

Beginning in late 1960, the author's research activities included a search for new chemical methods to crosslink ethylene polymers. Electron-beam radiation and peroxide treatment were already well known, but there were economic and safety problems, so the use of polar functional groups could be preferable. First experiments were with ethylene-vinyl acetate and a few promising reactions were found, but the crosslinking reagents were difficult to handle under commercial conditions. Attention was then focussed on ethylene-methacrylic acid which had been prepared on the commercial scale in a well-stirred reactor under the conditions specified by J. B. Armitage[11].

The use of epichlorohydrin as a difunctional reagent was one of the first approaches to be tried. If successful, the crosslink would be flexible and would contain a hydroxyl group. As a preliminary step, the ethylene/methacrylic acid copolymer was converted to its sodium salt by reaction with the stoichiometric quantity of sodium methoxide in xylene solution at about 90 °C. Addition of methanolic sodium methoxide to the stirred solution resulted in immediate gelation. The polymeric product was recovered from the gel by macerating it with a large excess of acetone in a Waring blender. A readily filterable precipitate was obtained, which was washed thoroughly and vacuum dried. Laboratory technician, C. A. Carrere molded a 1.5 mm slab for physical testing, and we immediately noted that it was clear, in contrast to the translucent starting material. Hand flexing indicated that the sodium salt was not only stiffer than the precursor but far more resilient and bouncy. It felt much more like a cured elastomer than a limp polyolefin. Infra-red spectroscopy gave a scan consistent with conversion of the free acid to the salt form.

Application of the standard melt index procedure[12] for polyethylene rheology revealed that the melt index of the sodium salt was very low (below 0.1 g/10 mins.), but a smooth, clear extrudate was obtained, and there was no indication of the fractured appearance typical of covalently crosslinked polyethylene. There was much speculation with respect to the type of crosslinking, and decarboxylation of the sodium salt was suggested. This question was resolved by heating a sample in xylene, which swelled but did not dissolve it and adding hydrochloric acid. The polymer then went into solution and after isolation and drying was found to be identical with the starting material in infra-red spectrum and melt index.

3   DEVELOPMENT OF IONOMER TECHNOLOGY AND APPLICATIONS

After discussion of these results, it was agreed that the ionically crosslinked polymer was so different from conventional polyethylene that it justified further study to establish its characteristics, the property limits, and possible end uses.

One of the positive factors contributing to rapid progress was the availability of large quantities of commercial quality ethylene/methacrylic acid copolymers. Three copolymers, containing 5, 10 and 18 % by weight of methacrylic acid, with melt index values of about 6.0 g/10 mins., had been produced in a commercial unit experimental run, so there was no supply problem for experimental work. Experiments on a heated 2 × 6 inch roll mill showed that neutralization could be effected very rapidly in the melt, with no necessity for workup or drying. The acid copolymer was banded on the mill at 125 °C and the metallic reagent added as an oxide, hydroxide or methylate, either dry or as a concentrated solution. As neutralization proceded, the melt usually became so elastic that characteristically loud snapping sounds were emitted. Homogeneity was assured by normal cutting and folding procedures.

The effects of varying the degree of neutralization on physical properties were investigated by the author, assisted by C. A. Carrere. Conventional measurement techniques used in the plastics industry, such as Instron Tensile tests at 2 inches per minute were applied to test specimens which were die-cut from compression molded sheets. The typical stress-strain curve was quite different from that of branched polyethylene, with stress increasing past the yield point (Figure 1). It combined features of elastomers with those of semicrystalline

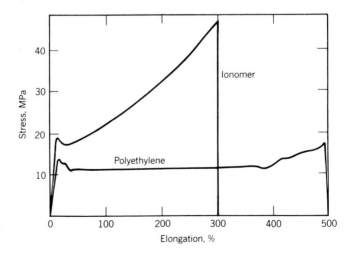

Figure 1 Stress-strain curves of ionomer and conventional polyethylene, density 0.920. Test speed is 5 cm per min

plastics. Stiffness increased with neutralization to a plateau at about 40 % (Figure 2). However, tensile strength continued to increase at higher levels of neutralization (Figure 3).

Work on extending ionic crosslinking to other cations was in progress at the same time. A value of about 77 % neutralization was selected for most of these cations, since the tensile strength had usually reached a plateau at this point. In Group I, soluble hydroxides were used successfully. Within Group II, magnesium and strontium hydroxides were effective reagents, but zinc presented a problem initially. Using zinc oxide in a milling experiment,

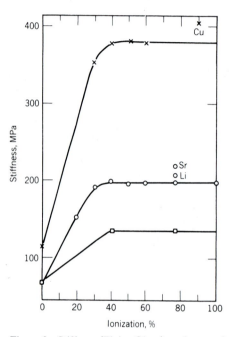

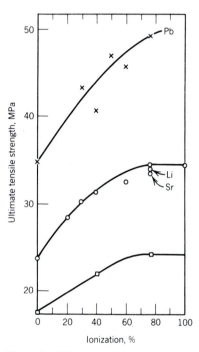

Figure 2   Stiffness (Tinius Olsen) vs degree of ionization (monobasic acid). The cation is sodium unless otherwise indicated. □ 1.7 mole % COOH, ○ 3.5 mole % COOH; × 5.9 mole % COOH

Figure 3   Ultimate tensile strength vs degree of ionization (monobasic acid). The cation is sodium unless otherwise indicated. □1.7 mole % COOH, ○ 3.4 mole % COOH, × 5.9 mole % COOH

some neutralization occurred smoothly, but unreacted zinc oxide was still present after extended periods of milling, as indicated by a white, opaque melt. Dr. D. L. Funck suggested the use of acetates as reagents, the acetic acid being removed by volatilization, and this approach was immediately successful. Acetates of zinc, lead, copper, barium, cobalt and nickel all gave clear melts and quantitative ionic crosslinking was achieved. Following up on this approach in the case of zinc, it was found that addition of a few drops of acetic acid to an opaque melt of acid copolymer/zinc oxide on the two-roll mill immediately resulted in a clear, elastic product[13].

Reviewing the data on the physical properties of Group II cations *vs* Group I, the similarity in solid-state and melt properties was striking and somewhat unexpected. Most of us had anticipated that the divalent cations would bind the chains together to give intractable products, but this was not the case, and a similar pattern of melt flow versus neutralization was established (Figure 4).

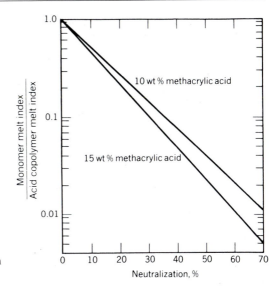

Figure 4   Effect of percent neutralization on melt index of ionomers

Early experiments on water adsorption were very simple in nature, involving boiling molded slabs for one hour. As shown below, the nature of the cation had a large effect:

Metal Ion	Weight gain [%] after 1 hour boil
None	0.13
Sodium	2.25
Potassium	2.35
Lithium	0.5
Magnesium	1.5
Zinc	0.22
Strontium	0.16
Lead	0.13

Although the full implication of water absorption on processing conditions, packaging requirements and performance would require much more detailed work, it was tentatively decided that products based on two cations, sodium and zinc, representing a large difference in water pickup, would be emphasized in future work. Hindsight reveals that this was a sound decision, since both sodium and zinc ionomers have been in the Surlyn® product line continuously since 1965.

Although small-scale tests in the melt indexer showed clearly that the ionically crosslinked copolymers were thermoplastic, their behavior in conventional plastics industry process equipment remained questionable. The roll-mill method was used to prepare a few pounds of sodium salt, and this was injection molded, using a simple 1 oz. plunger machine which injected into V-block molds, capable of being changed between shots. It was, therefore, possible to mold a variety of different articles, including test specimens, small gears, clothes pins, and chain links, (Example X, Ref 13). A few problems were identified, including a tendency toward mold sticking and excessively high melt viscosity. Also, the degree of clarity inherent in the polymers was not obtained in some moldings. It was observed that, as the melt cooled, it became hazy at about 70 °C and then cleared again as cooling continued.

In thick sections, this haze could be "frozen-in", so it was preferable to remove moldings at about 60 °C and complete cooling by immersion in an ice-water bath if good clarity was needed.

Similar small-scale work was done in the area of extrusion during mid 1961. A 1 inch diameter single-screw extruder was used to prepare tubular blown film from a 76 % neutralized sodium salt sample. The polymer temperature was set at 225 °C to keep the melt viscosity within reasonable limits. A stable bubble was obtained and thin 12 micron film produced which was quite glossy and transparent. Testing at the Du Pont Film Department laboratory revealed exceptional impact resistance, comparable with that of biaxially oriented PET (Example VIII, Ref 13). In addition, heat-sealing tests by C. A. Carrere and the author revealed that strong seals could be obtained over a wide range of conditions. Small packages were made and subjected to crude drop tests at intervals during the following months. Damage resistance appeared to be excellent.

Larger samples were subsequently converted into film by a variety of methods. Optical quality was well short of commercial standards, but the material was adequate to demonstrate that it would perform extremely well in skin packaging. The high melt strength of the polymer allowed it to be drawn down tightly around sharp objects without puncturing. Some spectacular exhibits were made by skin-packaging fish hooks on paper board backing, the film being drawn down so snugly around the hooks that it was invisible. Thus a key end-use for the Surlyn® products was recognized within the first year.

Additional fabricating work was done with thicker sheeting of polymers (0.6 mm). This sheet was extruded through a flat die and given a smooth surface by passage between the chrome-plated rolls of a "three-roll finisher". Frozen-food trays were molded, using a conventional vacuum forming device. It was observed that drawability was excellent, due to the high melt strength, so satisfactory parts were obtainable under a wide range of conditions.

In addition to the film and sheet areas, attention was directed to molded articles which could use the somewhat elastomeric characteristics of the new polymers. Work was in progress on a high performance, plastic golf ball, and it appeared that the impact toughness of the ionic copolymers might qualify them for this demanding application. A substantial amount of formulation work was carried out by the author, in collaboration with T. G. Smith and Mario Pagano, to obtain the desired density and resilience. This early work, in 1961-2, resulted in a one-piece ball which performed well on the golf course, but the "click" was much too loud and clearly unacceptable. Emphasis was then placed on softer compositions, containing other monomers to lower crystallinity. Later in the 1960's, the use of Surlyn® ionomers as golf ball covers was developed successfully by Ram Corp., in cooperation with Du Pont.

In view of the clarity and toughness of the ionically linked copolymers, these were evaluated as safety-glass interlayers, replacing poly(vinyl butyral). Early testing showed very good break-height performance relative to the commercial butyral of 1961, but adhesion was below acceptable limits. Internal haze also did not meet the stringent standards set by automotive customers. Further work showed that good break-height and adhesion could be obtained in a single product[14], but the problem of achieving satisfactory optical characteristics would require a lengthy development program.

Another potential automotive market application was featured in early research. In the era before widespread use of radial tires and front-wheel drive, the use of tire chains was well-nigh essential at some point during a North American winter, and the difficulties of grappling with these was well-known to most motorists. We had developed a polyurethane tire chain system and it was decided to try the new, injection-molded ionic copolymers as a substitute. A cheap casting mold was given minimal modification to transform it into an injection mold, and a series of strangely shaped chain segments was molded. In dry road tests the ionic copolymer chains outlasted their steel equivalents and ran much quieter. Winter-road tests revealed shortcomings with the chain design, so this development was useful only in terms of demonstrating ability to withstand unusual punishment.

As demands increased for larger quantities of "ionic copolymers" to be used in processing tests, efforts were directed to scale-up. V. C. Wolff extended the roll-mill techniques to large-scale equipment capable of producing 20 Kgs in a single run. A. A. McLeod developed a diffusion method which worked well for sodium salts. Pellets of the ethylene/methacrylic acid copolymers were submerged in aqueous or methanolic solutions of sodium hydroxide at 50–100 °C. The pellets swelled as diffusion proceeded, resembling "hominy grits" and the product was melt homogenized before use since there was a gradation in the degree of neutralization from outside to center[15]. An experiment on neutralization in an extruder by the author indicated that the ionic copolymer could be obtained, since reaction rate was very rapid, but efficient means were needed to remove volatiles from the melt. Further work by V. C. Wolff and R. L. Saxton on the extrusion-reaction concept resulted in a process which could be used to prepare a variety of ionic copolymers types in quantities up to 50 Kgs (Examples 27–34 of Ref. 15).

Since direct synthesis is usually preferable to post synthesis reactions from the economic standpoint, considerable effort in our studies was devoted to ethylene copolymerizations with salts of unsaturated acids. To obtain a partially neutralized copolymer most experiments involved ethylene, methacrylic acid and sodium methacrylate. High pressure, free radical polymerizations were carried out with vigorous agitation under conditions specified by V. C. Wolff and the author. High molecular weight polymers were obtained, but their properties were quite unlike those of the post-synthesis neutralized materials and were not attractive in any way. It was reluctantly concluded that reasonably uniform incorporation of the sodium methacrylate into the polymer could not be achieved under the conditions available to us. Some experiments on injection of sodium hydroxide into a polymerization reactor at the termination of the polymerization gave promising results (Example 58 of Ref. 15). The concept of "ionic mobility" was developed, predicting that the cation distribution would tend to become more uniform throughout the polymer melt over a period of a few minutes. This could be used to advantage in a large-scale process.

In the area of nomenclature, there were many changes during the first few years. The "ionic copolymers" were known successively as "Polymer A", "Arvon", Surlyn A and finally "Surlyn", the last being a registered trade mark. To differentiate these new products from polyethylenes, a new generic term, *Ionomer,* was proposed by W. B. Clark. This generic term was publicized at the time of new product announcement in 1964, and its significance described in a short paper by the author[16]. The word was immediately adopted by members of the academic community who were active in the field of ion-containing polymers, and is now a standard term in polymer science and technology.

4   EXTENSION OF IONIC CROSSLINKING TO OTHER POLYMER TYPES

Up to this point, the progression of Surlyn research based on the original type of copolymers: ethylene/methacrylic acid has been followed. During 1961, considerable effort was also devoted to ionomers derived from other carboxylated ethylene polymers. Many copolymers of ethylene with dicarboxylic acids were available as a result of pilot-plant work by V. C. Wolff. Some of the results are summarized in the following Table illustrating some unexpected responses to neutralization.

Mechanical Properties of Ethylene Unsaturated Acid Copolymers and Derived Ionomers

Comonomer	% by Weight	Cation	Melt Index (grs/10 min)	Modulus MPa	Ult. Tensile Strength MPa	Ult. Elong. %
Maleic Acid	3	–	44.5	169.6	12.4	450
Maleic Acid	3	Na$^+$	<0.01	115.8	20	260
Maleic Anhydride	3	–	305	124.8	8.1	200
Maleic Anhydride	3	Na$^+$	0.07	120	14	190
Maleic Anhydride	3	Sr^{++}	No-flow	125.5	10.7	250
Maleic Anhydride	3	Zn^{++}	No-flow	129	14.1	140
Maleic Anhydride	7	–	4.7	184.8	10.5	350
Maleic Anhydride	7	Na$^+$	<0.01	136.1	17.8	250
Methyl hydrogen maleate	6	–	7.8	130.3	13.6	520
Methyl hydrogen maleate	6	Na$^+$	<0.01	162	21.5	380
Itaconic acid	6	–	9.0	108.9	12.4	435
Itaconic acid	6	Na$^+$	0.003	181.3	18.4	320
Itaconic acid	6	Sr^{++}	No-flow	151.7	15.5	250

When the acids contained adjacent carboxyls, the polymers did not increase significantly in stiffness on neutralization, although tensile strength and resilience were enhanced. With non-adjacent carboxyls, as in itaconic acid, the expected stiffness increase was found. Neutralization with sodium reduced melt flow to very low levels, and when divalent ions were used with dibasic acids, the products exhibited zero melt flow under standard test conditions. In general, the properties of these ionomers were not outstanding in any way. Due to inherent properties of the monomers, it was quite difficult to obtain ethylene copolymers with maleic acid, maleic anhydride or fumaric acid at acid levels above a few weight percent. The decision to concentrate on copolymers with methacrylic acid was, therefore, quite straight forward. Comparisons of methacrylic with acrylic acid in the ionomer systems indicated that these two acids were almost indistinguishable.

Ionomers derived from graft copolymers also were studied in 1961. Technology had previously been developed for grafting mono or dicarboxylic acids on to high density, highly crystalline polyethylene. When these grafts were partly neutralized, the main property change was a large reduction in melt flow. No benefits in mechanical properties were seen as a result of partial neutralization, so the study was not continued.

An interesting extension of ionomer technology was the use of Portland cement as a combined filler/reagent in ethylene/methacrylic acid copolymers. In this work, performed by D. L. Funck in collaboration with R. M. Busche, the dry Portland cement was first blended with ethylene/methacrylic acid of the type already described[17]. At 25 % of cement by weight, the product still flowed well through the melt indexer. However, after a molded slab was boiled in water for a few hours, the melt index dropped to zero and other properties changed substantially, as shown below:

Material	Melt Index g/10 mins	Modulus MPa	Tensile Strength MPa	Ult. Elong. %
Acid Copolymer	6.0	62	21.3	480
Copolymers filled with 25% cement	4.3	118.6	14.5	330
Filled copolymers, water boiled-3hrs.	No-flow	380	20.2	180

In general, behavior suggested that the polymer was chemically bonded to the particulate filler following hydrolysis, giving a strong network. The products were similar in may ways to particle-reinforced cured elastomers. Extensive development of these "aquaset" polymers in building applications followed, during the 1960's and early 1970's, in view of their favorable economics and processing ease.

Early ionomer work included the use of terpolymers in which other polar monomers were present to depress the crystallinity. A series was obtained from V. C. Wolff and very interesting property combinations were obtained, as shown in the Table below:

Ionomers Derived from Terpolymer Precursors

Composition by Weight				Melt	Tensile		Wt.
Ethylene	Vinyl Acetate	Methacrylic Acid	Cation	Index (g/10 min.)	Modulus (MPa)	Strength (MPa)	Elong. (%)
70	20	10	–	9.0	13.8	10.3	530
70	20	10	Na$^+$	1.2	56	43.4	410
70	20	10	Mg^{++}	0.04	37.44	45	280
65	25	10	–	12.5	12.9	9.6	610
65	25	10	Na$^+$	1.7	18.5	20.9	410
65	25	10	Mg^{++}	0.007	37.4	37.1	300

Many of the terpolymer ionomers combined melt processability, low modulus and high tensile strength, so they were recognized as promising thermoplastic elastomers. Further research by T. C. Kogon, K. F. King and others confirmed the high strength and toughness, but also showed that resistance to compression set was poor, even at comparatively low temperatures. The ionic mobility resulted in reforming of the ionic crosslinks in the compressed samples, so that when the load was released, very little recovery occurred.

A typical experiment by I. C. Kogon consisted of milling a stoichiometric amount of magnesium oxide into a 65/25/10 ethylene/vinyl acetate/methacrylic acid terpolymer on a cold (25 °C) rubber mill, followed by compression molding at 140 °C. An attractive strong molding was obtained having a Yerzley resilience value of 67 %, while the compression set exceeded 100 % at 70 °C. Addition of SRF carbon black effected only a slight decrease in compression set. A white film composition containing titanium oxide and talc, neutralized with sodium, was calendered into attractive film having excellent resistance to dirt pickup and ozone. Development effort was focussed on end-uses requiring the toughness and flexibility of cured elastomers without the necessity for good compression set resistance. A strong tendency to creep under load has been found to be characteristic of several processable ionomeric ethylene copolymer elastomers and has also been reported in ionomeric butadiene copolymers[18].

In a study by K. F. King of chlorinated ionic copolymers, interesting solubility behavior was found. The chlorinated ethylene/methacrylic acid copolymers, containing about 30 % of chlorine, could be dissolved in xylene and converted to the potassium salt by addition of methanolic potassium hydroxide without phase separation. However, once isolated as films by evaporation of the solvent the ionic polymers could not be redissolved. This behavior was potentially advantageous for use in paints and other surface coatings.

The concept of using ionic crosslinking to improve compatibility was explored by the author during 1961-2. Acid-containing polymers of methyl methacrylate, styrene, acrylonitrile and other commercially important monomers were prepared by free-radical copolymerization. When these were blended with carboxylated ethylene polymers, strength properties were generally poor, due to gross incompatibility of the polymeric phases. Introduction of metal ions, by reaction with zinc acetate for example, increased strength by a factor of two to five[19]. In the case of methyl methacrylate/ethylene copolymer blends, partial neutralization yielded a clear, visually homogeneous material. This was not true in the case of styrene/ ethylene copolymer blends, but worthwhile improvements in strength were recorded.

Extension of ionic crosslinking to a broad spectrum of polymer types was investigated, as time permitted. Data on styrene/methacrylic acid and analogous copolymers were reported in U. S. Patent 3,322,734[20]. The elongation at break of an acidic styrene copolymer increased from 6 to 10 % as a result of partial neutralization with sodium. Likewise, in the case of methyl methacrylate copolymers, neutralization increased elongation from 3.5 to 6.0 %. Other mechanical properties were only slightly changed. In further work on acrylic system by K. L. Howe it was concluded that the effects of neutralization on physical properties were less dramatic in rigid, glassy polymers than in flexible, semicrystalline or elastomeric materials.

5   DIAMINE IONOMERS

A second family of ionically crosslinked polyolefins was under investigation simultaneously with the Surlyn® work. These interesting, reversibly crosslinked polymers were diamine salts of ethylene/methacrylic acid[21]. To prepare these a diamine was added to a well-stirred xylene solution of the polymers at about 130 °C. No gelation or viscosity increase occurred, and the product was recovered by methanol precipitation. Upon molding into a slab, the polymer was found to be clear and resilient, much like a sodium salt of the same polymer. The stiffness and yield point had increased substantially, while ultimate tensile strength and melt viscosity were unchanged. These effects are illustrated in the Table below:

Properties of Amine Ionomers Derived from Ethylene/Methacrylic Acid

% Acid by Wt.	Diamine	% Diamine Added	Melt Index	Modulus MPa	Tensile Strength MPa	Ult. Elong.
10	–	–	5.8	69	23.5	550
10	Hexamethylenediamine	10	5.8	262	23	390
10	Hexamethylenediamine	15	5.8	289	24.2	380
10	Hexamethylenediamine	10	5.0	216	22.9	340
10	Bis[p-aminocyclohexyl] methane	10	4.7	291	23.9	380
18	–	–	6.3	110	34.5	600
18	Hexamethylenediamine	10	6.3	345	33.2	480
18	Hexamethylenediamine	18	6.3	448	32	480
18	Diethylenetriamine	18	1.7	287	31	390

It was soon shown that the diamine salts could be prepared by injecting an amine, e. g. hexamethylenediamine, through a port into the melt of the acid copolymer while it was being pumped through the mixing section of a single screw extruder[22]. Thus substantial quantities of the polymer could be made, provided the maximum temperature was maintained below 190 °C. As freshly prepared, the polymer was transparent and water-white. However, after extended storage, a brown coloration developed due to oxidation of the diamine. Demonstration of good processability by conventional methods was rapidly accomplished. The problem of high melt viscosity encountered with the metal cations was absent. On the other hand, the desirable melt strength of the metal ionomers was lacking in the amine salts. Weathering studies showed that the hexamethylenediamine salts were much better than conventional ethylene polymers in resisting physical degradation by ultra-violet radiation, probably because the amine acted as a sacrificial antioxidant. These findings led to a development program conducted by R. Mullarkey aimed at flexible glazing for automotive and recreational uses. Some progress was made in identifying stabilizers for the system, but color development proved to be a persistent problem.

The relationship between diamine chain length, acid content and properties was explored and it was concluded that short diamines were effective only at high acid levels, while longer molecules such as decamethylenediamine could be used in all acid-containing polymers. This suggested that intramolecular bonding might be important. In the area of amine strength, it was concluded that dissociation constants above 10^{-8} were needed. Diamines containing ring structures, such as bis [p-aminocyclohexyl] methane, gave excellent properties. Heating the amine crosslinked polymers under vacuum split out water, resulting in covalent, non reversible crosslinks.

The diamine crosslinked polymers have not been commercialized due mainly to oxidative instability. They are of great theoretical interest as examples of perfectly reversible crosslinks. At room temperature, the ionic links result in substantially modified properties, while at the normal processing temperature of 190 °C, they seem to have completely dispersed. The academic community has not been active in studying these interesting polymers due, probably, to lack of availability. The monoamine salts also deserve further study, since they differ from the free acid precursor in transparency. This may be attributed to the bulky amine ions interfering with normal crystallization.

6   STRUCTURAL STUDIES ON IONOMERS

Following the early exploration of ionomer properties, interest developed during 1962-3 in obtaining a better understanding of their structures. The author conducted light microscopy experiments, assisted by R. P. Schatz, which showed that the crystallites seen in a 10 % methacrylic acid copolymer disappeared completely after neutralization. Samples were then supplied to Dr. H. A. Davis for transmission electron microscopy, and his micrographs confirmed the remarkable morphological change that accompanied neutralization. Dr. F. C. Wilson expressed interest in using x-ray diffraction to investigate ionomer structure, and his work on the same materials used in the light and electron microscopy uncovered many interesting phenomena. He observed the "ionomer peak" at 4°, corresponding to a spacing of about 25 A. Dr. Wilson also found that the level of crystallinity was not greatly effected by neutralization, despite the drastic difference in morphology. In discussions with the author, we agreed that his results, taken in combination with physical property data, suggested that ionic clustering was a probable feature of ionomer fine structure. The first brief publication on ionomers by the author also introduced the concept of clustering[16].

Other studies on the physical chemistry of ionomers included infrared spectroscopy by the author, DTA melting point measurements by D. L. Brebner, and torsion pendulum studies by E. T. Pieski.

Following publication of basic information on ionomer structure in 1965[23], interest within Du Pont was sufficiently high that a more detailed study was undertaken by R. Longworth, working in collaboration with F. C. Wilson, H. A. Davis and others. A symposium was held at the 1968 San Francisco ACS meeting at which the first of a lengthy series of debates on ionomer structure took place[24].

7   PRODUCT DEVELOPMENT

During the period of 1962-4, product development work by V. C. Long, D. DeVoe, R. L. Saxton, B. Borgerson and others resulted in a Surlyn® product line of sodium and zinc ionomers which formed the basis of a successful commercial venture. The early problem of excessively high melt viscosity was solved by lowering the molecular weight of the free acid precursors. It was found that a wide variation in the degree of neutralization was needed for diverse applications, so inevitably a rather extensive line of ionomer products evolved.

8   ACKNOWLEDGEMENTS

Although the development of Surlyn® and related products was never the subject of a vast industrial task force, important contributions were made by many individuals in addition to those mentioned above. Special recognition is due to D. J. Vaughan who was the Research Supervisor directly involved with ionomer activities during the first critical months, and R. H. Kinsey who was closely involved, both in Research and Marketing, for over twenty years and became Du Pont's leading expert on Surlyn® products.

References

1. U. S. Patent 2,377,753 (June 5, 1945), M. J. Roedel [to E. I. du Pont de Nemours & Co.]
2. U. S. Patent 2,497,291 (February 14, 1950), M. M. Brubaker, J. R. Roland and M. D. Peterson [to E. I. du Pont de Nemours & Co.]
3. U. S. Patent 2,397,260 (March 26, 1946), W. E. Hanford and J. R. Roland [to E. I. du Pont de Nemours & Co.]
4. U. S. Patent 2,468,954 (April 26, 1949), T. A. Ford [to E. I. du Pont de Nemours & Co.]
5. D. D. Coffman, P. S. Pinkney, F. T. Wall, W. H. Wood & H. S. Young, *J. Am. Chem. Soc.*, 74, 3391 (1952)
6. U. S. Patent 2,241,900 (April 26, 1938) M. M. Brubaker and J. Harman [to E. I. du Pont de Nemours & Co.]
7. A. Renfrew and P. Morgan, eds., *Polythene,* Interscience, New York, 1960, Chapter 13 by E. T. Pieski
8. M. J. Roedel et al., *J. Am. Chem. Soc.,* 75, 6110-6131 (1953)
9. U. S. Patent 4,076,698 (February 28, 1978), A. W. Anderson and G. S. Stamatoff [to E. I. du Pont de Nemours & Co.]
10. U. S. Patent 3,189,573 (June 15, 1965), A. Oken [to E. I. du Pont de Nemours & Co.]
11. U. S. Patent 4,351,931 (September 28, 1982), J. B. Armitage [to E. I. du Pont de Nemours & Co.]

12. ASTM D1238-79 condition E
13. U. S. Patent 3,264,272 (August 2, 1966) R. W. Rees [to E. I. du Pont de Nemours & Co.]
14. U. S. Patent 3,344,014 (September 26, 1967) R. W. Rees [to E. I. du Pont de Nemours & Co.]
15. U. S. Patent 3,404,134 (October 1, 1968), R. W. Rees [to E. I. du Pont de Nemours & Co.]
16. R. W. Rees, *Mod Plastics, 42,* 209 (Sept., 1964)
17. U. S. Patent 3,272,771 (September 13, 1966), R. M. Busche and D. L. Funk [to E. I. du Pont de Nemours & Co.]
18. A. V. Tobolsky, P. F. Lyons and N. Hata, *Macromolecules, 1,* 515 (1968)
19. U. S. Patent 3,437,718 (April 8, 1969), R. W. Rees [to E. I. du Pont de Nemours & Co.]
20. U. S. Patent 3,328,367 (June 27, 1967) R. W. Rees [to E. I. du Pont de Nemours & Co.]
21. R. W. Rees, *Polym. Prepr. Am. Chem. Soc. Div. Polym. Chem., 14,* 796 (1973)
22. U. S. Patent 3,471,460 (October 7, 1969) R. W. Rees [to E. I. du Pont de Nemours & Co.]
23. R. W. Rees & D. J. Vaughan, *Polym. Prepr. Am. Chem. Soc. Div. Polym. Chem., 6,* 287 (1965)
24. *Polym. Prepr. Am. Chem. Soc. Div. Polym. Chem., 9,* 515, 583 (1968)

Chapter 10B

RESEARCH ON IONOMERIC SYSTEMS

W. J. MacKnight, R. D. Lundberg

Contents

W. J. MacKnight, University of Massachusetts, Amherst, MA 01003
R. D. Lundberg, Exxon Chemical Company, Linden, New Jersey, NJ 07036

1   INTRODUCTION

In 1946 McAlevy[1] discovered a family of elastomers with a substantial degree of ionic cross-linking which was introduced commercially in the early 1950's by du Pont. It was based on the chlorosulfonation and chlorination of polyethylene. The materials, suitably cured with various metal oxides, gave rise to ionic, or a combination of ionic and covalent cross-links, depending on the system used, and were commercially available under the trade name Hypalon.

Brown, in 1954, presented a paper[2] on carboxylic elastomers such as butadiene-acrylonitrile-methacrylic acid vulcanized by metal salts. A terpolymer of this type containing about 0.01 equivalent of carboxyl per 100 rubber, vulcanized with 0.2 equivalents of zinc oxide per 100 rubber, showed a tensile strength of 62 MPa and elongation at break of 550 %. There were some adverse properties of these metal oxide vulcanizates related to high compression set and rapid stress relaxation.

The action of metal salts in cross-linking butadiene-methacrylic acid copolymers was discussed also by Brown[3, 4] in 1957 and 1963.

TABLE I   Examples of Commercial and Experimental Ionomers

Commercial Systems

Polymer System	Trade Name if Commercial	Comment
Ethylene/Methacrylic Acid Copolymer	Surlyn (E. I. DuPont)	Modified Thermoplastic
Butadiene/Acrylic Acid	Hycar (B. F. Goodrich)	High Green Strength Elastomer
Perfluorosulfonate Ionomers	Nafion (E. I. DuPont)	Multiple Membrane Users
Perfluorocarboxylate Ionomers	Flemion (Asahi Glass)	Chloralkali Membrane
Telechelic Polybutadiene	Hycar (B. F. Goodrich)	Specialty Uses
Sulfonated Ethylene/ Propylene Terpolymer	Ionic Elastomer (Uniroyal) (Development stage)	Thermoplastic Elastomer

Experimental Systems Polymer System	References	Comment
Sulfonated Polypentenamer	40,45	Model Ionomer System
Telechelic Polyisobutylene Sulfonate Ionomers	24–30	Model Ionomer System
Alkyl Methacrylate/ Sulfonate Copolymers	44	High Green Strength Elastomer
Acid-Amine Ionomer Reaction Products	53	Experimental

The first section of Chapter 10 is by R. W. Rees of du Pont entitled "Early Research – Surlyn and Related Polymers", in which Rees describes the early research in the 1960's leading to Surlyn. It is also notable that an article by Rees in 1964[5] contains the designation of these polymers, "Ionomers", coined by du Pont, and also importantly contains the first reference to clustering in ionomers. Two papers presented by Rees and Vaughan[6] in 1965 discussed the effect of ionic bonding on polymer structure and physical properties.

More recently, new families of ionic elastomers have emerged that possess a wide variety of properties leading to different applications. An overview of available ionic elastomers or flexible plastics is summarized in Table I.

In a recent review[7], we have described the manufacture/synthesis properties, and applications of a number of ionic elastomers, including many of those listed in Table I. In this chapter the material given in the earlier review will be updated and amplified and new polymers will be considered.

2 THEORY

The first successful theoretical attempt to deduce the spatial arrangement of salt groups in ionomers was that of Eisenberg[8]. In that work it was assumed that the fundamental structural entity is the contact ion pair. On the basis of steric considerations it was then shown that only a small number of ion pairs (the "multiplet") can associate without the presence of intervening hydrocarbon and that there is a tendency for multiplets to associate further into "clusters" which contain a considerable quantity of hydrocarbon material. This association is favored by electrostatic interactions between multiplets and opposed by forces arising from the elastic nature of the backbone chains. In the original formulation of the theory, Eisenberg assumed that the chains on average would undergo no dimensional changes as a result of the clustering phenomenon. Forsman[9] later removed this restriction and showed that the chain dimensions must actually increase as a result of association, a result confirmed by experiment[10]. There can be little doubt that the properties of ionomers can be interpreted on the basis of the existence of multiplets and clusters even though the precise structures of these units may remain obscure. Naturally, the ratio of the concentration of salt groups present as multiplets to that present as clusters differs with different backbones, acid types, and neutralizing species.

3 MORPHOLOGICAL EXPERIMENTS

3.1 Scattering Studies

3.1.1 X-ray Scattering

The X-ray scattering results have been of central importance in the interpretation of the structure of ionomers. Figure 1 compares the X-ray scattering observed for low-density polyethylene, an ethylene-methacrylic acid copolymer, and its sodium salt over a range of Bragg angles from $2\theta \cong 2°$ to $2\theta = 40°$. The presence of polyethylene-like crystallinity in all three samples is readily apparent from the 110 and 200 peaks arising from the orthorhombic polyethylene unit cell. The acid copolymer and the ionomer exhibit less crystallinity than the parent polyethylene but are quite similar to each other. The ionomer contains a new feature,

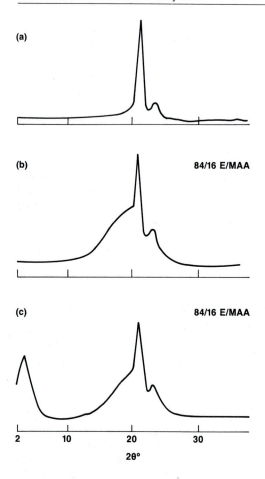

(a)

(b)   84/16 E/MAA

(c)   84/16 E/MAA

2   10   20   30

2θ°

Figure 1   X-Ray diffraction scans of (a) low density polyethylene, (b) ethylene-methacrylic acid copolymer (5.8 mole % acid), (c) the 100 % neutralized sodium salt of (b). From R. Longworth and D. J. Vaughan, Nature, *218*, 85 (1968)

however, consisting of a peak centered at approximately $2\theta = 4°$. This peak, which will be referred to as the ionic peak, appears to be a common feature of all ionomers which have been examined, regardless of the nature of the backbone and regardless of the presence or absence of backbone crystallinity. The ionic peak, in addition, possesses the following characteristics:

(1) The ionic peak occurs in all ionomers regardless of the nature of the cation, being present with lithium as well as heavy metals, divalent or trivalent cations, quaternary ammonium ions, etc.

(2) Both the magnitude and the location of the ionic peak are dependent on the nature of the cation. Thus the ionic peak occurs at lower angles for cesium cations of a given concentration than for corresponding lithium cations. In addition, the magnitude of the ionic peak is several thousandfold greater for cesium than for lithium.

(3) The ionic peak is relatively insensitive to temperature. Thus it was found that for the ionomer depicted in Figure 1 the ionic peak persisted to at least 300 °C.

(4) The ionic peak is destroyed or moved to lower angles when the ionomer is saturated with water. The scattering profile in the vicinity of the ionic peak in the water-saturated ionomer is different from that of the parent acid copolymer.

It is well known that the interpretation of any scattering data is model dependent. The procedure is to assume a reasonable model, fit the experimentally observed data and deduce model parameters from the best fit.

Several models for the distribution of salt groups in ionomers have been proposed based mainly on analysis of the ionic peak. Those appearing up to 1979 are summarized in reference[11]. They consist mainly of two approaches:

(1) that the peak arises from structure within a scattering entity;
(2) that the peak arises from interparticle interference effects.

As a representative of the first approach may be cited the "shell-core" model[12] originally proposed in 1974 and later elaborated[13, 14]. In essence the "shell-core" model, depicted in Figure 2, postulates that in the dry state a cluster of ∼ 0.1 nm in radius is shielded from surrounding matrix ions not incorporated into clusters by a shell of hydrocarbon chains. The surrounding matrix ions which cannot approach the cluster more closely than the outside of the hydrocarbon shell will be attracted to the cluster by electrostatic forces. This mechanism establishes a preferred distance between the cluster and the matrix ions. This distance is assumed to be of the order of 2 nm and accounts for the spacing of the ionic peak.

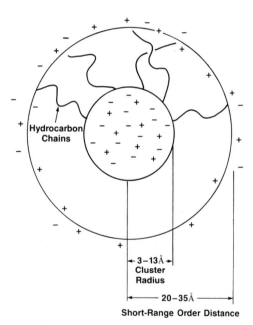

Figure 2   "Shell-core" model for Clusters with permission From ref. (12)

Figure 3 schematically illustrates the interparticle interference model where it is assumed that the peak arises from a preferred interparticle distance and the "shell-core" model and its variants such as the "lamellar shell-core model".

Recently, Yarusso and Cooper[15] have proposed a new interpretation of the ionic peak which rests on the liquid like scattering from hard spheres described originally by Fournet[16]. Yarusso and Cooper studied sulfonated polystyrene ionomers and concluded that the

1. Intercluster (lattice) (Cooper, Marx)

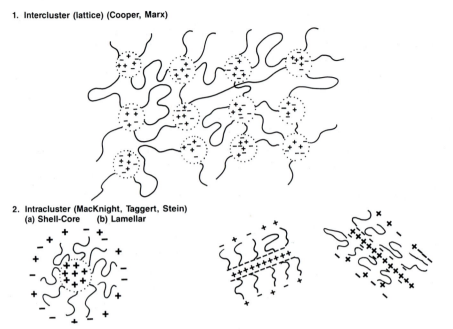

2. Intracluster (MacKnight, Taggert, Stein)
(a) Shell-Core   (b) Lamellar

Figure 3   Origin of SAXS Peak (1) Intercluster (lattice) (Cooper, Marx). 2 (a) shell core model and 2 (b) lamellar shell core model

Fournet model was quantitatively capable of modeling the ionic peak. They found that in the zinc neutralized polystyrene sulfonates about half of the ionic groups are aggregated in well-ordered domains ("clusters") with the remainder dispersed in the matrix ("multiplets"). The clusters are about 2.0 nm in diameter and clusters approach each other no more closely than 3.4 nm center to center. It is clear that this model, although based on quite different physical principles, yields structural parameters very similar to those obtained from the "shell-core" model and consistent with what may be termed the "standard model" for ionomer structure of multiplets and clusters.

3.1.2 Neutron Scattering

Small Angle Neutron Scattering (SANS) has assumed great importance in the investigation of polymer morphology. One of its most impressive accomplishments is the measurement of single chain dimensions in bulk. This is generally achieved by selectively labeling a small percentage of the polymer chains by replacing hydrogen with deuterium to take advantage of the much higher coherent neutron scattering cross section of the deuteron compared to the proton.

Several SANS studies of ionomers have appeared on both deuterium labeled and unlabeled systems[10, 17–20]. The earlier work[17] showed that an ionic peak, similar to that observed by X-rays and discussed above, could be discerned in some cases, especially when the sample was "decorated" by the incorporation of D_2O. It was also tentatively concluded[19] that the radius of gyration (Rg) of the individual chains is not altered when the acid is converted to the salt in the case of polystyrene-methacrylic acid copolymers. Subsequent SANS experiments were performed on sulfonated polystyrene ionomers over the range of 0–8.5 % sulfonation[10]. The samples were prepared by first mixing small amounts (up to 3 %) of anionically polymerized (narrow molecular weight distribution) perdeuteropolystyrene with polystyrene. The sulfonation reaction was accomplished subsequently by treating the blend with concentrated sulfuric acid and acetic anhydride in dichloroethane. This procedure insured that the deuterated and protonated polymers would contain exactly the same concentration and distribution of sulfonate groups, a result difficult or impossible to achieve by copolymerization. The neutron scattering data were treated by conventional means to obtain Rg's and apparent molecular weights. These results are collected in Table II. It is apparent from Table II that aggregation of ionic groups is accompanied by considerable chain expansion. As already noted, this is consistent with the theory of Forsman[9].

The molecular weights measured by neutron scattering listed in Table II are generally too high, even allowing for the fact that, they are weight average rather than number average values. This is unlikely to be the result of segregation of deuterium tagged chains since there are no trends in the molecular weight data for any of the derivatives and it has been well

TABLE II   Radius of Gyration, Rg, and Molecular Weight for Polystyrene Sodium Sulfonate Ionomers Obtained from Sans[a]

Mole % Sodium Sulfonate	Rg (nM)	$\overline{M}w \times 10^4$
0	8.6 ± 0.2	1.5
1.9	10.5 ± 0.5	2.3
4.2	11.1 ± 0.5	2.3
8.5	12.3 ± 0.9	2.7

[a] For the starting polystyrene, M_n = 90,000 with M_w/M_n = 1.05.
  For polyperdeuterostyrene M_n = 100,000 with M_w/M_n = 1.06. Reference 10.

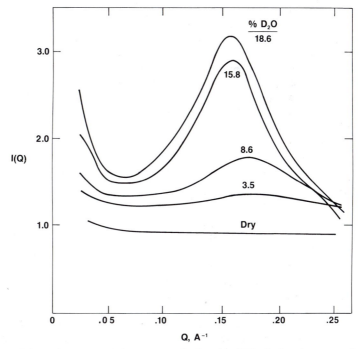

Figure 4   Neutron scattered intensity vs. scattering vector, Q, for the 17% Cesium ionomer of sulfonated polypentenamer. Numbers above each curve indicate weight percent D_2O; with permission[20]

established that poly(perdeuterostyrene) is molecularly dispersed in polystyrene of the same molecular weight. It is possible that inaccuracies in the molecular weights are caused by errors in the reference measurements or sample concentration together with difficulties in calculating the contrast factor K for the ionomer samples. In any case, the determination of R_g is independent of the absolute intensity calibration required in obtaining the molecular weight.

In a separate investigation, a series of polypentenamer sulfonate ionomers was studied[20]. In this case, contrast was achieved by adding measured amounts of D_2O to the samples. Figure 4 shows the results for the 17 mole % polypentenamer cesium sulfonate. For the dry film there is no evidence of a scattering maximum. However, as small amounts of D_2O are added the SANS peak becomes detectable. The Bragg spacing of the small angle X-ray ionic peak observed for the dry 17 % cesium derivative is essentially the same as the SANS peak at low D_2O concentrations. Above a D_2O/SO_3^- ratio of about 6, the SANS ionic peak moves markedly to lower angles. The results are consistent with a phase separated model where absorbed water is incorporated into the ionic clusters, remaining separated from the matrix even at saturation.

3.2   Electron Microscopy

Reference[11] reviews a number of electron microscopy studies of ionomer morphology in the period up to 1979. It may be stated that none of these studies made a convincing case for the direct imaging of ionic clusters. This is because of the small size of the clusters (< 5 nm based on scattering data) and difficulties encountered in sample preparation. The entire problem was reexamined in 1980[21]. In this study ionomers based on ethylene-methacrylic acid copolymers, sulfonated polypentenamer, sulfonated polystyrene and sulfonated Ethylene-Propylene-Diene Monomer (EPDM) Rubber were examined. The transfer theory of imaging was used to interpret the results. Solvent casting was found to produce no useful information about ionic clusters. Microtomed sections also showed no distinct domain structure even in ionomers neutralized with Cesium. However, microtomed sections of sulfonated EPDM appeared to contain 300 nm phase separated regions. Osmium tetroxide staining of these EPDM sections showed domains averaging less than 3 nm in size primarily inside those regions. Unfortunately, the section thickness prohibits an accurate determination of the size distribution or the detailed shape of these domains and hence the selection of the most appropriate model of domain structure.

3.3   Summary of Morphological Information

There is a considerable body of experimental and theoretical evidence that salt groups in ionomers exist in two different environments, termed multiplets and clusters. The multiplets are considered to consist of small numbers of ion dipoles (perhaps up to 6 or 8) associated together to form higher multipoles – quadrupoles, hexapoles, octapoles, etc. These multiplets are dispersed in the hydrocarbon matrix and are not phase separated from it. This means that in addition to acting as ionic crosslinks, they affect the properties of the matrix i. e., the glass transition temperature, water sensitivity, etc. The clusters are considered to be small (< 5 nm) microphase separated regions rich in ion pairs but also containing considerable quantities of hydrocarbon. They possess at least some of the properties of a separate phase including relaxation behavior associated with a glass transition temperature and have a minimal effect on the properties of the hydrocarbon matrix (they may have some reinforcing effect). The proportion of salt groups which resides in either of the two environments in a particular ionomer is determined by the nature of the backbone, the total concentration of salt groups, and their chemical nature. The details of the local structure of the clusters is not known and neither is the mechanism by which the clusters interact with low molecular weight polar impurities such as water. Up until the present time, attempts to image the clusters directly by electron microscopy have been unsuccessful.

4 RECENT DEVELOPMENTS – SYNTHESIS

Ionomers are typically prepared by copolymerization of a functionalized monomer with an olefinic unsaturated monomer or direct functionalization of a preformed polymer. Typically, carboxyl-containing ionomers are obtained by direct copolymerization of acrylic or methacrylic acid with ethylene, styrene, and similar comonomers by free-radical copolymerization. The resulting copolymer is generally available as the free acid, which can be neutralized to the degree desired with metal hydroxides, acetates, and similar salts.

The second route to ionomers involves modification of a preformed polymer. Sulfonation of ethylene propylene diene monomer, or EPDM, for example, permits the preparation of sulfonated EPDM with a content of sulfonic acid groups in proportion to the amount of sulfonating agent[7]. These reactions are conducted in solution permitting the direct neutralization of the acid functionality to the desired level. The neutralized ionomer is isolated by conventional techniques, i. e., coagulation in a non-solvent, solvent flashing, etc.

An alternate approach to modification of a preformed polymer involves a reaction conducted on a polymer melt as in an extruder[22]. The extruder sulfonation of EPDM has been described using the same sulfonating agents which are typically employed in solution. This continuous melt sulfonation was conducted on an oil extended EPDM at temperatures of 90–100 °C. The rapid reaction with the unsaturation in EPDM led to conversions of 80 to 100 % with residence times of about 6 to 12 minutes. Neutralization with metal stearates was conducted both in the extruder and on isolated EPDM-Sulfonic Acid product. Despite nonoptimal feed conditions, this extruder-reactor technique offers the advantages of shorter reaction times, elimination of solvent handling concerns, and simplification of polymer finishing steps. In addition, one patent has described alternate melt reaction schemes for Sulfo EPDM[23].

4.1 Halato-Telechelic Ionomers

Previously[7], we described the synthesis of carboxylated elastomers and sulfonated ethylene-propylene terpolymers. Here we shall discuss telechelic polyisobutylene sulfonate ionomers, Halato-telechelic carboxylate ionomers and sulfonated polypentenamer, and recent developments on direct copolymerization techniques as routes to sulfonate ionomers.

4.1.1 Telechelic Polyisobutylene Sulfonate Ionomers

Recent research on a new class of telechelic ionic polymers has been reported in a number of publications by Kennedy and Wilkes and their co-workers[24–30]. The synthesis procedure utilizes linear telechelic polyisobutylene diolefins

$$CH_2=\overset{\overset{\displaystyle CH_3}{|}}{C}\sim PIB\sim\overset{\overset{\displaystyle CH_3}{|}}{\underset{\underset{\displaystyle CH_3}{|}}{C}}-\langle\bigcirc\rangle-\overset{\overset{\displaystyle CH_3}{|}}{\underset{\underset{\displaystyle CH_3}{|}}{C}}\sim PIB\sim\overset{\overset{\displaystyle CH_3}{|}}{C}=CH_2$$

and radial star triolefins

Sulfonation is carried out in hexane solution at room temperature with excess acetyl sulfate generated in situ by the addition of sulfuric acid to acetic anhydride. After the reaction neutralization is accomplished in THF solution with ethanolic NaOH.

It is, of course, crucial to ensure that the sulfonation occurs only at the terminal olefin sites and that those sites are converted in a quantitative manner. To check this point, Kennedy et al.[24] first proved that no sulfonation occurred on the phenyl ring using the model compounds 1,4 di-tert butylbenzene (DTBB) and 2,4,4 trimethyl-1-pentene (TMP). A mixture of these hydrocarbons was reacted with excess acetyl sulfate in carbon tetrachloride and it was concluded on the basis of H^1 NMR spectroscopy that only the TMP was sulfonated under those conditions.

The quantitative nature of the terminal olefin sulfonation was determined by titration of the free acids and elemental sulfur analysis of the sodium ionomer. The success of those methods depends on there being no changes in polymer molecular weight upon sulfonation since all molecular weights were measured prior to sulfonation. Assuming this to be the case, the functionality determinations, especially those measured by titration, agree with the expected values of 2 for the diolefins, and 3 for the triolefins.

4.1.2 Halato-Telechelic Carboxylate Ionomers

The synthesis of low molecular weight difunctional carboxyl-terminated butadiene based polymers is well established and has been described in a recent review[31]. Anionic polymerization or free radical initiated polymerization processes are usually involved. The first route yields polymers of relatively narrow molecular weight distribution. However, in the molecular weight ranges which result in the best combination of properties (1500–6000), substantial amounts of organometallic catalyst are required. Free radical polymerization leads to broader molecular weight distributions, but being much cheaper it is generally preferred industrially. Chain transfer to solvent, which has an important effect on the final polymer functionality is minimized by selection of appropriate solvents.

Teyssie and co-workers have converted such carboxyl-terminated polymers to the salt forms, which they refer to as Halato-telechelic polymers, by neutralizing with metal alkoxides in appropriate solvents, commonly toluene[32–39]. They point out the necessity for the quantitative removal of low molecular weight reaction products such as methanol to drive the reaction to completion and fully realize the inherent ionomeric properties of the polymers. In particular, it was found that ionomers prepared in this fashion produced gel at about 2% solids in non-polar solvents. These gels are thermally reversible and the critical concentration for gel formation is related to chain molecular weight by the expression

$$C \text{ gel} = KMn^{-0.5} \tag{1}$$

where K is a constant depending on the polymer backone and solvent.

4.2 Sulfonated Polypentenamers

In general, sulfonation of highly unsaturated polymer backbones leads to crosslinking through a series of side reactions which are not well understood. Thus it has proved impossible to sulfonate polybutadiene without attendant crosslinking. The only report of successful sulfonation of a polymer in this category remains that of the sulfonation of polypentenamer $[(CH_2)_3CH = CH]_x$[40].

The reaction scheme may be summarized as follows:

$$[(CH_2)_3 CH = CH]_X + SO_3 : O = P(OEt)_3$$

$$\longrightarrow [(CH_2)_3 CH = CH]_Y [(CH_2)_3 \underset{\underset{SO_3^- Na^+}{|}}{CH} = CH]_Z$$

Na salt of sulfonated polypentenamer

The reaction proceeds in chloroform at room temperature.

It is possible to sulfonate above 20 mole % by this procedure without crosslinking, and, in fact, water soluble derivatives may be prepared.

Although the reason for a crosslinking side reaction attendant on sulfonation of poly-butadiene is not known, it may be suggested that it involves vinyl pendant groups which tend to be much more reactive than either cis or trans double bonds in the backbone. The virtual absence of such pendant vinyl groups in polypentenamer would then account for the possibility of sulfonating it without crosslinking. Further research is required, particularly mechanistic studies to determine the precise sequence of reactions involved in the sulfonation process as well as the structures of the products.

4.3 Copolymerization of Sulfonate Monomers

Nearly all of the ionomers based on carboxylates have been obtained by copolymerization of acrylic or methacrylic acid or related systems. Until recently there have been only a few publications covering the synthesis and characterization of sulfonate ionomers by direct copolymerization of a sulfonate monomer. In part this is because of the difficulties of copolymerizing many polar sulfonate monomers with relatively non-polar vinyl or diene monomers. The extreme insolubility of a metal sulfonate monomer in solvents other than water has impeded the synthesis of such materials.

A number of publications[41–43] have now shown that styrene sulfonates can be copolymerized with a variety of monomers in conventional emulsion polymerizations. In this respect the styrene derivative appears more suitable to successful copolymerization with non-polar comonomers than a variety of other sulfonate moieties. Recent papers[44] by McGrath and coworkers have shown that sodium styrene sulfonate is readily copolymerized with alkyl methacrylates through this approach. The resulting copolymers display thermoplastic character as shown in Figure 5. This figure shows the incorporation of metal sulfonate groups results in the formation of a network which persists to temperatures in excess of 200 °C as monitored by thermogravimetric analysis for a copolymer of n-butylacrylate and

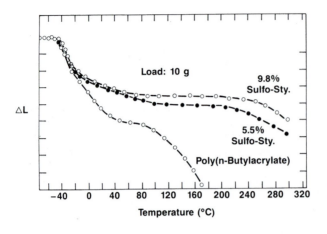

Figure 5 TMA Penetration Curves for n. Butylacrylate and Sulfonated Styrene Copolymers[44]

sodium sulfonated styrene. Figure 6 describes the stress-strain behavior of these copolymers. The substantial enhancement of tensile strength due to ionic group incorporation is especially evident at sulfonate levels of 5 mole percent.

It is apparent that in the series of methacrylate copolymers the amount of ionic comonomer required to achieve a high level of ionic crosslinking is significantly higher than that observed for ionomers based on low polarity polymer backbones such as Sulfo EPDM (approx. 0.5 to 1 mole % metal sulfonate content). This difference can be attributed to less uniform distribution of ionic groups within the polymer backbone or the diminished strength of ionic association in a polymer matrix of increased polarity.

Other recent papers[41], have described analogous emulsion copolymerizations of styrene and sodium styrene sulfonate and have demonstrated some differences in these polymer products compared with those prepared by direct sulfonation of polystrenes. While these systems are not elastomeric, the results suggest that emulsion copolymerization routes can lead to non-random incorporation of sulfonate groups in the polymer chain, clearly a result of the limited solubility of the very polar sulfonate monomer.

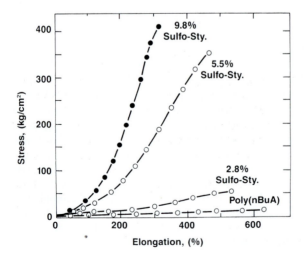

Figure 6   Stress-Strain Behavior of n. Butylacrylate Sulfonated Styrene Copolymers[44]. (Note: to convert to MPa multiply kg/cm² by 0.0981)

5   RECENT DEVELOPMENTS – PROPERTIES

5.1   The Glass Transition Temperature Tg

In general elastomeric halato-telechelic polymers exhibit glass transition temperatures which are insensitive to cation size and valence, degree of neutralization, and oligomer molecular weight. The situation is quite different with sulfonated polypentenamer. In a study of a series of sulfonated polypentenamers containing from 1.9 to 17.6 mol % pendent groups in the form of sodium salts, it was shown that the composition dependence of the Tg exhibits typical random copolymer behavior at low levels of sulfonation but deviates significantly from this behavior above 10 mol %[45], see Figure 7. Dynamic mechanical results indicate the presence of an ionic phase relaxation in addition to the Tg. This relaxation is only present in samples sulfonated above 10 mol % and is sensitive to the presence of polar impurities such as water. The most natural interpretation of this behavior is that above 10 mol %,

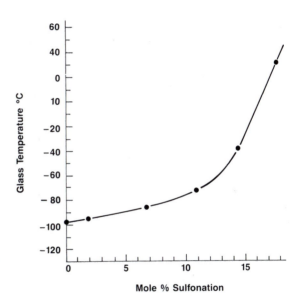

Figure 7   Composition dependent of DSC Tg's for sulfonated polypentanamers[45]

microphase separated clusters or ionic domains appear in significant concentration. Presumably the upturn in the Tg shown in Figure 7 is a result of such clusters acting as a combination of reinforcing fillers and highly functional crosslinks. This combined action results in a "bracing" effect on the chains of the matrix and hence elevates its Tg. Below 10 mol % in sulfonated polypentenamer and, by extension, in the halato-telechelic ionomer case, the salt groups exist as ion pairs, quartets, or multiplets which are not phase separated from the matrix.

5.2 Mechanical Properties

The properties of halato-telechelic elastomeric ionomers can be understood generally in terms of the formation of chain extension or pseudo-three dimensional networks by the aggregation of the ion-pair groups on the chain ends. The degree of aggregation and the thermal stability of the aggregates is a function of concentration, type of cation and anion, and perhaps placement of the ionic groups on the chain. Kennedy and Wilkes have carried out an extensive series of investigations with sulfonate terminated tri-armed stars of polyisobutylene neutralized with calcium and potassium hydroxides[25-30]. In experiments with oligomers of molecular weights below the critical molecular weight for entanglement formation of linear PIB ($< 9,000$), it was found that the simple rubber elasticity theory was capable of describing the stress strain behavior at low to moderate elongations.

$$\sigma = \frac{\varrho RT}{\overline{Mc}} \left(\lambda - \frac{1}{\lambda^2} \right)$$

(2)

where σ is the stress, ϱ the density, R the gas constant, T the absolute temperature, λ the extension ratio, and $\overline{M}_c$ the number average molecular weight between crosslinks.

Assuming only two ion pairs per ionic aggregate, $\overline{Mc}$ would equal the average molecular weight of two arms, i. e. $\overline{Mc} = 2/3 \overline{Mn}$. For a 9,000 $\overline{Mn}$ oligomer, $\overline{Mc}$ was found to be 6,700 from equation[2], which is quite close to the expected value of 6,000. Above extension ratios of 5, stress induced crystallization occurs with a concomitant upturn in the stress-strain curve, and equation[2] is no longer valid. The instantaneous permanent set is small, only 50–60 % even at 700 % elongation so that the networks possess considerable integrity.

In a later study[30], Kennedy and Wilkes examined a series of oligomers with different molecular weights both above and below the critical entanglement molecular weight. The results generally amplify and confirm those of the earlier study and it was concluded that tri-arm star PIB ionomers of $\overline{Mn}$ between 11,000 and 34,000 possess high tensile properties and low permanent set and hysteresis at ambient conditions. The presence of crystallinity at higher elongations helps to enhance mechanical properties. These ionomers can be thermally formed above 150 °C. A general finding was that excess neutralizing agent increases the tensile properties with a maximum at about 100 % excess agent.

The sulfonated polypentenamer ionomers have been studied by the dynamic mechanical relaxation technique[45]. The results provide strong evidence for the existence of microphase separated ionic aggregates or clusters above 10 mol % substitution. This evidence is in the form of an ionic phase relaxation which is present in samples above 10 mol % substitution and which increases in magnitude as the degree of sulfonation increases. This relaxation is sensitive to low molecular weight polar impurities such as water and decreases substantially in temperature when the ionomers are saturated with water.

The influence of the cation on ionomer properties has been examined in several ionomer systems. In the case of Sulfo-EPDM it was found[46] that physical properties such as tensile strength and melt flow were very dependent upon the choice of cation as shown in Table III. Interestingly, the monovalent cations such as lithium and sodium exhibited stronger ionic association, as manifested by melt viscosity measurements, than divalent cations such as zinc and lead. The observations coupled with the excellent tensile properties exhibited by the zinc ionomer have contributed to the selection of zinc sulfo EPDM as a primary ionic elastomer candidate for commercialization.

TABLE III   Effect of Cation on Flow and Physical Properties of Sulfo-EPDM[a, b]

Metal	Apparent viscosity[c], μPa-s[d]	Melt fracture at shear rate, Hz	Melt index (190 °C 3,3 MPa [e], 10g/min	Room temperature Tensile strength, MPa[e]	Elongation, %
Hg			disintegrated		
Mg	55.0	<0.88	0	2.2	70
Ca	53.2	<0.88	0	2.8	90
Co	52.3	<0.88	0	8.1	290
Li	51.5	<0.88	0	5.2	320
Ba	50.8	<0.88	0	2.3	70
Na	50.6	<0.88	0	6.6	350
Pb	32.8	88	0.1	11.6	480
Zn	12.0	147	0.75	10.2	400

[a] Based on ref. 46
[b] Sulfonate content: 31 meq/100 EPDM
[c] At 200 °C and 0.88s^{-1}
[d] To convert μPa·s to centipoise, divide by 1000
[e] To convert MPa to psi, multiply by 145

The response of these different cations to polymer flow and tensile properties indicates that ion pair association and the resulting network formation due to aggregation is more important than cation valency. Similar relationships were observed with carboxylate ionomers in Chapter 10 A.

6   PREFERENTIAL PLASTICIZATION

The fact that the ionic phase relaxation is sensitive to low molecular weight polar impurities suggests the possibility that the relaxation of the ionic aggregates can be controlled by the deliberate addition of an appropriate polar diluent and that such an additive would affect only the ionic groups leaving the properties of the matrix unchanged. Since the ionic aggregates act as physical crosslinks, it is clear that such an approach could lead to the control of the temperature and, presumably, the shear rate, necessary to induce flow, and hence to the possible development of a thermoplastic elastomer with desirable processing characteristics.

In a study of the modification of ionic associations in sulfonated ethylene propylene-diene ionomers, it was found[47] that a crystalline additive such as zinc stearate can strongly affect material properties in addition to being a highly effective preferential plasticizer for the ionic aggregates.

It was observed that zinc stearate is compatible with the ionomer even at high loadings (over 30 % by weight) and it enhances physical associations as reflected in mechanical properties and swelling characteristics. The morphological structure of the zinc stearate thus dispersed in the ionomer was found to be small microphase separated crystallites less than 500 nm in diameter. These entities act as reinforcing fillers below their melting points and greatly enhance the flow properties of the ionomer above their melting points. This behavior is thermally reversible.

Figure 8 summarizes some possibilities for varying the strengths of ionic interactions by utilizing different cations and preferential plasticizers. These modulus-temperature curves are a dramatic illustration of the versatility of the ionomer approach to controlling properties in thermoplastic elastomers.

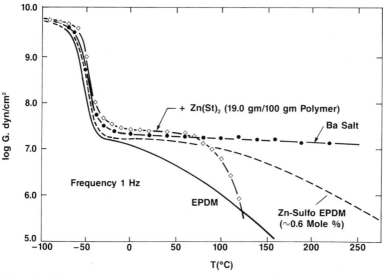

Figure 8   Temperature dependence of G' at 1Hz for sulfonated EPDM ionomers neutralized with various cations and containing preferential plasticizers as noted[65]

7   THERMALLY REVERSIBLE CROSS-LINKED STYRENE-BUTADIENE RUBBERS (SBR)

A new approach to ion containing polymers which form thermally reversible crosslinks is based on modification of the products from a styrene-butadiene emulsion copolymerization. In these studies[48–50] a coordinating monomer, N-isobutoxymethylacrylamide (IBMA), was directly incorporated in the monomer charge. The good oil solubility of this monomer permits effective incorporation in the final product at modest levels (0.7 to 5 weight percent). IBMA is a very effective ligand for metal coordination and permits the incorporation of metal cations such as calcium by two methods: (a) the latex product of styrene-butadiene-IBMA is coagulated directly into metal salt-containing aqueous solutions with modest stirring so that the IBMA containing polymers would coagulate; (b) a toluene solution of SBR-IBMA was heated with an aqueous salt solution under heterogeneous conditions followed by coagulation of the organic layer with an alcohol, such as isopropanol. In both cases the metal ions were incorporated and not removed by additional washing with isopropanol. Although calcium is frequently used, a variety of metals can be employed.

Evidence supporting strong metal coordination with the IBMA polymers was developed by several techniques. Infrared spectroscopy provided evidence of metal coordination as well as information concerning structures of the coordinated species.

The specific structures which have been postulated for these metal-ligand adducts are as follows[48]:

$$R = (CH_3)_2\,CH - CH_2 -$$

Two of these structures (II, III) are intramolecular complexes, and two of them (IV, V) are intermolecular complexes.

The solution properties of these polymers have been studied and reveal non-linear reduced viscosity-concentration behavior. The addition of polar cosolvents such as alcohols and amines also has a marked influence on the viscosity behavior, in a manner analogous to that observed with sulfonate ionomers.

In the bulk state these polymers exhibit thermally reversible crosslinking. The incorporation of the IBMA-Me^{2+} coordination enhances the green strength of compounded rubber and rubber blends, but these labile crosslinks dissociate at processing temperatures.

The amount of IBMA varied between 0.67–5.99 wt % in styrene/butadiene copolymer; therefore, Me^{2+} level increased proportionally to the IBMA level. For rubber blend applications, Ca^{2+} was incorporated. As the level of IBMA-Me^{2+} increased, the green strength rose.

The 0.67 wt % IBMA. Ca^{2+} containing SBR was blended with conventional SBR. Figure 9a shows the stress-strain curves for unaged SBR-IBMA-Ca^{2+} blends with different SBR levels while Figure 9b shows the stress-strain curves for the same blends after aging. Increasing IBMA level in the SBR blend enhances the green strength which improves further upon aging of the unvulcanized compound.

The unvulcanized SBR-IBMA elastomer itself showed very high elongation and tensile strength and these values increased as a function of the IBMA content.

The reversible cross-link technology was also applied to rubber filled polystyrene and poly(acrylonitrile-co-styrene)[49]. The blends of poly(styrene-co-IBMA) and poly(butadiene-co-IBMA) show a significant increase in the impact properties when compared to those of polystyrene and polybutadiene blends. Similar behavior was also observed for ABS type systems[50].

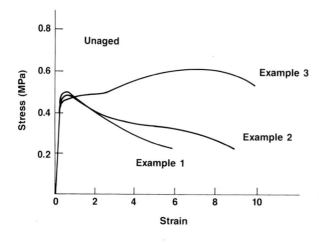

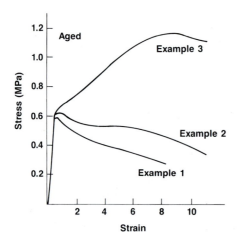

Figure 9 a   Stress-strain curves of unaged SBR blends with SBR-IMBA-Ca^{2+48}

Example 1:
80/70 SBR/IBMA.Ca^{2+}
Example 2:
60/40 SBR/IBMA.Ca^{2+}
Example 3:
40/60 SBR/IBMA.Ca^{2+}

Figure 9 b   Stress strain curves of aged SBR blends with SBR-IBMA.Ca^{2+}. Examples have same composition as in Figure 9 a

8   POLYURETHANE IONOMERS

While polyurethanes have been a important class of thermoplastic elastomers for many years, the modification of these systems with ionic functionalities has received relatively little attention. Several publications have described ionic polyurethanes and shown substantial enhancement of the mechanical properties compared to the base polyurethane[51, 52]. A recent article[52] has described the synthesis and characterization of polyurethane zwitterionomers, anionomers and cationomers. Typically, a polyurethane is prepared from prepolymer and a diisocyanate in the presence of a tertiary amine containing diol extender, such as N-methyl diethanolamine. The zwitterionomers are prepared by dissolving the polyurethane in dimethyl acetamide and adding the appropriate amount of γ-propane sultone. A ring opening reaction occurs on the sultone resulting in the formation of a quaternary ammonium ion closely linked to a sulfonyl anion; a zwitterion pair. From this point, reaction with the appropriate metal acetate results in a metal-sulfonyl ion pair and reduction to the tertiary amine of the ammonium ion with the generation of methyl acetate. The resulting ionomer is termed an anionomer since the charge on the polymer backbone is anionic.

The incorporation of ionic groups into polyurethanes can dramatically alter physical properties. Increasing the number of zwitterionic groups lowers the glass transition temperature correspondingly. This behavior is explained as a consequence of the decreasing compatibility between the polar hard segments and the non-polar soft segments in the polyurethane. Consequently, the soft segment segregates into a phase of greater purity and low glass transition. In effect the ionic functionality enhances phase separation of these systems.

Similarly the presence of ions primarily in the polar hard phase can strengthen those domains via coulombic interactions between the ionic species. Evidence of this behavior is seen in Figure 10, where a polyurethane based on polytetramethylene oxide glycol of 1000 molecular weight is functionalized by a variety of metal neutralized anionomers. As cation charge increases, the plateau modulus increases and softening temperature increases, due to increased ionic crosslinking.

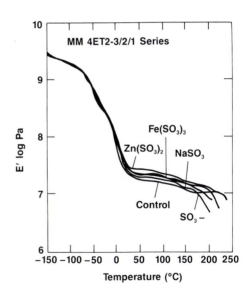

Figure 10 Storage Modulus versus Temperature for a nonionized control, a Zwitterionomer based on the control, and a series of metal neutralized polyurethane anionomers[52]

One immediate consequence of incorporation of ionic functionality in polyurethanes, therefore, is an increase in softening point of the hard segments as well as a higher modulus. Clearly this behavior will be manifested only if there is an interconnected hard domain morphology. If the polyurethane contains only a low level of hard segment ($\ll 50$ wt %) no significant impact on modulus is observed.

9   IONIC INTERACTIONS AS COMPATIBILIZING AGENTS

It is well known that most polymers of high molar mass are immiscible in the thermodynamic sense due to the very small increase in their conformational entropy upon mixing. Compatibility, meaning sufficient interaction between the blend components to produce useful properties, may be achieved by a number of different routes including the addition of compatibilizing agents such as block copolymers, the use of chemical techniques such as grafting, etc. A route to compatibilization involving ionomers has been described recently in a series of papers by Eisenberg and co-workers[53–55]. This involves the incorporation of specifically interacting acidic groups in one polymer with basic groups in the other to form ion pairs. Specifically, the blend of poly(styrene co-styrene sulfonic acid) (PSSA) and poly(ethyl acrylate-co-4 vinyl pyridine) (PEAVP) has been investigated. It was found that an approximately 4 mole percent functional group content is required for compatibilzation of this blend. In this case compatibility was assessed by examining the dynamic mechanical relaxation behavior in the glass to rubber (primary) relaxation region. It was found that, above the 4 mole percent concentration level mentioned above, only a single tan δ or G" peak associated with microbrownian motion accompanying the glass transition could be observed. Below this level of substituents, two peaks in these functions are clearly resolved. An increase in functional group content above 4 mole % has the effect of increasing the temperature of the glass-rubber relaxation in a manner similar to that observed with chemical crosslinks.

It is unlikely that the blends studied by Eisenberg are actually thermodynamically miscible, although this possibility cannot be entirely ruled out on the basis of the results available. They are certainly compatible in the operational sense and are of obvious scientific and technological interest.

The use of ionic interactions between different polymer chains to produce new materials with interesting properties dates back to at least the work of Michaels and Miekka[56], who prepared materials they referred to as "polysalts" by mixing solutions of acidic polyelectrolytes, such as poly(acrylic acid) with basic polyelectrolytes, such as poly(vinyl pyridine). The resulting materials were insoluble in all solvents although they would swell considerably in water. Their main areas of application involved membranes for reverse osmosis. Later, Otocka and Eirich[57] prepared similar materials and studied their mechanical properties. Due to their intractability, these materials have never been properly characterized.

Other specific interactions have also been utilized for compatibilization. Notable in this regard is the work of Pearce[60] and co-workers who have shown that the incorporation of short perfluorinated alcohol side chains into polystyrene results in compatible blends with poly(ethylene-oxide) (PEO). Hara and Eisenberg[59] have also demonstrated that poly(styrene co methacrylate) ionomers will interact with PEO via an ion-dipole mechanism to produce similar effects to those observed by Pearce in the hydrogen bonding systems alluded to above. Although one of these components (polystyrene) is a thermoplastic, compatibilization by this route with a low Tg second component can lead to materials with Tg's below room temperature. This is a possible route to new elastomeric compositions.

Relatively little exists in the literature concerning the properties of blends compatiblized by ionic interactions. The studies of relaxations accompanying the glass transition have been discussed already. Bazuin and Eisenberg[60], in a study of blends of PSSA and PEAVP, showed that greatly extended rubbery plateaus existed compared to blends of the unmodified parent backbones. However, the magnitude of the rubbery plateau modulus was more or less independent of ion content. It was not possible, under the experimental conditions employed, to observe a flow, or terminal zone of viscoelastic behavior.

There appear to be no morphological studies available bearing on the microstructure of blends with ionic interactions. Such studies, and much more extensive property investigations will be necessary before the true nature of such blends can be defined. From what is known at present, it may be that most of these blends fall into the rather ill-defined category of "interpenetrating networks".

10 APPLICATIONS OF IONOMERIC ELASTOMERS

Most ionomer applications exploit several characteristics which can be attributed to ionic aggregation or cluster formation, or the interaction of polar groups with ionic aggregates. Changes in physical properties caused by ionic aggregation in elastomeric systems or in polymer melts are most readily detected. Therefore, the marked enhancement in elastomeric green strength is a general characteristic of ionomer-based systems. The ionic aggregation is also apparent in enhanced melt viscosity. In the case of polyethylene-based metal carboxylate ionomers, the high melt viscosity is utilized in heat sealing. It also provides a particular processing advantage during extrusion operations. Under some conditions, however, high melt viscosity is a limitation, e.g., in injection molding. Other properties attributable to ionic aggregation include toughness and outstanding abrasion resistance, as well as oil resistance in packaging applications.

The interaction of various polar agents with the ionic groups and the ensuing property changes are unique to ionomer systems. This plasticization process is also important in membrane applications. A different application of ionic cluster plasticization involves the interaction of metal stearates with sulfo-EPDM to induce softening transitions. This plasticization process is required to achieve the processability of thermoplastic elastomers based on this technology.

One type of thermoplastic elastomer based on these concepts is Uniroyal's Ionic Elastomer. This elastomer is a metal sulfonated EPDM available in powdered form. It can be compounded with fillers, rubber-processing oils and selected polymers into a variety of elastomeric materials. Initially, two grades are available which can be formulated into a wide variety of compounds of interest in rubber applications. These include adhesives, impact modifiers, footwear applications such as unit soles, calendered sheet, garden hose, and similar rubber goods.

TABLE IV   Typical Property Range of Ionic Elastomer Compounds[a]

Property	Typical Range
Shore A hardness	49–90
100% Modulus, MPa	1.17–6.9
Tensile strength, MPa	3.4–17.2
Elongation, %	350–900
Tear strength, MPa	0.89–2.3
Specific gravity at ambient temperature	0.95–1.95
Compression set, %	30–35
Brittle point, °C	−57 to −46
Processing temperature, °C	93–260

[a] Uniroyal Technical Information Bulletin, 1982

These products differ from conventional vulcanized rubbers by the presence of metal sulfonate groups which provide a strong cross-link at ambient temperatures. However, when a suitable polar additive, such as zinc stearate, is incorporated, the elastomer becomes thermoplastic at elevated temperature permitting melt processing. Thus, by combining materials such as zinc stearate along with other formulation ingredients, a wide variety of products can be made based on several ionic elastomer gums. Typical physical property ranges of the elastomer compounds are shown in Table IV.

11 CONCLUSIONS

Although ionic interactions have been used to modify elastomer properties since at least the 1950's, the full potential of this technique has yet to be realized. Within the last five years, several important points pertaining to this subject have emerged.

Ionomeric associations dramatically modify polymer properties over a wide range of modulus, melt viscosity and transition temperatures. The reasons for this are only imperfectly understood due to a lack of knowledge of the degree of aggregation of ionic groups in the polymers under discussion and how structural variables affect them.

Multiple synthetic approaches to ionomeric elastomers exist and are commercially viable. Some of these have been discussed here and in our earlier review[7].

A wide range of potential applications exists for ionomers. Examples besides thermoplastic elastomers include foams, elastic fibers, polymer modifiers, and solution applications.

12 FUTURE DEVELOPMENTS

A recent report[61] has summarized the technical and patent literature in the field of thermoplastic elastomers (TPE's) from 1979 to 1984. Ionomeric thermoplastic elastomers led the field in terms of published articles over this time frame. Similarly ionomeric TPE's were the subject of more patents than any other TPE approach over the same period. The versatility of ionic crosslinking coupled with the wide variety of synthetic approaches which can be employed to achieve these systems serves to make ionomeric TPE's an attractive research area. The ability to moderate the degree of ionic crosslinking by the strength of the ionic crosslink, the number of such interactions, and the use of external ionic plasticizers to control the nature of this network offer unusual control over these systems. Several recent patents have suggested new uses for these ionomeric thermoplastic elastomers which vary from asphalt modification[62] to impact modification of engineering thermoplastics[63]. The use of Zinc Sulfo EPDM as a waterproof heat-sealable roofing membrane of exceptional tear strength has been described in a recent patent to Uniroyal[64].

Based on these developments, research on ionomeric TPE's will be concerned with the synthesis of new ionomeric candidates, additional characterization of the morphology and flow behavior of available systems, and new applications which specifically exploit the unique characteristics of ionic crosslinks.

References

1. A. McAlevy, Halogenated polyethylene, U. S. Patent 2,405,971, Aug. 29, 1946
2. H. P. Brown and C. F. Gibbs, "Carboxylic Elastomers"; presented at a Meeting of the ACS Rubber Division Sept. 1954; Rubber Chem. Techn. *28*, 937 (1955)
3. H. P. Brown, "Carboxylic Elastomers", Rubber Chem. Techn. *30*, 1347 (1957)
4. H. P. Brown, "Cross-linking Reactions of Carboxylic Elastomers"; presented at a Meeting of the ACS Rubber Division May 1963; Rubber Chem. Techn. *36*, 931 (1963)
5. R. W. Rees, "Chemistry of Surlyn A Ionomers", *Modern Plastics, 42*, 209 (1964)
6. R. W. Rees and D. J. Vaughan, "Surlyn® A Ionomers: I, The Effects of Ionic Bonding on Polymer Structure" and "II. The Effects of Ionic Bonding on Solid State and Melt Properties" *Polym. Prepr. Am. Chem. Soc. Div. Polymer Chem. 6*, 287, 296 (1965)
7. W. J. MacKnight and R. D. Lundberg, *Rubber Chem. and Techn., 57* (3), 652 (1984)
8. A. Eisenberg, *Macromolecules, 3*, 147 (1970)
9. A. Forsman, *Macromol., 15*, 1032 (1982)
10. T. R. Earnest, J. S. Higgins, D. L. Handlin and W. J. MacKnight, *Macromol., 14*, 192 (1981)
11. W. J. MacKnight and T. R. Earnest, Jr., J. of Polym. Sci.: *Macromolecular Reviews*, Vol. *16*, 41 (1981)
12. W. J. MacKnight, W. P. Taggart and R. S. Stein, *J. Polym. Sci., Polym. Symp. No. 45*, 113 (1974)
13. E. J. Roche, R. S. Stein and W. J. MacKnight, *J. Polym. Sci., Polym. Phys. Ed., 18*, 1035 (1980)
14. M. Fujimura, T. Hashimoto and H. Kawai, *Macromol., 15*, 136 (1982)
15. D. J. Yarusso and S. L. Cooper, *Macromol., 16*, 1871 (1983)
16. G. Fournet, *Acta Crystallzr., 4*, 293 (1951)
17. E. J. Roche, R. S. Stein and W. J. MacKnight, *J. Polym. Sci., Phys. Ed., 18*, 1035 (1980)
18. C. T. Mayer and M. Pineri, *J. Polym. Sci., Phys. Ed., 16*, 569 (1978)
19. M. Pineri, R. Dupliessix, S. Gauthier and A. Eisenberg, *IONS IN POLYMERS, Advances in Chem. Series 187*, ACS, Washington, 1980, p. 283
20. T. R. Earnest, Jr., J. S. Higgins and W. J. MacKnight, *Macromol., 15*, 1390 (1982)
21. D. L. Handlin, W. J. MacKnight and E. L. Thomas, *Macromol., 14*, 795 (1980)
22. R. Siadat, R. D. Lundberg, R. W. Lenz, *Polym. Eng. and Sci., 20*, No. 8, 530 (1980)
23. R. D. Lundberg, H. S. Makoski, J. Bock, T. Zawadski, U. S. Patent 4,157,432 Assigned to Exxon Research and Engineering Co., June 5, 1979
24. J. P. Kennedy and R. F. Storey, *Organic Coating and Appl. Polym. Sci. Procedings, 46*, 182 (1982)
25. Y. Mohajer, D. Tyagi, G. L. Wilkes, R. F. Storey and J. P. Kennedy, *Polym. Bull, 8*, 47 (1982)
26. S. Bagrodia, Y. Mohajer, G. L. Wilkes, R. F. Storey and J. P. Kennedy, *Polym. Bull., 8*, 281 (1982)
27. S. Bagrodia, Y. Mohajer, G. L. Wilkes, R. F. Storey and J. P. Kennedy, *Polym. Bull, 9*, 174 (1983)
28. S. Bagrodia, G. L. Wilkes and J. P. Kennedy, *J. Rheol., 28*, 474 (1983)
29. Y. Mohajer, S. Bagrodia, G. L. Wilkes, R. F. Storey and J. P. Kennedy, *J. Appl. Polym. Sci., 29*, 1943 (1984)
30. G. Tant, G. L. Wilkes and J. P. Kennedy, *Polym. Preprints, 26* (1) 32 (1985)
31. D. N. Schulz, J. C. Sandra and B. G. Willoughby; in "Anionic Polymerization: Kinetics, Mechanisms, and Synthesis", J. E. McGrath, Ed., *A.C.S. Symposium Series 166*, Chapter 27, p. 427 (1981)
32. G. Broze, R. Jerome and P. Teyssie, *Macromol., 14*, 224 (1981)
33. G. Broze, R. Jerome and P. Teyssie, *Macromol., 15*, 920 (1982)
34. G. Broze, R. Jerome and P. Teyssie, *Macromol., 15*, 1300 (1982)
35. G. Broze, R. Jerome, P. Teyssie and C. Marco, *Macromol., 16*, 996 (1983)
36. G. Broze, R. Jerome and P. Teyssie, *J. Polym. Sci., Phys. Ed., 21*, 2205 (1983)
37. G. Broze, R. Jerome, P. Teyssie and C. Marco, *Macromol., 16*, 1771 (1983)
38. G. Broze, R. Jerome and P. Teyssie, *J. Polym. Sci. letters, 21*, 237 (1983)
39. R. Jerome, J. Horrion, R. Fayt and P. Teyssie, *Macromol., 17*, 2447 (1984)
40. D. Rahrig, W. J. MacKnight and R. W. Lenz, *Macromol., 12*, 195 (1979)
41. R. A. Weiss, R. D. Lundberg and S. R. Turner, *J. Polym. Sci., Polym. Chem. Ed., 23*, 525, 535, 540 (1985)
42. B. Siadat, B. Oster and R. W. Lenz, *J. Applied Polym. Sci., 26*, 1027 (1981)
43. R. A. Weiss, R. D. Lundberg and A. Werner, *J. Polym. Sci. Polym. Chem. Ed., 18*, 3427 (1980)
44. J. E. McGrath et al., *Polym. Prepr. 24* (2) 37 (1983)
45. D. Rahrig and W. J. MacKnight, *Advances in Chemistry, Series No. 187*, A. Eisenberg Ed., American Chemical Society, 1980, Chapter 6

46. H. S. Makowski, R. D. Lundberg, L. Westerman and J. Bock, *Adv. Chem. Series 187,* 3 (1980)
47. (a) I. Duvdevani, R. D. Lundberg, C. Wood-Cordova and G. L. Wilkes, ACS Symposium Series, in press. (b) H. S. Makowski and R. D. Lundberg, *Adv. Chem. Soc., 187,* 37 (1980)
48. B. Z. Gunesin, D. N. Schulz, J. W. Kang, A. R. Chain and G. R. Hamed, *J. Polym. Sci., Polym. Chem. Ed., 22,* 353 (1984)
49. D. J. Dougherty, B. Gunesin and J. W. Spiewak, U. S. Pat. 4,338,425 (1982)
50. B. Z. Gunesin, U. S. Pat. 4,408,014 (1983)
51. D. Dieterich, W. Keberle, H. Witt, *Angew. Chem.* Intern. Edit. *9,* 40 (1970)
52. J. A. Miller, K. K. S. Hwang, C. Z. Yang and S. L. Cooper, *J. of Elastomers and Plastics, 15,* 174 (1983)
53. A. Eisenberg, P. Smith and L. L. Zhou, *Polym. Eng. and Sci., 22* (7) 1117 (1982)
54. P. Smith and A. Eisenberg, *J. Polym. Sci. Polym.* Letters, *21,* 223 (1983)
55. L. L. Zhou and A. Eisenberg, *J. Polym. Sci., Polym. Phys. Ed., 21,* 595 (1983)
56. A. S. Michaels and R. G. Miekka, *J. Phys. Chem., 65,* 1765 (1961)
57. E. P. Otocka and F. R. Eirich, *J. Polym. Sci., A2 6,* 921 (1968)
58. S. P. Ting, B. J. Bulkin and E. M. Pearce, *J. Polym. Sci., Polym. Chem. Ed., 19,* 451 (1981)
59. M. Hara and A. Eisenberg, *Macromol., 17,* 1335 (1984)
60. G. Bazuin and A. Eisenberg, *J. Polym. Sci., Polym. Phys. Ed.,* in press
61. N. R. Legge, Paper No. 73, 127th Meeting of Rubber Div., Los Angeles, April, 1985; *Elastomerics 117* (10), 19 (1985)
62. J. A. Cogliano, U. S. Patent 4,524,156, Assigned to W. R. Grace & Co., June 18, 1985
63. J. R. Campbell, P. M. Conroy and R. A. Florence, PCT Int. Appl. WO 85 01,056, Assigned to General Electric Co., March 14, 1985
64. A. U. Paeglis, U. S. Patent 4,480,062, Assigned to Uniroyal Inc., October 30, 1984
65. P. K. Agarwal, H. S. Makowski and R. D. Lundberg, *Macromol., 13,* 1679 (1980)

Chapter 11

THEORETICAL ASPECTS OF BLOCK COPOLYMERS

Dale J. Meier

Contents

Dale J. Meier, Michigan Molecular Institute, Midland, Michigan, USA

1   INTRODUCTION

Block copolymers demonstrate a number of unique properties as a result of morphological features which are unique to such systems. The unique features are the result of phase separation of the incompatible block components being restricted to a microscopic size scale. The resulting "microphases" have dimensions of the order of the dimensions of the constituent polymer molecules, and the microphases often develop a highly organized domain morphology. Such microphase separation in block copolymers was clearly established more than twenty years ago by Sadron and associates[1-3] at the (now) Institut Charles Sadron in Strasbourg (formerly C.N.R.S., Centre de Recherches sur les Macromolecules). However, the phenomenon remained an interesting curiosity until the discovery by Holden and Milkovich[4] that microphase separation in block copolymers of appropriate composition and architecture could yield materials having unique and useful properties. An explosion of interest in block copolymers resulted, since it then became obvious that molecular architecture was at least as important as were other molecular variables, e.g., composition, in governing properties, and that the design of polymers for specific end-use properties could be foreseen.

The existence of a form of phase separation between block components is not surprising since the dissimilar block components – as homopolymers – are typically incompatible with one another as a result of a positive heat of mixing, or as a result of crystallization of one or both components. The thermodynamically stable state of a simple mixture of two incompatible homopolymers is the gross separation of the components from one another so as to limit their interfacial contact, and with the phase sizes being limited only be the amounts of the components present.

Incompatibility still exists when such homopolymers are joined to from a block copolymer, and each would like to segregate itself from the other. However, the fact that they are joined together restricts their segregation to microscopic dimensions, i.e., to microphases having dimensions of the order of the molecular sizes of the blocks. In addition, the equilibrium morphological state of the microphases will be a highly organized domain structure. Thus there is a fundamental difference between phase separation in a system of incompatible homopolymers and that in a corresponding block copolymer system. In view of the fascinating and unique phase and morphological behavoir of block copolymers, it is not surprising that a number of investigators have attempted to develop theories to explain various aspects of such phenomena. This chapter will present a selective overview of this work, in which emphasis will be placed on discussing those theories which have enjoyed the greatest success in explaining or rationalizing the behavior of block copolymers. It will be impossible to reference all of the vast number of publications which discuss various aspects of block copolymer theories and properties, so it is hoped that those authors whose work is not included will understand.

This chapter will be organized in the following manner. Microphase separation and domain morphologies of pure block copolymers will be discussed in Section 2. This will be followed in Section 3 by a discussion of microphase separation and morphology in systems comprising block copolymers and a solvent (which may be homopolymer[s]). Both compatible and selective solvent systems will be covered, including micellar systems which form in dilute solutions of block copolymers in selective solvents. In general, the discussions will be restricted to phenomena involving the "simple" block copolymers, i.e., to either diblock or triblock varieties. This restriction is the result of the lack of suitable models for microphase separation in multi-block copolymers, particularly those containing crystallizable components such as the thermoplastic polyurethanes or polyether-ester block copolymers. In contrast to the ill-defined morphology of these systems, the morphologies which develop in di- and tri-block systems are particularly simple, a fact which has enabled realistic theoretical models to be developed for them.

2   MICROPHASE SEPARATION AND DOMAIN MORPHOLOGY

The development of theoretical models for microphase separation began almost immediately following the Holden-Milkovich disclosure[4] of the unique and useful properties of microphase-separated triblock copolymers, and a multitude of publications[5-19] describing these theories began appearing in the period 1969–1971. In the intervening years, these early theories have been modified or abandoned, and a multitude of new theoretical developments have appeared. It will not be the purpose of this chapter to discuss all of the various models and treatments which have been presented, rather the discussion will concentrate on two models which have had the greatest success. The first model to be discussed will be that in which the domain structure is modelled by random-flight chains being constrained by barriers. The barriers, of course, represent the effects of the incompatibility between the components and the resulting restriction of the components to segregated regions of space. This model, to be termed the "confined-chain" model, was first presented by Meier[7], and then modified and extended at various times by him and coworkers to its current form[20,21]. The other model to be discussed is a mean-field theory, first presented by Helfand and associates[22-29], and then embellished and applied to various block copolymers systems by Noolandi and Hong[30-32].

2.1   Domain Size and Interfacial Thickness by Confined-Chain Model

For simplicity at this point, the theory will be illustrated for an A-B diblock molecule having approximately equal volume fractions of the two block components. As will be shown in a following section, this stipulation forces the equilibrium microphase morphology to be lamellar. A cross section of a fully-developed lamellar domain structure is shown schematically in Figure 1. In the initial randomly-mixed state, the molecules have no spatial constraints, since they may occupy any portion of the total volume of the system. In

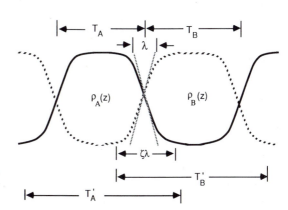

Figure 1   Segmental density profile of a block copolymer having a lamellar morphology

addition, since the molecules may occupy any portion of the volume, an interaction of the components occurs throughout the volume, giving an interaction energy or heat of mixing from all of the component segments. In contrast, in the domain or microphase-separated state, there are constraints on the placement of molecules and segments in space, and the interaction of unlike segments now occurs only between those segments in the interfacial region. Contributions to the free energy change associated with the spatial constraints and the interaction energy between the segments can be identified as follows[7]:

1. A change in the heat of mixing ΔH_m of the block components occurs when a random mixture tranforms into a microphase separated system, since following microphase separation the only contact between the components which remains is that in the interfacial region. It is this change in the heat of mixing which provides the driving energy for the microphase separation (provided the components mix with a positive heat of mixing).

2. The restriction on the placement of the A-B junction to the interfacial region in the microphase-separated state is responsible for a loss of entropy ΔS_p. Since the interfacial volume will (typically) constitute only a small fraction of the total volume of the system, this restriction on the placement of the molecules in space is responsible for a considerable loss of entropy upon microphase separation.

3. In the microphase-separated state, the A- and B-segments are segregated into their respective domains, i.e., into restricted regions of space. The constraints associated with this restriction on the location of segments also results in a loss of entropy ΔS_c.

The cross-section of a lamellar domain system displayed in Figure 1 shows the spatial density distribution of the A- and B-segments forming the lamellae. The location of the A-B junction and the (average) location of the chain ends in the lamellae is shown in Figure 2. If the interface between the A- and B-components is defined as the region where the components are mixed, then the junction between the blocks must reside in the interface, as shown in the Figure.

The above-listed contributions to the free energy change may be formulated in the following manner[7-8].

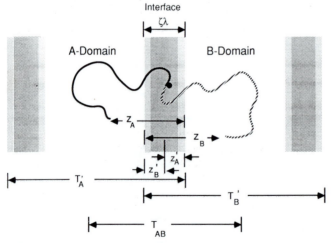

Figure 2   Cross-section of an A-B lamellar domain system showing the origin (A-B junction) of the A- and B-chains in the (shaded) interfacial region

2.1.1 Heat of Mixing and Interfacial Energy

The heat of mixing of segments in the random state ΔH_i will be assumed to be that given by the Flory-Huggins theory[33-34].

$$\Delta H_i = \frac{V \, \varphi_A \, \varphi_B \, \chi_{AB} \, k_B \, T}{\bar{v}_A} \tag{1}$$

where V is the volume of the system, $\bar{v}_A$ is molecular volume of an A-segment, φ_A and φ_B are the volume fractions of the A- and B-components, respectively, χ_{AB} is the interaction parameter between the components, k_B is the Boltzmann constant and T the temperature. The interaction term $\chi_{AB}k_BT$ is the energy change *per segment* of taking a chain of pure A and transferring it to an environment of pure B. The interaction parameter χ_{AB} is also formally related to the solubility parameters of the components by

$$\chi_{AB} = \bar{v}_A \frac{(\delta_A - \delta_B)^2}{k_B T} \tag{2}$$

where the δ's are solubility parameters. The mixing of the A- and B-components in the interfacial region results in a heat of mixing given by integrating the local heat mixing across the interfacial thickness

$$\Delta H_{int} = \frac{\chi_{AB} \, k_B \, T}{\bar{v}_A} \, S \int_{int} \varphi_A(z) \, \varphi_B(z) \, dz \tag{3}$$

where $\varphi_A(z)$ and $\varphi_B(z)$ are the volume fractions of the A- and B-components, respectively, $(\varphi_A(z) + \varphi_B(z) = 1)$. S is the area of the interface

$$S = \frac{2 \, N \, \bar{v}_A}{T_A} \tag{4}$$

where N is the number of A-B molecules and T_A is the thickness of an A-domain. The use of a local composition in the interface to evaluate the interfacial energy was introduced by Leary and Williams[12-13], albeit with an unrealistic segment density profile.

In those cases where the interfacial thickness is comparable to the range of intermolecular forces, an additional term[35] involving the gradient of the spacial composition must be added to Eq. 3 to account for "nonlocal interactions", i.e., the integrand becomes

$$\varphi_A(z) \, \varphi_B(z) + \frac{t^2}{6} \left(\frac{\partial \varphi}{\partial z} \right)^2 \tag{5}$$

where t is a measure of the range of intermolecular forces (approximately equal to the size of a segment, i.e. 5–10 Å). However, for most block copolymer systems the additional gradient term is not required since the interfacial thicknesses of most block copolymer systems will be considerably larger than 5–10 Å, making the influence of the gradient term negligible. The gradient term will not included in present presentation of the theory. To evaluate the value of the integral of Eq. 3, it will be necessary to specify the spatial dependence of the composition φ_A and φ_B in the interface. Although a theory[22-23] which includes the composition can be written, a solution of the resulting equations has been possible only for infinite molecular weight systems, i.e., those for which the placement of the chain ends can be ignored. It is fortunate that the integral in Eq. 3 is not particulary sensitive to reasonable choices of the spatial dependence, so the simple equation coming from the theory[44-45] for infinite molecular weight polymers will be used

$$\varphi_A(z) = (1 + \exp a'z)^{-1} \text{ and } \varphi_B(z) = 1 - \varphi_A(z) \tag{6}$$

where a' is related to the thickness of the interfacial region (to be determined by minimization of the free energy change). By substituting the spatial compositions of Eq. 6 into Eq. 3 and performing the integration over the interfacial thickness ($-\infty$ to $+\infty$), the interfacial energy ΔH_{int} becomes

$$\Delta H_{int} = \frac{N \chi_{AB} k_B T \lambda}{2 T_A} \tag{7}$$

where λ is the "linear" interfacial thickness

$$\lambda = \left(\frac{\partial \varphi}{\partial z}\right)_{z=0}^{-1} = \frac{4}{a'} \tag{8}$$

The change in the heat of mixing of components between the randomly-mixed state and the microphase-separated state then becomes from Eqs. 1 and 6

$$\Delta H_m = \frac{N \chi_{AB} k_B T \lambda}{2 T_A} - \frac{V \varphi_A \varphi_B \chi_{AB} k_B T}{\bar{v}_A} \tag{9}$$

2.1.2   Placement Entropy ΔS_p

The loss of entropy created by placing the A-B junction anywhere within the interfacial region is given by

$$\frac{\Delta S_p}{N k_B} = \ln\left[\frac{2\zeta\lambda}{T_A + T_B}\right] \tag{10}$$

where it is assumed that the A-B junctions are located within the distance $\zeta\lambda$ in the interface, with ζ being an adjustable parameter ($\zeta \sim 1$–2) characterizing the greater space available to the junction segments than is given by the measure of interfacial thickness λ. As Eq. 10 shows, the loss in placement entropy is simply related to the ratio of volume available to the placement of molecules in the microphase-separated state ($\sim \zeta\lambda S$), and that available in the randomly-mixed state ($\sim T_{AB}S$), where T_{AB} is the repeat spacing of the lamellar domain structure $T_{AB} = (T_A + T_B)/2$. Equation 10 allows the A-B junctions to be anywhere within the interfacial region, but it seems likely that the chain junctions will avoid one another (the region near the chain junctions will have a high segmental density) and become more-or-less equally spaced from one another in "cells". In this case, an additional term -1 should be added to Eq. 10.

2.1.3 Volume-Constraint Entropy ΔS_c

In order to evaluate the volume constraint entropy, we require the probability that the chains having one end in the interfacial region will have all segments within their domain space. In addition, the density distribution of segments must be such that space is uniformly filled with segments. The latter requirement follows from the very large stresses required to create a region of low density, i.e., to create a region having a density differing by only 10%

from the equilibrium value, would require a stress of about 10^8 Pa ($\sim$ 1000 Atm.) for most polymers. These large stresses ensure that whatever chain perturbations must occur to maintain a uniform density will be accommodated by the system.

In the microphase-separated state, each component chain is prohibited from being in the domain space occupied by the other, except in the interfacial region where both chain types intermingle. Referring to Fig. 2, the probability that an A- chain obeying random-flight statistics starting from the A-B junction position at z'_A within the interface region of thickness $\zeta\lambda$ will have the second (free) end at z_A (within dz_A) can be obtained from the diffusion equation

$$\frac{\partial P_A\,(z_A;z'_A)}{\partial n} = \frac{1^2}{6} \frac{\partial^2 P_A\,(z_A;z'_A)}{\partial z^2} \tag{11}$$

with appropriate boundary conditions[7]. In Eq. 11, n is the number of statistical elements of length l. The boundary conditions for the A-chains are $P_A(0;z'_A) = 0$ and $P_A(T'_A;z'_A) = 0$ (absorbing boundary conditions[36]). Similar boundary conditions apply for the B-chains. The solution for the A-chain is

$$P_A(z_A;z'_A) = \frac{2}{T'_A} \sum_{m=1}^{\infty} \sin \frac{m\pi z_A}{T'_A} \sin \frac{m\pi z'_A}{T'_A} \exp \left[-\frac{m^2\pi^2 \sigma_A\,1^2}{6T'_A{}^2} \right] dz_A \tag{12}$$

and for the B-chain

$$P_B(z_B;z_B') = \frac{2}{T'_B} \sum_{p=1}^{\infty} \sin \frac{p\pi z_B}{T'_B} \sin \frac{p\pi z'_B}{T'_B} \exp \left[-\frac{p^2\pi^2 \sigma_B\,1^2}{6T'_B{}^2} \right] dz_B \tag{13}$$

Thus from Eqs. 12 and 13 we obtain the joint probability $P_{AB}(z_A;z_B:z'_A)$ that each chain starting within the interface at z'_A, with the free end of the A-chain at z_A and that of the B-chain at z_B, and with all segments constrained to stay within their respective domain space of thickness T'_A and T'_B

$$P_{AB}(z_A;z_B:z'_A) = P_A(z_A;z'_A) \bullet P_B(z_A;\zeta\lambda - z'_A) \tag{14}$$

where the origin of the B-chain is at $(\zeta\lambda - z'_A)$ relative to its boundary condition. Since the origin (junction) of the chains can be anywhere within the interface, we integrate Eq. 14 over z'_A to obtain the probability $P_{AB}(z_A;z_B;\zeta\lambda)$ that allows the chain origins to be anywhere within $\zeta\lambda$

$$P_{AB}(z_A;z_B:\zeta\lambda) = \frac{1}{\zeta\lambda} \int_0^{\zeta\lambda} P_{AB}(z_A;z_B:z'_A)\, dz'_A \tag{15}$$

The integration gives

$$P_{AB}(z_A;z_B;\zeta\lambda) = \frac{4}{\pi\zeta\lambda} \sum_{m,p\,=\,1}^{\infty} \frac{\left(mT'_B \sin \frac{p\pi\zeta\lambda}{T'_B} - pT'_A \sin \frac{m\pi\zeta\lambda}{T'_A} \right)}{m^2 T'_B{}^2 - p^2 T'_A{}^2} \sin \frac{m\pi z_A}{T'_A} \sin \frac{p\pi z_B}{T'_B} \times$$

$$\exp \left[-\frac{\pi^2}{6} \left(\frac{m^2 \sigma_A 1^2}{T'_A{}^2} + \frac{p^2 \sigma_B 1^2}{T'_B{}^2} \right) \right] dz_A\, dz_B \tag{16}$$

Continuing, we must now obtain the joint probability that the free ends of the chains can be anywhere within their respective domain space. This is not simply the integral of $P_{AB}(z_A;z_B:\zeta\lambda)$ with respect to z_A and z_B over domain space, since the chains must not only occupy domain space but do so in a manner that maintains a uniform segment density, even though chain dimensions may be perturbed by, e.g., the presence of a solvent. This uniform-density constraint is introduced by specifying that the chain ends must occupy (on average) that relative position in space for which an unperturbed chain has an overall equal segment density throughout the domain (except, of course for the interfacial region where it is the sum of segment densities that must be uniform). Then, if domain dimensions are perturbed, a concomitant change in the relative position of the free chain end ensures that a uniform density will be maintained. Thus we require the average position of the free chain end in a domain which is of uniform density. In order to obtain this average position in space, we must first obtain segment densities as a function of domain and chain dimensions. Segment densities at points z are obtained by summing (integrating) the probabilities that sub-chains pass through points z. Thus the density of segments at a point z is

$$\varrho_\sigma(z;z') = \int_{n=1}^{\sigma} P_n(z;z')\bullet P_{\sigma-n}(T':z)\, dn \tag{17}$$

The first term within the integrand represents the probability that a subchain of n-statistical segments with its origin at z' will have its second end at z, while the second term is the probability that the remaining $(\sigma-n)$ elements of the chain originating at z (the terminal end of the n sub-chain) will be within the domain space T'. These probability functions are obtained as solutions to Eq. 11. With Eq. 17, segment densities are obtained for several spacial positions z across the domain $(0<z<T')$, and as a function of the ratio of domain dimensions to chain dimension, i.e., to the ratio $T'/(\sigma l^2)^{1/2}$. In this manner, that ratio which gives a constant density of segment throughout the domain (other than for the interface region) can be obtained. For the lamellar domain system in which space if filled from chains originating from both sides of the domain, the relationship of T' and σl^2 which gives the most uniform segment densities is[7-8] the simple

$$T'^2 \approx 2\,\sigma l^2 \tag{18}$$

The mean-square position $<z^2>$ of the free end of a chain in a lamellar domain having this value of $T'^2/\sigma l^2$ is obtained from

$$<z^2> = \frac{\displaystyle\int_0^{T'} z^2 P(z;z')\, dz}{\displaystyle\int_0^{T'} P(z;z')\, dz} \tag{19}$$

where $P(z;z')$ is the same as in Eq. 11, except that the chain index K is omitted since it is not required here. Evaluation of Eq. 19 gives

$$\frac{<z^2>}{T^2} = \frac{\sum_{m=1}^{\infty} \left(\frac{(-1)^{m+1}(m^2\pi^2-2)}{m^3} - 2\right) \sin\frac{m\pi z'}{T'} \exp\left[-\frac{\pi^2 m^2 \sigma l^2}{6T'^2}\right]}{\sum_{m=1}^{\infty} \left(\frac{(-1)^{m+1}+1}{m}\right) \sin\frac{m\pi z'}{T'} \exp\left[-\frac{\pi^2 m^2 \sigma l^2}{6T'^2}\right]} \tag{20}$$

This equation has been evaluated for values of $T'^2/\sigma l^2 = 2 \pm 0.5$, and for values of z'/T' ranging from 0 to 0.25, with results that are remarkably constant over these ranges of values, e.g., the r.m.s. position $<z^2>^{1/2}$ of the free end of the chain is $<z^2>^{1/2}T' = 0.50 \pm 0.02$. Thus the free end of a chain in a domain which is uniformly filled with segments is, on average, at the center of the domain. Taking $<z_K^2>^{1/2}/T'_K \equiv 0.5$, with K = A or B, the joint probability of finding the free ends of the A- and B-chains at these positions (in order to satisfy the uniform density requirement) is from Eq. 16

$$P_{AB}(z_A = T'_A/2; z_B = T'_B/2: \zeta\lambda) = \frac{4}{\pi\zeta\lambda} \sum_{\substack{m,p \text{ odd}}}^{\infty} (-1)^{(m+p+2)/2} \frac{\left(mT'_B \sin\frac{p\pi\zeta\lambda}{T'_B} - pT'_A \sin\frac{m\pi\zeta\lambda}{T'_A}\right)}{m^2 T'_B{}^2 - p^2 T'_A{}^2} \text{ x}$$

$$\exp -\frac{\pi^2}{6}\left[\frac{m^2\sigma_A l^2}{T'_A{}^2} + \frac{p^2\sigma_B l^2}{T'_B{}^2}\right] dz_A \, dz_B \tag{21}$$

and the entropy change associated with constraining the chains to their respective domains while at the same time satisfying the uniform density requirement is

$$\Delta S_c/Nk_B = \ln P_{AB}(z_A = T'_A/2; z_B = T'_B/2: \zeta\lambda) \tag{22}$$

2.1.4   Free Energy of A-B Domain Formation

From Eqs. 9, 10 and 21, we obtain ΔG_{AB}, the free energy change associated with the microphase separation from a homogeneous state to the domain-structured state of an A-B block copolymer

$$\frac{\Delta G_{AB}}{Nk_BT} = Z_A\chi_{AB}\left[\frac{(\alpha-1)}{2\zeta} + \frac{q}{p+1}\right] - \ln\frac{8\,\alpha\,\beta\,r^2}{\pi\,(q-1)} -$$

$$\ln\left[\sum_{\substack{m,n \text{ odd}}}^{\infty} (-1)^{(m+p+2)/2} \frac{m\beta \sin\frac{m\pi(\alpha-1)}{\beta} - p\alpha \sin\frac{p\alpha(\alpha-1)}{\alpha}}{m^2\beta^2 - p^2\alpha^2} \exp\left\{-\frac{\pi^2}{6}\left(\frac{\sigma_A l^2}{T_A{}^2}\right)\left(\frac{m^2}{\alpha^2} + \frac{cp^2}{\beta^2}\right)\right\}\right] \tag{23}$$

where, for convenience, the substitutions α, β, c and q have been made and are defined as follows

$$\alpha = \frac{T'_A}{T_A} = \frac{T_A+\zeta\lambda}{T_A} = 1+\zeta y, \quad \beta = \frac{T'_B}{T_B} = \frac{q+\zeta\lambda}{q}, \quad q = \frac{Z_B\bar{v}_B}{Z_A\bar{v}_A} \text{ and } c = \frac{(\sigma l^2)_B}{(\sigma l^2)_A} \tag{24}$$

where $q = Z_B\bar{v}_B/Z_A\bar{v}_A$ is the ratio of the molecular volumes of the two blocks.

From Eqs. 23 and 24, we see that the free energy change ΔG is a function of two independent variables, one associated with the domain thickness T_A or T_B and the other associated with the interfacial thickness λ (the parameter ζ can be treated as an adjustable parameter, although the value of $\zeta=2$ seems reasonable, both conceptually as well as giving agreement with experimental results, as will be shown). The equilibrium values of the domain and interfacial thicknesses are obtained by minimizing the free energy change with respect to these variables, e.g. by solving the set of simultaneous equations

$$\frac{\partial \Delta G_{AB}}{\partial \alpha} = 0 \quad \text{and} \quad \frac{\partial \Delta G_{AB}}{\partial ((\sigma l^2)_A / T_A^2)} = 0 \tag{25}$$

for a given set of molecular parameters, e.g., $(\sigma l^2)_A$, $(\sigma l^2)_B$, $\bar{v}_A$, $\bar{v}_B$, χ_{AB}, etc. The solution of these equations then allows the prediction of each domain dimension T_K (K = A or B), the domain repeat thickness $T_{AB} = (T_A + T_B)/2$ and the interfacial thickness λ.

Figure 3 shows the relative contributions to the free energy of domain formation (per chain) as a function of domain size. The interfacial energy ΔH_{int} decreases monotonically with an increase of domain thickness since the relative fraction of material in the interface then decreases. The placement entropy ΔS_p contribution (Eq. 10) to the free energy change increases monotonically with increasing domain size. In contrast, the constraint entropy contribution ΔS_c (Eq. 22) shows a minimum. This results from the interplay of the boundary constraints which favor an increase in the space available to the chains and the density constraint which forces the chains to uniformly fill space, i.e., an increase in domain thickness reduces the segmental densities in the center of the domain.

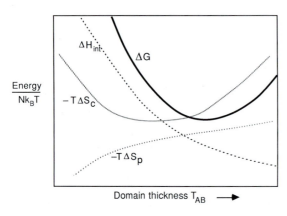

Figure 3   Relative contributions to the free energy of domain formation as a function of domain size. The contributions lead to a minimum in the free energy and establish the equilibrium domain size. See text for an explanation of the symbols

2.1.5   Comparison of Theory and Experiment for A-B Copolymer

Domain dimensions have been obtained by Hashimoto, Shibayama and Kawai[37], by Mayer[39] and by Hadziioannou and Skoulios[40] on various S-I block copolymers (poly[styrene-b-isoprene]) having lamellar morphologies which will allow comparison of domain dimensions with the predictions of the above theory. In addition, Hashimoto, Shibayama and Kawai[37] and Richards and Thomason[41] have presented data on the interfacial thickness of a number of S-I block copolymers, which can also be compared with the predictions of theory. In order to make the comparisons, the following molecular relationships are used in the theory

$$\bar{v}_K = \frac{M_K}{N_A \varrho_K} \quad \text{with } M_k = \text{molecular weight (K=S or I)}, \varrho_s = 1.05 \text{ g/cm}^3, \varrho_I = 0.92 \text{ g/cm}^3 \tag{26}$$

The unperturbed chain dimension are estimated from[37]

$$(\sigma l^2)_K = C_K^2 M_K \tag{27}$$
$$C_s = 0.67 \text{ Å}$$
$$C_I = 0.72 \text{ Å (for predominately 3,4-polyisoprene)}$$
$$C_I = 0.764 \text{ Å (for predominately 1,4-polyisoprene)}$$

The interaction parameter χ_{SI} determined by Rounds and McIntyre[38] will be used., i.e.,

$$\frac{\chi_{SI}}{\bar{V}_S} = \frac{(\delta_S - \delta_I)^2}{RT} = -900 + \frac{7.5 \times 10^5}{T} \text{ mol/m}^3$$
$$\text{or } \chi_{SI} = -8.57 \times 10^{-2} + \frac{71.4}{T} \text{ (per monomer unit)} \tag{28}$$

where $\bar{V}_S$ is the molar volume of a polystyrene monomer unit.

Since χ_{SI} is a function of temperature, there is a question of what temperature should be taken to evaluate χ_{SI} in order to compare the predictions of theory with experimental results. The experimental results were obtained on S-I block copolymer samples which were annealed at temperatures above the glass transition temperature of polystyrene in order to perfect the domain morphology. However, the domain dimensions were then obtained on samples cooled to room temperature. It is not apparent at which temperature the domain dimensions of an S-I block copolymer would become frozen as the sample is cooled from above to below the glass transition temperature of polystyrene, but it seems most reasonable to expect that the domain dimensions will be frozen for an S-I block copolymer at a temperature T′ near the glass transition temperature of polystyrene. Hence, even though the experimental data were obtained at room temperature, the domain dimensions would be those established at T′. However, in order to show the effect of the choice of temperature used to evaluate χ_{AB}, theoretical results will be presented for a temperature (30°C) approximately that used to obtain experimental data, and for 90°C, a temperature near Tg of polystyrene.

Table I shows the effects of the choice of the parameter ζ on calculated domain properties. As defined in an earlier section, ζ is a parameter which allows the block copolymer junction to occupy a greater volume of space ($\sim \zeta \lambda$) than that represented by the interfacial thickness measure λ. The data in Table I show that as ζ increases both the calculated interfacial thickness and the domain dimensions decrease. The value of ζ giving the best agreement between theory and experiment for the polymer of Table I is $\zeta \sim 3$. However, the value $\zeta = 2$ gives the best agreement overall when other experimental data are included, and hence this value is used for the data presented in Table II and in Figures 4–6. Table II shows a comparison of theory predictions and the experiment data of Hashimoto, Shibayama and

TABLE I   Effect of Choice of ζ on Domain and Interface Dimensions[a, b]

χ (T = 30 °C)			χ (T = 90 °C)		
ζ	T_{AB}, Å	λ, Å	ζ	T_{AB}, Å	λ, Å
1	580	20.8	1	570	26.4
2	552	18.4	2	537	23.3
3	529	16.8	3	511	20.7
4	512	15.6	4	492	18.9

[a] Calculations are for S-I diblock copolymer with $M_S + M_I = 102,000$ (20)
[b] T_{AB} is the domain thickness $(T_S + T_I)/2$, and λ is the characteristic interfacial thickness.

TABLE II   Comparison of Theoretical and Experimental Domain and Interface Dimensions

Reference	$(M_S+M_I) \times 10^{-3}$	Domain Thickness, T_{AB}, Å			Interfacial Thickness, λ, Å		
		Theory, 30 °C	Theory, 90 °C	Expt.	Theory, 30 °C	Theory, 90 °C	Expt.
37	21	198	187	172	27	32	` 17±2
37	31	263	252	243	25	29	17±2
37	49	353	341	319	23	27	19±2
37	102	552	537	503	19	23	17±2
37	94	513	514	527	19	24	
39	31		247	218			
39	40.5		286	286			
39	44		308	314			
39	51		343	364			
39	47.5		322	340			
39	64		406	440			

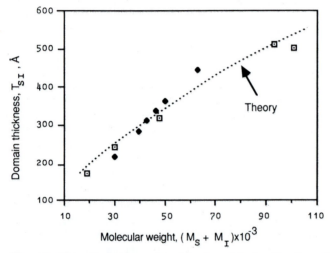

Figure 4   Theoretical and experimental values of the lamellar dimensions of S-I block copolymers as a function of molecular weight. The points labelled □ are from Reference 37 and those labelled ◆ are from Reference 39

Kawai[37] and of Mayer[39] for a series of S-I block copolymers. The domain thickness T_{SI} as a function of the block copolymer molecular weight $(M_S + M_I)$ is shown in Figure 4. The relationship between domain dimensions $T_{SI} = (T_S + T_I)/2$ and total block molecular weight which is predicted by theory is $T_{SI} \sim (M_S+M_I)^{0.65}$, and is shown by the line marked "Theory" in Figure 4. It is of interest to point out that theory predicts the domain thickness to be a monotonic function of the total block molecular weight, i.e., to be independent of the individual block molecular weights. The excellent agreement shown in Figure 4 appears to support this prediction, since the experimental data cluster about the theoretical line, even though the ratio of the block molecular weights of the individual polymers differ widely from one another. Figure 5 shows predicted domain sizes as a function of the experimental values. Again, these data show excellent agreement, with the data clustering about the line of unit slope. It will be noted in Figure 5 that the predicted values tend to be higher than the

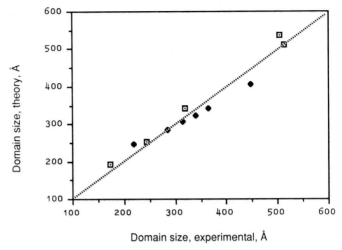

Figure 5   Comparison of theoretical and experimental value of the lamellar dimensions of S-I block copolymers. The experimental points are labelled as in Figure 4

experimental values of Hashimoto, Shibayama and Kawai[37], while being smaller than the experimental values of Mayer[39], i.e., most of the experimental data of Hashimoto et al. are above line, while most of those of Mayer are below.

A comparison of the predicted and theoretical values of the interfacial thickness λ is shown in Figure 6. The experimental data shown are the small-angle X-ray scattering (SAXS) results of Hashimoto, Shibayama and Kawai[37] and the small-angle neutron scattering (SANS) results of Richards and Thomason[41]. The S-I samples used by Hashimoto et al. had a lamellar morphology, while those of Richards and Thomason included samples with spherical, cylindrical as well as lamellar morphologies. The data for morphologies other than lamellar are included in Figure 6 since theories for the other morphologies indicate that the interfacial properties are essentially independent of morphology when the interfacial

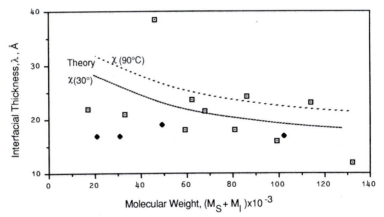

Figure 6   Theoretical and experimental values of the interfacial thickness of S-I block copolymers as a function of mulecular weight. The theoretical predictions are shown for 30 °C and 90 °C. The experimental points labelled ♦ are SAXS data from Reference 34 and the points labelled □ are SANS data from Reference 41

thickness is a small fraction of the domain size (narrow interface model). Other SAXS results on the block copolymer interface have been obtained by Siemann and Ruland[25] on (S-I-S) polymers, and by Roe, Fishkis and Chang[43] on di-and tri-block copolymers of styrene and butadiene (S-B and S-B-S). Their results are not included in Figure 6, but will be discussed in a following section.

The predicted and experimental results shown in Figure 6 show reasonable agreement, and probably better than one should expect from either the theory or the experiments. The major area of disagreement between the predicted and experimental values lies in the dependence of the interfacial thickness on molecular weight. The present theory clearly predicts a decrease (albeit slight) of the interfacial thickness with increasing molecular weight, whereas the results of Hashimoto, et al.[37] clearly do not show such a dependence. The results of Richards and Thomason[41] are somewhat scattered, but if the two extreme values (12 and 38Å) are excluded as being far outside the other values, the remaining data do show a slight dependence on molecular weight when analyzed statistically, but not as great as predicted by theory (the dependence on molecular weight would be greater if the two extreme values were included in the statistical analysis). The apparent disagreement between theory and experiment on this point presents a dilemma, since any theory which assumes a pair-wise interaction between components (as all existing theories do) will find that the energy of mixing in the interfacial region is directly proportional to the volume of the mixed region, i.e., to the thickness and area of the interfacial region. Also, the entropy change associated with localization of the junction segments of the block copolymer in the interfacial region introduces the logarithm of the interfacial thickness. Inclusion of these terms in the free energy of the system will produce a molecular weight dependence of the interfacial thickness when the free energy is minimized with respect to the thickness. The dilemma may be more apparent than real, since experimental data probably have not as yet been taken over a sufficiently wide range of molecular weights to prove or disprove the molecular weight dependence. The experimental determination of interfacial thicknesses by SAXS or SANS methods present a number of problems, of which one of the most important is the problem of subtracting out the background scattering in the high-Q region (Q is the scattering vector) where information concerning the interface resides. There is no absolute method of subtracting out the background scattering, so various empirical methods are used, and, depending on the method used, the calculated results will vary, a fact that is probably responsible for the wide variation in results of some investigators. More experimental data will be required before it is clear whether theory or experiment are in error. It should be noted that statements are often made[41] that the Helfand mean-field theory[22–29] (to be discussed in a later section) does not predict a molecular weight dependence of the interfacial thickness, and hence seems to agree better with experimental results than does the theory outlined above. However, the lack of dependence on molecular weight in the mean-field theory is simply the result of assuming that the interface has the same properties as corresponding pair of homopolymers of infinite molecular weight, and hence the possibility of a molecular weight dependence does not appear in the theory. The interfacial thickness is taken as that for infinite molecular weight block copolymers. It has been pointed out by Hashimoto, Shibayama and Kawai[37] that the interfacial thickness predicted by the theory outline above (with the inclusion of the term in Eq. 5 for non-local interactions) becomes identical with that of the Helfand theory[22–29] at infinite molecular weight.

In contrast to the results shown in Figure 6, Siemann and Ruland[42] find interfacial thicknesses of a series of S-I-S block copolymers to be in the range of 7–15Å, with an average of about 10Å. They also report major changes in interfacial thicknesses as a results of various annealing procedures, an effect not noticed or reported by other investigators. Their results showing such very small thicknesses seem anomalous, in that the values are hardly larger than the size of 1–2 segments of the polymer chain, and it is difficult to believe that the segmental composition across an interface could change so abruptly. Ruland has pointed out in a recent paper[46] another potential source of error in SAXS measurements, namely the possibility that the transition of composition in the interface may not be smooth, but rather has a statistical (non-smooth) structure. He concludes that if the interface does have statistical fluctuations in composition, SAXS results will underestimate interfacial widths. Roe, Fishkis and Chang[43] treated in a variety of ways the SAXS problem of the obtaining the appropriate variance σ of the Gaussian smoothing function used to evaluate data. They finally concluded that σ lies between 4 and 7Å, giving the interfacial thickness $\lambda = (12)^{1/2}\sigma$ between 14 and 24Å, a range encompassing the results shown in Figure 6. Their results were obtained on S-B and S-B-S samples having a sufficiently low molecular weight polystyrene block ($M_S = 7000$) that the domain structure (spherical) was sensitive to temperature and could be eliminated at high temperatures, i.e., at temperatures above the critical temperature for domain formation. They reached the interesting conclusion that the interfacial thickness of their samples was not a function of temperature, even though the domain structure itself became more and more diffuse at higher temperatures. This conclusion is not predicted by theory. It is possible that the experimental results on the spherical domain systems were affected by the systems being in non-equilibrium states – as all spherical domain systems will be (to be discussed in a later section). Further work with systems having a lamellar or cylindrical morphology would be helpful, since systems having these morphologies can attain equilibrium states. A number of attempts have been made to determine interfacial thicknesses in block copolymer systems by methods other than SAXS or SANS. In particular, Gronski and associates[48–50] have analyzed dynamic viscoelastic data by the Kerner model[51] for S-B-S copolymers and their hydrogenated versions to estimate interfacial properties. Although the absolute validity of the Kerner model might be questioned for such block copolymers, it is of interest that Gronski et al. do calculate interfacial thicknesses that are in the same range as those obtained by SAXS or SANS methods and shown in Fig. 6.

The use of NMR techniques to determine the fraction of material in the block copolymer interface (in di-, tri- and star-block copolymers of styrene and butadiene and tri-block copolymers of styrene and isoprene) has been reported by Tanaka and Nishi[52]. Their NMR method depends on resolving T_2 relaxation spectra into three T_2 contributions, one characteristic of polystyrene (rigid component), another characteristic of the polydiene (mobile component) and the third having intermediate properties (interfacial component). The authors estimate the interfacial thickness of all of the polymers they examined to be about 20Å, thus in the same range as that given by theory and by SAXS and SANS methods.

2.1.6   Criteria for Domain Formation

Critical molecular weights and interaction parameters for domain formation can be predicted by setting Eq. 23 for the free energy of domain formation equal to zero. The prediction is that the critical molecular weight for domain formation must approximately 3–5 times higher than for phase separation in a simple mixture of the corresponding homopolymers. For the S-I system considered above, the calculated critical molecular weight of the polystyrene block (as the minor component) is approximately 5000–6000. Although it is difficult to establish experimentally the actual onset of domain formation, data reported by Holden, Bishop and Legge[53] on the mechanical properties of a series of poly(styrene-b-butadiene-b-styrene) S-B-S thermoplastic elastomers supports this prediction. Their data show that the tensile strength of these polymers increased more than twenty-fold from 1.0 MPa to 23 MPa) when the molecular weight of the polystyrene block was increased from 6000 to 10000. Since the strength properties of such triblock thermoplastic elastomers depend on the existence of domains, the very large change in properties with a relatively small change in molecular weight is taken as evidence that domain formation occurred within this range of molecular weights. Although the predictions of theory are for S-I block copolymers, whereas the experimental data were obtained with S-B-S polymers, the comparison is considered valid since polybutadiene and polyisoprene appear to have essentially the same interaction parameter with polystyrene[38]. In addition, theories for A-B and A-B-A block copolymers (to be discussed) show the thermodynamic and domain properties are essentially the same if the triblock copolymer is treated as an A-B/2 diblock copolymer[12, 13, 21, 25]. It must be remembered that predictions of theory based on Eq. 23 are for the establishment of a full-developed domain system, and not for the onset conditions where aggregation of the block components just commences and where the effects of structure are minor. A criterion based on onset conditions will predict a lower value, as shown by the results of Leibler[54] and of Olvera de la Cruz and Sanchez[55] (to be discussed in a following section).

2.2   Domain Size and Interfacial Thickness by Mean-Field Model

As an outgrowth of his work on developing a mean-field theory for inhomogeneous polymer systems (polymer interfaces), Helfand presented in 1974 a mean-field theory for block copolymer lamellar microphases[23] which avoids some of the approximations (while introducing others) inherent in the "confined chain" theory presented and discussed above. In the intervening years, Helfand and associates have extended the theory[22–29], so that it is now also applicable to cylindrical and spherical morphologies. Noolandi and associates have developed a different formulation of a mean-field theory and have extended it to include the effect of solvents[30–32] and mixtures with homopolymers[32, 56]. Recently, Ohta and Kawasaki have presented a mean-field theory for the equilibrium morphology of block copolymer melts. Their formalism is similar to that used by Noolandi and associates and to that of Leibler[54] (to discussed in a later section). The essential point of departure of the mean-field formulation of theory from the "confined chain" approach outlined above is the generation of the barrier and density constraints by means of a modification of the diffusion equation used to generate chain statistics. This is done by including an additional term in the diffusion equation to account for the barrier constraints (polymer incompatibility) and for the requirement for uniform segment densities. Thus, in contrast to the confined chain model in which the interfacial barrier thickness and domain dimensions are introduced as terms whose values are determined by minimization of the system free energy, in mean field theory the solution of the diffusion equation should directly determine the interfacial thickness – as well as the domain dimensions. In the Helfand theory, the additional potentials into the modified diffusion equation arising from the barrier constraints and the density constraints are introduced as follows. A random-flight chain in a field-free region obeys the standard diffusion equation, Eq. 11. However, in the presence of a potential field, the diffusion equation must be modified to take account of the effect of the potential on chain statistics. In the presence of a potential field $U(r)/k_b T$, the modified equation becomes

$$\frac{\partial P_K(\bar{r},n,\bar{r}_o)}{\partial n} = \left[\frac{l^2}{6} \nabla^2 + \frac{U(\bar{r})}{k_b T} \right] P_K(\bar{r},n,\bar{r}_o) \tag{29}$$

where, as before, $P_K(\bar{r},n,\bar{r}_o)$ is the probability (non-normalized) of finding the n-th segment of the K-th chain at $\bar{r}$ when the first end is at $\bar{r}_o$. In a block copolymer microphase-separated (domain) system, there are two sources of the potential field acting on each unit of a chain. The first $U_{int}(\bar{r})$ is associated with the energetics of the interaction of the A- and B-units of a chain, i.e., to the interaction parameter χ_{AB}, and can be written[23] for the A-chains as $U_{int}(\bar{r})/k_B T = \chi_{AB}\varrho_B/\varrho_o$, where ϱ_B/ϱ_o is the fractional density of the B-component (ϱ_A is interchanged for ϱ_B for the B-chains). The second contribution to the potential field is associated with the density of segments, i.e., to a potential which attempts to maintain a uniform density of segments. This potential is given by Helfand[23] as

$$U_\varrho(\bar{r}) = \frac{1}{\varkappa} \left[\frac{\varrho_A(\bar{r}) + \varrho_B(\bar{r}) - \varrho_0}{\varrho_0^2} \right] \tag{30}$$

where $\varkappa$ is the volume compressibility of the system. Equation 29 for $P_K(\bar{r},n,\bar{r}_0)$ can then be written as

$$\frac{\partial P_K(\bar{r},n,\bar{r}_0)}{\partial n} = \left[\frac{l^2}{6} \nabla^2 + V_K(\bar{r}) \right] P_K(\bar{r},n,\bar{r}_0) \quad \text{with}$$

$$V_K(\bar{r}) = \chi_{AB} \frac{\varrho_{K'}(\bar{r})}{\varrho_0} + \frac{1}{\varrho_0 k_B T \varkappa} \left[\frac{\varrho_A(\bar{r})}{\varrho_0} + \frac{\varrho_B(\bar{r})}{\varrho_0} - 1 \right] \tag{31}$$

where $K' = B$ when $K = A$, etc.

The pair of equations represented by Eq. 31 are not sufficient to obtain solutions for the chain statistics since they contain the density profiles $\varrho_K(\bar{r})$. However, the density profiles are functions of the probability functions $P_K(\bar{r},n,\bar{r}_0)$

$$\varrho_K(\bar{r}) = \frac{N}{V\Gamma} \int\limits^{Z_K} dn \int\limits^{V} P_K(\bar{r}_K,(Z_K-n),\bar{r}) \, P_K(\bar{r},n,\bar{r}') P_{K'}(,\bar{r},Z_{K'},\bar{r}_{K'}) \, d\bar{r}' \, d\bar{r}_K \, d\bar{r}_{K'} \tag{32}$$

where N is the number of molecules in the volume V, $\bar{r}'$ is the common origin of the K and K' chains, and Γ represents the integral

$$\Gamma = \frac{1}{V} \int\limits^{V} P_K(\bar{r}_K,Z_K,\bar{r}') \, P_{K'}(\bar{r}',Z_{K'},\bar{r}_{K'}) \, d\bar{r}_K \, d\bar{r}_{K'} \, d\bar{r}' \tag{33}$$

The solution of Eqs. 31 and 32 to establish the segment density distributions $\varrho_K(\bar{r})$ must be done by computer in an iterative fashion, i.e., a trial distribution is used in Eq. 31 to find the terms $P_K(\bar{r},n,\bar{r}_0)$ required to evaluate Eq. 32. The solution of Eq. 32 in turn generates new density distributions $\varrho_K(\bar{r})$ which are then used to find new $P_K(\bar{r},n,\bar{r}_0)$, etc. If all goes well, the results converge to a self-consistent field $\varrho_K(\bar{r})$. The free energy of the system can then be written as[23]

$$\frac{G}{k_B T} = \int\limits^{V} \left[-\frac{\chi_{AB}}{\varrho_0} \varrho_A(\bar{r}) \, \varrho_B(\bar{r}) + \frac{1}{2\varrho_0^2 k_B T \varkappa} \left(\varrho_0^2 - \{\varrho_A(\bar{r}) + \varrho_B(\bar{r})\}^2 \right) \right] d\bar{r} - N \ln \Gamma \tag{34}$$

and from which equilibrium domain properties such as size and morphology are obtained by minimization.

In order to avoid the complexity involved in seeking self-consistent solutions to the above equations, Helfand introduced[23] the "narrow interphase approximation" for those systems where the interface represented a small fraction of the total system – an approximation that should be valid for block copolymer systems other than those of very low molecular weight or those on the verge of becoming homogeneous, e.g., at very high temperatures or diluted with solvent. He separated the various contributions to the free energy change associated with microphase separation in a manner somewhat similar to that done with the confined-chain model discussed in preceding sections. Thus his equation for the free energy change of domain formation, relative to a homogeneous mixture, is

$$\frac{\Delta G}{V\,k_B\,T} = 2\left(\frac{\chi_{AB}}{6}\right)^{1/2}\frac{\varrho_0}{T_{AB}} + \frac{\varrho_0}{Z_A+Z_B}\,\ln\frac{T_{AB}(6\chi)^{1/2}}{\pi l} + 0.13_9\,\varrho_0\,\frac{Z_A^{5/4}+Z_B^{5/4}}{(Z_A+Z_B)^{7/2}}\left(\frac{T_{AB}}{l}\right) -$$

$$\chi_{AB}\,\varrho_0\,\frac{Z_AZ_B}{(Z_A+Z_B)^2} \tag{35}$$

The first term in Eq. 35 represents the interfacial free energy (formulated in term of the interfacial tension of an infinite molecular weight homopolymer pair), the second term the free energy associated with the entropy loss associated with restricting the placement of the block junction in the interface region (corresponding to ΔS_p in the confined-chain model discussed above), the third term is an empirical term found to fit the computer calculations of the free energy associated with constraining the chains to be within their respective domain volumes (analogous to ΔS_c of the confined-chain model), while the last term is the heat of mixing of the homogeneous system. The domain dimensions calculated using Eq. 35 are almost exactly the same as indicated by the line labelled "Theory" in Fig. 4 (from the confined-chain model), and need not be reproduced again. The results predicted by this theory (in its "narrow interphase approximation" form) are in excellent agreement with experimental data. Although the results for domain dimensions of this mean-field theory and the confined-chain theory are essentially identical, there are differences in the predictive abilities of the two theories. As mentioned above and discussed in the earlier section dealing with interfacial thickness, this mean-field theory (Eq. 35) sets the interfacial thickness and interfacial energy as that of a corresponding pair of homopolymers of infinite molecular weight. Hence, it is not a theory from which the interfacial thickness can be predicted, e.g., as a function of block molecular weights.

The preceding discussions on domain sizes have concentrated on lamellar systems. However, Helfand and Wasserman have also extended the mean-field theory to include cylindrical and spherical morphologies[29, 70-71], and have provided a computer program[29] to enable computation of domain dimensions (for all three morphologies) given composition and molecular parameters. In general, the results of the theories for cylindrical domain systems are in good agreement with experimental data, but the same cannot be said for systems having spherical morphology. The reason for the lack of agreement for spherical systems has been obvious for some time[67]. Spherical domains can only change size by changing the number of block molecules in the spherical domain, but the number can only change by diffusional transport of the sphere-forming block component through the (incompatible) matrix of the other component. The barrier to such diffusion is such that it is unlikely to occur, and the system remains in a quasi-equilibrium state with the number fixed at that it had when the system underwent microphase separation at some solution concentration. This could be the equilibrium number under those conditions, but it generally would not be the equilibrium number (and hence size) when solvent was removed. In contrast, lamellar and cylindrical systems do not require diffusional transport through an incompatible matrix to change domain dimensions.

Discussion of the mean-field theories of Noolandi and Hong[30, 56] and of Ohta and Kawasaki[61] will be deferred until later sections, since the former is primarily applicable to systems containing solvent, and the latter to problems concerning morphology.

2.3   Onset Conditions for Microphase Separation

In section 2.1.6 the criterion used for domain formation was the free energy change being equal to zero. It was pointed out that this criterion was for the development of the fully segregated domain structure. Obviously, evidences of segregation and microphase order must occur before the fully-developed domain system forms. Onset criteria for this less structured state have been developed by Leibler[54] and by Olvera de la Cruz and Sanchez[55]. The theory developed by Leibler uses the "random phase approximation (RPA)" first introduced by de Gennes[57], while the theory of Olvera de la Cruz and Sanchez is based on the path integral methods of Edwards[58]. Both theories are quite complex when applied to block copolymers, and the details will not be covered here. The reader interested in the formalism and development for block copolymers is directed to the original papers[54, 55]. In spite of the complexity of the theories, the predictions from the theories regarding microphase separation are relatively simple. Thus in the theory of Leibler, the only relevant parameters in the theory (for A-B diblock copolymers) are the product $\chi(Z_A+Z_B)$ and the ratio Z_A/Z_B, where, as before, χ is the Flory-Huggins interaction parameter and Z_A and Z_B are the degreees of polymerization of the A- and B-chains. His formalism predicts that for a wide range of compositions (Z_A/Z_B) the onset of microphase separation will be to an ordered mesophase having the periodicity of a body-centered-cubic (bcc) lattice. In addition, the critical value of the product $[\chi(Z_A+Z_B)]_c$ for separation was determined to be $[\chi(Z_A+Z_B)]_c$ = 10.5. From Flory-Huggins theory, a binary mixture of homopolymers (of equal Z) will phase separate at a critical value of $[\chi(Z_A+Z_B)]_c$ = 4. Thus the joining of two homopolymers of equal size to form a block copolymer increases the critical value of the product $[\chi(Z_A+Z_B)]_c$ required for phase separation by a factor of 2.63, i. e., the molecular weight of the blocks must be 2.63 times larger than that required for simple phase separation of the corresponding homopolymer pair. Leibler constructed a phase diagram showing the critical values of $[\chi(Z_A+Z_B)]_c$ as a function of composition, but also showing that transitions from the onset bcc mesophase to other ordered mesophases would occur at certain values of $\chi(Z_A+Z_B)$, i. e., the morphology of the ordered mesophases will change as $\chi(Z_A+Z_B)$ increases. The predicted morphological transitions are bcc to hexagonal (cylindrical) and then to lamellar as $\chi(Z_A+Z_B)$ increases, with the actual values of $\chi(Z_A+Z_B)$ required being functions of composition. However, although the question of transitions in morphology of block copolymers is not in doubt (to be discussed in a following section), the validity of the random phase approximation to establish criteria for such transitions is in question when values of $\chi(Z_A+Z_B)$ are above the critical values and hence where strong segregation effects begin to occur. The predictions of the RPA theory depend on modeling the statistical properties of the block chains as Gaussian chains, but it is well established both theoretically[21, 59] and experimentally[60] that chains in a microphase environment are perturbed and deviate substantially from their usual Gaussian form, typically by being highly stretched in a direction normal to the domain boundary.

The theory of Olvera de la Cruz and Sanchez[55] extends the work of Leibler by considering block copolymers having a more complex molecular architecture than the diblock copolymers treated by Leibler. In particular, they investigated the phase stability criteria for simple graft copolymers, for star copolymers having equal number of A- and B-arms, and for n-arm star-block copolymers where the arms are A-B diblock copolymers. Their results with the simple A-B copolymers confirms Leibler's result, i.e., $[\chi(Z_A+Z_B)]_c$ = 10.5, a criterion which, surprisingly, is the same for star copolymers having equal numbers of A- and B-arms of equal size $Z_A = Z_B$. This result is independent of the number of arms. However, for star-block copolymers, the predicted critical values do depend on the number of arms n, i.e., if $Z_A = Z_B$ in each arm, $[\chi(Z_A+Z_B)]_c$ = 8.86, 7.07, 5.32 and 4.33 for n = 2, 4, 10 and 30, respectively. The result for n = 2 is particularly interesting, since the molecular architecture for n = 2 is the triblock A-B-B-A molecule, for which the predicted critical value compared to the precursor diblock molecule is 10.5/8.86 = 1.19, i.e., indicating that a triblock copolymer A-B-A is slightly more incompatible than the corresponding diblock copolymer of one-half the size A-B/2. The relatively small change in the critical conditions provides theoretical justification to the often-made comment that the domain properties of an A-B-A block copolymer are similar to those of the corresponding diblock copolymer of A-B/2 composition. The Olvera de la Cruz-Sanchez theory does not provide a prediction of the morphology of the microphases that form, as the Leibler theory[54] does for A-B polymers. As far as is known, the predictions of neither theory have been tested experimentally.

2.4   Domain Morphology

It has long been recognized that the morphology of the simple A-B and A-B-A block copolymers is a function of the volume ratio of the two components. The famous "Molau diagram"[62] shows a sequence of morphological transitions from A-spheres in B to A-cylinders in B to A- and B-lamellae to the inverted structures with B as the discontinuous phase as the A-component increases from being the very minor component to being the very major component. This pattern of morphological forms and regions of stability has been found, both experimentally and theoretically, to be essentially – but not completely – correct. The conclusion that there are only three basic morphological shapes – spheres, cylinders and lamellae – is not correct, for recent evidence [63–65] shows that a more complex morphology can develop in block copolymers of a particular composition or of star-block form. This morphology has been labelled "tetrapod"[63,64] and "double diamond"[65], and is a bi-continuous structure. Although the existence of this morphological type is now well established experimentally (also for small molecule systems[66]), no theory has yet been presented that deals with this morphology in block copolymers. Because of the nonexistence of a theory and because of the very specialized molecular properties that lead to this morphology, the discussion to follow will ignore it in favor of the three common morphological forms.

The first attempt to establish a theory showing regions of stability of the three morphological forms as a function of composition was by Meier[67]. The theoretical formalism used was similar to that outlined in Section 2.1.6 concerning the "confined-chain" model, with obvious changes being made to account for the different geometries. The results of the theory were in essential agreement with experiment, i.e., spheres were predicted to be the stable morphology at low volume fractions of the minor component ($\varphi < 0.2$), cylinders in the intermediate composition range ($0.2 < \varphi < 0.3$), and lamellae in the mid-range ($0.3 < \varphi < 0.7$). Although the composition ranges have been modified somewhat in more recent work[68], the essential conclusions from the theory remain unchanged. The major factor responsible for the transitions is simply the chain perturbations that arise when chains of different molecular volume are coupled and then forced to uniformly fill their respective domain space. The argument is as follows. Consider an A-B copolymer with equal molecular volumes $\bar{V}_A = \bar{V}_B$. Symmetry considerations alone establish the lamellar morphology as the equilibrium morphology, since a planar boundary (interface) of the lamellar morphology is the only boundary shape which has equal properties on each side of it, as required by the equal molecular volumes of the components. However, when the molecular volumes of the blocks begin to differ, then chain perturbations must occur in order to maintain a uniform density of segments. When the mismatch in molecular volumes becomes large enough, the system can avoid a further free energy increase from the chain perturbations by adopting a new morphology which relieves the space filling problem. Figure 7 shows this in a qualitative manner. With equal molecular volumes, the interface is planar, and the spacing of molecules in the interface is that necessary for the segment densities to appropriately fill space. However, if the volume of the B-block is then reduced, as shown, the chains then occupy less space and a region of low segment density results in between the B-chains – unless the B-chains are perturbed (stretched) laterally or the chain junctions are brought closer together, which would result in the A-chains being perturbed (stretched) normal to the interface. In either event, a mismatch in molecular volumes of the A- and B-chains must result in an

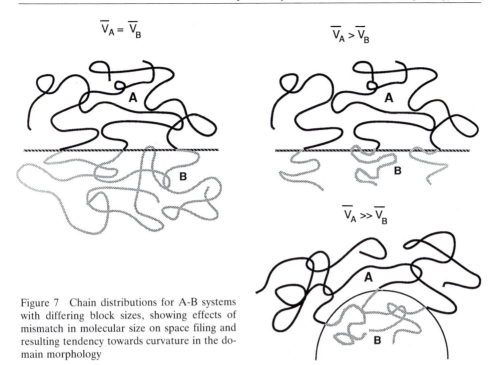

Figure 7 Chain distributions for A-B systems with differing block sizes, showing effects of mismatch in molecular size on space filing and resulting tendency towards curvature in the domain morphology

increase in free energy of the system as a result of the perturbation of chain dimensions. When the mismatch in molecular volumes becomes large enough, the system will change morphology to relieve the space filling problem. This is shown in Fig. 7, where it is seen that the introduction of curvature to the boundary between the components does help the smaller B-chains fill the intervening space and thus reduce the chain perturbations that would be required if the boundary remained planar. The introduction of curvature to the system changes the morphology from lamellar, first to cylindrical (curvature in one dimension) and then to spherical (curvature in two dimensions) when the mismatch in molecular volumes becomes very large.

That chain perturbations must occur when there are differences in the molecular volumes of the two components is quite easily shown (for simplicity, here for an A-B diblock copolymer). First, the ratio of domain dimensions is directly related to the block molecular volumes

$$T_A/T_B = \bar{V}_A/\bar{V}_B = M_A/M_B \quad \text{(assuming equal densities)} \tag{36}$$

On the other hand, both theory and experiment show that the domain spacing is also directly related to block molecular weights by

$$(T_A + T_B) \sim (M_A + M_B)^\beta \tag{37}$$

where β is very close to 2/3 (0.65 in the confined-chain model discussed earlier). The individual domain thicknesses are related to the (perturbed) chain dimensions by Eq. 18, i.e., $T \sim (\sigma l^2)^{1/2}$. With

$$(\sigma l^2)^{1/2} = \alpha (\sigma l^2)_o^{1/2} \text{ and } (\sigma l^2)_o^{1/2} = KM^{1/2}, \text{ where } (\sigma l^2)_o^{1/2} \text{ is the} \tag{38}$$

unperturbed chain dimension, α is the perturbation parameter relating perturbed and unperturbed dimensions, and K is an experimental constant. The perturbation parameters α' (relative to the case with $M_A = M_B$) can then be written as a function of the ratio of molecular weights M_A/M_B = x as

$$\alpha'_A = \frac{x^{1/2}}{(1+x)^{1/3}} \text{ and } \alpha'_B = \frac{1}{x^{1/2}(1+x)^{1/3}} \tag{39}$$

Table III shows values of α' as a function of the molecular weight ratios M_A/M_B. The chains become more and more perturbed as the ratio of block molecular weights departs from unity, with the higher molecular weight chains being expanded ($\alpha' > 1$ and the lower molecular weight chains being compressed ($\alpha' < 1$). The large chain perturbations arising from large mismatches in block molecular weights (volumes) are predominately responsible for the transitions that change the morphology from lamellar to cylindrical, and then to spherical.

TABLE III   Perturbation Parameters vs.
Molecular Weight Ratios

$\frac{M_A}{M_B}$ (= x)	α'_A	α'_B
1	1	1
2	1.24	0.62
3	1.37	0.46
4	1.47	0.37
5	1.55	0.31

Theories for the morphology of A-B and A-B-A block copolymers as a function of composition have been presented by Meier[67-68], by Helfand[13] and recently by Ohta and Kawasaki[61]. The theoretical formalisms used by each of the authors differ substantially, but the predictions of the theories for the stability of the various morphologies are similar (in the strong segregation or narrow interface limit), except for the spherical morphology in the Helfand theory. The theories agree in predicting the transition from lamellar to cylindrical morphology should occur at $\varphi \sim 0.33$. The Meier and the Ohta-Kawasaki theories place the transition from cylindrical to spherical at $\varphi \sim 0.20$, while the Helfand theory places the transition at $\varphi \sim 0.10$. Ohta and Kawasaki give a closed-form expressions for the free energy of each of the morphologies

$$F = Q\left[\frac{(1-\varphi)^2}{\varphi}\right]^{1/3} \qquad\qquad \text{lamellar} \tag{40}$$

$$F = 3^{1/3} Q (-1 + \varphi - \ln \varphi)^{1/3} \qquad \text{cylindrical} \tag{41}$$

$$F = 5.4 Q (2 + \varphi - 3 \varphi^{1/3})^{1/3} \qquad \text{spherical} \tag{42}$$

$$\text{where } Q = \frac{2^{1/2} \varphi}{3} (2^{1/2} \zeta \alpha)^{1/3} \tag{43}$$

$$\alpha = \frac{3}{R_g^4 \varphi (1-\varphi)} \text{ where } R_g \text{ is the radius of gyration} \tag{44}$$

and ζ is the interfacial thickness. Figure 8 shows the free energy (F/Q) given by Eqs. 41–43 as a function of volume fraction φ.

The predicted results for the morphological transitions can be compared with the experimental data of Hashimoto, Fujimura and Kawai[68], B. R. M. Gallot[69] and Kämpf, Hoffmann

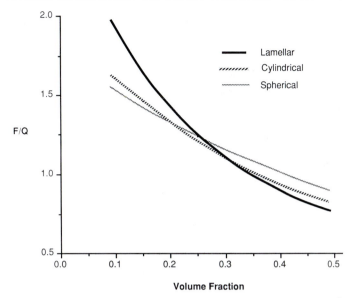

Figure 8   Free energy *vs.* volume fraction for various morphologies. Data from Ohta and Kawasaki[61]

and Krömer[17]. Experimentally it is found that the spherical to cylindrical transformation occurs at $\varphi = 0.20$–0.25, and the cylindrical to lamellar transformation at $\varphi = 0.35$–0.40. The experimental data reasonably well with the theoretical predictions of Meier[68] and of Ohta and Kawasaki[61] for both the spherical to cylindrical transition and the cylindrical to lamellar transition, and for the Helfand theory for the cylindrical to lamellar transition, although in all theories the predicted transition from cylindrical to lamellar morphology occurs at a somewhat lower volume fraction than is observed experimentally. However, a word of caution is in order with regard to comparisons of theory and experiment. The theories described are equilibrium theories, whereas the morphology of experimental samples is a function of the solvent used to cast films for examination (to be described in a following section), and quasi-equilibrium morphologies are often observed. It is extraordinarily difficult to ensure that an experimental sample has its equilibrium morphology, and particularly so in a transition region where the free energy difference between two morphologies is not large.

3   BLOCK COPOLYMERS AND SOLVENTS

This section will be divided into two main sections. The first section will deal with concentrated solution of block copolymers where microphase separation is still present. The second section will be concerned with block copolymers in dilute systems, where the block copolymer is present as an interfacially-active material (between pairs of homopolymers or where the block copolymer exists as a micellar aggregate (in a selective solvent). The topic of block copolymers in dilute solution as isolated molecules (in a non-selective solvent) will not be covered. Cowie[72] has published an excellent review of block copolymer/solvent systems, particularly covering experimental observations on the effect of solvents on various physical and mechanical properties. The interested reader is referred to that publication for details.

3.1   Block Copolymers in Concentrated Solutions

3.1.1   Domain Dimensions with Non-Selective Solvents

Experimental observations concerning the effect on domain morphology of a block copolymer by the addition of a non-selective solvent have presented a puzzle, since different groups have presented diametrically opposite data for nominally similar systems. The addition of toluene to an S-I block copolymer having lamellar morphology has been reported by Douy, Mayer, Rossi and Gallot[73] and by Ionescu and Skoulios[74] to *increase* the lamellar thickness, while the data presented by Shibayama, Hashimoto, Hasegawa and Kawai[75], also on an S-I/toluene system, show the lamellar thickness *decreases* with the addition of toluene.

Theories for the effect of solvent on domain dimensions have been presented by Noolandi and Hong[30] and by Meier[20, 68]. The theory of Noolandi and Hong is a mean-field theory somewhat similar to that discussed in an earlier section by Helfand[22–25], with modifications to take account of the presence of solvent and with a different method of introducing the constant-density constraint. Their theory[30–31] also begins with a modified diffusion equation for the polymer distribution function q_k

$$\frac{\partial q_k}{\partial t} = \frac{l_k^2}{6} \nabla^2 q_k - \omega_k q_k \tag{45}$$

where k refers to the polymer type and ω is an effective field. The quantity q_k is defined as

$$q_k(\bar{r},t) = \int d^3r_o \, Q_k(\bar{r},t;\bar{r}_o) \tag{46}$$

where $Q_k(\bar{r},t;\bar{r}_o)$ is the distribution function for a polymer chain of t repeat units which start at $\bar{r}_o$ and end at $\bar{r}$ (Q_k also obeys Eq. 45 with Q_k replacing q_k). Density distribution functions based on Q_k are essentially the same as given in Eqs. 32–33 with Q_k replacing P_K. The main point of departure of the Noolandi-Hong mean-field theory from that of Helfand is the introduction into the free energy functional the constant density constraint by means of a Lagrangian multiplier, rather than by use of a term involving directly the compressibility and the deviation from the average density. The density constraint is

$$\sum_p \frac{\varrho_p(\bar{r})}{\varrho_{op}} = 1 \tag{47}$$

where p refers to all components (polymer and solvent). The effective field ω is obtained by a gradient expansion of the potential energy[31], which gives

$$\omega_k = \Delta\mu_k - \frac{1}{Z_k}\left(\frac{\varrho_k}{\varphi_{ok}\,\varrho_{ok}}\right) - \frac{\varrho_{os}}{\varrho_{ok}}\left[\Delta\mu_s + \frac{1}{6}\sum_p \left(V_{sp'} - \frac{\varrho_{ok}}{\varrho_{os}}V_{kp'}\right)\nabla^2\varrho_{p'}\right] \tag{48}$$

where φ_{ok} is the overall volume fraction of polymer, $\Delta\mu_p$ is the shift of the chemical potential of a locally homogeneous system from a reference potential μ_p (uniform) of a macroscopically uniform system

$$\Delta\mu_p = \frac{\partial f_h}{\partial \varrho_p} + \frac{1}{\varrho_{op}}\left(f_h - \sum_p \varrho_{p'}\frac{\partial f_h}{\partial \varrho_{p'}}\right) - \mu_p \text{ (uniform)} \tag{49}$$

where f_h is the Flory-Huggins form of the locally homogeneous free energy. The $V_{kp'}$ terms of Eq. 47 are defined in terms of the interparticle potential

$$V_{kp'} = \int r^2\, U_{pp'}(\bar{r})\, d^3r \qquad (50)$$

Noolandi and Hong solved Eqs. 45–50 numerically to obtain the free energy difference between a lamellar domain system (with solvent) and a uniform system[30]. The results of this theory have been compared with experimental data by Shibayama et al.[75] for an S-I/toluene system. The agreement over the concentration range $\varphi_p = 0.25$–0.55 is excellent, both theory and experiment showing the domain thickness *decreases* with increasing solvent content.

In the confined-chain model (section 2.1), the free energy change associated with micro-phase separation and domain formation (Eq. 23) included a term for the interfacial energy, which was proportional to the Flory-Huggins interaction parameter χ_{AB} and to the volume of the interfacial region. This positive contribution to the free energy of domain formation can be minimized by reducing the interfacial volume, either by reducing the interfacial area and/or by reducing the interfacial thickness. An increase in χ_{AB} will increase a domain size T_{AB} since this reduces the interfacial area, and, conversely, a decrease in χ_{AB} will reduce domain dimensions. The effect of a non-selective solvent in the Meier theory[20–21] is simply to reduce the value of χ_{AB} in proportion to solvent concentration, i.e., $\chi_{AB}(\text{eff}) = \chi_{AB}\varphi_p$, where φ_p is the volume fraction of polymer. It is then not surprising that domain dimensions calculated using Eq. 23 decrease with increasing concentration of solvent (decreasing $\chi_{AB}(\text{eff})$). A comparison of the results of theory and experiment is shown in Figure 9, using the experimental data of Shibayama et al[75]. The results show a general agreement of theory and experiment, and, in agreement with the theory of Noolandi and Hong discussed above and with the experimental data, this theory also predicts that domain dimensions will decrease with increasing solvent content. Thus, although both theories and the Shibayama et al data are in agreement, a question still remains why other experimental data[73–74] show the opposite effect, namely an increase in domain dimensions with increasing solvent content. The answer probably resides in the ubiquitous non-equilibrium states that plague experimental observations on block copolymers, i.e., because of the constraints on segmental diffusion in a microphase separated system, long annealing times are required for a system to attain its equilibrium state.

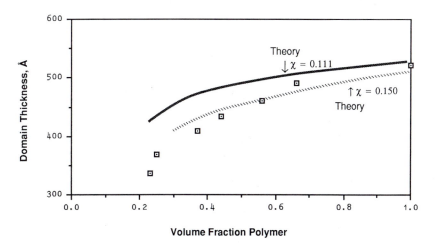

Figure 9   Effect of the addition of toluene (non-selective solvent) on the lamellar domain dimensions of an S-I block copolymer. The experimental points are from Ref. 75 and the theoretical lines are calculated from Eqs. 23–28

3.1.2   Domain Morphologies with Selective Solvents

In section 2.4 regarding domain morphology, it was pointed out that the predominate factor determining domain shapes was the relative volume fraction of the block components. With two different polymeric components in a block copolymer, the possibility exists of adding a selective solvent which is quite compatible with one component and quite incompatible with the other, thus changing the effective volume fractions of the components. This can be accompanied with a concomitant change in domain morphology. A theory for the effect of selective solvents on domain morphology has been published by Meier[68], and discussed by Cowie[72]. The relevant equations are complex and the interested reader is referred to the original publication for details. The results of the theory for one of the systems treated are shown in Figure 10 (other examples are shown in[72] and[20]). In Figure 10, the relative free energies of each of the domain shapes is shown as a function of the amount of selective solvent added wholly to the B-component (to the left) or to the A-component (to the right). In the absence of solvent, the equilibrium morphology of the polymer with $M_B/M_A = 2$ is lamellar. However, with the addition of a selective solvent, the equilibrium morphology can change, with the new morphology depending on the amount of solvent added and to which component. Thus, if solvent is added to the B-component in Figure 10, at a polymer volume fraction of approximately 0.9 the equilibrium morphology becomes cylindrical, and at a polymer volume fraction of approximately 0.5 the spherical morphology now has the lowest free energy. Such transformations are not unexpected, but the results do provide an explanation for the frequently reported (e.g.,[76–77]) effect of casting solvent on the mechanical properties of block copolymers. Assume that a polymer having the composition shown in Fig. 10 is dissolved in a selective solvent for the B-component in order to cast a film. As solvent is removed to form the film, the polymer concentration will eventually become high enough so that microphase separation will occur, with the critical concentration at which this occurs depending on the thermodynamic interactions among all of the components. If the critical concentration would be below about 0.3, the equilibrium morphology that would form would be spherical. The continued removal of solvent would eventually increase the concentration of polymer above 0.3, where the diagram indicates the cylindrical morphology would be the thermodynamically-stable form. However, the transformation from the spherical to cylindrical morphology would involve the diffusional transport of segments

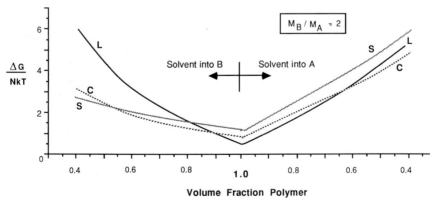

Figure 10   Free energy of domain systems with a selective solvent in either the A- or B-block component, showing regions of stability of the various morphological forms. The labels S, C and L refer to spherical, cylindrical and lamellar morphologies, respectively. The A-component is the dispersed component in the spherical and cylindrical systems

through an incompatible medium, thus establishing a kinetic barrier that precludes the transformation. The same reasoning would apply to the cylinder-lamella transformation that should occur at a polymer concentration of approximately 0.9. Thus the recovered cast film of this example would retain the spherical morphology it had when microphase separation first occurred. Depending on the particular concentration at which microphase separation established a domain morphology, the cast film from a sample having this composition could have any one of the three morphologies. The lamellar morphology is the equilibrium morphology for the film, but another morphology formed at the critical concentration for microphase separation could persist in a quasi-equilibrium state in the dried film and be essentially stable towards annealing. The mechanical properties of films having different morphologies would obviously be different, and thus the frequent observation (e.g.,[76–77]) of different mechanical properties of films recovered from different casting solvents is merely a manifestation of the control that a solvent has on block copolymer domain morphology by its specific interaction with the block components and by control of the critical concentrations for microphase separation.

3.2   Block Copolymers in Dilute Solutions

3.2.1   Block Copolymers in Homopolymer Blends

The idea that block copolymers are the polymeric analogues of low molecular weight surfactant molecules can be traced back to Mark[78] in the 1950's. However, it is only in recent years that the profound effects of block copolymers as interfacially-active molecules in polymeric systems have become widely recognized. Although many experimental observations concerning interfacial or surface activity of block copolymers have been published[78–91], theories of interfacial activity in homopolymer systems are quite limited. The work by Noolandi and associates[32, 56, 92–93] represents the major published work in this area. Cantor[94] has presented a theory of block copolymers as surfactants between immiscible low molecular weight solvents, but it will not be discussed here since it does not apply to homopolymer systems. The theory of Noolandi and associates for interfacial activity uses the general formalism for inhomogeneous multicomponent polymer systems developed by them and briefly described in Section 3.1.1. The theory provides a description of the interfacial profile (both block and homopolymer species) as well as the interfacial tension as a function of block copolymer concentration. Because of the complexity and length of the theory, it will not be described here and reader is directed to the original publications for details. Although the theory is formally applicable to concentrated systems, the equations of the theory must be solved by numerical methods which have limited the results to systems containing solvent (with the overall polymer concentration ~0.15–0.2). The most important result of the theory concerns the influence of the molecular weight of a block copolymer on its interfacial activity, i. e., on its presence in the interfacial region. Figures 11 and 12 show the calculated interfacial profiles for systems comprising polybutadiene and polystyrene homopolymers with added poly(styrene-b-butadiene) copolymer. The systems shown in Figs. 11 and 12 are similar, except the block copolymer of the system in Fig. 12 is of higher molecular weight than that in Fig. 11. These Figures show the very important effect the molecular weight of the block copolymer has on interfacial properties, namely the higher the molecular weight the greater the concentration of block copolymer in the interfacial region. The enhanced interfacial activity of higher molecular weight block copolymers is also predicted by Inoue and Meier[95], who have developed a theory for homopolymer/block copolymer blends based on the confined-chain model. This prediction is of considerable technological importance, since block copolymers are frequently used as "compatibilizing agents" in homopolymer blends, where it is important for economic reasons that the amount of (typically expensive) compatibilizing agent required be kept to a minimum. It is not clear whether the interfacial

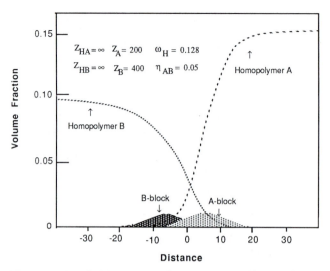

Figure 11   Interfacial density profiles of a blend of homopolymers A and B with added A-B block copolymer of relatively low molecular weight. ω_H is the total weight fraction of the homopolymers, η_{AB} is the weight fraction of the block copolymer with respect to one of the homopolymers. Z_{HA}, Z_{HB}, Z_A and Z_B are the degrees of polymerization of the A- and B-homopolymers and the A- and B-blocks of the copolymer, respectively. The figure is adapted from Ref. 56, with interaction parameters characteristic of a polystyrene/polybutadiene/n-heptane system. Distances are expessed in units of the average Kuhn length (6.95 Å)

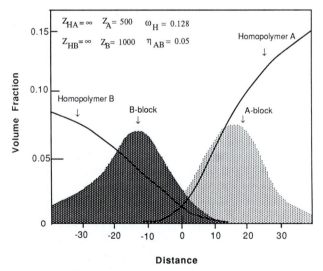

Figure 12   Interfacial density profile as in Fig. 11, but with higher molecular weight block copolymer. The symbols are the same as in Fig. 11

activity of block copolymers is a monotonic function of molecular weight, suggesting that the highest possible molecular weight would be desirable. Noolandi and Hong (56) have suggested that an upper limit does exist, based on the supposition that the block copolymers would prefer to form micelles at high molecular molecular weights rather than be at the interface. Granted that this possibility may exist, it is more likely from a technological point of view that an upper limit would be established by kinetics, i.e., by the time required for diffusional transport of higher molecular weight copolymers to the interface, which could be longer than the time available during processing operations.

3.2.2 Block Copolymer Micelles

When block copolymers are dissolved in solvents in which one of the block components is soluble and the other component insoluble, aggregation of the block copolymers may occur with the formation of micelles. An individual micelle is typically spherical in shape, having a core of the insoluble component surrounded by an outer "corona" of the soluble component. There is a vast number of publications dealing with the experimental aspects of block copolymer micelles (96–104 and references cited therein), and the review by Price[96] provides an excellent overview of this literature. However, there are very few publications dealing with the theoretical aspects of block copolymer micelles. Noolandi and Hong discuss a theory of diblock micelles in an environment of low molecular weight lyophilic solvent[105] or in a homopolymer medium[56], in which the micelle is modelled as having a uniform core of the insoluble block competent surrounded by a uniform shell of the soluble block component intermixed with solvent or homopolymer. Leibler, Orland and Wheeler[106] have developed a theory for the cirtical concentration for diblock micelle formation in a homopolymer medium, in which the micelle model is essentially the same as that of

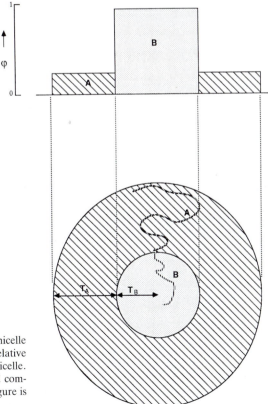

Figure 13 Cross section of a spherical micelle of a diblock copolymer showing the relative density distribution of segments in the micelle. The narrow interfacial region with mixed components and solvent is not shown. This figure is adapted from Ref. 105

Noolandi and Hong. A schematic diagram of the model is shown in Fig. 13. In the Noolandi-Hong (N-H) model with solvent[105], the region outside of the micelle is assumed to be pure solvent, whereas in their model with homopolymer[56] and in the Leibler-Orland-Wheeler (L-O-W) model[106] the outside is considered to have block copolymer molecules dissolved in the homopolymer. The latter allows both groups of authors to treat critical conditions for micelle formation in a homopolymer medium.

In both the N-H and L-O-W models, the micelles are considered to be monodisperse in size (an assumption which experimental data[104] show is valid), with the radius T_B of the central core and the thickness T_A of the surounding shell taken as the average end-to-end distances of the B- and A-block, respectively. The decrease in entropy of chains in the micelle (relative to a homogeneous mixture of components) is made up of contributions similar to those discussed in the confined-chain model for domain formation (Section 2.1), i.e., from confinement of the block junctions to the interface region (neglected by L-O-W), from confinement of the block chains to their appropriate regions of space, from the stretching or compression of the constrained chains and from the mixing of the A-chains with solvent (or homopolymer) in the outer A-shell (corona). The theories of the two groups differ in their treatment of the interfacial energy associated with the core-shell interface. Since the L-O-W theory deals only with polymeric components, the authors assume that the interface has the same interfacial tension as between the same incompatible homopolymers[107]

$$\gamma = (k_B T/l^2)\, (\chi/6)^{1/2} \tag{51}$$

whereas L-H formulate and introduce an interfacial tension (and interfacial width) for an interface having an asymmetric distribution of components

$$\gamma = \varrho_{os} k_B T \left[1/3\, (\varphi_A + \varphi_B)\, \Delta f \right]^{1/2} \tag{52}$$

where $\Delta f = \chi_{AB}\varphi_A\varphi_B + \chi_{As}\varphi_A\varphi_s + \chi_{Bs}\varphi_B\varphi_s + \varphi_s \ln\varphi_s$ \hfill (53)

N-H have minimized the free energy of micelle formation with respect to the various size variables and have compared results ₁with experimental data[108] for the poly(styrene-b-butadiene)/n-heptane system. The agreement between theory and experiment in very good, although the authors point out that even better agreement might be possible if the assumption of uniform density in the outer shell were relaxed. Both the theoretical and experimental results support a 2/3-power dependence of both the micellar core size and overall micellar size on the overall molecular weight Z_C of the copolymer (actually an exponent of 0.68 for the overall radius and 0.64 for the core radius is found). The authors present a simple scaling argument for the 2/3 exponent. The main contributions to the free energy are from contributions involving the interfacial free energy and the "stretching" free energy, which give

$$\Delta g \approx \frac{3\gamma T_B^2}{\varrho_o k_B T R^3} + \frac{\varphi_c^o}{2\, Z_c}\, \alpha_B^2 \tag{54}$$

where $\alpha_B = T_B/(Z_B\, l^2/3)^{1/2}$ is the degree of "stretching" of the core chain, and R is the core radius. Conservation of volume requires that

$$f_B\, \varphi_c^o\, (4/3)\, \pi\, R^3 = \varphi_B (4/3)\, \pi\, T_B \tag{55}$$

where φ_c^o is the overall concentration of copolymer and $f_B = Z_B/Z_C$.
Substituting Eq. 55 into 54 and minimizing the resulting expression with respect to T_B gives

$$T_B^3 = \frac{f_B^2 l^2 \gamma}{\varphi_B \varrho_0 k_B T} Z_c^2 \tag{56}$$

Thus Eq. 56 shows T_B scales as $Z_C^{2/3}$, in agreement with the more elaborate calculations of the N-H theory, and also in agreement with the L-O-R theory when the components are very incompatible.

4   SUMMARY AND CONCLUSIONS

In this overview of the theoretical aspects of block copolymers, an attempt has been made to indicate the current state of development of theories for certain interesting and unique properties of block copolymers. Space limitations have necessitated emphasizing certain selected topics, and these have generally been those concerned with various aspects of the microphase separation and the morphological consequences. As a result, theories dealing with a number of other interesting phenomena have been neglected, e. g., dilute (molecular) solutions, block copolymers as dispersants, mechanical and rheological properties, transport properties, etc.

In those areas discussed in this review, it is obvious that theory is able in most cases to provide a semi-quantitative (or better) description of the observed behavior of block copolymers. One can feel confident that future developments will bring improvements in the theoretical framework and theories will be extended to encompass new areas to expand our understanding of the unique structure/property relationships of block copolymers. The multitude of unique phenomena shown by block copolymers offers a endless horizon of opportunities for both the theoretician and experimentalist.

References

1. A. Skoulios, G. Finaz and J. Parrod, *Comp. Rend. 251,* 739 (1960).
2. C. Sadron, *Angew. Chem., Internation Edition 2,* 248 (1963).
3. B. Gallot, R. Mayer and C. Sadron, *Comp. Rend. 263,* 42 (1966).
4. G. Holden and R. Milkovich, U.S. Patent 3, 365, 765, Aug. 1964, Filed Jan., 1962.
5. T. Inoue, T. Soen, T. Hashimoto and H. Kawai, *J. Poly. Sci.: Part A–2 7,* 1283 (1960).
6. R. F. Fedors, *J. Poly. Sci.: Part C 26,* 189 (1969).
7. D. J. Meier, *J. Poly. Sci.: Part C 26,* 81 (1969).
8. D. J. Meier, *ACS Poly. Prep. 11,* 434 (1970).
9. L. Marker, *ACS Poly. Prep. 10,* 524 (1969)
10. S. Krause, *J. Poly. Sci.: Part A–2 7,* 249 (1969).
11. S. Krause, *Macromolecules 3,* 84 (1970).
12. D. F. Leary and M. C. Williams, *J. Poly. Sci.: Part B 8,* 335 (1970).
13. D. F. Leary and M. C. Williams, *J. Poly. Sci.: Poly. Phys. Ed. 11,* 345 (1973).
14. U. Bianchi, E. Pedemonte and A. Turturro, *J. Poly. Sci.: Part B 7,* 785 (1969).
15. U. Bianchi, E. Pedemonte and A. Turturro, *Polymer 11,* 268 (1970).
16. D. G. LeGrande, *ACS Poly. Prep. 11,* 434 (1970).
17. H. Krömer, M. Hoffmann and G. Kämpf, *Ber. Bunsenges. Phys. Chem. 74,* 859 (1970).
18. M. Hoffmann, G. Kämpf, H. Krömer and G. Pampus, in ACS *"Advances in Chemistry"* No. 99 (1970).
19. D. H. Kaelble, *Trans. Soc. Rheology 15,* 235 (1971).
20. D. J. Meier, in *Polymer Blends and Mixtures,* D. J. Walsh, J. S. Higgins and A. Maconnachie, Eds., NATO ASI Series, Martinus Nijhoff Publishers, 1985.
21. T. Hashimoto, M. Shibayama, H. Kawai and D. J. Meier, *Macromolecules 18,* 1855 (1985).

22. E. Helfand, *ACS Poly. Prep. 14*, 70 (1973).
23. E. Helfand, in *Recent Advances in Polymer Blends, Grafts and Blocks*, L. H. Sperling, Ed., Plenum Press, New York, NY, 1974.
24. E. Helfand, *Macromolecules 8*, 552 (1975).
25. E. Helfand, in *Polymer Compatibility and Incompatibility*, K. Solc, Ed., MMI Press, Midland, MI, 1982.
26. E. Helfand and Z. R. Wasserman, *Macromolecules 9*, 879 (1976).
27. E. Helfand and Z. R. Wasserman, *Polymer Eng. Sci. 17*, 535 (1977).
28. E. Helfand and Z. R. Wasserman, *Macromolecules 13*, 994 (1980).
29. E. Helfand and Z. R. Wasserman, in *Developments in Block Copolymers*, I. Goodman, Ed., Applied Science Publishers, London, 1982.
30. J. Noolandi and K. M. Hong, *Ferroelectrics 30*, 117 (1980).
31. K. M. Hong and J. Noolandi, *Macromolecules 14*, 727 (1981).
32. J. Noolandi, *Ber. Bunsenges. Phys. Chem. 89*, 1147 (1985).
33. M. L. Huggins, *J. Phys. Chem. 46*, 141 (1942).
34. P. J. Flory, *J. Amer. Chem. Soc. 10*, 51 (1942).
35. J. W. Cahn and J. E. Hilliard, *J. Chem. Phys. 28*, 258 (1958).
36. E. A. DiMarzio, *J. Chem. Phys. 42*, 2101 (1965).
37. T. Hashimoto, M. Shibayama and H. Kawai, *Macromolecules 13*, 1237 (1980).
38. N. A. Rounds, *Doctoral Dissertation*, University of Akron, (1970).
39. R. Mayer, *Polymer 15*, 137 (1974).
40. G. Hadziioannou and A. Skoulios, *Macromolecules 15*, 258 (1982).
41. R. W. Richards and J. L. Thomason, *Polymer 24*, 1089 (1983).
42. U. Siemann and W. Ruland, *J. Colloid & Polymer Sci. 260*, 999 (1982).
43. R.-J. Roe, M. Fishkis and J. C. Chang, *Macromolecules, 14*, 1091 (1981).
44. E. Helfand and Y. Tagami, *J. Poly. Sci., Part B, 9*, 741 (1971).
45. E. Helfand, *Macromolecules 8*, 295 (1975).
46. W. Ruland, *Macromolecules 20*, 87 (1987).
47. T. Hashimoto, M. Shibayama and H. Kawai, *Macromolecules 13*, 1237 (1980).
48. R. Stadler and W. Gronski, *J. Coll. & Polym. Sci. 261*, 215 (1983).
49. R. Stadler and W. Gronski, *J. Coll. & Polym. Sci. 262*, 466 (1982).
50. F. Annighöfer and W. Gronski, *J. Coll. & Polym. Sci. 261*, 15 (1983).
51. E. H. Kerner, *Proc. Royal Soc. (London) B 69*, 215 (1956).
52. H. Tanaka and T. Nishi, *J. Chem. Phys. 82*, 4326 (1985).
53. G. Holden, E. T. Bishop and N. R. Legge, *Proc. Internat. Rubber Conf. 1967*, Maclaren & Sons, London, 1968 p. 287–309; *J. Poly. Sci. Part C 26*, 37 (1969).
54. L. Leibler, *Macromolecules, 13*, 1602 (1980).
55. M. Olvera de la Cruz and I. Sanchez, *Macromolecules, 19*, 2501 (1986).
56. J. Noolandi and K. M. Hong, *Macromolecules 15*, 482 (1982).
57. P.-G. de Gennes, *Scaling Concepts in Polymer Physics*, p. 258, Cornell University Press, Ithaca, NY, 1979.
58. S. F. Edwards, *J. Phys. A, 9*, 1670 (1975).
59. D. J. Meier, *Prep. Polymer Colloq., Polymer Sci., Japan*, 83 (1977).
60. H. Hasegawa, T. Hashimoto, H. Kawai, T. P. Lodge, E. J. Amis, C. J. Glinka and C. C. Han, *Macromolecules, 18*, 67 (1985).
61. T. Ohta and K. Kawasaki, *Macromolecules, 19*, 2621 (1986).
62. G. Molau, in *Block Copolymers*, S. Aggarwal, Ed., Plenum Press, New York, NY, (1970), p 79.
63. H. Hashegawa and T. Hashimoto, *Poly. Prep., Japan Soc. Sci., 34*, 775 (1985).
64. H. Hasegawa, H. Tanaka, K. Yamasaki and T. Hashimoto, *Macromolecules*, in press.
65. D. B. Alward, D. J. Kinning, E. L. Thomas and L. J. Fetters, *Macromolecules, 19*, 215 (1986).
66. W. Longley and T. J. McIntosh, *Nature, 303*, 612 (1983).
67. D. J. Meier, *ACS Poly. Prep. 11*, 400 (1970).
68. D. J. Meier, in *Block and Graft Copolymers*, J. J. Burke and V. Weiss, Eds. Syracuse University Press, Syracuse, NY, 1973.
69. B. R. M. Gallot, *Adv. Polymer Science, 29*, 85 (1978).
70. E. Helfand and Z. R. Wasserman, *Macromolecules, 11*, 960 (1978).
71. E. Helfand and Z. R. Wasserman, *Macromolecules, 13*, 994 (1980).

72. J. M. G. Cowie, in *Development in Block Copolymers-1,* I. Goodman, Ed., Applied Science Publishers, London, 1982.
73. A. Douy, R. Mayer, J. Rossi and B. Gallot, *Molecular Crystals and Liquid Crystals, 7,* 103 (1969).
74. M.-L. Ionescu and A. Skoulios, *Macromol. Chem., 177,* 257 (1976).
75. M. Shibayama, T. Hashimoto, H. Hasegawa and H. Kawai, *Macromolecules, 16,* 1427 (1983).
76. D. M. Brunwin, E. Fischer and J. F. Henderson, *J. Poly. Sci., Part C, 26,* 135 (1969).
77. J. F. Beecher, L. Marker, R. D. Bradford and S. L. Aggarwal, *J. Poly. Sci., Part C, 26,* 117 (1969).
78. H. Mark, *Textile Research Journal, 23,* 294 (1953).
79. G. Riess, J, Nervo and D. Rogez, *Poly. Eng. Sci. 17,* 634 (1977).
80. D. J. Wilson, G. Hurtrez and G. Riess, in *Polymer Blends and Mixtures,* D. J. Walsh, J. S. Higgins and A. Maconnachie, Eds., NATO ASI Series, Martinus Nijhoff Publishers, Dordrecht, 1985.
81. H. B. Gia, R. Jerome and Ph. Teyssie, *J. Poly. Sci.: Poly. Phys. Ed. 18,* 2391 (1980).
82. R. E. Cohen and J. M. Tottadas, *Macromolecules 17,* 1101 (1984).
83. G. L. Gaines, Jr. and G. W. Bender, *Macromolecules 5,* 82 (1982).
84. A. R. Ramos and R. E. Cohen, *Poly. Eng. Sci. 17,* 639 (1977).
85. G. Riess, J. Kohler, C. Tournut and A. Banderet, *Makromol. Chem. 101,* 58 (1967).
86. D. J. Meier, *J. Phys. Chem. 71,* 1861 (1967).
87. D. H. Napper, *Polymeric Stabilization of Colloidal Dispersions,* Academic Press, New York, 1983.
88. Y. Ikada, F. Horii and I. Sakurada, *J. Poly. Sci.: Poly. Chem, Ed. 11,* 27 (1973).
89. J. J. O'Malley, H. R. Thomas and G. M. Lee, *Macromolecules 12,* 996 (1979).
90. M. J. Owen and T. C. Kendrick, *Macromolecules 3,* 458 (1970).
91. R. Fayt, R. Jerome and Ph. Teyssie, *Makromol. Chem. 187,* 837 (1986).
92. M. D. Whitmore and J. Noolandi, *Poly. Eng. Sci. 25,* 1120 (1985).
93. K. M. Hong and J. Noolandi, *Macromolecules 16,* 1083 (1983).
94. R. Cantor, *Macromolecules 14,* 1186 (1981).
95. T. Inoue and D. J. Meier, to be published.
96. C. Price, in *Developments in Block Copolymers-1,* I. Goodman, Ed., Applied Science Publishers, London, 1982.
97. T. Kotaka, T. Tanaka, M. Hattori and H. Inagaki, *Macromolecules 11,* 138 (1978).
98. C. J. Stacy and G. Kraus, *Poly. Eng. Sci. 17,* 627 (1977).
99. N. Ahmad, M. Kaleem and S. Noor, *Coll. and Poly. Sci. 261,* 898 (1983).
100. S. Krause and P. A. Reissmiller, *J. Poly. Sci.: Poly. Phys. Ed. 13,* 663 (1965).
101. C. Price, J. D. G. McAdam, T. P. Lally and D. Woods, *Polymer 15,* 227 (1974).
102. Z. Tuzar and P. Kratochvil, *Makromol. Chem. 160,* 301 (1972).
103. C. Konak, Z. Tuzar, P. Stepanek, B. Sedlacek and P. Kratochvil, *Prog. Coll. Poly. Sci. 71,* 15 (1985).
104. D. R. Smith and D. J. Meier, to be published (M. S. thesis of D. R. Smith, Case Western Reserve University).
105. J. Noolandi and K. M. Hong, *Macromolecules 16,* 1443 (1983).
106. L. Leibler, Henri Orland and J. C. Wheeler, *J. Chem. Phys. 79,* 3550 (1983).
107. E. Helfand and Y. Tagami, *J. Poly. Sci.: Part B 9,* 741 (1971).
108. J. Plestil and J. Baldrian, *J. Makromol. Chem. 176,* 1009 (1975).

Chapter **12**

RESEARCH ON THERMOPLASTIC ELASTOMERS

Section **1**

MODELING THE ELASTIC BEHAVIOR OF POLY(STYRENE-b-BUTADIENE-b-STYRENE) BLOCK COPOLYMERS

J. K. Bard, C. I. Chung

Contents

J. K. Bard* and C. I. Chung, Materials Engineering Departement, Rensselaer Polytechnic Institute, Troy, New York 12180–3590

* Present address: Hercules Inc., Research Center, Wilmington, Delaware 19894

1   INTRODUCTION

Many studies have been made of the mechanical properties of phase separated block copolymers. Attempts to model these properties have generally followed one of two routes. The first is to model the two phase structure as a composite and use expressions derived in composite theory to predict the mechanical behavior. The second approach, used for elastomeric block copolymers, is to consider the material to be like a filled elastomer. Concepts from the theory of rubber elasticity, modified to account for the presence of the phase separated structure, are then used to model the mechanical behavior. In this paper further development of the latter approach is presented.

The properties of elastomeric block copolymers of type ABA, such as poly(styrene-b-butadiene-b-styrene) (S–B–S) block copolymers, are understood to be caused by the presence of isolated glassy domains of block A in an elastomeric matrix of block B[1, 2]. The domains play the same role as chemical crosslinks, acting as junctions which create an elastomeric network structure. The simplest model of the mechanical behavior is thus to simply use the classical equation of rubber elasticity. This approach was taken in an early investigation[2], using the Mooney-Rivlin equation rather than the classical equation. Calculated stress values turned out to be an order of magnitude lower than the measured values. The investigators attributed this result to two factors not accounted for by a straightforward application of the Mooney-Rivlin equation. The first is the effect of the domains as filler particles. This effect was then accounted for by use of a multiplication factor derived by Guth and Smallwood[3, 4], $(1 + 2.5 \ \Phi_s + 14.1 \ \Phi_s^2)$, where Φ_s is the volume fraction of the polystyrene. The second factor is the presence of trapped entanglements. Their effect would be to change the molecular weight between crosslinks (M_c) from the center block molecular weight to some smaller value. Using experimental data for a poly(styrene-b-isoprene-b-styrene) block copolymer and the filler effect corrected Mooney-Rivlin equation, a value for M_c was calculated which was in reasonable agreement with measured values of the molecular weight between entanglements for homopolymer polyisoprene[2].

Several objections to this simple treatment were raised by later investigators[5, 6, 7]. The treatment of the entanglement effect was seen as being more of a curve fitting technique than a fundamental treatment, and doubts were also raised concerning the use of the filler effect term. The major objection was the simple application of rubber elasticity theory to block copolymers without considering the effect of the domains on the distribution function of the rubber matrix chains. In the derivation of the classical equation of rubber elasticity, it is assumed that the chain has a Gaussian distribution function. Use of this distribution function assumes that all space is accessible to a given chain. However, all space is not accessible to a matrix chain in a block copolymer because the domains take up space. Models taking this fact into account were developed by Meier[5] and by Gaylord and Lohse[6, 7]. Both models assume that the domains are non-deformable and that they exist as cubes on a simple cubic lattice. Matrix chains are assumed to run between the closest faces of nearest neighbor domains with their end-to-end vectors along one of the coordinate axes. An equal number of chains is assumed to run in each direction, as in the three chain model of rubber elasticity[8]. Chain distribution functions in these models account for the presence of the domains. Also, the effect of the domains on the strain in the matrix is accounted for by a simple strain amplification model rather than by the Guth-Smallwood filler effect term. However, no entanglement contribution is considered.

Much recent work in the area of rubber elasticity has concentrated on the contribution of chain entanglements to the equilibrium elastic behavior[9–17]. Although controversy remains regarding the nature and magnitude of such an entanglement contribution, this work can be applied to elastomeric block copolymers to provide a better means of modeling a possible entanglement contribution to their elastic behavior. Particularly useful is an equation developed by Graessley and co-workers[14, 15] for the shear modulus of a rubber in the limit of low strain. This equation considers two contributions to the modulus. The first is a contribution from chemical crosslinks, equivalent to that predicted by classical rubber elasticity theory. The second is a contribution from chain entanglements. The entanglement contribution is modeled empirically using the plateau modulus of the uncrosslinked material and Langley's trapping factor[18]. The idea behind this model is that a certain fraction of the entanglements, responsible for the existence of the plateau modulus in the uncrosslinked polymer, is "trapped" by crosslinking and contributes to the equilibrium elastic behavior as well. This model has been experimentally verified for polybutadiene[14], ethylene-propylene[15], and poly(dimethylsiloxane)[19].

In the work presented here, the entanglement model is applied to block copolymers by assuming that the domains serve the role of chemical crosslinks. The crosslink contribution is calculated by taking the center block molecular weight as the molecular weight between crosslinks. The entanglement contribution is calculated using the plateau modulus of the homopolymer corresponding to the center block. Contributions from the other factors discussed above, the filler effect of the domains and the change in chain distribution function of the center block, are also incorporated into the model.

The rubber-like behavior of elastomeric block copolymers is due fundamentally to the elastic nature of the center block. However, the models presented suggest several different factors which have possible influences on this behavior. These factors are network entanglements, the effect of the domains on the strain in the matrix, as described by either the Guth-Smallwood term or simple strain amplification, and a change in center block chain distribution function due to the constraint of the domains. It is the purpose of this paper to examine models based on these possible contributing factors, and to determine the validity and importance of the various factors by comparing their predictions with experimental stress-strain behavior.

2   THEORY

Three models for the mechanical behavior of S–B–S block copolymers have been developed. The first is obtained by a simple modification of the classical rubber elasticity theory to account for the filler effect of the domains, and it will be called the simple model. The second model makes use of the equations developed by Gaylord and Lohse[6, 7] to account for the change in center block chain distribution function due to the constraint of the domains. The final model is the most comprehensive of the three, and accounts for a possible contribution from trapped entanglements in addition to the factors considered by the other models.

Several assumptions are common to all of the models. The first is that the domains are non-deformable, so that only the matrix is strained. It is important to note that even though the domains are assumed to be non-deformable, they do contribute to the stress which develops in the material. Their most important function is to anchor the matrix chains into a network structure. In addition, the domains serve as filler particles and also affect the chain distribution function of the matrix chains. These effects are treated differently in the various models, but the assumption of non-deformable domains is common to all.

The second assumption common to all of the models is that the density of elastically effective chains in the rubber network should be calculated based on matrix volume rather than on total volume, since it is the stress developed in the rubber matrix which is of interest. This assumption is equivalent to replacing the S–B–S block copolymer with an equivalent network of PB in which there are no domains, but in which the effects of the domains, such as strain amplification, are present. The chain density in this network is equal to the number of elastically effective chains per unit volume of matrix in the two phase system. The center block molecular weight is taken as the molecular weight between crosslinks, with the domains serving as network junctions.

2.1 Simple Model

The first model considered is based on a straightforward application of classical rubber elasticity theory[8], with a modification for the filler effect of the domains. Two cases are examined, one in which the filler effect of the domains is modeled by the Guth-Smallwood filler effect term (equation (1) below) and the other in which the filler effect is modeled by assuming that the domains cause uniform strain amplification in the matrix (equation (2)).

$$\sigma = \frac{\nu}{V_m} kT \frac{<r^2>}{<r^2>_o} \left(\lambda - \frac{1}{\lambda^2} \right) (1 + 2.5\Phi_S + 14.1\Phi_S^2) \qquad (1)$$

$$\sigma = \frac{\nu}{V_m} kT \frac{<r^2>}{<r^2>_o} \left(\alpha - \frac{1}{\alpha^2} \right) \qquad (2)$$

In the above equations, σ is the stress, ν/V_m is the polybutadiene (PB) matrix chain density, k is Boltzmann's constant, T is the absolute temperature, $<r^2>/<r^2>_o$ is the ratio of the mean square end-to-end chain length in the undeformed PB matrix to the unperturbed value, λ is the applied macroscopic extension ratio, and α is the corresponding extension ratio in the matrix. In equation (1) the Guth-Smallwood term for the filler effect is derived by analyzing the strain distribution in a rubber (Poisson's ratio of 0.5) containing a non-deformable spherical filler particle. In equation (2) the filler effect is modeled by assuming that the domains cause uniform strain amplication in the matrix.

Both of the above equations use the classical equation of rubber elasticity[8] as a starting point. It is assumed in the derivation of the classical equation that the material deforms affinely. The network junctions are assumed to move as if embedded in a uniformly deforming medium. In another version of the classical theory, called phantom theory, the network junctions are free to fluctuate about their mean position[20] while the mean positions move affinely with strain. The form of the stress-strain equation is the same in both versions. In the phantom theory, however, the term $(1-2/f)$, in which f is the junction functionality, is also present. This term has been neglected in the present work for the case of the rubber network present in block copolymers for several reasons. The restrictions on the mobility of a PB chain end attached to a glassy domain are certainly great, limiting the ability of the S–B–S "network junction" to fluctuate. With increasing functionality, the term $(1-2/f)$ approaches one, and the phantom model approaches the affine model. Although they are not chemical crosslinks, the domains are equally effective and act as junctions of high functionality. In addition, in a study of the elastic behavior of PB, the value of a parameter which allowed for junction fluctuation was found to be essentially zero[14], indicating nearly complete suppression of junction fluctuations. Finally, according to Flory's recent model of rubber elasticity[9-12], affine behavior is to be expected at low strain. The mechanical behavior examined in this study is confined to low strain. These considerations all substantiate the use of the affine model. Knowledge of the "functionality" of the domains as crosslinks is not required in order to calculate the stress-strain behavior.

The value of v/V_m in the simple model is calculated by assuming that the molecular weight between crosslinks, M_c, is equal to the center block molecular weight. As a result, the effect of entanglements is not accounted for in calculations using the simple model. Also, only those PB blocks contained in triblock molecules are included in v/V_m. PB blocks in diblock molecules are not considered to be elastically effective in the simple model. Since several of the samples tested in this study have significant diblock fractions, this assumption has a noticeable effect on the predicted stress values.

A value of $<r^2>/<r^2>_o$ must also be obtained to use either equation (1) or equation (2). In conventional elastomers, the value of this ratio is generally assumed to be one. However, there are several reasons why the value of $<r^2>/<r^2>_o$ is greater than one for block copolymers, as discussed by Meier[21]. In triblock copolymers, the ends of the PB blocks can exist in only certain locations, namely, on the domain boundaries. In addition, the chains in the matrix must be positioned so as to maintain uniform density in the matrix. These constraints cause the PB chains in the undeformed state to be expanded in comparision with those in unperturbed state, as given by

$$<r^2>^{1/2} = \alpha_B <r^2>_o^{1/2} \tag{3}$$

in which α_B is the expansion parameter. Meier has presented values of α_B for several different morphologies and compositions[22]. Figure 1 is a plot of α_B versus fraction of A for A–B–A block copolymers based on the values given for a spherical domain morphology. Values of α_B for the block copolymers used in this study were obtained by drawing a smooth curve through Meier's values and determining the values of α_B corresponding to the fraction of A in the samples. Since Meier's calculations were based on random walk statistics, the fraction of A was calculated as the fraction of backbone bonds located in the A blocks. The value of $<r^2>/<r^2>_o$ was then calculated as α_B^2.

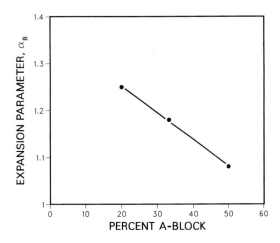

Figure 1   Meier Expansion Parameter (α_B) vs. percent A-block for a spherical domain morphology

Equations (1) and (2) represent two different approaches to modeling the effect of the domains as filler particles. Equation (1), containing the Guth-Smallwood term, is a result obtained by using a continuum mechanics approach and assuming linear elastic behavior. However, a question may be raised as to the applicability of continuum mechanics in this situation. When using continuum mechanics, it is assumed that details of the molecular structure are irrelevant and that the material may be treated as a continuum. In dealing with a phase separated material, this assumption requires the size scale of the heterogeneities considered in the analysis to be larger than molecular dimensions. In block copolymers, however, this is not the case. Molecular dimensions, such as the root mean square end-to-end chain length of the PB block, are similar to the dimensions of the heterogeneities, such as domain size and domain separation. The application of continuum mechanics in this situation is thus questionable.

One approach to this question has been presented by Arridge[23]. This approach is to determine the size of a representative volume element (RVE), that is, a region of large enough volume to be representative of the material as a whole. Above this size scale a continuum approach is valid, but below it, the molecular structure must be taken into account. At the molecular level, it is possible to define forces and displacements, but not stresses and strains. The problem is thus one of determining the size of the RVE, that is, the size scale for which stress and strain can be defined. In other words, what is the minimum size of a volume element in which, if it were possible, the stress and strain could be measured with reproducible results? Assuming a cubic RVE in amorphous polymers, Arridge argues that the mechanism of load transfer between cubes must be loads carried by chains which span the cubes. By assuming Gaussian chain statistics, it can be shown that the maximum probability that a chain will span the cube occurs for a cube having sides equal to about one-half the root-mean square end-to-end chain length. For a cube of this size, in any given direction, one chain out of seven runs between opposite cube faces. Arridge suggests therefore that a cube of this size is a good approximation of the RVE for amorphous polymers. Cubes of smaller dimensions will have fewer chains spanning the faces, and the exact force transferred between cubes will show greater variation due to the local molecular structure, in violation of the assumptions of continuum mechanics.

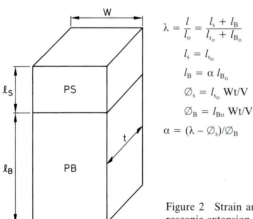

$$\lambda = \frac{l}{l_o} = \frac{l_s + l_B}{l_{s_o} + l_{B_o}}$$

$$l_s = l_{s_o}$$

$$l_B = \alpha \, l_{B_o}$$

$$\varnothing_s = l_{s_o} \, Wt/V$$

$$\varnothing_B = l_{B_o} \, Wt/V$$

$$\alpha = (\lambda - \varnothing_s)/\varnothing_B$$

Figure 2   Strain amplification model: relationship between macroscopic extension ratio (λ) and PB phase extension ratio (α)

Applying Arridge's result to block copolymers, it can be seen that the size of the RVE is on the same order of magnitude as domain dimensions. In other words, the size of a continuum "point" is about the same size as the structure present. This result suggests that use of continuum theory in this case, as represented by the Guth-Smallwood filler effect term, is questionable. Because of this uncertainty, a second approach to modeling the effect of the domains as filler particles was investigated. This approach is represented by equation (2). Equation (2) was derived by assuming that the effect of the domains is to cause uniform amplification of the strain in the matrix. As illustrated in Figure 2, the strain amplification is calculated by using a simple series model and stipulating that all deformation occur in the PB phase. A relationship can be derived between λ, the macroscopic extension ratio, and α, the matrix phase extension ratio, as shown in Figure 2. This relationship is

$$\alpha = \frac{\lambda - \Phi_S}{\Phi_B} \tag{4}$$

in which Φ_s and Φ_B are the volume fractions of PS and PB, respectively. To calculate the stress predicted using equation (2), the value of α is first calculated for the value of λ of interest. This value of α is then used in equation (2).

The modulus predicted by the simple model is also of interest. The value of the Young's modulus, E, is calculated by differentiating the stress-strain equations (equations (1) and (2)) with respect to strain and taking the limit as λ approaches one. The shear modulus, G, is calculated as (1/3) E. Using equation (1) with the Guth-Smallwood term, the equation for G becomes

$$G = \frac{\nu}{V_m} kT \frac{<r^2>}{<r^2>_o} \left(1 + 2.5\Phi_S + 14.1\Phi_S^2\right) \tag{5}$$

Using equation (2) for the case of strain amplification yields

$$G = \frac{\nu}{V_m} kT \frac{<r^2>}{<r^2>_o} \left(\frac{1}{\Phi_B}\right) \tag{6}$$

To summarize this discussion of the simple model, it should be remembered that the predictions of the simple model, as developed here, include no entanglement contribution. The domains alone are considered to act as crosslinks. The effect of the PS domains as filler particles is modeled either by the Guth-Smallwood term or by uniform strain amplification. The matrix chain distribution function is assumed to be Gaussian. No consideration is given to the possibility of a change in chain distribution function of the PB blocks due to the presence of the domains. However, a change in the PB block length in the undeformed state due to the presence of the domains is considered, as given in Equation 3.

2.2 Gaylord-Lohse Model

The Gaylord-Lohse model[6,7] is used to examine the effect on stress-strain behavior of a change in chain distribution function due to the presence of the domains. This model considers both those chains which run between domains (bridges) and those chains which end in the matrix (cilia). In block copolymers, these chain types correspond to triblock and diblock molecules, respectively. A direct comparison of the predictions of this model with experimental results has not been made before. In addition, several modifications of the model and the corresponding predictions are presented here. The stress-strain equations for a spherical PS phase morphology according to the Gaylord-Lohse model are given below. For bridges, the equation is

$$\left(\frac{\nu_B}{V_m}\right)^{-1} \frac{\sigma_B}{kT \frac{A}{3}} = -F^{-1} + B^{-1} - \frac{2Z}{3}\left\{B^{-3}\left[\frac{S1}{S2}\right] - C^{-3}\left[\frac{S3}{S4}\right]\right\} \tag{7}$$

and for cilia, the equation is

$$\left(\frac{\nu_C}{V_m}\right)^{-1} \frac{\sigma_C}{kT \frac{A}{3}} = -F^{-1} + B^{-1} - 2Z\left\{B^{-3}\left[\frac{S5}{S6}\right] - C^{-3}\left[\frac{S7}{S8}\right]\right\} \tag{8}$$

where $A = 1 + l/d$

$\quad\quad B = \lambda + (\lambda{-}1)l/d$

$\quad\quad C = 1 + (1{-}\lambda^{1/2})l/d$

$\quad\quad D = \lambda^{-1/2} + (\lambda^{-1/2}{-}1)l/d$

$\quad\quad F = \lambda + (\lambda{-}\lambda^{3/2})l/d$

$\quad\quad Z = (\pi^2/6)\,(d^2/{<}r^2{>}_o)$

$\quad\quad S1 = \sum_{m=1}^{\infty}(-1)^{m+1}\,m^4\exp(-m^2 Z/B^2)$

$\quad\quad S2 = \Sigma(-1)^{m+1}\,m^2\exp(-m^2 Z/B^2)$

$\quad\quad S3 = \Sigma(-1)^{m+1}\,m^4\exp(-m^2 Z/D^2)$

$\quad\quad S4 = \Sigma(-1)^{m+1}\,m^2\exp(-m^2 Z/D^2)$

$\quad\quad S5 = \Sigma(2m{-}1)^2\exp[-(2m{-}1)^2 Z/B^2]$

$\quad\quad S6 = \Sigma\exp[-(2m{-}1)^2 Z/B^2]$

$\quad\quad S7 = \Sigma(2m{-}1)^2\exp[-(2m{-}1)^2 Z/D^2]$

$\quad\quad S8 = \Sigma\exp[-(2m{-}1)^2 Z/D^2]$

$\quad\quad$(All Σ sum from m = 1 to m = ∞)

In these equations, σ_B is the stress contribution from bridges (triblock PB blocks), σ_B is the stress contribution from cilia (diblock PB blocks), v_B/V_m is the concentration of bridges in the matrix, v_c/V_m is the concentration of cilia in the matrix, l is the domain thickness, and d is the domain separation in the undeformed state. Gaylord and Lohse presented stress-strain equations for individual chains, and these equations have been multiplied by the chain densities to obtain equations (7) and (8). It is assumed in using these equations that all triblock molecules are bridges and all diblock molecules are cilia. The total stress is then calculated as the sum of σ_B and σ_c.

One major question to be answered in using this model is what is the value of d, the domain separation distance? The most obvious choice would seem to be the actual value measured by transmission electron microscopy (TEM) or small angle x-ray scattering (SAXS). However, use of the actual value is not proper due to the assumptions made in setting up the model. Of importance here is the assumption that a PB chain begins and ends in directly opposite walls of neighboring domains. This assumption is not realistic since a chain can end anywhere on a domain wall. For an S–B–S block copolymer of molecular weight 11,000-54,000-11,000, it can be shown that if the structure consists of cubes of thickness 100 Å (typical domain dimensions for this sample[24]) on a simple cubic lattice, the domain separation distance is about 54 Å. It can also be shown that the value of ${<}r^2{>}_o^{1/2}$ for the PB center block is about 150 Å. Since the value of d in the model is assumed to be equivalent to the value of ${<}r^2{>}^{1/2}$ which is still greater than ${<}r^2{>}_o^{1/2}$, use of the measured value d = 54 Å would be unrealistic.

In the Gaylord-Lohse model, d is actually used in two completely different ways at the same time. Because of this fact, the model was modified by making use of two different values of d at the same time to make it physically realistic. The first use of d is to compare the chain length in the undeformed state to that in the unperturbed state, as in the ${<}r^2{>}/{<}r^2{>}_o$ term in the simple model. This use of d occurs in the $d^2/{<}r^2{>}_o$ terms. For these terms, the value of ${<}r^2{>}/{<}r^2{>}_o$ calculated for the simple model was used. The model then becomes similar to the three-chain model[8] of rubber elasticity, in which one-third of the chains lies along each coordinate axis, and the chain lengths are equal to ${<}r^2{>}^{1/2}$ in the undeformed state. The only difference is that the classical three-chain model assumes a Gaussian chain distribution, while the Gaylord-Lohse model uses a chain distribution which has been altered to account for the presence of the domains. The second use of d is to account for the strain amplification which occurs in the matrix phase due to the assumption of non-deformable PS domains. The approach used by Gaylord and Lohse is the same as that presented in the discussion of the simple model, using the assumption of uniform strain amplification and a simple series model. The equation they used to relate α to λ is

$$\alpha = \lambda + (\lambda-1)l/d \tag{9}$$

If the actual value of d is used in equation (9), the strain amplification is greatly overestimated because of the use of the simple series model. Returning to Figure 2, use of the actual value of d corresponds to using $l_s = l$ and $l_B = d$ in the simple series model. This procedure overestimates the volume fraction of PS because it assumes continous layers of PS and PB, whereas the model actually considers isolated PS cubes embedded in a continuous PB matrix. A better approach to modeling the strain amplification is to consider volume fractions rather than domain dimensions. This approach can be taken by combining equation (4), the strain amplification equation already derived for the simple model, with equation (9) to give.

$$\frac{l}{d} = \frac{\Phi_S}{\Phi_B} \tag{10}$$

Since all the terms in equations (7) and (8) containing d other than the $d^2/<r^2>_o$ terms are present as l/d, equation (10) can be used to provide values of l/d in terms of volume fractions. The result of using equation (10) is that the strain assumed to exist in the matrix is the same for both the Gaylord-Lohse model and the simple model with uniform strain amplification (equation (2)) at a given macroscopic strain. A calculation was made to compare the stress predicted using a value of d obtained from equation (10) to that obtained using the actual domain separation distance. The value of d used for the latter case was 54 A, obtained as described earlier. The result was that the stress predicted using the actual domain separation distance was two orders of magnitude larger than that predicted by using equation (10). It was also almost an order of magnitude greater than experimental stress values.

The modulus predicted by the Gaylord-Lohse model is obtained by differentiating the stress-strain equations. That is,

$$E = 3G = \lim_{\lambda \to 1} \frac{d\sigma}{d\lambda} = \lim_{\lambda \to 1} \frac{d\sigma_B}{d\lambda} + \lim_{\lambda \to 1} \frac{d\sigma_C}{d\lambda} \tag{11}$$

It is useful at this point to review the factors considered by the Gaylord-Lohse model. Like the simple model, no entanglement contribution is considered. The effect of the domains as filler particles is modeled by assuming uniform strain amplification. The important feature of the Gaylord-Lohse model is that it considers the change in chain distribution function of the center block PB chains due to the constraints of the PS domains.

2.3 Entanglement Model

To model the effect of entanglements, the Langley-Graessley approach[14, 15, 18] to modeling conventional elastomers has been modified for the case of elastomeric block copolymers. This approach is represented in the following equation.

$$G = G_C + G_E \tag{12}$$

In equation (12), G is the total shear modulus, G_c is the contribution from chemical crosslinks, and G_E is the contribution from trapped entanglements. In S–B–S block copolymers, there are no chemical crosslinks. However, the domains serve the same role as chemical crosslinks, so that G_c corresponds to the modulus predicted if no entanglement contribution is considered. Both the simple model and the Gaylord-Lohse model meet this criterion. The prediction of the Gaylord-Lohse model is used here as G_c because it is more comprehensive than the simple model in accounting for factors which might influence the mechanical behavior.

The Langley-Graessley approach for modeling the entanglement contribution to the modulus is used here, with a modification for the effect of the domains as filler particles (assumed to cause uniform strain amplification). The equation for G_E is

$$G_E = T_E \, G_N° \, (1/\Phi_B) \tag{13}$$

in which T_E is the Langley trapping factor and $G_N°$ is the plateau modulus of homopolymer PB. The last term in the equation accounts for strain amplification in the matrix. The equation for the shear modulus using this entanglement model can thus be written as

$$G = G_C + T_E \, G_N° \, (1/\Phi_B) \tag{14}$$

The Langley-Graessley equation can be used to calculate the modulus at low strains only[14, 15]. It does not give the stress-strain relationship. In order to include the effect of strain amplification on G_E in an exact manner, knowledge of the stress-strain relationship is required. Since the stress-strain relationship is not known, multiplication of $(T_E \, G_N°)$ by $(1/\Phi_B)$ was used as an approximation to account for the effect of strain amplification on G_E. This procedure was motivated by equation (6), in which the effect of strain amplification on the modulus in the simple model was represented by $(1/\Phi_B)$.

Since equation (14) predicts the modulus only at low strains, there is no exact way to compare its predictions with experimental stress-strain behavior. To allow such a comparison to be made, it was assumed that the stress-strain behavior can be treated as linear, or $\sigma = E·\varepsilon$, in which ε is the strain. This approximation is reasonable for the low strains employed in this study. Although not strictly accurate, it allows for comparison of the entanglement model with the other models as well as with our experimental results to be made. The other theoretical models discussed here also give a virtually linear stress-strain relationship at low strains.

Values for T_E and $G_N°$ are required in this model. T_E is defined as the probability that all four strands leading from an entanglement are attached to the network, or, alternatively, the probability that both chains involved are part of closed loops in the network[15, 18]. For the case of block copolymers, this corresponds to the probability that both PB chains are in triblock molecules. The trapping factor can thus be defined as

$$T_E = (\text{Number fraction of triblock molecules})^2. \tag{15}$$

The value of T_E will be one if the sample consists entirely of triblock molecules. A value of $G_N°$ for homopolymer PB of similar microstructure to that found in the center block of the SBS block copolymers used in this study was given by Ferry[25]. This value for $G_N°$ is 1.23 MPa.

The entanglement model developed here is the most comprehensive of the models presented. It accounts for the filler effect of the domains by assuming uniform strain amplification in the matrix and, using the Gaylord-Lohse model to calculate G_c, it accounts for the effect of the domains on the PB block chain distribution function. The most important feature of the model, however, is the fact that it accounts for a possible contribution from trapped entanglements.

3   EXPERIMENTAL

The models discussed here make use of rubber elasticity theory to predict the stress-strain behavior of S–B–S block copolymers. Rubber elasticity theory predicts the equilibrium stress-strain behavior, that is, the stress which exists in a sample at a particular strain and temperature after any time dependent contribution has disappeared. Similar data must be obtained for S–B–S block copolymers to compare the theoretical predictions with actual material behavior. Stress relaxation experiments were carried out to measure the equilibrium stress-strain behavior of S–B–S samples.

Three different SBS samples provided by Shell Chemical Company were used in this study. The sample descriptions given below were provided by the company literature and private correspondence[26]. The three samples used were Kraton D1101 Thermoplastic Rubber, a commercial polymer containing 0.2 % anti-oxidant and having a molecular weight of 11,000–54,000–11,000 (11S–54B–11S), TRW–6–1087, with a molecular weight of 15,000–70,000–15,000 (15S–70B–15S), and 2445, with a molecular weight of 7,000–43,000–7,000 (7S–43B–7S). The microstructure of the PB block was about 51 % trans 1,4, 41 % cis 1,4, and 8 % vinyl 1,2. The 11S–54B–11S and 15S–70B–15S samples contained about 15 % diblock materials, while the 7–43–7 sample did not contain a substantial diblock portion. The diblock contents of the various polymers were qualitatively verified by size exclusion chromatography (SEC) in our Polymer Characterization Laboratory.

Solvent cast sheets were prepared by dissolving the polymers in a 30/70 mixture of cyclohexane and heptane, pouring the solution onto a glass plate covered with a Teflon (trademark) coated aluminium foil, and allowing the solvent to evaporate. An aluminium foil cover was placed over the plate to provide some measure of control over the evaporation rate. About 24 hours were typically required for sufficient evaporation to occur to allow removal of the sheet from the plate. The cast sheets were then dried under vacuum at room temperature to constant weight. This procedure generally took 7 to 10 days. The particular solvent mixture is preferential for PB, allowing the formation of an isolated PS domain structure. Such a structure is desirable because an isolated domain structure is assumed by the theoretical models. In a previous study, it was shown that a 50/50 mixture of cyclohexane and heptane produced an isolated domain structure in the 11S–54B–11S sample[27]. By using S–B–S samples having fairly low PS contents and casting from a solvent mixture preferential for PB, samples could be obtained having the isolated PS domain structures required by the theoretical models.

Rectangular stress relaxation samples of dimensions 5.72 cm long 1.52 cm wide, and 0.76 mm thick were cut from the solvent cast sheets. The gage length during testing was 2.54 cm. The exceptions were the 7S–43B–7S samples, which had dimensions of 8.26 cm long, 2.03 cm wide, and 0.76 mm thick and a 5.08 cm gage length. Stress relaxation measurements were made using the apparatus pictured in Figure 3. The main frame consists of four outer rods (two seen in the figure), and top and bottom plates which are fixed to the rods. The lower grip is attached to the bottom plate, serving as a fixed grip. The load cell, the travel plate, and the top grip are attached to the center rod assembly. Clearance holes exist in the load cell and the travel plate so that the center rod assembly is free to move up and down within the main frame. The top grip is thus a mobile grip. Strain is applied to the sample by rotating the load nut. This rotation moves the center rod assembly up relative to the main frame, causing a sample fixed between the grips to be extended. This simple method of strain application was used because measurement of the stress at long times, corresponding to the equilibrium stress of the sample, was the main objective of our

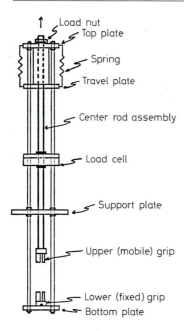

Figure 3   Stress relaxation apparatus

experiments. The time required for strain application was about 7 seconds. The apparatus was suspended in a clear plastic sample chamber and this was immersed in a water bath to maintain a constant temperature during each test. The water bath was kept at a temperature constant to within about 0.5 °C using a temperature controller/water circulation system. Sample temperatures were measured using a thermocouple attached to the bottom grip. Sample loads were measured using a 222 N (50 pound) load cell made by Precision Force Measurement, Inc. Strain measurements were made using a cathetometer. In this procedure, gage marks were placed at the sides of the sample and gage mark separation was measured before and after sample extension. The strain was then calculated from the change in distance between gage marks. Tests were conducted at a slightly elevated temperature of 29 °C to allow positive temperature control. The details of sample preparation, the stress relaxation apparatus, and test procedures used in this study may be found elsewhere[28].

4   RESULTS AND DISCUSSION

A complication in using stress relaxation measurements to obtain the equilibrium stress-strain behavior of S–B–S block copolymers arises from possible deformation in the PS glassy phase. The theoretical models assume that no deformation occurs in the PS phase, that only the PB rubbery matrix is deformed. Since deformation in the glassy phase would reduce the measured stress values by reducing the effective strain in the matrix, any such deformation would greatly complicate comparisons of experimental data with theoretical predictions. To avoid PS deformation, the stress relaxation experiments were conducted at low strains. It was hoped that at low strains, deformation in the PS phase would be negligible, and that a constant stress, corresponding to the equilibrium stress of the S–B–S network, could be obtained in stress relaxation experiments. However, the experimental results indicated that PS deformation was important even at low strains.

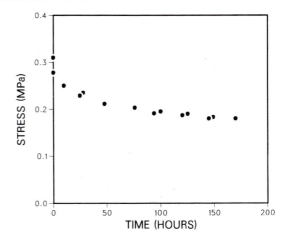

Figure 4 Stress relaxation of the 11S–54B–11S sample at 9.1% strain

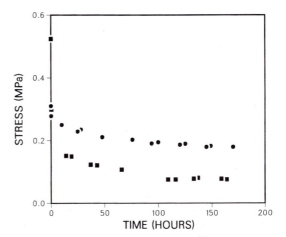

Figure 5 Stress relaxation of the 7S–43B–7S sample at 9.6% strain in comparison to the 11S–54B–11S sample at 9.1% strain on a linear time scale: 7S–43B–7S (■), 11S–54B–11S (●)

Figure 4 is the stress relaxation curve of an 11S–54B–11S sample tested at a strain of 9.1%. It can be seen that, on a linear time axis, the stress does appear to reach a constant level. Figure 5 shows the stress relaxation curve of a 7S–43B–7S sample tested at a strain of 9.6% compared to the 11S–54–B–11S sample shown in Figure 4. It can be seen that the 7S–43B–7S sample exhibits a higher initial stress, but then relaxes to a much greater extent, so that the final stress is lower than that of the 11S–54B–11S sample. Figure 6 shows the same curves in Figure 4 plotted on a log-log scale. It can be seen that the relaxation rate of the 7S–43B–7S sample is much faster than that of the 11S–54B–11S sample. Table I presents average values of the ratio of the relaxed stress to the initial stress for the three S–B–S sample used in this study. It can be seen that while this ratio was above 0.5 for the 11S–54B–11S and 15S–70B–15S samples, it was much lower for the 7S–43B–7S sample. The amount of relative relaxation which occurred in the 7S–43B–7S sample was much greater than that which occurred in the other two samples. These observations indicate significant deformation in the PS phase or pullout of the PS segments from the PS domains. If the PS domains were truly non-deformable, the only possible relaxation would be in the PB phase. In that case, such large differences in the relaxation rates would not be expected. These differences indicate that PS deformation or segment pullout is important even at the low strains used in

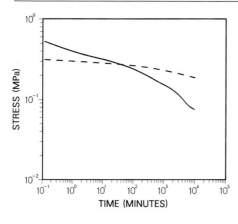

Figure 6   Stress relaxation of the 7S–43B–7S sample at 9.6 % strain in comparison to the 11S–54B–11S sample at 9.1 % strain on a logarithmic time scale: 7S–43B–7S (——), 11S–54B–11S (------)

TABLE I   Average Stress Relaxation

Sample	Relaxed Stress/Initial Stress
7S–43B–7S	.13
11S–54B–11S	.58
15S–70B–15S	.53

our tests. The difference between the 7S–43B–7S sample and the other samples is probably due to molecular weight, particularly the difference in the molecular weights of the PS end blocks. Domains of lower molecular weight PS in the 7S–43B–7S sample are no doubt weaker than those in the higher molecular weight samples, and are probably more susceptible to deformation and segment pullout. The effect of molecular weight on the mechanical behavior of S–B–S block copolymers was the subject of an investigation which used polymers having molecular weights of 7,000–43,000–7,000 and 16,000–85,000–17,000, and blends of the two[29]. Stress-strain, stress relaxation, solution, and swelling behavior similar to that found in this study were observed. The molecular weight dependence was explained in terms of changes in the interphase volume with molecular weight. Whatever the effect of molecular weight may be, it is clear that the stress relaxation behavior measured in this study is not simply due to relaxation of PB matrix chains anchored to non-deforming PS domains. Involvement of the PS phase in the relaxation behavior is of great importance.

Because the observed relaxation behavior includes significant relaxation in the PS domains, while the theories assume non-deformable domains, use of the stress measured after long relaxation times would be incorrect. To make a comparison of experimental results with the theoretical predictions, it was necessary to use the stress upon initial application of strain. It was assumed that the time required for application of the strain, about 7 seconds, was sufficient for most of the relaxation to occur in the PB phase, but not long enough for significant PS deformation to occur. In other words, the initial stress measured at about 7 seconds was used as an approximation to the equilibrium stress of an S–B–S sample assumed to have non-deformable PS domains. Neglecting PS deformation does not results in the neglect of a possible positive contribution to the modulus because the theoretical models already assume the maximum possible domain contribution by assuming nondeformable domains with infinite modulus.

Although use of the initial stress as the equilibrium stress is admittedly an approximation, there are at least two good reasons to justify this approximation. First, it is expected that most of the PB relaxation occurs at short times, while most of the PS relaxation occurs at longer times at room temperature since PB is rubbery while PS is glassy. The difference in molecular mobility is seen in values of the activation energy of deformation measured in various tests for S–B–S samples. The activation energy was calculated to be 35−40 kcal/mol, close to the value for homopolymer PS, at 0 °C from time-temperature superposition of stress relaxation data[30, 31, 32]. Time-temperature superposition of dynamic mechanical data, however, yields an activation energy of about 17 kcal/mol, closer to a value of 9 kcal/mol for homopolymer PB[32]. An interpretation of these results was that, during dynamic mechanical testing, with deformation times of a second or less, relaxation in the PB phase was the controlling mechanism, while in stress relaxation tests, with longer times of deformation, relaxation in the PS phase was the controlling mechanism[32]. It is thus not unreasonable to consider a stress value at some intermediate time as being representative of the stress in the S–B–S sample after most PB relaxation has occurred, but before PS relaxation becomes significant. Secondly, it is expected that 7 seconds is a sufficient time for most of the PB relaxation to occur. Examination of the stress relaxation results[33] for an end-linked PB network formed from PB molecules having a starting molecular weight given by $M_n = 4700$ and $M_w = 7500$ shows that the ratio of the equilibrium modulus to that at 7 seconds is about 0.94. Use of the 7 second modulus would thus be a fairly good approximation in this case. The above results indicate that use of the initial stress after 7 seconds as the equilibrium stress is a reasonable approximation for the purpose of this study, particularly in view of the large differences between the predictions of the various theories, as will be seen later.

Figures 7–9 compare the stress-strain behavior predicted by the theoretical models with the experimental behavior observed for the three SBS materials tested in this study. The simple model used in Figures 7–9 is the uniform strain amplification model (equation (2)). For all three samples, the stress predicted by the Gaylord-Lohse model is slightly higher than that predicted by the simple model. As discussed earlier, the Gaylord-Lohse model accounts for the change in chain distribution function of the PB center block due to the presence of the domains. This change is seen in Figures 7–9 to increase the stress at any given strain. An objection might be raised due to the inclusion of a contribution from diblock molecules in the Gaylord-Lohse model, while no such contribution is included in the simple model. A diblock contribution exists in the Gaylord-Lohse model due to the constraints imposed on the cilia by the presence of the domains. Figure 10 compares the stress-strain behavior predicted by the simple modsel to that predicted by the Gaylord-Lohse model considering bridge molecules only. It can be seen that the stress predicted by the Gaylord-Lohse model is still higher, indicating that a change in chain distribution function does indeed affect the stress-strain behavior.

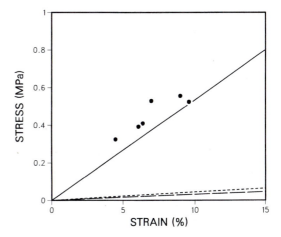

Figure 7 Stress vs. strain for the 7S–43B–7S sample: experimental (●), simple model with uniform strain amplification (— —), Gaylord-Lohse Model (------), entanglement model (—)

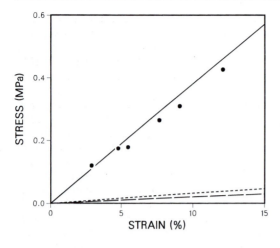

Figure 8 Stress vs. strain for the 11S–54B–11S sample: experimental (●), simple model with uniform strain amplification (— —), Gaylord-Lohse Model (------), entanglement model (—)

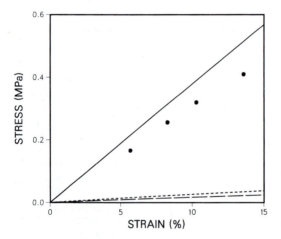

Figure 9 Stress vs. strain for the 15S–70B–15S sample: experimental (●), simple model with uniform strain amplification (— —), Gaylord-Lohse model (------), entanglement model (—)

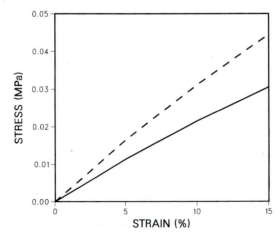

Figure 10 Stress vs. strain for the 11S–54B–11S sample: simple model with uniform strain amplification (—), Gaylord-Lohse model with bridge contribution only (— —)

Comparing the Gaylord-Lohse predicitions to the experimental results in Figures 7–9, it is obvious that, even though a change in chain distribution function results in increased modulus, if cannot account for the large deviation of the experimental results from the predictions of the simple model. However, the experimental results agree fairly well with predictions of the entanglement model, indicating the importance of the entanglement contribution to the mechanical behavior of S–B–S. In fact, the entanglement contribution is an order of magnitude greater than the contribution from the domains as crosslinks. This difference is not surprising considering that the plateau modulus of PB is relatively high, resulting in a large entanglement contribution, and that the PB center block molecular weight corresponding to M_c is high, resulting in a small crosslink contribution. Other studies have also found that the entanglement contribution could be several times larger than the chemical crosslink contribution in homopolymer PB and ethylene propylene rubber (EPR)[14, 15]. It might be argued that the large experimental stress values are due to the use of the initial stress value rather than a stress value obtained after a longer time of relaxation. This objection is answered by the fact that even the relaxed stress values are greater than the values predicted by the other theoretical models which neglect the entanglement contribution, as shown in Figure 11 for the 11S–54B–11S sample. The stress values in Figure 11 were measured after 7 to 10 days.

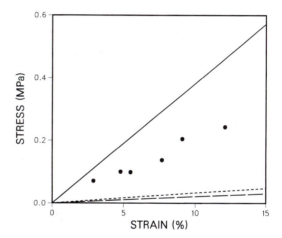

Figure 11   Stress vs. strain for the 11S–54B–11S sample: experimental stress after relaxation (●), simple model with uniform strain amplification (— —), Gaylord-Lohse model (-------), entanglement model (—)

Comparisons of the behavior of the different samples with each other also provides insight into the factors which affect the mechanical behavior. Figure 12 compares the predictions of the Gaylord-Lohse model for the three samples. This figure compares the crosslink contribution to the stress, that is, the contribution arising from considering the domains to be the only crosslinks. It is seen that the predicted stress increases with decreasing center block molecular weight. This result is not surprising since the center block molecular weight is taken as M_c in the Gaylord-Lohse model, and decreasing values of M_c correspond to increasing values of elastically effective chain density. Also of importance is the fact that the 11S–54B–11S and 15S–70B–15S samples have a 15 % diblock content. The density of bridge molecules is thus lower in these samples, further reducing the predicted stress values with respect to the 7S–43B–7S sample. The fraction of PS increases progressing from the 7S–43B–7S, to the 11S–54B–11S, to the 15S–70B–15S sample. This increase causes an increase in strain amplification in the matrix, which would result in an increase in modulus in the order listed above. This factor is not as significant as the change in chain density, however, so that the samples of lower molecular weight are predicted to have higher moduli than the samples of higher molecular weight even though they contain less PS.

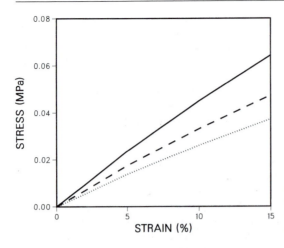

Figure 12 Stress vs. strain predictions of Gaylord-Lohse model: 7S–43B–7S (——), 11S–54B–11S (-------), 15S–70B–15S (. . . .)

Figure 13 compares the predictions of the entanglement model for the three samples. The experimental stress-strain results are also plotted. Comparing the theoretical predictions, it can be seen that the 7S–43B–7S sample is expected to have the highest stress values. This prediction is partially due to the crosslink contribution which is largest for the 7S–43B–7S sample. However, as already seen, the crosslink contribution is very small compared to the expected entanglement contribution. The 7S–43B–7S sample does not contain the large diblock fraction present in the other samples. The trapping factor is 1.0 for the 7S–43B–7S sample, while it is only 0.69 for the other samples. The entanglement contribution is thus much larger in the 7S−43B−7S sample than in the other samples. Comparing the theoretical prediction for the 11S–54B–11S sample with that of the 15S–70B–15S sample, it can be seen that the 11S–54B–11S sample is expected to have virtually the same modulus as the 15S–70B–15S sample. This is due to the difference in crosslink contribution between the two samples, seen in Figure 12, which is almost entirely compensated for by the effect of strain amplification since the 15S–70B–15S sample has a higher PS content. Comparing the observed experimental stress-strain results with the predictions of the theoretical models, it can be seen that the entanglement model best fits the data.

Table II contains the shear modulus values calculated and measured for the three samples. Analysis of these values leads to the same conclusions already reached by analyzing the

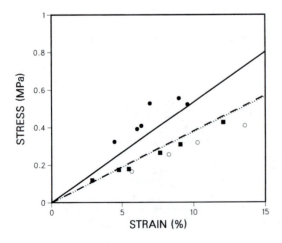

Figure 13 Stress vs. strain predictions of entanglement model: 7S–43B–7S (● experimental, —— model), 11S–54B–11S (■ experimental, --- model), 15S–70B–15S (○ experimental, ···· model)

TABLE II   Shear Modulus Values (MPa)

Model	7S–43B–7S	11S–54B–11S	15S–70B–15S
Simple (strain amplification)	0.121	0.081	0.063
Gaylord-Lohse	0.167	0.125	0.099
Entanglement	1.78	1.27	1.26
Experimental	1.95	1.14	1.02

stress-strain curves. The effect of the domains on the chain distribution function of the PB chains, considered in the Gaylord-Lohse model, increases the modulus over the simple model. The increases seen here are about 50 %, the same as reported by Meier[5]. However, comparison with the experimentally observed modulus once again indicates the importance of an entanglement contribution. The entanglement contribution is again seen to exceed the crosslink contribution by about an order of magnitude.

As discussed earlier, one of the functions of the domains is to serve as reinforcing filler particles. It is worthwhile at this point to explore this filler effect further. The effect of the domains as filler particles consists of two parts. The domains take up volume and, because they restrict the conformations available to the PB chains, they change the chain distribution function of the chains, as modeled by Gaylord and Lohse. The domains also alter the distribution of strain in the matrix. This effect has been accounted for in this study by use of either the strain amplification model or the Guth-Smallwood term. Figure 14 compares the stress-strain behavior predicted by the simple model for the 11S–54B–11S sample using the Guth-Smallwood term with that predicted using strain amplification. The choice of a model to describe the filler effect is seen to have an effect on the predicted stress. The difference between the two models of the filler effect is in the way that they describe the strain distribution in the matrix. The strain amplification model assumes that the strain in the matrix is uniform, while the Guth-Smallwood term assumes a strain distribution given by a continuum mechanics solution. Most likely, neither model is correct. This problem is complex, however, and will not be explored any further here. The important observation to make from Figure 14 is that, even though the choice of a filler effect model affects the calculated stress, the stresses predicted are still much lower than those measured. The contribution from trapped entanglements remains the most important factor.

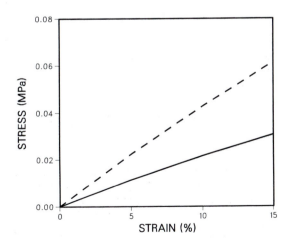

Figure 14   Stress vs. strain predictions for the 11S–54B–11S sample: simple model with uniform strain amplification (——), Guth-Smallwood term (— —)

One complicating factor is the shape or continuity of the PS phase. The theoretical models assume that the PS phase is the isolated domain phase in the PB matrix. Furthermore, the Gaylord-Lohse model and the Guth-Smallwood filler effect term are derived for spherical domains. Although domain shape most likely does make some contribution to the measured stress, it is probably not a major one, as can be seen from the variation in modulus with composition for the samples studied. The continuity of the PS phase increases with increasing PS content in S–B–S block copolymers. If this effect was dominant in the samples studied here, the measured modulus values would increase with increasing PS content. The 7S–43B–7S sample would have the lowest modulus and the 15S–70B–15S sample the highest. However, as seen in Table II, exactly the opposite trend is found. This result indicates that the domains in our samples cast from a solution preferential to PB are isolated enough that their exact shape is not of major consequence, and the mechanical behavior is controlled by the properties of the PB matrix.

5   CONCLUSIONS

The purpose of this study was to investigate the factors of importance in determining the mechanical behavior of elastomeric S–B–S block copolymers. By comparing experimental results with theoretical models which account for several factors in different ways, a determination of the importance of these factors could be made.

The presence of a two phase structure consisting of isolated glassy domains in a rubbery matrix is, of course, the primary reason for the elastomeric behavior of SBS block copolymers. The domains serve several roles. They serve in the place of chemical crosslinks, anchoring the PB chain ends. One contribution to the mechanical behavior comes from the PB network thus formed, with the domains as crosslinks and M_c equal to the molecular weight of the PB center block. The domains also serve as filler particles. One filler effect is a change in chain distribution function of the PB chains due to the constraints caused by the domains. This effect leads to an increase in modulus. Another filler effect is to amplify the applied strain to an effectively higher level in the rubbery matrix, also leading to an increase in modulus. These increases are not sufficient to explain the experimental data. As in conventional elastomers, entanglements in the PB phase are trapped by the formation of the network. The contribution from trapped entanglements was found to be very significant, almost an order of magnitude greater than that predicted by considering the domains as crosslinks only. Neglect of the entanglement contribution resulted in stress predictions which were far below the experimental values. The importance of entanglement contributions to the eleastic behavior of S–B–S block copolymers thus seems well established by this study.

6   ACKNOWLEDGEMENT

We wish to thank Dr. D. J. St. Clair of the Shell Chemical Company for providing S–B–S samples, and to acknowledge the support of Dr. Sonja Krause and Ms. Alice Granger in analyzing the samples using SEC. In addition, the support received in the form of a graduate fellowship from the Fannie and John Hertz Foundation is gratefully acknowledged by J. K. Bard.

References

1. J. V. Dawkins, in *"Block Copolymers"*, D. C. Allport and W. H. Janes, ed., Chapter 8B, John Wiley and Sons, Inc., (1973)
2. G. Holden, E. T. Bishop, and N. R. Legge, *J. Polym. Sci., Part C, 26*, 37 (1969)
3. E. Guth, *J. Appl. Phys., 16*, 20 (1945)
4. H. M. Smallwood, *J. Appl. Phys., 15*, 758 (1944)
5. D. J. Meier, *Polymer Preprints, 14*, 280 (1973)
6. R. J. Gaylord, in *"Multiphase Polymers"*, S. L. Cooper and G. M. Estes, ed., Chapter 12, ACS, Washington, D. C. (1979)
7. R. J. Gaylord and D. J. Lohse, *Polym. Eng. and Sci., 18*, 359 (1978)
8. L. R. G. Treloar, *"The Physics of Rubber Elasticity"*, Third Edition, Clarendon Press, Oxford (1975)
9. P. J. Flory, *J. Chem. Phys., 66*, 5720 (1977)
10. B. Erman and P. J. Flory, *J. Chem. Phys., 68*, 5363 (1978)
11. P. J. Flory, *Polymer, 20*, 1317 (1979)
12. P. J. Flory and B. Erman, *Macromolecules, 15*, 800 (1982)
13. G. Ronca and G. Allegra, *J. Chem. Phys., 63*, 4990 (1975)
14. L. M. Dossin and W. W. Graessley, *Macromolecules, 12*, 123 (1979)
15. D. S. Pearson and W. W. Graessley, *Macromolecules, 13*, 1001 (1980)
16. W. W. Graessley, *Adv. in Polym. Sci., 47*, 67 (1982)
17. G. Marrucci, *Macromolecules, 14*, 434 (1981)
18. N. R. Langley, *Macromolecules, 1*, 348 (1968)
19. M. Gottlieb, C. W. Macosko, G. S. Benjamin, K. O. Meyers and E. W. Merrill, *Macromolecules, 14*, 1039 (1981)
20. P. J. Flory, *Proc. R. Soc., London, A, 351*, 351 (1976)
21. D. J. Meier, *Polym. Preprints, 11*, 400 (1970)
22. D. J. Meier, *Appl. Polym. Symposium, No. 24*, 67 (1974)
23. R. G. C. Arridge, in *"Continuum Models of Discrete Systems 4"*, O. Brulin and R. K. T. Hsieh, ed., pg. 279, North-Holland Publishing Co., Amsterdam (1981)
24. P. S. Pillai, D. I. Livingston, and J. D. Strang, *Rubber Chem. Technol., 45*, 241 (1972)
25. J. D. Ferry, *"Viscoelastic Properties of Polymers"*, Third Edition, Chapter 13, John Wiley and Sons, Inc., New York (1980)
26. Private Communication, Dr. D. J. St. Clair, Shell Chemical Company
27. J. K. Bard, *"Structure-Property Relationships in Block Copolymers"* Masters's Thesis, Rensselaer Polytechnic Institute, December, 1981
28. J. K. Bard, *"Modeling the Mechanical Behavior of Elastomeric Styrene-Butadiene-Styrene Block Copolymers"*, Doctoral Thesis, Rensselaer Polytechnic Institute, August, 1983
29. Y. D. M. Chen and R. E. Cohen, *J. Appl. Polym. Sci., 21*, 629 (1977)
30. T. L. Smith, in *"Block Polymers"*, S. L. Aggarawal, ed., pg. 137, Plenum Press, New York (1970)
31. T. L. Smith and R. A. Dickie, *J. Polym. Sci., Part C, 26*, 163 (1969)
32. G. W. Kamykowski, J. D. Ferry, and L. J. Fetters, *J. Polym. Sci.: Polym. Phys. Ed., 20*, 2125 (1982)
33. G. W. Nelb, S. Pedersen, C. R. Taylor, and J. D. Ferry, *J. Polym. Sci.: Polym. Phys. Ed., 18*, 695 (1980)

Chapter 12

RESEARCH ON THERMOPLASTIC ELASTOMERS

Section 2

INTERFACIAL ACTIVITY OF BLOCK COPOLYMERS

G. Riess

Contents

G. Riess, Ecole Nationale Superieure de Chimie de Mulhouse, 3, rue Alfred Werner – 68200 Mulhouse (France)

1   INTRODUCTION

The various aspects on block copolymers, ranging from synthesis, fractionation, solution and solid state properties to applications, have been reviewed in a recent literature survey[1].

From the large number of publications, patents, specialized symposia published in this area during the last decade it appears that block copolymers represent one of the fastest growing areas in polymer science and that these polymers have gained considerable importance, both in scientific research and in industrial applications.

The interest in block copolymers is mainly because these copolymers have unique properties in solution and in the solid state as a consequence of their molecular structure. In particular, such block copolymers have sequences of different chemical composition which are usually incompatible and have therefore a tendency to segregate in space.

The amphiphilic properties in solution and microdomain formation in the solid state are directly related to this specific molecular architecture of block copolymers, which can be designed by using existing monomers or polymers.

The industrial applications of block copolymers and their potentials have been realized in polymeric material design, as in thermoplastic elastomers where the block copolymer is the major constituent of the material and in applications where it acts as an useful additive, e. g. surfactant, viscosity improver and "compatibilizer".

In this contribution, we intend to give a brief survey of our work related to block copolymers, which has been the main research area of our department for the last 25 years. This article will outline the synthesis of these copolymers, as well as their interfacial properties, especially with respect to their behavior as polymeric surfactants in solution and in the solid state.

These aspects will be approached by considering:

– some specific synthesis techniques to produce block copolymer with thermoplastic elastomer characteristics
– the surface activity and emulsifying properties of block copolymers, especially for the preparation of polymeric oil/oil emulsions, which are the starting point for polymeric two-phase systems
– their solid state properties relating to new mesomorphic structures and the extension possibilities of the thermoplastic elastomer concept (selective plasticization of block copolymers)
– the applicational possibilities of block copolymers in polymer blends, especially with respect to morphology regulation in polymeric two-phase systems.

2   SYNTHESIS

The polymerization methods leading to triblock or segmented block copolymers with thermoplastic elastomer characteristics are based on two general reaction schemes.

In the first one, $\alpha \omega$ active sites are generated on a polymer chain poly B which then initiate the polymerization of a second monomer B. Such a polymerization can be free radical, anionic or cationic and may be shown as follows:

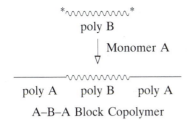

poly B

Monomer A

poly A   poly B   poly A

A–B–A Block Copolymer

Thus in typical block copolymers of thermoplastic elastomer type

— poly A is a hard segment such as polystyrene or poly (α methylstyrene)
— poly B is an elastomeric segment such as polybutadiene or polyisoprene.

The second method, which is usually called condensation, is the reaction between chemical functional groups present at the end of different polymers. Such a situation for the synthesis of a triblock copolymer can be shown as:

poly A   poly B   poly A

(A–B–A) Block Copolymer

where

Ⓧ is a functional group like OH, NH_2 ...

Ⓨ is a functional group like COCl, NCO ...

Ⓩ the reaction product of Ⓧ plus Ⓨ

As an illustration of our contribution in this area, two aspects will be mentioned:

– the preparation of functionalized triblock copolymers by anionic polymerization
– the synthesis of triblock copolymers by the so called "anionic-free radical" polymerization.

2.1 Preparation of Functionalized Triblock Copolymers by Anionic Polymerization

Anionic polymerization, since its re-discovery by Szwarc[2], and its wide use in the polymerization of high cis polyisoprene elastomers, has proved to be one of the most useful techniques for the preparation of monodisperse polymers and well-defined block copolymers. It differs from other methods, and especially from free radical polymerization, in that under necessarily stringent conditions required for polymerization, a termination or transfer step is absent; for this reason it is called "living anionic polymerization". The possibility of preparing almost pure block copolymers of a specific molecular weight, composition and structure, becomes realized by anionic polymerization. Monomers of a diene, nonpolar vinylic and cyclic ether nature may be polymerized by this technique.

An additional advantage is that functionalized block copolymers with specific end groups may be obtained by reacting a "living polymer" with suitable reagents.

Thus functionalized polystyrene-b-polybutadiene-b-polystyrene (S-B-S) have been obtained as indicated by the following reactions:

$$\text{————}^{\ominus} \quad + \quad \underset{O}{CH_2 - CH_2} \quad \longrightarrow \quad \text{————} CH_2 - CH_2 - OH$$

$$" \quad\quad + \quad R - \underset{\underset{O}{\|}}{C} - OR \quad \longrightarrow \quad \text{————} \underset{\underset{O}{\|}}{C} - R$$

$$+ \quad \text{(phthalic anhydride)} \quad \longrightarrow \quad \text{————} \underset{\underset{O}{\|}}{C} \text{—} \langle\ \rangle \quad COOH$$

$$+ \quad CO_2 \quad \longrightarrow \quad \text{————} COOH$$

$$+ \quad (CH_2)_n \underset{SO_2}{\overset{O}{\diagup}} \quad \longrightarrow \quad \text{————} (CH_2)_n - SO_3H \atop n = 3,4$$

$$+ \quad O_2 \quad \longrightarrow \quad \text{————} OOH$$

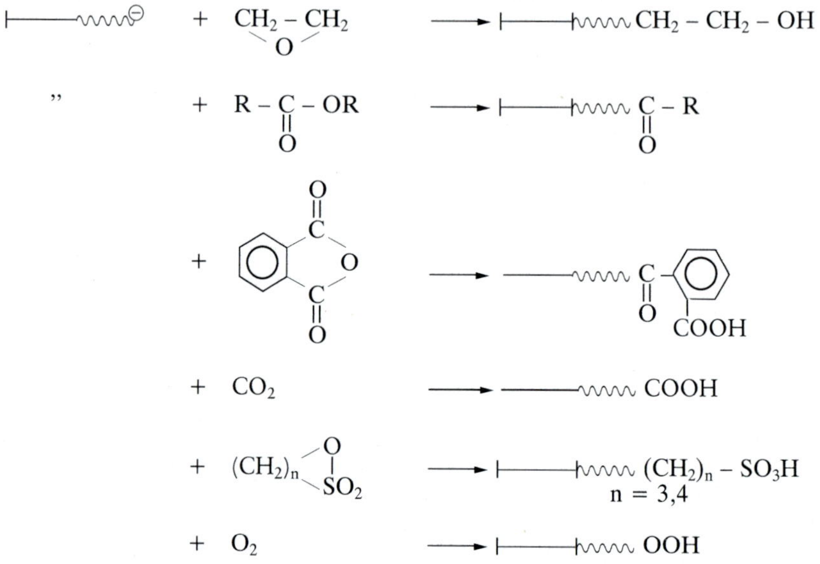

It appeared that these triblock copolymers with neutralized carboxy or sulfonic end groups provide an interesting approach for the design of thermoplastic elastomers with ionomer characteristics. Similar types of materials can also be obtained by chemical modification of S-B-S type block copolymers, e. g. by a carboxylation reaction, either with maleic anhydride or with thioglycolic acid, according to the following reaction scheme:

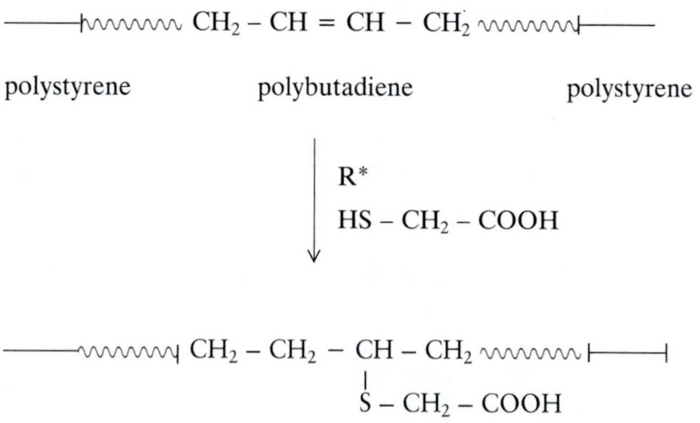

$$\text{————} CH_2 - CH = CH - CH_2 \text{————}$$

polystyrene   polybutadiene   polystyrene

$$\bigg\downarrow \quad \begin{array}{l} R^* \\ HS - CH_2 - COOH \end{array}$$

$$\text{————} CH_2 - CH_2 - CH - CH_2 \text{————} \atop \underset{S - CH_2 - COOH}{\big|}$$

2.2 Anionic – Free Radical Polymerization

Due to specific limitations of anionic, cationic or free radical polymerization, an alternative approach to the block copolymer synthesis is to devise processes whereby the polymerization mechanism can be changed at will to suit the monomers being polymerized sequentially.

Such "transformation reactions, e. g. from anionic to cationic polymerization or viceversa, have been reviewed by Richards et al.[3].

All transformations involving anions, cations and radical are possible; to show the potential area of interest, this principle will be illustrated by some examples of "anion to free radical transformation" developed in our laboratory. This type of transformation is based on the deactivation of a living anionic polymer with different reagents able to initiate the radical polymerization of a second monomer.

For example "living" polystyrene or polyisoprene have been deactivated with 4,4' bis (bromomethyl) benzoyl peroxide leading to a polymeric peroxide, thus

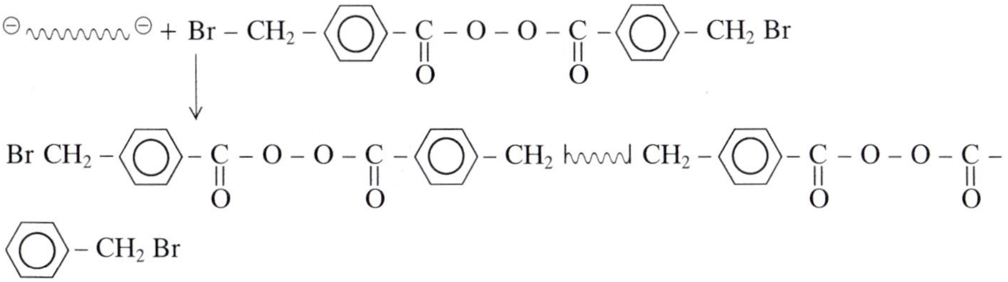

In an analogous way, peroxidized chain ends have been obtained by addition of a living polymer to a THF solution saturated in oxygen[4] or by reaction with 2,2' azobisisobutyronitrile[5]. The reaction using azobisisobutyronitrile may be depicted thus:

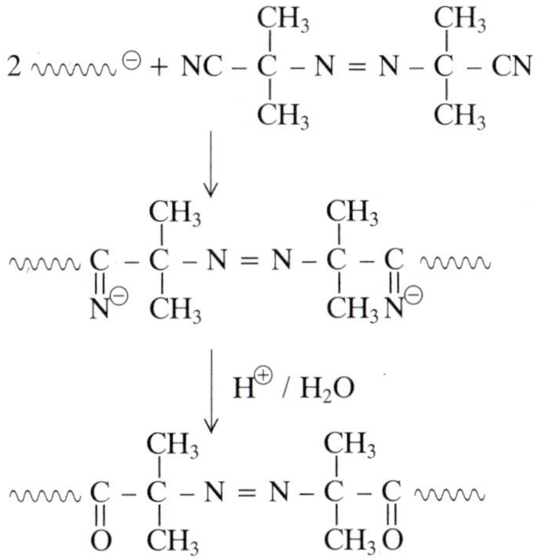

Starting with these polymeric peroxides or azo compounds, either by thermal or redox decomposition in the presence of a second monomer, diblock copolymers of the following types have been obtained:

polyisoprene – polymethylmethacrylate
polyisoprene – poly(styrene-alt-maleic anhydride)
polyisoprene – poly(styrene-co-acrylonitrile).

With respect to living anionic polymerization, these transformation reactions have a certain number of advantages as well as disadvantages. Thus, the main advantage is that triblock copolymers based on polar vinyl monomers become accessible. However, as expected from the inherent characteristics of free radical polymerization such as:

– an initiation efficiency f ≤ 1, with values of f decreasing with an increase in molecular weight of the polymeric initiator
– different types of chain termination (disproportionation or combination)
– various chain transfer reactions,

the resulting block copolymer is formed in a lower yield and its polydispersity (in structure, composition and molecular weight) is higher than those obtained by "anionic living" polymerization. Nevertheless, if this kind of copolymers might have certain limitations as thermoplastic elastomers, it appeared that they are very valuable as additives due to their interfacial activity.

3   INTERFACIAL ACTIVITY OF BLOCK COPOLYMERS IN THE PRESENCE OF SOLVENTS

To illustrate the surface and interfacial activity of block copolymers, we have to consider at first their behavior in the presence of solvents which leads us to subjects of micellization and formation of the various types of emulsions.

3.1 Micelles

Block copolymer may behave as a typical amphiphile in a selective solvent, that is a good solvent for one block but a precipitant for the other. Thus, at a lower concentration than the critical micellar concentration (CMC), the copolymer molecules have a tendency to saturate the air-solvent interface which in turn leads to a characteristic change for the surface tension of the solvent.

At a concentration higher than the CMC, the copolymer molecules aggregate reversibly to form micelles in a manner analogous to aggregation of classical surface active agents. Both monomolecular and multimolecular micelles may form and these species consist generally of a more or less swollen core of the insoluble block surrounded by a flexible fringe of soluble block(s) as shown schematically in Figure 1.

It is generally believed that such plurimolecular micelles, formed through a closed association process, are spherical in shape with narrow size distribution[6].

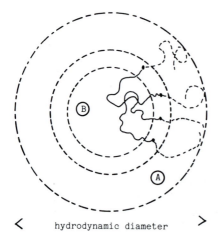

<   hydrodynamic diameter   >

Figure 1   Schematic representation of a plurimolecular block copolymer micelle in a selective solvent of poly A. Copolymer ABA: the insoluble blocks B are surrounded by the solvated A blocks

In addition to their shape and size, these micelles are also characterized by their average molecular weight, from which it becomes possible to determine the aggregation number, which is defined as the average number of copolymer unimers in a micelle. This aggregation number may for instance be calculated from the value of the hydrodynamic diameter in association with the corresponding viscosity data[6, 7].

A systematic study of the micellization has been performed for di- and triblock copolymers such as:

– poly(ethylene oxide) – *block* – poly(dimethylsiloxane) Cop PEO – PDMS
– poly(ethylene oxide) – *block* – polystyrene – *block* – poly(ethylene oxide) Cop PEO – PS – PEO

having hydrophilic/hydrophobic characteristics.

In the presence of water, a selective solvent for the PEO sequences, micelles may be formed having a PS or PDMS core and PEO fringes[8].

The determination of the hydrodynamic diameter $\overline{D}_h$, for instance by turbidity measurements or by photon correlation spectroscopy, showed that the average molecular weight of the micelles, and thus the aggregation number, are a function of:

– the molecular characteristics of the copolymer (molecular weight, composition and structure)
– the different parameters, for example temperature, determining the solvent/polymer interaction for the segments forming the micellar fringe.

A systematic study for a series of polystyrene-poly(ethylene oxide) di- and triblock copolymers has shown that a diblock copolymer has higher aggregation number than the corresponding triblock copolymer[8].

Another example of the influence of the molecular parameters, e. g. the molecular weight of the block copolymer at constant composition, on the micellar characteristics (hydrodynamic radius R_h and aggregation number N) is given in Table I for a series of polystyrene-polybutadiene diblock copolymers. A general feature that could be observed is that micelle size and aggregation number increase with the percentage of insoluble block and with the total molecular weight of copolymers. Usually the micelle size and aggregation number for the same block copolymer in heptane was higher in comparison to that in dimethylformamide (DMF)[7].

A characteristic feature of block copolymer micelles is their capability to solubilize insoluble substances within its core. Thus a given amount of homopolymer, corresponding to the insoluble block of the copolymer, can be solubilized in the micellar core.

TABLE I Micellar Characteristics of Polystyrene-b-Polybutadiene Copolymers; Hydrodynamic Radius (R_h) and Aggregation Number (N) as a Function of Molecular Weight*

Copolymer	$\overline{M}_n$ total	wt % PS total	Heptane		DMF	
			R_h (nm)	N	R_h (nm)	N
SB 7	46,000	51	32.5	204	14.5	61
410	68,000	48**	40.5	276	22.5	109
SB 6	72,000	52	48.0	312	21.0	74
TX 006	375,000	48	91.0	233	48.5	/

* Temperature : 25 °C; Selective solvents : heptane for the polybutadiene blocks, DMF for the polystyrene block (PS)
** Weight % block PS : 32%

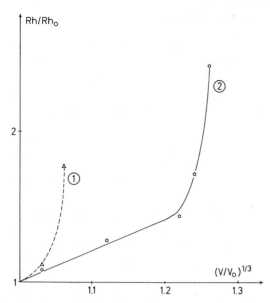

Figure 2   Solubilization of homopolymers within the core of micelles of a polystyrene-polybutadiene diblock copolymer; Variation of the relative hydrodynamic radius (Rh/Rh$_o$) as a function of the relative volume fraction v/v$_o$ of the core forming polymers (insoluble block + core solubilized homopolymers). ① Cop SB 51 wt % PS $\overline{M}_n$ = 46,000 + polystyrene $\overline{M}_n$ = 9,000 in heptane; ② Cop SB 51 wt % PS $\overline{M}_n$ = 46,000 + polybutadiene $\overline{M}_n$ = 20,000 in DMF

Figure 2 gives as an example the variation of the hydrodynamic diameter of the micelles having solubilized increasing amounts of the corresponding homopolymers. In agreement with Tuzar et al.[6, 9, 10] it appears that solubilization of homopolymers in a micellar system has several constraints:

– the molecular weight of the homopolymer to be solubilized must be lower than the molecular weight of the corresponding block copolymer sequence
– the amount of homopolymer solubilized has an upper limit which is dependant on its molecular weight, on the solvent and the molecular characteristics of the block copolymer.

In a similar way as Tuzar et al.[11], we have succeeded in stabilizing block copolymer micelles by crosslinking of the core. The most suitable system in this case is given by styrene-butadiene block copolymers forming micelles with a polybutadiene core in the presence of a selective solvent of polystyrene like DMF or dimethylacetamid (DMA). The crosslinking of the core is achieved by UV irradiation in the presence of benzoine ether type photo-initiators[12]. Such stabilized micelles proved to be resistant to temperature increase and remained intact as microgels in the presence of a good solvent for both blocks.

The concept of block copolymer micellization has furthermore been extended to A-B-C block copolymers, as for instance polystyrene-*block*-polyisoprene-*block*-polymethylmethac-rylate. In acetonitrile, which is a selective solvent for PMMA, "core-shell" type micelles are formed[13].

Starting with a poly(vinyl 2-pyridine)-*block*-poly(ethylene oxide) copolymer, we have shown that micelles can be formed having a core of metal complexed poly(vinylpyridine) and a stabilizing fringe of poly(ethylene oxide)[14].

3.2 Applicational Possibilities of Micellar Systems

With respect to their applicational possibilities, the surface-active properties of block copolymers render them suitable for use as stabilizers for a variety of colloidal dispersions.

A first example of this phenomenon is the stabilization of dispersed polymer particles formed as a result of emulsion or dispersion polymerization either in organic or aqueous media[15]. Thus polystyrene latices could be obtained by emulsion polymerization in the presence of hydrophobic-hydrophilic block copolymers like polystyrene-poly(ethylene oxide) di- and triblock copolymers. In this kind of application the rate of dissociation of micelles, as well as the diffusion rate of the copolymer molecules, play an important role in governing the effectiveness of the stabilizer. Thus the conditions must be carefully choosen to ensure that the block copolymer molecules have enough mobility to maintain adequate surface coverage of the latex.

Dispersed polymer particles with narrow size distribution and in a wide range of diameters can be obtained by carefully controlling the experimental conditions. In addition, these latices, due to stabilizing block copolymer anchored on their surface, exhibit interesting rheological properties, which makes them suitable for applications in paint systems, in fiber sizing, etc . . .

Figure 3 shows as an illustration the electron micrograph of a polystyrene latex obtained by using a polystyrene-poly(ethylene oxide) diblock copolymer as surfactant in a classical emulsion type polymerization.

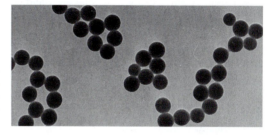

Figure 3   Electron micrograph of a polystyrene latex obtained by emulsion polymerization in the presence of polystyrene-poly-(ethylene oxide) diblock copolymer as surfactant. Magnification : 50,000

In a similar way, due to their steric stabilization action, block copolymers have also found applications in preparing pigment and filler dispersions, either in aqueous or organic medium.

The steric stabilization action of a AB block copolymer, with selective adsorption of the B block on the filler particle is schematically depicted in Figure 4a. As an extension of this principle, stabilization of filler suspensions can be achieved with ABC block copolymers according to a "flip-flop" mechanism. Thus by selective adsorption of the B block on the filler, either A or C block lead to the steric stabilization, depending on the specific interaction parameters of the A and the C with the suspending medium. This stabilization mechanism with ABC block copolymers is indicated schematically in Figure 4b.

As certain block copolymers, e. g. those based on poly(vinyl pyridine) form stable complexes with a number of metal ions, the corresponding micellar species may have potential in heterogeneous catalysis[14].

Finally it should be mentioned that

– polystyrene-hydrogenated polydiene block copolymers have been used as viscosity improvers for base lubricating oil[16, 17]

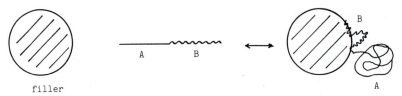

filler

Figure 4 a   A-B block copolymers as steric stabilizers for a filler particle in aqueous or organic medium. Schematic representation

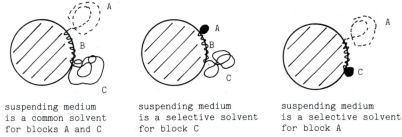

| suspending medium is a common solvent for blocks A and C | suspending medium is a selective solvent for block C | suspending medium is a selective solvent for block A |

Figure 4 b   A-B-S block copolymers as steric stabilizers for a filler particle. Schematic representation of the "flip-flop" mechanism

– poly(dimethylsiloxane)-poly(ethylene oxide) block copolymer systems have interesting gas solubilization properties, making them suitable for oxygen transport by means of colloidal dispersions[18].

3.3 Oil-Water Emulsions

An emulsion, defined as a liquid-liquid dispersion, is composed of two immiscible liquids, the one forming the continuous and the other the dispersed phase, stabilized by a suitable surfactant.

For oil-water systems, such emulsions can be of two types namely:

– oil droplets dispersed in water (o/w emulsions)
– water droplets dispersed in oil (w/o emulsions)

where hydrophilic-hydrophobic block copolymers are acting as emulsifiers.

Some typical examples for this kind of polymeric surfactants are given in Table II.

TABLE II   Block Copolymers as Polymeric Surfactants for Oil-Water Systems

Hydrophobic block	Hydrophilic block	Structure	Reference
polystyrene PS	poly(ethylene oxide) PEO	PS – PEO POE – PS – PEO	8
Poly(propylene oxide)	poly(ethylene oxide)	di and triblock	19, 20
poly(vinylpyridine)	poly(ethylene oxide)	diblock	14
polystyrene	poly(vinyl N alkyl) pyridinium bromide	diblock	21
polydimethylsiloxane PDMS	poly(ethylene oxide) PEO	PDMS – PEO	22

A systematic study of toluene-water and styrene-water emulsions, stabilized with polystyrene-poly(ethylene oxide) di- and triblock copolymers, has shown that the stability and the type of emulsion, which in turn depend on the particle size of the dispersed phase and on the viscosity, can be correlated to the concentration and molecular characteristics (composition, structure, molecular weight) of the block copolymer. For instance, stable oil/water emulsions with small droplet diameter are prepared preferably with di- or triblock copolymers having a poly(ethylene oxide) content of 60–80 wt %. In contrast, stable water/oil emulsions result with copolymers having a 60–80 wt % polystyrene content.

3.4   Oil-Oil Emulsions

With respect to classical surfactants, block copolymers have the unique property to act also under proper conditions as an emulsifier for oil-oil system. Thus block copolymers act as efficient emulsifiers for stabilizing emulsions composed of two immiscible organic liquids, generally when each of them is a selective solvent of one of the blocks of the copolymer. On the basis of this concept, we have investigated the emulsifying effect of polystyrene-polyisoprene block copolymers for dimethylformamide-hexane emulsions and of polystyrene-poly(methylmethacrylate) copolymers for cyclohexane-acetonitrile emulsions[23, 24].

From this study it was concluded that block copolymers, with a composition of about 50:50 and within the molecular weight range of 30,000 to 50,000, had the best emulsifying efficiency. This shows also that if oil-water emulsions can be obtained with relatively low molecular weight (1,000-10,000) block copolymers, the stabilization of oil-oil emulsions will require the use of block copolymers of higher molecular weight.

3.5   Polymeric Emulsions

These types of emulsions may be defined as two phase systems which consist of two incompatible polymers, poly A and poly B, in the presence of a common solvent S. The presence of a corresponding block or graft copolymers A-B acts as an emulsifier for both types of emulsions which exist, namely polymeric water/water and polymeric oil/oil emulsions.

A typical example of such a polymeric oil/oil emulsion we have studied in detail is the system consisting of polystyrene (PS) and polybutadiene (PBut) in a common solvent such as toluene or styrene[25, 26]. By adjusting the concentration of both homopolymers, phase separation occurs due to the incompatibility of the polymeric species; one phase has PBut as main polymeric component, the other polystyrene. Emulsification of this system can be achieved by addition of polystyrene-polybutadiene block copolymers.

In a systematic study, we have correlated the characteristics of such emulsions, e. g. stability, particle size of the dispersed phase, phase inversion etc., to the characteristics of the ternary system PS-PBut-styrene and to those of the PS-PBut block copolymer.

Thus in a typical phase diagram, shown schematically in Figure 5, the following characteristics of the ternary system PS-PBut-styrene have been established:

- the limit of phase separation which is the main requirement for the existence of polymeric emulsions
- the composition of the phases in equilibrium defined by the tie-lines (conjugated diameters) of the phase diagram
- the viscosity of the phases in equilibrium
- the interfacial tension γ_i, between the coexisting phases.

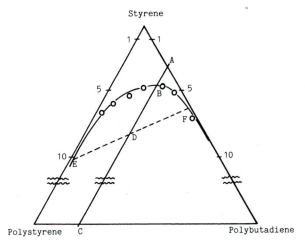

Figure 5   Phase diagram for the ternary system polystyrene, $\overline{M}_n = 130,000$, polybutadiene, $\overline{M}_n = 120,000$, and styrene at 25 °C. AC is the reaction path for the polymerization of styrene in the presence of 3 % polybutadiene; B is the phase separation limit; and EF is the tie line (conjugated diameter). Reproduced with permission (1)

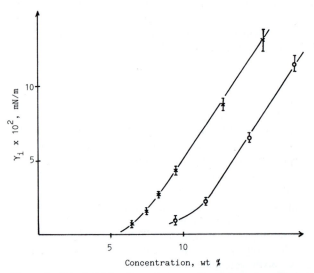

Figure 6   Interfacial tension γ_i between the phases at equilibrium, as a function of the total polymer concentration for phase-separated solutions of 50/50 (w/w) mixtures of polystyrene and polybutadiene in styrene at 25 °C. × –, system polystyrene ($\overline{M}_n = 76,200$) – polybutadiene ($\overline{M}_n = 120,000$) and o –, system polystyrene ($\overline{M}_n = 34,500$) – polybutadiene ($\overline{M}_n = 120,000$). Reproduced with permission (1)

As an example, we have given in Figure 6, the variation of γ_i, determined by the spinning drop technique, as a function of the total polymer concentration. In contrast to oil-water systems, it appears that the values of γ_i are relatively low (ca $10^{-1} – 10^{-3}$ mN/m) and that $\gamma_i \to 0$ by reaching the critical point or the phase separation limit.

It has been further observed that:

– an adapted block copolymer, in a given two phase system in equilibrium, has a tendency to decrease the interfacial tension, which is an additional proof of its surfactive properties

- the concentration of block copolymer necessary for stabilization of "polymeric emulsions" diminishes with the increase in overall polymer concentration of the system
- the stabilization action of the block copolymer is dependant upon its molecular characteristics, e. g. molecular weight, structure, composition, and upon the characteristics of the coexisting phases
- near the critical point or near the phase separation limit, it becomes difficult if not impossible to stabilize the emulsion
- the molecular weight of the stabilizing block copolymer has to be increased when the two-phase system approaches the critical point or the phase separation limit.

A mathematical model, based on Flory-Huggins[27] and Vrij's theory[28, 29] has been developed by Ossenbach-Sauter[14] for the interpretation of these results. By this relatively simple model it was thus possible to describe the characteristic features of the ternary system

poly A   poly B   solvent(s)

such as:

- the phase separation limit
- the critical conditions for phase separation
- the composition of the phases in equilibrium
- the interfacial tension between these phases
- the thickness of interfacial layer

as a function of:

- the degree of polymerization of the homopolymers $\overline{DP}_A$ and $\overline{DP}_B$
- the various interaction parameters (χ_{AS}, χ_{BS}, χ_{AB})

Figure 7a gives a typical concentration profile where $\chi_{AS} = \chi_{BS}$.

From this concentration profile it becomes possible to define an "interfacial thickness" designated by $\triangle$, where the two polymers poly A and poly B coexist. The corresponding variation of $\triangle$ as a function of the total polymer concentration is indicated in Fig. 7b.

It appears from these figures that for moderately concentrated systems (10 – 20 % total polymer concentration), $\triangle$ is in the order of 10 – 20 nm. Near the critical point however, or near the phase separation limit, $\triangle \rightarrow \infty$, which also corresponds to the limit where the interfacial tension $\gamma_i \rightarrow 0$.

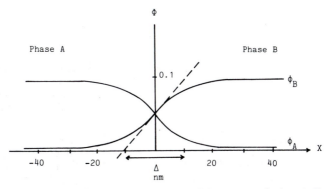

Figure 7a   Concentration profile for poly A and poly B at the interface of the system poly A, poly B and solvent S. Φ = volume fraction of poly A or poly B; X = distance from the center of the interface; $\triangle$ = thickness of the interface; $\overline{DP}$ of poly A = 1,000 : $\overline{DP}$ of poly B = 1,000; χ_{AS} = 0.4; χ_{BS} = 0.4; and χ_{AB} = 0.04. Reproduced with permission (1)

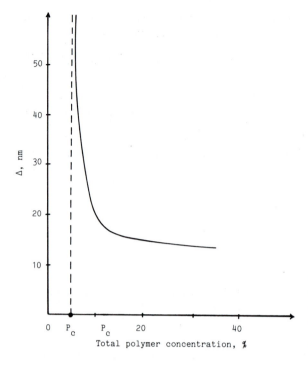

Figure 7b   Interfacial thickness Δ as a function of the total polymer concentration for system poly A, poly B and solvent S. $\chi_{AS} = 0.4$; $\chi_{BS} = 0.4$; $\chi_{AB} = 0.04$; $\overline{DP}_A = \overline{DP}_B = 1,000$

Ossenbach-Sauter[14] has completed this theoretical approach by calculating the free energy conditions required to place a diblock copolymer A-B at the center of the interfacial zone.

The conclusions about the stabilization of polymeric oil/oil by block copolymers derived from this model and in agreement with our experimental results can be summarized as follows:

– the necessary, but not sufficient, requirement is that the block copolymer Cop A-B is centered in the interfacial zone; this requirement is met if the composition of the copolymer is such that $\overline{DP}_A/\overline{DP}_B = \chi_{BS}/\chi_{AS}$, where $\overline{DP}$ corresponds to the blocks of the copolymer and χ to the respective interaction parameters
– the thickness Δ of the interfacial zone indicates that the block copolymer must have a high enough molecular weight to remain at the interface with a part of each block in the corresponding homopolymer-solvent phase.

In a first approximation it can therefore be assumed that the molecular weight of the block copolymer must be such as:

$$\overline{Rg_A} + \overline{Rg_B} \geqslant \Delta$$

where $\overline{Rg}$ are the radii of gyration of both blocks.

This fact explains why, upon dilution of a ternary sytem, which increases Δ by approaching the phase separation limit, block copolymers of higher and higher molecular weights must be used for the stabilization of polymeric emulsions.

As a general rule, the thickness Δ of the interfacial zone is in the following order:

polymeric emulsions > oil/oil systems > water/oil systems

which means that to stabilize polymeric emulsions, higher molecular weight block copolymers are needed than for the stabilization of oil/oil and oil/water emulsions.

At this point it is interesting to notice that for these systems the interfacial tensions (γ_i) vary in the reversed order such as:

water/oil system $>$ oil/oil system/polymeric emulsions

These studies clearly demonstrate that block copolymers, due to their amphiphilic character, largely surpass conventional surfactants and they are suitable for the various emulsion systems especially oil/oil and polymeric emulsions in which classical, low molecular weight surfactants lack emulsifying activity.

4   SOLID STATE PROPERTIES

Block copolymers with incompatible sequences exhibit characteristic morphological behavior and interesting properties, owing to microdomain formation in the solid state. The conditions for microphase separation and equilibrium domain size in the solvent free systems for the well known spherical, cylindrical and lamellar morphology of di- and triblock copolymers, are predictable in terms of the interaction parameters and the molecular characteristics of the copolymer[30, 31].

It has been established, especially by electron microscopy, small angle X-ray scattering (SAXS) and X-ray diffraction, that the segregated microphases can be spheres, cylinders or lamellae depending on the composition of the block copolymer. These mesomorphic structures have been studied extensively, particularly for styrene-diene block copolymers.

As an extension of these studies of microdomain formation, we have examined the mesomorphic structures

– for triblock copolymers of type poly A – block – poly B – block – poly C
– for functionalized block copolymers of the following type

$$\begin{array}{cc} \text{poly A} & \text{poly B} \end{array}$$

where $\bigotimes$ are – SO$_3$Na, COONa groups.

A typical example of an A-B-C triblock copolymer is that of polystyrene – block – polyisoprene – block – poly(methylmethacrylate) for which combined mesomorphic structures can be shown, as indicated schematically in Figure 8 and by the microphotograph given in Figure 9.

As demonstrated by Kotaka et al.[46] such A-B-C triblock or C-B-A-B-C pentablock copolymers might be a new approach to thermoplastic elastomers, as these kind of products exhibit interesting rheological and mechanical properties.

A similar type of a three phase system can be achieved with functionalized di- and triblock copolymers, where in addition to the mesomorphic structures formed by the poly A and poly B blocks, the ionic groups have a tendency to aggregate and thus to form ionic clusters, as it is well known from ionomer polymeric systems. This combination of the mesomorphic

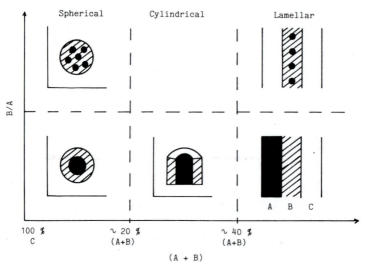

Figure 8   Schematic representation of the mesomorphic structures of A-B-C triblock copolymers as a function of composition; ■ phase formed by A blocks, ▨ phase formed by B blocks, □ phase formed by C blocks

$$\frac{B}{A} = \frac{\text{volume fraction B}}{\text{volume fraction A}} \quad (A+B) = \text{volume fraction of (A and B). Reproduced with permission (1)}$$

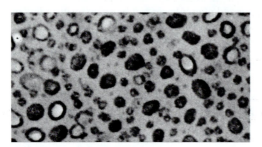

Figure 9   Core-shell morphology. Electron micrograph of an OsO_4-stained ultra-microtomed section of polystyrene-block-polyisoprene-block-poly(methyl methacrylate); $\overline{M}_n$ = 150,000. Composition : 72 wt % : polystyrene; 13 wt % polyisoprene; and 15 wt % poly(methyl methacrylate). Magnification : 126,500 (32) OsO_4 stained

structures, arising from the block structure of the copolymer, and the ionic clusters, formed by the association of $-SO_3Na$ or $COONa$ groups, are indicated schematically in Figure 10.

As another approach to a novel type of thermoplastic elastomers, which can be considered in some respects as model systems for oil extended S-B-S thermoplastic elastomers, we have examined the selective plasticization of A-B and A-B-A block copolymers, where A is poly(methylmethacrylate) and B polystyrene[33]. Because block copolymers form mesomorphic two-phase systems, it is possible to plasticize selectively either the continuous or the dispersed phase of the material.

With increasing amounts of selective plasticizer for the one or the other phase, we have the unique possibility to vary continuously the properties of the matrix or of the dispersed phase of the block copolymer system.

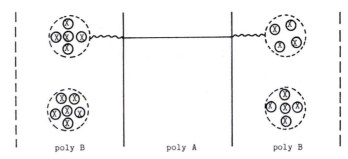

| poly B | poly A | poly B |

Figure 10   Functionalized di- and triblock copolymer

poly A   poly B

where $\otimes$ is SO$_3$Na, COONa, . . . Formation of ionic clusters in a mesomorphic block copolymer structure. Schematic representation of a lamellar structure containing ionic clusters

TABLE III   Characteristics of Selective Plasticizers for Polystyrene – Poly(methylmethacrylate) Block Copolymers PS – PMMA

Plasticizer type	Selectivity for	Molecular weight	Refractive index 25 °C	Melting point °C	Trade name
Di isobutyl azelate	PS	300	1.435	− 30	Hallco 3880 C.P. Hall Corp.
Ethylene glycol monobutylether stearate	PS	384	1.446	16 ± 1	KP 23 FMC Corp.
poly(oxypropylene)-*block*-poly(oxyethylene)	PMMA	3,000	1.46	16	Pluronic L 64 Wyandotte Chemical Corp.

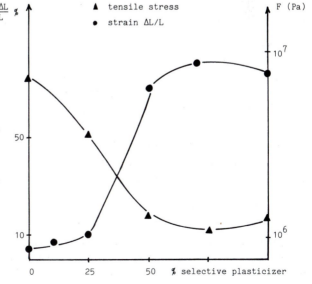

Figure 11   Tensile properties (tensile stress F at rupture and strain $\Delta L/L$) for a polystyrene-block-poly(methylmethacrylate) copolymer (Cop PS-PMMA) with a selectively plasticized PMMA phase. Cop PS-PMMA 39 wt % PS $\overline{M}_n$ = 330,000. Selective plasticizer : 0 to 100 % Pluronic L 64 with respect to the PMMA phase. Strain rate : 146 mm/min T = 25 °C. Reproduced with permission (33)

The characteristics of the selective plasticizers for polystyrene-poly(methylmethacrylate) block copolymers are given in Table III.

Figure 11 gives as an example the tensile properties of a polystyrene – block – poly(methyl-methacrylate) copolymer (Cop PS-PMMA) as a function of increasing amounts of selective plasticizer (Pluronic PL 64) for the PMMA phase.

5   POLYMER BLENDS – MORPHOLOGY REGULATION IN POLYMERIC TWO–PHASE SYSTEMS

The principle of polymeric oil/oil emulsions described previously can be considered as the starting point for the preparation of two-phase or multiphase polymer blends. In fact, blending of block copolymers with other polymers, either homopolymers or copolymers, is an industrially useful technique for the production of new polymeric materials, with desired physical characteristics.

Such blends can be classified as follows:

Binary systems	Ternary system
Cop (A, B) + poly A	Cop (A, B) + poly A + poly B
Cop (A, B) + poly C	Cop (A, B) + poly A + poly C
Cop (A, B) + Cop (A, B)'	Cop (A, B) + poly C + poly D
Cop (A, B) + Cop (A, C)	
Cop (A, B) + Cop (C, D)	

where:

– Cop (A, B) is a (A, B) diblock, triblock, or multiblock copolymer
– poly A is a homopolymer of same type as the A sequence of Cop (A, B)
– poly C is a homopolymer, compatible or incompatible with either the sequences of Cop (A, B)
– Cop (A, B)' is a random, graft or block copolymer having the same monomer units as in Cop (A, B)
– Cop (C, D) is a random, graft or block copolymer having different monomer units than in Cop (A, B).

Thus depending on the constituent polymers, two-phase or multiphase systems can be formed with these combinations.

For such two-phase or multiphase polymeric systems, block copolymers have as characteristic role:

– on the one hand, because of their interfacial activity, they act as emulsifiers, by means of which it is possible to regulate the particle size of the dispersed phase of the polymer blend
– on the other hand, as a block copolymer can be located at the interface of a two-phase systems, an *"anchoring"* between the phases can be achieved, leading generally to a dramatic improvement of the mechanical properties of the material.

In addition, as a result of the inherent property of block copolymers to form mesomorphic structures, it has become possible recently to design polymer blends with new and unique morphologies.

One of the first examples illustrating the emulsifying properties of block copolymer blends has been given for the ternary system

poly A + poly B + Cop (A, B)

where: poly A is polystyrene
poly B is polyisoprene or poly(methylmethacrylate)
Cop (A, B) is the corresponding di- or triblock copolymer[34, 35].

Figure 12 gives a typical representation of such a ternary system formed by polystyrene (PS), polyisoprene (PI) and the corresponding PS-PI block copolymer, which can be considered as a model system for rubber modified thermoplastics.

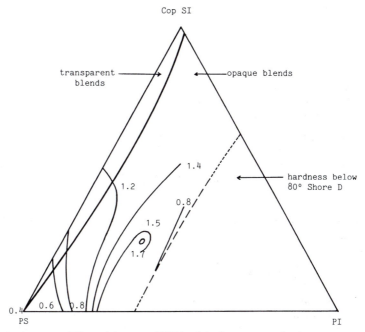

Figure 12   Properties of polystyrene (PS) – polyisoprene (PI) blends in the presence of polystyrene-block-polyisoprene (Cop PS-PI). Characteristics of ternary blends : polystyrene $\overline{M}_w$ = 91,000; polyisoprene, $\overline{M}_w$ = 50,000; and polystyrene-block-polyisoprene, $\overline{M}_n$ = 146,000; 59 wt % polystyrene (compression-molded samples after solution blending of the polymeric components). —, limit between transparent and opaque blends; –, contour lines corresponding to blends of the same impact resistance (Charpy method); impact resistance is indicated in arbitrary units; and ---, hardness limit corresponding to 80° Shore D. Reproduced with permission (1)

The emulsifying effect of block copolymers in such systems, appears on a qualitative level quite readily by checking the transparency of the polymer blend. In fact, transparency for a two-phase system, formed by two amorphous and incompatible polymers of different refractive indexes, can be achieved by reducing the particle size of the dispersed phase below a certain limit, generally below 500 to 800 nm, where the intensity of the scattered light becomes practically negligible.

More sophisticated techniques, such as electron microscopy with selective staining of one of the phases, SAXS, small angle neutron scattering (SANS) have confirmed the emulsifying properties of block copolymers in polymer blends[36, 37].

An additional proof that a block copolymer is usually located at the interface of the two polymer phases, and thus achieving an anchoring between these phases, has been given by UV fluorescence techniques[38].

Block copolymers of the following structure

$$
\begin{array}{c}
CH_3 \\
| \\
\text{——}(CH_2 - CH)\text{——}\text{ww}\, CH_2 - C = CH - CH_2 \,\text{ww}\, CH_2 - CH_2
\end{array}
$$

giving a blue UV fluorescence have been used in these experiments to demonstrate their interfacial activity in polymer blends.

Furthermore, it has been shown that the mechanical properties of such a two-phase polymer blend depend upon the characteristics of the matrix, the volume fraction and the viscoelastic properties of the dispersed rubber phase, the particle size and the size distribution, the morphology of the rubber phase and finally of the interfacial characteristics, particularly the "anchoring" between the phases which can be achieved by a block copolymer located at the interface. The parameters, morphology, size and interfacial characteristics, largely depend on the concentration and the type of block copolymer incorporated as so called "compatibilizer" in the polymer blend. It must, however, be kept in mind that the optimum efficiency for a block copolymer as surfactant and anchoring agent between the phases is obtained only by adjusting its characteristics (structure, composition, molecular weight) to the constituent polymers of the blend.

Concerning the morphology of two-phase blends, Holden[39] has already noticed, in the case of S-B-S and S-I-S blended with various polymers, that the preparation technique for blending has a tremendous influence on the final mechanical properties of the material. Because of differences in morphology, e. g. formation of discrete particles as dispersed phase or interpenetrating networks, compression-molded samples might not show the same mechanical properties as injection-molded or extruded samples.

In fact, concerning the preparation techniques of polymer blends, one has to consider:

– melt-mixing in an extruder or calendering
– solution blending, which is usually a laboratory technique
– *in situ* formation by polymerization of the one or the other components of the polymer blend.

This last technique, which is industrially applied in the preparation of rubber modified thermoplastics like "High Impact Polystyrene" (HIPS) or ABS resins, has the main advantage that by starting with a relatively low viscosity system it is easier to regulate the morphology and the interfacial characteristics of the blend, and thus its mechanical properties.

A typical example of *in situ* formed polymer blend is that of HIPS, which is generally prepared by starting with a solution of 4 – 10 % elastomer dissolved in styrene, followed by a free radical type polymerization. Owing to the incompatibility of polystyrene (PS) and polybutadiene (PB), a phase separation occurs shortly after the beginning of the polymerization leading to a typical polymeric oil/oil emulsion, with (PS + styrene) as the dispersed phase and (PB + styrene) as the continuous medium, which usually inverts during the course of polymerization.

The detailed procedure with its characteristic features, e. g. phase separation, phase inversion, *in situ* formation of graft copolymers, emulsifying effect of block and graft copolymers, has been given elsewhere[40]. The final product, after complete polymerization of styrene, consists of a continous PS phase and a discontinuous elastomer phase, generally of spherical shape with typical occlusions of PS particles.

A typical example of such classical HIPS structure is given in Figure 13.

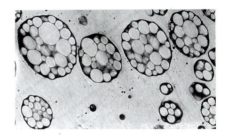

Figure 13   Electron micrograph of rubber modified polystyrene (HIPS). Magnification: 8,900. Courtesy of CdF Chimie (France)

More recently, it has been shown that the replacement of PB by styrene-butadiene di- and triblock copolymers in the HIPS procedure, leads to new types of elastomer modified polymers, having special two-phase morphologies.

A systematic approach of this morphology problem has been made by Echte[41], Riess et al.[40,42], and Eastmond et al.[43].

The typical morphologies obtained by using styrene-butadiene block copolymers of S-B-S and B-S-B type of various compositions are indicated schematically in Figure 14.

The structures indicated in Figure 14 can also be obtained with S-B or suitable combinations of two S-B block copolymers using techniques which cannot yet be disclosed in detail. Examples are given in Figure 15.

SBS   BSB

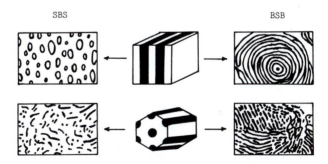

Figure 14   High impact polystyrene based on SBS and BSB block copolymers. Schematic representation of the different morphologies as a function of the mesomorphic structure of the block copolymer. – Polymerization in the absence of grafting reaction, also called "simulated polymerization". Figure drawn according to Echte et al.[41], with permission. Polybutadiene shown in black, polystyrene white

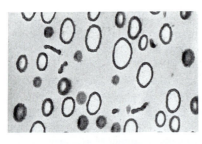

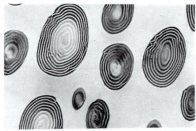

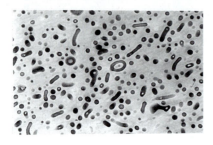

Figure 15   Electron micrographs of typical HIPS morphologies corresponding to Echte's scheme. Magnification : 25,500

(a) Core-shell morphology of HIPS. Sample prepared by polymerization of styrene in the presence of 10 % wt. S-B block copolymer. Polystyrene content of block copolymer 48 % wt., $\overline{M}_n$ = 225,000; initiator AIBN

(b) Onion skin morphology of HIPS. Sample prepared by solvent evaporation or polymerization in the absence of grafting (simulated polymerization). Final composition 75 % wt. polystyrene. 12.5 % wt. S-B block copolymers with 48 % wt. polystyrene $\overline{M}_n$ = 225,000. 12.5 % wt. S-B block copolymer with 52 % wt. polystyrene $\overline{M}_n$ = 78,000

(c) HIPS morphology obtained by polymerization of styrene in the presence of 25 % wt. S-B block copolymer with same characteristics as for 15 (a); initiator benzoyl peroxide
Polybutadiene stained black, polystyrene shows white.
Courtesy CdF Chimie (France), with permission[1]

The microphotographs in Figure 15 show some of these morphologies for HIPS prepared in the presence of styrene-butadiene block copolymers.

Some grades of these materials, in particular those of core-shell morphology, have already gained commercial importance, because these types of HIPS provide toughness and transparency, which is not the case for classical elastomer modified polystyrene.

For such HIPS with core-shell structure, which can also be obtained by suitable combinations of two styrene-butadiene block copolymers, in the presence of PS, it has been shown by Marti et al.[44] that the thickness (Δ) of the elastomer shell is directly related to the average molecular weight ($\overline{M}_n$) as follows:

$$\Delta = KM^{0.66}$$

where K is a constant taking into account the composition of the block copolymer system.

An interesting extension has been proposed by Tung et al.[45], who describes a procedure in which PS, as well as the styrene-butadiene block copolymers, are formed in situ during the free radical polymerization of styrene. Polybutadiene endcapped with – SH functional groups that act as chain transfer agents was used in this study.

6 CONCLUSIONS

This review illustrates at first the large range of techniques existing at present for the preparation of "tailor-made" block copolymers, which enable the control of the structure, the molecular weight and the composition. Of the variety of methods, anionic polymerization is, the most suitable leading to well-defined copolymers in good yield. Other techniques, such as cationic polymerization, polycondensation or free radical initiated polymerization via chain transfer, although having generally a lower yield, are of industrial interest. Yet for certain applications, e. g. polymeric two-phase systems, only small amounts of block copolymers might be required to achieve the desired properties of the final product.

Because of their amphiphilic characteristics, leading to unique surface-active properties, block copolymers largely surpass the possibilities of conventional emulsifiers. In fact, block copolymers are suitable for the preparation of a large variety of emulsion systems, such as oil/oil, polymeric oil/oil and polymeric water/water emulsions, in which classical low molecular weight surfactants lack emulsifying activity.

These special interfacial characteristics have rendered block copolymers very useful as dispersants, emulsifiers, wetting agents, solubilizers, etc., in many industrial applications, particularly in polymeric two-phase or multiphase systems. Many problems associated with two-phase systems, either liquid-liquid, liquid-solid or solid-solid can be approached with adapted block copolymers.

In addition to thermoplastic elastomers, where the block copolymer is the major component of the material, their importance is likely to increase with the development of applications as polymeric surfactants and as "building materials" for new types of polymer blends.

References

1. G. Riess, P. Bahadur and G. Hurtrez, *Encyclopedia of Polymer Science and Engineering, 2,* 324 (1985) Second Edition; John Wiley and Sons, New York
2. M. Szwarc, M. Levy and R. Milkovich, J. Am. Chem. Soc., *78,* 2656 (1956), see also A. F. Halasa, *Rubber Chem. and Techn. 54,* 627 (1981), M. Szwarc, *Polym. Chem. Div.* Preprints 26 (1) 198 (1985)
3. M. S. M. Abadie and D. H. Richards, *Inf. Chim., 208,* 135 (1980)
4. G. Riess and F. Palacin, *IUPAC Helsinki, 1970,* Preprint p. 123, *Inf. Chim., 116,* 9 (1973). J. Brossas, J. M. Catala, G. Clouet and Z. Gallot, *C. R. Acad. Sci. Ser. C 278,* 1031 (1974)
5. Y. Vinchon, R. Reeb and G. Riess, *Eur. Polym. J., 12,* 317 (1976) G. Riess and R. Reeb, *ACS Symp. Ser., 166,* 477 (1981)
6. Z. Tuzar and P. Kratochvil, *Adv. Colloid Interface Sci., 6,* 201 (1976)
7. L. Oranli, P. Bahadur and G. Riess, *Canadian J. Chem., 63* (10) 2691 (1985)
8. G. Riess and D. Rogez, *ACS Polym. Prepr., 23,* 19 (1982)
9. Z. Tuzar, P. Bahadur and P. Kratochvil, *Makromol. Chem., 182* 1751 (1981)
10. A. Rameau, J. P. Lingelser and Y. Gallot, *Makromol. Chem. Rapid Commun., 3,* 413 (1982)
11. Z. Tuzar, B. Bednar, C. Konak, M. Kubin, S. Svobodova and K. Prochazka, *Makromol. Chem., 183,* 399 (1982)
12. D. Wilson and G. Riess, *Polymer* in press
13. M. Schlienger, Thesis University of Haute-Alsace, Mulhouse, France (1976)
14. M. Ossenbach-Sauter, Thesis University of Haute-Alsace, Mulhouse, France (1981)
15. D. Rogez, P. Bahadur and G. Riess, *Int. Symp. on Copolymers and Emulsion Polymerization,* Lyon (France), March 6–9, 1984: CNRS: Preprint p. 138–140
16. C. Price, A. L. Hudd, C. Booth and B. Wright, *Polymer, 23,* 650 (1982)
17. C. Price, A. L. Hudd, R. B. Stubbersfield and B. Wright, *Polymer, 21,* 9 (1980)

18. G. Wegner, *Makromol. Kolloquium Freiburg* (FRG), March 1984
19. I. R. Schmolka, *J. Am. Oil Chem. Soc., 54,* 110 (1977)
20. A. A. Al-Saden, T. L. Whateley and A. R. Florence, *J. Colloid Interface Sci., 90,* 303 (1982)
21. J. Selb and Y. Gallot, *Makromol. Chem., 181,* 2605 (1980); *182,* 1491, 1513 (1981)
22. D. J. Wilson, private communication
23. J. Periard, A. Banderet and G. Riess, *Polym. Lett., 8,* 109 (1970)
24. J. Periard, G. Riess and M. J. Neyer-Gomez, *Eur. Polym. J., 9,* 687 (1973)
25. G. E. Molau, *J. Polym. Sci. Part A, 3,* 1263 (1965)
26. P. Gaillard, M. Ossenbach-Sauter and G. Riess, in K. Solc Ed., *Polymer Compatibility and Incompatibility,* Vol. 2, Harwood Academic, New York, 1982, p. 289
27. P. J. Flory, *Principles of Polymer Chemistry,* Cornell University, Ithaca, New York, 1953
28. A. Vrij, *J. Polym. Sci Part A 2,* 1919 (1968)
29. A. Vrij and G. J. Roeberson, *J. Polym. Sci. Polym. Phys. Ed., 15,* 109 (1977)
30. D. J. Meier, *J. Polym. Sci. Part C, 26,* 81 (1969)
31. D. J. Meier, in J. J. Burke and V. Weiss Eds., *Block and Graft Copolymers,* Syracuse University, Syracuse, N. Y., 1973, p. 105
32. G. Riess, M. Schlienger and S. Marti, *J. Makromol. Sci. Phys., 17,* 355 (1980)
33. J. Periard, A. Banderet and G. Riess, *Angew. Makromol. Chem., 15,* 37 (1971)
34. G. Riess, J. Kohler, C. Tournut and A. Banderet, *Makromol. Chem., 101,* 58 (1967)
35. J. Kohler, G. Riess and A. Banderet, *Eur. Polm. J., 4,* 173, 187 (1968)
36. T. Inoue, T. Soen, T. Hashimoto and H. Kawai, *Macromolecules, 3,* 87 (1970)
37. H. Kawai, T. Hashimoto, K. Miyoshi, T. Uno and M. Fujimura, *J. Macromol. Sci. Phys., 17,* 427 (1980)
38. G. Riess, *Ind. Chim. Belg., 37,* 1097 (1972)
39. G. Holden, *"Recent Advances in Polymer Blends, Grafts and Blocks"* Ed. L. Sperling, P. 269, Plenum (1974)
40. G. Riess and P. Gaillard, in K. H. Reichert and W. Geiseler Eds., *Polymer Reaction Engineering – Influence of Reaction Engineering on Polymer Properties,* Hanser, Munich, 1983, p. 221
41. A. Echte, *Angew. Makromol. Chem., 58–59,* 175 (1977)
42. S. Marti and G. Riess, *Makromol. Chem., 179,* 2569 (1978)
43. G. C. Eastmond and D. G. Philips, in D. Klempner and K. C. Frisch Eds., *Polymer Alloys,* Polymer Science Technology Series, *Vol. 10,* Plenum, New York, 1977, p. 147
44. S. Marti, A. Pavan and G. Riess, *Angew. Makromol. Chem.,* in press
45. L. H. Tung, G. Y-S. Lo and J. A. Griggs (Dow Chemical, Midland, Mich.), lecture present at Central Michigan University, 1982
46. K. Arai, T. Kotaka, Y. Kitano and K. Yoshimura, *Macromolecules, 13,* 1053 (1980)

Chapter 12

RESEARCH ON THERMOPLASTIC ELASTOMERS

Section 3

ORDER-DISORDER TRANSITION IN BLOCK POLYMERS

T. Hashimoto

Contents

T. Hashimoto, Department of Polymer Chemistry, Faculty of Engineering, Kyoto University, Kyoto 606, Japan

1   INTRODUCTION

The simplest (A–B) block copolymers such as poly(styrene-b-isoprene) (S–I) and poly(styrene-b-butadiene) (S–B) are amorphous and nonpolar. There exist only London's dispersive interactions among A–A, A–B and B–B interactions. The difference in the cohesive energy densities between the segments A and B results in the net repulsive interactions between A and B which are described in terms of Flory-Huggins thermodynamic interaction parameters in the mean-field approximation[1].

In the "ordered state" such block copolymers form "microdomains" with a long-range order having a spatial periodicity D of the order of the size of the polymer coil[2], as characterized by the radius of gyration of the block polymer R_g. They can also form a homogeneous structure in which the segments A and B are molecularly mixed in the "disordered state". The transition from the disordered state to the ordered state is a phenomenon known as "microphase separation" and, as a consequence of the microphase separation, the microdomain structures are evolved. The transition from the ordered state to the disordered state is known as a "microphase dissolution".

Nature of order-disorder transition of block copolymers has recently been explored quite extensively[3–9]. It is a fundamental problem from both industrial and academic view points.

Industrially it is associated with processability and performances of block copolymers as thermoplastic elastomers[10–13], pressure sensitive hot-melt adhesives[22], viscosity stabilizers for oils and so on[14]. At processing temperatures, e.g., typically 170 to 180 °C some block polymers can be in disordered state and in this case their melt viscosities are relatively low, which gives great advantage in processability and in the interfacial wetting between the adhesives and the substrates[22].

On the other hand, if they are in ordered state at processing temperature, they will exhibit high viscosity and quite remarkable non-Newtonian flow behavior[15–22], which causes difficulty in the processing. At service temperatures, they are in ordered state. The dispersed domains of polystyrene block chains act as reinforcing fillers for the elastomer phase[10–14] and hence improve the performances as elastomers and adhesives. When small amounts of similar block polymers are added to oil they are molecularly dissolved in the oil at higher temperature. This dissolution increases the viscosity of the oil and hence counterbalances the normal loss of viscosity of oils at higher temperatures. Upon lowering temperature, the block polymers form micelles or droplets. The transition from molecularly dissolved state to the micellar state reduces the viscosity of the oils and thus counterbalances the normal viscosity increase at lower temperature[14].

The order-disorder transition of block copolymers is important also from academic view points, because it is related to structure and structure evolution (ordering) and dissolution (disordering) in a cooperative system, a fundamental problem in equilibrium and non-equilibrium statistical physics in the condensed state. To predict the order-disorder transition of block copolymers, the physics developed for the cooperative phenomena in atomic or small molecular systems have to be generalized to properly take into account the connectivity between similar and dissimilar monomeric units, i.e., the connectivity of monomers A (B) in A (B) block sequence and the connectivity between the block sequence A and the block sequence B at their ends.

2   NATURE OF ORDER-DISORDER TRANSITION OF BLOCK COPOLYMERS

The order-disorder transition of the block copolymers is a thermodynamic transition which is controlled by counterbalancing two physical factors i.e., the energetics and the entropy. This is common to all the order-disorder transition in atomic or small molecular systems such as metallic alloys, lattice gas and ferromagnetic materials[36].

Figure 1 illustrates schematically the order-disorder transition in A–B diblock copolymers. In the ordered state A and B segments segregate themselves in A and B microdomains. However, because of molecular connectivity the segregation would not result in macroscopic phase separation into two coexisting macrosopic liquid phases as in the mixture of A and B but rather results in a regular periodic microdomain with a long-range order as schematically shown in Figure 1(a) (e.g., alternating lamellar microdomains[25]). On the other hand, in the disordered state A and B segments are molecularly mixed as depicted in Figure 1(b).

The characteristics of the ordered state are symbolically depicted in Figure 1(c), where the chemical junctions between A and B block chains are confined in the narrow interfacial region drawn by a series of vertical straight lines with the characteristic interfacial thickness

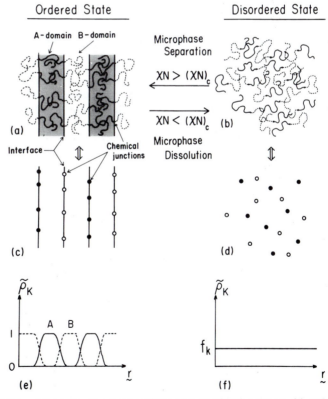

Figure 1   Schematic representation of the order-disorder transition of A–B diblock polymer. (a) and (b) are molecular packing, (c) and (d) are the spatial distribution of the chemical junctions, and (e) and (f) are the spatial distribution of segmental density in the ordered and disordered states, respectively

of about 20 Å for the S–I block copolymers[23, 24a, 24b]. Generally the average end-to-end vectors should orient normal to the interface. The solid and open circles differentiate the orientations of the end-to-end vectors of the block chains. The solid circles represent the junctions with their end-to-end vectors of A segments oriented right and conversly the open circles represent junctions with the A segments oriented left. Thus the block copolymers in the ordered state have the liquidcrystalline characteristics, although the block copolymer molecules themselves are the flexible chains without any mesogenic groups. On the other hand, in the disordered state, the chemical junctions are randomly distributed in space and the orientations of the end-to-end vectors for A and B block chains are also random, as schematically illustrated in Figure 1(d). It should be noted that the systems having the spherical and cylindrical microdomains in the ordered state have essentially identical characteristics to those described above.

The relevant order parameter in such systems may be a reduced spatial segmental density profile $\tilde{\varrho}_K$ (K = A or B) defined as

$$\tilde{\varrho}_K(\underline{r}) = \tilde{\varrho}_K(\underline{r})/\varrho_{Ko} \qquad (K = A \text{ or } B) \tag{1}$$

where $\varrho_K(\underline{r})$ is the spatial segmental density profile for the K-segments and ϱ_{Ko} is that for the pure K-homopolymers. The densities $\tilde{\varrho}_K$ satisfy

$$0 \leq \tilde{\varrho}_K(\underline{r}) \leq 1 \tag{2}$$

and

$$\tilde{\varrho}_A(\underline{r}) + \tilde{\varrho}_B(\underline{r}) = 1 \tag{3}$$

The latter conditions comes from incompressibility[26]. In the ordered state and in the strong segregation limit where D >> t (the characteristic interfacial thickness[23]), the order parameters $\tilde{\varrho}_K$ vary as shown in Figure 1(e), while in the disordered state they satisfy,

$$<\tilde{\varrho}_K>_T = f_K \qquad \text{(disordered state)} \tag{4}$$

where

$$f_K = N_K/(N_A + N_B) = N_K/N \tag{5}$$

where N_K and N are the polymerization indices of K-block chain and the total block polymer, respectively.

The energetics which originated from the repulsive interaction between A and B chains favors the ordered state since the interaction energy can be minimized by the segregation,

$$E_{AB} \alpha k_B T \chi \tilde{\varrho}_A(\underline{r}) \tilde{\varrho}_B(\underline{r}) \tag{6}$$

The segregation in the ordered state, however, has to pay penalty of loss of entropy. There are two kinds of entropy loss: (i) the placement entropy associated with the spatial arrangements of the chemical junctions (the solid and open circles in Figures 1(c) and 1(d) and (ii) the conformational entropy associated with the number of possible states for given chain molecules A and B in the confined domain space[33]. The entropy obviously favors the disordered state. If the energetics outweigh the entropy the systems attain the ordered state. On the other hand, if the entropy outweigh the energetics they attain the disordered state. The equilibrium structure is the one which minimizes the free energy should be "functional"

$$F = F\{\tilde{\varrho}_K(\mathbf{r})\} \tag{7}$$

Let us now consider the order-disorder transition in block copolymers. In the ordered state, the size of the microdomains parallel and perpendicular to the interfaces, the shape of the domains (spheres, cylinders, and lamellae), the thickness of the interfacial region between two coexisting microdomains, and the mixing of unlike segments in each microdomain should all be characterized. In the disordered state, the thermal concentration fluctuations should be characterized. A spectrum of thermal concentration fluctuations with wavelength $D = 2\pi/q$ where q is the wavenumber of particular Fourier component of the fluctuations can be generally analyzed from elastic scattering profiles of neutrons, X-rays and light. In the order-disorder transition, one should characterize the transition point, the kinetics, and the mechanism. In the bulk block copolymers the transition point is found to occur at

$$\chi N = (\chi N)_c \tag{8}$$

where $(\chi N)_c$ depends on f. If the third component S such as solvent, plasticizer, tackifying resin and so on exists in the system, $(\chi N)_c$ is a function of polymer volume fraction Φ_p and χ_{KS} (K = A, B) as well χ where χ_{KS} is the χ-parameter between K and S. It is also found that $(\chi N)_c$ depends upon fraction of the homopolymers A and/or B added to the A–B block polymers[28–31]. As for the mechanism one can think about spinodal decomposition and nucleation and growth as in mixtures of homopolymers[32].

3   EQUILIBRIUM ASPECTS OF ORDER-DISORDER TRANSITION

3.1   Theory

Pioneering work on prediction of the transition point were carried out by Meier[33, 34], Helfand[35], Noolandi and Hong[37]. Leibler[3] has carried out Landau analysis and developed most general theory on the transition point, and phase diagram in weak segregation limit where $D \simeq t$ and the deformation of polymer coils is not significant. He predicted also the thermal concentration fluctuations in the disordered state in the context of random phase approximation. Later on Noolandi and Hong developed the theory of phase equilibria for the mixtures of A–B with A (or B)[28, 37]. Here we will review Leibler's theory.

Figure 2 shows the phase diagram predicted by Leibler[3] for the symmetric A–B diblock polymers where A and B have identical polymerization indices ($N_A = N_B$), segmental densities ($\varrho_{A0} = \varrho_{B0}$), and Kuhn statistical segment lengths $a_A = a_B = a$. He predicted the first-order transition for $f \neq 0.5$ and the second-order transition for $f = 0.5$[65]. At a given χN, i.e., at a given T or N, he predicts morphological changes from spherical domains in body centered cubic lattice, hexagonally packed cylindrical domains, alternating lamellae and their phase-inverted domain structures as f increases from 0 to 1.

The critical point occurs at $f = f_c = \frac{1}{2}$ and $(\chi N)_c$ is equal to 10.5. In case of symmetric polymer/polymer mixture the critical point occurs also at $f_c = \frac{1}{2}$ but $(\chi N)_c$ has the value of 2. It should be noted here that for mixtures, N is defined as $N = N_A = N_B$. However, for the symmetrical block copolymer, N is defined as $N = N_A + N_B = 2N_A = 2N_B$.

Thus

$$(\chi N)_c = \begin{cases} 10.5 & \text{(block polymers, } N = N_A + N_B) \qquad\qquad (9) \\ \\ 2 & \text{(polymer/polymer mixtures, } N = N_A = N_B) \quad (10) \end{cases}$$

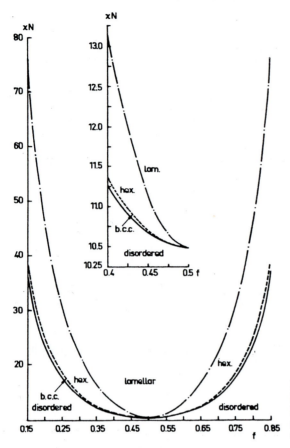

Figure 2 Phase diagram of A–B diblock polymer From Ref. 3, L. Liebler, Macromolecules *13* 1602 (1980), Copyright 1980 American Chemical Soc., with permission

The connectivity between A and B strongly affects the critical point $(\chi N)_c$ and enhances the miscibility of the polymers A and B.

Leibler also presented the theory for thermally induced concentration fluctuations of the block copolymers in the disordered state on the basis of random phase approximation[3]. The structure factor $\tilde{S}(q)$, which is a Fourier transform of the density-density correlation function is given by

$$I(q) \sim \tilde{S}(q) = \left[\frac{S(q)}{W(q)} - 2\chi\right]^{-1} \tag{11}$$

where $S(q)$ and $W(q)$ are given in terms of S_{ij}, the Fourier transform of the density-density correlation functions of the "ideal block copolymer chains" whose properties are given by Gaussian statistics,

$$S(q) = \sum_{i,j=1}^{2} S_{ij}(q) \tag{12}$$

$$W(q) = S_{11}(q)S_{22}(q) - S_{12}^{2}(q) \tag{13}$$

$S_{ij}(q)$'s are given in eqs. IV-2 to IV-4 in reference 3. The scattered intensity $I(q)$ is proportional to $\tilde{S}(q)$.

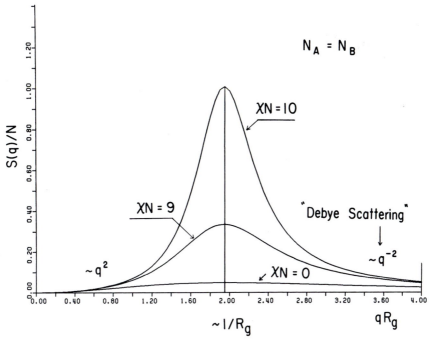

Figure 3   Calculated scattering profiles for A–B diblock polymer with $f = \frac{1}{2}$ ($N_A = N_B = N/2$) and for three different values of χN on the basis of Leibler's theory

Figure 3 shows the calculated structure factor $\tilde{S}(q)/N$ for the case of $N_A = N_B = N/2$, i.e., $f = \frac{1}{2}$ as a function of the reduced scattering vector qR_g where q is the scattering vector defined as

$$q = (4\pi/\lambda)\sin(\Theta) \tag{14}$$

λ and Θ are the wavelength and the scattering angle, respectively, and R_g is the radius of gyration of unperturbed chains

$$R_g^2 = Na^2/6 \tag{15}$$

Two important conclusions may be derived from Figure 3. (1) The scattering profiles exhibited a single scattering maximum at $q = q_m$ even in the disordered state. (2) The q_m value depends on f and R_g,

$$q_m = q_m(f, R_g) \propto 1/R_g \quad \text{(disordered state)} \tag{16}$$

but is independent of χ-parameter and therefore temperature,

$$q_m \propto \chi^0 N^{-1/2} \propto T^0 N^{-1/2} \quad \text{(disordered state)} \tag{17}$$

or

$$D = 2\pi/q_m \propto \chi^0 N^{1/2} \propto T^0 N^{1/2} \quad \text{(disordered state)} \tag{18}$$

If the theory is correct, one can estimate R_g from the peak position of q_m and the χ-parameter by best-fitting the experimental and theoretical scattering profiles and hence extract single chain properties from the thermal concentration fluctuations in bulk. Existence of the scattering maximum is a consequence of the connectivity between A and B. Further physical insight into this maximum has been given elsewhere[38, 31].

3.2   Characterization of Order-Disorder Transition by Scattering Techniques

The conventional techniques such as thermal analysis and volume analysis do not effectively characterize the transition. The small heat of the transition may be related to the molecular connectivity, i.e., a property attributed to the microdomains. Consequently the scattering technique seems to be the best technique for the characterization of the transition.

3.2.1 Principles of the Method

If temperature dependence of χ is given by

$$\chi = A_1 + B_1/T \tag{19}$$

as found in experimental results, then the temperature dependence of the scattered intensity is given by, from eqs. 11 and 19.

$$I^{-1}(q) \propto \frac{S(q)}{W(q)} - 2A_1 - \frac{2B_1}{T} \tag{20}$$

and hence in the disordered state I^{-1} should linearly decrease with T^{-1}. Deviations from linearity are a consequence of the onset of the ordering or the microphase separation. In the disordered state the wavelength of the dominant mode of fluctuations D should satisfy eq. (18) and be independent of T. The increase of D as T decreases is again a consequence of the onset of the transition[7]. Thus the transition point can be doubly checked from the crossover behavior of I^{-1} vs T^{-1} and D vs. T.

3.2.2 Experiments

Figure 4 shows typical small-angle X-ray scattering (SAXS) profiles from the block polymer samples having ordered structure (HS-10) and disordered structure (HK-17)[39]. Both HS-10 and HK-17 are the S–I diblock copolymers. HS-10 has number average molecular weight $M_n = 8.1 \times 10^4$, and $M_w/M_n = 1.13$, and the weight fraction of the polystyrene segment $w_S = 0.50$.

The SAXS profiles were obtained for the as-cast films at room temperature. Although the profiles were plotted on relative intensity scale, the intensity of HK-17 and HS-10 can be compared. HS-10 shows multiple-order scattering maxima from the single lamellar identity period D (= 452 Å)

$$2D \sin \Theta = n \lambda \tag{21}$$

or

$$sD = n \tag{22}$$

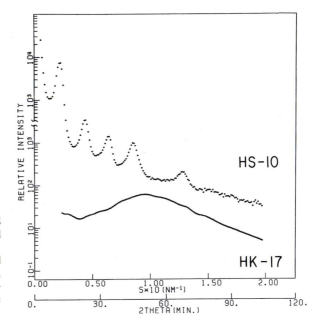

Figure 4 Comparison of the SAXS
profiles of HS-10 (ordered state) and
HK-17 (disordered state)
From Ref. 39, Mori, Hasegawa and
Hashimoto, Polym. J. *17* 799 (1985),
Copyright 1985, The Society of Poly-
mer Science, Japan, with permission

where s is defined as

$$s = q/(2\pi) = (2\sin\Theta)/\lambda \tag{23}$$

and 2Θ is the scattering angle. On the other hand HK-17 shows only the first-order
scattering maximum which is very broad and very weak compared with that of HS-10. The
analyses based on in eqs. 18 and 20 will prove that the scattering from HK-17 is typical to the
scattering from the disordered state.

Since f is about the same for the two polymers, the difference in the two SAXS profiles is
attributed to the effect of the polymerization index. For HK-17, N is small so that χN at
room temperature $(\chi N)_{RT}$ satisfies $(\chi N)_{RT} < (\chi N)_c$. Hence it is in the disordered state.
However, for HS-10, N is large so that $(\chi N)_{RT} > (\chi N)_c$. Hence it is in the ordered state. The
analysis shown in the next section indicates $(\chi N)_{RT} = 10.1$ for HK-17 and 33.5 for HS-10.

The change of the SAXS profiles above and below the order-disorder transition are shown in
Figure 5 for S–B–S triblock copolymer in dioctylphthalate (DOP). The S–B–S used in the
studies was the Shell copolymer KRATON D1102 Thermoplastic Rubber. This has $w_S =$
0.28 and segmental molecular weights of 10,000, 51,000 and 10,000. DOP is a good solvent
for both polystyrene and polybutadiene and is added to lower the order-disorder transition
temperature. The weight fraction of polymer in the solution was 0.6.

Figure 6 shows the behavior of $D = 2\pi/q$ vs. T and of I^{-1} vs. T^{-1} at various temperatures.

Above 90 °C, the system is in the disordered state where I^{-1} changes linearly with T^{-1} and D
is independent of T. Below 90 °C, the system is in the ordered state where the change of I^{-1}
with T^{-1} deviates from the linear relationship and D increases with decreasing T due to a
mechanism as will be clarified in the next section. The horizontal dotted line in Figure 5
indicates the criterion that the profiles above and below the line are those for the ordered
and disordered states, respectively.

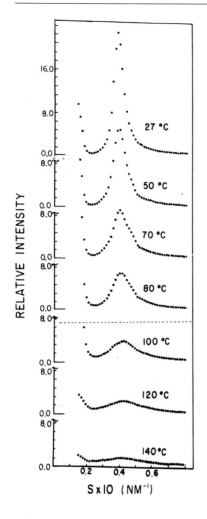

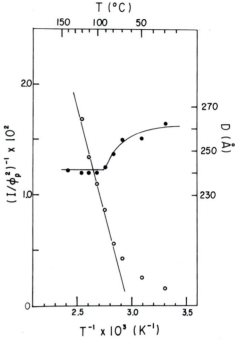

Figure 6   Reciprocal scattered intensity I^{-1} (relative intensity) and the wavelength D of the dominant mode of fluctuations as a function T^{-1} for the same sample as in Figure 5

Figure 5   Scattering intensity profiles for 60 wt % SBS triblock polymer (TR1102) in dioctylphthalate (DOP) at various temperatures. The order-disorder transition temperature T_r is 90 °C (see Figure 6)

The neutral solvent should decrease the effective interaction parameter χ_{eff} between the S and B segments,

$$\chi_{eff} = \chi \Phi_p \tag{24}$$

in the context of mean-field approximation where χ is the interaction parameter of the S and B segments in bulk. Thus in eq. 11 χ should be replaced by χ_{eff}, and the intensity I should be replaced by I/Φ_p for the concentrated solution in a neutrally good solvent. The factor Φ_p in I/Φ_p is associated with the correction for the change of the scattering contrast.

$$I(q)/\Phi_p \sim \left[\frac{S(q)}{W(q)} - 2\chi \Phi_p \right]^{-1} \tag{25}$$

Figure 7 shows the best-fit between the experimental (points) and theoretical SAXS profiles (solid line). The best fit was obtained for the volume fraction of f = 0.248 for the polystyrene phase calculated from w_S and the radius of gyration R_g = 105 A and χN = 30.86. The agreement between the theoretical and experimental profile is good except at small angles

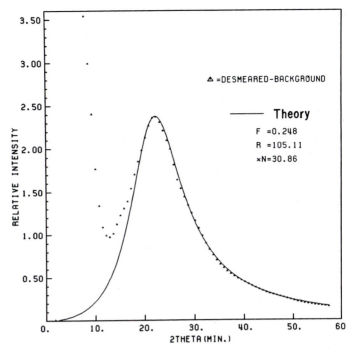

Figure 7   Experimental (dots) and calculated (solid line) scattering curve for the same sample as in Figure 5 at 120 °C. The calculated curve was obtained for $\chi N = 30.86$, $f = 0.248$, and $R_g = 105.11$ Å

where the experimental profile is accompanied by the excess scattering which probably arises from impurities. The effect of the solvent in lowering the order-disorder transition temperature can be estimated as follows,

$$\chi_c \Phi_p = \chi_{co} \tag{26}$$

or from eq. 19

$$\left(A_1 + \frac{B_1}{T_r}\right) \Phi_p = A_1 + \frac{B_1}{T_{ro}} \tag{27}$$

where χ_{co} is the critical value of χ and T_{ro} is the transition temperature when $\Phi_p = 1$, i.e., for bulk block copolymers.

Figure 8 shows temperature dependence of the order-disorder transition temperature measured for the S–B in n-tetradecane from the crossover behaviors of the intensity $I^{-1}(q)$ and D with T^{-1}. The measured T_r linearly increases with increasing polymer concentration Φ_p.

It is interesting to consider the transition temperature of the "tapered" block copolymers in which average monomer fraction of constituent monomer (e.g. A) continuously changes from unity to zero when it is scanned from one end of the block copolymer to the other. Such tapered block polymers are synthesized by a simultaneous copolymerization of styrene and isoprene or styrene and butadiene monomers in certain reaction media using "living" anionic polymerization. Quantitative studies on morphology, viscoelastic properties and polymerization mechanism indicated that they can be approximated by block copolymers with a A-rich random copolymer and a B-rich random copolymer[40-42]. A thermodynamic

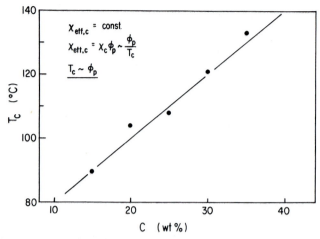

Figure 8   Concentration dependence of the order-disorder transition temperature T_c for SB diblock polymer in n-tetradecane. T_c in the figure is equal to T_r in the text. From Ref. 55, T. Hashimoto, et al, Macromolecules *19*, 754 (1986), Copyright 1986, American Chemical Society, with permission

property such as the order-disorder transition also confirms validity of this approximation; the tapered block polymers has much lower order-disorder transition temperature T_r than the pure block polymers with corresponding N and f.

Table I gives data on a tapered block copolymer of styrene and isoprene prepared by a simultaneous living-anionic polymerization in benzene with a trace amount of tetrahydrofuran. This polymer has $T_r = 150\,°C$, much lower than the corresponding ideal block polymer

TABLE I   Tapered & Ideal Block Copolymers

specimen	$\overline{M}_n \times 10^{-4}$	$\overline{M}_w/\overline{M}_n$	wt % of styrene	polymerization	$T_c(°C)$
Tapered Block	4.3	1.05	47	simultaneous polym. Benzene/THF	150
Ideal Block	4.9	1.13	45	Sequential Polym. THF	>220

Ideal Block: pure S-block/pure I-block
Tapered Block: "Styrene-rich" block/"Isoprene-rich" block

with comparable molecular weight and w_S and prepared by a sequential living anionic polymerization. T_r for the latter is over 220 °C. This is because the effective interaction parameter χ_{eff} between styrene-rich random copolymer (designated as A-block here) and isoprene-rich random copolymer (designated as B-block here) is smaller than χ value for the ideal S–I block[31],

$$\chi_{eff} = \chi(f_{AS} - f_{BS})^2 = \chi(f_{AI} - f_{BI})^2 \tag{28}$$

where f_{AS} and f_{AI} are the fraction of styrene and isoprene monomers in A-block and f_{BS} and f_{BI} are the corresponding fractions in B-block. Thus the T_r will be lowered by a factor associated with $(f_{AS} - f_{BS})^2$ or $(f_{AI} - f_{BI})^2$, i.e.,

$$(A_1 + \frac{B_1}{T_r})(f_{AS} - f_{BS})^2 = A_1 + \frac{B_1}{T_{ro}} \qquad (29)$$

where T_{ro} is the T_r for the ideal block for which $f_{AS} = f_{BI} = 1$ and $f_{AI} = f_{BS} = 0$. For the block polymers with $f_{AS} = f_{BS}$, χ_{eff} vanishes and therefore the ordered state cannot exist.

4 CHANGES OF SPATIAL CONCENTRATION FLUCTUATIONS ACCOMPANIED BY ORDER-DISORDER TRANSITIONS

In this section we discuss the spatial concentration fluctuations $\psi(\underline{r})$ in the disordered state and ordered state. The quantity $\psi(\underline{r})$ which is called as an "order-parameter" describes the thermodynamic state of the systems, since it determines free energy of the systems

$$F = F_o + \Delta F \{\psi(\underline{r})\} \qquad (30)$$

where F_o is the free energy of uniform system and ΔF is the free energy functional of $\psi(\underline{r})$ associated with excess free energy due to fluctuations. The order parameter is defined as the local fluctuation of the reduced segmental density $\bar{\varrho}_A(r)$ from the average reduced segmental density f

$$\psi(\underline{r}) = \delta\varrho_A(\underline{r}) = \bar{\varrho}_A(\underline{r}) - f \qquad (31)$$

The order-parameter $\psi(\underline{r})$ is expanded into a Fourier series,

$$\psi(\underline{r}) = \sum_{\underline{q}} \psi_{\underline{q}} = \sum_{\underline{q}} \psi_{(q)} \exp(i\,\underline{q}\cdot\underline{r}) \qquad (32)$$

where q is the wavenumber of the q-Fourier component.

The excess free energy due to the fluctuation ΔF can be also expanded in powers of the order parameter,

$$\Delta F = F - F_o$$
$$= \sum_{\underline{q}} F(\underline{q})\,|\psi_q|^2 + \Delta F_3 + \Delta F_4 + \ldots \qquad (33)$$

where the first term of the right hand side of eq. 33 is the second-order term, and ΔF_3, ΔF_4 etc. are the third-order and the higher-order term.

In the disordered state, the generation and dissolution of the fluctuations are in dynamic equilibrium and the thermal average of $\psi(\underline{r})$ and its Fourier components $\psi(\underline{q})$ become zero

$$<\psi(\underline{r})>_T = 0 \qquad (34)$$

or

$$<\psi_{\underline{q}}>_T = 0 \qquad (35)$$

where $< >_T$ denotes the thermal average. In the ordered state these two functions have infinite values.

From the scattering theory it is clear that the scattered intensity $I(q)$ at the scattering vector q is related to the intensity of Fourier components with the wavenumber q,

$$I(q) \propto <|\psi_q|^2>_T \tag{36}$$

For the systems which can attain thermal equilibrium, eq. 36 can be calculated on the basis of the Boltzmann statistics[43],

$$<|\psi_q|^2>_T = \int \psi_q^2 \, \exp[-\psi_q^2 F(q)/k_B T] d\psi_q \, /$$

$$\int \exp[-\psi_q^2 F(q)/k_B T] \, d\psi_q$$

$$= \frac{k_B T}{2F(q)} \tag{37}$$

Thus the measurement of the scattering profile $I(q)$ is equivalent to the measurement of the susceptibility, $F(q)^{-1}$, (i.e., the reciprocal of the free energy required to produce unit intensity of the fluctuations, $|\psi_q|^2 = 1$), as a function of q or to the measurement of the spectral distribution of the fluctuations $<|\psi_q|^2>_T$. It is obvious that $<|\psi_q|^2>_T$ is not zero even for the disordered state, though $<\psi_q>_T$ is zero.

4.1 Disordered State

The scattering profiles in the disordered state were presented and discussed to some extent earlier. Here we further extend the discussion for the bulk S–I block polymer designated as HK-17. Figure 9(a) shows the scattering profiles at various temperatures for this polymer[39].

The intensity profile at room temperature for this specimen was presented in Figure 4 using a semi-logarithmic scale, while the profile in Figure 9 for higher temperatures was plotted on a linear scale. Figure 9(b) shows the plots of I^{-1} vs T^{-1} and the wavelength of the dominant mode of the fluctuations $D = 2\pi/q_m$ vs T^{-1} to judge the state of order of the polymer. (The scattering vector q_m is the q at which the scattering intensity becomes maximum).

There are number of important observations which lead us to believe that the polymer sample is in disordered state over the observed temperature range: (i) q_m is independent of temperature, Figure 9(a), and the wavelength D is also independent of temperature, Figure 9(b), (ii) the reciprocal intensity I^{-1} linearly decreases with the reciprocal absolute temperature T^{-1} (the data point at 45 °C is an exception) and (iii) the measured profile are nicely fitted with the theoretical profiles (solid lines in Figure 9 (a)) calculated from eq. 11. The deviation of the data point at 45 °C from the linearity between I^{-1} vs T^{-1} turned out to be caused by vitrification of the disordered sample. In other words, the thermal fluctuations in the disordered state are frozen-in below its glass transition temperature T_g ($T_g \simeq 51$ °C),

$$I(q, T) \propto |\psi_q|^2(T)>_T \qquad \text{at } T > T_g$$
$$\propto |\psi_q|^2(T_g)>_T \tag{38}$$

Origin of the scattering maximum at $q = q_m$ is interpreted as a consequence that the connectivity between S and I segments invokes the minimization of $F(q)$ at $q = q_m$. D and q_m

(a)

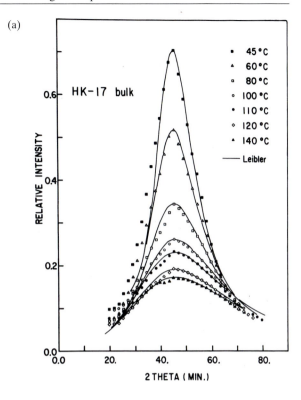

(b)

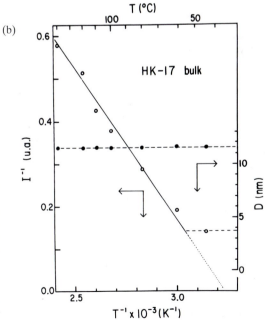

Figure 9   (a) SAXS profiles of HK-17 in the disordered state obtained at various temperatures. The data points and solid lines refer to the experimental and theoretical results, respectively. (b) Reciprocal intensity I^{-1} and the wavelength D of the dominant fluctuations as a function of T^{-1} for HK-17 in the disordered state. From Ref. 39, K. Mori, H. Hasegawa, and T. Hashimoto, Polym. J. *17*, 199 (1985), Copyright 1985, Soc. of Polymer Science, Japan, with permission

are then the most probable wavelength and wavenumber of the fluctuations, whose molecular interpretation will be given elsewhere[31, 38]. It should be noted that the mixtures of the polymers A and B have a minimum F(q) at q = 0, since the smaller the value q, the smaller the gradient free energy $(\nabla\psi(\underline{r}))^2$. Hence I(q) has a maximum at q = 0 rather than at q = q_m.

Fitting the experimental points to theoretical curves as in Figure 9(a) allows us to estimate temperature dependence of χ and R_g. Figure 10 shows the temperature dependence of χ on monomer units estimated by a best-fitting procedure[39]. The χ-value decreases with increasing temperature as shown in the figure in which the straight line is given by

$$\chi = -0.0937 + 66/T \tag{39}$$

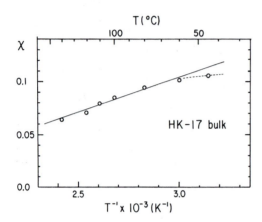

Figure 10   Temperature dependence of the interaction parameter χ on monomer units determined by the best fits of the experimental and theoretical SAXS profiles for HK-17 in bulk and in the disordered state. From Ref. 39, K. Mori, H. Hasegawa, and T. Hashimoto, Polym. J. *17*, 799 (1985), Copyright 1985, Soc. of Polymer Science, Japan, with permission

As the temperature is lowered, the χ-parameter increases and hence the thermal concentration fluctuations increase. Consequently the scattering intensity increases and becomes sharp as the temperature decreases to the order-disorder temperature T_c. However, if $T_c < T_g$, then when the temperature is lowered below T_g, the system cannot attain thermal equilibrium, and the thermal concentration fluctuations are frozen-in at T = T_g. This in turn gives rise to freezing-in of the thermal concentration fluctuations and hence the χ-value estimated by the fitting procedure are independent of temperature below T_g, as drawn by broken curve in Figure 10.

The χ-values and temperature dependences of χ determined here are in a reasonable agreement with those determined from the phase diagrams of corresponding oligomeric mixtures[44] or mixtures based on random copolymers[45]. However, the method presented here may be superior to others, because in the other methods the determination of the binodal line or the cloud point for the bulk specimen is usually difficult, and achievement of the thermal equilibrium is also difficult and time-consuming.

4.2   Ordered State and Transition

Here we consider the concentration fluctuations in the ordered state and their variation when the systems approach toward the disordered state or when the systems change from strong-segregation to weak-segregation regime.

Figure 11 shows a typical transmission electron micrograph showing a long-range order (super-lattice) of the microdomains for the alternating lamellar microdomains of an S–I

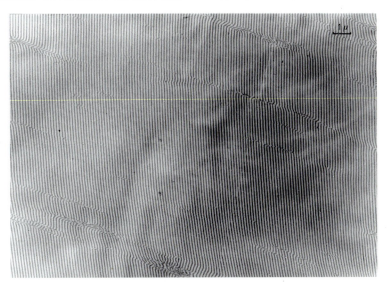

Figure 11   Typical transmission electron micrograph of ultrathin section stained with OsO_4 (SI with M_n = 5.2 × 10⁴, M_w/M_n = 1.16 and w_{PS} = 52).

diblock polymer HY-12 cast from toluene solution (the block polymer has M_n = 52.4 × 10⁴, M_w/M_n = 1.16 and w_S = 0.52). The transmission micrograph was obtained on the ultra-thin section stained by osmium tetroxide, and the bright and dark portions correspond to the unstained PS lamellae and the stained PI lamellae, respectively. Figure 12 schematically represents the spatial concentration fluctuations in the direction normal to the lamellar interfaces where $\tilde{\varrho}_K$ changes periodically with the spacing D, and extensive mixing of the unlike segments A and B occurs only in the narrow interfacial region with the characteristic interfacial thickness $t \simeq 20$ Å. D is the order of radius of gyration R_g of the total block polymer and is much larger than $t^{46, 47}$. Detailed analyses of SAXS also indicate that the

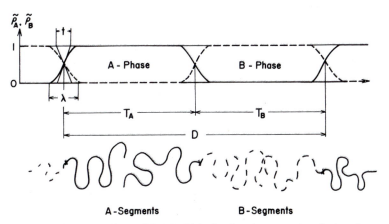

Figure 12   Reduced segmental density profile $\tilde{\varrho}_K$ (K = A, B) in the direction normal to the interface. t and λ are the parameters characterizing the interfacial thickness. From Ref. 46, T. Hashimoto, M. Shibayama and H. Kawai, Macromolecules *13*, 1237 (1980), Copyright 1980, American Chemical Society, with permission

distribution of the domain identity period is much narrower than that of the molecular weight of the block polymers[48], e.g.

$$D_W/D_N - 1 << M_W/M_N - 1 \tag{40}$$

where D_W and D_N are the weight- and number-average domain identity period.

The observations as described above are relevant to those for the strong-segregation limit. The fact that D-values are related to R_g-values originates from the segregation effect and incompressibility. The two physical factors, segregation and incompressibility, give rise to $\frac{2}{3}$ power law on dependence of the domain size on polymerization index.

$$D_A \propto N_A^{2/3} \tag{41}$$

$$D \propto (N_A + N_B)^{2/3} = N^{2/3} \tag{42}$$

where D_A is the size of the A-domain, and D is the domain identity period[46, 47]. The $\frac{2}{3}$-power law has been theoretically predicted by a number of workers[33, 34, 35, 37, 63, 64]. If the two block polymers with different molecular weights are miscible to form a single type of domain morphology, N_A and N are found to be replaced by number average polymerization indices $N_{A,n}$ and N_n, respectively[49].

Let us now consider what happens when repulsive interactions between A and B are weakened by raising the temperature T or by adding neutrally good solvents for both A and B, (i.e., by decreasing the polymer volume concentration Φ_p). In the strong segregation limit where T is low and Φ_p is high, the chains A and B segregate themselves into their respective domains, giving rise to the spatial segmental density profiles as shown in Figure 13(a)[7]. Owing to the repulsive interactions between the chain A and B, they are stretched normal to the interface as shown in Figure 13(b)[7], where the solid and dashed ellipsoids of revolution stand schematically for the segmental clouds of the chains A and B, respectively. The segmental cloud of each chain heavily overlaps those of the chains of the same neighboring polymers. This overlap is both lateral and longitudinal, assuring a uniform overall segmental density everywhere in the domain space.

The stretching of polymers normal to the interface gives rise to the increase of R_g normal to the interface, which, coupled with the incompressibility, gives rise to increase of D_1 and the decrease of the surface-to-volume ratio S/V. The stretching results in the loss of the conformational entropy and the loss of the placement entropy, i.e., the entropy associated with placing the chemical junction in the interfaces. The penalty of the entropy losses tends to be compensated by the gain in reducing the interaction energies associated with S/V.

When T is raised or Φ_p is lowered, χ_{eff} between A and B decreases. Now A-block chains tend to have some walks in the B domains, resulting in a larger value of the domain-boundary thickness t_2 and a smaller end-to-end distance. The latter, together with the incompressibility, results in a smaller domain size and interdomain distance D_2, as shown in Figures 13(d) and (e). The segmental density distribution for a given block copolymer chain is skewed at low T and high Φ_p, as shown in Figure 13(c). It becomes a more symmetric Gaussian-type distribution at high T and low Φ_p, as shown in Figure 13(f), resulting in increased conformational entropy of the block copolymer chains. The increased enthalpy of mixing caused by increasing S/V is outweighed by the increasing conformational entropy and placement entropy. It is important to note that the enthalpy of mixing decreases with increasing T and decreasing Φ_p because of the corresponding changes of χ_{eff} with T and Φ_p.

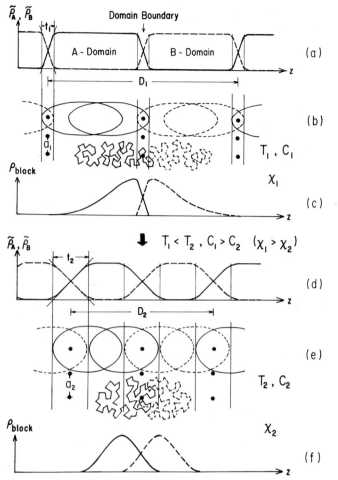

Figure 13   Schematic diagram showing concentration and temperature dependence of the domain size (D_1 and D_2), average nearest-neighbour distance of the junctions along the interface (a_1 and a_2), and spatial segmental density profile of a given block chain in a direction normal to the interface. From Ref. 7, T. Hashimoto, M. Shibayama, and H. Kawai, Macromolecules *16*, 1093 (1983), Copyright 1983, American Chemical Society, with permission

This decrease of the domain size from D_1 and D_2 involves the increase of the average distance between the junctions from a_1 to a_2 as shown in Figures 13(b) and (e).

The pyhsical insight gained above would suggest that the domain size, or the domain identity period D is primarily determined by the segregation power between the chains A and B, i.e., by the effective interaction χ_{eff} between A and B,

$$D \cong D(\chi_{eff}) \tag{43}$$

The greater the value χ_{eff}, the larger the value D. The value D depends also on the chain dimension R_g. However, the concentration and temperature dependence of R_g is much weaker than those of χ_{eff} in the concentration and temperature ranges to be discussed here[50]. For the neutrally good solvents and at higher polymer concentration.

$$\chi_{eff} = \chi\Phi_p \tag{44}$$

Moreover, if χ between A and B in bulk is given by eq. 19, and further approximated by

$$\chi \simeq B_1/T \tag{45}$$

it follows that

$$D \cong D(\Phi_p/T) \tag{46}$$

In this case, the D-value measured at various Φ_p and T should fall onto a single master curve when the D-values are plotted as a function of Φ_p/T. More generally D-values should be plotted as a function of $\chi\Phi_p$, and the increase of T is equivalent to the decrease Φ_p (see eq. 44).

When T is raised and/or Φ_p is lowered, χ_{eff} decreases and approaches to $(\chi_{eff})_c$. This is the weak segregation regime where D and the interfacial thickness become comparable or, in another words, the boundaries between the A and B microdomains are diffuse. If T is further raised and/or Φ_p is further lowered, $\chi_{eff} < (\chi_{eff})_c$, and the systems become disordered as discussed previously.

Figure 14 shows temperature dependence of SAXS[7] from (a) 50 wt % and (b) 40 wt % toluene solution of the S–I block polymer designated L-2 with $M_n = 3.1 \times 10^4$, $M_w/M_n = 1.13$ and $w_S = 0.40$, and Figure 15 shows similar data from a 60 wt % solution[7]. Temperature dependence of SAXS from 15, 20, 25, 29, 47 and 70 wt % toluene or DOP solutions were

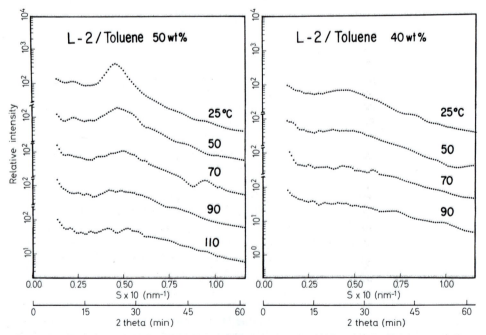

Figure 14   Variations of the SAXS profiles with temperatures for 50(a) and 40 wt % toluene solutions of L-2(b). From Ref. 7, T. Hashimoto, M. Shibayama, and H. Kawai, Macromolecules 16, 1093 (1983), Copyright 1983, American Chemical Society, with permission

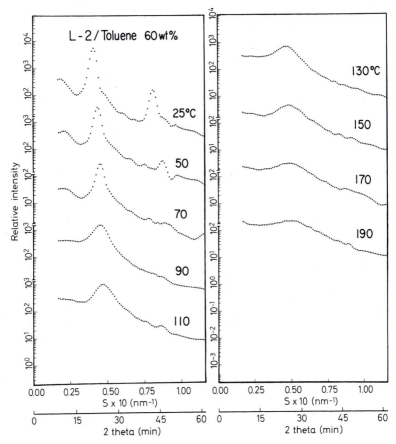

Figure 15   Variations of the SAXS profiles with temperature for a 60 wt % toluene solution of L-2. From Ref. 7, T. Hashimoto, M. Shibayama, and H. Kawai, Macromolecules *16*, 1093 (1983), Copyright 1983, American Chemical Society, with permission

measured also for the S–I block copolymer designated L-8. This has $M_n = 9.4 \times 10^4$ and $w_S = 0.50$. Figure 16 represents the wavelength of the dominant mode of fluctuations D of the block copolymer solutions at various Φ_p's as a function of T for (a) L-8 and (b) L-2[7], while Figures 17 and 18 represent the plots $(I/\Phi_p{}^2)^{-1}$ with T^{-1} to check the state of order for the solutions of these block copolymers[7]. In Figures 17 and 18, the intensity I denotes I(q) at q = q_{max} in arbitrary units, and T_c stands for the transition temperature.

In Figure 16 the D-values generally appear to first decrease with increasing temperature until they fall to a constant value which is independent of Φ_p but is dependent on molecular weight (cf. constant values D $\simeq$ 36 and 21 nm, for L-8 and L-2, respectively). The decrease of D with increasing T for a given Φ_p and the decrease of D with decreasing Φ_p at given T are the consequence of decreasing segregation power, see eq. 44 and Figure 13.

The regime where D = $2\pi/q_m$ is independent of T and Φ_p is the one where the block polymers are in the disordered state. This point is further confirmed in Figures 17 and 18. For example, for L-8 specimens I^{-1} linearly decreases with T^{-1} for 15 and 20 wt % solutions at all the temperature range covered and for 25 wt % solution at temperatures higher than

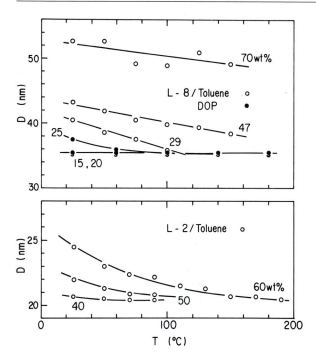

Figure 16   Temperature dependence of the wavelength D of the dominant mode of the fluctuations for 15, 20 and 25 wt % DOP solutions and 29, 47 and 70 wt % toluene solutions of L-8 (a) and for 40, 50 and 60 wt % toluene solutions of L-2(b). From Ref. 7, T. Hashimoto, M. Shibayama, and H. Kawai, Macromolecules 16, 1093 (1983), Copyright 1983, American Chemical Society, with permission

100 °C, see Figure 17. These temperature and concentration ranges are identical to those where the relation,

$$D = 2\pi/q_{m} \sim (\Phi_{p}/T)^{0} \quad \text{(disordered state)} \tag{47}$$

is observed in Figure 16(a). For L-2 specimen the linear decrease of I^{-1} with T^{-1} was observed over the whole temperature range for 40 wt % solution and at T > 90 °C for 50 wt % solutions. The relation of eq. 47 is again observed in Figure 16(b). From this behavior we conclude that in Figure 14(a) the profiles below and above 90 °C are those from the ordered and disordered states respectively, while all the profiles in Figure 14(b) are from

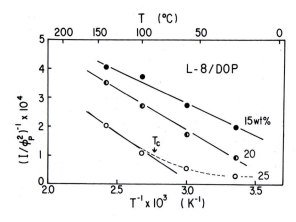

Figure 17   Variations of $(I/\Phi_{p}^{2})^{-1}$ with T^{-1} for 15, 20 and 25 wt % DOP solutions of L-8. T_{c} stands for the order-disorder transition temperature T_{r}. From Ref. 7, T. Hashimoto, M. Shibayama, and H. Kawai, Macromolecules 16, 1093 (1983), Copyright 1983, American Chemical Society, with permission

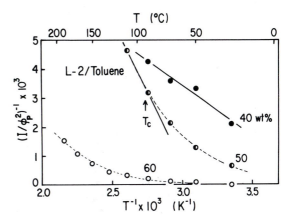

Figure 18   Variation of $(I/\Phi_p^2)^{-1}$ with T^{-1} for 40, 50 and 60 wt % toluene solutions of L-2. T_c stands for the order-disorder transition temperature T_r. From Ref. 7, T. Hashimoto, M. Shibayama, and H. Kawai, Macromolecules 16, 1093 (1983), Copyright 1983, American Chemical Society, with permission

the disordered state and all the profiles in Figure 15 are from the ordered state. The comparison of the wavelength D of L-8 and L-2 in disordered state should give dependence of D with $N^{1/2}$, which, together with eq. 47 predicts following scaling rule in the disordered state

$$D \propto N^{1/2}(\Phi_p/T)^0 \quad \text{(disordered state)} \tag{48}$$

Figure 19[7] shows a plot of D values for L-2 and L-8 at various values of Φ_p and T. In Figure 19(a) logarithms of D/b are plotted as a function of logarithms Φ_p/T and in Figure 19(b) logarithms of $D/bZ^{1/2}$ are plotted as a function of x/x_c where b is Kuhn statistical segment length, Z is the polymerization index (Z = N), and x and x_c are defined as follows:

$$x = \Phi_p/T \tag{49}$$

$$x_c = (\Phi_p/T)_c \tag{50}$$

As shown in Figure 19(a) for both polymers the D-values measured at various values of Φ_p/T nicely fall onto a single master curve when they are plotted as a function of Φ_p/T. D follows the relationship given by eq. 47 in the disordered state and in the ordered state

$$D \simeq (\Phi_p/T)^{1/3} \tag{51}$$

where thermal equilibrium is attainable, i.e., at $x < x_f = (\Phi_p/T)_f$. The molecular-weight dependence of D is found to be identical to that in bulk block copolymer and hence

$$D \propto N^{2/3}(\Phi_p/T)^{1/3} \quad \text{(ordered state)} \tag{52}$$

The value x_c corresponds to the order-disorder transition point. If $x > x_c$ the systems are ordered and if $x < x_c$ they are disordered.

The molecular-weight dependence of D and x can be rescaled by scaling D with the unperturbed chain dimension $bZ^{1/2}$ and x with x_c as in Figure 19(b). Thus we obtain following scaling rule

$$D/(bN^{1/2}) \simeq (x^*)^m, \quad x^* = x/x_c \tag{53}$$

where

$$m = \tfrac{1}{3} \quad \text{for } x^* > 1 \quad \text{(ordered state)} \tag{54}$$

$$m = 0 \quad \text{for } x^* < 1 \quad \text{(disordered state)} \tag{55}$$

and

$$x_c \sim N^{-1/2} \tag{56}$$

Figure 20 summarizes the temperature and concentration dependence of D in the disordered state and ordered states[7]. The crossover occurs at $x = x_c$ which has molecular weight dependence given by eq. 56. Thus the larger the molecular weight, the smaller the value of x_c and consequently the crossover takes place at lower concentrations and higher temperatures. The exponent $-\tfrac{1}{2}$ is not well understood but seems to originate from a chain-packing problem in locally oriented condensed phase. It is larger than -1, predicted for the critical point of the ternary mixture of polymer A, polymer B and solvent. At $x > x_f$ the system cannot attain thermodynamic equilibrium and the wavelength D is controlled by kinetics. Origin and effects of the nonequilibrium are discussed in detail elsewhere[51].

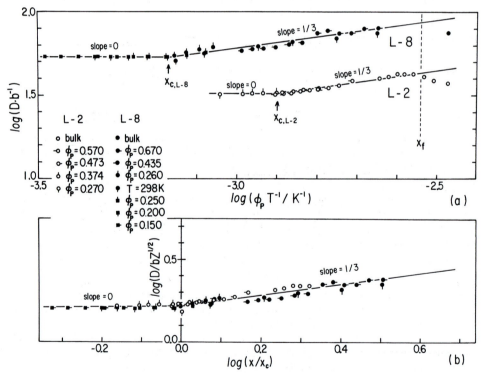

Figure 19   Master curves (a) between D/b and Φ_p/T and (b) between $D/bZ^{1/2}$ and $x^* = x/x_c$ where $x = \Phi_p/T$ and $x_c = (\Phi_p/T)_c$. Z is the polymerization index which is equal to N in the text. Note that the data points at $x > x_f$ in Figure (a) were neglected in the master curve shown in (b), because they are in the regime of "kinetic control" rather than in the regime of "thermodynamic control". From Ref. 7, T. Hashimoto, M. Shibayama, and H. Kawai, Macromolecules *16*, 1093 (1983), Copyright 1983, American Chemical Society, with permission

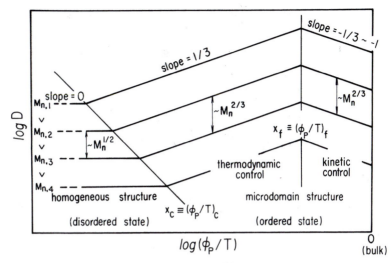

Figure 20   Summary of molecular weight, concentration, and temperature dependence of the wavelength D. The variations of log D with log (Φ_p/T) are plotted for four different molecular weights, M_{n1} to M_{n4}. From Ref. 7, T. Hashimoto, M. Shibayama, and H. Kawai, Macromolecules *16*, 1093 (1983), Copyright 1983, American Chemical Society, with permission

5   KINETIC ASPECTS OF ORDER-DISORDER TRANSITION

Here we briefly discuss kinetics of thermally induced disordering and ordering processes. The studies are of importance for molecular design of processability and to understand nonequilibrium statistical physics of polymers.

When the thermodynamic driving force for the phase separation is suddenly removed by temperature-jump (T-jump) above the order-disorder transition temperature T_r for the block polymers, they undergo the order-disorder transition (i.e., the disordering transition) according to a molecular mechanism as schematically illustrated in Figure 21[52–55]. A molecular process of the disordering may be envisioned by reptation of chain molecules across the interfaces. The reptation is a curvilinear diffusion of polymer molecules along its own contour in bulk or in concentrated solution[56, 57].

After T-jump, each molecules undergoes Brownian motion independently of others, and as a consequence the spatial distribution of the chemical junctions $h(\underline{r})$ becomes broader with time as shown in Figure 21(c). This process may be described by a random stochastic process. As the reptation takes place the segments loose their memories with respect to their positions and orientations, resulting in mixing of the unlike segments, increased interfacial thickness and eventually in an essentially uniform segmental density distribution characteristic for the disordered mixtures as shown in Figure 21(d).

The ordering process may not necessarily be a reversed process of the disordering process. However, the reversed disordering process can be a possible process of the ordering[53, 58]. That is, analogously to the spinodal decomposition of mixtures[59], after temperature drop (T-drop) below T_r concentration fluctuations of the junctions, Figure 21(c), or the segments,

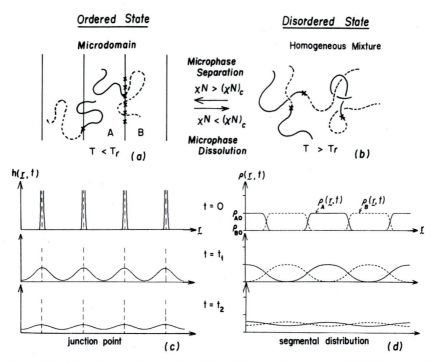

Figure 21   Ordered state (a), disordered state (b), and change of spatial distribution of chemical junctions (c) and segments $\varrho_K(\underline{r}, t)$ (K = A, B) (d) with time in the process of order-to-disorder transition (microphase dissolution). From Ref. 55, T. Hashimoto et al, Macromolecules *19*, 754 (1986), Copyright 1986, American Chemical Society, with permission

Figure 21(d), are built up throughout the whole sample space, and these fluctuations grow with time as depicted in Figures 21(c) and 21(d). An another possible process of the ordering may be envisioned to a process analogous to the nucleation and growth of mixtures; an ordered phase may be nucleated in the matrix of disordered phase by a thermal activation process[58]. Thus an intermediate structure is biphasic, in contrast to the single phase structure in the ordering process analogous to the spinodal decomposition. As times goes on, the ordered phase will grow at the expense of the disorderd phase to result eventually in completely ordered phase as depicted in Figure 21(a).

To gain some insights into the physics underlying the disordering process, let us further simplify our treatment by assuming that T is raised sufficiently high above T_r, so that the thermodynamic interaction between A and B polymers does not significantly affect the diffusion[52]. Under this condition, the change of the segmental density profile with time $\varrho_K(\underline{r}, t)$ should be governed by a Frickian mechanism

$$\frac{\partial \varrho_K(\underline{r}, t)}{\delta t} = D_c \, \nabla^2 \varrho_K(\underline{r}, t) \quad (K = A \text{ or } B) \tag{57}$$

where D_c is the diffusivity for the center-of-mass motion of the block polymer as a whole, which should be a function of the self-diffusivities of the constituent polymers, $D_{c,K}$. In case when T is not sufficiently high above T_r, eq. 57 should be modified to take into account an effect of finite value of $\chi(T)$. In such a case D_c may be replaced by D_{app} which is a product of D_c and the χ-dependent thermodynamic driving force for the disordering.

By solving eq. 57 or eq. 58

$$\frac{\delta h(\underline{r}, t)}{\delta t} = D_c \, v^2 \, h(\underline{r}, t) \tag{58}$$

for the spatial distribution of the chemical junctions, under appropriate initial conditions as shown in Figures 21(c) and (d) at t = 0, one obtains $\varrho_K(\underline{r}, t)$ and $h(\underline{r}, t)$. From these one can calculate the observable properties as a function of time. For example elastic scattering of X-rays, neutrons, and light as a function of time is given by

$$I(q,t; T) = I(q, t = 0; T)\exp\{-2R(q; T)\,t\} \tag{59}$$

$$R(q; T) = q^2 D_c(T) \tag{60}$$

Thus from the decay rate of the elastic scattered intensity one can determine D_c or D_{app}. The rate R(q) is the decay rate for the q-Fourier component of the fluctuations. The time required for the decay of q-Fourier component of the fluctuations is given by

$$\tau_q = R(q)^{-1} = q^{-2} D_c^{-1} \tag{61}$$

One can estimate the time τ_{qm} required for the decay of the wavelength $D = 2\pi/q_m$ of the dominant fluctuations from eq. 61

$$\tau_{qm} = q_m^{-2} D_c^{-1} = (D/2\pi)^2 D_c^{-1} \tag{62}$$

τ_{qm} is proportional to the mean-squared displacement, and therefore the larger the domain identity period D, the longer the time τ_{qm} required for the decay.

It should be noted that eq. 59 predicts $I(q, t = \infty ; T) = 0$. This is not correct because the intensity $I(q, t = \infty ; T)$ should be identical to the static scattered intensity at $T > T_r$ from the disordered state,

$$I(q,t = \infty; T) = I_s(q; T) \tag{63}$$

Eq. 59 may be modified to take this effect into account[54],

$$I(q,t;T) = [I(q,t=0;T) - I_s(q;T)]\exp[-2R(q;T)t]$$
$$+ I_s(q;T) \tag{64}$$

The theoretical treatment of the dynamics of the ordering process and on the effect of finite χ on the dynamics of ordering and disordering processes is developed[38] in the context of time-dependent Ginzburg-Landau formalism[36]. The connectivity between A and B in A–B diblock polymer is found to demand that a certain Fourier component of the fluctuations with wavenumber q_m (as given by eq. 65) has the maximum growth rate and these fluctuations become a dominant mode in the early stage of the ordering process.

$$q_m \simeq 1/R_g \tag{65}$$

Figure 22 shows an isometric display, demonstrating typical change of the SAXS profiles with time during the disordering process[53]. The disordering process was investigated for S–B diblock polymer solutions with n-tetradecane (C14) by a repetitive T-jump method described in detail elsewhere[54]. The block polymer has $M_n = 5.2 \times 10^4$ and $w_S = 0.30$ and its 35 wt % polymer solution has the order-disorder transition $T_r = 130\ °C$. Each curve was

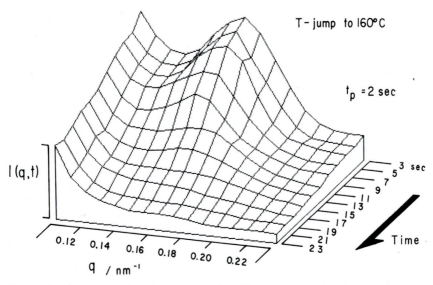

Figure 22   Isometric display of time-resolved SAXS profiles during order-disorder transition of 35 wt % SB in n-tetradecane. Each profile was obtained at a time interval of 2 s after T-jump to 160 °C. The order-disorder transition temperature of the solution is 130 °C. From T. Hashimoto (1985), Time resolved small-angle X-ray scattering studies on kinetics and molecular dynamics of order-disorder transition of block polymers. In: Physical Optics of Dynamic Phenomena and Processes in Macromolecular Systems, Proceedings 27th Microsymposium on Macromolecules, pp 233–243, Walter de Gruyter, Berlin, New York, with permission

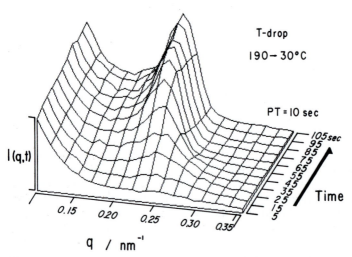

Figure 23   Isometric display of time-resolved SAXS profiles during disorder-order transition of 55 wt % solution of SBS in dipenentene. Each profile was measured at time interval 10 sec. after T-drop from 190 to 30 °C. The order-disorder transition temperature of the solution is 160 °C. From T. Hashimoto (1985), Time resolved small-angle X-ray scattering studies on kinetics and molecular dynamics of order-disorder transition of block polymers. In: Physical Optics of Dynamic Phenomena and Processes in Macromolecular Systems, Proceedings 27th Microsymposium on Macromolecules, pp 233–243, Walter Gruyter, Berlin, New York, with permission

obtained with 2 s time slicing after T-jump from room temperature to 160 °C. The scattered intensity is observed to decay with time, indicating that the microdomains are dissolved at a time scale of the order of a minute or less for this particular system.

The time-resolved SAXS studies were conducted as a function of polymer concentration and temperature [54, 55]. The apparent diffusivity, (D_{app}) of the order of 10^{-14} to 10^{-13} cm^2/s was estimated with this technique. The time required for the disordering is short, despite the very small D_{app}. This is because the distance $D = 2\pi/q_m$ required for the diffusion is very small. The concentration and temperature dependence of D_{app} were described in detail elsewhere[55]. D_{app} is expected to be a strong function of polymerization index N as well as f and type of the solvent.

Figure 23 shows an isometric display demonstrating typical evolution of the SAXS profiles with time during the ordering process of a 55 wt % solution of an S–B–S triblock polymer in dipentene, the S–B–S having $M_n = 5.8 \times 10^4$ and $w_S = 0.48$ and dipentene being a neutrally good solvent[53, 58]. The solution has $T_r = 160$ °C and the ordering was activated by the T-drop from 190 to 30 °C. The scattering maximum appears shortly after T-drop, maximum intensity increases, and the peak position q_m slightly shifts toward the smaller values with time. For this particular system the intensity increase tends to level off at about 80 s after T-drop. The ordering process typically occurs at the time scale of the order of 100 s. The rate should depend on N and f, as well as temperature, concentration, and type of the solvent.

6   CHANGES OF PROPERTIES ACCOMPANIED BY ORDER-DISORDER TRANSITION

The flow behavior of block polymers in bulk[15–17, 19–22] and concentrated solutions[18, 55, 60, 61] have been studied by a number of investigators. They reported the change of the flow behavior from non-Newtonian to Newtonian with increasing temperature and/or decreasing concentration, which was predicted to arise from the order-disorder transition. In the ordered state the flow is strongly non-Newtonian but in the disordered state the flow is Newtonian below a certain critical shear rate $\dot{\gamma}_c$.

The conclusions drawn from the rheological measurements were first proved, albeit qualitatively, by simultaneous observations of transmitted light intensity (Pico and Williams[18]) and SAXS (Widmaier and Meyer[21]). These conclusions were confirmed more quantitatively by the simultaneous observations of rheology and SAXS by Kraus-Hashimoto[22], and Hashimoto-Kotaka and their coworkers[60, 61]. Meier[62] proposed a theoretical interpretation on the non-Newtonian flow behavior in the ordered state and explained the experimental evidence of

$$\eta \sim \dot{\gamma}^{-1} \tag{66}$$

in terms of an excess energy dissipation associated with thermodynamic energy of mixing of the unlike segments during the flow process, an extra dissipation mechanism absent in single component and homogeneous systems.

We will discuss below an example encountered in the typical pressure sensitive adhesives based upon star-shaped (or radial type) block polymer[22]. Polymers selected for this study were the star-shaped block polymers $(S–B)_n x$ and $(S–I)_n x$ in which the block polymers S–B or S–I are chemically connected at the ends of the elastomer segments to star polymers with the mean arm-number n (see Figure 24). The polymers, designated as I and B have

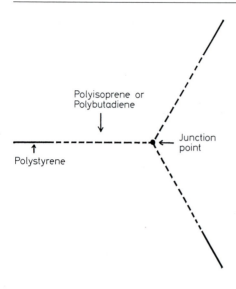

Figure 24   Radial block polymer of PS–PI (S–L) or PS–PB (S–B)

composition and molecular weight suitable for use in the pressure-sensitive adhesives, and their characterization data are shown in Table II. Adhesive formulations, designated as IA and BA are given in Table III.

Figures 25 and 26 show the steady flow viscosities at several temperatures for adhesives IA and BA[22]. At low temperature, flow is highly non-Newtonian over the entire range of $\dot{\gamma}$

TABLE II   Polymer Characterization Data

	Polymer I	Polymer B
Styrene, %	16	30
Comonomer, %	Isoprene (84)	Butadiene (70)
Inherent viscosity (THF, 25 °C)	1.44	0.90
$\overline{M}_w$	149,000	131,000
$\overline{M}_n$	103,000	118,000
M_s (styrene block length)	10,000	11,000
Free polystyrene, %	<1	2
Uncoupled diblock polymer, %	26	3
Mean functionality of branching (n)	3.1	3.5

From reference 22, G. Kraus and T. Hashimoto, *J. Appl. Polym. Sci., 27,* 1745 (1982) Copyright 1982 by John Wiley and Sons, Inc., with permission.

TABLE III   Adhesive Compositions

		IA	BA
Block polymer used		I	B
Parts:	Polymer	100	100
	Tackifying Resin	75[a]	88[b]
	Stabilizer	1[c]	1[c]

[a] Wingtack 95, polyterpene (Goodyear Chemical Co.)
[b] Picco Alpha 115, poly(α-pinene) (Hercules, Inc.)
[c] Irganox 1010 (Ciba-Geigy)
From reference 22, G. Kraus and T. Hashimoto, *J. Appl. Polym. Sci., 27,* 1745 (1982) Copyright 1982 by John Wiley & Sons, Inc., with permission

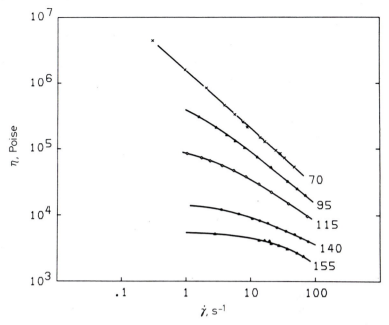

Figure 25   Steady flow viscosity of adhesive IA at various temperature in °C. From Ref. 22, G. Kraus and T. Hashimoto, J. Appl. Polym. Science, *27*, 1745 (1982), Copyright 1982. Reprinted by permission of John Wiley and Sons, Inc

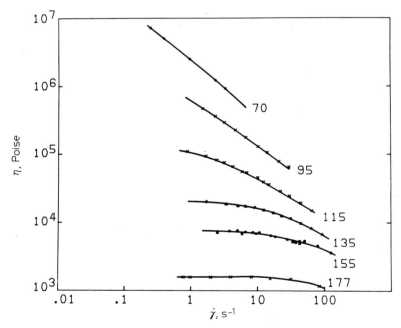

Figure 26   Steady flow viscosity of adhesive BA at various temperature in °C. From Ref. 22, G. Kraus and T. Hashimoto, J. Appl. Polym. Science, *27*, 1745 (1982), Copyright 1982. Reprinted by permission of John Wiley and Sons, Inc

examined, while at higher temperatures the curves exhibit a well-defined low shear Newtonian regime. Although this fact alone is sometimes taken as evidence of a structural transition from an ordered state to a disordered state, it is not sufficient to establish such a change. This is because even homogeneous, and thermorheologically simple melts show a similar tendency. A structural change would demand evidence of thermorheological complexity.

If there is a structural change, all the results should not be superimposed on a single master curve after applying time-temperature superposition principles but rather on a two-branch master curve as clearly shown by Widmaier and Meyer[21] (see Figure 27). Figure 27 shows their master curve on dynamic viscosity obtained for a S–B–S triblock polymer with $M_n = 4.5 \times 10^4$ and $w_S = 0.38$ at reference temperature $T_0 = 225$ °C. For reduced frequencies below a critical value $\omega_{r,crit}$ of about 70 rad/s at T_0, two branches are observed: (i) the lower one which results from the superposition at $T > T_0$ and the reduced viscosity is independent of ω_r (Newtonian behavior) and (ii) the upper one which corresponds to $T < T_0$ and shows ω_r-dependence of η_r (non-Newtonian behavior). SAXS measurements above and below T_0 indicate qualitatively that T_0 is near order-disorder transition temperature.

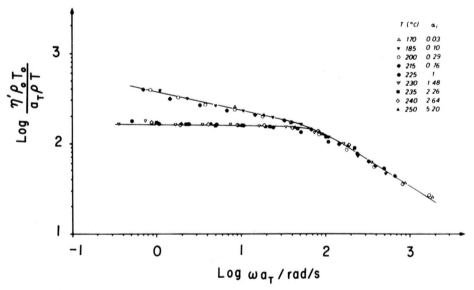

Figure 27   Reduced Viscosity ($\eta_r = \eta' \varrho_0 T_0 \lambda a_T \varrho T$) vs reduced frequency $\omega_r = \omega a_T$ at the reference temperature $T_0 = 225$ °C.
From Ref. 21, J. M. Widmaier and G. C. Meyer, J. Polym. Science, Polym. Phys. Ed. *18*, 2217 (1980), Copyright 1980. Reprinted with permission of John Wiley and Sons, Inc

For the particular specimens IA and BA, the superposition is unexpectedly successful, probably because there is not sufficient overlap in experimental points from different temperatures to reveal deviations from time-temperature superposition. Thus Figures 25 and 26 by themselves permit no conclusions regarding a structural transition. However, simultaneous measurements of SAXS profiles as a function of temperature permit unequivocal determination of the order-disorder transition temperature T_r as discussed by Kraus and Hashimoto[22].

In this paper the determination of T_r was somewhat arbitrary. They measured maximum intensity I_m as a function of temperature and determined T_r as a temperature at which I_m reaches to a certain weak intensity level. Rigorous assessment of T_r involves investigations of the crossover behaviors with I_m^{-1} and D as discussed previously. Figure 28 shows an example of a plot of I_m^{-1} vs. T^{-1} to determine T_r. The temperature T_r determined by analyzing the crossover behaviors is 120 °C for BA, 155 °C for IA, 200 °C for I and T_r > 230 °C for B. The temperatures T_r for BA and IA appear to correlate well with the temperatures at which the flow behavior changes from non-Newtonian to Newtonian. Thus this study suggests that the tackifying resin plays an important role in adhesives by lowering the transition temperature T_r as well as the reported effect of increasing the viscosity of the rubber matrix. This reduction is quite important in the enhanced processing of these adhesives at the processing temperatures since it allows them to flow more readily.

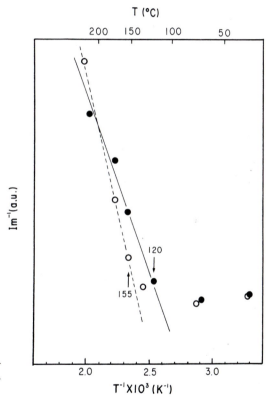

Figure 28   Reciprocal intensity I_m^{-1} in arbitrary units (au) vs T^{-1} for adhesives IA, open circles o; BA, closed circles.

The transition temperature of the star-shaped block polymer is primarily determined by the arm molecular weight and fraction of one component f. The difference of T_r between I and B is primarily due to the effect of f on T_r. If the molecular weight is the same, the sample having f close to ½ has higher T_r than the sample having f close to 0 or 1. The difference of T_r between IA and BA is primarily due to the effect of thermodynamic interaction between the tackifying resin and the constituent polymers. Thus choice of the resin is also important to control T_r.

References and Notes

1. P. J. Flory, *"Principles of Polymer Chemistry"*, Cornell Univ. Press, N.Y., 1967
2. T. Hashimoto, K. Nagatoshi, A. Todo, H. Hasegawa and H. Kawai, *Macromolecules, 7,* 364 (1974)
3. L. Leibler, *Macromolecules, 13,* 1602 (1980)
4. R. J. Roe, M. Fishkis, and C. J. Chang, *Macromolecules, 14,* 1091 (1981)
5. T. Hashimoto, M. Shibayama, and H. Kawai, *Polym. Prepr., Am. Chem. Soc., Div. Polym. Chem. 23,* 21 (1982)
6. T. Hashimoto, K. Kowsaka, M. Shibayama, and H. Kawai, *Polym. Prepr., Am. Chem. Soc., Div. Polym. Chem., 24,* 224 (1983)
7. T. Hashimoto, M. Shibayama, and H. Kawai, *Macromolecules, 16,* 1093 (1983)
8. T. Hashimoto, Y. Tsukahara, and H. Kawai, *Polym. J., 15,* 699 (1983)
9. F. S. Bates, *Macromolecules, 18,* 525 (1985)
10. S. L. Aggawal, Ed., *"Block Polymers"*, Plenum Press (1970)
11. G. E. Molau, Ed., *"Colloidal and Morphological Behavior of Block and Graft Copolymers"*, Plenum Press (1971)
12. N. A. Platzer, Ed., *"Copolymers, Polyblends, and Composites"*, Adv. Chem. Series, 142, Am. Chem. Soc. (1975)
13. S. L. Cooper and G. M. Estes, Eds., *"Multiphase Polymers"*, Adv. Chem. Series, 176, Am. Chem. Soc. (1979)
14. G. Kraus, in *"Block Copolymers:* Science and Technology", D. J. Meier, Ed., MMI press, Gordon & Breach Sci. Publisher (1983)
15. K. R. Arnold and D. J. Meier, *J. Appl. Polym. Sci., 14,* 427 (1970)
16. C. I. Chung and J. C. Gale, *J. Polym. Sci., Polym. Phys. Ed., 14,* 1149 (1976)
17. E. V. Gouinlock and R. S. Porter, *Polym. Eng. Sci., 17,* 534 (1977)
18. E. R. Pico and M. C. Williams, *Polym. Eng. Sci., 17,* 573 (1977)
19. C. I. Chung and M. I. Lin, *J. Polym. Sci., Polym. Phys. Ed., 16,* 545 (1978)
20. C. I. Chung, H. L. Griesbach, and L. Young, *J. Polym. Sci., Polym. Phys. Ed., 18,* 1237 (1980)
21. J. M. Widmaier and G. C. Meyer, *J. Polym. Sci., Polym. Phys. Ed., 18,* 2217 (1980)
22. G. Kraus and T. Hashimoto, *J. Appl. Polym. Sci., 27,* 1745 (1982)
23. T. Hashimoto, M. Shibayama, M. Fujimura, and H. Kawai, in ref. 14
24a. M. Shibayama and T. Hashimoto, *Macromolecules, 19,* 140 (1986)
24b. F. S. Bates, C. V. Berney and R. E. Cohen, *Macromolecules, 16,* 1101, (1983).
25. Five fundamental microdomain and morphologies have been found to exist depending upon volume fraction of A(f) in the two component block polymers; (i) A spheres in B, (ii) A cylinders in B, (iii) alternating A and B lamellae, (iv) B cylinders in A, and (v) B spheres in A.
26. Polystyrene and polyisoprene have compressibilities[27] of 220×10^{-6} and 515×10^{-6} MPa^{-1} above T_g, and hence polystyrene-polyisoprene has compressibility of about 3×10^{-4} MPa^{-1}
27. J. Bandrup and E. H. Immergut, Eds. *"Polymer Hand Book"*, Wiley, New York, 1975
28. K. M. Hong and J. Noolandi, *Macromolecules, 16,* 1083 (1983)
29. R. J. Roe and W. C. Zin, *Macromolecules, 17,* 189 (1984)
30. T. Hashimoto, H. Hasegawa, K. Mori, and H. Tanaka, in *"International Seminar on Elastomers"*, Pegasus House, Itoh, Shizuoka, Japan, Oct. 20–22, 1985, The Synthetic Polymer Research Assoc. and The Soc. of Rubber Industory, Japan
31. K. Mori, H. Tanaka, and T. Hashimoto, *Macromolecules, 80,* (1987) in press.
32. See for example, C. Domb and J. L. Lebowitz, Eds., *"Phase Transitions and Critical Phenomena* vol. 8", Academic Press, 1983
33. D. J. Meier, *J. Polym. Sci.,* Part C, *26,* 81 (1969)
34. D. J. Meier, *Prepr. Polym. Colloq., Soc. Polym. Sci., Jpn.,* Kyoto, 1977
35. E. Helfand, and Z. R. Wasserman, *Macromolecules, 9,* 897 (1976); *11,* 960 (1978); *13,* 994 (1980)
36. See for example, S. K. Ma, *"Modern Theory of Critical Phenomena"*, Benjamin/Cummings Pub. Co., Inc. 1976
37. J. Noolandi and K. M. Hong, *Ferroelectrics, 30,* 117 (1980)
38. T. Hashimoto, unpublished paper; T. Hashimoto, H. Tanaka, and K. Mori, Polym. Prepr., Jpn., *Soc. Polym. Sci. Jpn., 35,* 2970 (1986)
39. K. Mori, H. Hasegawa, and T. Hashimoto, *Polym. J., 17,* 799 (1985)

40. Y. Tsukahara, N. Nakamura, T. Hashimoto, H. Kawai, T. Nagaya, Y. Sugimura, and S. Tsuge, *Polym. J., 12,* 455 (1980)
41. T. Hashimoto, Y. Tsukahara, and H. Kawai, *Polym. J. 15,* 699 (1983)
42. T. Hashimoto, Y. Tsukahara, K. Tachi, and H. Kawai, *Macromolecules, 16,* 648 (1983)
43. Hereafter we restrict ourselves to the isotropic systems so that q can be replaced by q.
44. N. A. Rounds and D. McIntyre, cited in E. Helfand and Z. R. Wasserman, *Macromolecules, 9,* 879 (1976)
45. R. J. Roe and W. C. Zin, *Macromolecules, 13,* 1221 (1980)
46. T. Hashimoto, M. Shibayama, and H. Kawai, *Macromolecules, 13,* 1237 (1980)
47. T. Hashimoto, M. Fujimura, and H. Kawai, *Macromolecules, 13,* 1660 (1980)
48. T. Hashimoto, H. Tanaka, and H. Hasegawa, *Macromolecules, 18,* 1864 (1985)
49. T. Hashimoto, *Macromolecules, 15,* 1548 (1982)
50. It should be noted that the chain dimension in good solvents tends to decrease with increasing Φ_p because of the increasing screening of the excluded volume effects. Thus the domain size should decrease with increasing Φ_p if the excluded-volume effect is a dominant physical factor. However, in reality the excluded volume effect is outweighed by the segregation effect, resulting in the increasing D with increasing Φ_p
51. M. Shibayama, T. Hashimoto, and H. Kawai, *Macromolecules, 16,* 1434 (1983)
52. T. Hashimoto, Y. Tsukahara, and H. Kawai, *J. Polym. Sci., Polym. Lett. Ed., 18,* 585 (1980); *Macromolecules, 14,* 708 (1981)
53. T. Hashimoto, in *"Physical Optics of Dynamic Phenomena and Processes in Macromolecular Systems",* B. Sedlacek, Ed., Walter de Gruyter Co., Berlin, N.Y., 1985, pp. 233
54. T. Hashimoto, K. Kowsaka, M. Shibayama, and S. Suehiro, *Macromolecules, 19,* 750, (1986)
55. T. Hashimoto, K. Kowsaka, M. Shibayama, and H. Kawai, *Macromolecules, 19,* 754, (1986)
56. P.-G. de Gennes, *J. Chem. Phys., 55,* 572 (1971); *J. Phys. (Paris), 36,* 1199 (1975)
57. M. Doi and S. F. Edwards, *J. Chem. Soc. Faraday Trans. 2, 74,* 1789 (1978); *74,* 1802 (1978); *74,* 1818 (1978)
58. T. Hashimoto, S. Sakurai, M. Shibayama, and K. Kowsaka, to be published
59. J. W. Cahn, *J. Chem. Phys., 42,* 93 (1965)
60. H. Watanabe, T. Kotaka, T. Hashimoto, M. Shibayama and H. Kawai, *J. Rheology, 26,* 153 (1982)
61. T. Hashimoto, M. Shibayama, H. Kawai, H. Watanabe, and T. Kotaka, *Macromolecules, 16,* 361 (1983)
62. D. J. Meier, Invited lecture at 29th Rheology Symp., Soc. Rheology, Japan, Oct. 28–30, 1981, Kyoto, Japan
63. E. A. DiMarzio, C. M. Guttmann, and J. D. Hoffman, *Macromolecules, 13,* 1194 (1980).
64. T. Ohta and K. Kawasaki, *Macromolecules, 19,* 2621 (1986).
65. Block polymers with f = 0.5 are suggested to exhibit also the first-order transition if the Brazovskii effect is taken into considerations[3].

Chapter 12

RESEARCH ON THERMOPLASTIC
ELASTOMERS

Section 4

CHAIN CONFORMATION IN BLOCK COPOLYMERS BY SMALL ANGLE NEUTRON SCATTERING

J. A. Miller, S. L. Cooper

Contents

J. A. Miller*, S. L. Cooper, Department of Chemical Engineering, University of Wisconsin, Madison, WI 53706

---

* Present Address: Disposable Products Division, 3M Center St. Paul, MN 55144

1   INTRODUCTION

Small angle neutron scattering (SANS) has recently been used to examine chain conformation in bulk polymer samples. The great power of this technique comes from the difference
in the coherent scattering lengths between the two common hydrogen isotopes. By substituting deuterium for hydrogen in a polymer chain, one can provide a contrast mechanism for
the SANS experiments without altering the chemistry of the system being investigated. An
analogous labelling experiment for x-ray scattering invariably changes the chemical interactions present in the system. The first use of SANS to study the chain conformation in
polymer materials was by Ballard et al.[1] who found that polystyrene chains in a bulk,
amorphous sample were in the random flight or Gaussian conformation, confirming the
hypothesis of Flory[2]. Subsequent studies, which have been reviewed by Higgins and Stein[3],
on other amorphous polymers yielded the same conclusion.

Small angle neutron scattering more recently has been applied to phase separated block
copolymer systems. The chain conformation of the individual blocks can be obtained by two
different methods. The first method requires that the scattering samples possesses a well-
defined lamellar-microstructure. Hadziioannou et al.[4] (1982) investigated the conformation
of the polystyrene block in a very regular lamellar polystyrene/polyisoprene block copolymer. The polystyrene phase contained both purely deuterated and purely protonated chains.
When the plane of the lamellar surface was aligned either parallel or perpendicular to the
incident neutron beam, the interphase scattering due to the lamellae was nearly eliminated.
This left only the chain scattering from the labelled and unlabelled polystyrene chains, from
which the polystyrene chain conformation was obtained.

The second method for extracting the single chain scattering from a single block within a
two-phase block copolymer makes use of the scattering theory developed independently by
Koberstein[5] and by Jahshan and Summerfield[6, 7]. The basic principle of this theory is that the
single chain scattering function can be obtained by subtracting the scattering of one sample
from the scattering of a second sample. The first sample contains normal protonated chains
throughout and exhibits only interphase scattering. In the second sample, one of the
segment types has both protonated and deuterated chains and yields both interphase and
intrachain scattering. The interphase scattering from the second sample is subtracted by
using the scattering from the first sample as a reference for the interphase scattering. The
scattering from the first sample is weighted by a neutron contrast factor that depends on the
isotopic composition and density of each phase prior to the subtraction step.

2   THEORY

The expression governing the subtraction of the interphase scattering from a two-phase
system where one of the phases consists of a blend of labelled and unlabelled chains is given
by Koberstein[5] as

$$(R_L(q) - R_{inc,L}) - \left[\frac{\beta_A - x\beta_{BD} - (1-x)\beta_{BH}}{\beta_A - \beta_{BH}}\right]^2 (R_U(q) - R_{inc,U})$$

$$= \frac{4\pi}{V_S}(b_{BD} - b_{BH})^2 N_{BT} Z_B^2 \, x \, (1-x) \, P_B(q) \tag{1}$$

In this expression, R_L (q) and R_U (q) are the Rayleigh factors for a partially labelled sample and a completely unlabelled sample, $R_{inc,L}$ and $R_{inc,U}$ are the incoherent background scattering terms for the labelled and unlabelled sample, and P_B (q) is the single chain scattering function for the chains in the labelled B phase. The Rayleigh factor is defined as

$$R(q) = 4\pi \frac{d\Sigma(q)}{d\Omega} \tag{2}$$

In this expression, $d\Sigma/d\Omega$ is the absolute scattering intensity, which is defined in the usual manner. In Equation 1, β_A is the coherent scattering length density of pure A segments, β_{BH} and β_{BD} are the coherent scattering length densities for pure protonanted B segments and pure deuterated B segments, and x is the fraction of the B chains that are deuterated. The coherent scattering length density is the sum of all of the atomic coherent scattering lengths for all of the atoms within a unit volume. Coherent scattering lengths and incoherent neutron scattering cross-sections for various elements are listed in Table I. In Equation 1, V_s is the irradiated sample volume, b_{BH} and b_{BD} are the monomeric coherent scattering lengths for the protonated and deuterated B monomers, N_{BT} is the total number of B chains present in the scattering volume, and Z_B is the average degree of polymerization of the B segments. P_B (q) is the single chain scattering function, also known as the structure or form factor for the B segments or as the intramolecular interference function. P_B(q) contains the information on the chain conformation available from neutron scattering.

TABLE I   Neutron Scattering Lengths and Incoherent Cross-sections for Selected Elements[37]

Element	Coherent Scattering Length $\times\ 10^{12}$, cm	Incoherent Scattering Cross Section $\times\ 10^{24}$, cm
Hydrogen	−0.374	79.74
Deuterium	0.667	2.01
Carbon	0.665	0
Nitrogen	0.94	0.30
Oxygen	0.58	0
Fluorine	0.56	0
Sodium	0.36	1.80
Silicon	0.42	0
Sulfur	0.28	0.20
Chlorine	0.96	3.40

Equation 1 suggests that P_B (q) can be obtained by the subtraction of the scattering by an unlabelled sample from that of a labelled sample. The subtraction is weighted by the term in brackets that appears in the left hand side of Equation 1. For one particular value of x, the degree of deuteration of the B chains, this weighting factor is zero. This condition is known as the phase contrast matched condition. It is described by

$$\beta_A - x\beta_{BD} - (1-x)\beta_{BH} = 0 \tag{3}$$

When this condition is true for the labelled sample, there is no need to measure the scattering from an unlabelled sample. This makes the results of the scattering experiment easier to interpret and more reliable. There is no need to match the morphology of two samples exactly, which is a requirement for using Equation 1. This is often difficult for multiblock copolymer systems. Figure 1 shows scattering data from a labelled, phase contrast matched system and from an unlabelled sample of the same chemical composition.

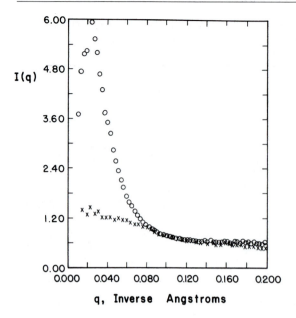

Figure 1   SANS data for a labelled, phase contrast matched sample and from an unlabelled sample

The samples shown are polyether-polyesters made from a 5/4/1 mole ratio of dimethyl terephthalate, butanediol, and poly(tetramethylene oxide). The most prominent feature in this figure is the absence of a peak due to interphase scattering in the phase contrast matched sample. The intensity of the maximum due to interphase scattering in the unlabelled curve is substantially larger than the magnitude of the intrachain scattering in this sample.

The phase contrast matching principle can be extended to include partial labelling of both phases. The restriction is that the coherent scattering length densities of both phases be the same. This requirement is met by a linear function of the degree of deuteration of both of the block types.

$$y\beta_{AD} + (1-y)\beta_{AH} = x\beta_{BD} + (1-x)\beta_{BH} \tag{4}$$

In this expression x and y are fractional deuteration of the soft and hard segments respectively. This expression implies that an increase in the hard phase coherent scattering length density caused by labelling the hard segments can be offset by deuterating the soft segments to a greater extent. Equation 3 is the special case of this constraint when the level of deuteration of the hard segments is zero.

For phase contrast matched samples with only the soft block being partially deuterated, the coherent portion of the scattering can be described by

$$R_{SS}(q) = 4\pi/V_S(b_{SD}-b_{SH})^2 N_S Z_S^2 x_{SS} (1-x_{SS})P_S(q) \tag{5}$$

Using this expression, the single chain scattering function for the soft segments can be obtained. If the single chain scattering from the hard blocks is desired, a four component sample must be used. The four components are the soft and hard blocks in the deuterated and protonated form. Such a sample, when it meets the phase contrast matching criterion of Equation 4, yields coherent scattering that obeys the following equation.

$$R_{HS}(q) = \frac{4\pi}{V_S} (b_{SD}-b_{SH})^2 N_S Z_S^2 x_{HS} (1-x_{HS}) P_S(q) \tag{6}$$

$$+ \frac{4\pi}{V_S} (b_{HD}-b_{HH})^2 N_H Z_H^2 y_{HS} (1-y_{HS}) P_H(q)$$

Figure 2 diagrams the procedure for obtaining the hard segment single chain scattering function. Starting with the unlabelled material, one deuterates the soft phase so as to raise the coherent scattering length density of the soft phase until it matches that of the hard phase. The soft segment single chain scattering function is obtained according to Equation 5 by performing the SANS experiment at this point. The soft phase is then deuterated to a greater extent, reestablishing a difference in the hard and soft phase coherent scattering lengths. The hard segments are now deuterated up to a point where the phase contrast matching condition again applies. The SANS data from this sample consists of two types of intrachain scattering, the soft segment single chain scattering and the hard segment single chain scattering. Having already obtained the soft segment single chain scattering function, the two contributions can be separated using Equation 6. Thus, this method involves using two phase contrast matched samples, one for obtaining the soft segment single chain scattering function and one for obtaining the hard segment single chain scattering function.

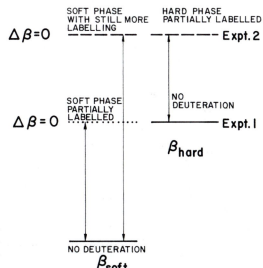

Figure 2   Diagram of the method for obtaining the hard segment single chain scattering function from a four component two-phase material

In Equations 5 and 6, the SS and HS subscripts refer to samples that are used primarily to obtain the single chain scattering functions for the soft segment and the hard segment respectively and to properties associated with these samples. $R_{SS}(q)$ and $R_{HS}(q)$ are the coherent scattering from the specified samples. The fraction of deuteration of the soft and hard segments are denoted by x and y respectively. $P_S(q)$ and $P_H(q)$ are the single chain scattering functions for the soft segments and for the hard segments.

3   LITERATURE REVIEW

Because of the complex morphology exhibited by block copolymers, analysis of the neutron scattering from these materials is complicated, and hence only a few reports have appeared concerning investigations of this type. Recently, the theoretical treatment of the scattering from block copolymer systems given by Koberstein[5] and Jahshan and Summerfield[6,7] provided a framework for using SANS to study block copolymers. Most of the reports in the literature concern chain conformation in diblock and triblock copolymers. Multiblock copolymers such as polyurethanes and polyether-polyesters have an even more complicated morphology than the triblock and diblock copolymers, and exhibit mixed phases, in contrast to most styrene-diene triblock and diblock materials. Only a few reports have appeared in the literature that discuss the small angle neutron scattering from multiblock copolymers.

Richards and Thomason[8] were the first to measure the chain dimensions of one of the blocks in a block copolymer using neutron scattering. They did this by measuring the scattering from two samples. The first sample was a nondeuterated polystyrene-polyisoprene block copolymer. The second sample was a blend of 4 % deuterostyrene-polyisoprene copolymer and 96 % polystyrene-polyisoprene copolymer. The single chain scattering from the styrene chains was obtained by subtraction of the two scattering curves. A conclusion from this study was that the conformation of the polystyrene chains in the spherical domains was identical to that of unperturbed polystyrene chains. However, Richards and Thomason failed to correctly account for the interphase scattering contribution. The subtraction of the scattering curves cannot be made directly, since the difference in the coherent scattering length density between the two phases changes when one of the phases is partially deuterated, and so the two samples have differing magnitudes of the interphase scattering.

Hadziioannou et al.[4] measured the conformation of polystyrene chains in a set of lamellar polystyrene-polyisoprene diblock copolymers in the directions perpendicular and parallel to the normal vector of the lamellar surface. This was accomplished by using samples with a very regular lamellar microstructure. When the lamellar surface was aligned parallel or perpendicular to the incident neutron beam, the interphase scattering vanished and only the single chain scattering remained. These researchers found that the chains were extended somewhat in the direction perpendicular to the lamellar surface but in the lateral direction were comparable in size to the unperturbed chain. Thus the polystyrene chain radius of gyration was found to be somewhat larger in the block copolymer than in the bulk homopolymer.

Bates et al.[9] used the subtraction method discussed previously to extract the single chain scattering for the polystyrene chains in a polystyrene-polybutadiene diblock copolymer that contained spherical polystyrene domains imbedded in a polybutadiene matrix. This was the first experimental confirmation of the theory of Koberstein[5]. Bates et al. found that it was difficult to apply the subtraction method directly, since subtraction of the interphase scattering is imprecise and small errors in the subtraction will lead to large errors in the single chain scattering date. They had more success in obtaining the single chain scattering data when they used a sample where the two phases had the same coherent scattering length density, which is the phase contrast matching principle described by Equation 3. Bates et al. reported that the polystyrene chains are in an unperturbed conformation, in accord with the results of Richards and Thomason[8].

Recently Hasegawa et al.[10] reported the results of a chain conformation study of a lamellar polystyrene-polyisoprene block copolymer using small angle neutron scattering. Like Hadziioannou et al.[4], these researchers attempted to eliminate the interphase scattering by using samples with a very regular lamellar structure. The morphology of their materials were not as regular as those of Hadziioannou et al., so some interphase scattering was present in the scattered signal. However, the residual interphase scattering was significantly lower in intensity than it would have been if the lamellae were randomly oriented. Hasegawa et al. then applied the method of Koberstein[5] to subtract the residual interphase scattering and thereby obtained the single chain scattering. By a combination of geometric elimination and subtraction, Hasegawa et al. were able to accurately measure the single chain scattering from the polystyrene chains in these materials. They found that the chains were extended somewhat in the direction perpendicular to the lamellar surface. The chains were also found to be contracted in the direction parallel to the lamellar surface when compared with the unperturbed state. The overall radius of gyration remained constant, in contrast to the results of Hadziioannou et al.[4]. This lateral contraction was attributed to the repulsive interactions between the unlike chain segments located in the interfacial region which restrict the positions available for the segments.

4   EXPERIMENTAL RESULTS ON POLYURETHANE ELASTOMERS

Miller et al.[11] extracted the single chain scattering data for the soft segment in a series of polyether polyurethanes using small angle neutron scattering. The materials studied consisted of a 3/2/1 mole ratio of methylene bis(p-phenyl isocyanate) (MDI), butanediol, and poly(tetramethylene oxide) (PTMO). The PTMO, which had a molecular weight of 1000, consisted of a blend of deuterated and protonated oligomers. The PTMO blends contained 0, 3, 5, 10, 20, and 30 % of the deuterated species. The materials were prepared in a two-step solution polymerization in dimethyl acetamide, and after purification and recovery were compression molded into disks for use in the SANS experiments.

The corrected Rayleigh factors for the set of samples are shown in Figure 3. The absolute level of the scattering in each of the samples decreases as the level of deuteration increases. The reason for this is that as the number of PTMO chains that are deuterated increases, the coherent scattering length density of the soft phase increases. Since the interphase coherent scattering is proportional to the square of the difference in coherent scattering length densities between the phases, reducing this difference by increasing the value for the soft phase causes a lower level of interphase coherent scattering. Table II lists the values for the coherent scattering length densities for each phase for each sample, assuming that no phase mixing occurs. These values are calculated from the densities of the samples and from the density of the PTMO homopolymer, which is 0.98 g/cm[11]. It can be shown that at a deuterated soft segment content of 32.5 %, the hard and soft phase coherent scattering length densities will be equal. Under these conditions, no interphase scattering occurs and only the single chain scattering appears in the coherent portion of the total scattering. The sample containing 30 % d-PTMO chains approaches this condition, as is seen in Figure 3.

To extract the single chain scattering from the data, equation 1 was used. Figure 4 shows the single chain scattering functions obtained from the samples containing 20 % and 30 % labelled d-PTMO chains. It is interesting to note the presence of the peak in the 20 % d-PTMO single chain scattering. This peak indicates that some interphase scattering is not being correctly subtracted. This does not imply that the subtraction equations are incorrect but rather points out the major difficulty in applying this technique, which is that it is very difficult to obtain two samples with different levels of labelling and exactly the same morphology. When the microstructures do not correspond exactly, small differences arise in

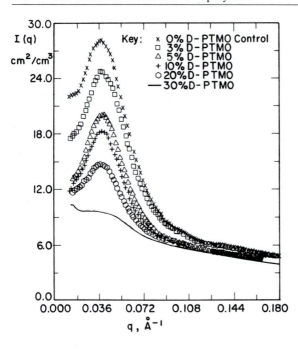

Figure 3   SANS Rayleigh factors for the 3/2/1 polyether polyurethanes containing 0, 3, 5, 10, 20 and 30 % deuterated PTMO soft segments

TABLE II   Coherent Scattering Length Densities for the Soft and Hard Phases for the Polyether Polyurethane Series

Sample	Soft Segment Coherent Scattering Length Density $\times 10^{-9}$ cm/cm^3	Hard Segment Coherent Scattering Length Density $\times 10^{-9}$ cm/cm^3
0 % d-PTMO	2.02	25.22
3 % d-PTMO	3.93	25.13
5 % d-PTMO	5.19	25.18
10 % d-PTMO	8.40	25.18
20 % d-PTMO	14.86	25.05
30 % d-PTMO	21.43	24.85

the scattering curves, which lead to artifacts in the data following subtraction, as observed in Figure 4.

For the samples containing 3 % and 5 % labelled chains, the single chain scattering function could not be extracted. There are two main reasons for this. First, the single chain scattering is obtained as the difference between two large numbers. At low levels of deuteration, the statistical noise in the original data tends to mask the contribution from the single chain scattering, because the level of single chain scattering in the total scattering is proportional to the product $x(1-x)$, where x is the percent deuterated PTMO. Second, especially at low levels of deuterolabelling, slight differences in sample morphology will lead to great difficulty in the extraction of the single chain scattering data.

To avoid the problems associated with the subtraction method, Miller et al.[12] utilized the phase contrast matching method to obtain the single chain scattering data for the soft segment in a polyether polyurethane. Two samples with the same molar stoichiometry (3/2/1

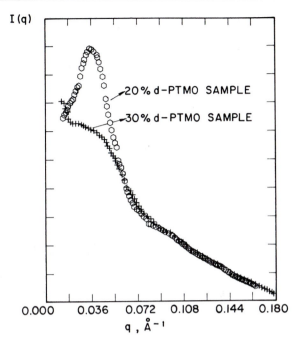

Figure 4 Single chain scattering data for the soft segment in a polyether polyurethane for 20 % deuterated soft segment and 30 % deuterated soft segment compositions

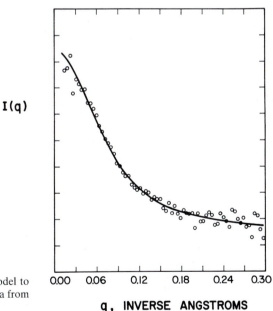

Figure 5 Model fit of the random coil model to the soft segment single chain scattering data from a polyether polyurethane

MDI/BD/PTMO) and degree of deuteration were prepared for this study. The degree of deuteration of the soft segments, 32.5 %, was chosen so that the samples would be phase contrast matched according to Equation 3. Figure 5 shows the absolute scattering intensity for one of these samples. The solid line is the scattering function for a random coil, which is given by Debye[13] as

$$F(q) = \frac{2}{t^2}(e^{-t} + t - 1) \tag{7}$$

where $t = q^2 R_g^2$ and R_g is the radius of gyration of the coil. This model has been found to be an excellent choice for amorphous bulk homopolymers. The excellent agreement between the best fit of the model and the actual scattering data do not imply that the soft segments are in a random coil conformation. Rather, the model is used to obtain the radius of gyration of the segments. In the low angle limit, the form factors for all particle shapes will approach the asymptotic limit of Guinier's law, and hence give the same radius of gyration.

$$\lim_{q \to 0} P(q) = e^{-q^2 R_g^2/3} \tag{8}$$

The radii of gyration measured as a function of temperature for these samples are shown in Figure 6. The error bars drawn are 95 % confidence limits generated by the nonlinear least squares fitting procedure. At room temperature, the radius of gyration of the average soft segment is approximately 15.3 Å, which is in agreement with the value obtained using Guiniers's law on the soft segment single chain scattering data shown in Figure 4. This value compares with a value of 12.1 Å obtained by SANS for the same deuterated PTMO oligomer measured in the bulk state[14]. Values from 11.5 Å to 12.3 Å are obtained when high molecular weight viscosity data for PTMO are extrapolated down to a molecular weight of 1000, and are summarized in the article by Miller and Cooper[14]. This implies that the soft segment chains are somewhat extended on the average at room temperature, as illustrated in Figure 7.

The average soft segment is found to be somewhat extended, but since neutron scattering measures an average of many chain segments, there is a range of segment extensions. One possible case would be a bimodal distribution of random coil chains and fairly taut chains. The presence of soft segments which are taut tie molecules has been used to rationalize the thermal mechanical behavior of polyether-polyesters[15–17]. It would not be unreasonable to expect to find such taut tie molecules in polyurethanes since the microstructure, chemical architecture, and thermal mechanical properties are similar for these two families of materials.

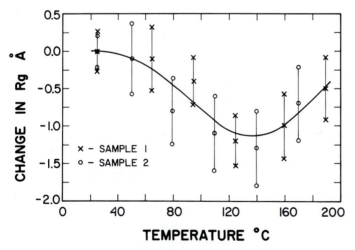

Figure 6   Plot of the change in the PTMO soft segment radius of gyration vs. temperature for a 3/2/1 polyether polyurethane

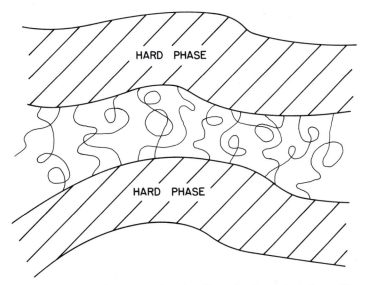

Figure 7   Average conformation for the soft segments in a lamellar polyether polyurethane. The conformation is somewhat extended relative to the bulk conformation

As the temperature increases, the radius of gyration of the soft segments initially decreases. Chee and Farris[18] have proposed a model for the kinetics of phase separation in two-phase polyurethane systems that states that as the temperature rises, the retractive force arising from the extended soft segment chains increases. This is especially true for the taut tie molecules that may be present in the material, and is also in agreement with the classical theory of rubber elasticity. This facilitates the pulling of hard segments out of the hard phase into the soft phase. The result of pulling a hard segment out of the hard phase would be to reduce the radius of gyration of the adjacent soft segments since after the hard segment is pulled from the hard domain, the soft segment is free to relax into a more nearly random coil conformation. This model, based only on a phase separation mechanism, supports the SANS results described above. This model also predicts that interphase mixing will increase as the temperature is increased, a phenomenon that has been observed experimentally using small angle X-ray scattering (SAXS)[19].

As the temperature is raised to 160 °C and above, a slight upturn in the soft segment radius of gyration is measured. This may be due to the presence of substantial phase mixing at higher temperatures, as discussed previously. Koberstein and coworkers[29, 21] have proposed a phase mixing/demixing transition in polyurethanes around 150 °C based on DSC and SAXS studies of the multiple endothermic properties of these materials. The SANS data of our experiment support this model, although the data do not prove the validity of the hypothesis. The interaction between the mixed hard and soft segments within the soft phase dominates any relaxation processes that may occur. This interaction causes the soft segment chains to have a larger radius of gyration than when there are few hard segment chains present. The chain conformation is nearly a random coil, but it is expanded somewhat, much as a homopolymer chain would be swollen by a good solvent.

5   EXPERIMENTAL RESULTS ON POLYETHER-POLYESTERS

Miller et al.[22] (1985) also investigated the conformation of the polyether soft segment and the polyester hard segment in a series of polyether-polyester block copolymers at intermediate polyester contents. The samples were prepared from 5/4/1 and 10/9/1 mole ratios of dimethyl terephthalate (DMT), butanediol, and PTMO-1000. The samples prepared are designated 5-SS, 5-HS, 10-SS and 10-HS for samples with 5 or 10 DMT units per ester sequence. The -SS samples are designed to yield the polyether soft segment conformation while the -HS samples are designed for examining the polyester hard segment conformation. The -HS samples contain deuterated and protonated soft segments and deuterated and protonated hard segments, while the -SS samples contained deuterated and protonated soft segments and protonated hard segments. All of the samples satisfy the phase contrast matching criterion of Equation 4.

Figure 8 illustrates the change in the soft segment radius of gyration as a function to temperature for the 5-SS and 10-SS samples. The radius of gyration of the soft segment at room temperature is 12.8 Å for the 5-SS sample and 13.4 Å for the 10-SS sample. A value of 12.1 Å is measured using SANS on a bulk oligomeric blend of protonated and deuterated PTMO of 1000 molecular weight[14]. This corresponds to a value of 11.8 Å for a segment with a molecular weight of 950. Thus the average soft segment is slightly extended at room temperature. The majority of the soft segments are in a random coil conformation, but a number of them are fairly elongated. As the temperature increases, the soft segment R_g decreases to 11.1 Å at 160 °C for the 5-SS sample and 11.5 Å at 210 °C for the 10-SS sample, a change of about 15 %. The mechanism responsible for this small change in the soft-segment R_g is the relaxation of stresses associated with the elongated segments. These elongated molecules have been termed taut tie molecules[23,24]. As the samples are heated above the glass transition temperature of the hard segment, which has been reported to be about 50 °C[25], the chains can more easily rearrange themselves to a lower energy state by minimizing the strain energy present in the elongated soft-segment chains. The chains that are firmly bound in hard-segment crystallites can only rearrange locally in the amorphous

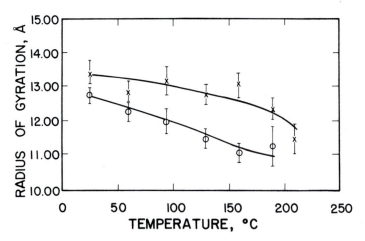

Figure 8   Change in the PTMO soft segment radius of gyration as a function of temperature in 5/4/1 (o) and a 10/9/1 (x) polyether-polyester block copolymer

part of the chain. This mechanism is consistent with arguments made by Bandara and Droscher[23, 24], who found that changes in the mechanical properties and the small-angle x-ray scattering behavior of polyether-polyester block copolymers could be brought about by changing the temperature at which the samples are prepared. The increase in the SAXS long spacing reported by Bandara and Droscher[23, 24] was partially attributed to the decrease in the number of taut tie segments, but the increase is mainly due to changes occurring in the crystalline hard domains.

Figure 9 shows the change in the hard segment radius of gyration as a function of temperature for the random coil model. The hard segments are probably not in a random coil conformation, since they are crystallized in the hard domains, but the radius of gyration obtained using a random coil model will agree well with the actual radius of gyration regardless of the true particle shape. The hard segment radius of gyration increases substantially with increasing temperature. For the 5-HS samples, R_g increases from 12.5 Å to 15.5 Å, a change of 25 %. This compares with a value of 18.0 Å for a hard segment consisting of 5 tetramethylene terephthalate (TMT) units in an extended crystal conformation as calculated from data given in a review of poly(tetramethylene terephthalate) crystal structure investigations by Desborough an Hall[26]. The hard segment R_g in the 10-HS sample increases from 12.8 Å to 25.8 Å at 190 °C. This compares with a value of 37.6 Å calculated for the extended crystalline conformation of a 10 TMT unit hard segment.

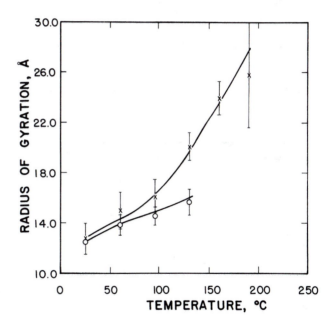

Figure 9   Radius of gyration of the polyester segments in the 5-HS (o) and the 10-HS (x) samples as a function of temperature for the random coil model

The results of the SANS experiments indicate that chain folding is occuring in the hard segments of these materials. At room temperature, the radius of gyration of the hard segments in both the 5-HS and 10-HS sample is about 12.5 Å. This is considerably smaller than would be expected if the hard segments were fully extended in the crystal. A fully extended segment that is 3 TMT units long and folds at the oxytetramethylene link would have a radius of gyration about 11.5 Å using an infinitesimal rod approximation. When the width of a folded segment is accounted for, the radius of gyration is expected to be around

11.9 Å for a folded 5 TMT unit structure and 12.4 Å for a folded 10 TMT unit structure. The close agreement of these figures with the measured values strongly supports the folded chain model. Van Bogart et al.[27] and Koberstein and coworkers[20, 28, 29] found evidence for chain folding of the hard segments in polyurethane block copolymers. Koberstein and Stein state that chain folding must occur in the hard segment in these materials based on SAXS measurements of the interdomain distance. The folding length suggested is three to four repeat units in the hard segment, which is similar to that suggested by the data reported by Miller.

When the temperature is increased, the hard segment radius of gyration also increases. Buck and coworkers[30, 31] reported that the long spacing measured by SAXS in similar materials increased with increasing annealing temperatures. The explanation given for this behavior was that the crystalline hard domain lamellae are thickening. The growth mechanism is similar to that proposed for semicrystalline homopolymers[32] where the thickening process occurs by the extension of folded chains through the melting of the higher energy multiply folded segments followed by a recrystallization of these melted segments into a more extended, lower energy state. The result of the present investigation supports the mechanism of thickening of the lamellar structure through an unfolding of the polyester segments in response to the annealing process. In the 5-HS case, the annealing seems to cause most of the crystallized hard segments to approach the extended crystalline conformation. The difference between the measured radius of gyration and that calculated for an extended chain (15.7 Å vs. 18.0 Å) can be attributed to the fact that the measured value is an average of the crystalline and amorphous configurations. If one assumes that 50 % of the ester sequence are located within the hard phase, the amorphous hard segment radius of gyration can be calculated to be about 13 Å. The 10-HS hard segments extend to a greater extent than do those of the 5-HS sample because the 10-HS hard segments start out with a greater amount of chain folding. When the presence of amorphous hard segments in the soft phase is accounted for, it can be concluded that there still is some chain folding in the 10-HS samples at elevated temperatures. Many of the hard segments are too long to reach an extended state.

Miller[33] also investigated the deformation response of the polyether soft segment in a 5/4/1 polyether-polyester. The PTMO had a molecular weight of 1900 for this study, and the sample was designated 5-SS-2. Two-dimensional SANS data were acquired for various degrees of elongation of the sample. Figure 10 shows contour plots of the uncorrected data for sample elongations of 0 %, 30 %, 100 %, and 200 %. The long axis of the ellipses in the plots corresponds to the direction perpendicular to the stretching axis. The contour plots show that as the degree of elongation increases, the eccentricity of the ellipses representing the scattering data increases as expected. The plots also have a wing on the left side of the beam center that is due to scattering from the beam stop. During the data reduction, this wing is corrected for by subtracting a background scattering pattern. The two-dimensional data in the contour plots were reduced to a simple $I(q)$ vs. q form in the directions parallel and perpendicular to the stretching direction and the data was fit to a Debye random coil model (Equation 7) to obtain the radius of gyration of the soft segment in the directions parallel and perpendicular to the stretching direction.

For the unstretched sample, the radius of gyration of the soft segment is 25.2 Å. The radius of gyration of an oligomer with a molecular weight of 1900 at theta conditions is expected to be 16.7 Å based on the results presented by Miller and Cooper[14]. The soft segments are therefore somewhat extended on the average. They are even more extended on the average than the 1000 molecular weight soft segments are in the 5-SS and 10-SS samples. This result is not surprising since it requires less energy to elongate the 2000 molecular weight segment a fixed percentage than it does to elongate a 1000 molecular weight segment by the same

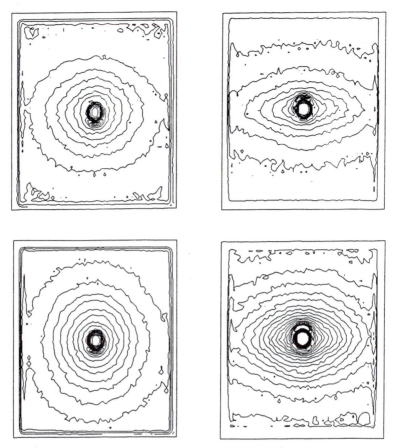

Figure 10   Contour plot for the two-dimensional SANS data for the 5-SS-2 sample at A. 0 %, B 30 %, C 100 % and D 200 % elongation. Stretching direction is horizontal.

percentage according to rubber elasticity theory[2]. Stated in equivalent terms, for the same distorting force on two coils of different sizes, the larger coil will deform more on a percentage basis.

Figure 11 shows the radius of gyration of the soft segment in the parallel direction plotted against the percent elongation of the sample. The error limits are within the size of each of the data point markers. The lines drawn on the figure are models which describe various deformation mechanism in terms of the change in the segment radius of gyration with elongation. The three models shown are the affine deformation model, the junction affine deformation model, and the phantom network model.

The affine deformation model states that the change in dimensions of the individual segments in a material are directly proportional to the changes in the overall sample dimensions. The parallel and perpendicular components of the radius of gyration in this model are given as

$$R_r/R_i = L/L_o \tag{9a}$$

$$R_p/R_i = (L/L_o)^{1/2} \tag{9b}$$

where R_i is the initial radius of gyration of a segment, L is the stretched length of the sample, and L_o is the initial length of the sample. R_r and R_p are the radii of gyration in the directions parallel and perpendicular to the stretching direction.

The junction affine deformation model comes from the standard form of the theory of rubber elasticity. In this model, the crosslink junctions in a network rather than the actual chain segments are assumed to deform affinely. Flory[2] gives the expressions for R_r and R_p for the junction affine model as

$$\frac{R_r}{R_i} = \left[\frac{L^2}{2L_o{}^2} + \frac{1}{2} \right]^{1/2} \tag{10a}$$

$$\frac{R_p}{R_i} = \left[\frac{L_o}{2L} + \frac{1}{2} \right]^{1/2} \tag{10b}$$

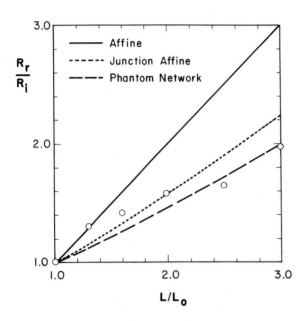

Figure 11   Plot of the change in the soft segment radius of gyration in the direction parallel to the stretching direction as a function of elongation for the 5-SS-2 sample. The solid line represents the affine deformation model, the dotted line represents the junction affine model, and the dashed line represents the phantom network model with a crosslink functionality of 8

The phantom network is the third model shown in Figure 11. The phantom network was first proposed by James and Guth[34, 35] and assumes that the chains in a network are free to move without any restrictions due to their neighboring chains. Only the crosslink points affect the motion of the segments. For this model, the mean positions of the crosslink points are assumed to deform affinely. For this model, R_r and R_p can be expressed as[36]

$$\frac{R_r}{R_i} = \left[\frac{1}{2} + \frac{1}{f} + \frac{L^2}{2L_o{}^2} - \frac{L^2}{fL_o{}^2} \right]^{1/2} \tag{11a}$$

$$\frac{R_p}{R_i} = \left[\frac{1}{2} + \frac{1}{f} + \frac{L_o}{2L} - \frac{L_o}{fL} \right]^{1/2} \tag{11b}$$

where f is the functionality of the crosslink junctions. Determing f for a block copolymer is not possible, since the crosslinking points, which are the phase boundaries, are not a single point in space as are crosslinks in a elastomer network. A value of f of 8 was used for the phantom network curves drawn in Figures 11 and 12.

The data shown in Figure 11 do not support any of the deformation models very well. The affine deformation model is certainly not the appropriate one. The junction affine or phantom network models may represent the proper deformation mechanism. The deviation from the predicted behavior of these models may be caused by the fact that in a block copolymer, the crosslink junction point is finite in size and that the hard phase which serves as the crosslink junction can deform, whereas in rubber elasticity theory crosslink points are assumed to be point-like and nondeformable.

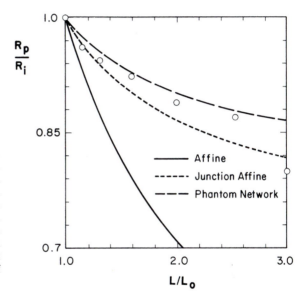

Figure 12   Plot of the change in the soft segment radius of gyration in the direction perpendicular to the stretch direction for the 5-SS-2 sample as a function of elongation. The solid line represents the affine deformation model, the dotted line represents the junction affine model, and the dashed line represents the phantom network model with a crosslink functionality of 8

Figure 12 shows the ratio of R_p to R_i plotted as a function of the sample elongation. This figure suggests that the deformation mechanism can be modelled by a phantom network model, at least up to 150 % elongation. Beltzung et al.[36] studied the deformation in a series of poly(dimethyl siloxane) networks using neutron scattering and found that the phantom network deformation model best described the data obtained. The materials they studied were closer to an ideal elostomer than the block copolymer used for this investigation, but their results suggest that the phantom network model is more appropriate than the other two models. A survey of the literature reveals that the phantom network model and the junction affine model describe the deformation behavoir of crosslinked networks fairly well, while the affine deformation model is more appropriate for uncrosslinked materials. The results of this study concur with other investigations of crosslinked materials, with the polyester domains acting as the crosslink junctions.

6   CONCLUSIONS

From the SANS investigations of chain conformation in diblock and triblock copolymers reported thus far, it appears that in lamellar materials the chain segments are somewhat extended in the direction perpendicular to the lamellar surface. For copolymers which exhibit an isolated spherical domain morphology, the chain conformation within the spherical domains is that of an unperturbed chain. The literature gives some indication that the phase contrast matching technique is better suited for extracting the single chain scattering data in block copolymers than is the subtraction method, since the subtraction method requires two samples of identical morphology.

At room temperature, the polyether soft segments in the polyurethane elastomer and in the polyether-polyester block copolymers are somewhat extended on the average relative to the bulk oligomer conformation. In the polyether-polyester with a lower hard-segment content, the soft segments are less extended than in the higher ester content material. A distribution of conformations occurs in these materials, with a majority of the soft segments being nearly in a random-coil conformation. A substantial number of segments are fairly taut, leading to an average conformation that is somewhat extended relative to the random coil conformation.

The soft-segment radius of gyration in the polyurethane material initially decreases with increasing temperature. As the temperature rises, the retractive force on the taut soft segments increases, thus facilitating the extraction of hard segments from the amorphous hard phase into the soft phase. One would expect that the degree of phase separation would decrease with increasing temperature due to such a mechanism, and in fact this is borne out by small-angle x-ray scattering studies[19].

The soft-segment radius of gyration in the polyether-polyester materials decreases smoothly with increasing temperature. This is primarily due to a decrease in the number of taut tie molecules present at elevated temperature[23, 24] caused by the rearrangement of the hard crystalline domains. In addition, relaxation of stresses introduced by molding these samples below the hard-segment crystalline melting temperature may contribute to the decrease in the soft-segment R_g.

The hard segments in the polyether-polyesters are chain-folded at room temperature. The average repeat distance is three to four DMT/butanediol segments. As the temperature is increased, the hard-segment radius of gyration increases. Two mechanisms are responsible. First, the tightly folded, higher energy chains are melting and recrystallizing in a more extended, lower energy conformation. Second, new hard-domain material is crystallizing out of the soft amorphous phase into an extended conformation. Thus one expects that the lamellae should thicken somewhat and grow laterally.

7   ACKNOWLEDGEMENT

The authors would like to acknowledge partial support of this research by the Polymer Section of the Division of Materials Research of the National Science Foundation under Grant No. DMR 81-06888.

References

1. D. G. H. Ballard, J. D. Wignall and J. Schelten, *Eur. Polym. J. 9* 965 (1973)
2. P. J. Flory, *"Principles of Polymer Science"*, Cornell University Press, Ithaca, New York (1951)
3. J. S. Higgins and R. S. Stein, *J. Appl. Cryst., 11,* 346 (1978)
4. G. Hadziioannou, C. Picot, A. Skoulios, M. L. Ionescu, A. Mathis, R. Duplessix, Y. Gallot and J. P. Lingelser, *Macromolecules, 15,* 263 (1982)
5. J. T. Koberstein, *J. Polym. Sci. Polym. Phys. Ed., 20,* 593 (1982)
6. S. N. Jahshan and G. C. Summerfield, *J. Polym. Sci., Polym. Phys. Ed., 18,* 1859 (1980)
7. S. N. Jahshan and G. C. Summerfield, *J. Polym. Sci. Polym. Phys. Ed., 18,* 2145 (1980)
8. R. W. Richards and J. L. Thomason, *Polymer, 22,* 581 (1981)
9. F. S. Bates, C. V. Berney, R. E. Cohen and G. D. Wignal, *Polymer, 24,* 519 (1983)
10. H. Hasegawa, T. Hashimoto, H. Kawai, T. P. Lodge, E. J. Amis, C. J. Glinka und C. C. Han, *Macromolecules, 18* 67 (1985)
11. J. A. Miller, S. L. Cooper, C. C. Han and G. Pruckmeyer, *Macromolecules, 17,* 1063 (1984)
12. J. A. Miller, G. Pruckmeyer, J. E. Epperson and S. L. Cooper, *Polymer, 26,* 1915 (1985)
13. P. Debye, *Phyzik, A., 28,* 135 (1928)
14. J. A. Miller and S. L. Cooper, *Makromol. Chem., 185,* 2429, (1984)
15. G. Perego, M. Cesari, and R. Vitali, *J. Appl. Polym. Sci., 29,* 1141 (1984)
16. G. Perego, M. Cesari, and R. Vitali, *J. Appl. Polym. Sci., 29,* 1157 (1984).
17. M. Droscher, *Adv. Polym. Sci., 47,* 119 (1982)
18. K. K. Chee and R. J. Farris, *J. Appl. Polym. Sci., 29,* 2529 (1984)
19. G. L. Wilkes and J. A. Emerson, *J. Appl. Phys., 47,* 4261 (1976)
20. L. M. Leung and J. T. Koberstein, *J. Polym. Sci. Polym. Phys. Ed., 23,* 1883 (1985)
21. J. T. Koberstein and T. P. Russell, *Macromolecules, 19,* 214 (1986)
22. J. A. Miller, J. M. McKenna, G. Pruckmeyer, J. E. Epperson and S. L. Cooper, *Macromolecules, 18,* 1727 (1985)
23. U. Bandara and M. Drosher, *Angew. Makromol. Chem., 107,* 1 (1982)
24. U. Bandara and M. Drosher, *Colloid Polym. Sci., 261,* 26 (1983)
25. W. Marrs, R. H. Peters and R. H. Still, *J. Appl. Polym. Sci., 23,* 1063 (1979)
26. I. J. Desborough and I. H. Hall, *Polymer, 18,* 825 (1977)
27. J. W. C. Van Bogart, P. E. Gibson and S. L. Cooper, *J. Polym. Sci. Polym. Phys. Ed., 21,* 65 (1983)
28. J. T. Koberstein and R. S. Stein, *J. Polym. Sci. Polym. Phys. Ed., 21,* 1439 (1983)
29. J. T. Koberstein and R. S. Stein, *J. Polym. Sci. Polym. Phys. Ed., 21,* 2181 (1983)
30. W. H. Buck and R. J. Cella, *ACS Polym. Preprints, 14,* 98 (1973)
31. W. H. Buck, R. J. Cella, E. K. Gladding and J. R. Wolfe, *J. Polym. Sci. Symp., 48,* 47 (1974)
32. A. Keller, *Rep. Progr. Phys., 31,* 623 (1968)
33. J. A. Miller, Ph. D. Dissertation, Department of Chemical Engineering, University of Wisconsin, Madison, Wisconsin (1985)
34. H. M. James and E. J. Guth, *J. Chem. Phys., 11,* 455 (1943)
35. H. M. James and E. J. Guth, *J. Chem. Phys., 21,* 1039 (1953)
36. M. Beltzung, C. Picot, and J. Herz, *Macromolecules, 17,* 663 (1984)
37. A. Maconnachie and R. W. Richards, *Polymer, 19,* 739 (1978)

Chapter **12**

RESEARCH ON THERMOPLASTIC ELASTOMERS

Section **5**

MODEL STUDIES TOWARD A MOLECULAR UNDERSTANDING OF THE PROPERTIES OF SEGMENTED BLOCK COPOLYETHERESTERS

G. Wegner

Contents

Gerhard Wegner, Max-Planck-Institut für Polymerforschung, D-6500 Mainz, West Germany

1   INTRODUCTION

Thermoplastic elastomers are generally prepared from two types of long chain segments such that they may be considered as multiblock copolymers[1]. One of the blocks consists of chain elements with low glass and melt transition temperatures, the other consists of chain elements which aggregate or crystallize to form rigid physical crosslinks. It is an open question as to what extent the details of the molecular structure such as the block length and block-length distribution or other molecular features affect the crystallization behavior and the mechanical properties of these materials.

Very large effects are seen, if, for example, a homopolyester such as poly(tetramethylene terephthalate) also commonly called polybutylene terephthalate (PBT) is compared in its melting behavior and mechanical properties with a segmented block-copolymer based on PBT as the hard segment and poly(tetramethylene oxide) (PTMO) as the soft segment[2-6]. A more subtle inspection of the available data does not reveal, however, to what extent the molecular structure of the copolymer, in terms of the concepts of the theory of rubber elasticity or because of other effects due to changes in the morphological superstructure of the sample, causes the change from a tough engineering plastic (pure PBT) to a hard elastic material (segmented copolymer)[7-10].

Even such seemingly straight forward determinations as the degree of crystallinity from measurements of density or enthalpy of melting are open to interpretation subject to the underlying model of the phase composition of the sample.

Another aspect of the materials properties of thermoplastic elastomers relates to the desired miscibility or compatibility of the chemically different segments in the melt phase. Ideally a complete miscibility at the processing temperature is desired to ensure extrusion or injection molding without problems. It is clear, however, that this can only be achieved within the limits of certain segment lengths or segment length distributions in which the melting of the crystallized segments occurs simultaneously with their dissolution in the non-crystalline matrix of different chemical composition.

To develop a better understanding of the material properties it is thus necessary to accumulate elementary data on the properties of the crystallizable and non-crystalline segments and their mixtures depending on chain-length and temperature. Moreover, block-copolymers with well defined segment length of the different blocks are interesting models to be compared with the industrially produced materials of the same composition but statistical segment length distribution. Finally, the analysis of the structure and performance of the commercially produced materials must be based on such numbers and observations obtained from the better defined models.

One well-known and commercially important example for such materials is provided by the segmented copoly(etherester)s based on poly(tetramethylene terephthalate) (PBT) as the hard segment and poly(tetramethylene oxide) (PTMO) as the soft segment[2-6]. These copolymers can be described as random copolymers of one acid and two alcohol components as depicted by Figure 1.

The poly(ether) component is derived from α-hydro-ω-hydroxyoligo(tetramethylene oxide) of number average molecular weight of 1000–2000. The hard segment average molecular weight ranges from 600 to 3000 in the copolymers of technical interest. The total molecular weight is around $2-4 \cdot 10^4$. The hard block segment length is determined by the ratio of PTMO to 1,4-butanediol, and assuming that the normal kinetics of polyester formation can be applied, a hard block length distribution will result which can be identified as the segment length distribution of T–B-units.

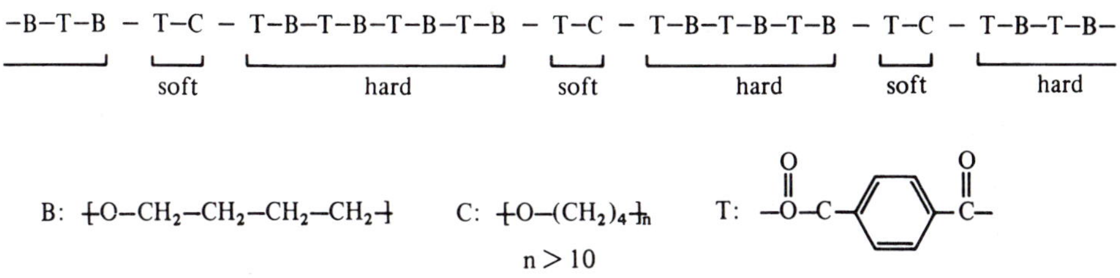

−B−T−B − T−C − T−B−T−B−T−B−T−B − T−C − T−B−T−B−T−B − T−C − T−B−T−B−

|_____| |__| |_____| |__| |_____| |__| |_____|
    soft   hard   soft   hard   soft   hard

B: ɟO−CH₂−CH₂−CH₂−CH₂ɟ   C: ɟO−(CH₂)₄ɟₙ   T: —O−C—⬡—C—
                                                    ‖O   O‖

n > 10

Figure 1   Schematical description of the molecular structure of a random segmented block-copolyester based on poly(tetramethylene terephthalate) and poly(tetramethylene oxide)

In the light of the above mentioned considerations it is thus necessary to investigate molecularly uniform oligo(oxytetramethylene)s, oligo(tetramethylene terephthalate)s and regularly built blockcopolymers from such segments. Finally, the structure of the technical material will be compared against such basic information.

2   SYNTHESIS AND PROPERTIES OF UNIFORM OLIGO(OXYTETRAMETHYLENE)S

2.1   Stepwise Synthesis of Oligomers

The strategy for the synthesis of monodisperse α-hydro-ω-hydroxyoligo(oxytetramethylene)s requires a stepwise chain extension reaction which works with high yields and without side reactions leading to other than the required end groups. The separation of higher oligomers with the same degree of polymerization but different end groups is such a difficult task that it should be avoided under all circumstances. This is one reason why the seemingly simple ether synthesis according to Williamson is not suitable except under special circumstances.

Bill, Dröscher and Wegner[11] chose the following strategy described by Scheme 1. The hydroxylterminated oligo PTMOs 1-n with degree of polymerization (DP) n ≤ 7 were obtained by reductive cleavage of the cyclic bisacetals 5-n which in turn could be synthesized by reacting 2,3-dihydrofuran with the appropriate oligomer of DP = n-2. The resulting mixture of oligomers differing in DP by ± 1 can be separated by fractional distillation up to n = 7. The synthesis of still higher oligomers requires a duplication or triplication method to produce mixtures of oligomers which differ by a sufficiently large but constant number of monomer units to allow chromatographic separation on a preparative scale. Bill et al. used reaction (8) described in Scheme 1, a modified Williamson-ether synthesis working under very mild conditions by phase transfer catalysis to prepare the desired mixtures of higher oligomers. After cleaving of the protecting end groups these mixtures could be separated by preparative column chromatography following the GPC principle. Alternatively, Baumgartner[12] showed that the dodecamer 1-12 can be obtained in high purity and with less steps from the bis-tosylate of 1-4 and the monosodiumalcoholate of 1-4 in THF at 40 °C. The separation of the resulting mixture could be achieved using preparative reversed phase HPLC.

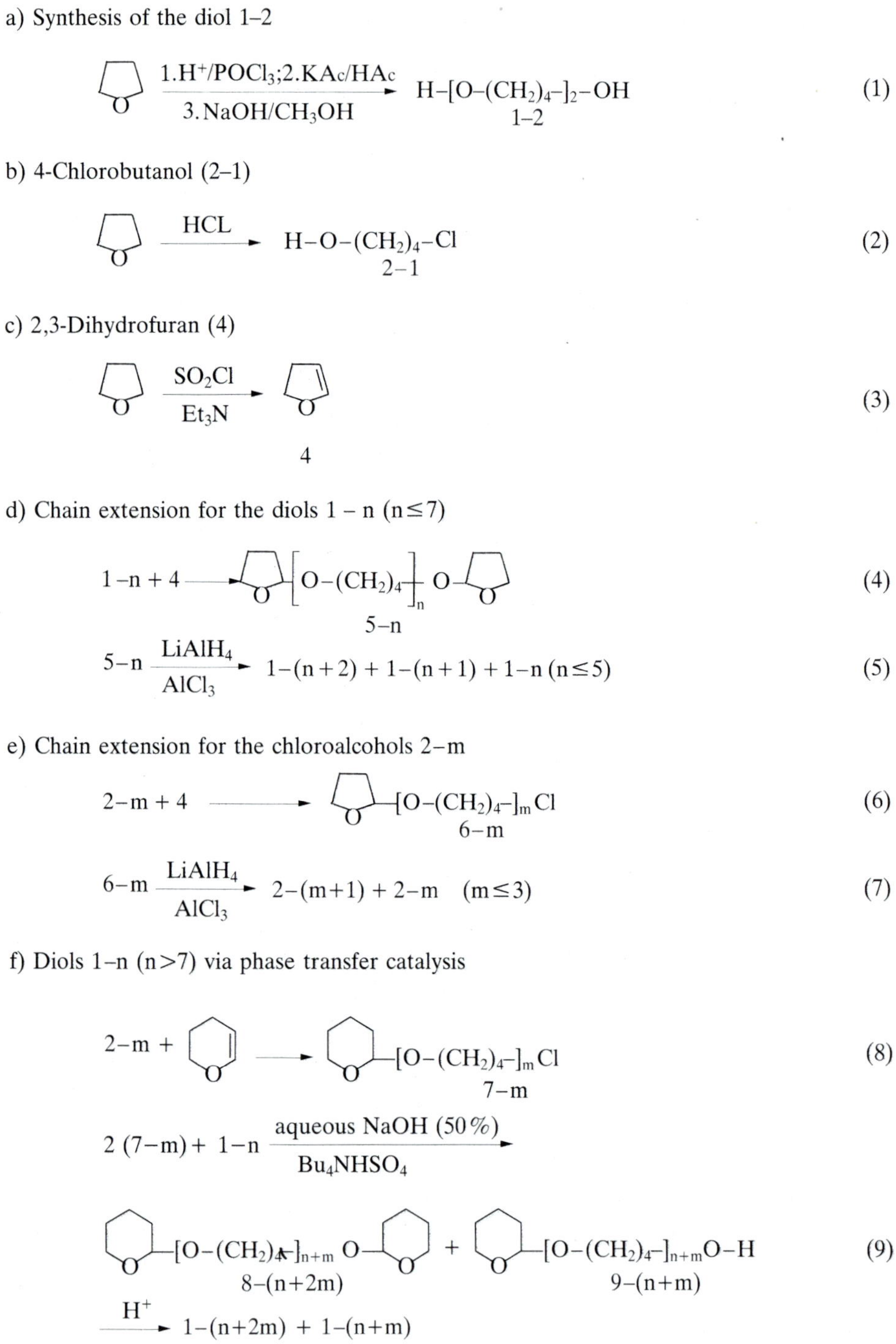

a) Synthesis of the diol 1–2

$$\text{(furan)} \xrightarrow[\text{3. NaOH/CH}_3\text{OH}]{1.\text{H}^+/\text{POCl}_3; 2.\text{KAc/HAc}} \text{H--[O--(CH}_2)_4\text{--]}_2\text{--OH} \qquad (1)$$
$$\underset{1\text{--}2}{}$$

b) 4-Chlorobutanol (2–1)

$$\text{(furan)} \xrightarrow{\text{HCL}} \text{H--O--(CH}_2)_4\text{--Cl} \qquad (2)$$
$$\underset{2\text{--}1}{}$$

c) 2,3-Dihydrofuran (4)

$$\text{(furan)} \xrightarrow[\text{Et}_3\text{N}]{\text{SO}_2\text{Cl}} \text{(dihydrofuran)} \qquad (3)$$
$$\underset{4}{}$$

d) Chain extension for the diols 1 – n (n≤7)

$$1\text{--n} + 4 \longrightarrow \text{(ring)}\Big[\text{O--(CH}_2)_4\Big]_n\text{O--(ring)} \qquad (4)$$
$$\underset{5\text{--n}}{}$$

$$5\text{--n} \xrightarrow[\text{AlCl}_3]{\text{LiAlH}_4} 1\text{--(n}+2) + 1\text{--(n}+1) + 1\text{--n (n}\leq5) \qquad (5)$$

e) Chain extension for the chloroalcohols 2–m

$$2\text{--m} + 4 \longrightarrow \text{(ring)}\text{--[O--(CH}_2)_4\text{--]}_m\text{Cl} \qquad (6)$$
$$\underset{6\text{--m}}{}$$

$$6\text{--m} \xrightarrow[\text{AlCl}_3]{\text{LiAlH}_4} 2\text{--(m}+1) + 2\text{--m} \quad (\text{m}\leq3) \qquad (7)$$

f) Diols 1–n (n>7) via phase transfer catalysis

$$2\text{--m} + \text{(ring)} \longrightarrow \text{(ring)}\text{--[O--(CH}_2)_4\text{--]}_m\text{Cl} \qquad (8)$$
$$\underset{7\text{--m}}{}$$

$$2\,(7\text{--m}) + 1\text{--n} \xrightarrow[\text{Bu}_4\text{NHSO}_4]{\text{aqueous NaOH (50\%)}}$$

$$\text{(ring)}\text{--[O--(CH}_2)_4\text{--]}_{n+m}\text{O--(ring)} + \text{(ring)}\text{--[O--(CH}_2)_4\text{--]}_{n+m}\text{O--H} \qquad (9)$$
$$\underset{8\text{--(n}+2\text{m})}{} \qquad\qquad\qquad\qquad \underset{9\text{--(n}+\text{m})}{}$$

$$\xrightarrow{\text{H}^+} 1\text{--(n}+2\text{m}) + 1\text{--(n}+\text{m})$$

Scheme 1   Strategy of the synthesis of monodisperse hydroxyl-terminated oligo(oxytetramethylene)s according to Bill et al.[11]

2.2 Melting Points and Other Characteristic Data

The melting and boiling temperatures as well as the enthalpies of melting of the homologous series are complied in Table I. There is a pronounced odd/even effect as similarly observed in paraffines[13]). The reciprocal melting points plotted vs. the reciprocal DP following equation 1[15] fall on different lines which both extrapolate to the same reciprocal melting point for infinite n. The melting point of perfectly crystalline poly(oxytetramethylene) is thus extrapolated to $T_m^°$ (PTMO) = 45 ± 2 °C in good agreement with the literature value

TABLE I   Boiling Temperature, Melting Temperature and Heat of Melting of the Hydroxy-Terminated Oligo(oxytetramethylene)s H[O–CH$_2$–CH$_2$–CH$_2$–CH$_2$]$_{\overline{n}}$OH (1 –n)

Compound	T_b/°C[a]	T_m/°C	ΔH_m/(kJ · mol^{-1})	Ref.
1 –2	108	5	24.4	12
1 –3	151	31	37.7	11
1 –4	183	23	48.7	12
1 –5	226	37	70.8	11
1 –6	253	31	69.0	11
1 –7	270[b]	42	101.4	11
1 –8	c	35	95.1	12
1 –9	c	41	108.7	11
1 –12	c	41[d]	158.1[d]	12
1 –14	c	38[e]	133.6	11

[a] Boiling Temp. at 0.01 mbar
[b] mixture containing 1 –6 and 1 –7
[c] cannot be distilled without decomposition
[d] the sample crystallized from n-pentane showed T_m = 43 °C, ΔH_m = 172.8 (kJ mol^{-1})
[e] the sample was only partially crystalline from the melt

of 43 °C[14]. The slope of the Flory-plot (equ. 1) for the even-numbered oligomers gives the enthalpy of melting of the perfect crystal of polymer $\Delta H_m^°$ (PTMO) = 14.8 (kJ mol^{-1}) in good agreement with the value of 14.4 (kJ mol^{-1}) given by Bowman et al.[16] and the average of the incremental increase $\Delta H_m/n$ calculated from the data of Table I of 13.8 (kJ mol^{-1}) counting the odd and even members of the series separately.

$$\frac{1}{T_m} = \frac{1}{T_m^°} + \frac{2R}{\Delta H_m^°} \cdot \frac{1}{n} \tag{1}$$

T_m: Melting temperature of oligomer with DP = n

$T_m^°$:   Equilibrium melting temperature of the perfect polymer crystal

R: Gas constant

$\Delta H_m^°$: Molar heat of melting per constitutive unit of the perfectly crystalline polymer

n: Degree of polymerization = number of constitutive units

2.3 Preparation of Narrow Fractions via Inclusion Complexes

Although pure hydroxylterminated oligo PTMOs can be directly synthesized as described above, their preparation on a larger scale as it is necessary to produce segmented polymers for mechanical studies meets with difficulties. In principle GPC or HPLC could be used to fractionate mixtures of oligomers as they are obtained from cationic polymerization of tetrahydrofurane. In practice this does not work on a preparative scale, if more than several grams of a desired fraction are required.

It was, however, found that a preparative fractionation can be developed based on the formation of urea-poly(oxytetramethylene) complexes[17]. These complexes are obtained by isothermal crystallization of a mixture of commercially available hydroxyl terminated polymers with urea in methanol. If a sample with broad molecular weight distribution is submitted to conditions of complex formation, the yield of the complex as well as M_n of the fraction to be included (and its distribution) will depend on the crystallization temperature provided the experiment is carried out under strictly isothermal conditions. The study of model inclusion complexes as well as data from actual fractionation of polymolecular mixtures provided the correlation between crystallization temperature T_c and DP of the oligomer to be included

$$T_c = 323.6 - 333.6 \cdot \frac{1}{n} \text{ (in methanol)} \tag{2}$$

As an example, the differences of crystallization temperature ΔT_c for the oligomer with n = 8 and 9, 18 and 19 or 28 and 29 are 4.6, 0.97 and 0.41 degrees, respectively. It is obvious that this fractionation method is very effective toward the low molecular weight tail of the total distribution of typical commercially available prepolymers. The polymer is easily retrieved from the complexes by extraction of their solution in water with trichloromethane. An actual example of a preparative fractionation is shown in Table II. Narrow fractions with $M_w/M_n \leqslant 1.06$ are obtained in a short time.

TABLE II   Characterization of Fractions from Successive Crystallization of a PTHF Sample[a] in the Form of Urea-PTHF Complexes[17]

Fraction #	Complex T_c[b] (K)	Yield (%)	T_m[c] (K)	Enclosed PTHF M_w[d] (g/mol)	M_n[d] (g/mol)	$(M_w/M_n - 1)$[d]	M_n[e] (g/mol)
1	312.5	12.0	412.8	2190	2087	0.049	2030
2	307.5	20.6	412.0	1687	1592	0.060	1480
3	303.0	12.9	407.5	1197	1159	0.033	1155
4	298.0	8.7	404.3	955	935	0.021	940
5	291.5	8.6	399.8	783	769	0.018	771
6[f]	–	17.1	–	–	–	–	465

[a] PTHF Sample $\overline{M}_n$ = 650 g/mol, M_w/M_n = 1.9 ± 0.1
[b] Crystallization temperature
[c] Decomposition temperature
[d] determined by HPLC analysis
[e] determined by VPO
[f] water-insoluble, non-complex forming residue

3   SYNTHESIS AND PROPERTIES OF UNIFORM OLIGO (BUTYLENETEREPHTHALATE)S WITH DEFINED END GROUPS

3.1   Synthetic Aspects

The synthesis of uniform oligo(butyleneterephthalate)s (systematic name: oligo(oxytetramethylenoxyterephthaloyl) with defined end groups provides the models to discuss the melting temperature and related phenomena of the segmented block copolyesters. Hässlin, Dröscher and Wegner[18, 19] developed a synthetic strategy which allowed the individual oligomers to be prepared in amounts of up to 20 grams and with end groups, so that they can be used as the building blocks for the synthesis of segmented copolyesters with uniform block length. The reaction sequences employed are sketched in Scheme 2 and the various

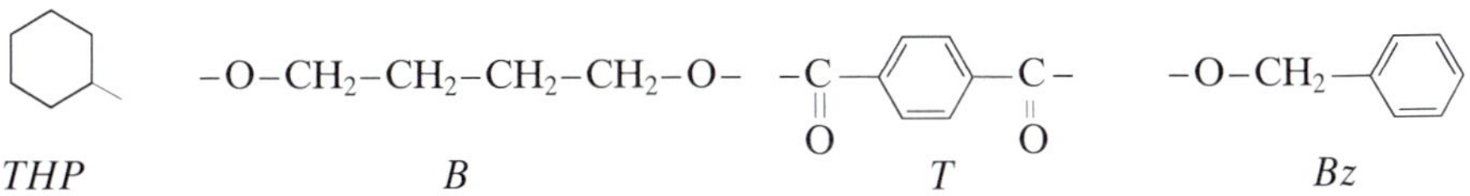

THP $-O-CH_2-CH_2-CH_2-CH_2-O-$ $-\overset{\|}{\underset{O}{C}}-\langle\bigcirc\rangle-\overset{\|}{\underset{O}{C}}-$ $-O-CH_2-\langle\bigcirc\rangle$

THP B T Bz

$Bz-T-B-H$ $THP-B-T-B-H$ $Bz-T-Cl$
1   2   3

a) $1+Cl-(T-B)_n-T-Cl \longrightarrow Bz-(T-B)_{n+2}-T-Bz \longrightarrow Cl-(T-B)_{n+2}-T-Cl$
4

b) $2+Cl-(T-B)_n-T-Cl \longrightarrow THP-(B-T)_{n+3}-B-THP \longrightarrow H-(B-T)_{n+3}-B-H$
5

c) $3+10\ H-(B-T)_n-B-H \longrightarrow Bz-(T-B)_{n+1}-H$

d) $4+THP-B-H \longrightarrow$ Transition from $-T-Cl$ to $-B-H$ end group

e) $5+3 \longrightarrow$ Transition from $-B-H$ to $T-Cl$ end group

Scheme 2   Synthetic route for the preparation of oligoesters with various end groups, comp. Table III for the various compounds prepared[18, 19]

compounds synthesized and investigated are tabulated in Table III. The details of the synthesis as well as analytical methods used to characterize the oligomers with regard to purity, chiefly elemental analysis, saponification number, hydroxyl number, HPLC with various combinations of columns and solvent systems, DSC, IR-, ^{1}H and ^{13}C-NMR spectra are found in reference 19 and 20.

TABLE III   Summary of the Uniform Oligo(butylene terephthalates)s with Defined Endgroups as Shown in Scheme 2

Name	Abbreviation	Notation	Degree of Polymerization n	Endgroups α	Endgroups ω
α-Hydro-ω-hydroxybutoxyoligo-(oxytetramethylenoxyterephthaloyl) (3-n)	Esterdiol	H-(B-T)$_n$-B-H	1, 2, 3, 5, 7	H-(O-	-O(CH$_2$)$_4$OH
α-(4-Benzyloxycarbonylbenzoyl)-ω-benzyloxyoligo(oxytetramethylen-oxyterephthaloyl) (4-n)	Dibenzylesters	Bz-(T-B)$_n$-T-Bz	0, 1, 2, 3, 4, 6, 8, 10	-C(=O)-⟨C$_6$H$_4$⟩-COCH$_2$C$_6$H$_5$	-OCH$_2$C$_6$H$_5$
α-Hydro-ω-benzyloxyoligo(oxytetra-methylenoxyterephthaloyl) (5-n)	Benzyl-butane-diolesters	Bz-(T-B)$_n$-H	1, 2, 3, 4	H-(O-	-OCH$_2$C$_6$H$_5$
α-(4-Carboxybenzoyl)-ω-hydroxy-oligo(oxytetramethylenoxytere-phthaloyl) (6-n)	Diacids	HO-(T-B)$_n$-T-OH	0, 1, 2, 3, 4, 6	-O(C=O)-⟨C$_6$H$_4$⟩-C-OH	-OH
α-Hydro-ω-tert-butoxyoligo(oxytetra-methylenoxyterephthaloyl) (7-n)	t-Butyl-butane diolesters	tB-(T-B)$_n$-H	1, 2, 3	H-(O-	-OC(CH$_3$)$_3$
α-(2-Tetrahydropyranyl)-ω-[4-(tetra-hydropyran-2-yloxy)butoxy]oligo-(oxytetramethylenoxyterephthaloyl) (8-n)	THP-Esterdiol	THP-(B-T)$_n$-B-THP	1, 2, 3	(tetrahydropyran-2-yl)-O-	-O(CH$_2$)$_4$O-(tetrahydropyran-2-yl)

From References 18 and 19

3.2   Thermoanalytical Characterization

Figure 2 shows the melting endotherms of the oligomeric dibenzylesters Bz(T–B)$_n$-TBz for n = 0,1,2,3,4,6,8 and 10 as observed by DSC. The true melting temperature for each oligomer was determined by measuring the DSC-trace for different heating rates and then extrapolating the peak temperature defined as T_m for zero-heating rate[21].

In a flory type plot, the melting temperatures plotted vs. degree of polymerization n following equation 1 are shown in Figure 3. Straight lines are obtained with a slope

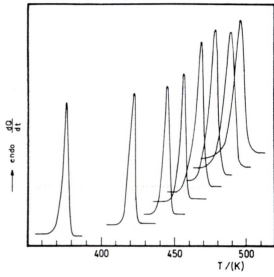

Figure 2   DSC-curves of the melting of the oligomeric dibenzylesters Bz(T–B) –TBz; from the left: n = 0, 1, 2, 3, 4, 6, 8 and 10. Heating rate was 20 (deg min^{-1}). The individual curves are shifted along the ordinate by arbitrary units for the sake of clarity

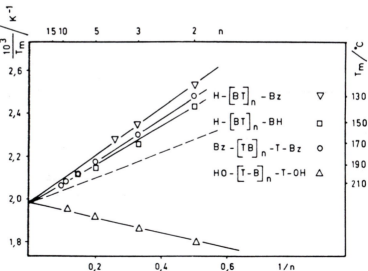

Figure 3   Plot of 1/T$_m$ vs. 1/n for the series 3-n, 4-n, 5-n and 6-n (comp. Table 3). Extrapolation to 1/n = 0 gives the reciprocal T$_m$° (PBT) = 509 ± K. The broken line is calculated for PBT according to equ. 1 with ΔH$_m$° (PBT) = 26 kJ mol^{-1}, T$_m$° (PBT) = 509 K

characteristic for each set of oligomers which extrapolate to a common crossing point on the ordinate, the reciprocal melting point of the pure crystalline phase of PBT. Thus $T_m°$ (PBT) is determined as 236 ± 4 °C in excellent agreement with the literature[22]. The meaning of n in Figure 3 needs some explanation. It is equal to the number of terephthalic ester residues per molecule since these units are the determining factor for the melting behaviour.

The different slopes are then caused by end group effects. Consequently a two-phase model can be adopted in which the end groups as defined in Table III do not contribute to the heat of melting but only occupy volume at the surface of the elementary crystallites consisting of the T–B units. Considering the large differences in the relative volume of the various end groups and in agreement with generally accepted theories in the thermodynamics of multicomponent systems, one can then rewrite equation 1 replacing the mole fraction of the end groups by their volume fraction. In the limits of v_e (volume fraction of end groups) $< v_m$ (volume fraction of T–B units) one may then write

$$\frac{1}{T_m} = \frac{1}{T_m^o} + \frac{2R}{H_m^o} \cdot \frac{v_e}{v_m} \tag{3}$$

v_e and v_m can be calculated from increments[23].

The melting points of the oligomers of the series 3-n, 4-n and 5-n fall indeed on the same line, if plotted according to equation 3 as shown in Figure 4. The oligomers with carboxylic end groups are an exception. Their data cannot be treated in this way because of effects of end group association which contribute significantly to the overall behavior.

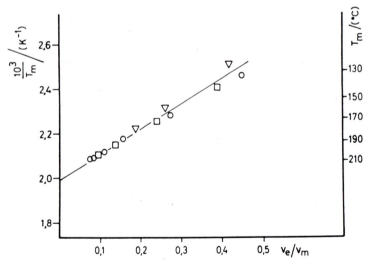

Figure 4   Plot of $1/T_m$ vs the ratio of the volume fraction of endgroups (v_e) and middle groups (v_m) of oligo (butylene-terephthalates); notation as in Figure 3

A value of $\Delta H_m°$ (PBT) = 28.7 kJ mol[-1] is determined from the slope of the line shown in Figure 4. This value is in reasonable agreement with the average of all incremental differences between the melting enthalpies of oligomers within the same series of 26 kJ mol[-1] and the value of 31 kJ mol[-1] reported by Illers[24].

3.3 X-ray Structure of the Oligomers

The crystal structure of PBT has been discussed by several groups. A critical discussion of the available data will be found in ref.[26]. The X-ray diagrams of the oligomers resemble those of the α-modification of PBT. As an example the unit cell parameters of the oligoesterdioles (series 3-n, Table III) are shown in Table IV[27]. These compounds are probably the best models for the crystalline fraction of the hard-segments in the block copolyesters. The length of the repeat unit (chain periodicity) is found as 1.159 nm from these data.

TABLE IV   Unit-cell Parameters of the Oligo(esterdiols) 3 -n[a] in Comparison to α-PBT

	α-PBT[25]	3 –5	3 –3	3 –2
a/nm	0.483	0.477	0.464	0.482
b/nm	0.594	0.589	0.575	0.592
c/nm	1.159	6.53	4.24	3.03
α/deg	99.7	98.4	104.9	102.4
β/deg	115.2	115.0	114.9	114.0
γ/deg	110.8	111.8	105.7	110.5
V/nm^3	1.261	1.462	0.895	0.672
p_c/gcm^{-3}	1.404	1.352	1.393	1.312

[a] From Reference 27, Table III

3.4 Binary Mixtures

It was of interest to study the phase diagrams of binary mixtures of oligomers with the same end group but differing in degree of polymerization. Care has to be taken in such studies to avoid effects due to transesterification in the melt which would lead to a multicomponent system. The oligoesterdiols 3-n (Table III) were sufficiently stable for such investigations. Binary mixtures were prepared, they were heated above the melting temperature in a DSC and the recrystallization behavior was then studied[27]. A sufficiently slow cooling rate has to be chosen to avoid effects due to supercooling.

The liquidus curves for three such mixtures are shown in Figure 5. The open symbols on the ordinate indicate the equilibrium melting point of the pure components. One realizes that even the pure components show some degree of supercooling which increases with increasing chain length. A eutectic composition is observed only for the mixture of trimer and pentamer at a mole fraction of pentamer of 0.03. The phase diagrams indicate that these oligomers do not cocrystallize and that the melt of the lower melting oligomer is a very poor solvent for the higher melting oligomer. One tends to predict from these observations that hard segments of different length are likely to undergo phase separation on crystallization when the corresponding block copolyesters are crystallized.

An interesting behavior was observed when the model oligomers 3-n were mixed with the corresponding block copolyesters of the structure indicated in Figure 1.

In all cases the blends of oligomer and polymer showed a much higher melting point than the pure block copolymer approaching nearly the value of pure PBT (495 K). The oligomer could be quantitatively extracted from such blends indicating that we deal with a purely physical effect. In agreement with the observed behavior of the block copolymers during annealing experiments, we tend to explain this observation by an equilibrium between the

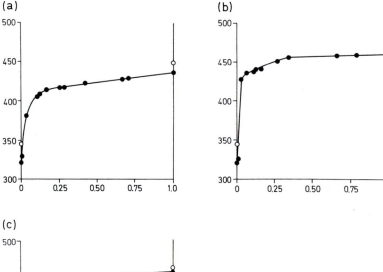

Figure 5   Phase diagrams of binary mixtures of the oligo esterdioles 3-n (n = 1, 3, 5) observed by DSC (cooling rate 1,25 K min). The open symbols are the equilibrium melting temperatures of the pure oligomers. a) *3*-1 and *3*-3; b) *3*-1 and *3*-1 and *3*-5; c) *3*-3 and *3*-5

ester segments crystallized and those dissolved in the amorphous matrix. This equilibrium will be established at the crystallization temperature. The amorphous matrix consists then of a mixture of non-crystalline ester segments dissolved in the ether segments. An admixture of further ester units to this amorphous volume will cause a crystallization of the least soluble component, i. e. the longest ester segments, until the total equilibrium concentration of ester segments in the amorphous volume is reestablished.

Finally, and investigation was made of the temperature dependence of the solubility of various oligoesters of the structure $n\text{-}C_4H_9TB_n\text{-}T\text{-}nC_4H_9$ in hydroxyl terminated oligo(oxy-tetramethylene)s in the temperature range 30–100 °C[28]. The solubility varies widely with the type of mixture and temperature.

As an example, the solubility of the ester with n = 5 is 0.26 gl^{-1} in the oligoether with n = 2, 0.5 gl^{-1} in the oligoether with n = 3 and 4 and 0.03 gl^{-1} in the oligoether with n = 5, all values being measured at 60 °C. As expected the solubility increases exponentially with increasing temperature according to

$$\ln c_{equ} = \frac{-\Delta H_L}{R} \cdot \frac{1}{T} + C$$

where c_{equ} is the solubility, ΔH_L is the enthalpy of dissolution, R is the gas constant and C is an integration parameter. The best investigated case is for mixtures of oligoester with n = 3 with various olioethers. A ΔH_L per repeat unit of oligoester of 21 kJ mol^{-1} has been found which is very close to the value of the enthalpy of melting of the ester segments. The data indicate an agreement with the experiment that the oligo(oxytetramethylene)s are good solvents for the oligoesters and consequently the hard segments of the block copolyesters at temperatures close and above the melting temperature of the latter.

4   SEGMENTED BLOCK COPOLYMERS OF UNIFORM LENGTH

The model ether- or ester-oligomers and/or combinations of both have been used to build up model block copolymers with defined segment length[28]. In other words, possible effects of the segment length distribution could be investigated. To this end the uniform hydroxyl terminated oligo(oxytetramethylene)s as described previously in this chapter were reacted with dimethylterephthalate and 1,4-butanediol following the general procedure of Hoeschele[29] and Witsiepe[30]. Alternatively, block copolyesters which had both a uniform distribution in soft and hard segment length were prepared from solution polycondensation of chloroterephthaloyl terminated model hard blocks with hydroxyl terminated soft blocks in pyridine as the solvent[28].

The melting behavior of all of these block copolymers was very similar to the one described by Wegner et al.[6], for the technically more important block copolyesters with most probable distribution of both type of segments. This behavior which will be described in more detail below is characterized by the fact that the peak temperature of the melting endotherm cannot be changed by annealing procedures, although the total shape of the endotherm may very well be a consequence of the thermal history of the sample under investigation. Thus the peak temperature of the endotherm can be used as characteristic data for the sample.

In the light of the previous discussion on the dependence of the melting temperature of oligomers on their degree of polymerization, it seems reasonable to treat the copolymers in the same way. In other words, the hard segments are considered as independent units with end groups consisting of the soft segments in discussion of the melting of the block copolymers.

The average block length, i. e. the average number of –T–B– units per hard block can be calculated for the block copolymers having a non-uniform block length distribution from the overall composition and considering the finite molecular weight of the polymer according to Sorta and Melis[31]. The observed melting temperatures can now be plotted vs. the degree of polymerization of the hard blocks following equation 1, where the average block length was used in the case of the non-uniform block copolymers.

Figure 6 shows the result of such data treatment for a total number of 84 different block copolymers including data from different groups of authors. Two regions can be clearly identified despite some scattering of the points. The points of all polymers with T–B_n n < 12 fall close to a line which extrapolates to the reciprocal value of 525 ± 6 K as the limiting value of the melting point. The polymers with n ≥ 12 show their melting temperatures close to another line which extrapolates to the reciprocal value of 502 ± 3 K. The latter value is close to the accepted value of the melting temperature for pure, perfectly crystallized PBT.

The slope of the lines cannot be directly used to calculate the enthalpy of melting in the light of the previous discussion on the effect of end groups onto the melting behavior (compare Figures 3 and 4), since it is not known how to take the fractional volume of the soft segments

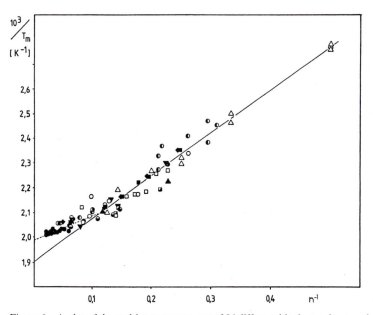

Figure 6   A plot of the melting temperatures of 84 different block-copolyesters (general composition as in Figure 1) vs. reciprocal number of (T–B) units in the hard blocks[28].
◪, □, ○, ◔, △: Data from Ref.[28]; ▲ from Ref.[5]; ◆ from Ref.[32]; ● from Ref.[33]; ■ from Ref.[34]; ◑ from Ref.[35]; ◐ from Ref.[2]. The number of repeat units in the soft (oxytetramethylene) blocks was in all cases $n \geqslant 4$

into account. Figure 6 should, therefore, only be regarded as a qualitative correlation waiting for further data treatment.

5   MORPHOLOGY OF SEGMENTED BLOCK COPOLYETHERESTERS

5.1   Light and Electron Microscopy

As in all semicrystalline solid polymers the polymer properties do not depend directly on the molecular structure but rather on the supermolecular structure sometimes also called morphology, which in turn depends in a rather complex way both on the molecular structure of the polymer and on the sample history.

Concerning segmented poly(etherester)s three different models of the morphology have been proposed in literature so far. Cella[2] assumes that these materials exhibit a morphology consisting of continuous and interpenetrating crystalline and amorphous phases. The crystalline phase is thought to consist of thin (approximately 100 Å in chain direction) lamellae interconnected by short length tie molecules in much the same way as they are found in semicrystalline homopolymers.

Seymour et al.[4] consider, however, a model more analogous to common semicrystalline thermoplastics than to block copolymer systems which undergo microphase separation. Based on experiments with small angle light scattering and polarized light microscopy these authors conclude that the copolyesters crystallize in a spherulitic superstructure with chain folding. According to their model the soft phase is embedded between radial crystalline fibrils of spherulites consisting of the hard segments. The amorphous phase is a mixture of the soft segments and non-crystalline hard segments showing a single glass transition region. In the framework of this model the soft segments serve merely to dilute and "soften" the surfaces and interlamellar regions of the normal PBT-superstructure.

Wegner et al.[6] described experiments aimed to better characterize the morphology and annealing behavior of such copolymers in the light of results on melting and mixing characteristics of well defined PBT-oligomers[18]. Their results of experiments on solution recrystallization indicated that dendritic growth structures seem to prevail, and that fractionation among the hard segments takes place during the crystallization. A sample morphology based on a fringed micelle model was assumed for the melt crystallized samples.

These morphological models proposed so far are all helpful in explaining some of the observed properties of these poly(etherester) elastomers, but they are contradictory in the details, if one believes that there exists only one supermolecular structure and, moreover, that this structure is predefined by the molecular design of the macromolecules rather than being effected by the crystallization and annealing procedures.

It was therefore important to investigate the effect of sample treatment and sample history on the observable morphological features for some model copolymers.

Zhu and Wegner[7] investigated three copolymer samples which were of approximately equal molecular weight and differed in their hard/soft-segment composition. The hard segment sequence length $\overline{P}_{n,H}$ was calculated from the known mole fraction x_H of the oxytetramethyleneoxyterephthaloyl units according to

$$\overline{P}_{n,H} = \frac{1}{1 - x_H}$$

Assuming that the segmented copolyesters under consideration can be regarded as random copolymers the fraction of all hard segments contained in sequences with $n \geq \overline{P}_{n,H}$ max be calculated. Their weight fraction $W_n{}^*$ is given by

$$\overline{W}_n^* = \frac{x_H^n(nx_s + x_H)m_H}{x_H m_H + x_s m_s} \tag{4}$$

where x_H and x_s are the mole fractions of hard and soft segments with molar weight m_H and m_s, resp.

In general the degree of crystallinity in these copolyesters, even if they are carefully annealed, has been found[6] to be much smaller than $\overline{W}_n^*$, thus indicating that only a very small fraction of all hard segments is able to crystallize. The characteristic data of the three samples investigated are compiled in Table V. In addition to the values describing the chain architecture, the temperature $T_m{}^{max}$ of the melting endotherm of each sample is recorded as measured after careful annealing as described in ref. 6, and it may be compared with the melting temperature of the appropriate model oligomers described previously.

All three samples A, B and C show the same overall features on isothermal crystallization from the melt. If the melt is rapidly quenched to the predefined crystallization temperature T_c, a well defined and reproducible density of nuclei is found. The nucleation occurs randomly and predominantly athermal and thus a finite number of growth centers is established after a short time compared to the total crystallization time. The nucleation density increases dramatically with decreasing T_c.

Once the nuclei are formed they develop rapidly into a globular form similar to a spherulite and continue to expand in size. They reach a constant size which depends on T_c without impinging on each other. Even after prolonged annealing at T_c a large nonbirefringent and thus amorphous volume remains around each growth center. Once the globular centers are formed subsequent crystallization takes place only within the skeleton of these initial semicrystalline domains of sperulite texture.

The finer details of the internal structure of these spherulites are obtained through a newly developed two-step staining technique[36]. Allylamine is first adsorbed preferentially to the internal phase boundaries between crystalline and amorphous regions which in the second step is reacted with OsO_4. Thus, the phase boundaries within the sample are preferentially made visible.

Figure 7 shows high-resolution electron micrographs obtained by this technique of a preparation of sample A. Figure 7a shows a portion of a spherulite which has grown in the amorphous surrounding. The sectional view of the lower, right part of Figure 7a, depicted in Figure 7b, demonstrates the excellent resolution of the details of the phase boundaries which appear as dark regions between the hard segment lamellar crystallites seen edge-on and the surrounding amorphous matrix.

In the light of the broad distribution of the hard segment sequence length in the copolymer it is surprising to see that the crystalline lamellae extend with little fluctuation in thickness over

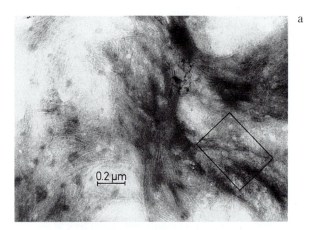

a

0.2 µm

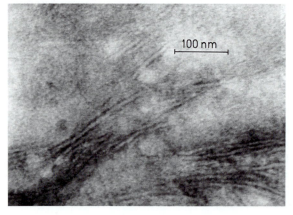

b

100 nm

Figure 7 Electron micrograph of sample A melt crystallized at 168 °C for 540 min and then stained by allylamine/OsO_4. (a): Portion of a spherulite; (b): sectional enlargement from reference 7

many 1000 Å. Remembering that the chain repeat of the hard segments is approximately 11 Å, the information contained in Figure 7b offers a direct evidence of the effective fractionation which takes place in these copolymers during crystallization. If hard blocks with widely differing length were able to crystallize in the same lamella or if they would form different crystals of their own species, it should be possible to recognize this under the limits of resolution indicated by Figure 7b. Note also that some of the individual lamellae are embedded into large noncrystalline regions. The average thickness of the crystalline (unstained) core of the lamellae in this sample preparation is of the order of 75 Å.

The birefringent domains formed at first on isothermal crystallization break up into smaller domains, if the samples are annealed below the initial crystallization temperature. More complicated structures due to internal reorganisation of the initially formed lamellar superstructure are observed by means of electron microscopy. Additionally dendritic overgrowth features are seen to develop at the edges of the original spherulites. The thickness of the lamellae remains, however, quite regular. Moreover, optical microscopy reveals that during the annealing the number of the sperulitic domains remains constant and equal to the number initiated at the isothermal growth stage. Consequently the increase of crystallinity observed during annealing occurs only inside these domains.

These results indicate that the segmented copolymers crystallize to form lamellar structures which are able to reorganize on annealing in much the same way as homopolymers. It may even be reasonable to discuss chain folded structures in which the fold surface is formed by the non-crystallizing soft segments and those hard segment sequences which are unable to crystallize because they are either too long or too short to fit into the crystals of the crystallizing fraction of the hard segment sequences. This agrees well with the previous assumptions[6] derived from DSC and SAXS data that only a small fraction of all hard segment sequences crystallize and that the crystals are built up preferably from those sequences which are present in the highest concentration within the sample.

A different kind of superstructure is formed on rapid quenching of the crystallizing melt film to room temperature as indicated by Figure 8. The nucleation density is very high and, contrary to the isothermal crystallization at low supercoolings where the crystallization is concentrated to spherulitic domains, the sample is transformed into an interpenetrating network of individual lamellae. It is again somewhat surprising to see that despite the irregular network-like aggregation of the lamellae their thickness is rather homogeneous throughout the sample. It is this type of supermolecular structure which has been described by Cella[2], while some features of the sperulitic structures mentioned earlier have been discussed by Seymour et al.[4].

Figure 8 Electron micrograph of sample A crystallized from the melt at $T_c = 150\ °C$ for a few seconds then quenched at once to room temperature (contrast by staining with molybdatophosphotungstic acid); from reference 7

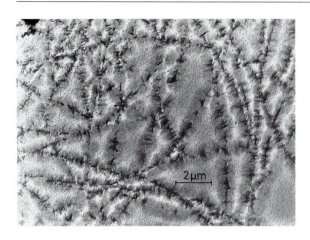

Figure 9   Electron Micrograph of sample B crystallized from the melt at T_c = 185 °C under shearing (shadowed by platinum); from reference 7

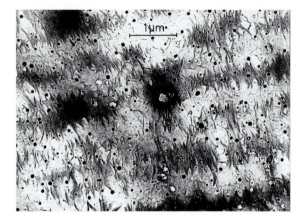

Figure 10   Electron micrograph of sample C crystallized from the melt at T_c = 195 °C under shearing (contrast after staining with $SbCl_5$); from reference 7

It is interesting to note and probably of technological significance that the segmented copoly(etherester)s can easily be crystallized in form of shish-kebab structures, if the crystallization is carried out under conditions of shear flow (Figs. 9 and 10). Shear conditions are established by crystallizing a thin melt film between two cover glasses and sliding the upper one against the lower one. An enhanced rate of crystallization and formation of extended shish-kebabs is observed under these conditions. Their occurence raises a number of questions with regard to the relation of the chemical structure of the chains and the internal structure of the shish as well as the density of the kebabs.

The formation of such shish-kebab structures may be relevant to the properties of materials which have been processed from these copolymers by extrusion or injection molding as well as by solid-state extrusion[37, 38].

Amorphous samples are obtained, if the melt films are rapidly quenched by immersion into liquid nitrogen. Such samples are transparent to light, they have no observable structure if investigated in the polarizing or electron microscope and they do not show a melting endotherm in the DSC experiment. When these amorphous samples are annealed at the same temperatures as described for the isothermal crystallization experiments, they crystallize as proven by the appearance of a melt peak in their DSC traces. The films remain, however, transparent to visible light and do not give rise to a discernible superstructure, if viewed in the polarizing microscope. This indicates that the nucleation density is very high under these conditions of crystallization and that crystalline domains of dimensions much smaller than the wavelengths of visible light had been formed. This behaviour is similar to the one described for pure PBT by Stein and Misra[39].

5.2 Small-Angle-X-ray Scattering (SAXS) and DSC

SAXS provides the means to qualitatively and quantitatively investigate the morphology and texture of semicrystalline samples. The analysis of the data is straight forward provided the sample consists of two phases only – usually a crystalline and an amorphous one – separated by sharp boundaries. Concommittant investigations by electron microscopy, DSC and density measurements are helpful to establish the correct model on which the data evaluation must be based. A thorough discussion of these considerations related to SAXS-data from segmented block copolyetheresters of the type described in this chapter will be found in reference 9.

The first step of the analysis is to fix the preparative and thermal history of a sample in an unambiguous way. DSC is a helpful tool to establish just that. This may be demonstrated for the case of sample C (Table V).

TABLE V   Sample Description[a] of the Three Block Copolyetheresters (Compare with Figure 1)

Sample	x_H	W_H	$\bar{P}_{n,H}$	$\bar{W}^*_n$	$\bar{T}_m{}^{max}/°C$	$T_m/°C$	$\Delta h_m/Jg^{-1}$	w_c^b	$w_c \cdot w_H^b$	$\varrho\ exp^b$
A	0.79	0.45	4.8	0.33	173	175/186	16	0.30	0.11	1.124
B	0.84	0.54	6.3	0.40	197	196	32.4	0.42	0.23	1.168
C	0.92	0.72	12.5	0.53	216	216	55.5	0.54	0.39	1.236

[a] x_H: mol fraction of the hard segments; W_H: weight fraction of the hard segments
$\bar{P}_{n,H}$: number average degree of polymerization of the hard segments
$\bar{W}^*_n$: weight fraction of all hard segments with $P \geq \bar{P}_{n,H}$
$\bar{T}_m{}^{max}$: highest melting temperature observed;
T_m: melting point of model oligomer of PBT[6] with $P_n = \bar{P}_{n,H}$ (for sample A two values are given for n = 3 and n = 4;
w_c: weight fraction of crystallized hard segments
$w_c \cdot w_H$: weight fraction of crystals in the total sample
[b] these values were determined for samples quenched from the melt and subsequently annealed 10 deg below $T_m{}^{max}$

If the sample is first quenched from the melt and then annealed for some time below the temperature of the peak maximum of the melting endotherm, multiple melting phenomena can be observed as shown in Figure 11. If the sample is however annealed very close to the melting temperature, a single and comparatively narrow melting endotherm is observed. It is typical for all these copolyesters that the melting point cannot be raised by annealing. It thus appears that domains of the hard segment of a certain length are formed on quenching the sample from the melt and that only the fraction of these domains and their perfection changes on annealing as indicated by the melting enthalpy Δh_m which increases from 35.8 to a maximum of 55.5 Jg^{-1} in the case of sample C, Figure 11.

The highest melting temperature observed $T_m{}^{max}$ and the maximum enthalpy of melting Δh_m observed after 24 h annealing time at the highest possible annealing temperature are compiled in Table V for the three different samples. Further annealing does not change the DSC behavior, and transesterification does not play any role in the observed facts[6].

Since the heat of melting stems from those hard segments which form the crystalline domains, their fraction w_c of all hard segments can be derived assuming that the enthalpy of

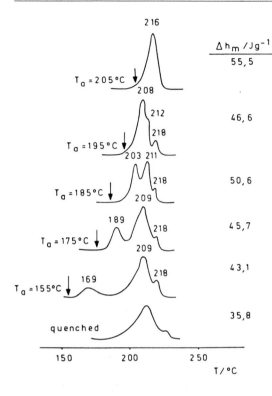

Figure 11   Effect of annealing on melting behavior of the sample A; annealing time was 24h at each temperature indicated by the arrow. A fresh sample quenched from the melt was used in each experiment. Heating rate was 20 deg.min⁻¹; from reference 6

melting Δh_m° of the unit weight of perfect domains is the same as of the unit weight of perfect crystalline PBT (144.5 Jg⁻¹).

$$w_C = \frac{\Delta h_m}{w_H \cdot \Delta h^\circ_m} \tag{5}$$

The values thus obtained and compiled in Table V show at once that the fraction of hard segments which form crystalline domains is surprisingly small and, moreover, that the total weight fraction of crystalline material in these samples is very small. The latter value is obtained by multiplying w_c with the total weight fraction of hard segments w_H.

That the values derived from the DSC-experiment describe the sample properties fairly well is also seen by comparison with values obtained by density measurements.

Since we know that the amorphous fraction of the samples consists of a mixture of hard and soft segments, its molar composition can be calculated and from that a theoretical density assuming additivity of the volumes of the constituents. The calculated and observed densities agree fairly well giving support to the conclusions derived from the melting behavior.

Another method to fix the thermal history of the samples consists in isothermal crystallization directly from the melt instead of first quenching to an amorphous or ill defined state at low temperature. That the two methods give different results in terms of morphology has already been demonstrated in the foregoing section. These differences are more clearly revealed by SAXS. Generally speaking all samples show a well resolved SAXS pattern.

Debye-rings are observed for the samples quenched from the melt indicating the isotropic distribution of the hard segment crystallites. If these samples are annealed, an exponential

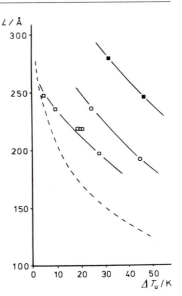

Figure 12   Long spacing L vs. supercooling $\triangle T_u$ for poly(ether ester)s crystallized under different conditions; the broken line refers to samples quenched from the melt and annealed subsequently as well as to samples drawn after quenching with subsequent annealing (comp. ref.[6]). The points refer to samples crystallized isothermally from the melt at temperature $T_m - \triangle T_u$; (■): sample A; (○): sample B; (□): sample C

increase in long-spacing is found as recorded in Figure 12. The long spacings of the different samples can be fitted by a single master curve, if plotted vs. supercooling $\triangle T$, here defined as the difference between T_m^{max} and the actual annealing temperatures T_t. Thus, the copolyesters behave surprisingly "normal" namely like a typical semicrystalline homopolymer rather than like a copolymer. In view of the rather short average sequence length of the hard segments especially in sample A, it is very surprising to see that long spacings up to 250 Å are easily reached and that neither hard nor soft segment sequence length seems to influence the annealing behavior in terms of the expected long spacing, if the supercooling is chosen as the relevant thermodynamic parameter.

Samples crystallized isothermally from the melt behave similarly in that the observed long spacing increases exponentially with the crystallization temperature T_c. There exist, however, a number of different features as indicated by the data in Figure 12.

First of all, much higher long spacings can be reached for all samples. Second, the samples differing by the hard segment block length differ strongly with regard to the long spacing which can be reached at a fixed value of $\triangle T_u$, although the general inverse correlation to $\triangle T_u$ is retained for each sample. Thus, the data for the three polymers A, B and C cannot be described anymore by a common curve. At given $\triangle T_u$ the long spacing increases in the sequence C<B<A, i. e. inverse to the average length of the hard segment blocks. In other words, the correlation between adjacent lamellae is a smooth function of the temperature.

A detailed and quantitative analysis of the SAXS intensity profiles of the samples A, B and C was undertaken by Bandara and Dröscher[9]. Among other things these authors show that the samples can be reasonably described in terms of a two-phase model and that the amorphous fraction behaves as expected from a liquid in terms of its contribution to the scattering intensity. The SAXS data are consistent with a lamellar model which is comprised of a crystalline core of thickness 3.5–4.5 nm, a diffuse boundary zone of width 0.9 nm and an amorphous layer which is varying strongly in thickness with sample composition and annealing temperature. These features of the model are sketched in Figure 13. The diffuse boundary zone arises due to lateral shifts of the PBT-segments forming the crystalline core of the lamellae. However, to explain the high crystallinity, especially of material C, one has

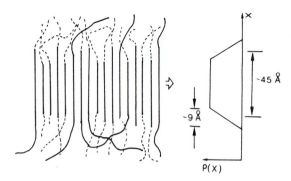

P(x)

Figure 13   A schematic model which represents the lamellar structure of bulk-annealed block copoly(ether ester); the sizes indicated have been estimated from SAXS results; from reference 9

to assume that there is a large number of longer hard-segments which contribute to the lattice by traversing the lamellae with segment folding. The multiple peak behavior observed in DSC, Figure 11, would then be explained by the presence of lamellae with different thicknesses.

From a fit of the experimentally determined one-dimensional correlation function to the assumed distributions in thickness for the crystalline and amorphous layers, it was further evaluated that the crystalline lamellae have a rather narrow distribution in thickness contrary to the amorphous layers. This in good agreement with the observations from electron microscopy described earlier.

5.3 Mechanical Properties

The impact of morphology on the mechanical performance of the blockcopolyetheresters is considerable. This was demonstrated by Zhu, Wegner and Bandara[8] by the following experiments making use of the model materials A, B and C already described in Table V.

One set of the samples A, B and C was crystallized by quenching melt films of the appropriate size to room temperature, the second set of samples A', B' and C' was isothermally crystallized as described in Table VI.

The relaxation spectra of the two sets of samples are shown in Figure 14. The spectra are in good agreement with previous data. The salient features such as the position and origin of the various relaxation peaks have been discussed earlier[4, 6.]

TABLE VI   Data of the Semicrystalline Samples as Related to Their Mechanical Behavior in the Hookean Range

Sample[a]	v_c[b]	$T_\alpha^{max}/°C$[c]	Modulus E/MPa	Yield stress σ^*/MPa
A	0,04	−50	32	5,8
A'	0,08	−60	64	8,2
B	0,15	−35	117	8,7
B'	0,18	−54	150	14,2
C	0,21	+24	186	14,2
C'	0,24	−18	340	19,6

[a] Samples A, B and C as quenched from the melt; samples A', B', and C' as isothermally crystallized (90 min) from melt. A': T_c = 150 °C (ΔT_u = 23 °C); B': T_c = 175 °C (ΔT_u = 22 °C); C': T_c= 200 °C (ΔT_u = 16 °C)
[b] v_c: volume fraction of crystallized hard segments in the total sample (based on DSC-data)
[c] T_α^{max}: temperature of the maximum of the loss peak in the glass transition region

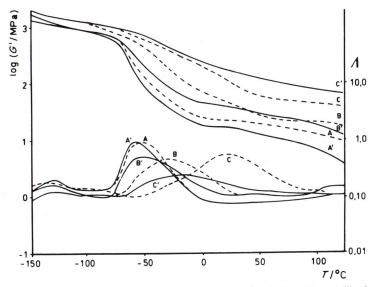

Figure 14   Relaxation spectra (torsion pendulum at 1 Hz) of two sets of samples A, B and C crystallized under conditions as described in Table VI

What is of interest in the present context is the marked effect of the thermal history of the sample on the mechanical-dynamical properties. The glass transition temperature, the value of which may be estimated from the peak position T_α^{max} of the logarithmic decrement Λ is found at much lower temperatures for the isothermally crystallized samples as compared to the samples crystallized by quenching. The effect is strongest for sample C, but even for sample A a difference of approximately 10 °C is clearly seen. In addition, the onset of the glass transition coming from the low temperature side becomes much sharper and the width of the glass transition region grows narrower, if the sample was isothermally crystallized

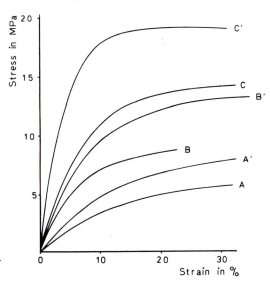

Figure 15   Stress-strain curves of the samples as described in Table VI

rather than quenched. This reflects mainly the higher degree of crystallinity of these samples and the better segregation between hard and soft segments resulting from the increase in crystallinity. The stress-strain behavior of the same samples was investigated at 30 °C, at which temperature all samples are well above their glass transition region with the exception of sample C. The latter is measured near its T_g, however.

The stress-strain curves obtained are shown in Figure 15. The region of linear response is covered as well as a part of the non-linear(flow-)behavior. All samples start to flow irreversibly at a strain higher than 5 percent. The slope of the stress-strain curves at zero-strain was taken as the value of the modulus E. A value for a yield stress σ* may be obtained by linear extrapolation of the irreversible part of the stress-strain curves which reflects the flow behavior of the samples under constant stress to the intersection with the ordinate. The data thus obtained are compiled in Table VI as well. A plot of log E vs. the volume fraction of crystallinity as shown by Figure 16 gives a straight line. Data which relate to the behavior of the pure PBT-homopolymer above its glass transition temperature (point X and Y) fit to the same curve as well. The coordinates of point X were taken from the literature[40], the point Y refers to a sample of PBT melt crystallized and measured at 70 °C.

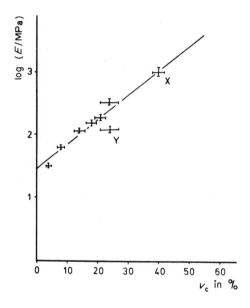

Figure 16   Relation between the stress-strain modulus E as derived from Figure 15 and the volume fraction of crystallinity v_c. Sample preparation as described in Table VI. Points X and Y refer to PBT-homopolymer samples

The data shown in Figure 16 suggest a relationship between the modulus E and the volume fraction of crystallinity v_c as represented by the purely empirical formula

$$\log E = v_c \log \frac{E_c}{E_s} + \log E_s \tag{6}$$

E_c and E_s are interpreted as the modulus of the crystalline and the amorphous fraction, resp. The values of $E_c = 1,95.10^5$ MPa and $E_s = 29.5$ MPa are derived from the slope and the intercept of the straight line in Figure 16.

A plot of similar kind is obtained relating the yield stress σ* to the volume fraction of crystallinity as shown by Figure 17 once again indicating the similarity of the samples despite

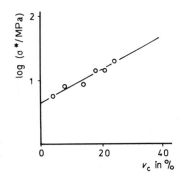

Figure 17   Relation between the yield stress σ* as derived from Figure 15 and the volume fraction of crystallinity v_c. Data from Table VI

the fairly large differences in their chemical composition. The present investigation refers strictly to isotropic samples in the range of the linear elastic response at $T>T_g$.

We believe that the results are fairly significant for the further interpretation of the properties of the segmented copolyesters and other segmented copolymers as well. It indicates that the strength of the material and its elastic response in the Hookean range at temperatures $T>T_g$, i. e. in the range of their technical application, is basically controlled by the degree of crystallinity which may be changed in an individual polymer sample by the crystallization and annealing conditions over a limited range. Moreover, these results suggest the conclusion that the variation in the chemical structure of the copolymer, in other words, the variation in the hard segment sequence length and length distribution, merely serves the purpose to control the degree of crystallinity and by this the mechanical strength over a larger range than this is possible to do with the pure homopolymer. This assumption is verified experimentally because the data of the homopolymer PBT (points X and Y in Figure 16) fit to the same relationship as the ones of the segmented copolyesters of different composition.

It becomes also clear that a treatment of the elastic behavior in terms of the therory of rubber elasticity cannot be a reasonable approach. This statement is even more valid for oriented samples of the same materials. Their properties were investigated by Bandara et al.[38], and it was shown that they exhibit a number of effects commonly observed in thermoplastics such as strain hardening and permanent set.

The common expression to describe the crystalline lamellae as "physical crosslinks" of the elastically active soft segments is certainly based on a much too simple and naive picture of the physical reality in these materials.

References

1. A. Noshay, J. E. Mc Grath, *Block Copolymers – Overview and Critical Survey,* Academic Press, New York 1977
2. R. J. Cella, *J. Polym. Sci., Polym. Symp. 42,* 727 (1973)
3. G. K. Hoeschele, *Chimia 28,* 544 (1974)
4. R. W. Seymour, J. R. Overton, L. S. Corley, *Macromolecules 8,* 331 (1975)
5. G. K. Hoeschele, *Angew. Makromol. Chem. 58/59,* 299 (1977)
6. G. Wegner, T. Fujii, W. Meyer, G. Lieser, *Angew. Makromol. Chem., 74,* 295 (1978)
7. Li-Lan Zhu, G. Wegner, *Makromol. Chem. 182,* 3625 (1981)
8. Li-Lan Zhu, G. Wegner, U. Bandara, *Makromol. Chem. 182,* 3639 (1981)

9. U. Bandara, M. Dröscher, *Colloid and Polymer Sci. 261,* 26 (1983)
10. J. A. Miller et al., *Macromolecules 18,* 1727 (1985)
11. R. Bill, M. Dröscher, G. Wegner, *Makromol. Chem. 182,* 1033 (1982)
12. M. Baumgartner, Diplomarbeit, Freiburg, 1983 and C. D. Eisenbach, private communication
13. M. G. Broadhurst, *J. Res. Natl. Bur. Stand, 66A,* 241 (1962)
14. H. Tadokoro, *J. Polym. Sci. Polym. Symp. 15,* 1 (1966)
15. P. J. Flory, A. Vrij, *J. Amer. Chem. Soc. 85,* 3548 (1963)
16. I. J. W. Bowman, D. S. Brown, R. E. Wetton, *Polymer 10,* 715 (1969)
17. G. Schmidt, V. Enkelmann, U. Westphal, M. Dröscher, G. Wegner *Colloid and Polymer Sci. 263,* 120 (1985)
18. H.-W. Hässlin, M. Dröscher, G. Wegner, *Makromol. Chem. 179,* 1373 (1978)
19. H.-W. Hässlin, M. Dröscher, G. Wegner, *Makromol. Chem. 181,* 301 (1980)
20. H.-W. Hässlin, Thesis, University of Freiburg, Freiburg, FRG, 1979
21. K. H. Illers, *Eur. Polym. J. 10,* 911 (1974)
22. A. Conix, R. van Kerpel, *J. Polym. Sci. 40,* 521 (1959)
23. M. L. Huggins, *Physical Chemistry of High Polymers,* Wiley, New York, 1958
24. K. H. Illers, *Colloid and Polymer Sci. 258,* 117 (1980)
25. M. Yokoushi, Y. Sakakibara, Y. Chatani, H. Tadokoro, T. Tanaka, K. Yoda, *Macromolecules 9,* 266 (1976)
26. I. J. Desborough, I. H. Hall, *Polymer 18,* 825 (1977)
27. M. Dröscher, Habilitationsschrift, Universität Freiburg, Freiburg 1973, FRG
28. H. G. Schmidt, Thesis, University of Freiburg, Freiburg 1984, FRG
29. G. K. Hoeschele, W. K. Witsiepe, *Angew. Makromol. Chem. 29/30,* 267 (1973)
30. W. K. Witsiepe, *Adv. Chem. Ser. 129,* 39 (1973)
31. E. Sorta, A. Melis, *Polymer 19,* 1153 (1978)
32. J. R. Wolfe, jr., *Adv. Chem. Ser. 176* (1979)
33. C. M. Boussias, R. H. Peters, R. H. Still, *J. Appl. Polym. Sci. 25,* 855 (1980)
34. J. R. Wolfe, jr., *Rubber Chem. Technol. 50,* 688 (1977)
35. A. Lilaonitkul, J. C. West, S. L. Cooper, *J. Macromol. Sci. Phys. B12,* 563 (1976)
36. G. Wegner, Li-Lan Zhu, G. Lieser, Hsuch-Li Tu, *Makromol. Chem. 182,* 231 (1981)
37. M. Dröscher, W. Regel, *Polymer Bull. 1,* 551 (1979)
38. U. Bandara, M. Dröscher, E. L. Thomas, *Colloid and Polymer Sci. 262,* 538 (1984)
39. R. S. Stein, A. Misra, *J. Polymer Sci. Polym. Phys. Ed. 18,* 327 (1980)
40. G. R. Davies, T. Smith, I. M. Ward, *Polymer 21,* 221 (1980)

Chapter 12

RESEARCH ON THERMOPLASTIC
ELASTOMERS

Section 6

COMPATIBILIZATION OF POLYMER BLENDS BY STYRENE/ HYDROGENATED BUTADIENE BLOCK COPOLYMERS

D. R. Paul

Contents

D. R. Paul, Department of Chemical Engineering and Center for Polymer Research, The University of Texas, Austin, Texas 78712

1   INTRODUCTION

The rate of introduction of new polymers into the market place has decreased in recent years owing to the high cost of research to develop new chemistry and processes compared to the probable return on this investment. As a result, increased attention has focused on blends or alloys of existing polymers to expand the spectrum of properties of established products and to meet new market needs. Most polymer pairs are immiscible and, therefore, form separate phases comprised essentially of the pure components when mixed[1-3]. Unfortunately, for many polymer pairs there is relatively poor adhesion between these phases[4,5] which precludes efficient transfer of stresses across the interface leading to inferior mechanical behavior of the mixture. This fact often precludes simple blending of polymer pairs which in principle might lead to interesting property combinations.

This situation has led to interest in blend additives which might somehow alter the interfacial problem mentioned above and circumvent the poor mechanical properties which result when most immiscible polymers are blended. Early work by Molau[6-9], Riess[10-16], and others[17-20] firmly established the fact that appropriately designed block or graft copolymers act as interfacial agents or emulsifiers for immiscible polymer mixtures. Ideally, a block copolymer will locate at the interface between phases A and B as shown in Figure 1 with its corresponding segments being associated with the appropriate phase. Since the block copolymer molecule traverses the interface, one expects greatly improved adhesion between the phases A and B owing to the strength of the covalent chain of this interfacial agent. Graft copolymers might be expected to function similarly.

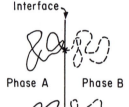

Interface

Phase A   Phase B

Figure 1   Ideal configuration of block copolymer at the interface between polymer phases A and B

A comprehensive review of this proposition was published in 1978[4], and the purpose here is to present a more focused review of results which have been published since then. This discussion will be limited to the use of styrene/hydrogenated butadiene block copolymers (S–EB–S) as the compatibilizing agent since this restriction fits the scope of the book and because these materials have been demonstrated to be quite successful for this purpose. The main body of experimental work considered here was developed in the laboratories of Teyssie[21-24], Heikens[25-29], and the author[30-32]. For easy reference, Table 1 summarizes the various block copolymers used in these publications. To facilitate reference to the original work, the copolymers are identified here by the designations used in these papers. Appropriate characterizing information as available has been included in Table I. The block structures include simple diblocks and triblocks plus some so-called tapered blocks. By control of the microstructure of the butadiene sequences during polymerization one can achieve after hydrogenation olefin-like segments which are essentially comparable to high

TABLE I   Description of styrene/hydrogenated butadiene block copolymers used as compatibilizers
[Note: S = styrene, B = butadiene, and Bh = hydrogenated butadiene units]

Designation	Composition	Block structure	Nature of hydrogenated butadiene block
SE-2[21,23] (Teyssie)	equimolar S/B	S–Bh $\overline{M}_n$ = 155,000	assumed to be 30 ethyl/1000 C
SE-4[23] (Teyssie)	equimolar S/B	S–(S/Bh)–Bh tapered block 26,000–22,000–22,000	assumed to be 30 ethyl/1000 C
SE-5[23] (Teyssie)	equimolar S/B	S–Bh $\overline{M}_n$ = 80,000	assumed to be 30 ethyl/1000 C
SE-7[24] (Teyssie)	equimolar S/B	S–(S/Bh)–Bh tapered block 22,000–22,000–26,000	assumed to be 30 ethyl/1000 C
H-7[24] (Teyssie)	–	S–Bh 10,400–39,000	5 ethyl/1000 C
none[22] (Teyssie)	–	S–Bh 75,000–80,000	30 ethyl/1000 C
none[29] (Heikens)	–	S–(S/Bh)–Bh tapered block 22,000–22,000–25,000	unknown
KRATON G 1652[30–32] Thermoplastic Elastomer® (Shell)	29% S by wt.	S–Bh–S triblock 7,200–64,000–7,200	equivalent to random ethylene-butene copolymer (essentially amorphous)

density polyethylene (HDPE), low density polyethylene (LDPE), or ethylene-butene random copolymers. This feature is quantified by the number of ethyl groups per 1000 carbon atoms in the hydrogenated butadiene segment and controls the level of crystallinity of this phase.

For the most part, we will be concerned with the addition of these block copolymers to mixtures of polystyrene (PS) with various polyolefins including LDPE, HDPE, and polypropylene (PP). Of course, the PS segment of these block copolymers should be entirely capable of mixing with the homopolymer PS while the olefin-like segment, depending on its structure, should be at least somewhat compatible with the various homopolymer polyolefins; although, complete miscibility may not exist in many cases[33–35]. We include one example for comparison where the block copolymer segments are not miscible with either homopolymer which are HDPE and poly(ethylene terephthalate) (PET) in which case the model shown in Figure 1 is clearly not applicable.

We begin by briefly reviewing some of the fundamental considerations applicable to the ideal notion embodied in Figure 1 and follow this with an extensive presentation of the efficacy of these block copolymers to improve mechanical properties. We conclude by considering the available experimental information related to the effect of these additives on phase morphology and interfacial adhesion. Throughout we attempt to reach conclusions concerning mechanisms and the optimum structure for a compatibilizing block copolymer.

2   FUNDAMENTAL CONSIDERATIONS

Optimal design of block copolymers for compatibilizing immiscible polymer blends requires consideration of a variety of issues beyond the intuitive notions embodied in Figure 1[4]. Under these circumstances will the block copolymer actually become a surface active agent? How long must the segments of the copolymer be in order not to simply slip from the homopolymer phases when the interface is stressed? Theories for such complex systems are being developed, but they are not yet able to answer such questions in detail. However, it is possible to understand some of the basic requirements[4].

As mentioned earlier in this book, the segments of block copolymers may segregate into separate phases if the segments are sufficiently long and the energy of mixing the unlike segments is endothermic. For the block copolymer to locate at the blend interface, it should have this propensity to segregate into two phases. Furthermore, the block copolymer should not be miscible as a whole molecule in one of the homopolymer phases. This tendency also depends on segmental interactions and molecular weights. The question of anchoring copolymer segments into homopolymer phases is a rheological one and would seem to be assured if the copolymer segments were sufficiently long to be entangled with surrounding chains.

Early considerations of ternary mixtures of homopolymer A/homopolymer B/block copolymers A-B were concerned with the issues of "solubilization" of the homopolymers into the pre-existing domains of the block copolymer. That is, given a phase separated block copolymer, will small amounts of added homopolymers enter these domains or from separate phases? Both theory and experiment indicated that significant solubilization can be expected only if the homopolymer molecular weight is comparable to or less than that of the corresponding segments of the copolymer[7–11, 13, 17–20, 36–38]. This forecasts a rather pessimistic view for efficient compatibilization of practical blend systems since the segments of block copolymers are usually relatively short (molecular weights range from under 10,000 to not more than 100,000 as seen in Table I) compared to industrially important homopolymers, e.g. commercial polystyrene generally has molecular weights of the order of several hundred thousands. However, it is our opinion that the notions of solubilization of homopolymers into block copolymer domains are not relevant to the question of compatibilization. The former is concerned with the perturbation of a copolymer morphology by adding small amounts of homopolymers; whereas, in the latter we are concerned with the perturbation of a blend of homopolymers by adding small amounts of copolymer. In other words, the real question is not the preservation of a block copolymer domain morphology or the accommodation of homopolymers into this structure, but will the block copolymer locate at the interface between homopolymer domains when added to this blend. For this question, the recent theories of Noolandi et al.[39–41] seem much more appropriate. The weight of the available theoretical and experimental evidence suggests that regardless of relative molecular weights block copolymers in the ideal case do generally locate at the interface, lower the interfacial tension, and reduce the size of the homopolymer domains as expected of an emulsifier. Molecular weights do play some role in the efficacy of these processes. Focused theoretical considerations of the general type developed by Noolandi could be extremely helpful in answering important questions about compatibilizer design. However, the results presented subsequently clearly show that the concept of Figure 1 is a very idealized one, and many useful compatibilizers do not function in this way at all.

3   MECHANICAL PROPERTIES

For the reasons outlined earlier, blends of immiscible polymers usually exhibit rather inferior mechanical properties relative to what might be hoped for based on the properties of the individual components comprising the blend. By this, we mean that when plotted versus composition, individual properties such as impact strength of a blend fall well below any expected additive behavior such as a simple tie line connecting the values for the pure components. This is especially true for failure properties and particularly those related to ductility of the material like elongation at break. Small deformation properties such as modulus are not usually very sensitive to the degree of interfacial adhesion between the components of the blend. Thus, in this section we will focus primarily on failure properties for a variety of immiscible blend systems which in most cases will consist of blends of polystyrene and various polyolefins. This selection is not so much related to any commercial importance or interest in these systems but is more related to the fact that available or easily synthesized block copolymers lend themselves to compatibilizing such pairs which have then been used by many laboratories as model systems.

To judge the efficacy of block copolymers as compatibilizing agents, it is consequently appropriate to examine how adding these materials improves the relationship between various mechanical properties and blend composition for a blend. In an ideal sense, an effective compatibilizer would raise a particular property from some low value up to one more closely representing an additive value. However, in a practical sense, this type of comparison is complicated by what effects addition of the compatibilizer to the individual blend components will have on their properties. For example, addition of most of the block copolymers given in Table I to polystyrene will result in a material which is less stiff and strong but more ductile. Thus, in judging the effects of compatibilization it is necessary to consider these issues, which is usually done by plotting the ternary blend data on the same coordinates as the original binary blend using a compatibilizer free basis for the composition coordinate and with various property curves for different levels of compatibilizer. In this scheme, zero percent compatibilizer indicates the property curve for the binary mixture.

3.1   Polystyrene – Low Density Polyethylene

Blends of LDPE and polystyrene with various block copolymers have been studied extensively in the laboratories of Teyssie[21, 23] and Heikens[25–29]. The former publications concentrate on failure properties obtained from tensile strain-strain diagrams which will be summarized here while the latter deal with a wider range of issues such as adhesion, dilatometric behavior, dynamic mechanical characteristics, and modelling which will be discussed in part in a later section.

The studies by Teyssie et al. compared effectiveness of the block copolymers identified as SE-2, SE-4, and SE-5 in Table I for compatibilizing this pair. Some key results from this work are reproduced here as Figure 2. The lower curves on the left and right illustrate the well below additive response of ultimate tensile strength and percent elongation at break for the polystyrene – LDPE binary and are typical of other data which have been reported for this system[42–47] and similar immiscible blends[48, 49]. The upper curves show how addition of these block copolymers improves strength and ductility when added to the binary. [Note: The original publications show these curves to go through the points for pure polystyrene and pure LDPE which cannot be the case as pointed out earlier. For this presentation, the curves have been redrawn accordingly, and, unfortunately, we do not know these properties for PS and LDPE containing 9 % block copolymer.] On an absolute scale, the improvements

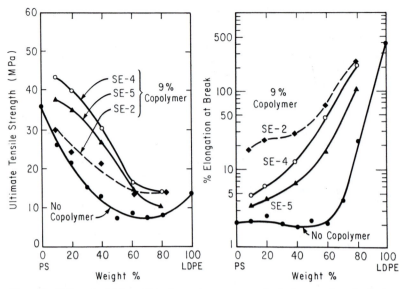

Figure 2   Effect of addition of block copolymers on mechanical properties of polystyrene – low density polyethylene blends. Reproduced with permission[23] John Wiley and Sons, Inc.

in both strength and ductility caused by adding these copolymers is impressive. The high molecular weight diblock copolymer, SE-2, causes the most improvement in elongation at break but the least improvement in strength. SE-4 and SE-5 have the same molecular weights but the former is a tapered block while the latter is a simple diblock. The tapered block gives slightly better strength and elongation at break than the diblock.

Teyssie et al.[21] conclude that block copolymers are far more effective as compatibilizers for this blend system than graft copolymers which had been used previously[45, 46]. These authors attribute the slightly better performance of the tapered block to a "graded" modulus profile at the domain interface that it is likely to produce. The hydrogenated butadiene segments of their block copolymers apparently have microstructures (see Table 1) quite similar to LDPE. It would be interesting to know about the crystallinity of the hydrogenated butadiene phase and the mechanical properties of the block copolymers to further analyze the interesting data presented.

3.2 Polystyrene – High Density Polyethylene

Blends of HDPE and polystyrene compatibilized with block copolymers have been studied in the laboratories of Teyssie[22, 24] and the author[30]. The former employed the copolymers SE-7, H-7, and the undesignated entry below these in Table I while the latter employed a commercial block copolymer, KRATON G1652 Thermoplastic Rubber. This is a poly(styrene-b-ethylene-co-butylene-b-styrene) and will be denoted as S–EB–S. It is marketed as part of Shell's family of thermoplastic elastomers. Ideally one could hope to compare the effectiveness of the quite diverse structural characteristics of these copolymers for compatibilization, but differences in the design of experiments in the two laboratories compromise such possibilities. The Teyssie studies were done on blends compounded on a two roll mill and compression molded into sheet; whereas, our blends were compounded in an extruder and injection molded into test bars. These choices reflect, in part, the differences in options

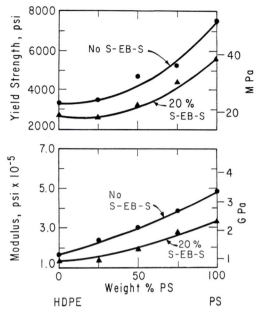

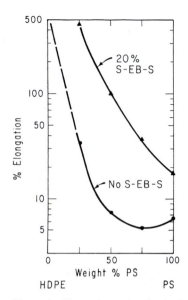

Figure 3   Strength and modulus of polystyrene – high density polyethylene blends with and without added block copolymer. Reproduced with permission[30] John Wiley and Sons, Inc.

Figure 4   Elongation at break of polystyrene – high density polyethylene with and without added block copolymer. Reproduced with permission[30] John Wiley and Sons, Inc.

when one works with laboratory quantities of specially synthesized compatibilizers versus materials available in commercial quantities. These processing differences influence mechanical properties enough that direct comparisons of properties cannot be made on an absolute basis. In view of this, our laboratory has subsequently examined the influence of processing methods and conditions on blend properties for some other systems[31, 32] as will be described in part later.

We will present some quantitative results from the rather extensive study by Lindsey in our laboratory[30] and make comparisons and contrasts where possible with the work reported by Teyssie et al. Figure 3 shows the yield strength and modulus for HDPE-PS binary blends and for ternary mixtures containing 20 % of the S-EB-S copolymer based on total blend mass irrespective of the HDPE/PS ratio. As expected, the yield strength of the binary is below the additivity level defined by a simple tie line, but the departure from additivity is not as severe as seen for roll milled/compression molded mixtures reported by Teyssie[22, 24]. The modulus for these blends shows a simple trend more closely approximating additive behavior. Since S-EB-S has lower strength and modulus than either HDPE or PS, its addition to mixtures of HDPE and PS lowers both properties in a rather systematic manner. In contrast, the diblock copolymers used by Teyssie et al. cause increases in blend strength – no modulus data were reported. This difference is probably due to the nature of the hydrogenated butadiene segments of these materials (which are undoubtedly crystalline) compared to the elastomeric nature of the EB midblock. These mechanical property differences in the block copolymers are translated into the corresponding characteristics of the ternary blends. Figure 4 shows the elongation at break of the compositions shown in Figure 3. The severe problems of incompatibility of HDPE and PS are quite evident for the

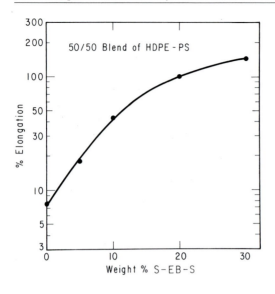

Figure 5 Effect of block copolymer on elongation at break for 50/50 blend of HDPE/PS. Reproduced with permission[30] John Wiley and Sons, Inc.

binary; however, the presence of the S-EB-S significantly improves this property for all ratios of HDPE to PS. Figure 5 shows for an equal weight ratio of HDPE and PS that ductility continues to improve as the amount of S-EB-S added increases, although a tendency to level off is apparent. The 50/50 binary blend prepared by Teyssie et al. has significantly lower elongation at break than those shown in Figures 3 and 4 owing to differences in processing; however, as a rough guide we can compare the factor by which this property is improved by addition of block copolymers for the two studies. Addition of 9 % of the various diblocks resulted in no improvement for H-7, about a factor of two improvement for SE-7, and about a factor of ten improvement for the undesignated diblock. The same amount of S-EB-S increased the elongation at break by about a factor of 4.5 in our studies.

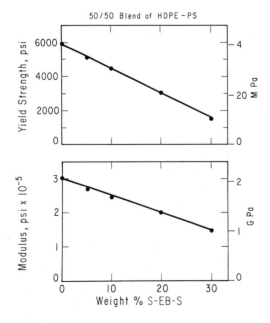

Figure 6 Effect of block copolymer on strength and modulus of 50/50 blend of HDPE/PS. Reproduced with permission[30] John Wiley and Sons, Inc.

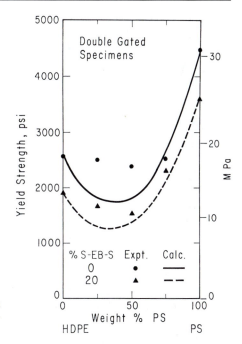

Figure 7   Strength of HDPE/PS blends injection molded to have a weld line. Reproduced with permission[30] John Wiley and Sons, Inc.

The principle advantage of diblocks in this case is the retention of strength whereas S-EB-S causes a loss as seen further in Figure 6. Owing to the many differences among the three diblocks in this example, it is difficult to draw any conclusions about the relative importance of overall molecular weight, segment length, microstructure, or tapering.

A quite serious problem for multiphase blends is weakness at weldlines in moldings originating from several mechanisms[49]. Figure 7 illustrates this with strength data for test bars made by injection molding with gating at both ends of the bar to give a weldline in the gage section. The lines drawn were computed from a simple model[49] allowing for the phase mismatch at the weldline. The point here is that addition of a compatibilizer does little to help this problem in the present case.

3.3   Polystyrene – Polypropylene Blends

The only work reported on block copolymer compatibilization of polypropylene blends with polystyrene to our knowledge is that by Bartlett from our laboratory[31] using the same S-EB-S mentioned earlier. Figures 8–11 show key results for blends made by extruder compounding followed by injection molding. As expected, there is a serious loss in mechanical properties on blending this pair as seen in Figure 8; however, addition of the S-EB-S greatly improves the ductility (see also Figure 9). As before, there is a loss in strength and stiffness, as seen in Figure 10, accompanying this improvement. These improvements in ductility do translate into substantial gains in notched Izod impact strength as seen in Figure 11. These are mainly caused by the toughening effect of S-EB-S on both PP and PS.

To illustrate the influence of processing technique and conditions on blend properties, Figures 12 and 13 show results for materials compounded at two different temperatures in a Brabender batch mixer and then compression molded. As may be seen, the lower mixing temperature gives somewhat poorer values of elongation at break than the higher mixing

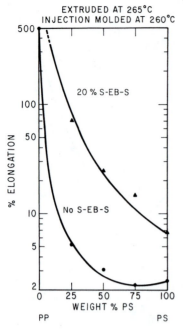

Figure 8   Elongation at break for polypropylene – polystyrene blends with and without added block copolymer. Reproduced with permission[31]

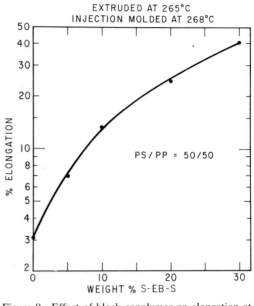

Figure 9   Effect of block copolymer on elongation at break for 50/50 blend of PP/PS blend. Reproduced with permission[31]

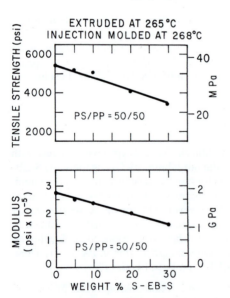

Figure 10   Effect of block copolymer on strength and modulus of 50/50 PP/PS blend. Reproduced with permission[31]

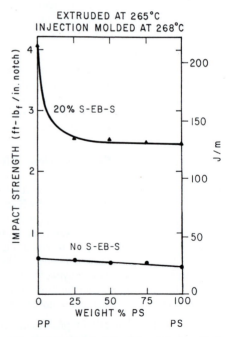

Figure 11   Notched Izod impact strength for PP/PS blends with and without block copolymer. Reproduced with permission[31]

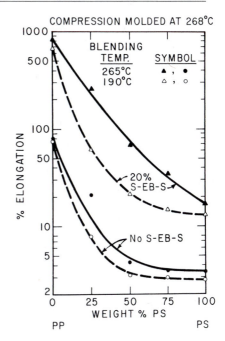

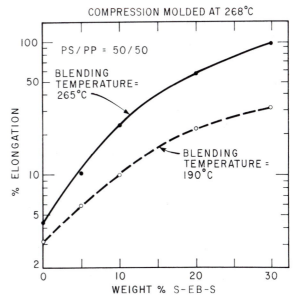

Figure 12 Effect of blending temperature on elongation at break of compression molded PP/PS blends with and with block copolymer. Reproduced with permission[31]

Figure 13 Effect of blending temperature and block copolymer content on elongation at break for 50/50 PP/PS blend. Reproduced with permission[31]

temperature probably due to differences in rheological characteristics and opportunities for interfacial knitting. Interestingly, a similar variation in molding temperature had little effect on mechanical properties. In contrast to the previous example involving HDPE, compression molding gave somewhat higher levels of ductility for PP than did injection molding at comparable processing temperatures.

In summary, S-EB-S is an effective compatibilizer for PP-PS blends based on the increases in ductility observed.

3.4 Poly(Ethylene-Terephthalate) – High Density Polyethylene

In the previous examples the blend components were either identical to one of the block copolymer segments, as in the case of polystyrene, or sufficiently similar, as in the case of the various polyolefins, that one could expect some level of compatibility if not miscibility. Here, we consider the work of Traugott from our laboratory[32] where polystyrene is replaced by poly(ethylene terephthalate) to see whether the same S-EB-S might produce any beneficial improvements in mechanical behavior in blends with HDPE. Clearly, there is no miscibility between PET and PS segments of the S–EB–S so the model of Figure 1 is not applicable.

Binary blends of PET and HDPE exhibit one of the most severe cases of mechanical property deterioration we have ever seen. Figures 14 and 15 show the pertinent values for binary blends plus those to which S-EB-S was added. As before, addition of the S-EB-S reduced strength and stiffness; however, relatively small amounts of S-EB-S caused remarkable improvements in ductility as seen in Figure 15. Those containing 20 % S-EB-S did not break within the full traverse of the Instron. The S-EB-S transformed the almost friable PET-HDPE blends into remarkably tough materials. One might ask whether addition of any elastomeric material might accomplish the same thing. To test this notion, blends were prepared using a commercial ethylene/propylene copolymer rubber (EPR), Epcar 847,

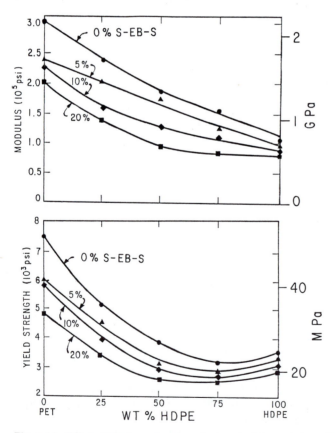

Figure 14   Effect of block copolymer content on modulus and strength of poly(ethylene terephthalate) – high density polyethylene blends. Reproduced with permission[32] John Wiley and Sons, Inc.

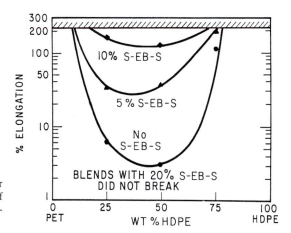

Figure 15 Effect of block copolymer level on percent elongation at break of PET-HDPE blends. Reproduced with permission[32] John Wiley and Sons, Inc.

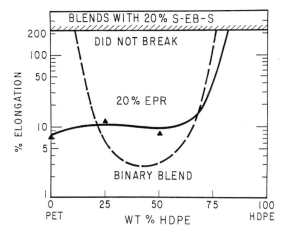

Figure 16 Demonstration that ethylene/propylene elastomer does not compatibilize PET-HDPE blends. Reproduced with permission[32] John Wiley and Sons, Inc.

instead with the results shown in Figure 16. These mixtures were substantially no better than the original blend demonstrating the uniqueness of the block copolymer character for this purpose.

Consequently, one must conclude that the beneficial "compatibilizing" effects of this type of block copolymer are not limited to the mechanism implied by Figure 1. Similar conclusions may be reached from the results presented elsewhere in this book by Davison, Gergen, and Lutz.

4   MORPHOLOGY AND ADHESION

There is extensive evidence complementing studies like those described above that properly chosen block copolymers significantly alter the morphology of the blends to which they are added[4–29, 32, 42–47]. Basically, the block copolymer appears to emulsify the immiscible mixture causing significant reductions in domain size. In some cases, the block copolymer appears to induce formation of an interpenetrating network of phases as described more fully elsewhere in this book by Davison, Gergen, and Lutz. Further indications of observations of fracture surfaces using scanning electron microscopy strongly support increased interfacial adhesion caused by addition of the block copolymer[4, 21–29, 32, 46, 47]. In summary, these facts leave no doubt that the block copolymer usually plays some interfacial role; although, it may, in some cases, have different origins than that implied by Figure 1.

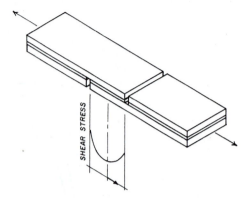

Figure 17   Schematic illustration of lap shear specimen from notched laminate. Variation of stress with position is indicated. Reproduced with permission[52] John Wiley and Sons, Inc.

One may anticipate that interfacial adhesion is a key element to the mechanical compatibilizing effect caused by any additive, and in the remaining part of this section information relevant to this point is reviewed. Much has been written about polymer-polymer interfaces and adhesion[50, 51]; however, rather little is directly applicable to the properties of blends. To obtain information about the relative adhesion at interfaces between polymer pairs in the blend systems of interest here, we have used the simple lap shear method shown schematically in Figure 17[5, 32, 52]. In this method, a three layer sandwich (A/B/A) is made by laminating sheets of polymers A and B by compression molding. Notches are cut so that symmetrical lap shear joints are created at the two interfaces when the specimen is pulled in an Instron. Table II gives some typical average stresses required to cause adhesive failure at the interfaces between various polymer pairs. As may be expected, adhesion between PS and HDPE, PS and PP, and PET and HDPE are relatively low. On the other hand, adhesion between the S-EB-S and each of these polymers is several fold larger. That this should be so is easy to understand for PS, HDPE, and PP since the end blocks of the S-EB-S are identical to polystyrene while the midblock of Kraton should be relatively compatible with HDPE and PP. The reasons for adhesion of S-EB-S to PET is less clear but probably relates to some affinity of the PS blocks with PET. This could be checked by

TABLE II   Average stresses at failure for lap shear adhesion test

Polymer pair (A/B)	Average shear stress at failure, KPa
PS/HDPE	110
PS/PP	248
PET/HDPE	234
S–EB–S/PS	1207
S–EB–S/HDPE	1986
S–EB–S/PP	1227
S–EB–S/PET	593

measuring the PET/PS pair which has not been done. In any case, the propensity of S-EB-S to mutually adhere rather well to each of the components in PS-HDPE, PS-PP, and PET-HDPE blends is believed to be a key to the ability of this block copolymer to compatibilize these blends. Most likely, the better affinity of S-EB-S to say PET and HDPE than of PET to HDPE, as indicated by this measure of adhesion, causes contacts between S-EB-S and each of the components during blending more likely than contacts between PET and HDPE. Thus, these results suggest an interfacial role of the S-EB-S in the blend even though the ideal configuration shown in Figure 1 may not be realizable. The results in Table II clearly demonstrate the value of adhesion data for interpreting blend mechanical properties.

There are several problems associated with the type of adhesion information given above. First, the actual values obtained are complex averages since there is a distribution of stresses in the joint formed[5] and may not readily reflect the stress at which joint failure initiates. Second, the values will depend on the laminating temperature, pressure, and time used to form the specimen. Third, the interfaces are not nascent or virgin ones such as those formed in the blend and may reflect some influences of contamination. Finally, one has no way to relate quantitative values, even if free of the above issues, to conditions of interfacial failure in blends owing to the complex stress conditions which develop at domain interfaces during mechanical property determination. A preferred approach would give some indication of in situ interfacial debonding during mechanical testing of the blend itself as this circumvents all of the problems outlined above. An attractive approach to this is measurement of volume dilation during mechanical stressing of the blend which has been pioneered by Heikens[26, 27, 29] using a relatively simple stress dilatometer.

Some results from the work of Heikens et al. along the lines mentioned above are described next. This group has measured the Poisson ratio, a measure of volume dilation at low strains, defined by

$$v = \frac{1}{2}\left[1 - \frac{1}{V}\frac{dV}{d\varepsilon}\right]$$

(where V is the sample volume and ε is the uniaxial strain) for blends of PS and LDPE with and without the block copolymer. This blend is the next to the last entry in Table I. The Poisson ratio can reflect events that a simple mechanical characteristic such as modulus cannot. This can be a powerful approach when coupled with modeling of the mechanical behavior in terms of theories for composites such as the Kerner equations[53]. Figure 18 shows the Poisson ratio and modulus for binary blends of LDPE and PS[29] as a function of the volume fraction of PS, $\varnothing_{PS}$, in the blend. The solid line represents the prediction of the Kerner equations while the broken curve is the prediction obtained when the shear and compression moduli of the ductile component are taken as zero. This approximately represents the situation of no interfacial adhesion. As may be seen, the measured Poisson ratio deviates considerably from the solid line at high PS contents. These values decrease, rather than increase as would be expected if adhesion occurred, as LDPE is added to PS. This trend may be explained by assuming little adhesion between LDPE and PS, since the experimental data deviate in the direction indicated by the dashed curve which represents the extreme limit of no adhesion at all. As may be seen, the modulus is rather insensitive to the extent of adhesion in the region of high PS contents. This approximate analysis does not apply to the LDPE rich region since the line for no adhesion assumes PS to be the continuous phase. Figure 19 shows the Poisson ratio and modulus for LDPE-PS blends to which various amounts of the block copolymer have been added. Here, $\varnothing_{PS}$ includes the homopolymer PS and the PS segments of the block copolymer. The remainder of the material is the LDPE and the hydrogenated butadiene segments of the block copolymer.

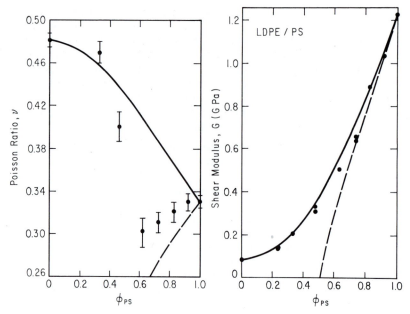

Figure 18   Poisson ratio and modulus of low density polyethylene – polystyrene binary blends. Curves explained in text. Reproduced with permission[29] Butterworth and Co. (Publishers) Ltd.

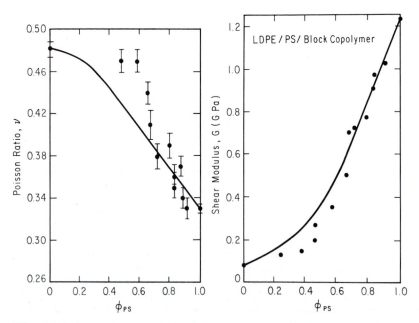

Figure 19   Poisson ratio and modulus of low density polyethylene – polystyrene blends to which block copolymer has been added. Curves explained in text. Reproduced with permission[29] Butterworth and Co. (Publishers) Ltd.

This division is appropriate since the two segments of the block copolymer have mechanical properties similar to those of PS or LDPE. In this compatibilized case, the Poisson ratio rises when LDPE is added to PS, in more or less good agreement with the Kerner prediction for good adhesion over the range of compositions this analysis might be expected to apply. Thus, the Poisson ratio, which reflects volume changes consequent to the complex stress state in the heterogeneous blend, indicates the improved adhesion between LDPE and PS resulting from the presence of the compatibilizing block copolymer.

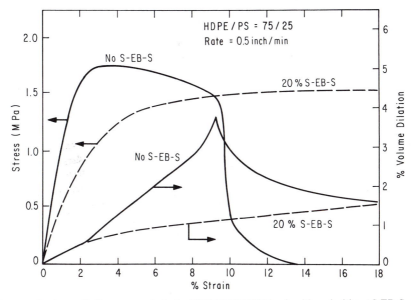

Figure 20   Stress and volume dilation versus strain for 75/25 HDPE/PS blends with and without S-EB-S block copolymer

We believe the above approach is a unique way to gain valuable information about the role of interfacial adhesion on mechanical behavior of immiscible blend systems. We have constructed a stress dilatometer in our laboratory similar to that developed by Heikens to aid our investigations. In contrast to the results presented above, we have concentrated on the volumetric changes during plastic deformation after the yield point where extensive debonding at the interface may occur. Some typical results from the work of M. C. Schwarz in progress in our laboratory are shown in Figure 20. The data are for a blend containing HDPE/PS in the ratio of 75/25 such that the ductile HDPE forms the continuous phase. Results are shown for samples with and without S-EB-S as a compatibilizer. For low strains below the yield point, both materials show a small volume increase resulting from the Poisson ratio effect. For the two blends this is essentially indistinguishable on this scale of comparison. However, when irreversible deformations set in beyond yielding (see the stress curves), there is a rapid increase in volume with strain for the blend with no S-EB-S. This increase results from voids formed at the interfaces between domains owing to the very low adhesion. When actual failure occurs these voids begin to collapse as indicated by the volume decrease with further strain. This process is actually a function of time and would occur even if the crosshead travel were stopped. On the other hand, the blend containing S-EB-S does not show this large volume dilation since apparently such voids are not formed owing to the improved adhesion between phases its presence causes. Further results of this study will be published in the future. It should be pointed out that such measurements can reflect other dilational processes like crazing which would obscure conclusions of this tpye; however, crazing was not present in the results shown in Figure 20 since the ductile polyethylene which formed the continuous phase yields by shearing mechanisms that produce insignificant dilation.

5   SUMMARY

This review has presented selected recent results which demonstrate that block copolymers containing segments of polystyrene and hydrogenated polybutadiene can cause significant improvements in the mechanical properties of immiscible blends or "compatibilize" them. It seems clear that this is the result of an interfacial role played by the block copolymer in the blend resulting in improved adhesion between the phases. In the most ideal case, this may be the result of the block copolymer acting as a surfactant with its segments penetrating deeply into the homopolymer domains in situations where complete miscibility exists. However, these copolymers function quite effectively also in systems where this idealized monolayer configuration (see Figure 1) cannot occur. We suggest that in these cases the block copolymer may form an *interphase* between the two components, as suggested in Figure 21, based on its mutual affinity to wet or adhere to each component which is greater than the affinity of the two components to each other. We do not doubt at all that many other issues are involved as well.

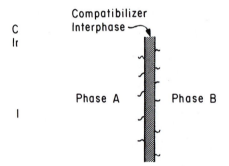

Figure 21   Illustration of compatibilizer forming an interphase between polymer phases A and B

At this time, it is quite impossible to state conclusively what the "best" block copolymer structure might be for a given application owing to the rather primative state of the literature on this subject.

6   ACKNOWLEDGEMENTS

Our work in this area was sponsored in its early stages by the Plastics Institute of America and more recently by a grant-in-aid from Hercules, Inc. Generous donations of S-EB-S polymer have been made by the Shell Chemical Co.

References

1. D. R. Paul and S. Newman (eds.), *"Polymer Blends, Vol. 1 and 2"*, Academic, New York, 1978
2. O. Olabisi, L. M. Robeson, and M. T. Shaw, *"Polymer-Polymer Miscibility"*, Academic, New York, 1979
3. D. R. Paul and J. W. Barlow, *J. Macromol. Sci. – Rev. Macromol. Chem. C 18*, 109 (1980)
4. D. R. Paul, Ch. 12 in *"Polymer Blends, Vol. 2"*, D. R. Paul and S. Newman (eds.) Academic, New York, 1978
5. J. W. Barlow and D. R. Paul, *Polym. Eng. Sci. 24*, 525 (1984)
6. G. E. Molau, in *"Block Polymers"* (S. L. Aggarwal, ed.), p. 79, Plenum, New York, 1970
7. G. E. Molau, *J. Polym. Sci. Part A-3*, 1267, 4235 (1965)
8. G. E. Molau and W. M. Wittbrodt, *Macromolecules 1*, 260 (1968)
9. G. E. Molau, *Kolloid Z. Z. Polym. 238*, 493 (1970)
10. G. Riess, J. Kohler, C. Tournut, and A. Banderet, *Makromol. Chem. 101*, 58 (1967)
11. J. Kohler, G. Riess, and A. Banderet, *Eur. Polym. J. 4*, 173, 187 (1968)
12. G. Riess, J. Periard, and Y. Jolivet, *Angew. Chem. Int. Ed. 11*, 339 (1972)
13. G. Riess and Y. Jolivet, in *"Copolymers, Polyblends, and Composites"* (N. A. J. Platzer, ed.), Adv. in Chem. Ser., Vol. 142, p. 243, Amer. Chem. Soc., Washington, D. C., 1975
14. G. Riess, J. Periard, and A. Banderet, in *"Colloidal and Morphological Behavior of Block and Graft Copolymers"* (G. E. Molau, ed.), p. 173, Plenum, New York, 1972
15. P. Gaillard, M. Ossenbach-Santer, and G. Riess, in *"Polymer Compatibility and Incompatibility – Principles and Practices"*, K. Solc (ed.), MMI Press Symp. Series, Vol. 2, Harwood Academic, New York, 1982, p. 289
16. G. Hurtrez, D. J. Wilson, and G. Riess, in *"Polymer Blends and Mixtures"*, D. J. Walsh, J. S. Higgins, and A. Maconnachie (eds.), NATO ASI Series E, Vol. 89, Martinus Nijhoff, Dordrecht, 1985, p. 149
17. T. Inoue, T. Soen, T. Hashimoto, and H. Kawai, *Macromolecules 3*, 87 (1970)
18. M. Moritani, T. Inoue, M. Motegi, and H. Kawai, *Macromolecules 3*, 433 (1970)
19. T. Inoue, T. Soen, T. Hashimoto, and H. Kawai, in *"Block Polymers"* (S. L. Aggarwal, ed.), p. 53, Plenum, New York, 1970
20. B. Ptaszynski, J. Terrisse, and A. Skoulios, *Makromol. Chem. 176*, 3483 (1975)
21. R. Fayt, R. Jerome, and Ph. Teyssie, *J. Polym. Sci.: Polym. Lett. Ed. 19*, 79 (1981)
22. R. Fayt, R. Jerome, and Ph. Teyssie, *J. Polym. Sci.: Polym. Phys. Ed. 19*, 1269 (1981)
23. R. Fayt, R. Jerome, and Ph. Teyssie, *J. Polym. Sci.: Polym. Phys. Ed. 20*, 2209 (1982)
24. R. Fayt, P. Hadjiandreou, and Ph. Teyssie, *J. Polym. Sci.: Polym. Chem. Ed. 23*, 337 (1985)
25. D. Heikens, N. Hoen, W. Barentsen, P. Piet, and H. Ladan, *J. Polym. Sci.: Polym. Symp. 62*, 309 (1978)
26. W. J. Coumans, D. Heikens, and S. D. Sjoerdsma, *Polymer 21*, 103 (1980)
27. W. J. Coumans and D. Heikens, *Polymer 21*, 957 (1980)
28. S. D. Sjoerdsma, J. Dalmolen, A.C.A.M. Bleijenberg, and D. Heikens, *Polymer 21*, 1469 (1980)
29. S. D. Sjoerdsma, A.C.A.M. Bleijenberg, and D. Heikens, *Polymer 22*, 619 (1981)
30. C. R. Lindsey, D. R. Paul, and J. W. Barlow, *J. Appl. Polym. Sci. 26*, 1 (1981)
31. D. W. Bartlett, D. R. Paul, and J. W. Barlow, *Modern Plastics, 58 (#12)*, 60 (1981)
32. T. D. Traugott, J. W. Barlow, and D. R. Paul, *J. Appl. Polym. Sci. 28*, 2947 (1983)
33. R. E. Robertson and D. R. Paul, *J. Appl. Polym. Sci. 17*, 2579 (1973)
34. H. W. Starkweather, *J. Appl. Polym. Sci. 25*, 139 (1980)
35. F. C. Stehling and G. D. Wignall, *Polym. Prepr. Amer. Chem. Soc. Siv. Polym. Chem. 24(2)*, 211 (1983)
36. L. Toy, M. Niinomi, and M. Shen, *J. Macromol. Sci. Phys. B 11*, 281 (1975)
37. M. S. Akutin, B. V. Andrianov, and V. S. Kulyamin, *Vysokomol. Soedin. Ser. B 17*, 457 (1975)
38. D. J. Meier, *Polym. Prepr. Amer. Chem. Soc. Div. Polym. Chem. 18(1)*, 340, 837 (1977)
39. J. Noolandi and K. M. Hong, *Macromolecules 15*, 482 (1982)
40. J. Noolandi and K. M. Hong, *Macromolecules 17*, 1531 (1984)
41. M. D. Whitmore and J. Noolandi, *Macromolecules 18*, 657 (1985)
42. D. R. Paul, C. E. Vinson, and C. E. Locke, *Polym. Eng. Sci. 12*, 157 (1972)
43. D. R. Paul, C. E. Locke, and C. E. Vinson, *Polym. Eng. Sci. 13*, 202 (1973)
44. C. E. Locke and D. R. Paul, *Polym. Eng. Sci. 13*, 308 (1973)

45. C. E. Locke and D. R. Paul, *J. Appl. Polym. Sci. 17,* 2597, 2791 (1973)
46. W. M. Barentsen and D. Heikens, *Polymer 14,* 579 (1973)
47. W. M. Barentsen, D. Heikens, and P. Piet, *Polymer 15,* 119 (1974)
48. J. R. Stell, D. R. Paul, and J. W. Barlow, *Polym. Eng. Sci. 16,* 496 (1976)
49. E. Nolley, J. W. Barlow, and D. R. Paul, *Polym. Eng. Sci. 20,* 364 (1980)
50. S. Wu, Ch. 6 in *"Polymer Blends, Vol. 1",* D. R. Paul and S. Newman (eds.), Academic, New York, 1978
51. S. Wu, *"Polymer Interface and Adhesion",* Marcel Dekker, Inc., New York, 1982
52. J. D. Keitz, J. W. Barlow, and D. R. Paul, *J. Appl. Polym. Sci. 29,* 3131 (1984)
53. E. H. Kerner, *Proc. Phys. Soc. (B) 69,* 808 (1956)

Chapter 12

RESEARCH ON THERMOPLASTIC ELASTOMERS

Section 7

NOVEL BLOCK COPOLYMERS, THERMOPLASTIC ELASTOMERS AND POLYMER BLENDS

R. Jérôme, R. Fayt, Ph. Teyssié

Contents

R. Jérôme, R. Fayt and Ph. Teyssié, Laboratory of Macromolecular Chemistry and Organic Catalysis, University of Liège, Sart-Tilman, B-4000 Liège, Belgium

1   INTRODUCTION

The coming of age of "macromolecular engineering" will certainly appear in the future as one of the prominent achievements of polymer science in the second half of this century. The design of a desired spectrum of final properties of polymers through a combination of geometric, molecular and interaction parameters followed by laboratory and large scale production has become a reality.

One of the best illustrations of that general trend is the fine tailoring of heterophase materials and of their overall morphology as demonstrated in the synthesis of block copolymers and the resulting thermoplastic elastomers in the 1960–1970 period. In this review we will illustrate the broad scope of this field of research through examples developed in our laboratory.

2   NOVEL BLOCK COPOLYMERS AS A SOURCE OF IMPROVED THERMOPLASTIC ELASTOMERS

The control of polymer properties allowed by anionic polymerization partly accounts for the impressive growth in commercial production of specialty polymers. Under suitable process conditions, termination-free and transfer-free polymerization is possible, allowing highly efficient synthesis of block copolymers. Thanks to the "living" nature of anionic polymerization, the sequential addition of monomers is a general method of preparing block copolymers and is readily adaptable to commercial production. Many block copolymers have been manufactured this way. The polydiene-polystyrene two-phase polymers containing three or more blocks and known as thermoplastic elastomers are especially noteworthy. Linear and radial elastomeric block copolymers, hydrogenated or not, have increasing uses in a variety of fields. One of the most significant is the use as impact resistance improvers when blended with polystyrene or polyolefins so that the thermoplastic forms the continuous phase. It is thus evident that anionic polymerization has been the key in discovering, and then producing on a significant industrial scale, in a relatively short time[1,2], such successful engineering materials as thermoplastic elastomers.

2.1   Block Copolymers of Soft Polydiene or Polysiloxane and Highly Cohesive Polyamide or Polyester

Recognizing that key role of living anionic polymerization in the production of thermoplastic elastomers, we have been interested in variations of the classical copolymers derived from monomers of dienes and vinyl aromatics to extend their range of service conditions. It is well known that these copolymers are generally confined to applications only requiring resistance to rather mild temperatures because of the softening of the glassy phases at higher temperatures. This deficiency can be improved by replacing the polystyrene blocks with high melting point semicrystalline blocks. Poly (ε-caprolactam) (or nylon-6) and poly(3,3-dimethyl-2-oxetanone) (or polypivalolactone) are candidates for this purpose since they exhibit a melting point of ca. 220 °C and 240 °C, respectively. Furthermore, these polymers can be prepared by anionic polymerization of cyclic monomers.

2.1.1 Anionic block polymerization of dienes and ε-caprolactam

The anionic polymerization of lactam is referred to as "activated monomer polymerization" because the monomer has to be metalated before its addition to the growing center which is an N-acyllactam group

$$(-CO-N-CO)$$
$$\{CH_2\}_n$$

Accordingly, the anionic polymerization of ε-caprolactam (ε-CL) is initiated by strong bases, e. g. (NaH, or LiAlH$_4$) added with a suitable cocatalyst or activator, e. g. acid derivatives or isocyanates) that easily reacts with the monomer to form the required N-acyllactam moiety. Quite interestingly, the activator residue is incorporated at the end of the growing poly-amide chains. Thus every polymer chain end-capped with one of the possible activators should promote the anionic block polymerization of ε-CL. To take advantage of this, the deactivation of living polydienyl anions by an excess of tolylene diisocyanate at low temperature has been recommended[3]. The reaction of diisocyanate with hydroxyl-termi-nated polydienes (previously prepared by anionic polymerization) is another approach that we have successfully applied[4] (Equation (1)).

$$Pol-OH + R(NCO)_2 \longrightarrow Pol-O-CO-NH-R-NCO \xrightarrow{+ \varepsilon-CL}$$

$$\underbrace{Pol-O-CO-NH-R-NH-CO-N-CO}_{}\qquad\qquad(1)$$
$$\underbrace{}_{carbamate}\quad\underbrace{}_{N\text{-acyllactam}}$$

As the carbamate and the N-acyllactam groups are formed together, and behave as potential activators, care has to be taken to avoid attack on the carbamate by the lactam salt, with release of the macroactivator and growth of homopolyamide chains (Equation (2)).

$$Pol-O-CO-NH-R-NH-CO-N-CO + {}^-N-CO \longrightarrow Pol-O^- +$$

$$OC-N-CO-NH-R-NH-CO-N-CO \qquad\qquad(2)$$

Models of carbamate and N-acyllactam activators have allowed us to define the best experimental conditions to obtain the reaction of Equation (1). At 105 °C, the carbamate is almost inactive, whereas the N-acyllactam is very reactive. Thus high yields of block polymerization (ca. 90 %) are reported for reactions initiated by NaH and proceeding at 105 °C in bulk[4]. The same reaction pathway can be exploited to block copolymerize ε-CL in a closed mold, or in a continuous polymerization system with microwave heating[5]. Conver-sions of about 95 % are obtained in reaction times shorter than one minute. Aliphatic isocyanates could be advantageously used to minimize the breaking of the carbamate linkage during the high temperature processing.

The very large difference between the solubility parameter of polydienes and that of nylon 6 gives these block copolymers a multiphase morphology which is stable even in the molten state well above the nylon melting point. Observations by transmission electron microscopy show that a solvent-cast film (m. cresol/chloroform 1.1) of such a triblock polymer (33 % of the central polydiene block) is phase separated at a very fine microscopic level. Small (~ 100 Angstroms) polydiene domains are evenly distributed in a continuous nylon matrix, Figure 1 a. After hot-compression molding (280 °C) and rapid quenching, the morphology is modified and highly oriented, Figure 1 b. Annealing at 230 °C (10 °C above Tm) has no effect on this feature and supports the retention of the two-phase system in the melt. This

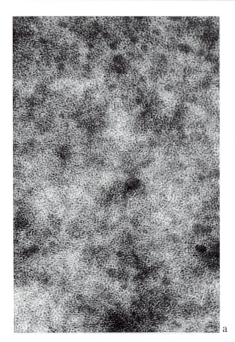

a   b

Figure 1   Electron micrographs of a poly (ε-caprolactam-b-butadiene-b-ε-caprolactam) containing 33 wt % of polybutadiene, (a) solvent-cast film, OsO$_4$ stained (X10^5), (b) ultramicrotomed film from a hot compression-molded sample, OsO$_4$ stained (X5 × 10^4). The darker areas are the polybutadiene phase. Reproduced with permission[4] from John Wiley and Sons, Inc.

raises obvious processing problems which are complicated by the poor thermal stability of the unsaturated rubber. Similar material characterized by a continuous polydiene phase can possibly be processed at room temperature[3]. Replacement of the polydiene block by a more stable polydimethylsiloxane (PDMS) block could be another answer to that problem. Unfortunately, a PDMS-type activator cannot be used because of the degradation of the polysiloxane under the usual conditions of ε-CL polymerization[6]. The preliminary hydrogenation of the starting polydiene to a saturated elastomer should solve these processability problems.

2.1.2 Anionic Block Polymerization of Cyclosiloxane and Pivalolactone

In accordance with the initial aim, we also investigated the synthesis of block polymers based on thermally stable PDMS and polypivalolactone (PPVL). Each type of block can be produced by living anionic polymerization of cyclic monomers; e.g. hexamethylcyclo-trisiloxane (D$_3$) and 3,3-dimethyl-2-oxetanone (DMO), respectively. Among the wide variety of nucleophiles able to initiate the ring-opening polymerization of DMO, only the tetraalkylammonium carboxylates promote a fast living propagation step[7]. Carboxy-terminated PDMS is accordingly the best precursor of block polymers based on PDMS and PPVL.

The desired A–B–A block polymers with PPVL as the A blocks and PDMS as the B block have been prepared by initiating the living polymerization of D$_3$ with ethyl, 6-lithiohexyl-acetaldehyde acetal followed with the coupling of the living PDMS chain. The complete hydrolysis of the acetal end-groups gives rise to α, ω-dihydroxyl PDMS, characterized by a hydrolytically stable linking (Si–C bond) of the hydroxyl end-groups to the PDMS chain. Subsequent reaction with succinic anhydride, in non anhydrous conditions, give the derived carboxy-telechelic polymer and avoids any significant chain extension. The final neutralization of the acid end-groups by tetramethylammonium hydroxide (NR_4OH) promotes the formation of a macroinitiator of the PVL polymerization. The initiation efficiency of the carboxylate end-groups seems, however, to be limited to about 70 %, leading to a blend of di- and triblock copolymers[8].

Diblock copolymer is known to reduce the performances of thermoplastic elastomers. To avoid this problem another pathway has been devised which uses more than one carboxylato group per chain-end. Poly (isoprene-b-dimethylsiloxane-b-isoprene) with a major PDMS content is easily prepared by sequential polymerization of isoprene and D_3, and coupling of the final living diblocks by $Si(CH_3)_2CI_2$. Several carboxylic acid groups are attached at both PDMS extremities by grafting β-mercaptopropionic acid on the very short polyisoprene (PI) end-blocks ($\overline{M}_n \simeq 1,000$ to $3,000$). When neutralized, these functional polymers behave as efficient promoters of block polymers displaying an unusual "palm-tree" structure of the polyester end-blocks. Equation (3).

$$
PI - PDMS - PI \xrightarrow[\text{AIBN}]{\text{HS(CH}_2)_2\text{–COOH}} \underset{\substack{| \\ (COOH)_n}}{PI} - \underset{\substack{| \\ (COOH)_n}}{PDMS} - PI \xrightarrow{NR_4OH}
$$

$$
\underset{\substack{| \\ (COONR_4)_n}}{PI} - \underset{\substack{| \\ (COONR_4)_n}}{PDMS} - PI \xrightarrow{DMO} \begin{array}{c} PPVL\text{~~} \quad \text{~~}PPVL \\ PPVL\text{~~}PDMS\text{~~}PPVL \\ PPVL\text{~~} \quad \text{~~}PPVL \end{array} \qquad (3)
$$

PPVL homopolymer is not produced when the mean number of carboxylates per PI block is higher than about three. A rough analysis of the product recovered after the selective degradation of the PI bridge shows an initiation efficiency of the carboxylate group of 40 %.

Interest in block copolymers containing PPVL components as thermoplastic elastomers is illustrated by the considerable research effort devoted to the attachment of PPVL segments to elastomeric polymers[9]. EPDM, polyacrylates, PI and polyisobutene have been grafted with PPVL segments and display physico-mechanical properties similar to those of the original elastomers when these have been chemically crosslinked and reinforced. Their strength increases markedly on orientation by drawing, and some of them show unusually low compression set values, especially after annealing. Block copolymers containing PI have been synthesized as block-graft polymers. Metalation of α, ω – dilithio-cis-1,4 PI followed with carboxylation at the anionic sites opens the way to block-graft PI. These polymers are easily melt spun into elastic fibers of good strength, high elongation, and high resilience when PPVL content amounts to 35 % or higher. At least 3 or 4 PPVL segments per PI chain appear desirable to obtain the best performances. The basic idea in the development of the "palm-tree" block PPVL-PDMS polymers and the block-graft PPVL-PI polymers is quite comparable, as it rests on the increase in the number of the PPVL segments per rubbery chain; in the first case, the PPVL blocks are gathered at both ends of the stable PDMS, while in the grafting approach the PPVL segments are randomly spaced along the PI chain.

2.2   Interfacial Coupling of Polymers Bearing Mutually Reactive End-Groups

Though anionic polymerization is the most efficient way to prepare block copolymers, its application is limited to the minority of monomers that respond to these types of initiators.

Compared to this "single-mechanism" method, any "mixed-mechanism" technique greatly increases the range of available products. In the latter case the first active end-group is converted quantitatively into another functional group able to promote the polymerization of a second class of monomers. Nevertheless, the coupling of two different polymers bearing mutually reactive end-groups [$PA(X)_m$ and $PB(Y)_n$ where X and Y are mutually reactive end-groups, m and n each being 1 or more] is theoretically the most versatile technique of block polymerization. This very simple idea meets, however, both kinetic and thermodynamic barriers. The kinetic restriction has its origins in the reduction in concentration of reactive end-groups, as molecular weight of the starting blocks increases. However, the decisive limitation is the thermodynamic immiscibility of the majority of polymer pairs as the molecular weight increases. Interfacial reaction can remove this limitation. The preferential location of the mutually reactive end-groups at the interface is an efficient way to bypass the deleterious effects of both the immiscibility of polymer pairs and the low overall concentration of the reactive end-groups. The key point of this new concept is to dissolve selectively the two functional polymers ($PA(X)_m$ and $PB(Y)_n$) in immiscible solvents in such a way that X and Y (or short segments onto which X and Y are attached) are less soluble in their own polymer solution than in the other one. When the experimental conditions (solvents, nature of end-groups) are well chosen the end-group(s) of PA are attracted to the solvent containing the prepolymer PB and vice-versa.

This new concept of interfacial block polymerization has been illustrated by the synthesis of multiblock poly (α – methylstyrene-b-ethylene oxide), starting from poly (α – methylstyrene) ($\overline{M}_n$:6,000) end-capped with – $(CH_2)_6 – N^+(Br)^-(CH_2)_6-N(CH_3)_2$ groups and poly-(ethylene oxide) ($\overline{M}_n$: 6,000) end capped with $-OCO-(CH_2)_x-Br$ groups. The α, ω-ditert. amino poly (α-methylstyrene) was dissolved in toluene (5 wt %), which is a non-solvating agent for the ammonium bromide ion pair close to the functional t-amino group. The α,ω-dibromo poly (ethylene oxide) was used in aqueous solution (5 wt. %) which is immiscible with toluene and interacts repulsively with the methylene segment-$(CH_2)_x$ – carrying the bromide function. The efficiency of the polymer coupling, via a quaternization reaction, was strongly dependent on the experimental parameters, especially the balance between the hydrophilic prepolymer and its hydrophobic end-groups. The block polymerization yield, at 60 °C, rose as high as 90 % when x = 5 but fell to 48 % and 6 % for x = 1 and 10, respectively. Temperature is also critically important since the copolymerization yield (x = 5) changed from 90 % to 43 % when the temperature decreased from 60 °C to 25 °C. Finally, the substitution of water by dimethylsulfoxide decreased the copolymerization yield ca. 75 %. These observations stress that the location of the reactive suppress end-groups and their opportunity for efficient collision and reaction can be changed by varying one or several of the parameters of the interfacial system. Therefore, the basic problem is the precise control of the formation of end-functionalized polymers having groups of the proper reactivity and philicity: fortunately this is a rapidly improving situation, and thus opens this block copolymerization technique to radical-generated polymers.

2.3   Diolefin Block Polymerization Promoted by Coordination Catalysts

Coordination-type catalysts are extremely helpful in controlling the chain-growth process, and especially the stereospecificity of polyolefins. The application of these catalysts is usually difficult because the very short active lifetime of the growing chains. Nevertheless, substantial progress has been reported, such as the succesful alternating block copolymerization of ethylene and propylene[10], the living polymerization of ethylene initiated by soluble macromolecular complexes based on Ti and Li[11], and the finely controlled polymerization of butadiene promoted by a new family of η^3-allyl-X-nickel complexes[12].

Bis [(η^3-allyl) (trifluoroacetato) nickel] or [(A)Ni(TFA)]$_2$ is an interesting coordination catalyst which ensures the "coding" of the living 1,4-polymerization of butadiene. Indeed it displays both excellent regioselectivity (ca. 1 % of 1,2 units), and stereoselectivity (from 99 % cis to 99 % trans units), depending on the choice of proper ligands and kinetic conditions. For instance, the addition of ligands such as triphenyl phosphite (TPP: an electron donor) or chloranil (CA: an electron acceptor) is able to promote a living 1,4-polymerization of butadiene over the whole stereoselectivity scale controlled by the molar ratio of ligand to Ni[13]. This unique behavior allows the synthesis of stereodiblock poly [cis-1,4-butadiene-b-trans-1,4-butadiene][14]. In this polymerization a solution of [(A) Ni (TFA)]$_2$ in n. heptane initiates the living cis-1,4-polymerization of butadiene. After completion, the addition of TPP (TPP/Ni = 0.8) is sufficient to polymerize a second monomer feed with formation of a trans-1,4 block. This is the first example of a block polymer prepared from one monomer in a "single-mechanism" method through a coordinative pathway. It is significant that these block copolymers combine a soft segment (Tg of cis-1,4-PBD = −98 °C) and hard semi-crystalline segment with a high melting temperature (T$_m$ of trans-1,4-PBD = 127 °C). The corresponding multistereoblock copolymers are expected to behave as thermoplastic elastomers. The synthesis of these materials takes advantage of the well known sensitivity of the coordination catalysts to any change in temperature, solvent and ligand (as demonstrated above). Similarly, it is also possible to produce block copolymers from one monomer by taking advantage of the microstructure changes in the anionic polymerization of butadiene that are produced by variations in the amounts of polar modifiers and the temperature at different stages of the reaction[2]. Hydrogenation of block copolymers of 1,4 and 1,2 units substantially improves the mechanical strength of the material.

The synthesis of poly(cis-1,4-butadiene-b-styrene) has been achieved by the "living" polymerization of butadiene initiated by [(A)Ni(TFA)]$_2$. The hydrogenation of this diblock yields an interesting poly(ethylene-b-styrene) which is useful as an emulsifier for blends of high-density polyethylene and polystyrene[15]. A later section of this chapter will focus on polymer blending, which is now a field of growing interest.

3   CARBOXYLATO-TELECHELIC POLYDIENES: NEW ELASTOMERS WITH A DYNAMIC MULTIBLOCK STRUCTURE

Multiblock structures combining soft segments and strongly interacting hard segments have been successfully commercialized as new types of thermoplastic elastomers, (e. g. HYTREL polyether-ester and ESTANE segmented polyurethanes). The replacement of the polymeric hard segments by single groupings able to promote strong mutual interactions could give more versatile versions of the classical multi-block structures.

The properties of well-known ionomers suggest use of this technique. Ion pairs randomly spaced onto a nonpolar polymeric backbone spontaneously associate into aggregates (multi-plets and/or clusters), which are responsible for crosslinking and reinforcement. Although stable at normal temperatures, the ionically stabilized polymer network may be softened sufficiently by heating to allow processing[16]. Ionomers can be visualized as graft polymers, in which the hard grafted segments are represented by salt groups involved in strong mutual interactions. Similarly the association of ionic groups attached at both ends of linear rubbery chains should give these polymers morphological and macroscopic properties quite compar-able to those of multi-block thermoplastic elastomers. This concept has led to the synthesis of non polar linear chains end-capped with salt groups, for which the name "halato-telechelic polymers" has been coined (telechelic and halato have Greek roots meaning α, ω – difunctional and saltlike respectively). The salt groups can be either neutralized acidic, neutralized basic or quaternized amino groups. Representative polymers of this type have been made by the end-neutralization of α, ω-dicarboxylato polydienes[17], α, ω-disulfonato polyisobutenes and similar triarms[18, 19]. The telechelic polymers with carboxylic or sulfonic acid end groups are excellent prepolymers for tailor-made elastomers after addition of compounds of di- or multi-valent metals. The "inifer technique" introduced by Kennedy et al. has allowed the preparation of sulfonic acid end-capped PIB[20]. The living anionic polymerization initiated by a difunctional promoter and stopped by CO_2 is an efficient way to prepare carboxy-telechelic polydienes[21].

Both the quantitative functionalization of the prepolymer and the complete neutralization of the acid end-groups are key parameters for obtaining optimum physico-mechanical proper-ties. A highly controlled method for neutralization of carboxy telechelic polydienes has been reported using stoichiometric amounts of very reactive metal alkoxides or alkyls[21]. The latter technique is most versatile, provided that the alcohol formed as a byproduct is completely eliminated both to displace the reaction equilibrium and also to avoid the ion-pair solvation. Carboxylato-telechelic polydienes with a large range of polydiene molecular weights and cation moieties have been prepared in this way.

Dynamic mechanical analysis indicates that the end-neutralization of very short length α, ω-dicarboxylic polydiene ($\overline{M}_n \simeq 5,000$) by alkaline – earth alcoholates produces thermorevers-ible cross-linking and reinforcement of the elastomer[22, 23]. For the first time, the relaxation of the ion-pair aggregates has been observed and thoroughly investigated. The mechanism shows Arrhenius-type behavior and its activation energy is strongly dependent on the ion-pair features. If the prepolymer molecular weight is higher than the critical entaglement value, the rheological behavior shows WLF-type of temperature dependence, which means that the ion-pair association stabilizes a network of entangled chains by aggregates too small to be detected[24].

The metals used in the cation moieties can be classified into three categories, depending on their effect on the viscoelastic properties of the carboxylato-telechelic polydiene ($\overline{M}_n < 5,000$)[17]. The first class consists of alkaline and alkaline-earth metals. In these systems the ionic strength of the carboxylates promotes the formation of highly interacting ion-pairs giving virtual crosslinking of the elastomer. At constant ionic radius, the strength of the polymer network was higher when elastomers based on earth cation were compared to analogs based on alkaline ones. Tetravalent transition metals (Ti, Zr . . .) form the second class[25]; here the metal-carboxylate bonds are mainly covalent and their mutual electrostatic interactions are noticeably less. A crosslinking effect is observed only when an excess of alkoxy groups is used in the neutralization step and subsequently hydrolyzed. The resulting carboxylato-oxo-metal groupings provide an elastomer network which shows an interesting stability towards polar compounds and contains nascent inorganic domains. This last feature could favor a very fine, homogeneous and stable dispersion of fillers such as calcium carbonates or talcs. Trivalent metals such as Al constitute the third class. They are versatile interlinking elements between those produced by tetravalent transition metals and those produced by alkaline and alkaline-earth metals. In all cases the prepolymer molecular weight and the nature of the metal ions are the key parameters in the control of the viscoelasticity of the elastomer network. It is noteworthy that SAXS supports the multiphase character of the metal carboxylato-telechelic polydienes[26]. The principal factor governing the organization of the ionic aggregates in the organic matrix is likely to be the root mean square end-to-end distance of the prepolymer[27]. EXAFS highlights a high degree of local order around cations within the aggregates[28].

Halato-telechelic polymers have the great advantage that the network points are well defined at the chain ends and also that all chain segments should contribute to the load-bearing capabilities of the material. The stress-strain behavior of α, ω-metal disulfonato polyisobutene and triarm counterparts agrees with a three dimensional "network-like" behavior[18, 19]. Networks generated from three-arm star polyisobutene of low molecular weight (9,000) contain covalent and ionic junction points, and exhibit strain induced crystallization at higher elongations. At room temperature the physio-mechanical properties of these materials compare favorably with conventional elastomer networks linked by covalent bonds. They can be easily processed at reasonably low temperature due to the thermoreversibility of the ionic junctions and the low molecular weight of the prepolymer. As expected the networks formed from tri-arm polymers are much stronger than those formed from the linear difunctional polyisobutene, because of higher average functionality and density of "network junction points". These mechanical properties of model ionomer networks convincingly support the suggested analogy to the classical thermoplastic elastomers.

4 THE CONTRIBUTION OF THERMOPLASTIC ELASTOMERS IN POLYMER BLENDS

Polymer blending has become the more attractive and versatile means to generate new materials from already known polymers, as well as to improve some deficiencies of common thermoplastics. In particular, thermoplastic elastomers have been blended with other polymers. In some cases they are the minor components and serve as impact modifiers for production of new toughened plastics. In others they are the base resin to which thermoplastics are added to improve some physico-mechanical or rheological characteristics of the thermoplastic elastomer. All these features have been reviewed recently by Kresge[29].

Two interesting new products lately developed in our laboratory are presented here as an illustration of the potential offered by thermoplastic elastomers in the field of polymer blends. This area has been broadly explored as reported in the current literature, and a special mention must be made of the outstanding work performed by Shell's scientists[30, 31]. (See Chapter 14)

4.1   Development of New "ABS" Type Resins Using Block Copolymer Emulsifiers

Most ABS resins are prepared by a graft copolymerization process in the presence of an elastomer. Melt-blending SAN with the elastomer should be a more versatile and simpler route towards similar materials, since it should directly allow a continuum of compositions to be obtained at will during processing. However, it requires that a number of demanding features such as good interfacial adhesion, adequate crosslinking of the elastomer, and optimum particle size can be achieved during the blending. The problem of obtaining the desired crosslinking during the blending process can be overcome or minimized by using a thermoplastic elastomer such as a poly(styrene-b-butadiene-b-styrene) or S–B–S since this material is physically crosslinked by formation of PS domains. Pure blends of SAN with an S-EB-S (EB = poly ethylene-co-butylene) triblock copolymer (KRATON G1651 Thermoplastic Rubber from Shell) or with a star-shaped block copolymer, $(S–B)_4$ (SOLPRENE 411 from Philips) do not have either good tensile or good impact properties, (see Table I). This situation results both from the difficulty of achieving a fine dispersion of the elastomer phase and also from the lack of interfacial adhesion due to the incompatibility between the blended polymers. This problem can be alleviated by the addition to the blends of well tailored block copolymers which behave as polymeric emulsifiers[32]. The validity of this concept and its applicability have been demonstrated in extensive work in this laboratory[33-40]. Results in Table I show that the addition of a PB-PMMA diblock copolymer to $SAN/(S–B)_4$ blends or of a hydrogenated PB-PMMA copolymer to SAN/S–EB–S blends gives very significant improvements in the impact resistance of these blends, leading to impact values even higher than those of a classical commercial ABS. Interestingly enough, this is not achieved at the expense of the modulus E.

Figure 2   Scanning electron micrographs of fracture surfaces from a Charpy impact test, (a) 70 SAN/30 $(S–B)_4$ (X1250), (b) 66,5 SAN/23,5 $(S–B)_4$ / 10 PB–PMMA (X1250), (c) ABS (X2500)

TABLE I   New ABS Type Resins from SAN – Thermoplastic elastomer (TPE)

SAN %	TPE %	Copolymer %	TPE % of Total[a]	Young's E MPa	Stress at Yield MPa	Stress at Break MPa	Elongation at Break %	Impact Charpy KJ/m²	Resistance Izod Ft. Lb/in.
SAN K17 –	–	–	–	2000	–	66	6	–	–
ABS –	–	–	30[b]	1490	43.5	34	19	19.1	5.48
71.4	28.6 S–EB–S	–	28.6	–	–	–	–	6.7	0.79
69	26 S–EB–S	5HPB–PMMA	28.5	–	–	–	–	16.9	–
63.5	27.5 S–EB–S	9HPB–PMMA	31.8	–	–	–	–	22	2.03
66.5	23.5 S–EB–S	10HPB–PMMA	28.5	1510	32.2	30.1	51.9	–	1.91
70	30 (S–B)₄	–	30	1230	–	33.2	7.2	6.8	–
80	20(S–B)₄	10PB–PMMA	22.7	1640	39.7	33.5	23.5	16.8	7.46
66.5	23.5(S–B)₄	10PB–PMMA	28.5	1590	35.9	29.9	23.4	31.8	8.51

Blends were prepared on a laboratory two-roll mill at 200 °C for 5 min. and then compression molded at 200 °C for 3 min.
Tensile tests performed on specimens DIN 53448 at a cross-head speed of 2 cm. min.⁻¹.
Charpy impact tests performed on specimens DIN 53453 (0.3 mm notch).
(a) % total rubber includes the PB or HPB block of the PB–PMMA or HPB–PMMA copolymer
(b) rubber portion of the ABS

That situation obviously results from the important surface activity of the PB–PMMA or HPB–PMMA diblock copolymers; the PB or H PB block interacts strongly with the PB or EB block (forming the continuous phase of the $(S-B)_4$ or S–EB–S respectively) whereas PMMA is known to develop good interactions with SAN. Scanning electron microscopy, Figure 2 a, b or c, shows the beneficial effect of PB-PMMA copolymer in a SAN/$(S-B)_4$ blend, Figure 2 a, b; the fracture surface clearly features an excellent phase adhesion even better than in a classical ABS, Figure 2 c. HPB–PMMA behaves similarly in SAN/S–EB–S.

These results demonstrate unambiguously that the very high impact performances can be obtained from simple blending of a SAN resin with a suitable thermoplastic elastomer and a polymeric emulsifier. Still more interestingly, they suggest possible ways to modify the impact fracture history[41].

4.2   New Blends Based on Thermoplastic Elastomers and Halato-Telechelic Polymers

Thermoplastic Elastomers can play an important role in the development of new interpenetrating networks (IPN). These IPN's are defined as a combination of two polymer networks, synthesized or crosslinked in the presence of each other[42, 43]. Thermoplastic S–EB–S IPN's of thermoplastic elastomers with several other polymers (e. g. polyamides, polyesters . . .) have been studied by Davison and Gergen[44, 45]. Other types of IPN's can also exist, including those containing multiblock copolymers, semi-crystalline polymers and polymers bearing ionic groups[46]. In our work we were interested in the blending of classical thermoplastic elastomers (the $(S-B)_4$ and S–EB–S described in the preceding section) with a halato-telechelic polybutadiene (PBD) resulting from neutralization of a carboxy-terminated PBD (HYCAR CTB from B. F. Goodrich) with different metal ions.

Table II illustrates that simple blending of thermoplastic elastomers with CTB itself resulted in very poor tensile properties, at every composition which could be processed and tested. When CTB was neutralized with a Zr-alkoxide, the resulting Zr-carboxylates formed ion aggregates which allowed the material to also exhibit a thermoreversible network behavior. This gave significant increases in both tensile strength and elongation of the final blend. The nature of the telechelic polymers, the neutralizing ions and their molecular characteristics as well as those of the thermoplastic elastomer component, are among obviously important

TABLE II   Tensile Properties of PB Hycar-TPE Blends (Before and After Zr-Neutralization of CTB)

Hycar CTB[1] %	Zr-neutralized: Hycar %	Thermoplastic Elastomers %	Tensile Stress at Yield MPa	Tensile Stress at Break MPa	Elonga-tion at Break %
75	–	25 S–EB–S	not	measurable	
–	75	25 S–EB–S	0.8	1.7	160
50	–	50 S–EB–S	not	measurable	
–	50	50 S–EB–S	1	3.7	340
25	–	75 S–EB–S	1.3	3.65	360
–	25	75 S–EB–S	1.5	11.2	430
25	–	75 $(S-B)_4$	not	processable	
–	25	75 $(S-B)_4$	5	5	160

Blends were prepared on a laboratory two-roll-mill at 200 °C for 5 min and then compression molded into sheets at 200 °C for 3 min

Tensile tests were performed on specimen DIN 53448 at a cross-head speed of 2 cm. min^{-1}

[1] Carboxy-terminated polybutadiene, B. F. Goodrich

parameters which are available for optimizing the behavior of these new and versatile blends and for generating original morphologies.

5 CONCLUSIONS

We believe that the foregoing discussion of our work on the heterophase polymers, their synthesis by a wide variety of techniques, and their morphologies amply illustrates the potential of macromolecular engineering. It is evident that these synthesis techniques have broad application in block copolymer research and development.

References

1. H. L. Hsieh, R. C. Farrar, and K. Udipi, *"Anionic Polymerization. Kinetics, Mechanism and Synthesis"*, J. E. McGrath, Ed., ACS Symposium Series 166, Washington, D. C., 1981, p. 389
2. A. F. Halasa, *"Anionic Polymerization. Kinetic, Mechanisms and Synthesis"* J. E. McGrath, Ed., ACS Symposium Series No. 166, Washington, D. C., 1981, p. 409
3. W. L. Hergenrother, and R. J. Ambrose, *J. Polym. Sci., Polym. Chem. Ed. 12*, 2613 (1974)
4. D. Petit, R. Jérôme and Ph. Teyssié, *J. Polym. Sci., Polym. Chem. Ed. 17*, 2903 (1979)
5. W. T. Allen, and D. E. Eaves, *Angew. Makromolek. Chem. 58–59*, 321 (1977)
6. P. M. Lefèbvre, R. Jérôme, and Ph. Teyssié, *Makromol. Chem. 183*, 245 (1982)
7. Y. Yamashita, Y. Nakamura and S. Kojima, *J. Polym. Sci. 11*, 823 (1973)
8. P. M. Lefèbvre, R. Jérôme, and Ph. Teyssié, *J. Polym. Sci., Polym. Chem. Ed. 21*, 789 (1983)
9. W. H. Sharkey, *"Ring-Opening Polymerization. Kinetics, Mechanisms and Synthesis"*, J. E. McGrath, Ed., ACS Symposium Series 286, Washington, D. C., 1985, p. 373
10. P. Prabhu, A. Schindler, M. H. Theil, and R. D. Gilbert, *J. Polym. Sci. Polym. Lett. Ed. 18*, 389 (1980) – *J. Polym. Sci., Polym. Chem. Ed. 19*, 523 (1981)
11. A. Siove, and M. Fontanille, *Makromolek. Chem. 181*, 1815 (1980)
12. M. Julémont, and Ph. Teyssié, *"Aspects of Homogeneous Catalysis"*, R. Ugo, Ed., D. Reidel Publ. Comp. 1981, p. 99.
13. P. Hadjiandreou, M. Julémont, and Ph. Teyssié, *Macromolecules 17*, 2455 (1984)
14. P. Hadjiandreou, Ph. D. Thesis. University of Liège (Belgium), 1980 – IUPAC International Symposium on Macromolecules, Bucharest, 1983
15. R. Fayt, P. Hadjiandreou, and Ph. Teyssié, *J. Polym. Sci., Polym. Chem. Ed. 23*, 337 (1985)
16. A. Eisenberg, and M. King, *"Ion-Containing Polymers"*, *"Polymer Physics, vol. 2"*, R. S. Stein, Ed., Academic Press, New York, 1977
17. R. Jérôme, and G. Broze, *Rubber Chem. Techn. 58*, 223 (1985)
18. Y. Mohajer, D. Tyagi, G. L. Wilkes, R. F. Storey, and J. P. Kennedy, *Polym. Bull. 8*, 47 (1982)
19. S. Bagrodia, Y. Mohajer, G. L. Wilkes, R. F. Storey, and J. P. Kennedy, *Polym. Bull. 8*, 281 (1982), and *9*, 174 (1983)
20. J. P. Kennedy, L. R. Ross, J. E. Lackey, and O. Nuyken, *Polym. Bull. 4*, 67 (1981)
21. G. Broze, R. Jérôme, and Ph. Teyssié, *Macromolecules 15*, 920 (1982)
22. G. Broze, R. Jérôme, Ph. Teyssié, and C. Marco, *Macromolecules 16*, 996 (1983)
23. G. Broze, R. Jérôme, Ph. Teyssié, and C. Marco, *J. Polym. Sci., Polym. Phys. Ed. 21*, 2205 (1983)
24. G. Broze, R. Jérôme, Ph. Teyssié, and C. Marco, *Macromolecules 16*, 1771 (1983)
25. G. Broze, R. Jérôme, Ph. Teyssié, and C. Marco, *Macromolecules 18*, 1376 (1985)
26. G. Broze, R. Jérôme, Ph. Teyssié, and B. Gallot, *J. Polym. Sci., Polym. Lett. Ed. 19*, 415 (1981)
27. C. E. Williams, T. P. Russell, R. Jérôme, and J. Horrion, *Macromolecules, 19*, 2877 (1986)
28. R. Jérôme, G. Vlaic, and C. E. Williams, *J. Physique – Lettres 44*, L-717 (1983)
29. E. N. Kresge *"Polymer Blends"*, D. R. Paul and S. Newman, Ed., Academic Press, New York, 1978, vol. 2 chap. 20

30. W. P. Gergen, Paper presented at the ACS Rubber Div. Meeting, April 1985
31. W. P. Gergen, S. Davison, and R. G. Lutz, Paper presented at the ACS Rubber Div. Meeting, April 1985
32. D. R. Paul, *"Polymer Blends"*, D. R. Paul and S. Newman Ed., Academic Press, New York, 1978, vol. 2, chap. 12.
33. R. Fayt, R. Jérôme and Ph. Teyssié, *J. Polym. Sci. Polym. Lett. Ed., 19,* 79 (1981)
34. R. Fayt, R. Jérôme and Ph. Teyssié, *J. Polym. Sci. Polym. Phys. Ed., 19,* 1269 (1981)
35. R. Fayt, R. Jérôme and Ph. Teyssié, *J. Polym. Sci. Polym. Phys. Ed., 20,* 2209 (1982)
36. R. Fayt, P. Hadjiandreou and Ph. Teyssié, *J. Polym. Sci. Polym. Phys. Ed., 23,* 337 (1985)
37. R. Fayt, R. Jérôme and Ph. Teyssié, *Makromol. Chem., 187,* 837 (1986)
38. R. Fayt, R. Jérôme and Ph. Teyssié, *J. Polym., Sci., Polym. Lett. Ed., 24,* 25 (1986)
39. T. Ouhadi, R. Fayt, R. Jérôme and Ph. Teyssié, *J. Polym. Sci. Polym. Phys. Ed., 24,* 973 (1986)
40. T. Ouhadi, R. Fayt, R. Jérôme and Ph. Teyssié, *J. Appl. Polym. Sci., 32,* 5647 (1986)
41. R. Fayt and Ph. Teyssié, *Macromolecules, 19,* 2077 (1986)
42. D. A. Thomas and L. H. Sperling, *"Polymer Blends"*, D. R. Paul and S. Newman, Ed., Academic Press, New York, 1978, vol. 2 chap. 11
43. S. C. Kim, D. Klempner, K. C. Frisch, N. Radigan and H. L. Frisch, *Macromolecules 9,* 258 (1976)
44. S. Davison, W. P. Gergen, U. S. Pat. 4.041103 (1977)
45. W. P. Gergen, S. Davison, U. S. Pat. 4.101605 (1978)
46. D. L. Siegfried, D. A. Thomas and L. H. Sperling, *J. Appl. Polym. Sci., 26,* 177 (1981)

Chapter 12

RESEARCH ON THERMOPLASTIC ELASTOMERS

Section 8

THERMOPLASTIC ELASTOMERS STUDIES 1966–1986

J. E. McGrath

Contents

J. E. McGrath, Department of Chemistry and Polymer Materials and Interfaces Laboratory, Virginia Polytechnic Institute and State University, Blacksburg, VA 24601

1 INTRODUCTION

The writer appreciates the opportunity provided by the editors to review research in the area of thermoplastic elastomers over about the last twenty years. This review will not stress the many contributions of other workers in this field, but will rather focus on research of groups with which the author has been associated. References 1–19 describe books, reviews and original articles which provide many references to the outside literature. Indeed, readers of this monograph may find those references of some additional utility in pursuing the literature of thermoplastic elastomers. It has been convenient to subdivide these efforts into three areas, namely the diene-containing block copolymers, the urea and urethane systems, and the siloxane-containing block copolymers. Highlights of our efforts in each of these areas are included in this review.

2 DIENE CONTAINING BLOCK COPOLYMERS

Essentially all of the work in the literature dealing with the subject area is based upon polymerizations of butadiene, isoprene, and, to some extent, the hydrogenated derivatives as the soft blocks in thermoplastic elastomeric compositions. As has been pointed out earlier in this book, the idea of a microphase separation in these soft diene materials copolymerized with hard regions is, indeed, critical to the utilization as thermoplastic elastomers. It is perhaps worthwhile to utilize Figure 1 to remind us of this situation. Single phase systems show the behavior indicated in the upper portion of the figure and the unusual and more desirable behavior of multiphase structural formation is demonstrated in the lower portion of the figure. The essential feature, as is well known, is the retention of the two glass transition temperature intervals corresponding to each of the microphases. The concept of microphases is both a function of the block length and the polymer-polymer interaction parameters. Proper compositional design allows for an elastomeric type moduli between the

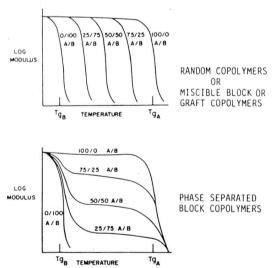

Figure 1   Generalized modulus temperature behavior of homogeneous and microheterogeneous copolymers

transition temperatures. Furthermore, to generate the hard-soft-hard physical network structure, it is necessary to provide terminal glassy or semi-crystalline regions. Living polymer processes may entail only initiation and propagation steps and can be essentially devoid of terminating reactions. This feature allows the synthesis of predetermined and well-controlled structures which is a valuable asset in the preparation of block copolymers. Although various living polymerizations can now proceed via anionic, cationic, and coordination mechanisms, historically, at least, the anionic route was inherently freer from terminating reactions as a result of the greater stability of the carbanion growing ends. Therefore, this technique was investigated as the preferred method for synthesizing diene-containing block polymers. The best route available for synthesizing well-defined block polymers utilized anionic living polymer techniques in high vacuum systems. Alkyl lithium initiators were well known to be suitable for these types of processes. The general synthesis of a diblock is illustrated in Scheme I. The chemistry demonstrated in Scheme I can quantitatively produce a diblock structure. Additional blocks could then be formed by sequential addition of monomer or alternatively, coupling agents such as the silyl halides or divinyl benzene might be utilized. The high vacuum technique for conducting these operations has been well discussed in the reference cited in this article as well as other chapters of the book. For the sake of completeness, interested readers may wish to investigate references 1, 2, 6–9, 23–26. The well-defined diblocks indicated in Scheme I were readily prepared utilizing appropriate purification techniques and slowly gained expertise

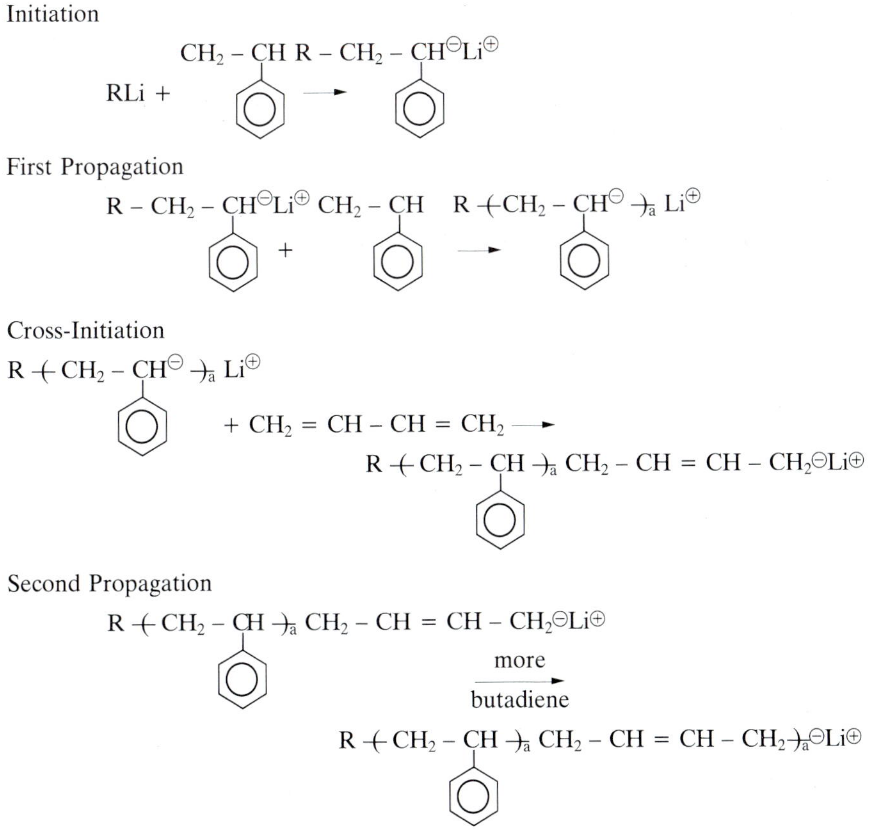

Initiation

$$RLi + \underset{\bigcirc}{CH_2 = CH} \longrightarrow \underset{\bigcirc}{CH_2 - CH \; R - CH_2 - CH^{\ominus}Li^{\oplus}}$$

First Propagation

$$R - CH_2 - \underset{\bigcirc}{CH^{\ominus}Li^{\oplus}} \; + \; \underset{\bigcirc}{CH_2 = CH} \longrightarrow R \underset{\bigcirc}{(CH_2 - CH^{\ominus})_a} \; Li^{\oplus}$$

Cross-Initiation

$$R \underset{\bigcirc}{(CH_2 - CH^{\ominus})_a} \; Li^{\oplus} \; + \; CH_2 = CH - CH = CH_2 \longrightarrow$$

$$R \underset{\bigcirc}{(CH_2 - CH)_a} \; CH_2 - CH = CH - CH_2^{\ominus}Li^{\oplus}$$

Second Propagation

$$R \underset{\bigcirc}{(CH_2 - CH)_a} \; CH_2 - CH = CH - CH_2^{\ominus}Li^{\oplus} \xrightarrow[\text{butadiene}]{\text{more}}$$

$$R \underset{\bigcirc}{(CH_2 - CH)_a} \; CH_2 - CH = CH - CH_2)_a{}^{\ominus}Li^{\oplus}$$

Scheme I

with a high vacuum system. However, the question of how to form the third block consumed much more experimental time than now seems to have been needed. The kinetics of cross initiation were known to be somewhat unfavorable for either butadiene or isoprene chain anions initiating styrene in a sequential addition. Therefore, for several months, various coupling methods were investigated. The initial problem was to devise ways to quantitatively couple the living ends. Finally, it was decided to neglect possible kinetic problems and experimentally try simply adding the third batch of highly purified styrene.

The results were very gratifying and in early 1966 it was possible to prepare nearly monodisperse triblock systems of predictable molecular weights which had very high 1,4 microstructure. Some concern was also expressed regarding the distribution of molecular weight in the initial hard block (e. g. polystyrene). At that time, principally n-butyl lithium and the crystallizable ethyl lithium had been investigated. Ethyl lithium was favored for several good reasons. The most critical of these, perhaps, was that it could be crystallized and thus highly purified. However, there were already some indications that the branched alkyl lithiums might initiate more efficiently than their linear chain counterparts. The utilization of minor amounts or aromatic ethers was pursued extensively to modify the initiation step. Indeed, aromatic ethers, such as anisole or even diphenyl ether, were found[20–23] essentially able to enhance the initiation rate without reducing substantially the ~ 90 % 1,4 microstructure of the polydienes.

Methods for characterizing block polymers were extremely primitive in 1966, although rapid membrane osmometry was used extensively. Fortunately, the technique of gel permeation chromatography, now often called size exclusion chromatography (SEC), had just been invented at DOW by J. C. Moore. Several units were available in the Akron area and a few early samples were subjected to GPC analysis. By this approach, it was possible, perhaps for the first time, to clearly distinguish between homopolymer, diblock, and well-defined triblock systems. Some of these early results were published later[23]. Of course, the technique has advanced dramatically since those times, but some of the earliest demonstrations of the technical utilization of GPC grew out of this work with the diene-containing block polymer

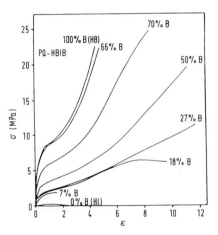

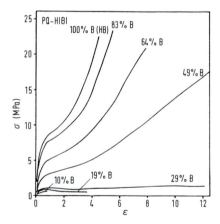

Figure 2 a   Comparison of the stress-strain properties of the press-quenched films of HBIB to those from the homopolymers HB and HI. Composition of each polymer is denoted by the butadiene content next to the curve

Figure 2 b   Comparison of stress-strain properties of the press-quenched films of HIBI block copolymers to those of homopolymers HB. Butadiene content is next to the curve

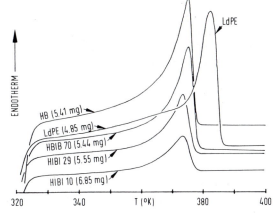

Figure 3 Comparison of the Differential Scanning Calorimetry (DSC) thermograms of the homopolymer HB and various block copolymers to that of the LDPE. Weight of each polymer sample is indicated in parentheses. The instrument range is 2 mcal/s for all the runs

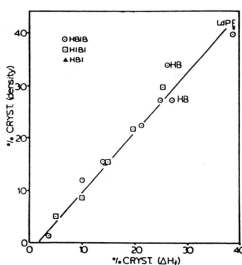

Figure 4 A Comparison of percent crystallinity obtained from density to that obtained from ΔH_f for the various block copolymers

systems. The first presentation of the above results was reference 20 which was part of the Rubber Division meeting held in May of 1967 at Montreal. Many of these early results just commented upon could be found in that paper which emphasized, in fact, the isoprene-based block polymers. In time Dr. Juliano made many contributions principally working on butadiene-based systems. As is well known now, the butadiene-based systems are quantitatively quite different in their physical behavior from the isoprene materials. Later, aspects of the copolymerization of butadiene were investigated[24–29]. Butadiene and isoprene copolymerized in substantially a block-like manner, quite analogously to the better known situation for styrene and butadiene. The copolymerization has been analyzed in some detail[24–29]. It was reasoned the pure block 1,4-polybutadiene should be converted to polyethylene-like structures if they were completely hydrogenated, whereas the corresponding isoprene systems would produce an amorphous rubber-like model ethylene-propylene rubbery segment. Indeed, in cooperation with Professors Wilkes and Ward, this was proved to be the case, both with chemical hydrogenation[26,28] and catalytic hydrogenation[30,32]. Tough, transparent block polymers that are more chemically resistant than the styrene-based systems were generated and discussed extensively in the literature[26–28]. Typical stress strain behavior, DSC and crystallinity-density correlations are provided in Figures 2–4.

The chemistry of endlinking also was not neglected. Others have demonstrated the utility of divinyl benzene as a linking agent for preparation of star-shaped macromolecules. However, working with Dr. Martin[25], it was discovered that the DVB system could be remarkably well controlled under the proper reaction conditions. Divinyl benzene has a number of advantages relative to the chlorosilanes. One does not have to have the stoichiometry exactly correct to make a perfectly linked star block polymer. Secondly, hydrogenation catalysts are able, in some cases, to cleave carbon silicon bonds and, hence, disrupt the structure. It was shown that the aluminium alkyl/nickel octoate system, which was well known in the patent literature, is quite effective at quantitatively hydrogenating dienes such as butadiene and even isoprene to a saturated material with no apparent loss in structural integrity[30,37].

Some of the current work has investigated the interesting block polymers derived from tertiary butyl styrene with either isoprene or butadiene. In this case, the TBS hard block shows some partial miscibility with the isoprene center segment. However, upon hydrogenation, one can lower the solubility parameter of the diene block and effectively transform a partially miscible copolymer into a substantially microphase separated copolymeric material. The resulting change in the physical properties is quite dramatic[30,32–35].

Another area of current common interest in the diene-based systems, has been to investigate difunctional organolithium initiators[36–39]. The system chosen was basically an outgrowth of research reported by Dr. Tung and coworkers at the DOW Chemical Company. Dr. Broske, at Virginia Tech, has particularly shown that, under the right conditions, one may get a perfectly soluble difunctional initiator which can produce block copolymers of high 1,4 microstructure without the need of any polar additives. The system works best for butadiene and is somewhat less effective for isoprene and styrene. This is believed to be related to the competition between initiation and propagation. Fortunately, butadiene has a low enough propagation rate constant that the chains can be effectively initiated with this difunctional initiator. With butadiene, predictable molecular weights and narrow molecular weight distributions are obtained. Moreover, block polymers can be made in one step which show excellent physical properties. Further publications and detailed kinetic investigations are in progress with this polymerization system.

3   UREA AND URETHANE SYSTEMS

Polyurethane systems have been of interest since the early discoveries in Germany and later at the B. F. Goodrich by Schollenberger, et al. as discussed in Chapters 1 and 2 previously. Polyurethanes may be, of course, either linear or crosslinked depending on the reaction functionality and conditions utilized. Most commonly, they are derived from relatively low molecular weight (1–3,000), aliphatic polyethers such as polypropylene oxide or polytetramethylene oxide. Alternatively, many polyester polyols based upon poly(butylene adipate) or polycaprolactone are used. These polyols comprise the soft segment of the resulting copolymer which is usually synthesized with a symmetrical diisocyanate such as MDI and a suitable short chain diol "chain extender" such as 1,4-butane diol. Synthesis of these materials has been termed earlier by the author as an "in situ" preparation, wherein the hard block is generated in the presence of the soft polyol segment. Very few examples in the literature have produced perfectly alternating segmented polymers although in principle this is possible. The result is that in most thermoplastic polyurethanes, the sequence length of the hard segment increases as its weight or volume fraction is increased. These variables, in turn, influence the extent and rate of microphase separation in these important copolymers.

The reproducible solution synthesis of linear model thermoplastic polyurethane (TPU) copolymers of this type has proved to be a problem for many investigators. In this regard a useful experiment was developed which is summarized here. This utilizes a mixture of an azeotropic solvent, e. g. toluene, with a polar amide solvent such as dimethylformamide (DMF). The polyol and the diol are dissolved in the solvent mixture and heating is initiated. The toluene/water azeotrope is quite effective at drying both the polyol and the diol reactants. In addition, it is effective at removing traces of amines that are serious impurities found in amide solvents such as DMF. After a suitable portion of the toluene is removed via, for example, the Dean Stark trap, purified MDI may be added at a suitable temperature, e. g. 90 °C with no catalyst, or lower in the presence of suitable catalysts, e. g. stannous octanoate. Such a procedure can be followed viscometrically or by GPC until appropriate molecular weights are achieved. This procedure has been not only an interesting demonstration, but also a useful way to evaluate new intermediates for polyurethanes.

Although urea systems have been known for many years and, indeed, widely utilized in high performance materials such as spandex fibers, they have not been as important as the carbamate systems until recently. However, it is known that the urea systems have much higher cohesive energy density parameters than the corresponding urethanes. As such, they tend to separate more easily into microphases in these copolymer systems and also retain their thermal mechanical integrity to significantly higher temperatures. Current studies in these areas have focused on the preparation of urea urethane copolymers and completely urea linked segmented systems. For the latter situation, one needs first to generate an amine terminated polyol. Commercially available systems have relied primarily upon chemical transformations of the secondary hydroxyl functionality with, for example, ammonia and various transition metal catalysts. Another approach is to functionally terminate stable coordination polymerization chain ends with suitable reagents. Some of this work has been presented recently[67].

The urea urethanes, on the other hand, may be made by a variety of methods which involve first capping the hydroxyl terminated polyol with excess diisocyanate and then chain extending the material to generate the urea hard segments. In the classical approach, this utilizes the addition of diamines such as ethylene diamine in polar solvents. The reaction is known to be very rapid and is often difficult to control. Similarly, so-called "water extended" urea systems involve the utilization of trace amounts of water, to produce carbamic acid functionality which decomposes to yield CO_2 and amines. Recent efforts[41–43] have focused on an unconventional route for the generation of polyureas. A method has been developed which uses tertiary alcohols, such as cumyl alcohol or t-butyl alcohol to first cap the terminal

$$ \underset{\displaystyle CH_3}{\overset{\displaystyle CH_3}{\bigcirc\!\!-\,\overset{|}{\underset{|}{C}}\!-\,OH}} \qquad \text{(Cumyl Alcohol)}$$

isocyanate units to form hindered carbamates. These experiments suggest that at higher temperatures, or in the presence of suitable catalysts, these hindered carbamates dissociate, followed by elimination of CO_2 and generation of amine functionality, which then rapidly produces urea segments. The chemistry is described in references 41–43. Typical stress-strain curves, dynamic mechanical behavior and thermogravimetric analysis data for these systems are illustrated in Figures 5, 6 and 7. The interest in polyureas is continuing, particularly via efforts at synthesizing amine functional poly(alkylene ethers).

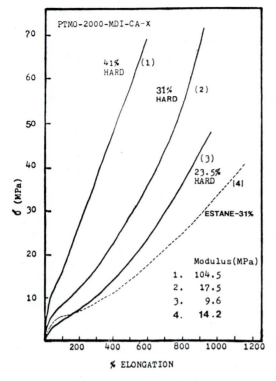

Figure 5   Effect of the hard segment contents on the stress-strain behavior of the PEUU's

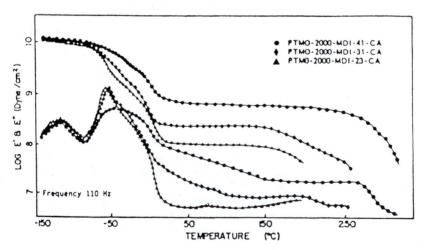

Figure 6   Dynamic mechanical spectra. Frequency 110 Hz

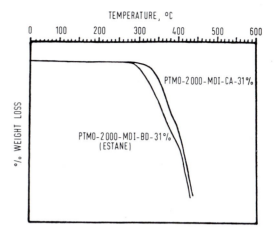

Figure 7   TGA curves for the polyether-urethane-urea and Estane

4   SILOXANE CONTAINING BLOCK COPOLYMERS

Much of the early effort on siloxane systems has been summarized in Reference 1. In the synthesis of organosiloxane copolymers, one has the choice of introducing either a silicon-oxygen-carbon link or a silicon-carbon link between the two dissimilar segments. In small molecules, quite distinctly different hydrolytic stability is observed. For example, one often uses silicon-oxygen-carbon bonds as protecting groups which are stable under anhydrous neutral or basic conditions but quickly revert when treated with aqueous acidic environments. Noshay and coworkers developed an interesting route for the preparation of stable perfectly alternating siloxane poly(arylene ether sulfone) copolymers which is reviewed in Reference 1. A large variety of different hard segments were incorporated into the resulting copolymers. It was observed that, in fact, the processibility of these copolymers was very dependent upon the differential solubility parameter between the hard segment and the nonpolar polydimethyl siloxane block[44]. In some cases, the microphase separation was apparently so well developed that the materials developed an extremely high viscosity in the melt, rendering them essentially non-processible, even though they were linear chains and, indeed, solvent castable from a variety of appropriate organic liquids. This effect is general with microphase separated systems but was particularly pronounced for the organosiloxane materials[44]. Despite some of the melt fabrication problems, the organosiloxane systems produced by the silyl amine hydroxyl reaction[1] produced interesting perfectly alternating copolymers from a variety of hard segments. Polycarbonates were investigated[46–48] as well as aromatic polyesters[49, 50]. The chemistry is illustrated in Scheme II.

The perfectly alternating copolymers developed very uniform morphology[7] reminiscent of the triblock styrene-diene materials. Typical stress-strain and dynamic mechanical behavior is shown in Figures 8 and 9. By contrast, if the copolymers were prepared by either a randomly coupled route or an in situ generation of the hard-block[45, 47] the morphology was not regular and, indeed, the physical properties of both elastomeric and rigid compositions were quite different from the perfectly alternating systems. The copolymers have considerable interest as multiphase damping materials[49] due to the fact that two, three or even more relaxations can be designed into these copolymers as a function of block length and composition. Indeed, significant loss peaks ranging from −120 to well over 200 °C have been achieved[49,50]. The chemistry for synthesizing the functional oligomers has been reviewed in

Block Copolymers

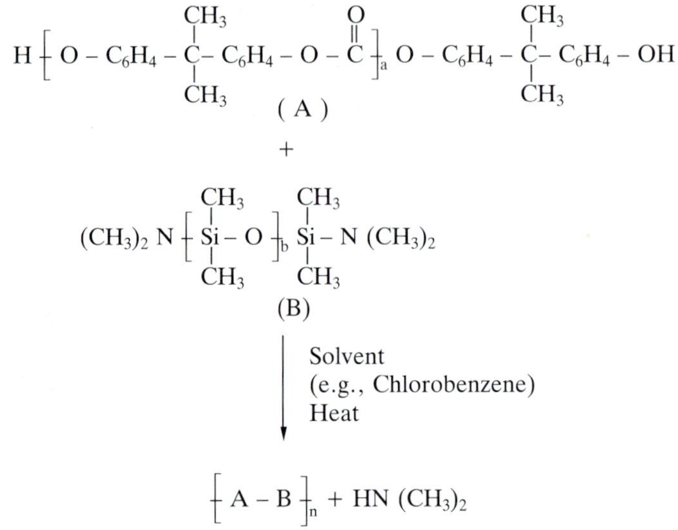

$$H \left[O - C_6H_4 - \underset{\underset{CH_3}{|}}{\overset{\overset{CH_3}{|}}{C}} - C_6H_4 - O - \underset{}{\overset{\overset{O}{\|}}{C}} \right]_a O - C_6H_4 - \underset{\underset{CH_3}{|}}{\overset{\overset{CH_3}{|}}{C}} - C_6H_4 - OH$$

(A)

+

$$(CH_3)_2 N \left[\underset{\underset{CH_3}{|}}{\overset{\overset{CH_3}{|}}{Si}} - O \right]_b \underset{\underset{CH_3}{|}}{\overset{\overset{CH_3}{|}}{Si}} - N (CH_3)_2$$

(B)

Solvent
(e.g., Chlorobenzene)
Heat

$$\left[A - B \right]_n + HN (CH_3)_2$$

Scheme II

Reference 51 and more recently, in Reference 3. Most generally, one prepares silicon carbon linked functionalities by conducting hydrosilylation reactions between SiH functional groups and the corresponding unsaturated functional end group. In some cases, the functional end group must first be protected or further reacted after the hydrosilylation to produce the desired functionality. The benefit of the silicon-carbon bond is that it is significantly more hydrolytically stable than the silicon-oxygen-carbon bond. However, Noshay, Matzner and coworkers[1] showed that the silicon-oxygen-carbon bond in hy-

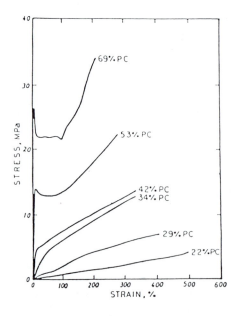

Figure 8   Stress-strain curves of polycarbonate-polydimethylsiloxane block copolymers (Cross-head Speed: 5 cm min.)

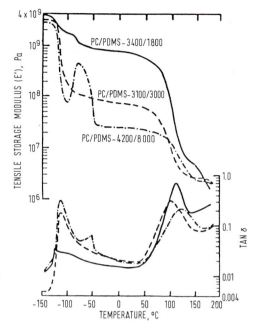

Figure 9   Storage moduli and loss tangents versus temperature for three typical block copolymers: Frequency: 11 Hz; M_n of blocks expressed in g mole

drophobic high molecular weight copolymers was much more stable than would have been predicted from small molecule considerations. Apparently the hydrophobic environment protects the potentially hydrolyzable group.

Recent work here has focused on a variety of thermoplastic elastomers based on the aminopropyl end functionality in suitably equilibrated polydimethyl siloxane. Characteristic of these are the urea linked materials described in References 54–57. The chemistry is summarized in Scheme III. A characteristic stress-strain curve and dynamic mechanical behavior for the urea linked systems is provided in Figures 10 and 11. It was of interest to note that the ultimate properties of the soluble, processible urea linked copolymers were equivalent to some of the best silica reinforced chemically crosslinked silicone rubber

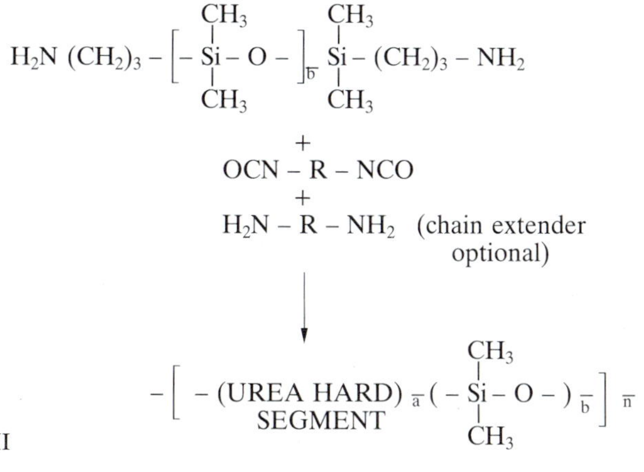

$$H_2N\,(CH_2)_3 - \left[-\underset{\underset{CH_3}{|}}{\overset{\overset{CH_3}{|}}{Si}} - O - \right]_{\overline{b}} \underset{\underset{CH_3}{|}}{\overset{\overset{CH_3}{|}}{Si}} - (CH_2)_3 - NH_2$$

$$+$$
$$OCN - R - NCO$$
$$+$$
$$H_2N - R - NH_2 \quad \text{(chain extender optional)}$$

$$\downarrow$$

$$-\left[-(\text{UREA HARD SEGMENT}) _{\overline{a}} (-\underset{\underset{CH_3}{|}}{\overset{\overset{CH_3}{|}}{Si}} - O -)_{\overline{b}} \right]_{\overline{n}}$$

Scheme III

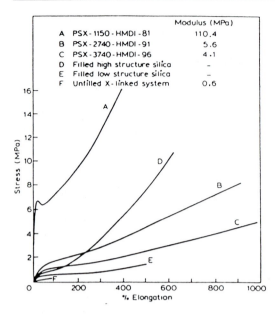

Figure 10   Stress vs % elongation behavior for siloxane-urea segmented copolymers from H-MDI as a function of molecular weight of oligomer used and the hard segment content at 25°C

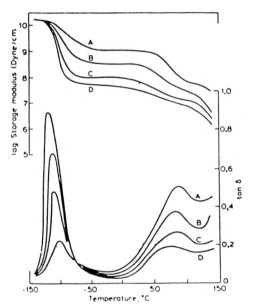

Figure 11   Dynamic mechanical behavior of siloxane-urea copolymers prepared from H-MDI, curve (A): PSX-1150-HMDI-81; curve (B): PSX-1770-HMDI-87; curve (C): PSX-2770-HMDI-91; curve (D): PSX-3680-HMDI-94

materials described in the literature. Various other fundamentally oriented studies which describe the kinetic mechanism of the synthesis of these oligomers are provided in the references herein. A number of other hard segments such as the imides and amides have also been investigated. There was a good correlation between the intensity of the hydrogen bond formation and the ultimate mechanical properties at room temperature. In this regard, the urea linked system were preferred. On the other hand, the thermal stability was best for the polyimide systems.

Brief discussion of the novel surface properties in these elastomers is appropriate. The bulk microphase separation characteristics of thermoplastic elastomers has been studied in great detail and is very important. However, less information is known about the surface structure in these two phase materials. A number of investigators have been interested in these areas. Some of the first work, described in Reference 58, focused on the (at that time) surprising siloxane enhancement at the air/vacuum surface in pure copolymers and even in homopolymer-block copolymer blends. Essentially, the polydimethyl siloxane displays very low surface energy which provides a thermodynamic driving force for migration to the air or vacuum interface. In contrast to the homopolymer, the siloxane segment is chemically linked and cannot *macro*scopically phase separate. Photoelectron spectroscopy studies (XPS or ESCA) conducted demonstrated that the surface structure was predominantly siloxane, even when the bulk siloxane compositions were relatively low. An important criteria, though, was the development of microphase structure in the bulk, which apparently allows the siloxane microphase to migrate to the air or vacuum interface more readily. Many other studies of this phenomenon have appeared in the literature since that time. In the cases of the siloxane modified polyimides, it is great interest in both the area of oxygen plasma processing and atomic oxygen resistance in space applications. In these cases, apparently the siloxane structure on the surface is converted to an organosilicate-type ceramic-like materials which provide protection for the etching process. Further discussion of this phenomena is provided in Reference 62.

Although most of the thermoplastic elastomer studies have utilized the readily available cyclic tetramer (D_4) structure as a starting monomer[3], there has also been interest in materials derived from the cyclic trimer D_3. The cyclic trimer has the advantage that one can produce predictable molecular weights and narrow distribution due to the ability for the cyclic trimer to produce living lithium siloxanolate chain ends. This has been described by an number of authors[1]. Recently polymers based upon t-butyl styrene and D_3[70] have been studied. These materials, again, rely somewhat upon the lower solubility parameter associated with the t-butyl styrene group relative to styrene. As a result, the subsequent block polymers that were prepared process more easily and may lead to attractive specialty elastomeric and rigid copolymers.

In summary, it has been possible to prepare a variety of organosiloxane copolymers which demonstrate useful mechanical properties but also provide a variety of other interesting properties such as hydrophobic character, high gas permeability, thermal and UV stability, atomic and oxygen plasma resistance, and biocompatibility, which is related to the hydrophobic surfaces that are prepared. The synthesis and characterization of these materials is continuing.

5   THE FUTURE

Current and future studies are continuing to investigate the areas already described which include the diene-containing materials and hydrogenated derivatives, the urea-urethane systems and the siloxane-containing copolymers. All three of these areas have a number of interesting developments that are being pursued here and elsewhere.

In addition, acrylic thermoplastic elastomers have been a dream of a large number of investigators over the past twenty years. However, several limitations have prevented the development of such materials. The application of the anionic processes to methacrylate polymerizations had been hindered by a variety of side reactions involving the carbonyl group. These have been discussed somewhat in Reference 1 and, more recently, in References 13, 14 and 63–66. Some of these deficiencies have been addressed by the recently developed Group-Transfer Polymerization Process from the DuPont Laboratories. Other approaches here have continued to focus on techniques for anionically preparing well defined alkyl methacrylate systems. In particular, it has been demonstrated that high purity anionic polymerization grade monomers can be prepared via titration methods utilizing trialkyl aluminium agents[65]. In addition, very significant enhancement of the lifetime of the carbanion has been achieved by altering the alkyl group from methyl to t-butyl[64,66]. Thus, it is possible to prepare living poly(t-butyl methacrylate) even at room temperature; such behavior was unheard of until very recently. The t-butyl ester group in these methacrylate systems easily allows several transformation reactions to take place. Conversion of the bulky ester groups into corresponding carboxylic acid can be made essentially quantitative simply by refluxing in the presence of appropriate acid catalysis. Simple thermal treatments have also been demonstrated to allow dehydration to the corresponding anhydride. The anhydride system can then be easily hydrolyzed back to a polymeric carboxylic acid. Several useful applications of these facts to thermoplastic elastomers can be cited. For example, very clean block polymers of predictable molecular weights, narrow distributions and very low homopolymer systems even at room temperature[66]. The initial hydrocarbon polymers were aromatic materials based on either polystyrene or poly(t-butyl styrene). Current research[68] is aimed at synthesizing butadiene and isoprene di- and triblock materials that are terminated by well-defined links of t-butyl methacrylate. The availability of the t-butyl ester and blocks allow simple quantitative conversion to the corresponding polymethacrylic acid and to, of course, the ion-containing derivatives. The latter ion-containing elastomers should allow, for the first time, a definitive evaluation of carboxylate association. For example, they may be contrasted with the usual randomly copolymerized carboxylic acid systems which, upon neutralization, must then traverse long portions of the macromolecule to associate into multiplets and/or clusters[13]. In these new ion-containing elastomers, the sequences are adjacent to each other and one might expect that that association into rather well-defined structures should be enhanced.

Another variation on the all-acrylic thermoplastic elastomer systems is to combine sequences of isotactic and syndiotactic structures. The isotactic alkyl methacrylates, for example, can have remarkably low glass transition temperatures. For example, highly isotactic poly (2-ethylhexyl methacrylate) has a glass temperature of $-40\,°C$, well in the range of elastomeric blocks. Initiation of this monomer in hydrocarbon solvents with the stable t-butyl methacrylate, enolate ion, is being pursued as a route of all-acrylic systems[69].

References

1. A. Noshay and J. E. McGrath, *Block Copolymers: Overview and Critical Survey,* 520 pages, Academic Press, New York, 1977
2. J. E. McGrath, Editor, *Anionic Polymerization: Kinetics, Mechanism and Synthesis,* 592 pages, ACS Symposium Series, No. 166, November 1981
3. I. Yilgor, J. S. Riffle and J. E. McGrath, *Advances in Organosiloxane Copolymers, Adv. Poly. Sci.,* Springer-Verlag, Heidelberg 1987
4. J. E. McGrath, Editor, *Ring Opening Polymerization: Kinetics, Mechanisms and Synthesis,* ACS Symposium Series, No. 286 (1985)
5. B. M. Culbertson and J. E. McGrath, Editors, *Advances in Polymer Synthesis,* Vol. 31, Plenum Press, New York (1985)
6. J. E. McGrath, M. Matzner, A. Noshay and L. M. Robeson, *Encyclopedia of Polymer Science and Technology* (Wiley, New York). Review an Block and Graft Copolymers – Supplement 2, 1977, p. 129–158

7. J. E. McGrath, *Encyclopedia of Chemical Technology Volume 8*, Third Edition, John Wiley & Sons. Inc. (1979), p. 446–1459

8. J. E. McGrath, *Block Copolymers*, D. J. Meier, Editor, MMI Press (1983), p. 1–2

9. J. E. McGrath, *Pure and Applied Chemistry, 55(10)*, 1573–85 (1983)

10. I. Yilgor, J. S. Riffle and J. E. McGrath, *Reactive Oligomers*, F. Harris, Editor, ACS Symp. Series, No. 282, 1985

11. J. E. McGrath, *Ring Opening Polymerization: Kinetics, Mechanisms and Synthesis*, J. E. McGrath, Editor, ACS Symposium Series, No. 286 (1985)

12. P. M. Sormani, R. J. Minton and J. E. McGrath, *Ring Opening Polymerization: Kinetics, Mechanisms and Synthesis*, J. E. McGrath, Editor, ACS Symposium Series, No. 286 (1985)

13. R. D. Allen, I. Yilgor and J. E. McGrath, *Coulombic Interactions in Macromolecular Systems*, A. Eisenberg and F. E. Bailey, Editors, ACS Symp. Series No. 302, 1985

14. R. D. Allen, T. E. Long and J. E. McGrath, *Advances in Polymer Synthesis*, J. E. McGrath and B. M. Culbertson, Editors; Vol. 31, 347–362, Plenum Press, New York (1985)

15. M. Matzner, J. E. McGrath, et al., *Appl. Polymer Symposia, No. 22*, 143–156 (1973)

16. J. E. McGrath, M. Matzner, L. M. Robeson and R. Barclay, Jr., *J. Polymer Science*, Polymer Symposium 60, 29–46 (1977)

17. J. E. McGrath, *Adv. in Engineering Science, 1*, 37–46 (1976)

18. M. Matzner, A. Noshay, D. L. Schober and J. E. McGrath, *Ind. Chim. Belg. 38*, 1104–1118 (1973)

19. J. E. McGrath, *J. Chem. Education, 58*, 914–921 (1981)

20. M. Morton, J. E. McGrath and P. C. Juliano, *ACS Rubber Division CIC Meeting*, May 4, 1967 (Montreal)

21. J. E. McGrath, M. Morton and P. C. Juliano, *Symposia on Block Copolymers*, Pasadena, California, June 5, 1967

22. M. Morton, J. E. McGrath, P. C. Juliano and F. C. Schwab, *4th International Synthetic Rubber Symposium*, London, October 2, 1969

23. M. Morton, J. E. McGrath, and P. C. Juliano, *J. Polymer Sci., Part C, No. 26*, 99–115 (1969)

24. I. C. Wang, Y. Mohajer, T. C. Ward, G. L. Wilkes, and J. E. McGrath, *Anionic Polymerization: Kinetics, Mechanisms, and Synthesis*, J. E. McGrath, Editor, ACS Symposium Series, No. 166, 529–555 (1981)

25. M. K. Martin, T. C. Ward, and J. E. McGrath, *Anionic Polymerization: Kinetics, Mechanisms, and Synthesis*, J. E. McGrath, Editor, ACS Symposium Series, No. 166, 557–580 (1981)

26. Y. Mohajer, G. L. Wilkes, I. C. Wang, and J. E. McGrath, *Polymer (London), 23(10)*, 1523–1536 (1982)

27. S. Abouzahr, Y. Mohajer, G. L. Wilkes, and J. E. McGrath, *Polymer (London), 23(10)*, 1519–1523 (1982)

28. Y. Mohajer, I. C. Wang, G. L. Wilkes, and J. E. McGrath, *Elastomers and Rubber Elasticity*, J. Lal and J. E. Mark, Editors, Polymer Symposium Volume Series, p. 120–154 (1982)

29. D. J. T. Hill, J. H. O'Donnell, P. W. O'Sullivan, J. E. McGrath, I. C. Wang and T. C. Ward, *Polymer Bulletin, 9(6/7)*, 292–298 (1983)

30. J. M. Hoover, T. C. Ward and J. E. McGrath, *Advances in Polyolefins*, ACS Symposium Series, T. Cheng, Editor (1986)

31. M. K. Martin and J. E. McGrath, *Polymer Preprints, 22(1)*, 212–214 (1981)

32. J. M. Hoover, T. C. Ward, and J. E. McGrath, *Polymer Preprints, 26(1)*, 253–254, 1985; see also *Polymer Preprints 27 (1)*, 183 (1986)

33. M. M. Sheridan, J. M. Hoover, T. C. Ward, and J. E. McGrath, *Polymer Preprints, 25(2)*, 102–104 (1984)

34. M. M. Sheridan, J. M. Hoover, T. C. Ward, and J. E. McGrath, *Polymer Preprints (26(1)*, 186–188 (1985)

35. A. M. Walstrom, J. M. Hoover, T. C. Ward, and J. E. McGrath, *Polymer Preprints, 26(1)*, 193–194 (1985)

36. A. D. Broske, T. L. Huang, J. M. Hoover, R. D. Allen and J. E. McGrath, *Polymer Preprints, 25(2)*, 85–87, 1984; *Adv. in Anionic Polymerization*, T. E. Hogen-Esch and J. Smid, Editors, in press, 1986

37. A. D. Broske and J. E. McGrath, *Polymer Preprints, 26(1)*, 241–243, 1985; A. D. Broske, Ph. D. Thesis, VPI&SU (1987)

38. A. D. Broske, T. L. Huang, J. M. Hoover, R. D. Allen and J. E. McGrath, *ACS Southeastern Regional Meeting*, Raleigh, North Carolina, October 24–26, 1984

39. A. D. Broske, R. A. Patsiga, J. M. Hoover and J. E. McGrath, *ACS Southeast/Southwest Regional Meeting,* Memphis, TN, October 9–11, 1985

40. D. Tyagi, J. P. Armistead, G. L. Wilkes, B. Lee and J. E. McGrath, *Polymer Preprints, 26(2),* 12–15 (1985)

41. B. Lee, D. Tyagi, G. L. Wilkes and J. E. McGrath, *Sagamore Conf. on Elastomers,* R. D. Singler, Editor, in press, 1986

42. B. Lee, D. Tyagi, G. L. Wilkes and J. E. McGrath, *Polymer Preprints, 27(1),* 100, 1986: *Unconventional Mechanism of Polymerization,* S. Shalaby, Editor, ACS Symp. Series, 1986: B. Lee, Ph. D. Thesis, VPI&SU (1987)

43. D. Tyagi, G. L. Wilkes, B. Lee and J. E. McGrath, *Advances in Elastomer and Rubber Elasticity,* J. Lal and J. E. Mark, Editors (1986)

44. M. Matzner, A. Noshay and J. E. McGrath, *Trans. Soc. Rheology 21/22,* 273–290 (1977)

45. J. S. Riffle, R. G. Freelin, A. K. Banthia, and J. E. McGrath, *J. Macromol. Sci.-Chem., A15(5),* 967–998 (1981)

46. S. Tang, E. Meincke, J. S. Riffle and J. E. McGrath, *Rubber Chem. and Tech., 54(5),* 1160, 1980: J. S. Riffle, Ph. D. Thesis, VPI&SU, 1981

47. T. C. Ward, D. P. Sheehy, J. S. Riffle, and J. E. McGrath, *Macromolecules, 14(6),* 1791–1797 (1981)

48. S. Tang, E. Meinecke, J. S. Riffle and J. E. McGrath, *Rubber Chem. and Tech., 57(1),* 184 (1984)

49. P. J. Andolino-Brandt and J. E. McGrath, *SAMPE Proceedings (Anaheim), Vol. 30,* 959–971 (1985)

50. P. J. Andolino-Brandt, C. S. Elsbernd and J. E. McGrath, *J. Polym. Sci.,* in press, 1987; P. J. Andolino-Brandt, Ph. D. Thesis, VPI&SU, June 1986

51. I. Yilgor, J. Riffle, and J. E. McGrath, *Reactive Oligomers,* ACS Symposium Series, No. 282, 161–174 (1985)

52. P. M. Sormani, R. J. Minton, and J. E. McGrath, *Ring-Opening Polymerization,* ACS Symposium Series, No. 286, 147–160 (1985)

53. J. E. McGrath, J. S. Riffle, I. Yilgor, A. K. Banthia and G. L. Wilkes, *Initiation of Polymerization,* ACS Symposium Series, No. 212, 145–173 (1983)

54. I. Yilgor, J. S. Riffle, G. L. Wilkes, and J. E. McGrath, *Polymer Bulletin, 8,* 535–542 (1982)

55. D. Tyagi, I. Yilgor, G. L. Wilkes, and J. E. McGrath, *Polymer Bulletin, 8,* 543–550 (1982)

56. I. Yilgor, W. P. Steckle, Jr., D. Tyagi, G. L. Wilkes and J. E. McGrath, *Polymer, London, 25(12),* 1800–1806 (1984)

57. D. Tyagi, I. Yilgor, J. E. McGrath and G. L. Wilkes, *Polymer, London, 25(12),* 1806–1814 (1984)

58. D. W. Dwight, A. Beck, J. S. Riffle and J. E. McGrath, *Polymer Preprints, 20(1),* 702–706, 1979; *Macromolecules,* in press, 1987

59. I. Yilgor, E. Yilgor, J. Eberle, W. Steckler Jr., B. C. Johnson, D. Tyagi, G. L. Wilkes and J. E. McGrath, *Polymer Preprints, 24(1),* 167–170 (1983)

60. I. Yilgor, E. Yilgor, B. Johnson, J. Eberle, G. L. Wilkes and J. E. McGrath, *Polymer Preprints, 24(2),* 78–80 (1983)

61. I. Yilgor, B. Lee, W. P. Steckle, Jr., J. S. Riffle, D. Tyagi, G. L. Wilkes and J. E. McGrath, *Polymer Preprints, 24(2),* 35–37 (1983)

62. B. C. Johnson, I. Yilgor and J. E. McGrath, *Polymer Preprints, 25(2),* 54–56, 1984: *Polymer Sci.,* in press, 1986; B. C. Johnson, Ph. D. Thesis, VPI&SU, 1984; J. D. Summers, C. A. Arnold, R. H. Bott, L. T. Taylor, T. C. Ward, and J. E. McGrath, *Polymer Preprints, 27(2),* 403 (1986)

63. R. D. Allen and J. E. McGrath, *Polymer Preprints, 25(2),* 9–11 (1984)

64. R. D. Allen, S. D. Smith, T. E. Long, and J. E. McGrath, *Polymer Preprints, 26(1),* 247–248 (1985)

65. R. D. Allen, T. E. Long and J. E. McGrath, *Polymer Bulletin, 15(2),* 127–134 (1986)

66. T. E. Long, R. D. Allen, J. E. McGrath, *Polymer Preprints, 27(2),* 54 (1986)

67. Y. Yoo and J. E. McGrath, *ACS S. E. Meeting,* Louisville, 1986; *Polymer Preprints, 28(1),* (1987)

68. J. E. McGrath, P. M. Sormani, C. S. Elsbernd, and S. Kilic, *Symposium on Ring Opening Polymerization,* Blois, France, June 1986; *Makromolekulare Chem.,* in press, 1986

69. T. E. Long and J. E. McGrath, unpublished results

70. S. D. Smith and J. E. McGrath, *Polymer Preprints, 27(2),* 31, 1986; *J. Polymer Sci.,* in press (1987)

Chapter **13**

APPLICATIONS OF THERMOPLASTIC ELASTOMERS

G. Holden

Contents

G. Holden, Shell Development Co., Houston, Texas

1   INTRODUCTION

Thermoplastic elastomers are materials which combine the processing characteristics of thermoplastics with the physical properties of vulcanized rubbers. Those based on segmented polyurethanes were first introduced in the early 1950's. In 1965, the announcement[1] and commercial introduction of products of this type based on styrenic block copolymers generated much interest in the rubber industry. Since then they have gained considerable importance. Their first applications spanned two industries – rubber and thermoplastics. At first the growth of these new products and of the pioneering thermoplastic polyurethane elastomers was slow. At that time the rubber industry had little thermoplastic know-how or processing equipment. The thermoplastics industry had this know-how and equipment but lacked knowledge of which rubber products to aim at or of how to sell into the rubber market. However, the unique feature of thermoplastic elastomers – their ability to provide products with most of the physical properties of conventional vulcanized rubbers, but without going through the process of vulcanization – is so attractive that they became commercially successful.

Because of their excellent impact strength, some thermoplastic elastomers were used to replace thermoplastics. However, the first area in which thermoplastic elastomers became commercially important was as replacements for vulcanized rubbers. In this application, the economic advantages of eliminating the compounding of rubbers with fillers, plasticizers and vulcanizing agents, as well as avoiding the slow and costly process of vulcanization, led to a rapid growth. The diversification of the major rubber (i.e., tire) companies into plastics ventures such as PVC aided considerably in this growth, which was predicted to take about 15 % of the non-tire rubber market by 1986[2]. Recently it was estimated that thermoplastic elastomers would displace at least an additional 200 million pounds of vulcanized rubber parts by the end of 1990.[3] In some areas, for example footwear, the market for thermoplastic elastomers is now relatively mature but others are still experiencing rapid growth.[4,5]

The unique feature of thermoplastic elastomers can be best appreciated by comparing their properties to those of those of other commercial polymers, as in Figure 1. In this figure, polymers are compared using two criteria – their mechanical properties at room temperature (either hard, flexible or rubbery) and the means by which they are formed into the final product (thermoset or thermoplastic). Six classes result – hard thermosets, flexible ther-

	THERMOSET	THERMOPLASTIC
RIGID	Epoxy, Melamine-Formaldehyde, Sheet Molding, Compounds	Polypropylene, High Density Polyethylene, Polystyrene
FLEXIBLE	Highly Vulcanized Rubber	Low Density, Polyethylene, Ethylene-Vinyl, Acetate Copolymer, Plasticized PVC
RUBBERY	Vulcanized Rubber	Thermoplastic Rubbers

Figure 1   Classification

mosets, rubbery thermosets, hard thermoplastics, flexible thermoplastics and rubbery thermoplastics. The first five classes have been known for many years and the introduction of the thermoplastic elastomers completed the picture. The fact that the thermoplastic elastomers do not require vulcanization is of course the key point. In the terminology of the plastics industry, vulcanization is a thermosetting process. As such, it is slow, irreversible and takes place on heating. In contrast, in thermoplastic elastomers, the change from a fluid, processible melt to a solid rubbery article is fast, reversible and takes place on cooling. Additionally, in some thermoplastic elastomers, a similar reversible transition from a solid to a fluid can take place on the addition and removal of a solvent. These transitions are shown diagrammatically in Figure 2.

This ability of thermoplastic elastomers to become fluid on heating and then solidify on cooling gives manufacturers the ability to produce rubberlike articles using the fast proces-sing equipment (injection molders, blow molders, extruders etc.) which have been developed for the plastics industry. The intensive (and expensive) compounding and vulcanization steps or conventional rubber processing are eliminated, as are the vulcaniza-tion residues in the final product. Scrap can usually be reground and recycled. Output is greatly increased and manpower reduced. However, because these materials are *thermo-plastic* elastomers, they have some deficiencies. In the softer grades of materials such properties as compression set (particularly at elevated temperatures), upper service temper-ature and resistance to solvents and oils are often not as good as with conventional vulcanized elastomers. Thus soft thermoplastic elastomers have not found many applications as replacements for vulcanized rubbers in such areas as automobile tires, fan belts or radiator hose. However, they have found many other such applications in areas where these properties are less important (e.g., footwear, wire insulation and milk tubing). They have also found many applications in areas entirely away from conventional vulcanized rubber technology. These include such rapidly growing markets as adhesives, sealants, polymer modification and asphalt blending. The harder products, particularly those based on polyurethanes, polyethers and polyamides (see later) usually have much better resistance to oils and solvents and also to compression set. Thus they are used in such applications as brake hose and automobile grease boots for steering or drive train linkages.

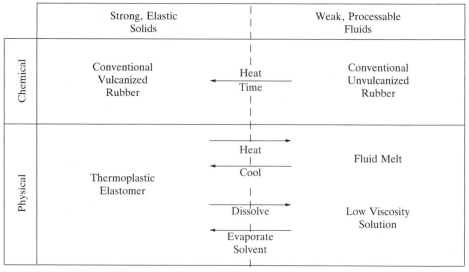

Figure 2   Chemical and Physical Changes

2   COMPOSITION

The applications of thermoplastic elastomers are numerous and varied. They are of course dependent on the properties of the individual types, which in turn are determined by their compositions.

Five classes of thermoplastic elastomers are commercially important. They are:

Polystyrene/elastomer block copolymers
Polyurethane/elastomer block copolymers
Polyether/elastomer block copolymers
Polyamide/elastomer block copolymers
Hard thermoplastic/elastomer blends

2.1   Phase structure

All these thermoplastic elastomers have one feature in common – they are phase separated systems in which one phase is hard and solid at room temperature while another phase is an elastomer. The hard phase gives these thermoplastic elastomers their strength. Without it, the elastomer phase would be free to flow under stress and the polymers would be unusable. When the hard phase is melted, or dissolved in a solvent, flow can take place and so the thermoplastic elastomers can be processed. On cooling, or evaporation of the solvent, the hard phase solidifies and the thermoplastic elastomers regain their strength. Thus, in a sense, the hard phase in a thermoplastic elastomer acts in a similar manner to the sulfur crosslinks in conventional vulcanized rubbers and the process by which it does so is often referred to as physical crosslinking.

2.2   Molecular Structure

Although the first four classes of thermoplastic elastomers listed above are all block copolymers, they have important structural differences. Most of the polystyrene/elastomer class have the general formula S-E-S, where S represents a polystyrene block and E an elastomer block. Others have a branched structure with the general formula $(S-E)_nx$, where x represents a multifunctional junction point. In contrast, the next three classes have the general formula H-E-H-E-H-E . . . or $(H-E)_n$, where H represents a hard thermoplastic block, either polyurethane, polyester or polyamide. In these three classes of block copolymers, the molecular weight distributions of both the individual blocks and the polymer as a whole are very broad. The last class, the hard thermoplastic/elastomer blends, are usually intimate mixtures of the two phases, although in some cases grafting of one polymer onto the other can take place.

2.3   Phase Properties

Since thermoplastic elastomers are phase separated systems, the physical properties of the polymers which constitute the separate phases also influence the properties of the thermoplastic elastomers. Thus, thermoplastic elastomers show many of the characteristics of the individual polymers which constitute the phases. For example, each phase has its own glass transition temperature (T_g), (or crystal melting point (T_m), if it is crystalline), and these in turn determine the temperatures at which the thermoplastic elastomer goes through transitions in its physical properties. Thus, when the modulus of a thermoplastic elastomer is

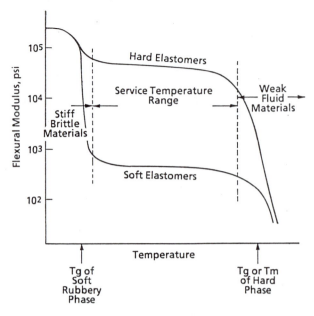

Figure 3   Stiffness of a Typical Thermoplastic Elastomer at Various Temperatures

measured over a range of temperatures, there are three distinct regions (see Figure 3). At very low temperatures, both phases are hard and so the material is stiff and brittle. At a somewhat higher temperature the elastomer phase becomes soft and the thermoplastic elastomer now resembles a conventional vulcanizate. As the temperature is further increased, the modulus stays relatively constant (a region often described as the "rubbery plateau") until finally the hard phase softens. At this point, the thermoplastic elastomer becomes fluid. Thus, thermoplastic elastomers have two service temperatures. The lower service temperature depends on the T_g of the elastomer phase while the upper service

TABLE I   Glass Transition and Crystal Melting Temperatures[a]

Thermoplastic Elastomer Type	Soft, Rubbery Phase Tg (°C)	Hard Phase Tg or Tm (°C)
Polystyrene/Elastomer Block Copolymers		
S–B–S	−90	95 (Tg)
S–I–S	−60	95 (Tg)
S–EB–S	−60	95 (Tg)
		165 (Tm)[b]
Polyurethane/Elastomer Block Copolymer	−40 (polyether) −60 (polyester)	190 (Tm)
Polyester/Elastomer Block Copolymers	−65 to −40	185−220
Polyamide/Elastomer Block Copolymers	−65 to −40	120−275 (Tm)
Hard Thermoplastic/Elastomer Blends[c]	−60	165 (Tm)

From reference 10 with permission
[a] Measured by Differential Scanning Colorimetry
[b] In compounds containing polypropylene
[c] Values quoted are for Polypropylene/EPDM blends

temperature depends on the T_g or T_m of the hard phase. Values of T_g and T_m for the various phases in some commercially important thermoplastic elastomers are given in Table I. (Since the hard phase in the thermoplastic elastomer begins to soften below its T_g or T_m, practical upper service temperatures are somewhat below the values given in Table I. They also depend on the stress applied. An unstressed part (e.g., one undergoing heat sterilization) will have a higher upper service temperature than one which must support a load. Similarly, practical lower service temperatures are somewhat above the T_g of the elastomer phase. The exact value depends on the extent of hardening which can be tolerated in the final product.

Other effects of the properties of the individual phases on the properties of the thermoplastic elastomers are as follow:

2.3.1 Hard Phase

The choice of polymer in the hard phase strongly influences the oil and solvent resistance of the thermoplastic elastomers. Even if the elastomer phase is resistant to a particular oil or solvent, if this oil or solvent swells the hard phase, all the useful physical properties of the thermoplastic elastomer will be lost. Thus, the polystyrene/elastomer block copolymers have little or no resistance to most organic solvents unless they are blended with solvent resistant polymers such as polypropylene or polyethylene. However, this feature also allows polystyrene/elastomer block copolymers to be applied from solution, an important feature in many of their applications as adhesives and coatings (see later). In the next three classes of thermoplastic elastomers, the crystalline hard phases (polyurethane, polyester and polyamide), together with the relatively polar elastomer phases, give the products good resistance to oils and solvents. Commercial materials in the last class (the hard phase/elastomer blends) usually have a crystalline polymer (typically polypropylene) as the hard phase. This also gives them some oil resistance.

2.3.2 Elastomer Phase

In the polystyrene/elastomer block copolymers, the elastomer phase controls both the stability and the stiffness of the products. Three elastomers are commonly used in the commercial versions of these materials – polybutadiene, polyisoprene and poly(ethylene-co-butylene). The corresponding block copolymers are denoted S-B-S, S-I-S and S-EB-S. Poly(ethylene-copropylene) or EP is also used in a few materials. It is very similar to poly(ethylene-cobutylene). The elastomer segments in S-B-S and S-I-S block copolymers are unsaturated and contain one double bond per original monomer unit. Typical S-B-S and S-I-S block copolymers have one thousand or more double bonds in each elastomer chain. These double bonds are an obvious source of instability and so limit the use of these polymers in applications where they are exposed to high temperatures, ultraviolet light or ozone. In contrast, S-EB-S block copolymers are saturated and thus much more stable. If degradation of these polymers takes place, S-B-S block copolymers crosslink and eventually become hard, insoluble and infusible. Under similar conditions, S-I-S block copolymers undergo chain scission and so become softer and weaker. As noted, S-EB-S block copolymers are much more resistant to degradation, but if it does occur, they also undergo chain scission. Another important point is the difference in stiffness between block copolymers based on these three elastomers. Because of differences in the molecular weights between entanglements in the elastomer phase (see Chapter 3),[5] S-I-S block copolymers are softer than corresponding S-B-S block copolymers and these in turn are softer than corresponding S-EB-S block copolymers. All three of these elastomers are readily swollen by hydrocarbon oils. If the oils used are low in aromatics, they are not compatible with the polystyrene segments and so the elastomer network remains effective. Oils of this type are used as compounding ingredients with S-I-S, S-B-S and S-EB-S block copolymers. Another important difference is in cost. S-B-S block copolymers are the least expensive. Prices of S-I-S equivalents are about 15 % higher and the S-EB-S block copolymers are about double the price of the similar S-B-S block polymers.

The next three types of thermoplastic elastomers, (polyurethane/elastomer block copolymers, polyester/elastomer block copolymers and polyamide/elastomer block copolymers) share several features and so can be considered together. All are linear alternating copolymers with a very broad distribution both of the size of the individual segments and also of the number of such segments in the polymer molecule. The segmental molecular weights are relatively low compared to those of the polystyrene/elastomer block copolymers. All can be made with polyether elastomer segments. In the polyurethane/elastomer block copolymers, polyesters (including poly-caprolactones) are also used. The polyamide/elastomer block copolymers can be made with polyester elastomer segments also. The polymers having polyester elastomer segments are tougher and more resistant to oils, solvents and thermal degradation whereas analogs with polyether elastomer segments have better hydrolytic stability and are more flexible at low temperatures. The polyurethane/elastomer block copolymers with polycaprolactone elastomer segments have better resistance to hydrolysis than those with the other polyester segments and are considered to be premium products. All three types have good electrical properties.[6]

In the last class (the hard phase/elastomer blends) the elastomer is usually an ethylene/polypropylene random copolymer (EPR) or a similar material with a small amount of out-of-chain unsaturation (EPDM). These elastomers are stable but are readily swollen by oils and solvents. The elastomers can be crosslinked during mixing (a process referred to as dynamic vulcanization). Hard phase/elastomer blends based on EPDM have been available for some time. Similar products based on nitrile rubbers and on ethylene – vinyl acetate have recently been announced and are claimed to have excellent oil resistance (see later).

2.3.3 Hard Phase/Soft Phase Ratio

Not surprisingly, thermoplastic elastomers with a high proportion of hard phase are themselves relatively hard and stiff. As the proportion of hard phase is further increased, the products lose their elastomeric character and instead become leathery. Finally, with still further increases in the proportion of hard phase, they become hard thermoplastics, usually with high impact resistance. Polystyrene/polybutadiene block copolymers with high styrene content have been commercialized under the trade name K-RESIN (Phillips Petroleum Co.).

3   COMMERCIAL END USES OF THERMOPLASTIC ELASTOMERS

Since their commercial introduction, many types (and grades within types) of thermoplastic elastomers have been produced to meet specific end use requirements. Two fairly recent books have discussed them in detail.[7,8] At least twenty manufacturers have entered the field. Trade names of some of the commercial products are listed in Tables II, III and IV.

TABLE II   Some Trade Names of Thermoplastic Elastomers Based on Polystyrene/Elastomer Block
Copolymers

Trade Name (Mfgr)	Type	Hard Segment	Soft Segment	Notes
KRATON® D and CARIFLEX TR (Shell)	S–B–S, S–I–S and (S–B)$_n$x	S	B or I	
SOLPRENE 400^a (Phillips)	(S–B)$_n$x			
FINAPRENE (Fina)	(S–B)$_n$x			
STEREON (Firestone)	S–B–S	S	B	General purpose, soluble
TUFPRENE & ASAPRENE (Asahi)	S–B–S			
EUROPRENE SOL T (ENICHEM)	S–B–S or S–I–S	S	B or I	
KRATON G (Shell)	S–EB–S	S	EB	Improved stabiltiy, soluble when uncompounded
ELEXAR® (Shell)	S–EB–S	S	EB	Wire and cable
C-FLEX (Concept)	S–EB–S and silicone oil	S	EB	Medical applications

^{a} No longer made in the U.S.A.

3.1 Polystyrene/Elastomer Block Copolymers

Like most conventional vulcanized rubbers – and unlike most thermoplastics – the polysty-
rene/elastomer block copolymers are never used commercially as pure materials. To achieve
the particular requirements for each end use, they are compounded with other polymers,
oils, resins, fillers, etc. In almost all cases, the final products contain less than 50 % of the
block copolymer. The applications can be divided into three classes.

3.1.1 Replacements for Vulcanized Rubber

These applications have been described in several recent articles.[9,10] In this end use the
products are manufactured by machinery originally developed to process conventional
thermoplastics. Examples are injection molding, blow molding and extrusion. S-I-S block
copolymers have not been used very much in this application but there are many applications for compounded products based on S-B-S and S-EB-S block copolymers. Products can
be produced with a very wide of hardness, as soft as 35 Shore A to as hard as 55 Shore D. A
list of some of the compounding ingredients and their effects on the properties of the
compounds is given in Table V. Quite large amounts of these compounding ingredients can
be added and the final products often contain only about 25 % of the S-B-S or S-EB-S block

TABLE III   Some Trade Names of Thermoplastic Elastomers Based on Polyurethane/Elastomer, Polyether/Elastomer and Polyamide/Elastomer Block Copolymers

Trade Name (Mfgr)	Type	Hard Segment	Soft Segment	Notes
ESTANE (B. F. Goodrich) ROYLAR[a] (Uniroyal) TEXIN (Mobay) PELLETHANE (Upjohn) RUCOTHANE (Hooker) PLASTOTHANE (Thiokol)	Multiblock	Polyurethane	Polyether, Polyester, or Polycapro-lactone[c]	Hard, abrasion and oil resistant high cost
HYTREL (DuPont) GAFLEX (GAF) LOMOD (GE)	Multiblock	Polyester	Polyether (Amorphous)	Similar to polyurethane, but can be harder. Better at low temp.
PEBAX (Atochem) OREVAC (Atochem)[d] MONTAC (Monsanto)[d]	Multiblock	Polyamide	Polyether	Similar to polyurethanes but can be softer. Very good at low temp.
ESTAMID[b] (Upjohn)	Multiblock	Polyamide	Polyester	

[a] Now sold to B. F. Goodrich
[b] Now sold to Dow
[c] Only Pellethane has polycaprolactone segments
[d] For hot melt adhesives

copolymers. From an economic point of view, this is most important. For example, it enables compounds based on S-EB-S block copolymers to compete with those based on polypropylene/EPDM blends, even though the S-EB-S alone is several times more expensive than the EPDM.

Polystyrene is often used as a compounding ingredient for S-B-S block copolymers. It acts as a processing aid and makes the products stiffer. Oils are also processing aids but make the products softer. Naphthenic oils are preferred and oils with high aromatic contents should be avoided, since they plasticize the polystyrene domains. Crystalline hydrocarbon polymers, such as polyethylene or ethylene-vinyl acetate copolymer, improve the solvent and ozone resistance. Polypropylene has similar effects and also improves the upper service temperature of the compounds. Large amounts of inert fillers such as powdered chalks, talcs and clays can also be added. They have only a small effect on physical properties but reduce cost. Reinforcing fillers such as high structure carbon blacks are not needed and in fact usually worsen the properties of the final product, producing stiff, "boardy" materials.

S-EB-S block copolymers can be compounded in a similar manner to their S-B-S analogs. One important difference is that for S-EB-S block copolymers, polypropylene is a preferred additive, acting in two different ways to improve the properties of the compounds. Firstly, it gives the compounds better processability. Secondly, when the compounds are processed under high shear and then quickly cooled, (as for example in injection molding or extrusion), the polypropylene and the S-EB-S/oil mixture form two continuous phases. Polypropylene is insoluble and has a relatively high crystal melting point (about 165 °C). This continuous polypropylene phase significantly improves both the upper service temperatures and also the solvent resistance of these compounds. In these S-EB-S based compounds, paraffinic oils are preferred, because they are more compatible with the EB center segments than the naphthenic oils used with similar S-B-S based compounds. Blends with silicone oils are used in some medical applications.[11] Once again, hydrocarbon oils with

TABLE IV   Some Trade Names of Thermoplastic Elastomers Based on Hard Thermoplastic/Elastomer Blends

Trade Name (Mfgr)	Type	Hard Segment	Soft Segment	Notes
TPR (Reichhold-Cook)[a]	Blend	Polypropylene or polyethylene	EPDM (crosslinked)	
SANTOPRENE (Monsanto)	Blend	Polypropylene	EPDM (crosslinked)	Low density, hard, not highly filled
REN-FLEX (Research Polymers, Inc.) POLYTROPE (Schulman) SOMEL (Colonial) TELCAR (Teknor-Apex) FERROFLEX (Ferro) ETA (Republic Plastics)	Blend	Polypropylene	EPDM	
ALCRYN (DuPont)	Blend[b]	Polyvinylidene Chloride	Crosslinked Polyvinyl Acetate Copolymer	Soft Oil Resistant
GEOLAST (Monsanto)	Blend	Polypropylene	Nitrile Rubber	Oil Resistant
ELASTAR (Nippon Zeon)	Blend	PVC	Nitrile Rubber	Oil Resistant
RIMPLAST (Petrach Systems)	Blend	Blend of other Thermoplastic Elastomers with Silicone Rubbers		Medical Applications

[a] Now sold to BP Performance Polymers
[b] Also contains 10% carbon black

TABLE V   Compounding Styrenic Block Polymers

Component	Hardness	Processability	Effect on Ozone Resistance	Cost	Other
Oils	Decreases	Increases	None	Decreases	Decreases U.V. resistance
Polystyrene	Increases	Increases	Some Increase	Decreases	—
Polyethylene	Increases	Variable	Increases	Decreases	Often gives satin finish
Polypropylene	Increases	Variable	Increases	Decreases	Improves high temperature properties
EVA	Small Increase	Variable	Increases	Decreases	—
Fillers	Some Increase	Variable	None	Decreases	Often Improves surface appearance

high aromatic contents should be avoided. The same inert fillers used in the S-B-S based compounds can also be used with the S-EB-S analogs.

Compounds based on both S-B-S and S-EB-S thermoplastic elastomers require some protection against oxidative degradation and in some cases, against sunlight also, depending on their end use. Hindered phenols are effective antioxidants and are often used in combination with thiodipropionate synergists. Benzotriazoles are effective UV stabilizers and they are often used in combination with hindered amines. If the product does not have to be clear, titanium dioxide or carbon black pigments give very effective protection against sunlight.

Compounding techniques are relatively simple and standard. There is one important generalization – the processing equipment should be heated to a temperature at least 20 °C above the upper service temperature of the block copolymer (see Table I) or the melting point of the polymeric additive, whichever is greater. The use of cold mills, etc. can result in polymer breakdown, which is not only unnecessary but also detrimental to the properties of the final product.

Unfilled or lightly filled compounds can be made on a single screw extruder fitted with a mixing screw. The length/diamter ratio should be at least 24:1. A twin screw extruder can also be used to mix compounds of this type. If large amounts of fillers are to be added, these are best dispersed on a closed intensive mixer. This discharges into an extruder, which in turn feeds a pelletizer. This can be either a strand cutting or an underwater face cutting system. If the first type is used, it is important to remember that rubbery compounds must be cut rather than shattered. Thus, the blades of the cutter should be sharp and the clearance between the fixed and the rotating blades should be minimized. With this type of pelletizer, the strands must be thoroughly cooled before they enter the cutter. A chilled water bath can be used to give high production rates.

Trial batches or small scale production runs can be made using a batch type closed intensive mixer. Mixing times of about five minutes are usually adequate. After this mixing, the hot product is passed to a heated two roll mill. When it has banded, it is cut off, allowed to cool and finally granulated. In this case also, the granulator blades must be sharp and clearances minimized.

S-B-S and S-EB-S block copolymers with high molecular weight polystyrene segments and/ or high styrene contents are very difficult to process as pure materials. Oiled versions with oil contents of from about 25 % to about 50 % are commercially available. These process much more easily and of course more oil can be added during mixing.

Many end users prefer to buy pre-compounded products and numerous grades have been developed for the various specialized end uses. Representative examples and some details of their properties are given in Table VI. The end uses covered include milk tubing, shoe soles, sound deadening materials, wire insulation and flexible automotive parts. After priming, the latter can be coated with paints which are also flexible. The products then match the appearance of painted sheet metal but do not dent on impact.

The physical properties of compounded thermoplastic elastomers based on both S-B-S and S-EB-S block copolymers are sensitive both to processing conditions and to processing equipment. Thus, it is most important to make test samples under conditions and on equipment similar to those which will be used in production. Misleading results will be obtained if, for example, prototype parts or test pieces are compression molded when the actual products will be made by extrusion or injection molding.

Conditions for processing these compounds by injection molding, blow molding, extrusion, etc. have been discussed in some detail in a recent publication.[12] As a generalization,

TABLE VI Properties of Compounded Styrenic Block Copolymers

Product	KRATON® D2109	KRATON D2705	KRATON D3202	KRATON D5119	KRATON D5152	KRATON D5239	KRATON G7150	KRATON G7720	KRATON G7880	ELEXAR® 8313	ELEXAR 8451	ELEXAR 8614
Application	Milk Tubing	Medical	General	Footwear Direct Moulded	Footwear Unitsole	Footwear Crepe Look	Sound Deadening	Automotive Soft Parts	Automotive Bumper Cover	Automotive Primary Wire	Wire & Cable Flexible Cord	Wire & Cable Fire Retardant Control Cable
Properties												
Hardness Shore A or D	44A	55A	65A	47A	47A	36A	36D	60A	42D	54D	80A	95A
Tensile Strength MPa (psi)	6.5 (950)	7.6 (1100)	5.9 (850)	4 (580)	3.9 (560)	4.8 (700)	4.8 (700)	6.2 (900)	14.5 (2100)	24 (3500)	14 (2000)	14 (2000)
100% Modulus MPa (psi)	1.7 (240)	1.7 (240)	3.3 (480)	2.5 (360)	1.9 (275)	1.0 (140)	3.5 (500)	2.1 (300)	9 (1300)	13 (1900)	4.1 (600)	9.7 (1400)
Elongation, %	800	700	500	380	550	820	250	600	450	550	500	500
Melt Flow, gm/10 min Condition E or G	15(G)	—	14(E)	27(E)	26(E)	20(E)	—	—	—	—	22(G)	3(G)
Specific Gravity	0.94	0.9	1.0	1.09	1.0	0.98	1.94	1.20	1.05	1.28	1.0	1.2

compounds based on S-B-S block copolymers are processed under conditions suitable for polystyrene while those based on S-EB-S block copolymers are processed under conditions suitable for polypropylene. These compounds usually have relatively high surface friction. Ejection of the molded parts can be difficult, espicially with softer products. Use of a release agent or a Teflon coating on the mold makes for easier ejection and if possible the mold should be designed so that the ejection can be air assisted. Tapering the sides of the mold is also helpful, as is the use of stripper rings. The use of small diameter ejection pins should be avoided, since they tend to deform the molded part rather than eject it.

Ground scrap from molding is reusable and is usually blended with virgin product. Grinding is relatively easy if the conditions required for successful pelletization are met, i.e., if the grinder blades are kept sharp and the clearances minimized.

3.1.2 Adhesives, Sealants and Coatings

This is one of the most important applications for polystyrene/elastomer block copolymers and probably the fastest growing. Again, the products are always compounded and the subject has been extensively covered.[13, 14] The effects of the various compounding ingredients depend on what region of the phase structure they associate with. There are four possibilities. The added ingredients can either go into the polystyrene phase, into the elastomer phase, into both phases or into neither phase. Those in the first group are usually styrenic resins with high softening points. They increase the upper service temperature of the product (or at least, do not lower it). Since they increase the volume fraction of the polystyrene phase, they make the product harder. Similar materials with low softening points, and aromatic oils, are not used because they plasticize the polystyrene phase. Conversely, if the added ingredients go into the elastomer phase, they make the product softer. Since there are three different elastomers used in these block copolymers, each has particular resins and/or oils with which it is most compatible. Details of the various resins and oils suitable for each of the elastomers are given in Table VII. Ingredients which go into both phases are usually avoided, since they make the phases more compatible with each other, which weakens the product. Polymers which go into neither phase (e.g., polypropylene) are used in some hot melt applications (see later), where they stiffen the products and improve upper service temperatures. Fillers can also be added to reduce cost.

TABLE VII   Resins Used to Formulate Adhesives, Sealants, etc. from Styrenic Block Copolymers

Resin Type	Segment Compatibility[a]
Polymerized C$_5$ Resins (Synthetic Polyterpenes)	I
Hydrogenated Resin Esters	B
Saturated Hydrocarbon Resins	EB
Naphthenic Oils	I, B
Paraffinic Oils	EB
Low Molecular Weight Polybutenes	EB
Aromatic Resins	S

From reference 5 with permission
[a] I – Compatible with polyisoprene segments
  B – Compatible with polybutadiene segments
  BB – Compatible with poly(ethylene-butylene) segments
  S – Compatible with polystyrene segments

The products can be applied either as solutions or as hot melts. Since the molecular weights of these block copolymers are relatively low (typically less than 100,000), the solutions can be made at high solids content. Some details of the behavior in various solvents are given in a recent publication.[15] Hot melt application is preferred in many cases since it avoids many of the problems associated with solvents, such as flammability, toxicity and air pollution. In this case, the molten resins and/or oils can be regarded as taking the place of the solvents. Application rates of hot melt products are usually faster than those of solvent based analogues because the time for a product to cool is much less than the time for a solvent to evaporate. Some details of the various end uses are as follows:

Pressure Sensitive Adhesives   This is probably the largest single end use for polystyrene/elastomer block copolymers. The products, are usually applied as hot melts although solvent application is possible and takes advantage of the low solution viscosity of these polymers. The end uses include various kinds of tapes and labels, as well as adhesive fasteners such as diaper tabs. The mechanism by which the resins and the thermoplastic elastomer combine to give tacky products has been described.[16, 17] According to this theory, the resins have two functions. Firstly, they mix with the elastomer phase in the thermoplastic elastomer and so soften the product. This softening allows the adhesive to conform to the substrate. This is considered as the "bonding" stage of adhesion and is relatively slow. Next is the removal of the adhesive from the substrate, the "disbonding" stage of adhesion. This is much faster. Here the function of the resins is to adjust the glass transition temperature of the elastomer phase so that the adhesive stiffens up during this fast stage and so resists removal from the substrate.

Since a soft product is necessary to from the adhesive bond, softer block copolymers are preferred as the materials from which to formulate pressure sensitive adhesives. These soft block copolymers usually have low polystyrene contents and a relatively high content of diblock (i.e., S-I, S-B or S-EB). This diblock content is non-load-bearing. It, and the resins in the elastomer phase, weaken the adhesive. However, this weakening can be tolerated so long as it is not carried to the point where it causes cohesive failure of the adhesive during service.

Products have recently been developed that can be crosslinked after being applied to the tape.[18] This process gives the adhesive improved solvent resistance, which is important for applications such as masking tapes.

Assembly Adhesives   S-B-S and S-EB-S block copolymers are preferred for this application and again hot melt application is more usual than application from solution. Tack is not important (it may even be undesirable) and so harder products are satisfactory. These adhesives are usually formulated to contain both resins that are compatible with the polystyrene phase and also resins (and possibly oils) that are compatible with the elastomer phase. The relative proportions of the two types of resin determines the hardness of the adhesive, while the total amount of resin added determines the viscosity of the final product.

Sealants   This application is dominated by S-EB-S block copolymers. Both hot melt and solvent based applications are important. Hot melt sealants are applied in a variety of manufacturing processes, frequently by robotics. They can also be processed as foamed products. Often they are used as formed-in-place gaskets. Another application is their use as cable filling compounds. These fill the voids in "bundled" telephone cables and prevent water seepage.[19] In contrast, the solvent based products are limited to the building industry where they are applied on site, both during the initial construction and also during subsequent maintenance and repair. Diblock polymers are often part of both hot melt and solvent based sealants, since they reduce the viscosities of the hot melt products or allow the solvent based products to be formulated at higher solids content. The diblock polymers also reduce the strength of the sealant to the point where it fails cohesively during peel, which is a requirement in many sealant specifications. Again, both types of resins are normally used and oils are frequently a part of the composition. Unless clarity is a requirement, quite large amounts of fillers such as calcium carbonates can also be added. Suggested starting formulations for both hot melt[20] and solvent based sealants[20, 21] have been published.

Coatings   Chemical milling of metals is the most important application for coatings based on the polystyrene/elastomer block copolymers. In this process, a protective film is first applied to the whole surface of the metal sheet and then selectively peeled away from areas from which metal is to be removed. The sheet is then immersed in an etchant bath, which dissolves away the unprotected areas. The two most common metals processed in this way are aluminum and titanium. Aluminum is etched under alkaline conditions and can be protected by coatings based on S-B-S block copolymers. Titanium, however, is etched by strongly oxidizing acids and so coatings based on S-EB-S block copolymers must be used. Both types of protective coatings are probably formulated with the usual resins, fillers, etc. but details of the compositions have not been published.

Asphalt Blends   This application is slightly different from those discussed previously in that the polystyrene/elastomer block copolymers are used to modify the properties of asphalts and bitumes. In the other applications the opposite is true, i.e., the additives (resins, oils, etc.) modify the block copolymers. The block copolymer content of these blends is usually less than 20 % and even as little as 2 % can make significantly change the properties of asphalts. The polystyrene/elastomer block copolymers make the blends more flexible (especially at low temperatures) and increase their softening point. They decrease the penetration and reduce the tendency to flow at high service temperatures, such as those encountered in roofing and paving applications. They also increase the stiffness, tensile strength, ductility and elastic recovery of the final products. Melt viscosities remain relatively low and so the blends are still easy to apply. As the polymer concentration is increased to about 5 %, an interconnected polymer network is formed. At this point the nature of the blend changes from an asphalt modified by a polymer to a polymer extended with an asphalt. It is important to choose the correct grade of asphalt; those with low asphaltenes content and/or high aromaticity in the maltene fraction usually give the best results.[22] Applications include road surface dressings such as chip seals (these are applied to hold the aggregate in place when a road is resurfaced), slurry seals, asphalt concrete (this is a mixture of asphalt and aggregate used in road surfaces), road crack sealants, roofing and other waterproofing applications.[23-25] Because of their lower cost, S-B-S block copolymers are usually chosen for this application, but in roofing and paving applications the S-EB-S block copolymers are also used because of their better UV oxidative and thermal stability.

3.1.3 Polymer Blends

The polystyrene/elastomer block copolymers are technologically compatible with a surprisingly wide range of other polymers, that is the blends show improved properties when compared to the original polymers. Impact strength usually is the most obvious improvement, but others include tear strength, stress crack resistance, low temperature flexibility and elongation. Both thermoplastic and thermoset polymers can be modified in this way.

Thermoplastics   Thermoplastics elastomers have several advantages in this application. The other elastomers that can be blended with thermoplastics to improve their impact resistance (e.g., SBR, EPDM and EPR) can normally be used only in the unvulcanized state – the vulcanized products usually cannot be dispersed (an exception is the process of vulcanization *during* dispersion – see Chapter 7). Since these unvulcanized elastomers are soft and weak, they reduce the strength of the blends and so only limited amounts can be added. However, thermoplastic elastomers are much stronger, even though they are unvulcanized, and so there is no such limitation on the amounts that can be added. Blending is usually be carried out in the processing equipment (injection molders, extruders, etc.), especially if a thermoplastic elastomer with low viscosity is used. The thermoplastic elastomers form a separate phase and so do not change the T_g or T_m of the thermoplastic into which they are blended. Thus, these blends maintain the upper service temperature of the original thermoplastic. Three large volume thermoplastics – polystyrene, polypropylene and polyethylene (both high and low density) – can be modified using polystyrene/elastomer block copolymers.[26, 27] Again, because of the price considerations, S-B-S block copolymers are most commonly used with these thermoplastics. In polystyrene there are two important applications – upgrading high impact polystyrene to a super high impact product and restoring the impact resistance which is lost when flame retardants are mixed into high impact polystyrene. Polypropylene has very poor impact resistance at low temperatures. This also can be improved by adding styrene/elastomer block copolymers. Blends with polyethylene are mostly used to make blown film, where they have improved impact resistance and tear strength, especially in the seal area. Polystyrene/elastomer block copolymers are also blended with engineering thermoplastics such as poly(butylene terephthalate), poly(phenylene oxide) and polycarbonate. S-EB-S block copolymers are often used in these blends because of their better stability.

A slightly different application is the use of polystyrene/elastomer block copolymers to make useful blends from otherwise incompatible thermoplastics. Polystyrene, for example, is completely incompatible with polyethylene or polypropylene and blends of this type form a two phase system with virtually no adhesion between the phases. Thus when articles made from them are stressed, cracks easily develop along the phase boundaries and the products fail at low elongations. Addition of a low molecular weight S-EB-S block copolymer changes this behavior and converts the blends to more ductile materials.[28, 29] Similar results were obtained on blends of polyethylene and poly(ethyleneterephthalate).[30] In another example, a higher molecular weight S-EB-S was used in a blend with a polycarbonate and a polypropylene. Compared to the pure polycarbonate, the blend had almost as good an upper service temperature combined with improved solvent resistance, lower cost and lower density.[31]

Thermosets   Sheet molding compounds (SMC) are thermoset compositions containing unsaturated polyesters, styrene monomer, chopped fiber glass and fillers. They are cured to give rigid parts that are often used in automobile exteriors. Special types of polystyrene/elastomer block copolymers have been developed as modifiers for these compositions and give the final products improved surface appearance and better impact resistance.[32–34]

In an entirely different application, thermoplastic elastomers are blended with silicone rubbers containing either vinyl or silicone hydride functional groups. The silicone rubbers containing the vinyl groups are pelletized separately from those containing the silicone hydride groups. When melted and mixed together in the processing equipment, the two groups react under the influence of a platinum catalyst to form an interpenetrating network of the silicone rubber and the thermoplastic elastomer. The products are useful in medical applications. This end use was originally developed using polyurethane/elastomer block copolymers and other thermoplastics. It has now been extended to other thermoplastic elastomers including S-EB-S and polyester/elastomer block copolymers.[35, 36]

3.2 Polyurethane/Elastomer Block Copolymers

These block copolymers were developed before the polystyrene/elastomer block copolymers. Their properties are complementary in that the polyurethane/elastomer block copolymers are generally harder, tougher, more expensive and more resistant to oils and solvents.
A full discussion of their manufacture, structure and properties is given in Chapter 2 and in
some recent publications.[6, 37] Their structure is an alternating series of hard and elastomeric
segments. The hard segments are polyureas or polyurethanes and are usually crystalline.
The amorphous elastomeric segments are either polyethers or polyesters (usually adipates,
but polycaprolactones can also be used). The polymers with adipate polyester elastomer
segments are tougher and have better resistance to abrasion, swelling by oils and oxidative
degradation. Corresponding polymers with polyether elastomer segments have much better
hydrolytic stability (this is probably the main weakness of the polyester based materials) and
are more resistant to fungus growth. They are also more flexible at low temperatures and
more resilient. Thus they give less heat increase under repeated cyclic stress. Those with
polycaprolactone elastomer segments are premium grades with a combination of superior oil
and solvent resistance and quite good hydrolytic stability. Properties of some typical grades
are given in Table VIII.

TABLE VIII   Properties of Polyurethane/Elastomer Block Copolymers

Product	ESTANE 58113	ESTANE 58013	ESTANE 58880	TEXIN 480A	PELLE-THANE 2102–90A	PELLE-THANE 2103–70A
Type	Polyester	Polyether	Polyether	Polyester	Polycapro-lactone	Polyether
Hardness, Shore A or D	55D	86D	80A	86A	90A	70A
Tensile Strength, MPa (psi)	35 (5000)	30 (4300)	24 (3500)	31 (4500)	48 (7000)	24 (3500)
100% Modulus, MPa (psi)	13 (1900)	4.5 (650)	4.5 (650)	4.8 (700)	10.7 (1500)	3.5 (500)
Elongation, %	500	630	600	600	500	700
Specific Gravity	1.22	1.18	1.10	1.20	1.20	1.06

3.2.1 Replacements for Vulcanized Rubber

This is the most important end use of the polyurethane/elastomer block copolymers. In this
application the materials are fabricated into the final article by the typical processing
techniques developed for conventional thermoplastics, i.e., injection molding, blow molding, extrusion, etc. They are usually not compounded, although calcium carbonates and
radiopaque fillers can be added.[38]

It is most important that polyurethane/elastomer block copolymers are dried before processing. If they are not, water will be released when the hot, molten polymer is being processed
and the final article will contain bubbles and will possibly be degraded. Drying times of from
one to two hours at temperatures of about 100 °C are recommended and reground polymer
or color concentrates should be dried also. During processing, hot, dry air should be

circulated through the hopper in which the dry polymer is held, to prevent water being reabsorbed. After processing has been completed, the finished parts may be annealed by heating overnight at about 115 °C. This improves their physical properties.

In both molding and extrusion, the melt temperature should be about 200 °C. For injection molding applications, mold release can be a problem, as it is with most soft thermoplastic elastomers. The possible solutions are covered in the similar section dealing with the applications of the polystyrene/elastomer block copolymers (see above). Recommended conditions for extrusion include the use of relatively high compression screws (about 3:1 compression ratio) with length to diameter ratios of at least 24:1. Profile, blown film and sheet extrusion can all be used with these polymers. They can also be laminated to fabric backings.

The final articles can be metallized or painted. Special elastomeric paints have been developed which match the appearance of painted automotive sheet metal. Parts painted in this way are used in car bodies. Most other applications take advantage of the abrasion resistance and toughness of these polymers. They include rolls, gears, footwear (including ski boots), wheels, timing and drive belts, tire chains and industrial hose. The polymers with polyether elastomer segments have significant medical applications, including their use in body implants.[39]

3.2.2 Adhesives, Sealants, and Coatings

This is a relatively small application for these polymers. They are usually applied as hot melts, although some grades can be applied from solutions in such polar solvents as methyl ethyl ketone or dimethyl formamide. They have some uses in footwear, including attaching the shoe soles to the uppers, and also in coextrusion, where they act as adhesive interlayers between dissimilar polymers.

3.2.3 Polymer Blends

Polyurethane/elastomer block copolymers have been blended with a wide range of other thermoplastics and elastomers.[40] Non-polar polymers such as polyolefins were about the only class of materials tested which showed little or no compatibility. Probably the most important blending material is plasticized PVC, although other elastomers (including S-B-S and S-I-S thermoplastic elastomers) or polar thermoplastics such as polycarbonates can also be used. In the PVC blends, the polyurethane/elastomer block copolymers improve the flex life and abrasion resistance of footwear products.

Like S-EB-S block copolymers, polyurethane/elastomer block copolymers can be blended with reactive silicone rubbers to give products intended for medical applications.[35,36] In fact, they are probably the most important thermoplastic elastomer in this end use.

3.3   Polyester/Elastomer Block Copolymers

These polymers were developed later than the polyurethane/elastomer block copolymers but share many of their characteristics. Structurally, they are alternating block copolymers in which the blend segments are crystalline polyesters and the soft segments are amorphous polyethers or polyesters. Their properties and structure are described in Chapter 8 and also in some recent articles.[11,41,42] The harder versions are somewhat harder than the corresponding polyurethane/elastomer block copolymers. However, the softer versions are not as soft. Like the polyurethane/elastomer block copolymers, they are tough, oil resistant materials with high tear strength. They have excellent resistance to compression set and flex cracking. At low strain levels, they show very little hysteresis, that is, they behave almost like a perfect spring. Compared to polyurethane/elastomer block copolymers of the same hardness, they have higher modulus (i.e., they are stiffer), better resistance to creep and show less variation of modulus with temperature. This is claimed to give them a wider service temperature range. Some work has been reported on the use of plasticizers in these materials.[43] Those tested were suitable for use with PVC and were most compatible with the softer grades of the polyester/elastomer block copolymers. At least 50 parts of some of these plasticizers could be added to 100 parts of the polyester/elastomer block copolymer. The products were softer and more processible. Flame retardants can also be mixed with these polyester/elastomer block copolymers and some flame retardant grades are commercially available. The properties of some representative grades of polyester/elastomer block copolymers are given in Table IX.

TABLE IX   Properties of Polyester/Elastomer Block Copolymers

Product	HYTREL 40xy[a]	HYTREL 55xy[a]	HYTREL 63xy[a]	HYTREL 72xy[a]	GAFLEX 547	LOMOD B0100
Hardness Shore A or D	40D 92A	55D	63D	72D	47D	35D
Tensile Strength						
MPa	26	38	39	39	32	17
(psi)	(3700)	(5500)	(5700)	(5700)	(4500)	(2500)
25 % Modulus						
MPa	7.5	14	17[b]	26[b]	11	—
(psi)	(1100)	(2000)	(2500)[b]	(3800)[b]	(1500)	—
Elongation, %	450	450	350	350	750	685
Specific Gravity	1.17	1.20	1.22	1.25	1.18	1.16

[a] xy denotes a two digit identifier for the individual grades
[b] Yield point

3.3.1 Replacements for Vulcanized Rubber

This is the most important application for these thermoplastic elastomers also. They are particularly useful as replacements for oil resistant rubbers such as neoprene because they have better physical properties (e.g., tear and tensile strengths) at temperatures up to about 150 °C. They can be processed by the techniques originally developed for thermoplastics – e.g., injection molding, blow molding and extrusion. They can also be processed as blown films.[44] Processing is generally easier than with the polyurethane/elastomer block copolymers because thermal degradation is less of a problem and this gives the polyester/elastomer block copolymers a wider processing window. One important point is that the recommended processing temperature of the polyester/elastomer block copolymers varies with the hardness of the material.[41] Grades suitable for all these processing techniques have been developed. Applications include flexible couplings, seal rings, automotive steering boots, hydraulic hose, ski boots and outer coverings for wire and for optical fiber cables.

3.3.2 Polymer Blends

Polyester/elastomer block copolymers can be blended with PVC, (both plasticized and unplasticized) and with chlorinated PVC (CPVC) also.[45] Compared to the plasticized PVC alone, the blends have better flexibility, (particularly at low temperatures) and improved abrasion resistance. In unplasticized PVC and CPVC, the polyester/elastomer block copolymers act as polymeric plasticizers. They can also be blended with thermoplastic polyesters such as poly(butylene terephthalate) to give relatively hard, impact resistant products.

3.4   Polyamide/Elastomer Block Copolymers

These are one of the newer developments in thermoplastic elastomers and are covered in some detail in Chapter 9. Like the previous two classes, they are block copolymers with alternating hard and soft segments. The hard crystalline segments are polyamides while the soft segments are either polyethers or polyester. One notable feature is that there are many different polyamides from which to make a choice. These include nylon-6, nylon-6,6, nylon-11 and nylon-12 and also polyamides containing aromatic groups. These all have different melting points and degrees of crystallinity and so quite a wide range of property variations are available.[46] When these are combined with the various polyethers and polyesters, the range of property variations becomes even wider. Quite soft materials can be produced (as low as 65 Shore A hardness), as can harder counterparts (up to 70 Shore D). Those with polyester soft segments have excellent resistance to thermal and oxidative degradation while those with polyether soft segments are more resistant to hydrolysis and more flexible at lower temperatures. Moisture uptake is normally quite low, but hydrophillic products which can absorb up to 120 % of their weight of water have been produced.[46] As far as resistance to deformation is concerned, the upper service temperature depends on the choice of polyamide segment and can be as high as 200 °C. Resistance to oils and solvents is also good. The properties of some representative grades are given in Table X.

TABLE X   Typical Properties of Polyamide/Elastomer Block Copolymers

Product	PEBAX 2533	PEBAX 4033	PEBAX 6333	ESTAMID 90A
Hardness Shore A or D	25D 75A	40D —	63D —	— 93A
Tensile Strength MPa (psi)	29 (4200)	33 (4800)	49 (7100)	27 (3900)
100 % Modulus MPa (psi)	4.3 (630)	10 (1450)	19 (2700)	14 (2000)
Elongation, %	350	620	680	320
Specific Gravity	1.01	1.01	1.01	1.14

3.4.1 Replacements for Vulcanized Rubber

This is by far the most significant use of these polymers at the present time. They are processable on conventional plastics equipment (injection molders, extruders, etc.) and also can be melt spun to give textile fibers. They are suitable for overmolding metallic and thermoplastic inserts and can be compounded with fillers, fiberglass, etc. The recommended processing temperatures are about 60 °C above the melting points of the polyamide segments and processing techniques are similar to those used with other polyamides, such as nylon-6. The polymers should be dried before processing and kept dry while in the hopper of the processing equipment. The main applications are in footwear, particularly sports shoes and ski boots. Others include blow molded bellows and automotive steering boots, belting, cable covers and hose.

3.4.2 Adhesives, Sealants and Coatings

Grades intended for use in hot melt adhesives are in the developmental stage.

3.4.3 Polymer Blends

The polyamide/elastomer block copolymers can be blended with a number of other polymer, including polypropylene, nylon and plasticized PVC. However, so far these blends have not been commercialized.

3.5 Hard Thermoplastic/Elastomer Blends

A very large number of these blends have been investigated[47] and are described in more detail in Chapters 6 and 7. They are produced by intensively mixing the elastomer and the hard thermoplastic together. In some cases, crosslinking agents are added so that the elastomer phase is vulcanized under intensive shear to give a fine dispersion of the crosslinked elastomer in the hard thermopolastic. This process is known as "dynamic vulcanization"[48] and gives the products better resistance to deformation at high temperatures. Blends of polypropylene (and in a few cases, polyethylene) with EPDM and EPR are by far the largest commercial application for these products. They have been available for about ten years and at least eleven manufacturers produce them in the United States (see Table IV). They are believed to have the second largest share of the market for thermoplastic elastomers, after the polystyrene/elastomer block copolymers[38] and have numerous applications, particularly in the automobile industry and in wire insulation. When suitably pigmented and stabilized, they have good resistance to oxidative and hydrolytic degradation and to weathering. Detailed compositions have not been described, but judging from values given for their densities,[49] most products are not highly filled although some grades intended for sound deadening applications are claimed to contain up to 65 % by weight of filler.[38] Hydrocarbon oils can be used in as compounding ingredients, but the amount which can be added is limited by the fact that the rubber phase is already relatively weak (especially when compared to block copolymers such as S-EB-S) and so significant loss of strength cannot be tolerated. Much effort has been devoted to developing specialized grades for the various applications,[50] including flame retardant products. The products can vary quite widely in hardness, from 60 Shore A up to 55 Shore D. Details of the properties of some of these thermoplastics rubbers are given in Table XI.

Three new hard thermoplastic/elastomer blends have recently been described. One is stated to be a fine dispersion of crosslinked nitrile rubber in polypropylene,[51] prepared by "dynamic vulcanization" (see above). It is expected to be the first of a series of products using this technology. Compared to similar polypropylene/EPDM blends, it has much better oil resistance and is available with hardness down to 80 Shore A. The second new product has been described as a blend of poly(vinylidene chloride) hard thermoplastic with a crosslinked elastomer which may be a copolymer of ethylene and vinyl acetate. The product is also said to contain about 10 % carbon black.[3] Quite soft grades are available (as low as 60 Shore A) and the oil resistance is stated to be good.[52] The third is claimed to be blend of PVC hard thermoplastic with an ionically crosslinked nitrile-butadiene rubber.[53] Several grades are available. Like the previous two materials, it is claimed to have improved oil resistance and all three are expected to compete with Neoprene.[53]

TABLE XI Properties of Hard Thermoplastic/Elastomer Blends

Product	RENFLEX 826	REPUBLIC 3041	REPUBLIC AB 6053[a]	FERRO FF 100	SANTOPRENE 101–73 201–73	SANTOPRENE 101–40 203–40	GEOLAST 701–80	GEOLAST 701–87	ALCRYN R–1101B 70A
Hardness Shore A or D	50D	40D	40D	68A	73A	50D	80A	87A	70A
Tensile Strength, MPa (psi)	11.7 (1700)	16.5 (2400)	8.4 (1200)	4.2 (600)	8.4 (1200)	19 (2750)	11 (1600)	14.2 (2050)	13.2 (1900)
100 % Modulus, MPa (psi)	10.5 (1500)	9.5 (1400)	— —	3.0 (450)	3.2 (470)	10 (1250)	5.4 (785)	6.9 (1000)	5.1 (740)
Elongation, %	450	500	75	1500	375	600	310	380	280
Specific Gravity	0.91	0.94	1.89	0.90	0.98	0.95	1.09	1.07	1.21

[a] Grade intended for sound deadening application

3.5.1 Replacements for Vulcanized Rubber

This is by far the most significant end use for these materials. Automotive parts, wire insulation and weatherstripping are the major applications for the polypropylene/EPDM blends and the product are generally pre-compounded by the manufacturer to meet the requirements of the end user. Processing conditions are similar to those used for polypropylene and since the products are relatively stable, degradation during processing is rarely a problem. Scrap can easily be reground and reworked (see the suggestions for grinding soft products previously given in the section on polystyrene/elastomer block copolymers) and unless the products are highly filled, predrying is usually not necessary. If the products are to be painted, an undercoat is normally needed, although some directly paintable grades have been introduced.[50] Ejection of injection molded parts can be a problem, particularly with the softer grades (again, see the suggestions given in the section on polystyrene/elastomer block copolymers).

The three newer materials will probably have their first applications in areas which will take advantage of their excellent oil resistance, such as wire insulation (particularly under the hood) and hose.

3.5.2 Polymer Blends

This is not a large application for these elastomers although grades have been developed for use as impact modifiers in blends with polypropylene and polyethylene.[49] Their use to upgrade scrap polypropylene has also been suggested.[11] They are not compatible with more polar polymers such as polystyrene.

4   ECONOMICS AND SUMMARY

The economic aspect of thermoplastic elastomers is not simply a function of their price. If it was, they would have achieved little commercial success, since their raw material cost is significantly above that of conventional vulcanized rubbers. Equally (and perhaps more)

TABLE XII   Price and Property Ranges for Thermoplastic Elastomers[a]

	Approximate Price, Range (¢/lb)	Specific Gravity	Hardness Range[a]
Polystyrene/Elastomer Block Copolymers			
S−B−S (Pure)	90− 95	0.94	60A−90A
S−I−S (Pure)	100−110	0.92	30A−40A
S−EB−S (Pure)	172−215	0.91	65A−75A
S−B−S (Compounds)	65−110	0.93−1.1	35A−45D
S−EB−S (Compounds)	95−175	0.9−1.2	
Polyurethane/Elastomer Block Copolymers	200−250	1.05−1.25	70A−70D
Polyester/Elastomer Block Copolymers	235−325	1.15−1.45	35D−75D
Polyamide/Elastomer Block Copolymers	240−450	1.0−1.15	75A−65D
Polypropylene/EPDM Blends	75−150	0.90−1.1	60A−75D

From reference 5 with permission

[a] These price and property ranges do not include fire retardant grades or highly filled materials for sound deadening

important are the cost savings they bring because of fast processing, scrap recycle, etc. Another significant factor is the new processing techniques which they have introduced to the rubber industry. These include blow molding, hot melt coating of pressure sensitive adhesives and direct injection molding of footwear. Thus rather than a simple cost comparison based on raw material prices, the "value in use" of thermoplastic elastomers should be considered when they are being evaluated as possible replacements for more conventional materials. Bearing this caveat in mind, the price ranges of the various types of thermoplastic elastomers are summarized in Table XII. This table also includes data on the specific gravity and hardness of the products. The former is particularly important when used in conjunction with the price, since the multiple of the two gives the relative price per unit of volume, and this (rather than the price per unit of mass) is the quantitiy which determines the cost of the end product.

References

1. J. T. Bailey, E. T. Bishop, W. R. Hendricks, G. Holden and N. R. Legge, paper "Thermoplastic Elastomers" presented at the ACS Rubber Division Meeting, Philadelphia, PA, October 1965. *Rubber Age, 98* (10), 69 (1966)
2. J. F. Auchter, *Rubber World 185*(5), 21 (1982)
3. G. E. O'Connor, paper presented at ACS Rubber Division Meeting, Cleveland, OH, October, 1985
4. N. R. Legge, paper presented at the ACS Rubber Division Meeting, Los Angeles, CA, April 1985. *Elastomers 177*(10), 19 (1985)
5. G. Holden, Article "Elastomers, Thermoplastic" in *Encyclopedia of Polymer Science and Engineering,* 2nd Ed., Vol. 5, J. I. Kroschwitz, ed., John Wiley & Sons, Inc., New York, 1986, p. 416
6. H. W. Bonk in J. Agranoff, ed., *Modern Plastics Encyclopedia 1984–85,* McGraw-Hill, Inc., New York, 1985, p. 100
7. B. M. Walker, ed., *Handbook of Thermoplastic Elastomers,* Van Nostrand Reinhold, New York, 1979
8. A. D. Thorn, *Thermoplastic Elastomers – A Review of Current Information,* Rubber and Plastics Research Assoc. of Great Britain, Shawbury, Shrewsbury, Shropshire SY4 4NR, Great Britain, 1980
9. G. Holden in I. Rubin, ed., *Handbook of Plastics and Related Materials,* John Wiley & Sons, Inc., New York, in press
10. G. Holden in *Rubber Technology,* 3rd Ed., M. Morton, ed., Van Nostrand Reinhold, New York, 1987
11. *Modern Plastics 60*(12), 42 (1983)
12. Technical Bulletin SC:455–81, Shell Chemical Co., Houston TX, 1981
13. D. J. St. Clair, *Rubber Chem. Technol. 55,* 208 (1982)
14. Technical Bulletin SC:198–83, Shell Chemical Co., Houston TX, 1983.
15. Technical Bulletin SC:72–85, Shell Chemical Co., Houston TX, 1985
16. G. Kraus, K. W. Rollman and R. A. Gray, *J. Adhesion 10,* 221 (1979)
17. S. G. Chu and J. Class, *J. Appl. Poly Sci. 30,* 805 (1985)
18. J. R. Erickson, *Rubber Plast. News,* p. 16 (Sept. 9, 1985)
19. D. M. Mitchell and R. Sabia, Proceeding of the 29th International Wire and Cable Symposium, November 1980, p. 15
20. G. Holden and S. S. Chin, Paper presented at the Adhesives and Sealants Conference, Washington, D.C., March 1986
21. G. Holden, Paper presented at the Adhesives and Sealants Council Seminar, Chicago IL, Oct. 1982
22. E. J. van Beem and P. Brasser, *J. Inst. Pet. London 59,* 91 (1973)
23. Technical Bulletin SC:57–84, Shell Chemical Co., Houston TX, 1984
24. Bulletin TR-18, Shell International Chemical Co., London, 1984
25. J. H. Collins and W. J. Mikols, paper presented at the 60th Meeting of the Association of Asphalt Paving Technologists, San Antonio, TX, Feb. 1985
26. Technical Bulletin SC:165–77, Shell Chemical Co., Houston TX, 1977

27. A. L. Bull and G. Holden, *J. Elastomers and Plastics 9,* 281 (1977)
28. C. R. Lindsey, D. R. Paul and J. W. Barlow, *J. Appl. Poly. Sci. 26,* 1 (1981)
29. D. W. Bartlett, D. R. Paul and J. W. Barlow, *Modern Plastics 58*(12), 60 (1981)
30. T. D. Traugott, J. W. Barlow and D. R. Paul, *J. Appl. Poly. Sci. 28,* 2947 (1983)
31. G. Holden, *J. Elastomers and Plastics 14,* 148 (1982)
32. C. L. Willis, W. M. Halper and D. L. Handlin Jr., *Polym.-Plast. Technol. Eng. 23*(2), 207 (1984)
33. Technical Bulletin SC:449–84, Shell Chemical Co., Houston TX, 1984
34. Technical Bulletin SC:789–84, Shell Chemical Co., Houston TY, 1984
35. B. C. Arkles, *Medical Device and Diagnostic Industry, 5*(11), 66 (1983)
36. B. C. Arkles (to Petrach Systems), U. S. Patent 4, 500, 688 (Feb. 19, 1985)
37. S. Wolkenbreit in Ref. 7, Chapt. 5
38. R. School, *Rubber Plast. News, 49* (May 7, 1984)
39. M. Szycher, V. L. Poirier and D. Demsey, *Elastomerics 115*(30), 11 (1983)
40. H. W. Bonk, R. Drzal, C. Georgacopoulos and T. M. Shah, paper presented at the 43rd Annual Technical Conference of the Society of Plastics Engineers, Washington, DC, 1985
41. S. C. Wells, in Ref. 7, Chapt. 4
42. A. S. Wood, *Modern Plastics 62*(3), 42 (1985)
43. Hytrel Bulletin HYT-302(R1), E. I. Du Pont de Nemours & Co. (1981)
44. Hytrel Bulletin HYT-452, E. I. Du Pont de Nemours & Co. (1981)
45. Hytrel Bulletin IF-HYT-370,025. E. I. Du Pont de Nemours & Co. (1976)
46. G. Deleens, paper presented at the 39th Annual Technical Conference of the Society of Plastics Engineers, Boston, MA, 1981
47. A. Y. Coran, R. Patel and D. Williams, *Rubber Chem. Technol. 55,* 116 (1982)
48. A. M. Gessler, (to Esso Research and Engineering Co.), U. S. Patent 3,037,954 (June 5, 1962)
49. H. L. Morris, in Ref. 7, Chapt. 2
50. S. E. Avery, *Modern Plastics 62*(4), 74 (1985)
51. *Modern Plastics 62*(9), 14 (1985)
52. J. G. Wallace, W. R. Abell and J. F. Hagman, paper presented at the ACS Rubber Division Meeting, Los Angeles, CA, April 1985
53. *Chemical Week* p. 28 (September 25, 1985)

Chapter **14**

HYDROGENATED BLOCK COPOLYMERS IN THERMOPLASTIC ELASTOMER IPNs

W. P. Gergen, R. G. Lutz, S. Davison

Contents

William P. Gergen, Robert G. Lutz and Sol Davison, Shell Development Company, Westhollow Research Center, Houston, Texas

1   INTRODUCTION

The commercial introduction of Styrenic block copolymer thermoplastic elastomers occurred two decades ago. The first polymers were linear triblock copolymers with polystyrene hard blocks and polybutadiene elastomer blocks (S-B-S) or polyisoprene elastomer blocks (S-I-S), both formed by anionic polymerization. Ten years later, a second generation of linear triblock copolymers, in which the polybutadiene center blocks were hydrogenated, was brought to the market.

The hydrogenated block copolymers which we will discuss are linear triblock copolymers with terminal polystyrene blocks and elastomeric center blocks. The elastomer block consists of a copolymer of ethylene and butylene (S-EB-S) which is derived from a butadiene precursor by hydrogenation. These blocks, at sufficiently high molecular weight, have a sharp compositional boundary; the blocks are pure polystyrene or pure elastomer. Since the polymeric blocks are immiscible they phase separate into domains of polystyrene in a matrix of the elastomer. At less than about 50 % polystyrene the domains are dispersed.

The concept behind all thermoplastic elastomers is to provide in the same polymer the mechanical performance of a vulcanized rubber and the facile processing of thermoplastics. This is achieved over a limited range of service conditions in the thermoplastic elastomers which we know today. Indeed, it is the dream and the goal of researchers in this area to widen the window of service conditions to eventually equal that of vulcanized rubbers. It was this goal that drove the development of hydrogenated block copolymers a decade ago. The experience with EPR and EPDM rubbers clearly showed the advantages of saturated polymers in providing resistance to degradation from exposure to high temperatures (in air) and to UV radiation. Lack of resistance to degradation was a clear limitation of the unsaturated block copolymers and hydrogenation of these polymers gave the same measure of resistance to degradation as found in the olefin rubbers.

Clearly, the improvements expected from hydrogenation were achieved. Of even greater importance, however, it was found that the inter-relationships governing phase separation were so strongly changed by hydrogenation that a different quality of block copolymer resulted, one having dramatically different properties. The unique rheology of these polymers, together with their high temperature stability inevitably led to a new class of blended compounds, consisting of interpenetrating co-continuous polymer phases, the thermoplastic IPNs[1,2]. The ability to form co-continuous morphologies is a result of the network structure of the block copolymers in the melt and the consequent yield phenomena in a flow field during mixing. The network structure "templates" the surrounding phase while the yield stress prevents spontaneous demixing.

Styrene has been the chosen building block for the hard phase of block copolymers. Although it is one of the most readily available, anionically polymerizable monomers, its special utility in hydrogenated block copolymers arises from other factors to be discussed in detail. The chosen building block for the elastomer segment of the commercial hydrogenated block copolymers has been ethylene-butylene, derived from butadiene, rather than ethylene-propylene, derived from isoprene. Originally, this choice was made primarily on the basis of traditional cost and availability of the monomers, although there are other decision factors involved.

The first part of this chapter discusses in detail the chemical and physical structure of hydrogenated block copolymers with emphasis on the differences from their unsaturated analogues and the properties that result. The second part deals with the role of such polymers in the formation of thermoplastic IPNs and the properties of such blends. An experimental section is provided at the end, in which the materials and the experimental methods and testing procedures are outlined briefly.

2   HYDROGENATED DIENE BLOCK COPOLYMERS

2.1   Chemical Structure

It is possible to hydrogenate styrenic block copolymers completely, including the aromatic unsaturation of the polystyrene blocks. This leads to a certain class of polymers which we will discuss shortly. However, it is usually the case that only the elastomer block is hydrogenated. Most of the art of the commercial process involves both this often-times difficult selective hydrogenation and also controlling the precursor block copolymer micro-structure.

The hydrogenation of polyisoprene polymerized through the 1,4 carbons yields an olefin type rubber, an ethylene-propylene copolymer with perfectly alternating ethylene and propylene sequences. These polymers are completely free of polyethylene-like crystallinity and have low Tg, about -55 to -60 °C.

Isoprene Monomer

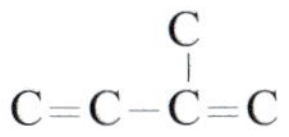

$$C=C-\overset{\overset{\displaystyle C}{|}}{C}=C$$

1,4-Polyisoprene/3,4-PI

$$[\,C-C=\overset{\overset{\displaystyle C}{|}}{C}-C\,]\qquad[\,C-\overset{\overset{\displaystyle C\diagdown\ \diagup C}{C}}{}\ \ C\,]$$

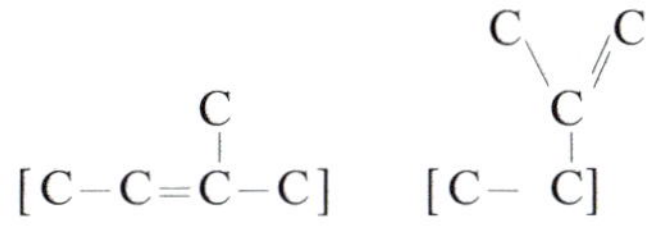

1:1-Ethylene-Propylene/3-Methylbutene

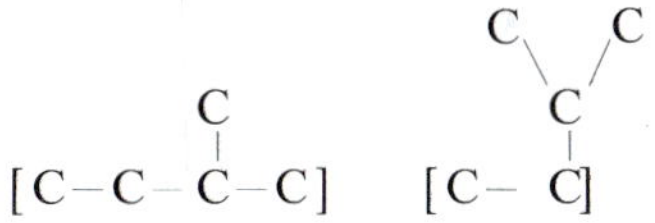

$$[\,C-C-\overset{\overset{\displaystyle C}{|}}{C}-C\,]\qquad[\,C-\overset{\overset{\displaystyle C\diagdown\ \diagup C}{C}}{}\ \ C\,]$$

Each isoprene monomer addition to the growing chain incorporates two methylene and one propylene sequence (or one ethylene and one propylene). Although some of the isoprene can also polymerize through the 3,4 carbons, the resulting hydrogenated structure, which has an isopropenyl side group, does not allow any crystallinity nor does it substantially increase Tg. In practice, in making block copolymers with ethylene propylene blocks the 3,4 addition reaction usually is supressed as much as possible. The important point is that incorporation of each monomer unit enchains four "back-bone" carbon atoms and includes a propylene or branched monomer unit. Runs of polyethylene are impossible, regardless of the type of addition, and the chain is truly a rubbery polymer.

When butadiene is the rubber block monomer, the situation is somewhat more complex;

Butadiene Monomer $C=C-C=C$

1,4/1,2-Polybutadiene $[\,C-C=C-C\,]\qquad[\,C-\overset{\overset{\displaystyle C}{\|}\ \overset{\displaystyle C}{|}}{C}\,]$

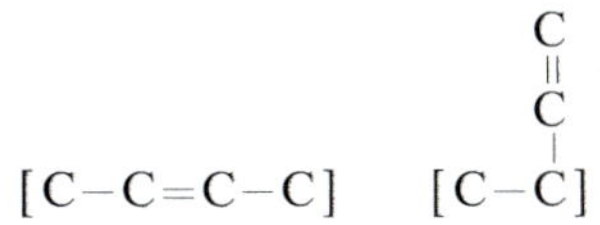

$$
\text{Ethylene/Butylene} \qquad [\,C-C-C-C\,] \qquad [\,C-\underset{\underset{C}{\mid}}{\overset{\overset{C}{\mid}}{C}}\,]
$$

In the synthesis of polybutadiene, polymerization can proceed through the 1,4 or the 1,2 double bonds. The random balance of 1,4 and 1,2 addition during polymerization can be controlled very readily in the range of about 8 to 70 per cent 1,2 addition. Hydrogenation of these chains then yields either a polyethylene sequence from the 1,4 addition or a polybutylene sequence from the 1,2 addition. Each monomer can enchain in the backbone either four (a tetramethylene sequence) or two (an alpha-butylene sequence) carbon atoms. Hydrogenated pure 1,4 polybutadiene would be indistinguishable from linear high-density polyethylene, whereas hydrogenated pure 1,2 polybutadiene would yield atactic poly 1-butene. The random mixtures resulting from hydrogenation of anionic butadiene polymers produce elastomeric ethylene-butylene copolymers. (Such EB copolymer chains are not identical in molecular structure to those formed from random polymerization of ethylene and butylene, due to the absence of certain forbidden sequences. This arises from the enchainment of two ethylene units for each 1,4 addition. However, common physical properties apparently are not affected by this subtle difference.)

The elastomer segment composition in these block copolymers must be designed to adequately supress polyethylene crystallinity, by interrupting polyethylene-like sequences with butylene monomer units. However, the T_g of polybutylene is around -18 °C, high for a good quality elastomer, so that too much enrichment with butylene will substantially raise

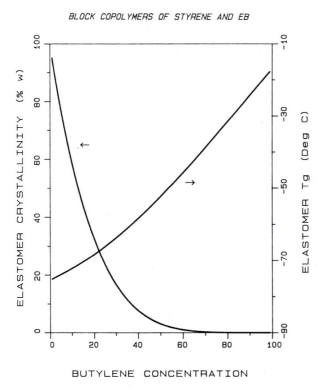

BLOCK COPOLYMERS OF STYRENE AND EB

Figure 1   The Effect of Butylene (1,2 Addition in the Precursor) Concentration on the Crystallinity and Tg of the Elastomer Phase in S-EB-S Polymers

T_g. This balance is a requirement that is well known to manufacturers of Ziegler polymerized EPR or EPDM rubbers. The purpose is to obtain a saturated olefin elastomer block with the lowest possible T_g and the best elastomeric characteristics. Thus, the optimal composition will minimize the increase in T_g arising from butylene monomer incorporation and also minimize crystallinity by interrupting polyethylene sequences.

As the composition becomes rich in tetra-methylene sequences arising from the hydrogenated polybutadiene 1,4 additions, the probability of runs of polyethylene-like sequences becomes higher and the crystallinity shows an increase displayed by the left-hand curve in Figure 1. This curve matches a calculated relationship assuming that 20 methylene sequences, which would be produced by five sequential 1,4 additions to the chain, are capable of joining polyethylene crystallites at ambient temperature. Crystallization reduces the amorphous phase volume and reinforces the elastomer, overlaying and masking the T_g relationship on the left-hand side of the composition diagram. When crystallinity is completely supressed, in the vicinity of 50 per cent 1,2 addition, T_g is strongly increased by further butylene enchainment.

2.2 Microphase Separation in Block Copolymers

The phase separation of block copolymers both in solution and in the solid state has been developed from thermodynamic principles by a number of authors[3, 4, 5]. All start from the thermodynamic equation of mixing for polymer pairs and involve summations of two main terms, the enthalpy of mixing and the change in entropy.

$$\Delta G = \Delta H - T\Delta S \tag{1}$$

Phase separation will occur when the Free Energy of Mixing (ΔG) is positive. The enthalpy (ΔH) is equal to the the heat of mixing and is related to the Flory-Huggins interaction parameter (X_{ab}) which in turn, is a function of the difference in solubility parameters ($\delta_a - \delta_b$) between the block segments and the molecular weight and density (M_a, ϱ) of the "a" segments.

$$\Delta H = f(X_{ab}) \tag{2}$$

$$X_{ab} = \frac{(\delta_a - \delta_b)^2 \, M_a}{\varrho_a \, RT} \tag{3}$$

The change in entropy is due mainly to the reduction in entropy from constrained A-B block junctions. One can view the equation describing microphase separation in block copolymers as one which describes the conditions under which phase separation will occur or alternatively as an expression of the energy level which must be overcome to dissociate the blocks (i.e. provide homogeneous mixing of the segments). Phase separation leads to a domain structure consisting of areas of pure A block composition, areas of pure B block composition, and an area of mixed composition which we call the interface region or interface volume. If the polymer architecture allows ties between domain areas (such as a tri-block ABA copolymer) a phase separated network structure results.

The interface constitutes a volume which is quantitively dependent on the driving force for phase separation. It is very important because it is a region of gradient composition which can actually lower the interfacial tension between different polymer pairs[6]. Figure 2 shows the relationship between the interface volume and the interaction parameter between blocks (M being the molecular weight and δ the solubility parameter in the figure)[7]. The figure

PHASE-MIXING IN BLOCK COPOLYMERS

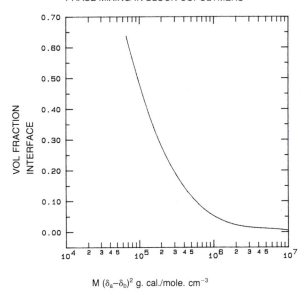

Figure 2   The Volume Fraction of Polymer Homogeneously Mixed at the Interface as a Function of the Product of Molecular Weight and the Squared Difference in Solubility Parameter in (AB) Block Copolymers. Drawn from relationship derived by Meier

shows that unless the polymer pairs are sufficienty different chemically, or molecular weight is sufficiently high, a very substantial volume of the polymer will be homogeneously mixed.

Figure 3 shows a map of solubility parameters for the most common pairs of polymers which make up anionically polymerized block copolymers. Both ordinate and abscissa are scaled in units of solubility parameter; polymers used as hard-blocks or end-block are plotted on the abscissa while polymers used as the elastomer-block are plotted on the ordinate. Values of T_g, and in one case (polyethylene) T_m, are indicated on the labels. Diagonal lines indicate the squared difference between ordinate and abscissa values and therefore describe the Flory-Huggins interaction parameter between polymer pairs which are located at intersections of the plotted polymers on the map at constant molecular weight. Solubility parameters are calculated by the method of group contributions[8]. Polymers which are either commercially manufactured or extensively synthesized are indicated by the crosses and symbols at the intersection of the respective polymers. The end-block polymers are based on polystyrene, alkylsubstituted polystyrenes, poly α methyl styrene (aMS), poly paramethyl styrene (pMS) and poly tertbutyl styrene (tBS), hydrogenated polystyrene (polyvinylcyclohexene, VCH) or polyethylene (PE), which results from the hydrogenation of predominantly 1,4 polybutadiene and has a range of melting temperatures (Tm) depending on the level of 1,2 addition in the precursor. The elastomer blocks are 1,4 polyisoprene (1,4 I) and its hydrogenated polymer (HI 1,4); 1,4 polybutadiene (1,4 B) (typically with 5–10% 1,2 content), and hydrogenated polybutadiene of about 40% 1,2 content (EB$_{40}$).

The criteria for microphase separation into the domain network structure, the interface volume, and the consequent dissociation energy of the block copolymers are dependent on the interaction parameter, i.e., on the squared difference in solubility parameter. Further, the processing rheology and the mechanical property set, especially time-dependent and temperature-dependent properties, also will be very dependent on this dissociation energy, which is the level of energy holding the polymer material in a network structure. So, to judge the criticality of this parameter, we can reference all of the block copolymers on this map to

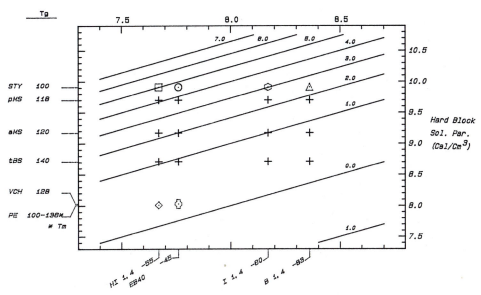

Figure 3   Map of Hydrocarbon Block Copolymers. Solubility parameters are calculated from group contributions for the rubbery state, corrected to 25 °C. Diagonal lines indicate locus of squared difference in solubility parameter. ⊙ S-EB-S, ☐ S-EP-S, ⊘ S-I-S, △ S-B-S, ◇ HY(B-I-B), ⊕ VCH-EB-VCH

the S-B-S polymer shown. This S-B-S is easily processed, shows a network structure at reasonable molecular weights, has high strength and reasonable creep rate at 23 °C, however, it has excessive creep at 50 °C. We can, therefore, say that the interaction parameter represented by this copolymer is a minimum value for useful block copolymers of ordinary molecular weight. Polymers which have squard difference in solubility parameter lower than that of S-B-S, would have insufficient driving force for separation and therefore a greatly inferior property set. This is primarily why the alkyl-substituted polystyrene polymers, which have higher Tg values then polystyrene, are not used in commercial block copolymers. They would exceed the minimum interaction parameter only in the case where the elastomer block was hydrogenated. The advantages of stronger phase separation far outweigh the advantages of higher hard-block Tg. Polystyrene remains the choice for any amorphous hydrocarbon block copolymer. This last fact is clearly demonstrated in the case of the fully hydrogenated VCH-EB-VCH polymer. The interaction parameter is so severely reduced by hydrogenation that at only slightly elevated temperatures the polymer loses all strength and appears to be homogeneously mixed at ordinary melt temperatures.

The polymer labeled Hy(B-I-B) is a special case. In this polymer the end block is a hydrogenated 1,4 polybutadiene and therefore is a "linear" polyethylene. The elastomer block is polyisoprene and on hydrogenation becomes a 1:1 ethylene propylene copolymer. If the quality and molecular weight of the polyethylene end-blocks is such that rapid crystallization can occur, phase separation is the result of polyethylene crystallizing out of the homogenously mixed segments. Crystallinity in these polymers can be measured by DSC although the crystallites cannot be seen by light or electron microscopy[9]. The reason these and similar polymers are not commercially made is because the polyethylene made this way is not very "linear", i.e. the precursor 1,4 polybutadiene has a substantial 1,2 content which breaks up the crystallizable segments. Current anionic polymerization technology does not allow reduction of 1,2 content below about 5 %. Also, without adequate phase separation in the melt, crystalline domains are not well developed and therefore are not a strong as spherulite phases in ordinary high crystallinity polyethylene.

Thus, the principal commercial offering of hydrogenated polymers is S-EB-S, a polymer with polystyrene end-blocks, and ethylene-butylene rubber blocks. In this polymer the interaction parameter is at least two-and-one-half times the critical base case for S-B-S because of the shift to lower solubility parameter of the 1,4 and 1,2 polybutadiene segments upon hydrogenation. The effect of this shift on the property set of S-EB-S compared to S-B-S is quite dramatic. To illustrate this shift, properties of two S-EB-S polymers (I and II) are now compared to those of an S-B-S. Further details of all three polymers are given in the Experimental Section.

The hydrogenated polymers typified by S-EB-S I have such a high association energy that they will not spontaneously dissociate above the polystyrene Tg, nor will they dissociate in response to a rather strong mechanical stress field. Figure 4 shows the apparent melt viscosity of such a polymer as a function of shear rate and temperature from 200 to 300 °C. The polymer melt viscosity is extremely non-Newtonian, resembling that of a solid (a solid would have a slope of -1 in this plot), with a slope of -0.98 at the lowest temperature. The slope changes only slightly with increasing temperature. At 260 °C the slope has decreased

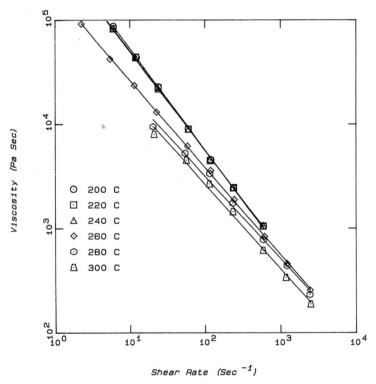

Figure 4   Melt Viscosity of S-EB-S I Hydrogenated Block Copolymer. The slope of the viscosity/shear-rate curve is nearly 1.0 up to 260 °C

to only about −0.89. This is a result of the intact network structure which persists in the so-called "melt" and prevents the development of dissipative flow in the shear field. At least up to 260 °C, flow is not temperature activated, an apparent contradiction in terms for a thermoplastic material. This same type of behavior is shown by covalently crosslinked rubbers and by some types of ionomers.

2.3 Morphology and Strength

The equilibrium morphology of styrenic block copolymers, where the "A" phase volume fraction is lower than that of the "B" phase, consists of phase separated "A" domains in the form of spheres, cylinders, or lamellae dispersed in a matrix of the "B" phase, Figure 5. The geometric form will be that which minimizes the surface free energy between phases. The typical morphology of the polymers studied here is dispersed cylinders. If the polymer architecture is tri-block or multiblock, the mechanism of network structure is bridging between domains by molecules whose "A" blocks enter different "A" domains. This creates a barrier to shear flow just as covalent crosslinking does. The mechanisms of failure and flow in a stress field then, are very closely related, arising from the pulling-out of bridging chain "A" blocks, and are of comparable energy. In the "melt" state this energy is low, whereas in the "solid" state it is comparable to that of covalently crosslinked systems. The creation of sheared interfaces results in the formation of new units located in the stress field.

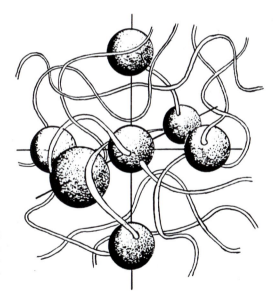

Figure 5 Spatial Domain and Network Structure for the Case of Spherical Domain Geometry. A network, incapable of flow, is created when a few inter-domain cross-links are formed

The tensile behavior of the three polymers is shown in Figure 6. Both S-EB-S polymers (only one of which is shown) are stronger and have higher modulus than that of the S-B-S. This again is attributable to the higher association energy and the absence of substantial interface volume in the S-EB-S. The elongation of the S-EB-S polymers is lower because the contour length of the S-EB-S is lower than that of the S-B-S (40 % 1,2 versus 8 % 1,2) and therefore stress transfer to the dispersed domain structure occurs at lower strain. In line with this, the higher association energy is obvious in Figure 7, an Arhenius plot of the tensile

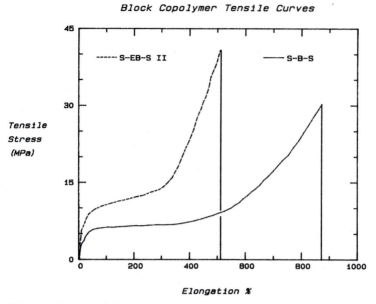

Figure 6   Stress-strain Relationship in Tension for Saturated and Unsaturated Block Copolymers

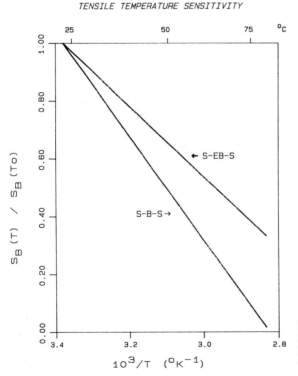

Figure 7   Arhenius Plot of Tensile Strength of S-EB-S II and S-B-S. Breaking stress is normalized to the value at 23 °C.

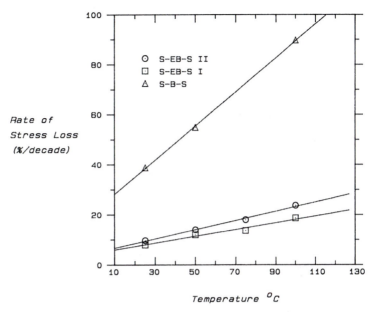

Figure 8   Rate of Stress-Relaxation as a Function of Temperature

strength normalized to 23 °C. The rate of tensile loss in the S-EB-S with an increase in temperature is far less than that of the S-B-S analog polymers. As shown in Figure 8, the rate of stress relaxation increases with temperature to a far lesser degree in the S-EB-S materials and is even comparable at this level of strain to that of vulcanized polymers.

2.4 Dynamic Mechanical Properties

One of the problems common to both Ziegler-polymerized EPR or EPDM polymers and the S-EB-S polymers is the effect of polyethylene crystallinity on the elastic properties of the elastomer (i.e. resilience, rebound, recovery, etc.). To overcome this problem it is necessary that almost all methylene runs that otherwise would be large enough to join the PE crystal must be interupted. As was shown in Figure 1, a balance between reduction of crystallinity and increase in Tg is achieved at a 1,2 content of about 35 %. Figure 9 shows that the dynamic hysteresis is minimized at about this same level. The curve was derived from a large amount of data which is not reported here but used somewhat different techniques. Values of dynamic hysteresis measured for the S-B-S polymer and the two S-EB-S polymers are shown in Table I.

Conventional vulcanized natural rubber gum compounds have values in this test of less than 5 % while clay filled SBR compounds have values of about 25–30 %, so these polymers are quite "rubbery" by comparison to standard rubbers.

The dynamic mechanical spectra of the three polymers are shown in Figures 10, 11 and 12. The first difference that we focus on lies with the rubber block. This peak in the S-B-S sample, Figure 12, has an intensity of 1.4 tan delta and a width of about 40 °C centered at

BLOCK COPOLYMERS OF STYRENE AND EB

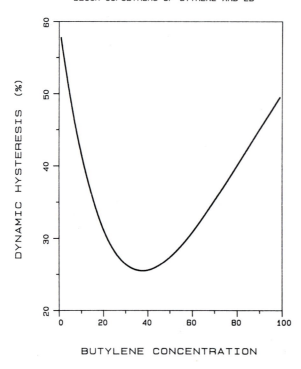

Figure 9   Dynamic Hysteresis as a Function of Butylene Concentration. Taken from process development data, continuous function shown is an empirical model

TABLE I   Hysteresis of Block Copolymers

Sample	Dynamic Hysteresis 23 °C, 150 % Elongation
S–B–S	8.8
S–EB–S I	9.6
S–EB–S II	15.5

about −84 °C. On the other hand, the EB peaks in the S-EB-S samples, Figures 10 and 11, have intensities of about 0.3 and a width of 70 °C or more and are centered at −45 °C with a marked shoulder in the loss peak. This indicates a broader distribution of relaxation times, likely due to the existence of amorphous runs of ethylene and butylene and a small amount of crystallinity.

The modulus level in the rubbery plateau region is dependent primarily on the hard-block (polystyrene) concentration, being highest for the S-EB-S I sample. Since material in the interface will have transitions between those for pure A and pure B, the level of losses in the rubbery plateau region will be increased by the volume in the interface[10]. These data show that the S-B-S sample has the higher level of losses in this region (tan delta ~ 0.06 compared to tan delta ~ 0.04 for the two S-EB-S polymers). The S-B-S polymer also has lower modulus than its hydrogenated analog because of the decreased volume of pure A phase which determines the dynamic modulus level in this region.

In all three materials the loss peak associated with the polystyrene phase appears to be located at about 110 °C (somewhat higher for the S-EB-S I sample, which has higher

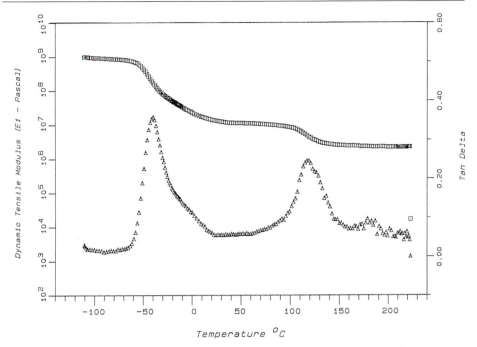

Figure 10   Dynamic Mechanical Spectrum at 11 Hertz for S-EB-S I. Modulus (squares) and tan delta (triangles) as a function of temperature

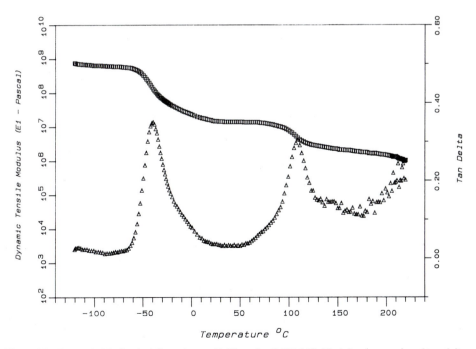

Figure 11   Dynamic Mechanical Spectrum at 11 Hertz for S-EB-S II. Modulus (squares) and tan delta (triangles) as a function of temperature

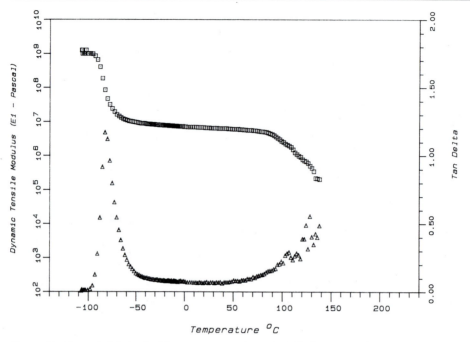

Figure 12   Dynamic Mechanical Spectrum at 11 Hertz for S-B-S. Modulus (squares) and tan delta (triangles) as a function of temperature

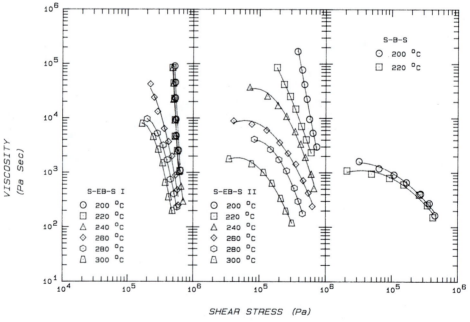

Figure 13   Corrected Melt Viscosity as a Function of Shear Stress and Temperature for the Three Block Copolymers Studied

molecular weight). However, from the modulus curve one can see that the onset of this transition occurs at about 75 °C in the S-B-S material and not until about 95 °C in S-EB-S II, and 100 °C in the S-EB-S I polymer. In addition, the plateau region above the transition is highest and flattest in the S-EB-S I sample, and does not even exist in the S-B-S sample. These phenomona are the result of the much stronger phase separation in the S-EB-S materials, recall Figure 3. The volume of pure A phase is highest and the interface volumes lowest in the S-EB-S samples and dissociation above the end-block transition does not occur at the strain levels of this test. There is a measurable yield stress above the styrene Tg which is related to the interaction parameter between the block segments and in both S-EB-S samples is high enough to maintain the integrity of the material.

The lack of any dissipative processes in the "melt" regime suggests that the S-EB-S polymers are rather intractible. The melt viscosity as a function of shear stress in shown in Figure 13 for the 3 samples studied here. The S-B-S sample on the right is typical of well-developed flow in a thermoplastic polymer. The analogous S-EB-S II polymer fails to reach a comparable level of flow even at 100 °C higher temperature although it does show some flow processes. In the higher molecular weight S-EB-S I materials, there is extremely little flow over its melt temperature range. This "melt" behavior is very similar to that of covalently crosslinked rubbers. Both the dynamic modulus in the plateau region above the styrene Tg from the dynamic data and the shear yield stress from the capillary measurements are of the same magnitude as that of a vulcanized, particulate-filled SBR material.

3 THERMOPLASTIC IPN FORMATION AND PROPERTIES

3.1 Concept of Thermoplastic IPNs

Interpenetrating Polymer Networks (IPNs) have received a great deal of attention since they were first proposed by Klempner, Frisch and Frisch in 1971[11]. The rationale behind the concept of IPNs was that normally immiscible polymers could be locked together in a catenated structure by covalent crosslinking once an interpenetration of entangled chain segments was achieved. Crosslinking would provide a kinetic barrier to gross phase separation or reversion to the lower free energy, demixed condition. The ideal state was visualized as two infinite networks, everywhere interlocked but having no mutual chemical attachment.

In the period since the IPN concept was introduced, a great many conventions and much specific terminology have developed dealing with the emerging technology. For the most part, these conventions are perceived from the point of view of the practitioner who is attempting to produce the structure. There is a very methodical, descriptive terminology which differentiates IPNs on the basis of the sequence of steps intended to achieve the interdispersed networks[12, 13]. Although thermoplastic IPNs have a great deal of conceptual commonality with thermosetting IPNs, at present they are synthesized in an entirely different way[14]. Therefore, it is difficult for thermoplastic IPNs to fit this increasingly accepted terminology convention that is being applied to thermoset IPNs.

It must be granted that chemical or "covalent" crosslinking is not an absolute requirement in the production of a network structure. Consider a material consisting of a polymer that has gelled in a solvent under some set of conditions. If one can note in the gel a resistance to some kind of disruptive field, a macroscopic stress field for instance, one then presumes that this resistance arises from a network structure. In the gel there is spatial connectivity of every element of the polymer phase; the polymer is continuous throughout the macroscopic volume. Spatial connectivity also applies to the solvent. The mechanism of stabilizing the gel after the instant of its formation need not be interchain chemical crosslinking. Such gels just as well could be locked into place through a reversible, physical mechanism and, in fact, quite commonly are. Block polymers of certain architecture form networks with some measurable level of association, just as crosslinking forms networks with a measurable level of association. Both types of network will dissociate if this level of energy is exceeded[7].

The conceptual structure evoked by the original IPN theory is that of co-continuous polymer networks or interdispersed gels, interpenetrating on some finite scale of mixing. In one theoretical extreme, the scale of mixing is small enough to be at the level of thermodynamic solubility of polymer chain segments. Interpenetration then could be traced only along the backbone of individual polymer chains. However, if there is association of like chains at a level greater than molecular scale, then the components begin to take on characteristics familiar to their species and the gel network is an interpenetration of polymer phases. In this case, interpenetration could be traced by a number of possible routes within any element of the network. Crosslinking within these phases can proceed but it constitutes an ordinary internal network, quite apart from the macro-network which constitutes that particular IPN.

The existence of identifiable phases clearly prevails in thermoplastic IPNs, although there may be some doubt in certain thermoset IPNs. The overall structure is rendered metastable by the formation, within one or more phases, of a persistent, micro-network structure, continuous within the macroscopic phase volume in all dimensions. This internal network, whether arising from covalent bonding or reversible physical interaction, indeed is a vital element of the structure but it does not define the IPN. It is the final, persistent, macro-topological structure of the phases that defines an IPN, regardless of the chemical or physical route by which it was created.

We define IPNs as equilibrium blends of two or more polymers in which at least two of the components have three-dimensional spatial continuity. Implicit in this definition, especially for thermoplastic IPNs, is the notion that each component is a polymer phase, generally with its own internal network-like structure from which its properties arise. In a binary mixture, the surface of each of the phases is an exact topological negative of the other, that is, they are "antitropic". It is obvious in that case that only one of the two phases need be spatially fixed to completely stabilize the entire framework. This definition, of course, is a morphological description of physical structure, not of the route by which an experimenter chose to create it.

Nature is replete with examples of materials that possess bicontinuous structure (our definition of IPN), from sandstone, open-celled sponges, and various naturally occurring biological membranes, to the polymer blend structures that result from spinodal decomposition above a lower critical solution temperature. Many writers, artists and scientists have envisioned stylistic IPN-like frameworks, for example the co-eating apple worms of George Gamow, "Double Planetoid" by Maurits Escher and the "Olympic Gels" of P. deGennes.

Scriven has very elegantly described space-filling topologies which are equillibrium bicontinuous structures and which are illustrated by the models of periodic minimum-surface structures of Schwarz and Neovius[15, 16, 17]. The requirements of bicontinuous structure are spatial (mathematical) connectivity, positive genus (multiply connected), with each sub-volume intersecting (touching) each outer surface in more than one place. Scriven proposes that such bicontinuous structures can exist as an equilibrium morphology in water-oil emulsions which contain an amphiphile at the point in the phase-diagram where inversion occurs.

We can now postulate that blends of two polymers which contain no additional phases, fall into three major morphological types depending on the scale of interdispersion and the continuity of the phases. With binary mixtures of polymers A and B one can have:

1. Miscible blends or combinations where the scale of mixing is at the magnitude of the molecular dimensions. The components lose their individual identity and characteristics of a new hybrid material are expressed.
2. Matrix-disperse blends where either A is dispersed in a matrix of B or the opposite case, B dispersed in A. The components retain their individual identity but the properties of the matrix are predominantly expressed.
3. Co-continuous blends or IPNs where each of the two polymers has three-dimensional continuity. The components retain their individual identities and thus the properties of both are fully expressed.

As one considers variations in the morphology of the individual polymeric phases of an IPN, as we will point out later, it becomes apparent that there are a number of morphological variants which are more subtle than phase connectivity. Both thermodynamic and kinetic factors are involved in determining which specific morphology will occur in a certain mixture. In binary thermoplastic IPN systems, in most cases, one can form the co-continuous structure at least as a transient structure, through the application of correct methods of mixing. Interfacial tension between the incompatible polymer components drives the system toward minimum surface free energy, that is to phase growth. It is then the function of network structure within one or both continuous phases to kinetically inhibit retraction. This inhibition may be achieved by chemical or physical crosslinking. The possibilities include covalent bonding, ionic or phase association, domain formation, crystallization and vitrification. All thermoplastic IPNs contain an internal network in at least one of the co-continuous polymer phases. Ideally, perhaps, for the ultimate in stability and properties, covalent bonds would have to be broken for phase disengagement to occur, or alternatively some process of comparable energy dissipation would have to take place.

3.2   Formation of the IPN Structure

Intensive mixing of viscous incompatible polymer pairs in the melt can result in the development of an IPN structure in the shear field. The most efficient mixing of two components into a finely divided interdispersed structure can be achieved when the viscosities and the volume fractions of the two components are equal, Figure 14. This situation, termed "iso-viscous" mixing, maximizes coupling of adjacent fluid elements and assures an even distribution of the imposed shear field during mixing. Equal volume fractions maximizes the opportunity for maintaining connectivity since neither component is present in a minor amount. As the viscosity of the components diverge, the efficiency of shear stress transfer across an element of the lower viscosity phase is progressivly reduced, requiring a reduction in its volume fraction to compensate for the reduced stress coupling. This mechanism of IPN formation describes the structure in the melt state, in the mixing shear field, and does not require the network characteristics we have illustrated for the S-EB-S I material. Such structures may survive to varying degrees after the shear field is removed and while the melt is being transferred prior to solidification. Rapid quenching of an IPN melt, prior to retraction, will preserve the structure by crystallization or vitrification. In the quiescent melt, however, the morphology will be transient in the absence of a kinetic barrier to flow such as would be provided by the block copolymer.

An example of a transient, unstabilized IPN was seen in blend BL1, a blend of polypropylene and polybutylene, two similar, linear polymers. Upon mixing, these polymers readily

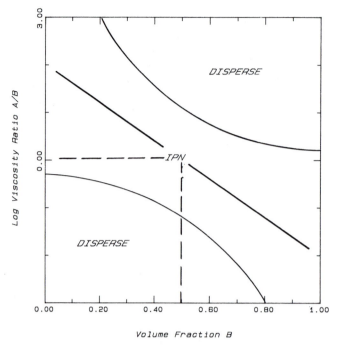

Figure 14   IPN Mixing Relationship Showing the Line Along Which Co-continuity is Easily Obtained with Two Components which Have Similar Viscosities. The permitted region is considerably expanded when block copolymers are used

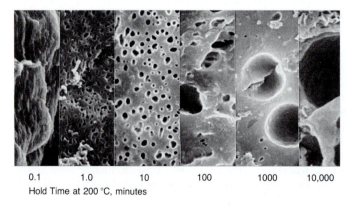

Figure 15   Phase Growth of a Polypropylene (70) / Polybutylene (30) IPN Blend. SEM at 5000X shows the increase in phase size as time at 200 °C increases to 10,000 minutes (one week)

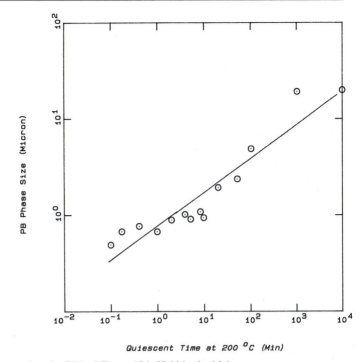

PB Phase Size (Micron)

Quiescent Time at 200 °C (Min)

Figure 16   Phase Size Measured as the IPN of Figure 15 is Held in the Melt

formed an extremely fine "celled" IPN that was preserved by quenching the material immediatly after it cleared the extruder die. The small size, on the order of 0.1μ, attests to the facility of interdispersing components of similar solubility parameter. When held quiescent in the melt (200 °C) this blend underwent gradual but extensive phase growth, Figures 15 and 16, while retaining continuity of the phases, revealed by extraction and electron microscopy examination. The chemical similarity of the two polymers results in a low interfacial tension, the predominant driving force for phase growth or phase "retraction". Phase retraction in this system was an extremely slow process, with the phase size increasing about one-hundred-fold over the period of a week. This IPN blend is sufficiently stable to retain fine cell size under practical melt fabrication and conditions. We conclude that low interfacial tension, facilitates IPN formation and reduces the rate of retraction.

When polypropylene is blended with the S-EB-S I polymer, as in IPN-B2, a structure on the order of 0.2 micron is obtained. This structure shows no phase retraction or growth even after 1000 hours at 200 °C, Figure 17 a. In this case the low interfacial tension is assisted by the network characteristics of the S-EB-S polymer, which provides the kinetic barrier to phase retraction. The same stabilization is shown when only 10 % of the S-EB-S I is added to IPN-B1 resulting in a stable ternary IPN mixture. When the polypropylene level is increased to 50 % as in IPN-B3, Figure 17 b, the characteristic cell size of the mixture is somewhat higher, one-half to one micron. As we go to polymers which are less chemically similar to the S-EB-S polymer, the binary IPNs from these polymers have increasing phase size. This is shown in the IPN-B4, Figure 17 c, a blend of S-EB-S with nylon 12, and in IPN-B5, Figure 17 d, a blend of S-EB-S with polyethersulfone.

The structure which can be seen in these photographs is typical of the thermoplastic IPN structure. It is more chaotic than any perceived minimal surface which might be present, for

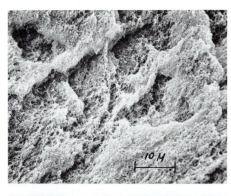

Figure 17 a   Fracture Surface SEM of Extracted Sample of an IPN Blend Containing 22 % Polypropylene and 78 % S-EB-S I Block Copolymer. The S-EB-S has been extracted (2000X)

Figure 17 b   Fracture Surface SEM of Extracted Sample of an IPN Blend Containing 50 % Polypropylene and 50 % S-EB-S I Block Copolymer. The S-EB-S has been extracted (2000X)

Figure 17 c   Fracture Surface SEM of Extracted Sample of an IPN Blend Containing 25 % NYLON 11 and 75 % S-EB-S I Block Copolymer. The S-EB-S has been extracted (2000X)

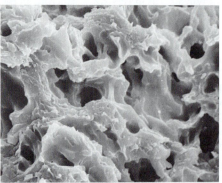

Figure 17 d   Fracture Surface SEM of Extracted Sample of an IPN Blend Containing 50 % Polyethersulfone and 50 % S-EB-S I Block Copolymer. The S-EB-S has been extracted (2000X)

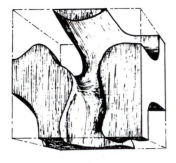

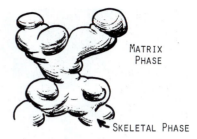

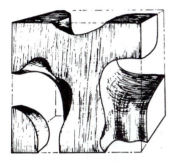

Figure 19   Model of the Skeletal Element of the IPN. The components with the higher surface tension or the higher viscosity becomes the skeletal component with convex surface. The "antitropic" phase is the co-continuous matrix phase

Figure 18   Model of the IPN Structure Based on SEMs of a Large Number of Blends. Interlocking halves are separated and both convex and concave surfaces can be observed. Model is depicted at about 25,000X

instance, in phases that are a result of a spinodal growth mechanisms above the lower critical solution temperature Complementary phases, which are deduced by SEM are depicted in the model in Figure 18. This model is a conception resulting from the careful examination of a great number of IPN structures by SEM. The model shows both concave and convex surfaces and interlocking and continuous phases. In a binary IPN, the co-continuous phases have some topological characteristic differences; one phase, usually the phase having network structure in the melt, seems to be primarily convex, forming a "skeletal" structure, while the second phase then occupies the space around that phase and has a "matrix" characteristic. This skeletal and matrix phase character is depicted in Figure 19. The skeletal phase characteristic emphasized in this element is the rounded convex surface which maintains a "limb-like" connectivity to other elements and constitutes a template for the matrix phase. The matrix is the surrounding phase, which takes the opposite, concave surface at the interface. These structural identities are easily seen in Figure 20 a showing a deeply extracted nylon/S-EB-S IPN residue. The void areas clearly show the form of the sketal S-EB-S phase and the antitropic nylon matrix. These characteristics are also seen in the SEM of IPN-B6, Figure 20 b a polypropylene/S-EB-S IPN which was etched with an oxygen plasma and viewed at a 120 degree angle. The small nodes or nodules at the etched surface are "skeletal" S-EB-S continuous phase. (Since PP etches faster, the residue in the unshielded area is the S-EB-S.)

Figure 21 shows the the cell size of binary blends as a function of the squared solubility parameter difference (the thermoplastic resin and the EB block). As the difference increases, or as interfacial tension increases, the cell size of the IPN shows a very rapid increase. The higher the interfacial tension, the greater will be the work required to increase the interfacial area between the phases. (These blends were not made with the high molecular weight S-EB-S polymer and result from ordinary viscous mixing.)

As we mentioned earlier, the S-EB-S I polymer shows no measurable true shear flow, no apparant temperature activation of flow and is capable of templating the IPN structure. This

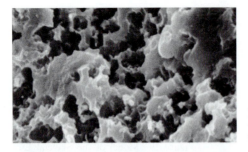

Figure 20 a   SEM of a Nylon / S-EB-S IPN Mixture. The skeletal structure of the extracted rubber can easily be seen in the nylon residue

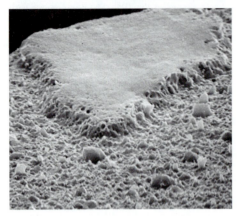

Figure 20 b   View of SEM of an Oxygen-Plasma-Etched Sample of PP and S-EB-S. Area at the top of the micrograph was shielded from the plasma. Since the PP etches faster in the plasma, protuberances in the unshielded area are the S-EB-S skeletal phase

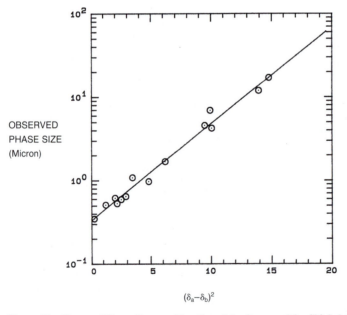

Figure 21   Observed Phase Size as a Function of the Square of the (D) Solubility Parameter Difference Between the Resin IPN Component and the Elastomer Block of the S-EB-S Component

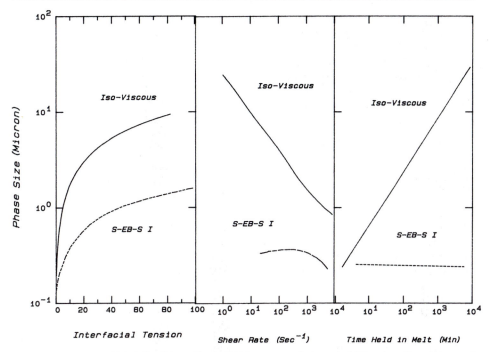

Figure 22   Factors Which Affect Phase Size in IPN Structures, the Interfacial Tension, Shear Rate, and Melt Residence Time. The response is different for the iso-viscous case and the case where high molecular weight S-EB-S is used as the IPN former

polymer, in its gel-like state, fragments in the blending device only along shear planes when mixing with an incompatible resin, and easily forms the skeletal continuous structure while the thermoplastic resin then takes up the antitropic continuous structure. This can take place by reversibly removing a few terminal blocks from domains, while retaining a "flow unit" structure of a size distribution that is consistent with the shear field.

The cohesive strength of the intact block polymer network structure prevents the breakup of the block polymer phase into droplets which would form a disperse phase; the reformation of the continuous phase then can occur by the restoration of the same number of chain segments that were breached in forming the macroscopic flow unit. This mechanism is analogous to dynamic vulcanization except that in the case of the block copolymer templated IPN the particles have the possibility to reconnect through the reversible network structure. This is the point in which S-EB-S diverges from all other network polymers, which merely serve to stabilize the IPN once formed by ordinary viscous mixing. The result is freedom from the constraints of the viscosity/composition ratio relationship and the interfacial tension relationship. High molecular weight S-EB-S polymers consistently form fine phase size IPNs independently of these factors.

We have seen that factors important to IPN structure formation and stability are the viscosity ratio, compositional ratio, and solubility parameter difference. These control the interfacial tension and network structure. Other factors of importance are the absolute melt viscoelastic characteristics, viscosity and melt strength, and the degree of mixing or the energy field input in the mixing device. Figure 22 shows the effect of interfacial tension, of shear rate in the mixing field, and of quiesent phase retraction time on IPN phase size (in the case of isoviscous mixing) and the lack of effect (in the case of S-EB-S templating). High shear-rate in the mixing device will reduce the cell size up to a limit of the ability of the polymer pairs to resist degradation and to the practical limit of even the most intense mixing devices of about 2000 to 3000 inverse seconds. In addition to factors which are related to the shear field and the relationship between the IPN components, the individual components of the IPN mixture must resist breakup in elongational flow as the mixture is carried forward in the mixing extruder so as to maintain the connectivity which is developed in the shear field[18].

3.3 Mechanical Properties of IPNs

The benefit of a co-continuous structure versus a dispersed structure is that the properties of a co-continuous structure can generally can be described by an additive relationship. This effect for a polycarbonate/S-EB-S blend is shown in Figures 23 and 24. In the first case there is only a hydrodynamic effect of the volume of polycarbonate used on the modulus. At the S-EB-S polystyrene glass transition temperature the small increase in modulus disapears. In the second case, the co-continuous case, the modulus is increased in proportion to the polycarbonate volume fraction and thus the blend is still load-bearing up to the Tg of the polycarbonate rather than up to that of the polystyrene. Therefore, with co-continuous resin phases that are capable of withstanding high temperatures, the S-EB-S compounds are able also to provide stiffness and strength at temperatures well above the Tg of polystyrene.

In the IPN blends with co-continuous polymer phases, the components express their individual characteristics to the extent of the fraction of the total volume occupied by that phase. There is a load-path continuity which accompanies the structural phase co-continuity. In terms of intuitive continuum mechanical models, the IPNs resemble most closely a parallel combination of elements such as is employed for uniaxial, long fiber reinforcement in composites. The most important points in the application of any model relating properties of IPNs to the structure are the independence of the contribution of the components and the three-dimensional spatial connectivity of the elements.

The upper bound solutions in most continuum mechanical models (e.g. composite relationships developed by Kerner, Uemura and Takayanagi, Nielson, Sato and Furukawa, Coran and Patel, or Hapin and Tsai) resolve to simple linear additive relationships for the case of perfect adhesion and perfect connectivity in one dimension[19-24]. This is usually referred to as the "rule of mixtures" where strain is constant in each element. Lower bound relationships describe a series arrangement of elements where stress is constant in each element. The upper and lower bounds in blend modulus are given from the component moduli by:

Upper Bound: $M_c = M_a\theta_a + M_b(1 - \theta_a)$ $\qquad\qquad$ (4)

Lower Bound: $M_c = 1 / (\theta_a/M_a + (1 - \theta_a)/M_b)$ $\qquad$ (5)

$\qquad\qquad$ M_c = Modulus of the Blend
$\qquad\qquad$ θ_a = Volume Fraction of Component A
$\qquad\qquad$ M_a = Modulus of Component A
$\qquad\qquad$ M_b = Modulus of Component B

The IPN "unit cell", consisting of binary combinations with parallel elements with perfect adhesion, under a macroscopic stress field provides three load paths, one each through each component phase, and one via a series combination of the two materials. The latter load path, as a series element, is a consequence of the three-dimensional co-continuity of the IPN system. A somewhat more flexible model for this situation is a logarithmic rule of mixtures (the linear "rule of mixtures" is a special case of such a model with an exponent of 1.0). This is proposed by a number of workers to model the complex dielectric behavior of composites.

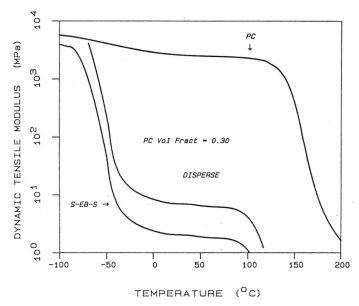

Figure 23   Dynamic Modulus / Temperature Spectrum for S-EB-S I Materials, Polycarbonate, and a Blend of the Two in Which the PC is a Particulate Dispersed Phase. Blend was made from powdered constituents far below the iso-viscous temperature. The Tg of the polystyrene end-blocks in the S-EB-S I is at 110 °C

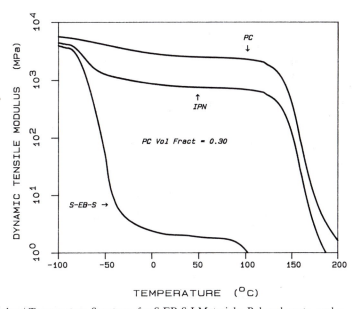

Figure 24   Dynamic Modulus / Temperature Spectrum for S-EB-S I Materials, Polycarbonate, and a Blend of the Two in Which the PC is a IPN Co-continuous Phase. Blend was made from powdered constituents above the iso-viscous temperature and with a long residence time in the melt

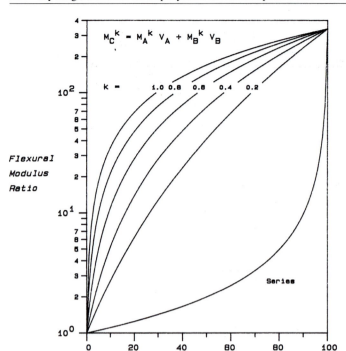

Figure 25   Logarithmic Model of IPN Blend Modulus. This modulus is expressed as a ratio of the blend modulus to that of the softest component. Exponents in the model are given for various cases

Proposed by Looyenga with exponent weighting of 0.5 and later by Davies (with a weighting of 0.2) it is postulated to be a more rational model than the rule of mixtures for composites with three dimensional phase continuity[25]. The model given below is shown plotted for a series of weighting exponents in Figure 25.

$$M_c^K = M_a^K \theta_a + M_b^K (1 - \theta_a) \tag{6}$$

In Figure 26 is shown a number of binary mixtures of S-EB-S polymers with various resins (listed in the experimental section) at several levels. The measured blend modulus is expressed as a modulus ratio compared to the modulus of the S-EB-S I block copolymer, which is a component of all these blends. Each of these resins has about 350 times the modulus of the S-EB-S I polymer. The measured modulus data is shown plotted on the same grid as in Figures 25 and 26 again shows the various logarithmic models. The data are located within a band in the upper region of this plot below the rule of mixture. They are described by weighting exponents in the range of 0.2 to 0.6 in the logrithmic mixture equation. It appears as if no single exponent is applicable to all the IPN systems.

In Figure 27, the dynamic moduli measured at 205 °C for a series of binary mixtures of S-EB-S and PBT are shown. The lower solid curve is the Davies equation with exponent of 0.2. The data appear to fall in a range between this equation and the upper bound, with an exponent of about 0.6. Figure 28 shows the dynamic modulus of binary mixtures of S-EB-S and polycarbonate. These data are fit with a logarithmic model with an exponent of 0.5. Noteworthy in these data is the complete masking of the polystyrene glass transition of the

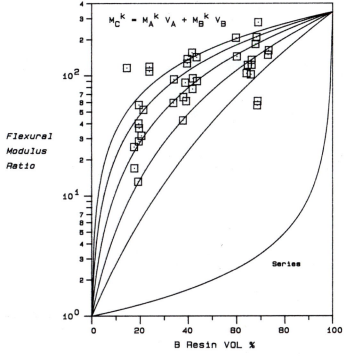

Figure 26   Binary Blends of Resins Described in the Experimental Section. Resin grades with modulus ratio (to that of the S-EB-S) of about 350 were used in this comparison. Data falls in the range of the logarithmic model with exponents in the range 0.2 to 0.6

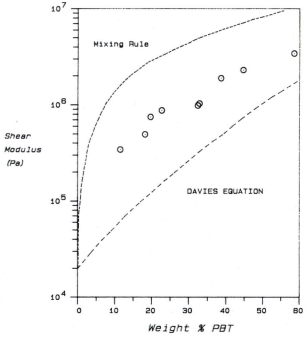

Figure 27 Dynamic Modulus (Obtained From a Rheometrics Mechanical Spectrometer) in Shear at 205 °C, (a common bake oven temperature for curing painted high performance materials). The data appear to be fit by an exponent in the logarithmic model of 0.5

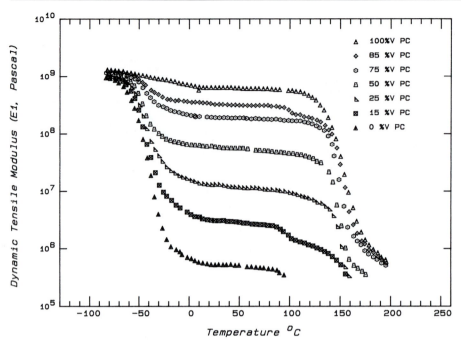

Figure 28   The Dynamic Tensile Modulus of IPN Mixtures of S-EB-S and Polycarbonate. The increase in modulus can be modelled by the logarithmic model over the entire temperature range

S-EB-S by the polycarbonate continuous phase. Such mechanical property response can provide quite outstanding high-temperature integrity in blends at moderate stress levels with only moderate amounts of the high-temperature resin. For instance, amorphous resins can significantly raise the heat distortion temperature of thermoplastic crystalline resins.

Figure 29 shows the effect of temperature on the dynamic modulus of a number of IPN blend compositions, two vulcanized rubbers and a plasticized PVC. In every IPN blend the high-temperature resin, either polypropylene or polybutylene terephthalate masks the polystyrene Tg of the S-EB-S and provides structural integrity up to the resin melt temperature. In the case of the blend containing both PP and PBT, modulus level above the PP melt temperature is equivalent to that of the vulcanized tread rubber. In this ternary IPN blend, the modulus level can be adjusted up or down by the PP content while the PBT provides some resistance to deformation up to a temperature of 225 °C, where it also melts. The IPN blends show a true rubbery plateau, not quite as flat as that of the vulcanized rubbers but much better than that of the PVC. They also provide the same level of integrity up to the same failure temperatures shown by the vulcanized rubbers. The NR gum rubber degrades by losing rigidity at about 150 °C while the SBR begins to crosslink and embrittle at about the same temperature.

The relationships discussed for describing the modulus at very small deformations appear to adequately fit the co-continuous IPN blend modulus. The same rationale for modeling such high strain properties as tensile strength, would be applicable only if the components had identical tensile response, a very unlikely situation. A useful analogy is found, however, in models of the tensile failure of macroscopic blends of textile fibers[26]. If we propose an IPN blend of two components or "fibers", one with higher breaking strain than the other, the

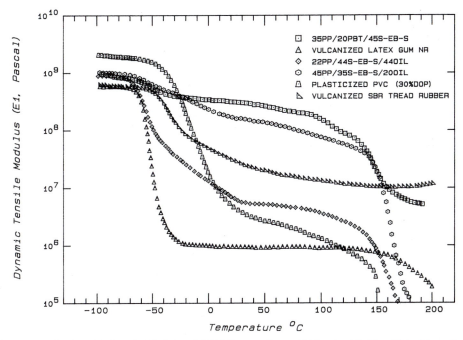

Figure 29   The Dynamic Tensile Modulus of IPN Mixtures, Several Vulcanized Rubber Materials, and Plasticized PVC. The IPNs have structural integrity at high temperatures (>100 °C) similar to that of the vulcanized rubbers and far superior to PVC

fiber model proposes that if these fibers are clamped in parallel in a tensile fixture and pulled, then at the point of breaking elongation of the first fiber, the load supported by both fibers will be transferred to the remaining fiber. If this load represents a stress in excess of the breaking stress for the remaining fiber, the remaining fiber will also break, short of its breaking strain. This analysis presumes that the response of each fiber is independent of the other, and that there is no adhesion between fibers. The model is illustrated in Figure 30. The fiber pairs are in uniaxial tension on the right and the stress-strain response is shown in the curve on the top left. As the strain causes breaking in fiber A, (at elongation X_1) the load is transfered to the remaining fiber B at the corresponding point on its stress strain response. The load is then borne by the remaining fiber B. The macroscopic stress across both fibers just before rupture consists of contributions from the strength of fiber A multiplied by its volume fraction and from the stress in fiber B at the point of fiber A rupture. Therefore the stress can be considered as the sum of these independent contributions.

The contributions can be represented as functions of the stress-strain response in the individual fibers and the volume fraction in the blend as shown in the lower curve in Figure 30. It must be emphasized again that this is a no-adhesion situation; when the A fiber breaks, its contribution ceases. When the two phases adhere, fiber A can still be load bearing after it breaks at one point by coupling through fiber B. The profile of non-adhering IPN blends would be expected to follow the model in this figure as a function of composition.

Figure 31 shows the measured stress-strain response of polycarbonate neat resin and polypropylene neat resin. The breaking stress of ternary IPN blends of these two resins made with varying amounts of S-EB-S polymer (shown included with PP in the volume %) is

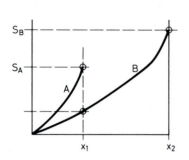

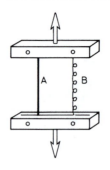

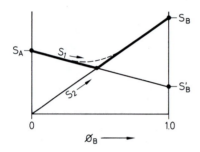

$$x_1 : \varnothing_A\, S_A + \varnothing_B\, S'_B = S_1$$
$$x_2 : \varnothing_B\, S_B = S_2$$

Figure 30   Tensile Fiber Mechanical Model with No Adhesion

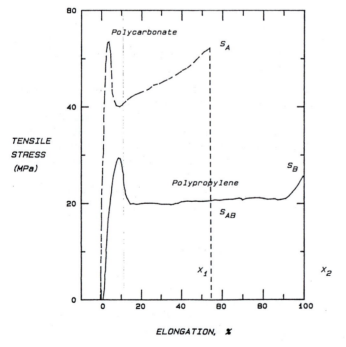

Figure 31   Stress-strain Curves at 23 °C for Polycarbonate and Polypropylene. The point of stress transfer in a parallel pulling of fibers of these materials is at XI with transfer stress of S_{AB}

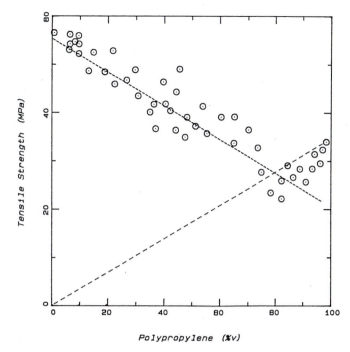

Polypropylene (%v)

Figure 32   Construction of the Fiber Mechanical Model From the Data of Figure 31. The data points are from Binary IPN blends of PP and PC (iso-viscous) and from ternary blends of PP, PC, and S-EB-S I. The S-EB-S concentration varied but in every case is included as part of the PP concentration in the figure

shown in Figure 32 along with the construction of the Fiber Tensile Model from the component stress-strain data. The data appear to fit the model consistently. The apparent upturn near the right of the curve (pure PP) would tend to support the model rather than a dilution in the higher strength component.

While the mechanical characteristics of properties which are manifest at low strain are certainly encouraging for IPN structures, the properties at higher strain are clearly interior to those of the blend components. This is a result of the lack of adhesion between the phases in the IPN blends. Inter-phase adhesion can be obtained in blend with sufficiently small phase size, (high interfacial area). Small phase size can be achieved in a number of ways as previously discussed, but with a certain difficulty which always reduces the degrees of freedom in blending. We expect to see in the next step in this field of thermoplastic IPN blending, a new technology which will satisfy the need for strong interfacial adhesion while at the same time, retaining the excellent characteristics of co-continuous IPN structure at low strain.

4   EXPERIMENTAL

4.1 Materials and Blend Compositions

The polymers which we report here, S-EB-S I, S-EB-S II, and S-B-S, are similar to those made in Shell Chemical Company's commercial block polymer plant by proprietary processes of polymerization and hydrogenation. Molecular weights are nominal values which would be obtained by GPC number average using a polystyrene calibration. Polystyrene contents are calculated from the molecular weights. Polybutadiene (PB) microstructures are nominal values as would be obtained from thin-film infra-red spectrographic measurements. The 1,4 microstructure of the polybutadiene is about half trans 1,4 and half cis 1,4. The block copolymers are described in Table II.

The thermoplastic resins used in blends were commercial materials obtained from the manufacturer in the form of conventional thermoplastic resin pelletized product. The resins used in the studies are listed in Table III.

The compositions of many of the blends are given in the figures. Several blends ohich are specifically discussed are given in Table IV.

TABLE II   Characteristics of Block Copolymers Studied

Sample	MW A–B–A	%w A	PB 1.2 Content
S–B–S	10S/50B/10S	29.4	8.0
S–EB–S I	30S/130B/30S	33.3	40.0
S–EB–S II	10S/50B/10S	29.4	40.0

TABLE III   Thermoplastic Resins Used in IPNs

Thermoplastic Resin		Supplier
Polypropylene	P-5520	Shell Chemical Co.
Polybutylene	PB-0200	Shell Chemical Co.
Nylon 6	CAPRON-8027	Allied Chemical
Nylon 6/6	ZYTEL 101	DuPont
Polybutylene terepthalate	VALOX 340	General Electric
Polycarbonate	MERLON M40	Mobay Chemical
Polyacetal	DELRIN 100	DuPont
Polyethersulfone	PES	ICI
Polyurethane	PELLETHANE	Upjohn

TABLE IV   IPN Blend Compositions

Blend No.	A Resin	Conc. %w	B Resin	Conc.
IPN B1	PP	70,0	PB	30,0
IPN B2	PP	78,0	S–EB–S I	22,0
IPN B3	PP	50,0	S–EB–S I	50,0
IPN B4	Nylon 11	25,0	S–EB–S I	75,0
IPN B5	Poly(Ethersulfone)	50,0	S–EB–S I	50,0
IBN B6	PP	70,0	S–EB–S I	30,0

4.2   Blending and Testing

All moisture sensitive resins were extensively dried before use following the manufacturers' recommended technique. Dry mixtures of ground components were blended on a 30 mm twin screw Baker-Perkins MP mixer, extruded at various temperatures and shear stress, cooled in water, and where appropriate dried and then stored over a desiccant. Samples for physical property tests were injection molded on a 6-ounce reciprocating screw injection molder into standard ASTM plastic specimens.

Dynamic hysteresis was measured by repeated stretching of straight specimens between 0 and 150 % elongation on an Instron tester at 10 inches/minute. It is defined as the fractional energy loss per cycle after at least five cycles, converted to percent.

Dynamic mechanical spectra were determined using an Autovibron Dynamic Mechanical Spectrometer. Specimens were in the form of films of about 0.4 mm. thickness. The Autovibron programs which control and calculate various dynamic properties were extensively modified to correct for instrument compliance, for transducer temperature drift, and for the change in creep rate for very low-modulus materials. As a result the dynamic spectra of very soft materials could be followed using the same specimen at temperatures well above upper transitions and to stress levels of less than 0.1 MPa.

Melt rheology of polymers and their blends was studied with an Instron Capillary Viscometer at shear rates ranging from 1 to 3000 inverse seconds. Shear rates were corrected using the Rabinowitch correction.

Tensile properties were measured on ASTM "D" Die specimens with an Instron Tester using an Instron high-temperature chamber and optical extensometer. Pulling rate was 10 inches/minute for materials having modulus lower than 60 MPa and 1 in/min for materials with modulus greater than 60 MPa.

Stress relaxation was measured by stretching the specimen to 150 % elongation at a rate of 50 inches/minute, stopping the crosshead and digitally recording the decay curve for a period of about 100 minutes. The computer then calculated the decay curve as a function of logarithmic time by ratioing the observed stress to the stress at the moment of cessation of crosshead motion. Only data whose decay curve fitted a regression line with an index of determination of at least 0.999 were used.

Phase retraction or phase growth was studied by maintaining a number of thin samples of the blended material in a closed mold in a press at 200 °C for periods of time up to 10,000 minutes (about one week). Some degradation was evidenced by discoloration around the outer edges and this portion was discarded. Samples were removed from the press periodically, cryogenically fractured, extracted and examined by Scanning Electron Microscopy. Polybutylene was extracted from the polypropylene with xylene at 95 °C. Phase size was estimated from measurements made on the electron micrographs.

Extraction of the block copolymer phase from the blends generally was done using toluene in a Soxholet extractor. In most cases, extraction followed freezing in liquid nitrogen and fracture, so that it was necessary to extract only a small depth to illuminate the structure. In several cases thin films of about 0.4 mm. were extracted until all of the block copolymer was recovered to prove complete phase continuity. Retention of shape in the residue indicated a continuous structure in the remaining phase.

References

1. S. Davison and W. P. Gergen, US 4,041,103 (1977)
2. W. P. Gergen and S. Davison, US 4,079,099; 4,079,100; 4,080,356; 4,080,357; 4,080,403; 4,081,424; 4,085,163; 4,088,626; 4,088,627; 4,088,711; 4,090,996; 4,096,204; 4,101,605; 4,102,854; 4,107,130; 4,107,131; 4,110,303; 4,111,894; 4,111,895; 4,111,896; 4,119,607; 4,126,600 (1978)
3. D. J. Meier, *J. Polym. Sci, Part C 26* (1969)
4. S. Krause, *Macromolecules 11* (1971)
5. E. Helfand, *Rubber Chem. and Tech. 49* (#2) 237 (1976)
6. I. C. Sanchez, *Poly. Eng. and Sci. 24* (#2) 79 (1984)
7. D. J. Meier, *ACS Polymer Preprints 11* 400 (1970)
8. D. W. Van Krevelen, *Properties of Polymers,* Elsevier Publishing, N.Y., 1976, p. 142
9. M. Morton, N. C. Lee and E. R. Terrill, *Elastomers and Rubber Elasticity,* ACS Symposium Series #193, p. 101, J. E. Mark and J. Lal, Eds., American Chemical Society, Washington, D. C.
10. C. P. Henderson and M. C. Williams, ACS *Polymer Preprints 21* (#2) 249 (1980)
11. D. Klempner, H. L. Frisch and K. C. Frisch, *J. Elastoplastics 3* (1971) p. 2
12. J. A. Manson and L. H. Sperling, *Polymer Blends and Composites,* Plenum Press, N.Y. (1976) Ch. 8
13. D. A. Thomas and L. H. Sperling, *Polymer Blends,* Paul and Newman, Eds., Academic Press, N.Y. (1978) ch. 11
14. D. R. Paul, *Polymer Blends* Vol. 1, ch. 1
15. L. E. Scriven, *Micellization, Solubilization, and Microemulsions,* Vol. 2, p. 877, K. L. Mittal, Ed., Plenum Press, N.Y. (1975)
16. H. A. Schwarz, *Gesammelte Mathematische Abhandlung,* Vol. 1, p. 6–125, Springer, Berlin (1890), from Reference 15
17. E. R. Neovius, *Bestimmung zweier spezieller periodischer Minimalflächen,* J. C. Fenkel, Helsing-Forest (1883), from Reference 15
18. G. N. Avqeropoulos, et. al., *Rubber Chem. and Tech. 49* 93 (1976)
19. E. H. Kerner, *Proc. Physical Soc. London, 69B* 808 (1956)
20. S. Uemura and M. Takayanagi, *J. Polym. Sci. 10* 113 (1966)
21. L. E. Nielson, *J. Appl. Phys. 41* 4626 (1970)
22. Y. Sato and J. Furukawa, *Rubber Chem. and Tech. 36* 1081 (1963)
23. A. Y. Coran and R. Patel, *Rubber Chem. and Tech. 53* 141 (1980)
24. S. W. Tsai, *Formulas for the Elastic Properties of Fiber-Reinforced Composites,* AD845861 Nat. Tech. Information Service, Springfield, VA, (1986)
25. W. E. A. Davies, *J. Physics Part D: Applied Physics 4* (1971) p. 318
26. B. C. Goswami, J. G. Matindale and F. L. Scardino, in *Textile Yarns, Technology, Structure, and Applications,* John Wiley and Sons, N.Y., (1977) p. 350

Chapter 15

FUTURE TRENDS

H. E. Schroeder, N. R. Legge

Unreal, unduly optimistic forecasts of future research and development are all too prevalent, especially in chapters like this where the writers do not have to pay the piper – but who could look at thermoplastic elastomers without adopting a rosy view of the future? Here is an unusual combination of a fertile scientific field, of great academic and industrial interest, with much to be learned, and an eagerly receptive market awaiting the fruits of discovery.

For over fifty years new thermoplastic elastomer (TPE) materials have been emerging, many of them as surprises, well before the physical science had advanced paradigms which could explain and predict their properties. It has been that way too with most new polymerization systems. This situation is beginning to change, one of the reasons which led the editors to believe that this volume was indeed timely. With the growth in understanding that TPEs all owe their essential properties to the presence of at least two polymeric phases, one fluid and the other solid (in the normal operating range), plus the realization that these phases can be combined in very many ways, both physical and chemical, the possibilities for new useful TPE structures appear almost boundless.

To create these new thermoplastic elastomers we have at our disposal a very broad choice of polymerization reactions and catalysts which can be used to enchain the most diverse of monomers, polar and non-polar, in almost any ratio. We are learning how to control monomer ordering and even chirality. Control of molecular weight and of molecular weight distribution is no longer a mystery. There is also a wealth of fluid or elastomeric structures and even more hard, glassy or crystalline polymers to combine with them. The rapidly developing science of the rheology of these systems is beginning to explain polymer flow properties and the relationships between processing characteristics and chain structure, chain length, branching and molecular weight distribution. Morphological research on these fascinating products is showing us the bases for physical and mechanical properties. Present knowledge of the chemical structures can explain solubility, stability to solvents and chemicals, and resistance to degradation by heat, light and oxidation. With such assets at our disposal it is now possible to undertake material research problems with the expectation that particular property goals can be approximated. The day is approaching when we will be able to predict processing behavior and physical properties. So why should we not be positive in assessing this future?

The content of the preceding chapters supports this thesis. The extent of our understanding is remarkable, yet in no case does it appear that the subjects is exhausted. Rather, the explications of the authors all seem to presage an interesting future. The real question is not whether, but where, the new TPE products will appear. Of course, this leaves open the question of economics insofar as practical products are concerned. Here again, experience has shown innumerable compounding modifications, or selection of use areas, which can

H. E. Schroeder, Consultant, 74 Stonegates, 4031 Kennett Pike, Greenville, Delaware 19807
N. R. Legge, Consultant, 19 Barkentine Rd., Rancho Palos Verdes, CA 90274.

provide success. Against this background we propose to look at the future by touching, first on the properties that might appear desirable, the possibilities of achieving these, and then on the supporting sciences.

Thermoplastic elastomers have been welcome in the marketplace because they are easy to process and give excellent properties economically. They have quickly filled many product requirements formerly held by conventionally cured rubbers. They have been particularly welcome where the physical properties are adequate and the resistance to deformation at elevated temperatures, conveyed by a chemical (covalent) crosslink, is not needed, for example, in certain wire coatings, shoe soles and adhesives. We expect that with some limitations we shall see the TPEs fill out the entire continuum of properties now provided by the conventional cured rubbers. This continuum now goes from the softest silicone to the ultrastable perfluoroelastomers and includes products with extraordinary chemical and solvent resistance. In addition, we expect the TPEs to offer properties which cannot be achieved with the usual cured rubbers. Certainly they will fill out the territory between the hardest conventional rubbers and the high-impact plastics. This area has been partially occupied already by the so-called "engineering" high modulus TPEs such as the polyurethanes and the copolyesters. We believe that the TPEs will meet the developing needs of the hard, resilient materials more easily and more economically than the cured rubbers.

Certain characteristics are associated with the families of cured rubbers. These include:

Elasticity – long range extension and retraction, snap, softness, resilience – the domain of natural rubber and the general purpose synthetics (SBR, IR and EPDM), plus polychloroprene and the silicones.

Solvent resistance plus most of the above characteristics – the realm of almost all of the "general purpose" specialty rubbers ranging from butadiene/acrylonitrile rubbers (NBR) to the more oxygen or heat stable polychloroprene, on to chlorosulfonated polyethylene and related polyethylene derivatives and polyacrylates.

Thermal and oxidative stability – province of the ethylene copolymers, ethylene/propylene/diene (EPDM) elastomers, the silicones, acrylates, and for more extreme demands – the various fluoroelastomers.

Chemical resistance – the hydrofluoroelastomers, fluorosilicones, fluorophosphazenes, and the *per*-fluorocarbon elastomers.

Abrasion resistance, toughness – found in most cured rubbers to varying degrees but outstanding in the cross-linked polyurethanes.

Resistance to creep, permanent set, compression set – load bearing capacity, the hallmark of all cured elastomers.

Stability to deformation at elevated temperatures – characteristics of all cured rubbers up to the limit of thermal stability of crosslinks or polymer chains.

Clues to discovery of thermoplastic elastomers to match properties of cured rubbers lie in the very structures which convey the desired properties. Elastomer type molecules quite naturally will be first choice for the fluid matrix (elastomeric phase) but many other fluids with low Tg are quite suitable. Similarly, selection of the hard or physical crosslinking segment will depend on a fit between properties sought and the hard polymer structure known to convey them. In these two categories there are hundreds of available polymers and more keep coming. The problems, of course, are in the coupling reactions to form the particular segmented copolymer molecules desired, for example, tripolymer, randomly segmented block copolymer, ionomer, polymer blend, etc.

For snappy, elastomeric characteristics, experience as delineated in the preceding chapters seems to show best prospects are in structures where the fluid phase has a very low Tg, and is high in proportion to the hard phase. The latter should be discrete, separate and not continuous, without solubility in the fluid phase because this raises the Tg.

Triblock copolymers with shorter, higher melting glassy, or crystalline blocks will offer one approach to improved resilience. The higher melting hard blocks should also raise the heat distortion temperature significantly and convey increased resistance to creep and set. Where sequential anionic polymerization does not yield the desired structure, capping reactions followed by coupling should. In addition, there is always the possibility of new methods of enchainment such as the recently discovered Group Transfer Polymerization. Stability in the elastomeric phase will be obtained by further use of the polyolefin structures rather than the simple polydienes. Silicones and other new chains of diverse sorts with heteroatoms such as phosphazines offer opportunities to improve low and high temperature performance.

These same comments could also apply to the multi-segmented copolymers $(A–B)_n$, such as the polyurethanes, copolyetheresters, polyether amides, etc. It does not appear possible to take this specific approach with melt mixed blends, dynamically vulcanized, although steps in this direction can be taken with blends of very high melting thermoplastics and elastomers with incorporation of a suitable A–B diblock copolymers as an interfacial adjunct to convey compatibility and processability as well as enhanced physical properties.

Ionomers would seem to offer a unique opportunity to imbed very small "hard" ionic clusters in an elastomer matrix and thus achieve a very soft rubber with good properties. This is probably the closest we can come to the model of the cured elastomer, one covalent link per 100–200 chain length atoms. Ionomers based on the fusible Na, K, NH_4, etc., salts unfortunately show excessive creep, probably because of a very low energy barrier to the dislocation of some ions in the cluster. Higher melting or infusible salt combinations, such as the Pb, Zn or Ca salts used in the SURLYN development, may be applicable with a temporary fluxing agent or salt to enable processability. On a more speculative level is the possibility of using thermally dissociating bonds which recombine as the melt is cooled, for example, diene adducts, or groupings which on heating dissociate to relatively unreactive free radicals which recombine on cooling.

Resistance to swelling by solvents is not easily achieved with the copolymers accessible through the relatively inexpensive anionic polymerizations used in triblock copolymers. While the copolyesters and polyurethane TPEs all show good resistance to non-polar and many polar solvents because the crystalline hard segments are so insoluble, the intermediates are more costly. As shown by ALCRYN and other blends, this goal is probably attainable at lower cost by melt blending hard and soft polymers, with or without dynamic vulcanization and technical compatibilization. This approach to TPEs is particularly attractive to industrial managers because so many commercial polymers with desired properties are available for blending. Investment in new plant is minimal. In contrast a new polymer requires a long and costly development and large amounts of capital. The rapidly increasing knowledge of the rheology and morphology of polymer blends as well as the availability of polymeric (A–B) dispersants and compatibilizers further expands the product possibilities.

Chemical, solvent and high temperature resistance of the highest order is likely not a good practical goal for thermoplastic elastomers. First, the concept of thermoplastic processing is antithetical to stability at very high temperatures. For example, a silicone or hydrofluoroelastomer is stable for long periods at 225 °C and resists short excursions to over 275 °C. Appropriate hard segments are not easily found. An aromatic polyamide, ether, or ester melting above this point would present some very interesting processing problems, somewhat like those involved in perfluorocarbon resins. Even if temporary fluxing or plasticizing agents were found, the aromatic polyamides, esters and ethers do not possess the stability of a fluorocarbon chain to corrosive chemicals, water and acids at high temperatures.

On the other hand, chemical and temperature resistance in the intermediate range should be an attractive goal for thermoplastic elastomers. There are many polycondensation reactions available and new ones are often discovered. The condensation polymers can be designed to possess many of the desired properties without greatly increasing cost. In addition, new intermediates for condensation reactions could be created from substituted polyolefins by equipping them with end groups for attachment of hard segments to form various sorts of segmented copolymers. The discovery of Group Transfer Polymerization (GTP)[1-8] brings many acrylic monomers into the picture for the creation of tri- and poly-block copolymer structures: straight chain, star-shaped, and branched. GTP is a true living polymer system which enables the polymerization of monodisperse copolymer blocks and would be particularly useful. To illustrate, a difunctional monomer such as ethylene dimethacrylate could be converted via the silyloxy reagent to difunctional initiator. This in turn, on reaction with methyl or butyl acrylate, could yield a monodisperse, elastomeric polyacrylate segment. Further treatment with an acrylic monomer, such as methyl methacrylate or acrylonitrile, could give higher melting segments. As research on GTP continues there will undoubtedly be many more monomers which will work. It is to be expected that, in addition to new elastomer sections, both glassy and crystalline hard segments will be accessible.

Abrasion resistance and toughness are no problem for thermoplastic elastomers and accordingly setting these properties as new product objectives will not be hindered. The suitability of S–B–S triblock copolymers for shoe soles, and utility of the polyurethane and copolyester TPEs in industrial wheels, gears, and uninflated tires attests to their quality.

Of course, they are not suitable for applications where they are exposed to temperatures at which the hard segments melt. For example, polyurethane TPEs will melt or depolymerize if, in tire form, they are subjected to a panic stop skid which results in high temperatures from frictional forces.

Creep resistance, permanent set, and compression set resistance of the thermoplastic elastomers of various classes are not usually equivalent to the corresponding cured rubbers over the normal service temperature range of the latter. When subjected to excessive extending or compressive forces, slippage of the polymer molecules in the hard segments occurs. Crystalline hard segments will often draw or orient to form more perfect crystals. Prospects for improving these characteritics are reasonably good. Copolyester and polyurethanes, TPEs with a high concentration of hard segments, have very good resistance to creep or set. We believe that these traits can be improved and even extended somewhat to softer TPEs by improving the crystallinity. This means using either more crystallizable (higher melting) hard segments or monodisperse hard segments which are able to form more perfect crystals. To illustrate, in a copolyetherester, polybutylene terephthalate crystallizes more quickly and more perfectly than it does in polybutylene terephthalate homopolymer. Also when a copolyetherester is annealed under tension it draws, with increase in crystallinity and corresponding improvement in resistance to set and creep.

There would appear to be little hope that a thermoplastic elastomer could attain the ability to withstand deformation at elevated temperatures in the highest part of the range to the extent shown by cured rubbers. Yet by the use of high melting hard segments remarkable properties are within reach. A copolyester with 75 % butylene terephthalate hard segments has better mechanical properties at 150 °C than almost all cured rubbers. It is to be expected that this property would be greatly improved by the use of high melting aromatic polymer segments. Processability requirements will, however, dictate very careful study of the soft segment accompanying structures. In this area of polymer properties it is interesting to note (in Chapter 5) that the comb-graft copolymer of short grafts of polypivalolactone (PPVL) on an EPDM backbone showed mechanical properties closely resembling those of a chemically vulcanized rubber in many respects. The PPVL appeared to exist in discrete crystalline domains of size in the range of 10–100 nm. The graft copolymers were very strong and resistant to compression set.

Future research must also consider the potential of compounding new products to result in required properties and to broaden the economic range of these products as well. There are many examples in the preceding chapters, such as the effects of oils and plasticizers, in adjusting the phase volumes in melt-mixed blends of EPDM and polypropylene, dynamically vulcanized (Chapter 7); the addition of isotactic polypropylene to semi-crystalline propylene/α-olefin copolymers to provide improved properties via co-crystallization (Chapter 5); the blending of polystyrene, resins, and oils with the S–B–S triblock TPEs to broaden their range of physical properties, and the blending of polypropylene with S–EB–S (Chapters 3 and 13). On the other end of the spectrum, we have seen the significant effects of 20 % of S–EB–S on the physical properties of blends of two thermoplastics (Chapter 12, Section 6), and the influence of less than 5 % of S–B–S on the properties of asphalt (Chapter 13).

In addition to Group Transfer Polymerization, there are two other preparative techniques we wish to draw to your attention. The second is the Carbocationic polymerization described by Kennedy[9]. These inifer systems can yield linear or three-arm star polyisobutylenes (PIB) from which one can proceed to macromers, ionomers, block copolymers and telechelics. Kennedy has described model PIB based polyurethane networks from hydroxy-terminated PIB.

The third of these processes is entirely different, as claimed by Falk and Van Beck[10]. The product is a thermoplastic elastomer prepared by a sequential emulsion polymerization to give a core-shell system. The rigid thermoplastic core, for example, a styrene-acrylonitrile copolymer lightly cross-linked, is polymerized as a latex. A transition layer is then formed by adding the monomers of the core and the shell, butylacrylate, to the emulsion polymerization simultaneously, thus surrounding and encapsulating the core. Finally, the monomers of the shell are added and polymerized to form the encapsulating outer shell. Small amounts, 5 %, of functionally reactive monomers are added to the core (acrylic acid), and to the shell (2-hydroxyethyl methacrylate) with the intent that these will link the core and shell lightly during melt mixing. The approximate proportion of the components were: core 20 %, shell 30 %, transition 50 % by weight of the total polymer. The presence of the core, transition layer and shell is essential for TPE properties. Omitting the transition layer, or the functional linking monomers, results in a soft, low strength gum. Compounding the product with 0.1 to 1 % of a metal oxide, such as zinc oxide, improves extrusion and molding operations. The core-shell polymer is processable in normal thermoplastic operations. Although the physical properties of these polymers are not equal to those of many of the current TPE base copolymers, they are, nevertheless, those of a TPE. If this approach can be optimized to provide improved physical properties it would have a major impact on the thermoplastic elastomer area.

To sum up – there are large numbers of possible structures of new thermoplastic elastomers. The essential principle, now well known, is the requirement of at least two polymeric phases, one fluid (above its Tg) and one solid (below its Tg or Tm), at normal operating temperatures, with some interaction between them. A good guide for future R&D would be to avoid a prior mind-set on a given polymer structure, for example $(A–B)_n$, or $(A–B–A)$, but to select polymer segments to achieve the properties desired. In reviewing elastomeric property ranges, one may conclude that the trend toward TPEs with stability at higher temperatures will continue. Another area of significant effort will be aimed at chemical, oil, and temperature resistance, with emphasis on the melt-mixing of blends of polymers. In the triblock copolymer TPEs, new polymerization techniques can lead to polyolefin center blocks with crystalline end blocks. In the next decade we expect that new thermoplastic elastomers will begin to fill in the entire range of conventional crosslinked rubbers. Undoubtedly there will limitations, which we have discussed here; however, we view the scope and utility of TPEs as being much broader than generally considered today. In the preceding chapters we have seen a wealth of information on the TPE systems which we believe will be applied to expand this product area. Everything points to a research area that is fast moving and rewarding – and which will become more so!

References

1. O. W. Webster, et al., *Polymer Preprints, 24 (2)* 52 (1983); *J. Am. Chem. Soc. 105* 5706 (1983), US 4,544,724, Oct. 1, 1985 (to Du Pont)
2. D. V. Sogah, O. W. Webster, *Polymer Preprints, 24 (2)* 54 (1983)
3. D. V. Sogah, O. W. Webster, *Macromolecules 19,* 1775 (1986)
4. O. W. Webster, *Polymer Preprints 27 (1)* 161 (1986)
5. D. Y. Sogah, *Polymer Preprints 27 (1)* 163 (1986)
6. W. R. Hertler, *Polymer Preprints 27 (1)* 165 (1986)
7. W. B. Farnham and D. Y. Sogah, *Polymer Preprints 27 (1)* 167 (1986)
8. F. Banderman, H. D. Sitz and H. D. Speikamp, *Polymer Preprints 27 (1)* 169 (1986)
9. J. P. Kennedy, *Polymer Preprints 26 (1)* 33 (1985); F. Faust and J. P. Kennedy *Living Carbocationic Polymerization I Initial Investigation with Isobutylene,* Paper No. 29, presented at the Sept. 1985 Meeting of the ACS Polymer Division; R. Faust and J. P. Kennedy, *Living Carbocationic Polymerization II, Introduction to the Polymerization of Isobutylene,* Paper No. 13, presented at the April 1986 Meeting of the ACS Polymer Division.
10. J. C. Falk and D. A. Van Beck, US 4,473,679, Sept 25, 1984, filed Dec. 12, 1983, (to Borg-Warner Chemicals, Inc.)

INDEX

The editors draw your attention to the unusual form of the index. This was necessary because the comprehensive nature of the book, which covers all types of thermoplastic elastomers, would not be well served by the normal indexing which provides long lists of page numbers for each major subject indexed.

The following index is arranged by chapter number. Under each chapter heading we have listed the sub-sections by title in the same numerical order as found in each chapter of the text. Within each sub-section we have listed the keywords alphabetically with a page number for each one.

We believe that this index will aid the readers in using the book as a reference volume.

Chapter 2

THERMOPLASTIC POLYURETHANE ELASTOMERS

Chapter 3

THERMOPLASTIC ELASTOMERS BASED ON POLYSTYRENE-POLYDIENE BLOCK
COPOLYMERS

Chapter 4
RESEARCH ON ANIONIC TRIBLOCK COPOLYMERS

Chapter 6
ELASTOMER-THERMOPLASTIC BLENDS AS THERMOPLASTIC ELASTOMERS

Chapter 7
THERMOPLASTIC ELASTOMERS BASED ON ELASTOMER-THERMOPLASTIC
BLENDS DYNAMICALLY VULCANIZED

Chapter 8
THERMOPLASTIC POLYESTER ELASTOMERS

Chapter 9B
POLYETHER BLOCK AMIDE THERMOPLASTIC ELASTOMERS

Chapter 10A
IONOMERIC THERMOPLASTIC ELASTOMERS EARLY RESEARCH –
SURLYN AND RELATED POLYMERS

Chapter 10B
RESEARCH ON IONOMERIC SYSTEMS

Chapter 11
THEORETICAL ASPECTS OF BLOCK COPOLYMERS

Chapter 12/1
MODELING THE ELASTIC BEHAVIOR OF POLY(STYRENE-b-BUTADIENE-b-
STYRENE) BLOCK COPOLYMERS

Chapter 12/2
INTERFACIAL ACTIVITY OF BLOCK COPOLYMERS

Chapter 12/3
ORDER-DISORDER TRANSITION IN BLOCK COPOLYMERS

Chapter 12/6
COMPATIBILIZATION OF POLYMER BLENDS BY STYRENE/HYDROGENATED
BUTADIENE BLOCK COPOLYMERS

Chapter 12/7
NOVEL BLOCK COPOLYMERS, THERMOPLASTIC ELASTOMERS AND
POLYMER BLENDS

Chapter 12/8
THERMOPLASTIC ELASTOMERS STUDIES 1966–1986

Chapter 13
APPLICATIONS OF THERMOPLASTIC ELASTOMERS

Chapter 14

HYDROGENATED BLOCK COPOLYMERS IN THERMOPLASTIC ELASTOMER IPNs

Chapter 15
FUTURE TRENDS 541

BIOGRAPHIES

N. R. Legge

Dr. Legge obtained the degrees of B. Sc. (Honors Chem.) and M. Sc. (Phys. Chem.) from the University of Alberta and did his doctoral research at McGill University.

He entered the elastomers research field at Polymer Corp., Sarnia, Ontario, in 1945. There he led research projects on oil extended SBR and cold (5 °C) polymerized acrylonitrile-butadiene (NBR) rubber. In 1951 he was appointed Director of Research and Development for Kentucky Synthetic Rubber Corp. in Louisville, and directed research projects sponsored by the Office of Rubber Reserve.

Dr. Legge joined Shell Development Company, Emeryville, California, Laboratory in 1955 and spent the last 23 years of his career with the Shell Companies. He led research and development on high cis-polyisoprene (IR), high cis-polybutadiene (BR), ethylene-propylene (EPR) rubbers. He is best known as leader of the Shell team which discovered and developed, in the years 1961 to 1972, the triblock styrene-diene thermoplastic elastomers.

After retiring from Shell he has been active as a consultant in polymers. In 1987 he received from the Rubber Division of the American Chemical Society the Charles Goodyear Medal for his research in thermoplastic elastomers.

G. Holden

Geoffrey Holden was born and educated in England. After receiving the degrees of B. Sc. Tech. and Ph. D. from the University of Manchester, he came to the United States in 1958 and joined the staff of the Elastomers Technical Center of Shell Chemical Company, Torrance, California. In 1974 he spent a year at Shell's Plastics laboratory in Delft, The Netherlands, and since 1975 has been at the Shell Development Company, Westhollow Research Center in Houston, Texas.

Dr. Holden's particular interests have been in the properties of thermoplastic elastomers and the relation of these properties to the structure of the styrenic triblock copolymers, especially the domain theory. He holds, with others, several of the basic patents on styrenic block copolymer thermoplastic elastomers, and has written, from 1965 to date, numerous articles and papers on the relationships between physical properties and copolymer structures.

H. E. Schroeder

Following completion of his undergraduate and graduate studies at Harvard University in 1938, Dr. Schroeder began a 42 year career with the du Pont Company that culminated in 17 years as Director of Research and Development for the Elastomer Chemicals Department. Before his retirement in 1980 Dr. Schroeder contributed to the development of a variety of specialty elastomers, including: the first good (vinyl pyridine copolymer) adhesive for bonding nylon to rubber, du Pont's pioneering work on polyetherurethanes and the thermoplastic polyetherester Hytrel, the fluorelastomer Viton, the ethylene/acrylic rubber Vamac, and Nordel, the first sulfur-curable ethylene propylene-diene rubber.

Since retiring he has served as consultant on material science for art conservation at several museums and also been active as an industrial consultant and lecturer. In 1979 Dr. Schroeder was honored by the International Institute of Synthetic Rubber Producers for his many contributions to the rubber industry and in 1984 he received the Charles Goodyear Medal in recognition of a lifetime dedicated to the field of specialty elastomers.